# DICTIONARY OF
# BRITISH POLITICS

KT-431-650

WQEIC
Th

WITHDRAWN

Wyggeston QE I

00382600

Published in our
centenary year
~ 2004 ~
MANCHESTER
UNIVERSITY
PRESS

# DICTIONARY OF BRITISH POLITICS

Bill Jones

Manchester University Press
Manchester and New York

distributed exclusively in the USA by Palgrave

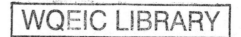
WQEIC LIBRARY

Copyright © Bill Jones 2004

The right of Bill Jones to be identified as the author of this work has been asserted by him in accordance with the Copyright, Designs and Patents Act 1988.

*Published by* Manchester University Press
Oxford Road, Manchester M13 9NR, UK
*and* Room 400, 175 Fifth Avenue, New York, NY 10010, USA
www.manchesteruniversitypress.co.uk

*Distributed exclusively in the USA by*
Palgrave, 175 Fifth Avenue, New York,
NY 10010, USA

*Distributed exclusively in Canada by*
UBC Press, University of British Columbia, 2029 West Mall,
Vancouver, BC, Canada V6T 1Z2

*British Library Cataloguing-in-Publication Data*
A catalogue record for this book is available from the British Library

*Library of Congress Cataloging-in-Publication Data applied for*

ISBN    0 7190 4957 1  *hardback*
EAN    978 0 7190 4957 6

ISBN    0 7190 4958 X  *paperback*
EAN    978 0 7190 4958 3

First published 2004

13 12 11 10 09 08 07 06 05 04          10 9 8 7 6 5 4 3 2 1

Typeset
by R. J. Footring Ltd, Derby
Printed in Great Britain
by CPI, Bath

This book is dedicated to the many members of the Extra-Mural Wednesday Current Affairs Discussion Group from 1977 onwards, especially two of its original members, Mrs Hilda Turner and Mrs Sheila Gardner.

# About the author

Bill Jones was born on the Welsh border in Oswestry and educated at the Priory Grammar School for Boys, Shrewsbury, before studying international politics at University College of Wales, Aberystwyth, where he was awarded his doctorate in 1975. He was an administrative-class civil servant for two years in the Ministry of Defence in Whitehall before he joined the University of Manchester as its staff tutor in politics. He was made Director of Extra-Mural Studies 1986–91 but was forced to retire after a stroke, incurred while jogging, in 1992. He continues to teach at the university and to write books and articles on British politics, several for Manchester University Press but also including *Politics UK* (now in its fifth edition) for Pearson Education. He was Vice Chairman and Chairman of the Politics Association 1979–83 and still organises conferences for the PA in concert with the University of Salford. He has been twice married, has two children and lives in Stockport, Greater Manchester.

# Contents

Acc No.

WITHDRAWN

Class No.
320·03 JON

# Preface

There are plenty of dictionaries of politics on the market that deal with definitions or analytical terms, but very few reference books that focus squarely on the subject of British politics itself. Students, teachers and members of the public are often mystified by some term, event or personality they have read or heard about, and it seemed to me that a ready source of reference would be very useful. There is another, personal source for the book's provenance: my mother always used to scold me for asking questions which should have been looked up in dictionaries or other reference books. I realise that, in consequence, I have become that somewhat pedantic 'anorak' type of person who always likes to nail down the query.

The *Politics Today* series is dedicated to the publication of accessible books that are good value for money, on a wide range of political topics. As the series includes some reference volumes, Manchester University Press thought it a good idea to produce within it a reference work on the broad subject of British politics. As my choices of entry appeared, on occasions, to be a little eccentric, my publishers thought Graham Thomas and Adrian Sackman would bring some welcome objectivity as well as fresh perspectives and accuracy. I am pleased to say that they have both done so, as well as contributed helpfully to the text.

As the *Politics Today* series has a volume on the constitution, written by the late Colin Pilkington, constitutional matters are not covered here in great detail. Otherwise, I have tried to include every entry that is likely to be of interest and importance to both the teacher and the student of British politics, as well as those many people who have a thirst for the details of public life and current affairs. Ultimately, however, the selection has reflected personal choices. And, as Colin Pilkington wearily agreed, 'even though there are lots more entries one could add, one *has* to stop somewhere'. I must apologise in advance to any readers who have failed to find the reference they were sure they would find in this book. Please forward to the publisher any suggestions for entries in a future edition.

In essence the book aims to cover:
1  the most memorable political events since 1945;
2  the most important political institutions and offices;
3  in the biographical section, those people – politicians, journalists, academics, civil servants and others – who have had a formative influence on British politics since 1945, and, more selectively, before that too.

I have tended to avoid entries on political concepts except where they relate specifically to the British case.

The structure of this book is simple. It is divided into two principal sections, 'Politics' – for events, institutions, concepts, places and so on – and 'People'. Within each, entries appear in word-by-word alphabetical order (including prepositions and conjunctions) and numbers appear where they would be if spelt out as words. A bibliography is provided for those who wish to follow up entries with more in-depth reading. Websites are given within entries for specific bodies, but a list of more general political sources is provided at the end of the book.

Bill Jones
*Manchester, summer 2004*

# Acknowledgements

Part of my impulse to write this book came from the Extra-Mural Wednesday Current Affairs Discussion Group which I initiated in the 1970s as a Staff Tutor in Politics for Manchester University, in the days when it – together with the Department of Education – had the excellent sense to fund extra-mural departments in British universities. These classes have been among the best and most interesting I have taught in a working lifetime of university teaching. Adult students bring their experience, intellectual energy and special knowledge to such forums and make them chock full of humour, friendly disputation and the lust for more knowledge. It is to this changing, dynamic group over 20 years or more that I dedicate this book; they have nourished my own love of the subject and have activated the part of my brain 'ordinary' teaching (with no disrespect to undergraduates) fails to stimulate.

More particularly, I would like to thank a number of people for their help with this enjoyable project. The late Colin Pilkington wrote a reference book on the British constitution in the *Politics Today* series and helped me considerably, as well as sharing with me the intractabilities of being unable to include the totality of the political universe in a single book like this. My friend Andrew McLaughlin, who was with me when the idea of the book first dawned, has been very helpful and imaginative in identifying entries.

I must also thank: Nicola Viinikka, formerly at Manchester University Press, who encouraged me warmly and wisely on this project from the outset; Tony Mason, her successor – ably assisted by Lucy Nicholson – has nursed the project through to completion; and Richard Delahunty, who, while at the Press, was also endlessly supportive. I would in addition thank Philip Norton (or Professor the Lord Norton of Louth, to give him his full title) for his typically generous responses to my many queries. I thank Jon Tonge for his help on Northern Ireland items and Duncan Watts for his thoughtful and helpful suggestions on several matters. But most of all among colleagues, I must thank Graham Thomas, my friend and fellow textbook author for Manchester University Press, who has been a tower of strength in editing early drafts so meticulously and accurately. Also engaged in similar labour was my friend David Hesp, a long-time teacher of politics and someone blessed with a much better memory than I. Copy-editors are seldom given the credit they deserve for the meticulous line-by-line work they do in preparing a manuscript for publication. In this case the contribution to the book made by Ralph Footring was immense and I mention it with gratitude. The careful attentions of the last named led to the rectification of many errors in the drafts. I owe all of the above a considerable debt. Any mistakes, misinterpretations or omissions are not their responsibility but mine. Also helpful have been Bob Franklyn, Kate Morrison, Richard Kelly and Simon Bulmer. My son Markus kindly assisted with the bibliography.

# Politics

## abdication crisis, 1936

Edward VIII acceded to the throne in January 1936. By November he had decided to marry an American divorcee, Mrs Wallis Simpson. Given his role as spiritual head of the Church of England, his marriage to a divorcee was widely seen as inappropriate. A crisis ensued which culminated in the king's abdication on 10 December 1936. He was succeeded by his brother (who became George VI) and was made Duke of Windsor. In June 1937 he married Mrs Simpson. He was governor of the Bahamas from 1940 to 1945. Some 60 years later there was speculation that Elizabeth II might abdicate in favour of her son Charles, but it seemed that she was determined to carry on as monarch.

## absolutism

Form of government characterised by one-person rule, unrestricted by law, institution or constitution. Britain has probably not seen such a ruler since King John was forced to accede to the restrictive demands of his nobles in 1215, when he signed the Magna Carta. In the 16th century Thomas Hobbes elaborated arguments in favour of absolute monarchical power, using the justification that only such a 'Leviathan' could prevent human beings becoming lawless.

*See also* Magna Carta; Hobbes, Thomas.

## accountability

The requirement to take responsibility for one's actions and make redress when appropriate. In British politics five forms of accountability apply:

1 *Electoral accountability.* National governments are accountable at general elections, which must take place at least once every five years. Moreover, individual MPs are also accountable to their constituents at election time (and to their parliamentary party through the system of whips). Local councillors are elected for four-year terms.

2 *Administrative accountability.* Hierar-chies exist in which civil servants are answerable to their political masters. In turn, government ministers must account for their actions to parliament through such procedures as debates and question time. The government is answerable to the electorate at general elections, thus creating the chain of democratic accountability and legitimacy on which British government rests. Within parliament the accountability of the executive was enhanced by the extension of select committees in 1979.

3 *Public accountability.* Newspapers and broadcasters investigate and question government actions and contribute to public debate on the issues of the day.

4 *Judicial accountability.* The govern-ment is not above the law and can be held accountable in court for actions which exceed the powers granted to it by statute law, or if it fails to fulfil obligations laid upon it by parliamentary statute or international treaty.

5 *Service standards.* Professionals in the public services, such as the National Health Service and education, must now demonstrate to the consumer the effective use of public money and quality of service through transparent systems

1

of accountability, including independent inspection regimes, performance league tables, and the 'naming and shaming' of poorly performing services.

## act of parliament

Otherwise known as a statute – a legislative proposal, or bill, which has passed all stages of the parliamentary procedure. Most bills can be introduced in either House (the first reading), although those involving finance must start their life in the House of Commons.

1  The first reading is little more than an announcement of an intention to pass the bill.
2  The second reading is a full-scale debate on underlying principles, as well as the detail.
3  It then passes on to its committee stage, where a standing committee considers every clause and proposes amendments.
4  Any changes are announced at the report stage, when the amendments are voted on.
5  Next comes the third reading, in which the amended bill is again subject to a full debate.

A similar procedure takes place in the House of Lords. After the bill has cleared both chambers, it receives royal assent and becomes law.

The stages usually take several months, enough to allow time for debate and amendment, although, if necessary, for example in time of national crisis or war, the legislative process can be telescoped into a few hours. By virtue of the Parliament Acts of 1911 and 1949, the House of Lords cannot delay the legislation for more than 12 months. Money bills – that is, those concerned with taxation or public expenditure – always start their passage in the House of Commons and cannot be delayed or amended by the House of Lords (although the Lords nonetheless may influence the government as a result of its debate). The Parliament Act can be invoked in cases of disagreement between the two chambers to ensure the will of the elected House prevails.

*See also* legislative process; money bill.

## Act of Settlement 1701

Act which provided that a Protestant (not a Catholic) must accede to the throne. It stipulated that the monarch must take communion with the Church of England (and to this day the sovereign must be a member of that church). A change in the constitution would be required to permit a Roman Catholic to become king or queen. The act meant that, in the event of William III or Anne dying without a surviving heir, the succession would pass to Sophia, Electress of Hanover, or her Protestant descendants. It also required the sovereign to seek the consent of parliament before making war or protecting foreign possessions, and barred foreigners from office or parliament. It ensured the Hanoverian succession, thus neutralising the claims of the Stuarts. On the death of Anne in 1714 George I of Hanover succeeded her to the throne of Great Britain.

## Act of Union 1536 (Wales)

Merged all Welsh territory with that of England when Henry VIII was on the throne, who was himself descended from the Welsh house of Tudor. Wales was given parliamentary representation and English was made the language of legal and administrative affairs.

## Act of Union 1707 (Scotland)

After James VI of Scotland succeeded Elizabeth to become James I of England in 1603, the crowns of the two countries became unified. However, the kingdoms remained legally separate for another century. In 1707 it became strategically necessary to effect a legal union with Scotland because of the danger that France might re-establish an alliance with Scotland, which was a major concern due to the Franco-British war of the time. Scotland was not as fully absorbed into the Union as Wales had been and retained distinctive legal and educational features as well as its Presbyterian church.

## Act of Union 1800 (Ireland)

This last act of union joined Ireland to Great Britain, creating the United

Kingdom of Great Britain and Ireland, on 1 January 1801. The reason once again was defensive, with Britain fearing that France would exploit a disaffected Ireland in the Napoleonic Wars. The act was revoked in 1922 with the setting up of the Irish Free State.

## Adam Smith Institute (ASI)

www.adamsmith.org

An independent non-profit-making think tank, which explores new ways of 'extending choice and competition into public service'. It was founded in 1977 by two graduates of St Andrews University, Madsen Pirie and Eamonn Butler. The ASI designs 'practical policy strategies' and introduces 'innovative ideas into the public policy debate'. It is claimed to have inspired: the Education Reform Act 1988; the reduction of higher levels of tax; the policy of contracting out services in the public sector; and the citizens' charter. Following the political demise of Margaret Thatcher, not to mention the victory of New Labour in 1997, most commentators believe the ASI lost much of its influence. In the autumn of 1997 it produced a highly flattering assessment of New Labour's first 200 days.

## additional member system (AMS)

A hybrid electoral system combining proportional representation with first past the post. It is most notably used in Germany, where voters have two votes: one to elect half the members of the Bundestag as constituency representatives and another to elect the other half from regional party lists across the country. It is the proportion of the vote won by a party in the latter vote which determines its overall seat entitlement, its constituency seats being 'topped up' from the regional list pool. AMS is also used, in an amended form in the UK, for elections to the Welsh assembly and Scottish parliament and for the Greater London Authority.

## adjournment debate

A debate in the House of Commons prompted by the motion that 'This House

do now adjourn'. There are four types of adjournment debate.

1  In the main House, there are those proposed by a backbench MP (who is chosen by ballot) at the close of business for the day. A government whip moves the motion and then the MP speaks for 15 minutes, usually on a topic close to the heart, and a government minister replies.

2  In Westminster Hall on a Thursday afternoon, either a report of a select committee (selected by the Liaison Committee) or a government motion is debated. The debate which led to Winston Churchill replacing Neville Chamberlain was of this latter type – and is attractive to the government because no amendments to the motion can be tabled, no decision can be made except to adjourn and usually there is no vote.

3  Adjournment debates in Westminster Hall also occur on Tuesday and Wednesday mornings, when MPs are again selected by a speaker's ballot the week before.

4  Emergency adjournment debates are held under standing order 24 on matters of great moment. Few applications are successful under this standing order – perhaps only one a session. Usually 24 hours' notice is given but the debate can take place on the evening of the day on which it is requested.

Some 25 per cent of the time of the House is taken up by debating adjournment motions.

*See also* half-hour adjournment.

## administration

A term with a number of meanings. It can refer to the civil service or bureaucracy which advises ministers and coordinates and implements government policy. It can also refer to elected politicians who hold government office (the executive), or to the period of government led by a particular person, as in 'the Thatcher administration'.

## administrative class

The elite stream of the civil service, recruited mostly from the best university graduates to provide the 'intellectual' leadership recommended by the Northcote–Trevelyan report of 1854. The 'executive' and 'clerical' classes were intended to provide lesser support. In theory the administrative class is open to all applicants, but Oxbridge graduates have in practice dominated the administrative class. In 1968 the Fulton report urged changes and the somewhat broader administration group resulted, open to people with a first or upper second degree. This group advises ministers, including the prime minister, on policy options and courses of action and numbers about 4,000 above the rank of 'principal'. In the 1980s the majority of recruits still came from Oxbridge. The term has fallen into disuse in recent decades.

*See also* civil service; Fulton report; Northcote–Trevelyan report.

## administrative court
*See* administrative law.

## administrative law
The rules governing relations between the individual and the state. If a government agency acts in a way that is not sanctioned by the law, a court may judge it to be ultra vires. This may not be easy, as government has a fairly wide degree of discretion. The scope of administrative law has widened with the extension of government activity, especially with the emergence of the welfare state. The Queen's Bench Division of the High Court acts as the administrative court, which considers, for example, cases arising from immigration and tribunal judgements. Compared with that of the USA or France, the UK's administrative law is poorly developed.

*See also* ultra vires.

## Admiralty
Body responsible for the Royal Navy from 1832 to 1964, when the Admiralty Board was merged into the Ministry of Defence.

## adversarial politics
A bipolar system of politics where an incoming government, after unceasing attack in opposition, reverses the major policies of its predecessor. A two-party system plus a simple majority voting system encourages adversarial politics. However, in practice, reversals by Conservatives in the 1950s of Labour's measures were few, although in the 1980s the Thatcher governments used privatisation to reverse Labour's postwar nationalisations. After its 1997 victory, Labour, in keeping, perhaps, with a 'third way' pragmatism, reversed remarkably few of the Conservative measures it had bitterly attacked during the previous 18 years, such as privatisation and trade union legislation. Advocates of proportional representation argue that it would end dangerous swings in government policies by encouraging the formation of more cooperative coalition governments.

## advisor
*See* political advisor.

## Advisory, Conciliation and Arbitration Service (ACAS)
www.acas.co.uk
Body founded in 1974 by the Employment Protection Act. ACAS seeks to 'promote the improvement of industrial relations'. In practice, it engages substantially in the conciliation of industrial disputes and the provision of arbitration and mediation facilities, as well as giving advice to employers and employees. In the 1970s it was very much in the headlines, but once the Conservatives came to power in 1979 ACAS assumed a much lower profile.

## Afghanistan
After the terrorist attacks on the USA on 11 September 2001 George Bush attacked Afghanistan after its Taliban regime refused to hand over the Saudi Arabian dissident Osama Bin Laden, who was alleged to be behind the attacks. Tony Blair declared he was standing 'shoulder to shoulder' with his US ally and travelled the globe doing his best to construct a worldwide coalition in favour of Bush's anti-terrorist action. As further justification for this support, he told the Labour

Party conference in October 2001 that 90 per cent of the heroin on British streets originated in Afghanistan. British troops were available but used sparingly during the successful military action; they assumed a more prominent role in the wake of the war as a peacekeeping force in Kabul.

## Age Concern
www.ace.org.uk
A classic sectional pressure group representing older people. Founded in 1940 this body comprises 98 representatives of national organisations plus 107 from Age Concern organisations. Its function is to promote the welfare of elderly people and coordinate 1,600 branches, which work with volunteers. It liaises with government departments and agencies.

## ageing population
When the proportion of older people in a society is increasing. On 28 July 2004 the Office for National Statistics announced that the number of people aged over 80 years would grow from 2.5 million in 2002 to 4.9 million in 2031, peaking at 7 million by 2050. The number of those over state pension age would increase from 10.9 million in 2002 to 12.2 in 2011. By the middle of the century older people will outnumber children by a large margin and the rise in the number of those who are of working age will not match the rise in number of those who are older.

## agency
See executive agency.

## agenda setting
Media selection of news stories. News organisations select their stories on the basis of a set of news values. These prioritise some issues, events and personalities over others. Although it does not determine what people think, agenda setting can influence what people think about, that is, the 'important' issues of the time. For example, throughout 2000 the news media gave extensive coverage to 'mad' or 'bad' doctors, thus setting the agenda for increased

regulation of the medical profession. Political parties and government now make extensive use of spin doctors and public relations advisors, who attempt to influence the process of agenda setting. It was also alleged that during the 1980s the tabloid newspapers succeeded in determining the topics debated during election campaigns.

See also mass media; news values; political agenda; power.

## agriculture
See Department for Environment, Food and Rural Affairs; Ministry of Agriculture, Fisheries and Food.

## alderman
Senior councillor who was elected by fellow councillors to serve six years. The aldermanic system of representation applied to county and county boroughs before the 1974 reorganisation of local government. The office was established in 1835. The system fell into disrepute due to corruption and the fact that local citizens were excluded from the process. The Local Government Act 1972 abolished it.

See also local government.

## Alliance
Name given to the collaboration in September 1981 between the Social Democratic Party (SDP) and the Liberal Party. The Alliance fought the 1983 election on a joint manifesto, with Roy Jenkins as 'prime minister designate'. It garnered just over a quarter of the vote (25.4 per cent) but only 23 seats (3.5 per cent). In 1987 it fought under the joint leadership of David Owen and David Steel, when it gained a smaller share of the vote (20.6 per cent) and only 22 seats. In January 1988 the two parties formally merged to form the Social and Liberal Democratic Party.

See also gang of four; Liberal Democrats.

## Alliance Party of Northern Ireland
www.allianceparty.org
One of the smaller Northern Ireland parties, historically important since it bridges

the sectarian and thus political divide between Catholics and Protestants. It supports the unionist line on the constitution but attracts some Catholic support, especially among middle-class voters. The party has regularly gained 10 per cent of the vote in elections and strongly supports the power-sharing arrangements established by the Good Friday Agreement in 1998.

### all-party group
Type of parliamentary body established to address an issue of interest, such as particular countries or regions, AIDS or adult education. In 1995 there were 130 such groups. The disability group is especially effective as, allegedly, are the parliamentary reform and scientific groups; the football group has over 100 members. Many of the groups have links with relevant bodies outside parliament but they seldom exert much influence within parliament.

### alternative vote
Majoritarian electoral system in which voters rank order their preferences from a list of candidates. If no candidate achieves half of the first preferences, the one with the least votes is eliminated and the second preference votes on those ballot papers are distributed. If no candidate has reached the 50 per cent threshold, then the next weakest is eliminated, second preferences redistributed and so on until a winner is achieved. The Australian system of alternative vote has some support in Britain, where over half of MPs are elected on minorities of the votes cast.

*See also* alternative vote 'top-up'; Jenkins report; proportional representation.

### alternative vote 'top-up' (also known as AV plus)
Sometimes referred to as 'limited AMS' (additional member system). Alternative vote 'top up' was the system recommended by the Jenkins report in 1998. This operates on the principle whereby 80–85 per cent of seats are decided via the alternative vote, with the remaining 15–20 per cent to be decided by a second vote for parties,

which are used to achieve a degree of proportionality. Its supporters claim the system is fairer and more democratic. However, the Labour government, which commissioned the report, buoyed up by its landslides in 1997 and 2001, sidelined discussion about electoral reform.

### Amalgamated Engineering Union (AEU)
*See* Amicus.

### amendment
*See* legislative process.

### Amicus
www.amicustheunion.org
A union that resulted from the merger between the Amalgamated Electrical Engineering Union (AEEU) and the Manufacturing, Science and Finance Union in 2001. The name is the Latin word for 'friendly'. It has well over a million members, which makes it the second biggest union in Britain and the biggest within the private sector. The union has been generally supportive of Tony Blair's Labour government. During the 1970s the Amalgamated Engineering Union (AEU) under Hugh Scanlon was one of the most powerful unions in the country, ever eager to advise, disagree with and confront the government. The AEU merged with the Electrical, Electronic, Telecommunications and Plumbing Union (EETPU) to become the AEEU. In June 2004 Amicus general secretary Derek Simpson urged Blair to find a 'reverse gear', warning that if he was 'not for turning, then we'll have to turn him out'.

### anarchism
An approach to politics which rejects the need for the state and its coercive institutions. The view can be traced back to the Frenchman Pierre-Joseph Proudhon and the Englishman William Godwin, who suggested that governments would disappear as human beings acquired reason and judgement. Not unsurprisingly, there are different forms of anarchist theory. For

example, anarcho-syndicalism proposes that trade unions should replace the state. Some major anarchist thinkers include Max Stirner, Michael Bakunin, Peter Kropotkin and Leo Tolstoy. There are also elements of anarchist thinking in the writings of Karl Marx, who argued that the state would 'wither away' after the overthrow of capitalism and the establishment of socialism. Despite the occasional outbreaks of anarchist activity at demonstrations, sometimes peaceful, sometimes not, Britain has generally been free from this form of politics. However, an element of anarchistic activity was apparent in the May Day anti-capitalist protests of 2001. Anarchist groups issued leaflets in advance of those protests which identified stores like Tesco in the Old Kent Road and gave comments like: 'encourages intensive monocrop agriculture', 'upsets eco-systems' and 'forces third world peasants to grow for export'.

*See also* political culture.

### Anglo-Irish Agreement
Agreement between Margaret Thatcher and Garret FitzGerald (the Irish Taoiseach, or prime minister) signed at Hillsborough in 1985. The agreement represented yet another attempt to find a solution to the problems of Northern Ireland. Its main provisions were: that there should be no change in the constitutional status of Northern Ireland without majority consent; that no majority for change existed in the province; that the Republic of Ireland was to be given a consultative role in Northern Ireland via a permanent intergovernmental conference. Unionists and republicans both opposed the agreement but did not succeed in destroying it.

### Animal Liberation Front (ALF)
*See* animal rights protest.

### animal rights protest
Campaigns on behalf of suffering animals, and in particular those used for scientific research. The Animal Liberation Front (ALF) is the most high profile and arguably the most radical of such organisations.

Its methods include regularly picketing university laboratories, forcible entry into premises and, on occasion, violence against individuals. In July 1998 activists released 6,000 mink into the New Forest area but the ploy backfired as the mink then killed many native animals. In the autumn of 2000 the home secretary, Jack Straw, announced plans to curb the unacceptable tactics of groups, such as intimidation and other activity which the police find difficult to prosecute. In January 2001, the government announced that it would introduce tougher powers to deal with violent animal rights protestors, such as those who were demonstrating outside the Cambridgeshire animal-testing firm Huntingdon Life Sciences and who violently attacked some of its staff.

*See also* political violence.

### Anti-Corn Law League (19th century)
Usually cited as one of the first effective pressure groups in British politics. It was established by radical factory owners under the leadership of future radical Liberals Richard Cobden and John Bright, to oppose the laws which protected landed interests by levying charges on imported grain. Robert Peel was eventually persuaded by the League's arguments and repealed the Corn Laws in June 1846, thus ending his career and splitting the Conservative Party.

### Anti-Nazi League (ANL)
www.anl.org.uk
Body set up to resist the growth of Nazism in Europe in the 1970s. It was established mainly by far-left socialists, especially members of the Socialist Workers' Party, but relaunched in 1992 at a time when the far right was seen to be making inroads in eastern Europe, Germany, Belgium, Norway and Austria. The ANL seeks to campaign by demonstrating against the British National Party and events like the visit of the French far-right leader Jean-Marie Le Pen in April 2004. Sometimes the clashes have become violent as the ANL argues that such threats have to be met in kind.

## antisocial behaviour order (ASBO)

One of the principal elements of home secretary Jack Straw's Crime and Disorder Act 1998, which gave local agencies the power to prohibit for a period of two years violent or racist behaviour in local communities. Developed by Straw in liaison with police on housing estates in his Blackburn constituency, the order is targeted at, among others, the 'neighbours from hell' who make life a misery for those who live near them. At first few ASBOs were issued but slowly cities like Manchester and Liverpool began to use them and by 2004 they were perceived as a useful weapon against yobbish behaviour.

## apathy

Low levels of participation in political activity, especially voting. Commentators have been worried at times about Britain's civic culture, as it reveals a high degree of apathy. This is most clearly expressed in low turnout at election times. While general election turnout used to be well over 70 per cent, in 2001 it slumped to under 60 per cent (see below), the lowest since universal franchise was introduced in 1918. Even worse, the figure has been as low as 30–40 per cent for local elections, with some wards polling as few as 10 per cent of eligible voters. For European elections in 1999, the UK figure was the lowest in the European Union, at a mere 24 per cent; one ward in Sunderland registered only 1.5 per cent of voters turning out. In September 1998, the Home Affairs Committee urged a debate on the low level of participation in elections, and called for weekend voting and easier voter registration. In the 2001 general election the question of apathy achieved front-page importance when only 59.1 per cent turned out to vote. Labour won the election easily but only one in four of the electorate voted for the party. A BBC/ICM recall poll produced some interesting reasons for choosing not to vote: 53 per cent said they thought the result was a foregone conclusion; 77 per cent said there was no point in voting as 'it would not change anything'; and 65 per cent said

they did not trust politicians. On 12 June 2001 Professor Patrick Dunleavy in the *Guardian* pointed out that the 2001 general election turnout was even worse than the low of 1918, as the latter election involved 'around 60 per cent completely unused to voting'. The 2001 election, he opined, represented the 'nadir in our history as a liberal democracy'. Based on recent research he judged 'the public do not believe they possess the power they want through conventional politics and are increasingly sympathetic to direct action'.

*See also* civic culture; political participation.

## appeasement

The policy adopted in the late 1930s by the national government of Neville Chamberlain, and supported by much of the press and public, in an attempt to defuse Hitler's aggression in eastern Europe. It reached its climax at the signing of the Munich Agreement on 30 September 1938, when Chamberlain, the French leader Daladier, Hitler and Mussolini agreed to the handing over to Germany of the Sudetenland, the German-speaking part of Czechoslovakia. Chamberlain returned to Britain, with a 'piece of paper signed by Herr Hitler' to pronounce 'Peace with honour … peace in our time'. By March 1939 Hitler had marched into and occupied the rest of Czechoslovakia, making the Munich Agreement the symbol of pusillanimity in the face of aggression. Henceforth the term 'appeasement' has become part of the vocabulary of political abuse, used to upbraid opponents who, in the eye of the accuser, lack moral courage. An example of this was just before the outbreak of the Falklands War in 1982, when Margaret Thatcher answered critics with: 'Britain does not appease dictators'.

## Appellate Committee of the House of Lords

A committee of the House of Lords that is most closely analogous to the US Supreme Court. It currently has 12 lords of appeal in ordinary (i.e. law lords), all of whom must have held senior judicial office to qualify. They are members of the Lords and remain so even after they have ceased to hold this judicial office. This is Britain's highest court of appeal and is the last resort after the Court of Appeal. Decisions on cases and points of law are made by the lord chancellor and the law lords plus those members of the Lords who have held high judicial office. In the summer of 2003 Tony Blair announced as part of a cabinet reshuffle that the office of lord chancellor was to be phased out and that a new Supreme Court was to be created with its own premises, separate from the Lords.

## Appointments Office
Part of the machinery of the prime minister's office. It deals with those appointments, especially to the Church of England and universities, which are the premier's responsibility.

## aristocracy
In his classification of constitutions, Aristotle (*c.* 383–322 BC) defines 'aristocracy' as 'rule by the best citizens'. In practice, however, and in Britain, it has meant rule by the landed nobility, who dominated government up until the late 19th century, when they were challenged by the emergent upper middle classes. The reforms to the House of Lords in 1911 symbolised the decline of the aristocracy, but their influence continued nevertheless. Between 1884 and 1924 they filled 43 per cent of cabinet posts and even during 1933–64 they sustained 26 per cent of its membership. Once Labour returned to office in 1997 the days of the hereditary element in the House of Lords were limited and in 1999 they were reduced to a rump of 92. However, the influence of the aristocracy lingers on, especially in the Conservative Party, where, for example, Michael Ancram, heir to the Marquis of Lothian, has served as MP and minister as well as party chair and who stood in the leadership election following the Conservatives' 2001 general election defeat. He declined to use his honorary

title the Earl of Ancram while sitting in the Commons.

*See also* House of Lords reform.

## armed forces
Term that covers the Army, Royal Navy and Royal Air Force (RAF). The UK's main armoury includes four Vanguard-class submarines carrying nuclear weapons, which are on constant patrol. Before the conflicts in Afghanistan and Iraq the biggest military deployment was an armoured division in Germany. From 109,144 personnel garrisoned overseas in 1975, the number fell to 48,841 in 1997. The defence budget is well over £20 billion, 3.1 per cent of the UK's gross domestic product, or £586 per head of the population, compared with the USA's £1,048. The total number of personnel is 225,000: 48,000 in the Royal Navy, 112,000 in the Army and 65,000 in the RAF. In addition there are 114,000 civilians and 116,000 non-industrial staff.

The RAF was formed in 1918 when the Royal Air Naval Service merged with the Royal Flying Corps. It was central to the country's survival in the Second World War, especially through its role in the Battle of Britain (1940), when it resisted the German aerial onslaught known as the Blitz. It is run by the Air Force Board, which is chaired by the secretary of state for defence. The RAF is organised into three commands: Strike (operational), Personnel, and Training and Logistics. The RAF's equipment includes 78 Tornados and 59 Harrier GR7 aircraft.

The Royal Navy was founded in the 9th century by Alfred the Great. In the 19th century it was the most powerful navy in the world and helped make Britain briefly the most powerful country. In the Second World War the Navy was essential in helping the country survive the attacks of the German U-boats and maintaining lifelines to the USA and to the USSR. After the war the Navy was overshadowed by those of the two superpowers but its force of nuclear submarines carried Britain's nuclear deterrent in the form of Trident missiles. The Navy is run by the Admiralty Board and its chief officer is called the first lord of the Admiralty. In addition to its submarines, the Royal Navy has 35 frigates and destroyers, as well as three small aircraft carriers equipped with Sea Harrier aircraft, 12 hunter killer submarines with cruise missiles and two large aircraft carriers as well as two amphibious assault ships.

The Army has five mechanised brigades, eight tank regiments and six armoured brigades.

In July 2004 it was announced that a 1.4 per cent increase would be given to defence over 2004–07 but a short time later the cutback implications of this below-inflation award were spelt out: for the RAF, three Jaguar fighter-bomber squadrons to be disbanded, plus a Tornado T3 one, and 7,500 jobs to go; for the Navy, three frigates and three destroyers to go, plus six other smaller vessels; for the Army, four infantry battalions to go, 90 Challenger tanks to be withdrawn and 1,500 jobs to be axed.

### arms to Africa affair
*See* Sandline affair.

### arms to Iraq affair
*See* Matrix Churchill case; Scott report.

### Army
*See* armed forces.

### Arthur Andersen Accounting
Worldwide accountancy firm. It first attracted attention in British politics in 1982, when the Conservative government blamed the company for enabling US businessman John De Lorean to extract £70 million from taxpayers to fund a poorly implemented plan to establish a sports car production plant in Northern Ireland. In November 1997 the Labour government abandoned legal proceedings against the firm in exchange for £21 million, a fraction of what the government had claimed. Questions were asked regarding 'cash for access' in January 2002, when it transpired that Andersen had audited the faulty accounts of the defunct energy conglomerate Enron.

It was pointed out that the company had provided advice and staff to New Labour free of charge and claimed that in exchange it had received government contracts worth millions of pounds.

### Arts Council
www.artscouncil.org.uk
(Arts Council England)
www.scottisharts.org.uk
(Scottish Arts Council)
www.artswales.org
(Arts Council of Wales)
www.artscouncil-ni.org
(Arts Council of Northern Ireland)
Body responsible for the allocation of public funding for the arts. There are separate Councils for England (with nine regional offices), Scotland, Wales and Northern Ireland. The Arts Council of Great Britain was founded in 1945 but was reconstituted in 1994 as the separate councils, and the devolved assemblies now take care of arts funding in their areas. The function of the Councils is to use an annual grant to develop and improve knowledge, understanding and practice of the arts and to increase public accessibility to them. The budget includes substantial funding from the National Lottery.

### assassination
Murder for political cause. Britain has not been noted for assassinations; certainly, it is less dangerous for politicians than the USA, although not always. In 1812, the prime minister, Spencer Perceval, was shot in the lobby of the House of Commons by a Liverpool broker, John Bellingham, who was later hanged for his crime. In 1920, Sir Henry Wilson was shot in London by a Sinn Fein activist. More recently, Conservative politicians and other members of the British establishment have been targeted by the Provisional IRA and other terrorist groups. Tory MP Airey Neave was killed by a car bomb at the Commons in 1979 by the Irish National Liberation Army; Earl Mountbatten was assassinated while on holiday in the Republic of Ireland in 1979; and Ian Gow (Conservative MP

and former minister) was killed when a bomb exploded at his Sussex home in 1990. Margaret Thatcher and her husband Dennis narrowly escaped without physical injury when the IRA tried to blow up the British cabinet at the Grand Hotel in Brighton in 1984. However, others were less lucky, including Sir Anthony Berry, MP, who was killed, and Norman Tebbit's wife Margaret, who, among others, was badly injured by the bomb blast.

**assembly**
*See* Northern Ireland assembly; regional assembly; Scottish parliament; Welsh assembly and executive.

**assisted places scheme**
Introduced by the Conservative government after 1979 to give financial support to bright children from under-represented socio-economic groups to attend private schools. Labour opposed the policy in opposition and phased out the scheme when it came into office in 1997, using the funds thereby freed to help reduce class sizes.

**asylum seeker**
A person applying to live in Britain in order to escape persecution in the home country. Britain has long been a home for people fleeing from oppression in other countries: the Huguenots in the 16th century, the Jews in the 19th and 20th centuries in the face of pogroms in Russia and anti-Semitism in Germany, especially during the 1930s, when the Nazis persecuted Jews. More recently refugees have poured out of the trouble spots in the world – in Africa, eastern Europe and the Middle East – and have sought political asylum in Britain. However, at the same time thousands of poor people from the third world have been keen to enter the country to improve their economic prospects and enjoy the benefits of a western lifestyle. It is the latter group who have caused a political problem. Britain is a favourite target for asylum seekers, as the welfare system is relatively generous, work as an 'illegal' is

quite easy to acquire and most big cities have a potentially welcoming community of immigrants of just about every variety.

Britain has been relatively free of racial tension and support for the British National Party (BNP) has been scant compared, for example, with France's Front National. However, evidence of racial tension sometimes surfaces in the form of riots, beatings and murders, and the government has been keen to limit the number of immigrants, whether economic migrants (many of whom are in great demand, especially skilled workers) or asylum seekers. Politically, the Conservatives have been more willing to identify 'bogus asylum seekers' and to support the somewhat fevered exaggerations of the tabloid newspapers about how much the government spends on supporting asylum seekers while their applications are being considered. Labour has tended to take a more liberal view in theory but to be just as strict as the Conservatives in practice. (Indeed, Labour insider Peter Mandelson in September 2002 even suggested Labour address the subject more rigorously to prevent the far right from making the issue its own, potentially with dire political consequences.) The problem with the asylum laws was that it was possible for people to arrive in the country, apply for asylum and then disappear into their minority ethnic havens: it was calculated that nearly 200,000 such 'illegals' had entered the country in this way by January 2003. It is true that Britain has proved the most popular destination for asylum seekers and there is evidence to suggest the less liberal a country's immigration laws and procedures, the less likely it is to be the desired destination.

In September 2002 Tony Blair, interviewed on BBC2's *Newsnight* programme, agreed that the number of applications, at nearly 9,000, was too great; he hoped new measures would reduce this figure by 30 per cent within a few months and by 50 per cent within a year. By October 2003 applications had reduced to 4,225. In the queen's speech for that year even tougher measures were announced, including:

restrictions on the rapidly increasing bill
for legal aid for asylum appeals; a more
restricted appeals procedure; possible jail
for immigrants who travelled by air and
destroyed their passports upon landing to
make it impossible to discover their country
of departure; and the possible taking into
care of the children of immigrants denied
leave to stay but who refused to take
advantage of free air tickets to their home
country.

## Athenian democracy

The world's first direct democracy, which
existed between c. 500 and 321 BC. In
contrast to representative democracy, the
political system of Athens made use of an
assembly of all citizens, which excluded
women, slaves and foreigners, and council
and citizen juries, which were in charge
of the day-to-day government of the city.
The membership of the assembly and
juries was decided by selection through a
'lottery' of all the citizens. In general terms,
any Athenian male citizen could become
directly involved in the political system of
the city state. Clearly, Britain is too highly
populated to allow an Athenian form of
direct democracy, but advocates of more
democracy, notably Tony Benn, urge its
introduction into all forms of national and
social life.

## attorney general

www.lslo.gov.uk
The government's principal legal advisor.
The attorney general, along with other law
officers (the solicitor general and the lord
advocate), is part of the government and
has the following functions:

1  to represent the government in civil and
   criminal proceedings, as either plaintiff
   (for example in relation to alleged
   breaches of the Official Secrets Act) or
   defendant;
2  to head the Crown Prosecution Service
   and the Serious Organised Crime
   Agency, which play a major role in the
   criminal justice system;
3  to refer cases to the Court of Appeal,
   if in the eyes of the prosecution the

sentence is deemed too lenient (a
function acquired in 1989).

The attorney general is accountable to
parliament, as is any minister; however,
according to received wisdom, the legal
function is exercised independently of
government.

## audit

The process whereby the purpose of government expenditure is measured against
its end result. There has been a dramatic
increase in such activity and most public
services are now subject to external scrutiny
and an audit culture.

See also National Audit Office.

## Audit Commission

www.audit-commission.gov.uk
Examines local government and health
expenditure to ensure it has taken place
as intended. The Commission was set up
under the Local Government Finance Act
1982; it also has a remit to improve the
efficiency and effectiveness of local government.

## Auld report, 2001

A report by Sir Robin Auld, an appeal
court judge, into the criminal justice system.
He suggested a new, unified, three-tier
system: a crown division with a judge and
jury to try serious cases; a district division
for cases eligible for up to two years in
prison; and the magistrates to deal with the
lesser cases. A separate youth court would
hear cases involving young defendants. His
proposal to make juries more representative was welcomed but his suggestion that
defendants should lose the right to choose a
jury trial where this option currently exists
was widely criticised and finally dropped as
a serious government intention in 2002.

## authoritarianism

A highly directive system of government
where rulers make decisions without the explicit procedural consent of the population.
This is not to say that authoritarian systems
do not make use of popular sentiment, but
rather that no extensive consultation or

dialogue exists between government and the governed as is the case with representative democracy. Authoritarian regimes often fill the gap when the social, political and economic conditions do not exist for full liberal democracy. Individual politicians have often been described as authoritarian in style, for example Oswald Mosley in the early years of the last century and in the latter part, most notably, Margaret Thatcher.

## authority

The legitimate use of power. The term can be applied to an individual office holder (for example the authority of the prime minister or a police officer), a collective of individuals, or an institution (for example the authority granted to a government by the mandate obtained at a general election). A useful distinction is made between 'authority' and 'power' whereby someone with a gun can command compliance and an unarmed police officer can do the same. The difference is that citizens of a country accept the right of the police officer to give orders, who consequently has 'authority', while they obey the person with the gun only through fear, who consequently has 'power'.

Max Weber, the German political economist, proposed three types of authority: charismatic, traditional and legal rational. The first is based upon some special characteristic, such as a great sporting, sexual or personal prowess (for example Adolf Hitler). Traditional authority is based upon custom and practice and often the hereditary principle applies (as in the case of the monarchy). Finally, Weber argues that legal rational authority is associated with the development of the modern state and the associated large bureaucracies (the civil service), who staff its key institutions.

Changes of government are effected by the application of abstract rules and procedures; for example, the authority of a governing party in Britain is based upon it having obtained – usually – a majority of seats in the House of Commons following a general election.

*See also* leadership.

## awkward squad

The leaders of the big four unions (Transport and General Workers' Union, Unison, GMB and Amicus), who coordinated a campaign in the summer of 2004 to 'reclaim the Labour Party' and return it to more traditional values of public ownership, strengthened employment rights and more building of council houses. With organised labour still commanding half of Labour Party conference votes, a united stand by the unions was not something Tony Blair could easily countenance, especially as his party was relying on the unions to donate £20 million over the years 2004–06 to fund election and other expenses.

# B

## backbencher

Name given to MPs who do not hold ministerial office or have a shadow cabinet portfolio. Many such MPs seek greater influence as members and chairs of the 20 or so select committees. Failed, disgraced or politically rejected ministers are often consigned to the backbenches, where they may seek rehabilitation or merely seethe with rebellious frustration.

## backwoodsman

Name given to a member (usually hereditary) of the House of Lords who took little active part in the day-to-day proceedings of the upper chamber but who turned up to vote on key issues for the Conservative Party. (Many defenders of the hereditary principle nonetheless used to argue that the Lords acted as a safeguard of the constitution and was above party politics.) The abolition in 1999 of the right to sit of all but 92 hereditary peers means that the term 'backwoodsman' is now essentially a historical one.

## Bains report, 1972

Report that attempted to bring streamlined corporate management to the over-complex world of local government committees. The idea of this approach, borrowed from the business world, was to weaken the heads of departments in favour of a collective approach. This centred on a form of local government 'cabinet', to be called the policy and resources committee, which coordinated council policies and priorities; there would also be a chief executive to head a chief officer's management team. Over time a lot of Bains' recommendations were adopted by many local authorities.

## balance of payments

The gap between the overall value of the country's imports and exports. During the 1960s this measure of the economy's performance was closely scrutinised and a bad set of figures, shortly before polling day, was believed to have damaged Labour's election hopes in 1970. However, it receded in importance during subsequent decades as other, more potent indexes superseded it, such as inflation, interest rates, the growth in gross domestic product and the money supply. Nonetheless, in early 2001 concern was expressed by economic commentators that the balance of payments was beginning to widen excessively, especially that relating to the manufacturing sector, which fell into recession during that year, and it reached record levels by 2004. However, trade in 'invisibles' – investment income, fees for financial services and so forth – usually serves to lessen the gap.

## Balfour declaration, 1917

Important early statement on the formation of a Jewish state. Arthur Balfour, when foreign secretary, wrote to the Zionist leader Lord Rothschild in November 1917 stating his support for the establishment of a Jewish 'national home' in Palestine. He included the proviso, however, that non-Jewish people's civil and political rights should not be prejudiced. These terms were embodied in the League of Nations' 'mandate' for Palestine, which Britain undertook. Some saw the move as an attempt to win support from American Jews as part of Allied attempts to bring the USA closer to the anti-German effort in the First World War. The declaration was crucial in making Palestine the focus of Jewish resettlement during the interwar years and subsequently.

## ballot

An election in which secret votes are cast for two or more candidates. The ballot box is the box into which votes are placed before counting. Ballot rigging is the attempt to interfere with the voting process by fraudulent means. The Ballot Act 1872 introduced measures to counter corruption and intimidation; one of the most important of these measures was the requirement that voting was to take place in secret.

*See also* Reform Act; voting behaviour.

## Bank of England

www.bankofengland.co.uk

Britain's central bank. Incorporated by statute in 1694 to provide finance for William III's French wars, the Bank of England was forbidden to lend money to the government without parliamentary approval, but was given the right to issue notes against the security of its loan to the government. It became the principal banker to government departments when it took over the administration of the national debt in 1750. In 1833 its notes became legal tender and it assumed a monopoly over the issue of English bank notes in 1844. From 1928 the Bank was no longer obliged to redeem bank notes in the form of gold coin. The Bank was nationalised in 1946, since when it has acted as an agent of and advisor to government financial policies. Chancellor Nigel Lawson wanted to set the Bank free of government controls and allow it to set interest rates to control inflation, but Margaret Thatcher believed this would be 'abdicating responsibility'. When Gordon Brown became chancellor in 1997 he did give the Bank autonomy to set interest rates. A team of professional economists in the Monetary Policy Committee is now responsible for interest rates, which it must set to meet an inflation target stipulated by government; minutes of its monthly meetings are made public. However, Brown also stripped the Bank of certain of its regulatory powers over financial institutions.

*See also* Monetary Policy Committee.

## Barnett formula

Formula devised by Joel Barnett, chief secretary to the Treasury under James Callaghan, for distributing central government funds to Scotland and Wales. The aim of the formula was to allow for the fact that both countries had lower incomes per head than England. So for every £85 by which public expenditure on England rose, it would rise by £10 in Scotland and £5 in Wales. Despite the fact that gross domestic product per capita has risen in these areas to not much less than England's, the Barnett formula still provides the basis for financial distribution, and spending per head still exceeds England's by 23 per cent in Scotland and 16 per cent in Wales.

## Battle of the Boyne

Battle fought on 12 July 1690 that was decisive in the aftermath of the Glorious Revolution, 1688–89. The problem of Northern Ireland has its roots deep in history, the Battle of the Boyne being one of the more notable dates in the calendar of sectarianism. The Battle is still celebrated on 12 July in Northern Ireland by Protestants as symbolic of the crushing of the Irish Catholics. In the battle, the army of the Protestant William III (William of Orange) crossed the River Boyne near Drogheda to outflank and defeat the army of the exiled James II. James thereafter fled to France and resistance in the rest of Ireland soon crumbled.

*See also* Orange Order.

## BBC

*See* British Broadcasting Corporation.

## beacon (authorities, schools, etc.)

Adjective used by New Labour to describe outstanding local authorities and schools which have demonstrated excellence in the provision of public services. Such bodies usually receive additional resources and increased autonomy from central government control.

## *Belgrano*

*See General Belgrano*.

## best value

New Labour's approach to local government finance and service provision. Enacted in the Local Government Act 1999, best value replaced the Conservative policy of compulsory competitive tendering (CCT). Its advocates claim that, unlike CCT's reliance on the operation of crude free market forces in local government services, best value provides a locally based set of priorities which more properly meet local needs. In particular, it has the following four elements: service targets based on the Thatcherite three 'E's (economy, efficiency and effectiveness); annual plans which take into account past performance and future targets; new external audit and inspection mechanisms; procedures for public consultation.

*See also* compulsory competitive tendering; market testing.

## Beveridge report, 1942

The *Report on Social Insurance and Allied Services*. This historic work by William Beveridge established the basis for Labour's welfare state legislation after the Second World War. It identified five 'giants' to be slain: illness, ignorance, disease, squalor and want. It proposed a scheme of social security together with a national health service, family allowances and a policy of full employment.

## bicameral system

A two-chamber parliament. Britain has an unbalanced bicameral legislative system, in that the House of Commons (the lower chamber) is much more powerful than the House of Lords (the upper chamber). British politicians tend to believe the second chamber is useful and merely needs to be reformed. The US Congress provides the contrasting example of a balanced bicameralism, where the House of Representatives and Senate play an equal part in the legislative process.

## bill
Name given to a legislative proposal before it is passed through its stages in parliament and receives the royal assent, after which it becomes law.

*See also* act of parliament; hybrid bill; money bill; private bill; public bill.

## Bill of Rights, 1689
One of the most important documents of the British constitution. It resulted from the Glorious Revolution 1688–89, when William III and Mary II were installed as monarchs to take the place of James II. It is a statute limiting the power of the sovereign but was called a bill as it was originally passed by a convention. It was only after that convention had been converted into the first parliament of William and Mary that it was possible to enact it as a statute but it has remained ever since 'the Bill of Rights'.

It limited the authority of monarchs so that they could not rule without the consent of parliament. It also established free and regular elections to parliament as well as freedom of speech for those speaking in parliament. The consent of parliament was required for any changes in taxation. The Bill also forbade the maintenance of a standing army in peacetime without parliament's consent. The Bill of Rights is often described as the nearest thing to the written constitution which Britain (famously) does not have.

Constitutional reformers believe Britain's dependence on common law as a substitute for a modern bill of rights is insufficient in a time when the power of government has increased to the extent where, according to many critics, it now represents a serious threat to civil liberties. Proponents of reform suggest that basic rights should be entrenched in such a way that no government with a parliamentary majority can remove them. The Labour government of 1997 incorporated the European Convention on Human Rights into British law in 1998, and thus provided the citizen with an easier form of redress of grievance against the state than was previously the case. The entrenchment provided, in the eyes of some experts, another written element of the uncodified British constitution.

## bipartisanship
Consensus within two-party politics. British party politics is based on the principle of conflict between opposing 'camps' of supporters; however, on some issues political differences give way to a united or 'bipartisan' approach. For example, on Northern Ireland the major parties tend to respect a consensus regarding policy, and on foreign affairs, too, there is a general (though by no means invariable) tendency to ignore party differences, especially when ministers are travelling abroad.

## Birmingham Six
Infamous instance of a miscarriage of justice, in which six suspected IRA terrorists were tried at Lancaster Castle and convicted in 1974 of placing a bomb in a Birmingham pub. After a long campaign, led by MP Chris Mullin and journalist Paul Foot, their convictions were found to be unsafe and were quashed by the Court of Appeal in 1991. The behaviour of the police in helping to obtain the original flawed convictions was roundly criticised.

*See also* Guildford Four.

## bishop (Anglican)
The two Anglican archbishops of Canterbury and York sit in the House of Lords together with the 24 senior bishops of the Church of England, making up the 'lords spiritual' in that chamber. They tend to confine themselves to ethical and moral issues and generally refrain from party political debate.

## Black report, 1980
Report on inequalities in health published in April 1980. It was deliberately given a low profile by the then Thatcher Conservative government, which viewed with suspicion its emphasis on the social

causes of ill-health. Inevitably this exercise in 'under-promotion' backfired and the findings achieved wide publicity. They were that the lower down the social scale one is: the less likely one is to derive sufficient benefit from the National Health Service; the less healthy one is likely to be; the less likely one is to survive into old age; the more likely one's children are to suffer injury, sickness and death. Most disturbing was the conclusion that this effect begins in the womb: twice as many babies born to mothers in social class 5 (working class) were found to die compared with those born in social class 1 (professional class). The inquiry which led to the report was chaired by Sir Douglas Black.

### Black Rod (Gentleman Usher of the)

Officer of the House of Lords. The post dates back to 1350. His duties include the maintenance of order in the Lords as well as security, and he also has some respon-sibility for ceremonial events. He is known chiefly for his annual duty of summoning the Commons to the Lords to hear the queen's speech. On this occasion he knocks three times on the door of the Commons with his ebony staff of office, which is topped with a gold lion's head. After his first knock the door is slammed in his face, which symbolises the Commons' right to be free from interference. In March 2002, in the wake of the Queen Mother's funeral, it was alleged by a number of publica-tions – principally the *Spectator* – that the holder of the post, Sir Michael Willcocks (a former UK representative to NATO), was approached by a member of the staff at Number 10 seeking to enhance the role to be played by Tony Blair in the funeral ceremonies. Number 10 complained to the Press Complaints Commission but in June dropped the matter, claiming it had been 'resolved', although Boris Johnson MP, editor of the *Spectator*, described this as a 'humiliating climb-down'.

### black section

Special unit of the Labour Party for black members. Calls for special representation

in the Labour Party for members of ethnic minorities surfaced at the annual confer-ences in 1983, 1984 and 1985. This was in response to the low levels of participation in the party, which resulted in the election of only one black candidate in the 1983 general election. However, most members of the parliamentary party opposed the idea, as did the Labour leader, Neil Kinnock. Ironically, Diane Abbott, a black Oxford-educated woman, who was one of the most enthusiastic supporters of the idea, defeated the sitting MP Ernie Roberts in the stand-ard selection procedure for the safe seat of Hackney and Stoke Newington.

### Black Wednesday

Wednesday 16 September 1992. On that day, international speculators, most notably George Soros, began to sell the pound relentlessly on the foreign exchange markets. Despite the Bank of England raising interest rates up to 15 per cent and buying sterling massively in attempts to maintain the value of sterling within the European Exchange Rate Mechanism (ERM), chancellor Norman Lamont was forced to take the pound out of the ERM. This was a huge reverse, as membership of the ERM was then the foundation of prime minister John Major's economic policy. Leaving the ERM effect-ively devalued the pound by 20 per cent. After this debacle, a 'black hole' appeared in the government's macroeconomic policy and serious damage was done to the reputation of the Conservative Party as a competent manager of the nation's finances. Major was unsure if he could continue in government after such a reverse but did so, although this event, along with splits over Europe, marked the start of a period of terminal decline of the Conservative government – the party's position in the polls never recovered after this economic policy disaster. The sharp devaluation, however, helped the economy to begin a slow recovery.

### Blitz

Short for *Blitzkrieg* (lightning war). This was the all-out bombing attack on London from autumn 1940 to spring 1941. It is calculated 40,000 civilians were killed during this period plus 46,000 injured and 1 million homes destroyed or damaged. As well as London other cities were attacked including Coventry, Liverpool, Southampton and Birmingham.

### block grant
The name given to central government funding of local government services. Originally such funding was specific to each local authority service, but after the Second World War they were brought together into a single rate support grant or block grant, which the local authority could spend according to its needs. These grants were replaced by the more tightly controlled revenue support grant in 1980.

*See also* local government finance; rate support grant.

### block vote
The casting of a large number of votes by a single delegate at a conference. At the Labour Party annual conference, trade union leaders once cast the votes of all members who paid a political levy, itself a somewhat negotiable figure for some large unions. This meant, in practice, that the four or five of the largest unions were able to determine the outcome of important policy debates. Many both inside and outside the party were uneasy about this lack of democracy for individual party members; moreover, it provided Conservative opponents with easy ammunition. Therefore, at the 1993 party conference, John Smith, as party leader, carried the proposal to introduce one member one vote (OMOV), accompanied by a reduction of the union vote from 70 per cent to 50 per cent of those cast. Tony Blair was the first Labour leader to be elected on the principle of OMOV.

### Bloody Sunday
Sunday 30 January 1972. On that day, a banned civil rights demonstration in Londonderry (or 'Derry' to those from a Catholic or republican tradition) was fired upon by British soldiers. As a result 13

civilians were killed and 17 wounded, creating a dramatically symbolic injustice which still causes immense ill-feeling against the British. It provoked intense sectarian violence and consequently direct rule was imposed on Northern Ireland in March 1972. The Widgery report (April 1972) into the tragedy cleared the British soldiers of wrong-doing but the issue would not go away and from 2000 the long-running Saville inquiry expended huge efforts to find the truth. In 2002 an influential film, *Bloody Sunday*, pointed the finger of blame at the military commanders on the spot.

*See also* Saville inquiry.

### Blundell–Gosschalk classification
System to classify the political persuasions of members of the public. In December 1997 a report by the Institute of Economic Affairs resulting from a collaboration between pollsters MORI and authors Blundell and Gosschalk offered a new classification of political positions. The following groups were identified (with percentages of respondents indicated):
1   conservative (pro free market but with ethical controls), 36 per cent;
2   libertarian (maximum personal freedom), 19 per cent;
3   socialist (big government with controls on market), 18 per cent;
4   authoritarian (anti-personal/anti-economic freedom), 13 per cent
5   centrist (some economic and social freedom), 15 per cent.
*See also* left–right continuum; third way.

### boom and bust
A phrase used to describe the tendency of the British economy to experience a cycle of rapid inflationary growth, often triggered by governments in advance of an election (for example Nigel Lawson's 1986 budget), followed by a recession, after interest rates have been increased to bring inflation under control, as occurred under the chancellorship of Norman Lamont in the early 1990s. Gordon Brown, New Labour's first chancellor, claimed he was breaking out

of this tendency by letting the Monetary Policy Committee of the Bank of England set interest rates on purely economic criteria. Evidence in 2001, an election year, suggested that this policy had been successful, albeit with a temporary rise in rates to 7.5 per cent in 1998. However, rates declined subsequently and Labour was able to claim it had halved mortgage rates since 1997. During the 2001 general election campaign Labour made great play of how the economy had remained stable under its stewardship. Interest rates remained low after 2001 but began to rise in 2004 in an attempt to curb the housing boom which such rates had initiated.

*See also* political business cycle.

## borough
Term originating from the Saxon *burh*, meaning settlement, but in British history a town awarded a charter endowing it with certain legal privileges. In the Middle Ages it denoted a town that elected a member of parliament. In the late 19th century boroughs became important units of local government and were run by elected councils. In 1972 boroughs outside Greater London were abolished, although the status may still be conferred by royal charter upon a district.

## Boundary Commission
www.statistics.gov.uk/pbc
(Boundary Commission for England)
www.bcomm-scotland.gov.uk
(Boundary Commission for Scotland)
www.boundarycommission.org.uk
(Boundary Commission for Northern Ireland)
www.bcomm-wales.gov.uk
(Boundary Commission for Wales)
A body that draws up constituency boundaries and revises them regularly (at least every 15 years). There are separate Commissions for England, Wales, Scotland and Northern Ireland. The Commissions aim to produce constituencies of roughly equal size – about 65,000 voters, which follow existing county and natural boundaries as far as possible. Three of the four

Commissions are based in London and the Scottish one is based in Edinburgh. They also drew up the boundaries for the European elections of June 1999, a task made more complex by the need to create larger constituencies for the regional list system introduced in that year. Most recent revisions of constituency boundaries have tended to reflect the move of people from the inner-city areas out to the suburbs and to the disadvantage of the Labour Party, as its vote tended to be less in suburban areas than the Conservatives' vote. The number of MPs was increased from 651 to 659 for the 1997 general election. The Commissions are chaired formally by the speaker of the House of Commons, although in practice by a High Court judge, who acts as deputy chair. The two other members of the English Boundary Commission are nominated by the home secretary and the environment secretary. On 6 February 2002 the Scottish Boundary Commission announced that Scottish seats would be reduced from 72 to 59 in the wake of devolution, which had given Scotland authority over its domestic affairs and thus reduced the need for Westminster representation. The changes affected Labour seats for the most part and initiated a rush among Scottish Labour MPs for new seats in the redrawn political map of their country.

*See also* Boundary Committee for England.

## Boundary Committee for England
www.lgce.gov.uk
Successor to the Boundary Commission for Local Government. This body regularly reviews ward boundaries under the Political Parties, Elections and Referendums Act 2000. Boundaries are drawn up by an official of the Committee after consultation with interested parties, who may include political parties, community groups, the local authority and individuals. There are two rounds of consultation but no public inquiry: the first round produces a draft plan after consultation; the second round involves further consultation on the draft

POLITICS

before decisions are made and boundaries are set for the next 10–15 years.

**bourgeoisie**
Name given by Karl Marx to the property-owning creators of capitalism who extracted surplus labour value from workers and in so doing 'exploited' members of this class. Those adopting the concept have reckoned it to comprise the middle or especially upper middle classes – basically those running all the economic and political institutions of the state and almost always voting Conservative. The 'petit bourgeois' were, accordingly, the small shopkeepers and those who aspired to full membership of the upper middle classes. The term was never popular with middle-of-the-road Labour MPs and was generally used only by those on the Marxist left.
*See also* class.

**bovine spongiform encephalopathy (BSE)**
'Mad cow disease'. An outbreak of bovine spongiform encephalopathy (BSE) occurred in Britain during the late 1980s. Its danger lay in the ability of the incredibly resistant infecting agent to transfer from cows to humans, when it would take the form of the terminal Creutzfeldt–Jakob disease (CJD). The first officially documented case of BSE was in 1986 but it was not until 1996 that it was confirmed that BSE could cause CJD. The disease is caused by giving cows feed containing the spine and brain of infected animals, thought to have originally been sheep with scrapie. Initially the government was reassuring but when the scale and severity of the problem became clear it introduced in 1989: a policy of slaughtering all potentially infected animals, numbered in millions (and for which farmers received only 50 per cent compensation); restrictions on the composition of animal feed; and measures to protect people from eating contaminated meat. Despite costing a total of £4 billion, this initially failed to reassure Britain's trading partners, many of which, especially in the European Union (EU), banned British beef. Slowly

confidence was renewed and the EU bans were lifted in November 1998 but, given the ignorance over the incubation period for the disease, the full extent of the problem was still unclear, even when the ban was lifted. In July 2000 a report indicated that British beef exports, especially to France, were only a fraction of what they were before the crisis began. In October 2000, a report accused former Conservative ministers of not acting with sufficient speed or candour on the issue.

**Bow Group**
www.bowgroup.org
A centre-right think tank formed in 1951 and with close links to the Conservative Party. The Group urges the acceptance of the postwar consensus on the welfare state and a mixed economy. It convenes a number of policy groups and publishes the journal *Crossbow*. It boasted a membership of 1,000 in the mid-1990s.

**boycott**
A form of direct action by people who wish to protest by withdrawing support from a product, service or gathering. For example, in the 1970s many students boycotted Barclays Bank because of its investments in apartheid South Africa; less successfully, in August 2000, an action group opposed to the high levels of excise duty on petrol organised a boycott of filling stations.

**Bradford**
*See* Ouseley report.

**Brighton bomb, 1984**
The IRA bombing of the Grand Hotel, Brighton, in 1984, during the Conservative Party conference. Patrick Magee, an IRA member, stayed in the hotel a month before the conference and concealed a time bomb weighing 20–30 pounds in a bathroom wall. It exploded at 2.45 a.m. on 12 October 1984, killing five (including Sir Anthony Berry, MP for Enfield Southgate) and injuring 34. Margaret Thatcher and her husband narrowly missed being affected by the blast, as did most of her cabinet, but Norman Tebbit was injured and his

wife paralysed. Magee was sentenced to
eight life sentences, was transferred to the
Maze Prison in 1994 and then released
under the Good Friday Agreement in 1999
after serving only a third of his sentence.
Michael Howard, former home secretary,
called it a 'disgrace'; Tony Blair said it was
'very hard to stomach' but the manager of
the Grand Hotel said he would forgive and
forget and Magee would be welcome to stay
as a paying guest.

## British Broadcasting Corporation (BBC)

Established by royal charter in 1927 out
of a company set up in 1922 by a group
of radio manufacturers. It was eventually
granted a monopoly over radio broadcasting in Britain and became financed through
an annual licence fee. Another landmark in
the Corporation's history arrived in 1936,
when the world's first television service
was introduced, in the London area. Its
first director general was John (later Lord)
Reith, a high-minded moralist who wanted
the Corporation to 'inform, educate and
entertain', a formula which was later to
become known as the 'public service' tradition in broadcasting. During the 1960s
the BBC shed its grey image and began to
express some of the energy and rebellion
characteristic of that decade, most famously
perhaps in the form of the late Saturday
night programme *That Was the Week That
Was*, which transfixed the country for a
while before it was discontinued for stretch-
ing the moral and censorship boundaries.

The BBC is run by a board of governors
with a chair appointed by the government.
It is often accused by politicians of media
bias in the reporting of political issues,
especially those affecting the government;
Winston Churchill thought it was full of
communists, Margaret Thatcher that it
contained 1960s liberals and advocates of
permissiveness. Labour ridiculed such accusations but echoed them when in power,
especially with criticism of the *Today* programme. Recently politicians have accused
the Corporation of 'dumbing down' in an
attempt to attract audiences.

## British constitution

According to Philip Norton – one of
the foremost experts on this subject – a
constitution is a set of rules which defines
the 'composition and powers of organs of
the state and regulates the relations of the
various state organs to one another and
those of the state organs to the private
citizen'. Some constitutions are very long
and include exhortations as to how citizens
should behave.

The British constitution is famously unwritten. This is not strictly correct, in that
large parts of it comprise written statutes. It
is uncodified but has written and unwritten
elements. There are four of these:

1 *Common law*. This is made up of those
   legal principles which have evolved since
   Saxon times regarding the powers of the
   monarch and parliament.
2 *Conventions*. These are not legally binding
   laws but are rules of behaviour which are
   considered binding by those in authority.
3 *Works of authority*. There are a number
   of such works (for example those by A.
   V. Dicey), which are extremely influential
   in the interpretation of the constitution.
4 *Statute law*. This is the most authoritative
   element of the constitution as a direct
   result of the doctrine of the sovereignty of
   parliament. The English Bill of Rights
   in 1689 defined the powers of parliament
   and the crown such that parliament had
   the sole source of authority or power to
   make or alter any law. The corollary of
   this is that parliament cannot bind itself
   but can rescind any law that it passes. In
   practice, given the fading of royal power
   at the end of the 17th century, 'sovereign
   power' passed to the executive (i.e. the
   government of the day).

There is no special procedure whereby
the constitution is amended – the standard legislative stages that are required for
any law apply also to constitutional ones.
Consequently all the following amendments
were passed in the normal way:

1 In 1972 Britain joined the European
   Economic Community and thereby
   made its laws subject to the superior law
   of that organisation.

POLITICS

2 The European Convention on Human Rights was embodied in British law in 1998 and came into effect on 2 October 2000. This provides in effect the kind of bill of rights for which reformers have long argued.

3 After 1997 separate assemblies were established for Wales and Scotland and later a new elected authority for Greater London plus an elected mayor.

4 In 2000 all but 92 of the hereditary members of the House of Lords were expelled from the legislature.

## British Gas

www.house.co.uk

Formerly the British Gas Board and a nationalised industry since the Second World War. It became a candidate for privatisation by Margaret Thatcher. Its chair, Sir Dennis Rooke, fought the transition but the Thatcher government had too much political will. The privatisation raised £7.3 billion in 1987. The reputation of the company was damaged by the huge personal salary received by its chair, Cedric Brown, whose name was given to a live pig mascot used by protestors who demonstrated against the alleged greed of the chair and company. Centrica is now the parent company of British Gas.

## British Medical Association

www.bma.org.uk

The professional body for over 100,000 doctors in Britain. It has some 30 com-mittees representing the various 'crafts' or clinical specialties and is run by a 57-strong elected council, which oper-ates via a finance and general purposes committee and an executive committee. The Association meets annually to debate motions concerned with professional mat-ters like conditions of work and pay but also ethical matters like genetic engineering and euthanasia. After the war it fought hard to resist the establishment of the National Health Service but has become its ardent supporter in subsequent decades.

*See also* General Medical Council.

## British National Party

www.bnp.org.uk

Either of two postwar far-right parties. The first was formed in 1960 under the leadership of Colin Jordan. The grouping had anti-Semitism and anti-immigration as basic tenets. By 1967 there were 1,000 members but, in common with left-wing political fringe groups, the British National Party (BNP) was rife with personality feuds, especially between Jordan, John Tyndall and Martin Webster.

The second BNP formed out of a then declining National Front in 1982. It displayed a more fanatical approach, and was rumoured to have contacts with neo-Nazi groups abroad. John Tyndall was its autocratic leader, until he was challenged and succeeded by Nick Griffin in 1999.

Halting immigration by non-white people has always been central to the beliefs of the BNP and often disguises other kinds of underlying racialism, like anti-Semitism and the idea of a 'Zionist conspiracy'. The party made little headway in electoral terms; in 1997 its 57 candidates mustered less than 2 per cent of the vote in all constituencies in which they stood. However, a major revival occurred in 2001, when it cleverly exploited racial tension in Oldham. Here riots occurred during the May/June general election campaign, partly stirred by incoming right-wing activ-ists. In the election Nick Griffin stood in Oldham West and mustered 6,552 votes (16 per cent). In the neighbouring Oldham East constituency the BNP candidate, Michael Treacy, received 5,091 votes (11 per cent) and in Burnley the BNP also did well, polling over 4,000 votes (over 11 per cent). At an average of 3.9 per cent of the vote where candidates stood, 2001 saw the best ever performance by the party in general elections and was a worrying result for those who value toleration and a liberal political culture. To put the result in context, though, right-wing parties did negligibly compared with similar parties in Austria, Italy and France. Nick Griffin, a Cambridge graduate, aimed to attract the 'neglected and oppressed white working class', possibly former Conservative voters. One of the slogans of the party was 'Defend Rights for Whites'. It subsequently won council seats in Burnley and, in January 2003, a 'sink' estate close to Halifax. For the May 2003 local elections the party fielded 221 candidates. It managed to win eight seats in Burnley, thereby becoming the second largest party on the council, and five others nationwide, including in Stoke-on-Trent.

See also National Front.

## British Rail
See Network Rail.

## British Telecom (BT)
www.bt.com
Originally part of the General Post Office (GPO), but came into being after an act separated the postal side of the GPO from the telephone operation. The bill to privatise BT lapsed in 1983 at the end of the parliament but Margaret Thatcher reintroduced it in changed form after the election and it became law in April 1984. BT was thus the first big privatisation undertaken by the Conservatives after 1979. The outcome of the process was somewhat different to the intended aim of reintroducing competition.

The flotation on the stock market produced £4 billion but within two years the value of its shares had doubled and most of the individual shareholders had sold their stock at a profit. BT shares ultimately reached around £15 each but during 2000, in common with other information technology stocks, they crashed to one-third of that figure, the principal reason being the high level of debt the company had incurred in trying to invest in new technologies. Chairman Sir Ian Vallance was forced to retire and a former chairman of the BBC, Sir Christopher Bland, took his place.

## British Union of Fascists
Party founded in 1932 by Oswald Mosley. Its provenance lay in Mosley's attempts to inject dynamism into British socialism after his own Labour government post and his

brief flirtation with the 'New Party' failed. It sought to offer a mixture of fascism and racism to the British voter, particularly anti-Semitism. It organised the paramilitary Blackshirts, who participated in violent street demonstrations in the East End of London. The Public Order Act 1936 placed legal limits on its activities and it was banned in 1940, when Mosley was imprisoned. In retrospect the party was probably merely a vehicle for Mosley, who was seeking to emulate continental fascist leaders and to achieve political power. When the British voter proved unmoved, the attempt unravelled.

## Broadcasting Act 1990
Act that introduced a number of changes to the regulation of independent broadcasting in Britain. Primarily it was concerned with opening up the 'cosy' world of commercial franchises to the stiff wind of market forces which, according to Margaret Thatcher, one of the act's chief supporters, increase choice and quality. Under the act the Independent Broadcasting Authority was replaced by the Independent Television Commission (which included cable in its jurisdiction) and the Radio Authority; these bodies awarded television licences to bidders – usually to the highest bidders but with some quality controls. Channel 5 was set up, along with three national commercial radio stations and new local radio stations. Since the act, according to many critics, there has been an increased concentration of ownership in fewer hands, and television companies fight to attract audiences, and thus advertisers, by offering mass market and in some cases down-market programming. This in turn led to claims that, despite the act's intentions, audiences for independent television, and thus by extension audiences for the BBC, which must compete to justify the licence fee, have now been offered more of the same, and less real choice. The act was superseded in some respects by the creation of Ofcom in 2003.

See also Office of Communications (Ofcom).

## Bruges Group

www.brugesgroup.com
Anti-European group of Conservative
MPs set up in 1989 after the speech
made by Margaret Thatcher in that city
in September 1988 in which she outlined
her doubts about European integration.
Thatcher was its original president and it
attracted much support from Eurosceptics
in the early and mid-1990s.

## Bruges speech, September 1988

A speech made to the College of Europe by
Margaret Thatcher in which she expressed
her anger and frustration at the creeping
encroachments of European integration, as
envisaged (especially) by Jacques Delors,
president of the European Commission.
The speech was heavily modified by
Foreign Office senior officials to make it
less offensive to partner countries. It contained the key sentence which summed up
Thatcher's objections to the European idea:
'We have not rolled back the frontiers of the
state in Britain only to see them re-imposed
at a European level with a European
super-state exercising a new dominance
from Brussels'. The speech also invoked the
'Atlantic Community – our noblest inheritance and our greatest strength'.

## BSE

*See* bovine spongiform encephalopathy.

## budget

The most well known part of the budgetary process, by which spending plans of
government departments and taxation
are adjusted each year. The budget is an
announcement of the result of this process
and is presented to the House of Commons
each March or April. Originally it was a
statement of how revenue was to be raised
but now is a major economic instrument
and is much analysed, although in recent
years the chancellor's autumn statement
has reduced the importance of the spring
announcements. It is prepared with great
secrecy and the Commons is supposed to
be the first to hear its contents but in recent
years the government has leaked proposals
as a way of trailing them and gauging
public reaction. The chancellor's statement – during which he sometimes sips,
by tradition, from a glass of whisky and
water – lasts about an hour or more and
is followed by an extempore comment by
the leader of the opposition. The government's taxation proposals usually come into
effect immediately, although the legislative
authority comes only with the passing of
the subsequent Finance Act, usually in the
early summer. Some measures are delayed
by up to a year or more.

## Bulger case

In 1993 a two-year-old boy from Liverpool
was tortured and killed by two 10-year-
olds, Robert Thompson and Jon Venables.
The crime shocked the nation and helped
shift the emphasis in penal policy further
to the right. Michael Howard, the home
secretary, declared they should serve a
minimum of 15 years but the European
Court of Human Rights over-ruled this
decision and the boys were released on
parole after serving eight and a half years.
The mother of James Bulger was outraged
and many in her native city supported her
attempts to rescind the Parole Board's
decision. Labour's home secretary David
Blunkett agreed with the Parole Board's
decision. The two boys have been given
new identities and locations, although
many fear they will be hunted down and
harmed by vigilantes sympathetic to the
Bulger family.

## bureaucracy

A term (first used in 1818) used to refer
collectively to the civil servants who assist
and advise ministers. It is often used in a
pejorative sense to suggest officials are inefficient. The Duke of Wellington captured
this sense when he referred to officials as
'malevolent quill drivers'. The German
sociologist Max Weber saw bureaucracy as
a characteristic of modern society, based
on rational rules, as opposed to his other
identified sources of legitimacy – tradition
or charisma.
*See also* civil service.

POLITICS

## Business for Sterling

www.bfors.com

A group, formed out of several smaller ones, that opposes Britain's adoption of the euro. It was set up in June 1998, in the House of Lords. Its aim is to attract funds and support from businesses that may have been repelled by some of the more radical Eurosceptics in the past. Headed by ex Labour minister turned crossbencher Lord (Richard) Marsh, it also has the support of the electronics magnate Sir Stanley Kalms, the retired chairman of the Dixons group. Other corporate supporters include McAlpine, Matheson, Forte and Great Universal Stores, as well as Paul Sykes, the maverick millionaire who funded anti-European MPs in the 1997 election. The Institute of Directors also favours the anti-euro camp, as well as the Federation of Small Businesses. The *Sun* newspaper supports the 'anti' camp in accordance with the views of its owner, Rupert Murdoch.

## Butler report, 2004

*The Review of Intelligence on Weapons of Mass Destruction*, resulting from the Butler inquiry. In the wake of the Hutton inquiry and report into the death of David Kelly, Tony Blair opposed any formal inquiry into the much criticised intelligence upon which the decision to invade Iraq in 2003 was made. He changed his mind, however, after US president George Bush set up such an investigation in early February 2004. Blair chose former cabinet secretary Lord Robin Butler as the chair of the inquiry team; many immediately criticised the choice of such an impeccably establishment (though undeniably able) figure. Similar criticisms were made of the other members of the inquiry team: Ann Taylor, former Labour chief whip; Lord Inge, former chief of the defence staff; Sir John Chilcott, former permanent secretary to the Northern Ireland Office; and Michael Mates, former Conservative junior minister and before that an army officer. The Liberal Democrats refused to serve in the team, as they claimed its terms of reference were too narrow and should have addressed all the possible reasons for going to war. The Conservatives also withdrew but Mates insisted that he remain a member.

Lord Butler's eagerly awaited report was couched in polite and calm language but contained some substantial criticisms of the intelligence services, the infamous September 2002 dossier and Blair's informal style of decision making. Its key findings were as follows:

1 Intelligence on Iraq was thin and unreliable; the September dossier nevertheless was based upon it.
2 The claim that Saddam could attack the British forces within 45 minutes was wrong and only included because of 'its eye-catching character'.
3 The separation between intelligence and policy had not been maintained.
4 The dossier and the intelligence were laid out side by side, showing how the qualifiers and caveats were removed in a dossier which rang with certainties.
5 The prime minister's style of government was based on unminuted oral briefings and not on pre-circulated papers.
6 The shift in policy on Iraq followed policy in Washington.

However, no single person was identified as responsible:

1 The shortcomings of the dossier were attributed to collective failures, a 'group think' which reflected a prevailing view that Saddam had stockpiles of weapons of mass destruction.
2 John Scarlett, chair of the Joint Intelligence Committee (JIC), had been too close to the policy process. He was not criticised but rather praised and his appointment to head MI6 defended. However, it was recommended that in future chairs of the JIC should not be vulnerable to career pressure and should preferably be in their final post.
3 No cabinet member was singled out, nor any of Blair's aides, who had seemed so active in creating the debacle when giving evidence to the Hutton inquiry. Nor was the good faith of any such people questioned.

POLITICS

In the following debate in the House of Commons Blair was able to declare he was responsible for the errors while appearing not to be to blame for them.

> I have been briefed in detail on the intelligence and am satisfied as to its authority. (Blair's foreword to the dossier, 24 September 2002)

> Intelligence on Iraq's weapons of mass destruction and ballistic missiles programmes is sporadic and patchy. (JIC assessment, 15 March 2002)

> I am in no doubt that the threat is serious and current. (Blair's foreword to the dossier)

> Intelligence remains limited and Saddam's own unpredictability complicates matters. (JIC assessment, September 2002)

*See also* Hutton report.

**by-election**
Single-constituency election held when a vacancy arises in the House of Commons through the death or retirement or elevation of the sitting MP to the Lords. If the government is unpopular by-elections can provide a partial snapshot of how the public perceives it. They often also include a number of frivolous candidates attracted by the high media profile such elections command. These tests of public opinion can often give a misleading picture because supporters of a party often use them as an opportunity to chastise a government for unpopular policies; however, many may return to the fold during a general election campaign. Tony Blair's New Labour government began to lose by-elections seriously in the autumn of 2003, when the Liberal Democrats received a massive swing to win Brent East. This was repeated on 15 July 2004, when they won Leicester South with a 21 per cent swing and nearly won Birmingham Hodge Hill with a 27 per cent one. In all three cases the Conservatives came third.

A little-known practice, until 1921, was the convention that cabinet ministers recontest their constituencies upon being appointed. Usually such contests were formalities but Winston Churchill actually lost his Oldham seat (albeit narrowly) in 1908 to William ('Jix') Joynson-Hicks.

**by-law**
*See* delegated legislation.

# C

**cabinet**
The supreme committee of government, chaired by the prime minister. This body originated in the time of Charles II, when he consulted only a few of his over-large Privy Council in his private rooms: his 'cabinet'. As parliament increased its power at the expense of the monarchy, senior ministers became more important and their forum, the cabinet, accordingly grew in importance. Majorities had to be organised in parliament to ensure the flow of taxation to sustain the armed forces. Under Queen Anne the term 'cabinet' became the official title for this committee. With King George I, whose English was very poor, the monarch stopped attending cabinet meetings and the first lord of the Treasury became the intermediary and hence, effectively, the prime minister. Further restrictions of royal power in subsequent centuries delivered effective power to the prime minister and cabinet. The prime minister decides the composition of the cabinet. This usually entails a judicious blend of: ideology (left/right, wet/dry, Europhile/sceptic); administrative experience; regional balance; and gender. The cabinet – usually 20–24 in number – comprises the main departmental ministers – chancellor, home and foreign secretaries, chief whip, lord chancellor and party chair plus a few individuals with non-departmental portfolios, like chancellor of the Duchy of Lancaster, who tend to chair cabinet committees and do the prime

minister's bidding. Lesser departmental ministers stay outside cabinet but may be invited to attend on specific issues.

In theory, the cabinet is the supreme committee of government, coordinating policy, deciding the big policy questions and resolving disputes between departments. Doubtless all these functions are performed in the present day but the nature of cabinet government has undeniably changed. Some commentators have discerned a process whereby the cabinet has lost real power to its committees and to the prime minister, and have concluded that we now have 'prime ministerial' or 'quasi-presidential' government. There is much to support this view. However, opponents argue that this depends on the personal style of individual premiers; in the case of the most powerful post-war example, Margaret Thatcher, her resignation followed a virtual vote of no confidence by members of her own cabinet. Premiers have varied according to how they have run cabinets. Winston Churchill used to talk to the cabinet eloquently during the war but it was his deputy, Clement Attlee, who managed to work the cabinet through the agenda during the great man's absences. Most prime ministers listened to colleagues before signalling the taking of collective decisions but Thatcher seemed so concerned to advance her own agenda that she often led the discussion as well as summing up. She also 'fixed' the agreement of small groups in advance, thus tending to reduce the role of cabinet. Tony Blair is somewhat similar in style to Thatcher, preferring small ad hoc meetings outside cabinet with key ministers (especially Gordon Brown), plus advisors (notably Alastair Campbell before his resignation). Some commentators suggest that Blair's full cabinets are as brief as half an hour, when he merely reports decisions made elsewhere. In the wake of the Butler report Peter Hennessy described the Labour cabinet of that time as 'The weakest since the Second World War'.

*See also* cabinet committee; prime minister; Privy Council.

## cabinet committee

Any subcommittee of the cabinet. Because of the volume of work in cabinet, much is delegated to committees. These have the authority of cabinet decisions when their members are in agreement; if they fail to agree, the matter – at least in theory – will go to the full cabinet. The full extent of cabinet committees and their remits used to be kept secret but the veil has been raised in recent years. There are standing committees, which are given a code letter, and ad hoc ones to deal with specific problems (these are not given a code letter but the records are filed as 'miscellaneous'). The prime minister usually chairs the most important ones, on the economy and defence and overseas policy. There were over 400 cabinet committees in the early 1970s but they were halved under James Callaghan and reduced still further, to 135, under Margaret Thatcher (25 standing and 110 ad hoc committees). In July 2001 it was announced that a new overarching Domestic Affairs Committee was to be chaired by deputy prime minister John Prescott. Reporting to it would be nine subcommittees covering domestic issues, including adult basic skills, active communities and families, drugs, equality, fraud, energy, older people and social exclusion. The idea was to innovate and produce coherence across the departments.

## Cabinet Office

www.cabinet-office.gov.uk

Civil service body that coordinates cabinet briefings on matters of highest policy: the security and intelligence services; international meetings; appointments in Whitehall; and honours. It also informs departments of decisions taken and ensures that appropriate action has been taken. It was established by Lloyd George in 1916. It is not merely bureaucratic in its function: as Bernard Donoughue (a prime ministerial advisor and later junior minister) commented, it 'establishes the agenda for policy discussion ... thus shaping the structure, balance and timetable of policy debate'.

The Office operates via six secretariats: Economic; Overseas and Defence; European; Home Affairs; Science and Technology; and Security and Intelligence. The Social Exclusion Unit was set up after 1997 with the cross-departmental task of monitoring the extent of poverty and seeking ways of alleviating its effects. In addition a Policy and Innovation Unit was set up to fight 'departmentalism' and to promote government objectives.

In July 1998 the Office was strengthened further when it absorbed the Office of Public Service and its head was given a wide-ranging brief across Whitehall to ensure policy objectives were achieved. Initially this 'enforcing' job was assumed to be destined for Tony Blair's advisor and favourite, Peter Mandelson, but it surprisingly went in the July 1998 reshuffle to Jack Cunningham instead. Since then the job declined in importance under Mo Mowlam but revived after Blair's victory reshuffle in June 2001, when John Prescott was assigned to it assisted by Lord (Gus) MacDonald ('progress chaser in chief' according to David Walker in the *Guardian*, 18 June 2001), Charles Clarke, junior minister Barbara Roche and Blair's former political secretary (raised to peerage) Sally Morgan. The Future Strategy Unit (FSU) was also set up, headed by Geoff Mulgan and including Lord (John) Birt, formerly director general of the BBC, who was asked by Blair to produce a study on long-term transport policy in January 2002. Most commentators have concluded that, under Blair, the Cabinet Office has developed into a de facto prime minister's department. Some observers, unsurprisingly, have criticised the proliferation of special units and diagnose a lack of coordination.

#### cabinet secretary

Head of the Cabinet Office and head of the civil service. 'The prime minister's permanent secretary' is how Sir Burke Trend described his office to Harold Wilson in 1964 but, as the Labour prime minister observed, he owed an equal loyalty to the cabinet as a whole. The office was founded in 1916 and the first incumbent was Sir Maurice Hankey during the First World War; the job proved so useful it was continued into peacetime and is now the most powerful civil service appointment. The cabinet secretary is in essence the prime minister's principal advisor. However, Sir John Hunt, though he saw himself in this light under both Wilson and James Callaghan, did not have constant access to the prime minister but had to ring the parliamentary private secretary to receive clearance to come through the locked door between the Cabinet Office (on Whitehall) and Number 10. In April 2002 Sir Richard Wilson, the retiring cabinet secretary, told the Commons Public Administration Committee that new incumbents would be interviewed by trained psychologists and a report submitted to the prime minister. Sir Andrew Turnbull, formerly of the Treasury and Margaret Thatcher's private office, was given the job in 2002.

#### Calcutt reports, 1990 and 1993

Reports from an inquiry by Sir David Calcutt, QC, set up following deep concern that the press, and especially the tabloid press, was too intrusive and irresponsible. Calcutt recommended that the industry-dominated Press Council be converted into the Press Complaints Commission, with stronger lay representation. The warning was given that this was the last chance the industry would have for self-regulation. However, the subsequent Calcutt review of the Commission in 1993 recommended a statutory framework to enforce responsibility. Andrew Neill, editor of the *Sunday Times*, complained this would make the press the 'poodle of the establishment'; this received further support from Lord Wakeham, the then chair of the Commission, and the proposals were rejected by government. The tabloids still break the rules of the Commission and self-regulation clearly does not work; however, government control is fraught with problems and, arguably, is not consistent with British political culture.

## Campaign for Nuclear Disarmament (CND)

www.cnduk.org

Anti-nuclear movement formed in 1958 by a number of intellectuals, including Bertrand Russell, Michael Foot and Canon John Collins. Its aim was the unilateral abandonment by Britain of its nuclear weapons. Its annual march from Aldermaston to London, culminating in a Trafalgar Square rally, attracted huge numbers of sympathisers in the 1960s. In 1960 CND effectively captured the Labour Party conference, which passed a unilateralist resolution, but this was reversed the following year when the party adopted a policy of multilateralism (i.e. disarmament via collective negotiations with other nuclear powers). The Partial Test Ban Treaty in 1963 took away some of CND's momentum but it gathered huge support again in the 1980s when NATO decided to site a new generation of nuclear weapons in Europe. Membership rose from 10,000 to 100,000 at the time of the women's protest against cruise missiles at Greenham Common. By the end of the 1990s, however, in the wake of the fall of the communist bloc, the movement was a shadow of its former self.

## Campaign Group

Left-wing Labour group set up in 1982 by 23 Labour MPs. It advocated familiar left-wing themes such as more spending on welfare services and more government control of the economy plus constitutional changes such as the abolition of the House of Lords and the abolition of the royal prerogative by 'proxy' by the prime minister. It eventually attracted 40 members and was very active early on, under the Thatcher Conservative governments, but has kept relatively quiet since. Its decline is yet another sign of New Labour's success in damping down ideological debate within the party.

## campaign strategist

An umbrella term for an advisor, usually an unelected media, marketing and public relations professional, who provides information, analysis and guidance on how a political party should present itself to the electorate. Well known strategists include Tim Bell of Saatchi and Saatchi, Gordon Reece and Christopher Lawson, who were closely associated with the Conservative campaigns of the 1980s, and Philip Gould and Peter Mandelson were key figures in the reconstruction of the Labour Party's image after the 1983 defeat. However, a number of political scientists have argued that the practice of employing campaign strategists who embrace a political marketing perspective can be dated back to the Representation of the People Act 1918, which trebled the electorate to 21 million. For example Sidney Webb, joint author of the Labour Party's 1918 constitution, argued in 1922 that Labour should use 'stratified electioneering', an early form of dividing up the electorate into separate groups which could be targeted by political propaganda. In the 1990s and early 2000s campaign strategists made themselves an indispensable part of the political scene, communicating with key groups in the electorate, which raised questions about a democratic deficit created by their lack of individual accountability to voters. Some more traditional politicians criticise the construction of political strategies on the basis of opinion-consulting techniques; they argue that the role of politicians is to lead public opinion, not merely follow it.

*See also* Campbell, Alastair; Mandelson, Peter; Reece, Gordon.

## campaigning

The concentrated efforts party activists make at election time to persuade people to vote their way and to encourage their supporters to turn out on the day. At the local level campaigns take the form of face-to-face encouragement (canvassing), leafleting and local meetings. The last have become less common as national campaigns have assumed higher prominence and meetings have been changed to all-ticket party rallies along US lines. Access to the national media – especially television – has become critical in modern campaigns and parties do their best to intrude symbolic photo-calls of their leaders into news bulletins. Such images include the leader driving a tank (tough on defence), visiting hospital patients (caring about the National Health Service) or kissing babies (genuinely 'normal and nice' person). Similarly, they seek to win airtime for pithy one-line statements (sound bites). However, some experts point out that campaigns do not always have a large effect: in 1983 and 1987 the Labour Party under Neil Kinnock ran superb campaigns but managed to increase its vote by only 3 and 3.6 per centage points, respectively.

**candidate for parliamentary election**
Person standing for election as a member of parliament. To be eligible to stand for parliament a prospective candidate has to be a British citizen, a resident citizen of another Commonwealth country or of the Irish Republic, and be aged 21 or over. Candidates must be nominated by 10 voters and pay a deposit of £500, which is forfeited if less than 5 per cent of the vote is polled. In order to succeed, it is generally necessary to be nominated by a political party, and preferably one which has a chance of attracting a substantial number of votes, as the British electoral system (first past the post) does not favour independents or small parties with thin support. Those not allowed to stand include: members of the House of Lords who remain peers, bankrupts, ordained priests (though not nonconformist or non-Christian priests), holders of certain public offices, those suffering from severe mental illness and those serving prison sentences.

There were 3,000 candidates in the 1992 election, nearly all affiliated to political parties. However, in 1997 Martin Bell, an independent, unseated Neil Hamilton, in the safe Conservative constituency of Tatton. In 2001 Dr Richard Taylor was returned as an independent for Wyre Forest, after standing on the issue of the retention of a hospital in Kidderminster.

The parties select candidates in different ways. Labour begins its process by circu-lating a list of candidates approved by its National Executive Committee to all nominating bodies, including ward and branch parties, affiliated trade unions, socialist societies and the constituency Labour party (CLP) executive committee, all of which can nominate one candidate. The CLP makes up the shortlist and since 1993 selection has been decided by one member one vote (OMOV). At least one woman has to be on the shortlist. The NEC then has to endorse the candidate; in theory it can intervene at this point but such power is used sparingly, as it provokes so much local dissent.

For the Conservatives a central list of approved candidates is kept, from which constituencies can select. A subcommittee of the constituency association executive draws up a shortlist of about 20; after interviews, this is reduced to a list of no less than three. The executive then interviews the candidates and recommends two to the general meeting of the association – comprising paid up members – to make the final choice. Central Office would like to intervene from time to time to increase the number of ethnic and women candidates as well as to exclude those of whom it does not approve but local associations jealously guard their independence.

The Liberal Democrats' procedure is similar to the Conservatives', with the addition of at least one woman on the shortlist.

**cannabis legalisation**
Calls for the legalisation of cannabis have been made since the 1960s but both main parties have shied away from even discussing it, for fear of offending a voting public alarmed at the spread of drug taking, principally among young people. Jack Straw when home secretary was determined to preserve the status quo, even when a strong case was made for the legalisation of cannabis for medical purposes. At the Conservative conference in 2000, Ann Widdecombe called for a 'zero' tolerance attitude to the substance but when the police condemned this as unenforceable she lost credibility. Influential elements of the police – especially the Met – favoured

a relaxation of the laws on smoking 'pot' as it tends currently to be seen as a relatively harmless recreational drug, possibly less harmful than alcohol. In July 2001 Mo Mowlam, former cabinet minister, called for the decriminalisation of cannabis. She advocated that it be controlled by the government like alcohol and tobacco and proceeds used to fund public services. Surprisingly Peter Lilley, former deputy leader of the Conservatives and cabinet minister, called for the legalisation of cannabis in July 2001 on the grounds that this would remove the 'gateway' from soft to hard drugs which the illegal pushers of cannabis provide. Prohibition had become unenforceable, he claimed, and so should be replaced by government-controlled off-licences selling the substance. In early July 2001 several peers came out in support of reform, including Roy Jenkins and Kenneth Baker. However, Melanie Phillips, in a well argued piece in the Sunday Times (8 July 2001), insisted the medical evidence was against cannabis and that foreign experience warned against legalisation – she cited The Netherlands and Sweden in support of her arguments. In 2001 the government marked the possible beginning of decriminalisation of cannabis by deciding to give only cautions to those in possession of cannabis for personal use, though technically possession remains an offence. On 10 July 2002 David Blunkett, home secretary, downgraded cannabis to a 'class C' drug but increased penalties for dealers. Some criticised the change for giving a mixed message and the Conservatives attacked the policy as wrongheaded. The aim of the declassification was to give police time and resources to focus on class A drugs such as heroin and crack cocaine.

### Cantle report, 2001

Report entitled *Community Cohesion* produced by the Home Office Independent Review Team chaired by Ted Cantle. The approach to race relations in Britain that embraced a degree of separate identity for different cultures was shaken in the summer of 2001 by riots in the northern inner cities.

The report called into question the practice of allowing single ethnic groups to dominate schools in areas of high immigrant settlement. The report, published in December 2001, recorded the team's shock at the 'depth of polarisation' in housing, education, community and voluntary bodies, places of worship, languages and social networks. The team also suggested that the government practice of 'pump-priming' money into specific projects had exacerbated these polarising tendencies. The review called for a 'national debate' and an end to the non-discussion of sensitive matters involving race and ethnicity.

### capital punishment

*See* death penalty.

### capitalism

Term used by Karl Marx to describe an economic system comprising a relatively unregulated market, private property, investment in future projects and a workforce who produce profit for the owner in return for wages. Britain had the archetypal capitalist economy in the 19th century as the home of the industrial revolution and the so-called 'workshop of the world'. Marx argued that the private ownership of capital exploited workers ('wage slaves'), who would eventually rise up and overthrow the system that oppressed them. However, history has demonstrated that capitalism, rather than being destroyed, has prospered, albeit in a different form, and has been adopted by a number of previously communist states. Some commentators argue that 'globalisation' represents the final or 'monopoly capitalism' stage predicted by Marx. Francis Fukuyama, the US writer and theorist, argued in his controversial 'end of history' thesis that liberal capitalism had emerged from the conflict with communism as the victor and the template for the indefinite future.

*See also* Marxism.

### cash for questions scandal

Concern over the payment of money to Conservative MPs to ask parliamentary questions in 1994. On 20 October 1994 the *Guardian* newspaper accused Neil Hamilton, a junior trade minister, of accepting cash from Harrods owner Mohamed al Fayed in exchange for asking questions in the House of Commons. His co-accused, Tim Smith, admitted the offence and resigned, but Hamilton fought it together with lobbyist Ian Greer. Five days later Lord Nolan's Committee on Standards in Public Life was set up, which was destined to change the nature of British politics in a number of profound ways. Hamilton dropped his libel case against the *Guardian* a year later, citing lack of cash as the reason. The newspaper responded with a banner headline above Hamilton's photograph branding him: 'A Liar and a Cheat'. The BBC news reporter Martin Bell stood against him in the Tatton constituency in May 1997 and won by a huge majority.

*See also* Committee on Standards in Public Life; sleaze; Hamilton, Neil.

## Catalyst

www.catalystforum.org.uk

Left-wing think tank established in 1997 by former Labour Party director of policy Roland Wales. It seeks to stimulate new thinking on such issues as forms of government and political processes but talks of 'policies of redistribution of wealth, power and opportunity' – very Old Labour ideas – and it is not surprising to see Lord Hattersley as its editorial chair.

## catch-all party

Term associated with political scientist Otto Kircheimer, who pointed to the transformation of mass ideological parties into political organisations which assembled coalitions of support from a disparate range of voters. It is arguably the case that New Labour's 'third way' and 'big tent' approach to politics marked Labour's move towards this catch-all type of party.

## Catholic emancipation

Catholics suffered discrimination from the 16th century onwards. The situation eased in the late 18th century, when many of the penal laws were repealed, but they were still barred from sitting in parliament (though not from standing as a candidate) until 1829 as a consequence of the anti-Catholic oaths MPs were required to take. In 1828 Daniel O'Connell was elected to represent County Clare and the strength of his support led to a fear of civil disturbance such that even the (Iron) Duke of Wellington decided to give way to the pressure and accept that Catholics could now stand for all public offices. It still remains a fact, however, that despite the repeal of anti-Catholic measures the British monarch, according to the Act of Settlement 1701, must not be a Catholic or marry one.

## cause group

A subdivision of pressure groups. The term is used by political scientists to indicate either: sectional groups, which defend and promote specific social groups (for example Age Concern for the elderly, Shelter for the homeless and Child Poverty Action for the children of poor families); or attitude groups, which share common views on a particular issue and seek to change social attitudes (for example the Howard League for Penal Reform, Charter 88 on constitutional reform and the Lord's Day Observance Society).

## central–local relations

Relations between Westminster and local government. Local government has always operated by virtue of laws passed in parliament and so its powers and to varying extents its funding originate at the centre. This means relations between the centre and local authorities have traditionally been problematic. When the Conservatives were elected in 1979 they wanted to curb public spending and reduce the powers of what soon became Labour-dominated local government. In 1986 the Greater London Council and the metropolitan counties, set up by the Local Government Act 1972, were abolished. Attempts by local authorities to raise more funds from the rates were countered first by 'rate capping' and then by imposition of the ill fated 'poll tax'.

Further reforms ensured tension between centre and periphery continued long into the 1990s. Devolution for Wales, Scotland and Northern Ireland, together with plans for elected heads of city authorities (for example Ken Livingstone in London), suggest that the domination of the centre may not be as powerful now as in the past.

*See also* community charge; local government; rates.

## Central Office

Headquarters of the Conservative Party, previously based in Smith Square but now in Victoria Street, London. The party's bureaucracy proved instrumental in the fall of Iain Duncan Smith in November 2003, when squabbles fuelled discontent with the soon to be deposed leader. Once Michael Howard became leader it was announced that the Smith Square building was to be sold in order to save money.

*See also* Smith Square.

## Central Policy Review Staff (CPRS)

Civil service body popularly known as the 'Think Tank'. It was set up by Edward Heath in 1970 to assist the cabinet with strategic policy making. Its task was generally to 'think the unthinkable', but more particularly: to present briefing papers on issues free from departmental bias; to research 'horizontal issues' – those for which responsibility ran across several departments; and to assess how well government objectives were being achieved. Headed by the eminently suitable Lord Rothschild, it drew its youthful personnel half from 'outsiders' such as business people, academics and members of the professions, and half from 'insiders' – civil service high-flyers. It considered a number of subjects over the years, for example airships, computers, Concorde, low-energy cars, the coal industry and worker participation. In its first two years the CPRS was influential, largely because of its charismatic head, but after that it began to decline until Margaret Thatcher, convinced she knew the way forward without lengthy discussion documents, put an end to it in 1983. However,

her Policy Unit was substantially similar to the defunct Think Tank. Some saw resemblances to the Think Tank in Tony Blair's Strategy Futures Group located in the Cabinet Office and headed by Geoff Mulgan.

*See also* Policy Unit (Downing Street).

## centralisation

The concentration of power and authority in a single place. Critics of the unitary state, with its headquarters in London, have been vocal for many decades and have two main criticisms: first, local decisions are made away from the areas with which they are concerned (though devolution of powers to Scotland and Wales partially answered this); and second, power is overly concentrated in the hands of the executive, particularly the prime minister and a small group of key ministers and advisors. An example of centralisation was when Michael Heseltine, as deputy prime minister (1995–97), contrived to centralise a great many of the controlling threads of government in his own oversized office (he was given the chairmanship of four major cabinet committees and membership of all the others and he was in charge of industrial strategy as well as having a wide-ranging remit to promote competitiveness). Despite constitutional changes such as Scottish and Welsh devolution, many commentators have pointed to increased centralisation under Tony Blair's government, for example in education and health, although efforts to regionalise National Health Service administration were announced in spring 2001. An enduring problem of government seems to be the tension between the need for a democracy to devolve power yet the tendency for politicians to keep the reins of power in their own hands.

## Centre for Management and Policy Studies (CMPS)

www.cmps.gov.uk

This body was set up in 1999 and incorporated the Civil Service College, which had been set up in the wake of the Fulton report in 1970 and which had established a good name for itself as a provider of courses for senior civil servants – its course for assistant under-secretaries had been particularly well regarded and recognised as part of the transition to promotion. In 1995 the College narrowly missed being privatised and its ethos became more akin to the private sector, in keeping with the new managerialism of the civil service. In 1999 the Labour government set up the CMPS to 'be responsible for corporate civil service training and development'.

### Centre for Policy Studies
www.cps.org.uk
One of the most influential right-wing think tanks. It was founded by Margaret Thatcher in the 1970s, and it formulated or elaborated many of the constituent elements of 'Thatcherism'. However, by the early 1990s, with John Major in Number 10, like similar bodies, it was all but silent and, according to *The Economist*, had 'moved to a drabber address'.

### centre party
Term used to describe political parties in the middle of the accepted left–right political continuum. On the proposed continuum parties on the right favour free enterprise, low public spending and tough law and order policies, while those on the left favour higher public spending, public sector activities and policies more sympathetic to the offender's rights. Centre parties, for example the Liberal Democrats, tend to advocate a judicious blend of free enterprise and public sector policies. However, Tony Blair avowed that his government's 'third way' politics broke out of this false dichotomy. By 2001 many commentators saw the Liberal Democrats as a centre party which had staked out a position to the left of Labour. Indeed, during the 2001 general election the Liberal Democrats boldly committed themselves to increasing taxation to pay for better public services.

### chancellor of the Duchy of Lancaster
Title created by Henry III in 1267 for his son Edmund. The crown continues to hold the Duchy's revenues and its chancellor sits in the cabinet with this title held in an honorary capacity; the assigned duties are ceremonial and the office holder usually performs a specific task for the prime minister. For example, in 1998 Jack Cunningham as chancellor was in charge of the Cabinet Office and was responsible for coordinating government policy (the media dubbed him Tony Blair's 'enforcer').

### chancellor of the exchequer
Title that originated in the time of Edward the Confessor as the name for the king's chief secretary, keeping the great seal and presiding over the Chancery. In the modern day the chancellor is the chief finance minister of the government, presenting budgets and controlling the nation's overall financial strategy, as well as having responsibility for expenditure and the raising of revenue from taxation. After the prime minister the chancellor is the most important figure in the cabinet and is often seen as a likely successor to the prime minister. Two recent examples demonstrate the central role of this office. When Nigel Lawson resigned from the cabinet in 1989, it was seen as a disaster for Margaret Thatcher and was the beginning of the end for her tenure in power. More recently Gordon Brown quickly assumed the role of a political colossus after 1997, master of the all-controlling Treasury and architect of New Labour's reputation for economic competence; indeed, he was seen by many as the next Labour leader and future prime minister should Tony Blair stand down. Furthermore, the chancellor relies especially upon the political support of the prime minister (and vice versa) and the relationship between these two key people often decides the fate of a government. Some noteworthy examples include Lawson's 1986 budget, which laid the economic foundations for Thatcher's 1987 general election victory.

### Chancery
*See* High Court.

## Channel 5
www.channel5.co.uk
Television channel established by the
Independent Television Commission in
1995 when it handed the Channel 5
Broadcasting Consortium the right to
broadcast on a fifth terrestrial channel. It
began doing so in January 1997 and quickly
acquired a reputation for a decidedly down-
market style of programming, adding fuel
to the debate about the 'dumbing down'
of terrestrial broadcasting as a result of
the Broadcasting Act 1990. Some media
watchers feared the Labour government
might be trying to free the channel for purchase by Blair-supporter Rupert Murdoch.

## Channel 4
www.channel4.com
Television channel set up in 1982 with a
brief to encourage innovation and cater for
minority interests. Initially it was funded
by contributions from other television
companies but in the late 1980s it became
a public corporation funded by its own advertising. It was especially successful, under
the executive leadership of Michael Grade,
in collaborating with film companies,
and this helped to initiate a new wave of
creativity in British film. Some programmes
proved too avant garde for some tastes and
they attracted protest from those wishing to
keep television suitable for 'family view-
ing', while others criticised it for 'dumbing
down'. In 2001 arts and media commentators reacted with horror to William Hague's
suggestion that a future Conservative
government would privatise Channel 4.
Channel 4 News has established itself as an
authoritative source of news and comment.

## Channel Islands
Crown dependencies close to the French
coast. They were occupied by Germany
during the Second World War. Jersey has
150,000 inhabitants; St Helier is its capital. Along with Guernsey it has been part
of England since 1106. Alderney, Great
and Little Sark are also part of the same
group of islands. They are legally part of
the UK and, though not represented in

Westminster, they are ruled directly by
the crown. British acts of parliament do
not affect the islands unless specifically
indicated, although the British government is responsible for external affairs.
The Channel Islands are not part of the
European Union de jure.

## Channel Tunnel
Rail tunnel linking England to France.
Mooted since the time of Napoleon, a
tunnel under the English Channel was
not constructed until the time of Margaret
Thatcher, a famously Eurosceptic politician. Ironically, the tunnel joining Britain
to the European continent has become a
kind of monument to her years in power.
She insisted it should not be built from
public funds so mostly private finance was
sought for it. It opened in 1996. Britain, it
could be argued, is now physically as well
as politically part of Europe.

## charisma
Natural leadership quality which commands attention or even obedience. British
politicians have seldom had such qualities,
although Winston Churchill and possibly
David Lloyd George can be said to fall into
this category. The charisma alleged to have
been possessed by Margaret Thatcher and
Tony Blair probably owed as much to clever
public relations as to the genuine quality.
  *See also* authority.

## Charter 88
www.charter88.org.uk
Pressure group for constitutional change.
It was set up in 1988 to commemorate the
Glorious Revolution 300 years earlier,
which had inaugurated the emergence of
parliamentary government out of monarchical rule. The organisation captured
the support of the leading left-leaning
intellectuals of the day and its agenda of
devolution, reform of the House of Lords
and the voting system was virtually taken
over by the Labour government coming
into power in 1997. Much of it was implemented but Charter 88 still awaits reform
of the voting system.

## charter mark

A means of rewarding outstanding service in the public sector and fostering the consumer approach to public service provision. It was introduced by John Major in 1993. The charter mark was supplementary to the citizens' charters introduced at the same time but, like these, never really made a deep impression on the public consciousness. They were replaced by the service mark after 1997, which also failed to impress itself on the nation's mind.

*See also* citizens' charter.

## Charter Movement

www.tory-charter.org.uk

Conservative Party group that has as its aim the democratisation of the party. It was set up by party activists in the early 1980s and it aims to replace the hegemony of the leader with more member votes. For example, it called for a new Policy Committee answerable to the Central Council and a fusion of the National Union of Party Activists with Central Office by giving activists the right to vote for a party chair in a postal ballot. In 1997 William Hague introduced some of the reforms long called for by Charter members.

*See also* Conservative Party.

## Chartist

A supporter of the popular movement for political reform in the 19th century. The People's Charter, drafted by William Lovett, demanded: annual parliaments, universal male suffrage, equal electoral districts, an end to property qualifications for MPs, voting by ballot and payment of MPs. Feargus O'Connor and James O'Brien were the demagogic leaders of the movement. In July 1839 parliament rejected a petition bearing over a million signatures and did the same to one with three million signatures in May 1842. The Chartists became disunited over strategy after these setbacks and failed to agree a general strike. When the government reacted with the threat of military action to the attempted third petition in 1848 the movement crumbled and faded away, although most of its objectives were achieved within the next century.

## Chicago School of Economics

Associated chiefly with the name and ideas of Milton Friedman, though close also to the ideas of Friedrich von Hayek. Two key ideas lie at the heart of the School's approach: that government should be as much as possible non-interventionist; and that it should restrict its activities to controlling the supply of money in the economy on the grounds that an uncontrolled money supply leads inevitably to inflation. All else would be looked after by the 'hidden hand' of an unfettered market. Friedman's brand of monetarism influenced both Margaret Thatcher and Nigel Lawson, although its predicted remedial effects were hard to discern during the 1980s.

## chief secretary to the Treasury

The most important Treasury brief after the chancellor of the exchequer. It is a high-profile job because the chief secretary is the 'scrooge' of the nation's finances since he (there has never been a female holder of the office) is responsible for controlling public spending (especially monies granted to local government), ensuring public services deliver value for money and scrutinising and controlling pay in the public sector. The post holder also chairs cabinet committees on public expenditure and future legislation. All these functions come together in the annual spending round, when the chief secretary manages negotiations between the Treasury and spending departments and chairs the PX and QFL cabinet committees. John Major was a successful chief secretary before becoming chancellor in 1989: none of his negotiations had to be referred to the informal 'Star Chamber' which adjudicated on such matters.

*See also* Star Chamber.

## chief whip

Appointed by all parties to manage the teams of whips. Whips are an important mechanism of intra-party control and communication in both houses of parliament. In particular, the chief whip's greatest power comes through the role of advising the party leader on appointments to front-bench jobs and thus career advancement. Equally, the chief whip can advise on demotion, perhaps as a punishment for failing to follow the party line on a compulsory party vote ('three-line whip'). The government chief whip (or parliamentary secretary to the Treasury) is close to the centre of power, with a seat at the cabinet table; the office at Number 12 Downing Street, however, is no more. The parties have traditionally seen the whips' office as a 'nursery' of future ministerial talent and some chief whips – such as Edward Heath – have gone on to become prime minister.

*See also* whip.

### child benefit
Established by the Child Benefits Act 1975 to replace family allowances.

### Child Poverty Action Group (CPAG)
www.cpag.org.uk
Pressure group founded in 1963 that exists for the 'relief, directly or indirectly, of poverty among children and families with children'. It 'works to ensure that those on low incomes get their full entitlements to welfare benefits' and campaigns via public education, lobbying and demonstrations. One of its former directors, Frank Field, became a Labour minister for social security in 1997, but resigned shortly afterwards, claiming his ideas were being ignored.

### Child Support Agency (CSA)
www.csa.gov.uk
Set up in 1993 in order to calculate and collect child maintenance from parents (generally fathers) who had left their families. The Agency epitomised the Conservative idea that people should be responsible for their actions. The huge growth in the proportion of children born outside the traditional two-parent family (over a quarter in the mid-1990s), plus the related problem of increasingly large welfare demands on the agencies of the state, all combined to support the creation of the CSA. However, the practice was not in line with the theory and the CSA soon became exceptionally unpopular, not only for delays and other administrative failings, but also for the fact that fathers willing to pay were allegedly charged crippling rates while those who prevaricated seemed to get away with it as before. Press stories abounded of fathers driven to nervous breakdown or even suicide. The government, in line with the 'naming and shaming' of civil servants, responded by changing the chief executive from Ros Hepplewhite to Ann Chant in 1994. The CSA continues its work as part of the Ministry of Work and Pensions but not without continuing controversy.

### Chiltern Hundreds
An Anglo-Saxon unit of local government. If any MP wishes to resign his seat he must apply for one of two stewardships: of the Chiltern Hundreds (the better known) or of the Manor of Northstead, in Yorkshire. The arcane constitutional reason is that since 1707 any paid officer of the crown may not sit in parliament. There are three Chiltern Hundreds: Stoke, Desborough and Burnham.

### Christian socialism
An important strand within British church history, especially Methodism, and the Labour Party. Many Labour politicians claim that Christ and his teachings represent a more powerful element of party doctrine than does Marx and dialectical materialism. In essence, it stresses the importance of social responsibility, especially towards the poor and the duties of employers towards their workers. State education holds a special place in this strand of thought. Some have suggested that this is a form of 'gentle capitalism' or capitalism with a caring face, although it must be said that Christian socialism does point towards alternatives such as cooperatives and other voluntary associations. Tony Blair, among others in the Labour Party, can claim a link with this tradition, and stated in a speech before the 1997 election that he was his 'brother's keeper'.

## Church of England

www.cofe.anglican.org

The 'official' or national church of the United Kingdom, established in the 16th century during the Reformation (a breakaway from the Church of Rome occasioned by the Pope's refusal to sanction Henry VIII's divorce from Catherine of Aragon). In 1563 the Articles of Religion laid out the basic doctrines of the Church, at the behest of Elizabeth I, which are still in force today. During the Civil War the Church was suspended until the Restoration in 1660. The attempts by James II to introduce pro-Catholic reforms contributed to the Glorious Revolution of 1688. 'Low Church' practices, closer to Presbyterian thinking, and 'High Church', closer to Catholicism, became a feature of religious life. The monarch is the supreme governor of the Church of England and the Archbishop of Canterbury traditionally performs coronations in Westminster Abbey. Some bishops of the Church of England – the 'lords spiritual' – are entitled to sit in the House of Lords.

It is thought to be an advantage politically to profess Christianity and many politicians attempt to identify themselves with the Church; Tony Blair is a high-profile and active member of the Church of England, who espouses its beliefs as an article of personal faith and who also occasionally attends communion at Catholic churches, the faith of his wife, Cherie.

*See also* bishop; Glorious Revolution.

## citizens' charter

An attempt by John Major in November 1991 to combat bureaucratic inefficiency and indifference. The idea was to provide standards of service across the public sector and then measure how the various agencies were performing. Some 38 charters were published, including British Rail's Passenger Charter and the National Health Service's Patients' Charter. Charter mark awards were given to those agencies judged to have performed especially well. Cynics observed that the idea involved no extra resources and others claimed that

this, the only 'big idea' from the Major government, failed to capture the public imagination.

*See also* charter mark.

## citizenship

Term referring originally to an inhabitant of a city, later applied to native or naturalised members of a state who have certain rights and reciprocal obligations. Citizenship has been a potent idea behind political education: that people need to learn something of the workings of a democratic system in order to participate effectively. Bernard Crick has been a leading thinker in this field and chaired a working party on citizenship after Labour won the 1997 election. In formal or legal terms British citizenship has changed markedly as a result of the British Nationality Act 1981, the Immigration Act 1988 and the British Nationality (Hong Kong) Act 1990. Further changes occurred when Britain signed the 1992 Treaty on European Union, which granted UK citizens a number of rights (residence, work, voting and freedom of travel) in European Union countries and reciprocal ones for European Union nationals in Britain. Citizenship has now entered the school curriculum.

## City (the)

The area of London where the most important financial transactions take place. Often called 'the square mile', this ancient area of the capital city is located on the north bank of the Thames between Tower Bridge and London Bridge. It includes the Bank of England, the London Stock Exchange, Lloyds Insurance and the headquarters of most of the important banks, insurance companies and other financial institutions. 'The City' is often used as a catch-all term for foreign markets and for large corporate interests.

## civic culture

Term originating in Almond and Verba's study of political culture that appeared in 1963. It defined the civic culture as a majority acceptance of the authority of the state and a commitment to participation in public duties. The authors saw Britain as having the ideal political culture, in which citizens trusted their ruling elites, believed in a degree of participation and accepted the validity of the laws of the land. This moderate, non-ideological culture is believed to have protected the country from extremist ideas, whether of the fascist right or the Marxist left. Margaret Thatcher sought passionately to change the British culture, to be more self-reliant, more opposed to high levels of taxation and more entrepreneurial. Survey evidence suggests she was unsuccessful and that the majority of respondents still believed in higher social expenditure, even if this meant higher taxes. However, high poll responses for such measures did not prevent the voters electing Conservative governments in 1987 and 1992. The civic culture thesis has been subject to much criticism, especially the view that it is based on data collected during the late 1950s, a particularly quiescent period of British political and social history.

*See also* apathy; civil society.

### Civil Contingencies Secretariat
www.ukresilience.info
Civil service body set up in 2001 to provide early warning of impending problems. The secretariat is staffed by 100 civil servants based in the Cabinet Office, where it reports to the prime minister through the cabinet secretary. Its remit is to 'scan the horizon' as an early warning system and then to coordinate departments to ensure their response is effective. This initiative emerged from the debacle involving foot and mouth disease, when it was widely perceived that the Ministry of Agriculture, Fisheries and Food had not performed these jobs properly.

### civil law
Law that governs the rights of individuals and organisations and their dealings with each other. It is also called 'private' as opposed to 'public' and 'criminal' law and stipulates, for example, the principles of commercial transactions, family, property

and inheritance. Civil disputes are heard in civil courts. The police are not involved and there is no question of punishment. One of the key legal differences between the two kinds of law is that the civil courts require a lower standard of evidence: in criminal law the case against the accused has to be 'beyond reasonable doubt' while in civil courts it has to be on 'the balance of probabilities'.

### civil liberties
Those rights and freedoms so precious they are thought to underlie liberal democratic government. Most of the freedoms focus on the protection of the individual from the coercive power of the state executed by political or legal authorities. The rights include: freedom of speech; freedom of religion and thought; freedom of movement; freedom of association; right to a fair trial; and freedom of the person. Economic freedom – the right to buy, sell and make a profit – is central to the liberal democratic tradition of Britain and the USA. In Britain civil liberties do not receive any special constitutional protection and many have argued that they have been eroded in recent times. For example, the right to remain silent when arrested and not have this held against you was abolished by the Criminal Justice and Public Order Act 1994, and ethnic minorities believe that they suffer disproportionately from the police power to stop and search people. The pressure group Liberty is an enthusiastic campaigner for the protection of civil liberties in Britain. The Human Rights Act 1998 provided for the first time statutory defence of basic human rights in British courts.

### civil list
The annual grant given by parliament to the royal family to run the royal households. It was distinguished from other public monies in 1698, when parliament decided to limit the monarch's ability to control public funds by exerting control itself over all funds except for those required by the monarch for day-to-day expenses. By the early 20th century the sum was £700,000,

but it had risen to £7.9 million per annum by 2000. Prince Charles is excluded from the list as he has income from estates owned from his position as Duke of Cornwall. In 1993 the queen announced she was willing to pay income tax for the first time and removed all members of the royal family from the civil list except for herself, the Duke of Edinburgh and the late Queen Mother. Upkeep of royal castles and the royal train are met from the relevant departments but the Royal yacht, *Britannia*, was decommissioned in 1997 after Labour (in opposition) refused to support a government scheme to build a £60 million replacement.

### civil rights

An umbrella term for the rights of a disadvantaged group, usually suffering racial or religious discrimination, which is campaigning for equal treatment in economic, political and social life. Although mainly associated with the US civil rights movements of the 1960s, the Northern Ireland Civil Rights Association campaigned against the religious discrimination practised against Catholics in Ulster before the troubles. Civil rights movements traditionally use non-violent methods of protest, such as marches and civil disobedience. Legislation has since outlawed many forms of discrimination on the grounds of sex, race or religion and the incorporation of the European Convention on Human Rights into UK law provides extra protection for individuals and minority groups.

### civil servant

*See* civil service.

### civil service

www.civil-service.gov.uk

All those employed by central government to run its administration. The civil service is the workhorse of central government and is responsible for carrying out the wishes of the legislature as interpreted by the ministers who head up departments of state. In the early 1980s there were over 700,000 civil servants but by 1996 this figure had shrunk – as a result of privatisation and the

Next Steps reforms – to under 500,000. This reduction was both an attempt to decentralise the administration and to reduce the workforce, as well as to relieve overload on Whitehall by hiving off the routine aspects of government to executive agencies. Policy was still to be formulated by ministers, who in turn were to be advised by some 4,000 elite 'administrative class' civil servants. In 1968 the Civil Service Department was set up to run the public service but this was abolished in 1981 and its functions were replaced by the Office of Public Service in 1995.

One of the abiding debates in the study of British politics is the extent of civil servants' influence on the formation of policy. The comic *Yes, Minister* and *Yes, Prime Minister* series on television and radio suggested that the clever Sir Humphrey Appleby almost always outwitted the somewhat dim minister Jim Hacker, although expert commentators assert that decisive ministers will usually prevail if they know their subject and their own minds.

One of the most important developments since 1979 has been a decline in the traditional formula that civil servants should be anonymous, neutral and permanent. Margaret Thatcher put up Sir William Armstrong to defend the government in the attempt to prevent the book *Spycatcher* by Peter Wright from being published, for example. Clive Ponting, on the other hand, decided to ignore the conventions of Whitehall and sent confidential information regarding the *General Belgrano* affair to MP Tam Dalyell. Other civil servants have been 'named and shamed' by senior politicians, arguably trying to escape their responsibilities, as in the case of Ros Heppelwhite of the Child Support Agency or Derek Lewis of the Prisons Agency.

Tony Blair's government has also left its mark on the service. Not only have traditional higher-flying bureaucrats been joined by media-savvy special advisors, but all government departments must now adopt a customer-friendly approach to their client groups, similar to the customer service ethos now common in retailing and other service industries. In addition, the civil service has been redirected to be more focused on 'delivery': the priority Blair faced once it became clear voters were dissatisfied with the state of the public services. In the autumn of 2001 Lord Birt was appointed part-time to the new Forward Strategy Unit (FSU) in Number 10 to help reform the civil service, which was widely perceived as failing to deliver the results required by government. In July 2004 chancellor Gordon Brown, as part of that year's comprehensive spending review, announced planned cuts of 84,000 in the civil service to save over £20 billion in expenditure.

> As I learnt very early on in my life in Whitehall, the acid test of any political question is: what is the alternative? (Lord (Burke) Trend, secretary to the cabinet, 1975)

*See also* administrative class; executive agency; modernisation.

## Civil Service College
*See* Centre for Management and Policy Studies; Office of Public Service.

## Civil Service Department
*See* Office of Public Service.

## civil society
The non-political relationships in society – those of family, business and, especially, voluntary organisations. These relationships, it is argued, provide the 'glue' which cements society together and instruct people in the arts of compromise, responsibility, self-discipline and leadership. The concept was originally related to the 17th-century notion of the 'state of nature' which humans supposedly inhabited before entering the confines of the state. The idea was crucial in that it enabled thinkers like John Locke to argue that citizens had the right to overthrow a government which failed to live up to its 'contract' with citizens. It has been suggested that the lack of strong or 'thick' civil society in eastern Europe hindered its transition to democracy after the collapse of

communism. Studies have found substantial group membership in Britain: 16 per cent church; 14 per cent trade unions; 17 per cent sporting bodies; and 5 per cent environmental groups. However, the poor turnouts in national, local and European elections suggest civil society in Britain is 'thinner' than is healthy for the body politic as a whole. Some social observers believe the *Bowling Alone* thesis of Robert Putnam (1995) applies to Britain as well as to the USA. He argues that the dramatic decreases in citizen participation rates in social and voluntary activity represent a worrying decline of civil society. Data collected in 1999 by the US scholar Peter Hall, however, suggested British civic culture or 'social capital' is healthier than the US one. Sheffield University's social audit seemed to reinforce Hall's findings, despite the poor turnout in the 2001 general election.

*See also* apathy; civic culture.

## Civil War
*See* English Civil War.

## class
A combination of economic, occupational and social status and identity. Class is an emotive question in Britain, which is famously obsessed with it. Interestingly, the subjective classification of class in Britain differs markedly from the objective. A survey published in the *Daily Telegraph* (25 September 1998) revealed that 70 per cent of respondents still saw themselves as 'working class', even though at least half of them would be classified as middle class.

Generally speaking, definitions of class fall into two broad categories: the two-class model developed by Marx; and the multi-class system associated with Max Weber. Karl Marx saw society as stratified into two major and antagonistic classes based on their relationship to the productive process: the proletariat (working class) and the bourgeoisie (middle-class owners of means of production). He believed the proletariat would eventually realise the bourgeoisie was exploiting it and rise up to establish a new classless socialist society. History has suggested that such a revolution is far from the inevitable conclusion of social interaction which Marx believed it would be. Political scientists prefer more specific classifications, developed from Max Weber's distinction between class and occupational or status groups. A number of different classifications are in use in Britain, three of the most common being the ABC scale of the British Market Research Association (BMRA), John Goldthorpe's salariat system and the eight-point classification used by the Office for National Statistics (ONS). In November 1998 the ONS issued a report based upon an Economic and Social Research Council (ESRC) study into class categories. Existing class categories were based on a six-fold division: professional, managerial and technical, skilled non-manual, skilled manual, partly skilled and unskilled. The report argued that changes in 'the nature and structure of both industry and occupations have rendered [current classifications] both outmoded and misleading'. The new system is based to a greater extent upon job security and career prospects.

*The ABC scale*

A   Upper middle – professional, higher managerial (3 per cent of households)
B   Middle – middle managers (16 per cent)
C1  Lower middle – junior managers, routine white collar (26 per cent)
C2  Skilled – plumbers, carpenters, mechanics (26 per cent)
D   Semi-skilled and unskilled – manual workers (17 per cent)
E   Residual – dependent on long-term benefit (13 per cent)

*The salariat scale*

Higher salariat (12 per cent)
Lower salariat (16 per cent)
Routine clerical (24 per cent)
Petty bourgeoisie (7 per cent)
Foremen and technicians (5 per cent)
Skilled manual (11 per cent)
Unskilled manual (25 per cent)

*ONS scale*

1    Higher managerial and professional
1a   Employers and managers in large organisations
1b   High professionals – lawyers, doctors, dentists, civil servants, professors, teachers and airline pilots
2    Lower managerial and associate professionals – police sergeants and constables, prison officers, fire-fighters, journalists, nurses and professional sports people
3    Intermediate occupations – computer engineers, dental technicians, secretaries, flight attendants, driving instructors
4    Small employers and own account workers – self-employed non-professionals
5    Lower supervisory, craft and related occupations – electricians, car mechanics and engine drivers
6    Semi-routine occupations – drivers, shop assistants, traffic wardens and postal workers
7    Routine occupations – car park attendants, cleaners, road workers, refuse collectors, labourers, road sweepers
8    Never worked and long-term unemployed

**classical liberalism**

One of the most important traditions of political thought of the last 200 years. These ideas can be traced back to the writings of John Locke and Adam Smith, among others, and evolved into the laissez faire or free enterprise economics of the 19th century. Adam Smith was a key early economic theorist; he believed that the government should eschew all subsidies and anything likely to distort markets, that is, he advocated the free play of the forces of supply and demand in the market. He also advocated that business people should be allowed to produce goods to meet market demand, employ labour to produce goods at the rate that the market dictates, take profit in accordance with their efficiency and competitiveness, and invest profits in other enterprises. According to Smith, this capitalist system would, if left unaided, prove to be the most efficient means of producing goods possible. In the 19th century the Liberals espoused this doctrine while the embryonic labour movement became increasingly hostile to its inegalitarian tendencies. Socialist critics maintained that free enterprise inevitably created huge disparities of wealth and poverty, destroyed the idea of craftsmanship and created an alienated urban population.

Allied to Adam Smith's economics were the philosophical ideas of Jeremy Bentham, James Mill and John Stuart Mill. Bentham inaugurated the idea of utilitarianism. James Mill and his son went on to add to classical liberalism the basic arguments for representative government. Richard Cobden and John Bright completed what is usually perceived as classical liberalism with the idea that the extension of trade worldwide would naturally incline nations towards peace rather than war.

In the 20th century the Conservative Party under Margaret Thatcher rediscovered classical liberalism and absorbed it into party policy. Labour was in turn influenced by these developments and adapted them. This has led some to claim, with some justification, the long-term triumph of classical liberalism's advocacy of capitalism.

### clause four

The 'nationalisation' clause of the Labour Party's constitution. The constitution was drafted by Arthur Henderson and Sidney Webb in 1918 and clause four established as a benchmark of British socialism that it was the party's intention to achieve the 'common ownership of the means of production, distribution and exchange'. However, in practice the party never attempted to achieve a comprehensive 'common ownership' and tacitly accepted a capitalistic private sector as the engine of the economy. Anthony Crosland's widely accepted revisionist reformulation (*The Future of Socialism*, 1956) arguably made the clause unnecessary in any case. Hugh Gaitskell tried to change it formally in 1959 but was defeated by indignant left-wingers. Tony Blair used its reform, however, as a demonstrative sign he meant business when modernising Labour. His campaign was supremely successful and a special conference in April 1995 accepted a reformulation which spoke of 'a dynamic economy' in which the 'enterprise of the market' is joined with the 'forces of partnership and cooperation'. Veteran Old Labourites like Arthur Scargill protested in vain: clause four, as traditionally understood, was no more.

### cleavage

Term used to denote major divisions in society. Britain is generally believed to lack many of the cleavages which cause problems in other societies, like religion (apart from in Northern Ireland). The main cleavage in British society is normally thought to be class, but even class divisions have become blurred over the past half century.

*See also* class; voting behaviour.

### closed shop

The system whereby all employees in an enterprise are obliged to join a specified union or unions. Usually in such circumstances the employer is in agreement, as it is advantageous to deal with as few bodies as possible that represent workers. However, such agreements prevent the employment of workers who do not wish to join unions and the Conservative government passed legislation in the early 1980s to weaken the closed shop by insisting that such agreements receive in a secret ballot the support of 80 per cent of those covered by them. This measure was moderated by the Employment Relations Act 2000, which obliges employers to recognise unions for negotiation purposes, provided a majority of workplace members are in favour.

### coalition government

When two or more political parties combine to form a joint government, usually (in Britain's case) in the face of war or some other crisis. There have been a number of occasions when such governments have been formed. In 1915 Herbert Asquith formed one to conduct the war. David Lloyd George took over as its leader in 1916 and its mandate was reaffirmed in 1918 until it fell in 1922. The next example was in 1931, when Ramsay MacDonald split the Labour Party and was elected as head of the national government, which was re-elected and was technically still in office in 1940 when the Conservatives, under Winston Churchill, formed his wartime coalition government with Labour and the Liberals. Since 1945 governments have always been single-party ones, although between 1976 and 1978 Labour needed Liberal MPs to support them in votes in order to survive (the 'Lib–Lab pact'). Close electoral contests, as in 1992, often encourage speculation that either Labour or the Conservatives may do a deal with the smaller third party and govern in coalition. However, the possible reform of the voting system to a system of proportional representation would certainly make such arrangements more likely. Despite Liberal Democrat hopes of a referendum on this topic after 1997, Labour hostility to the idea led to it being shelved.

*See also* national government.

### code of conduct for MPs

Drawn up by the Standards and Privileges Committee in 1995 in the wake of the 'cash for questions' scandal and approved by the House of Commons in July 1995. It laid out the duties of MPs to serve their constituents, obey the law and observe the principles of 'selflessness, integrity, objectivity, accountability, openness, honesty and leadership'. Observance of the code is monitored by the parliamentary commissioner on standards and the Standards and Privileges Committee.

*See also* Committee on Standards in Public Life; ministerial code of conduct; parliamentary commissioner for standards; parliamentary privilege; Standards and Privileges Committee.

### Cold War

The name given to the period of tension after the Second World War when the USSR began to impose its influence upon eastern Europe, especially Poland, Bulgaria, Romania, Hungary and Czechoslovakia. The degree of tension and armed preparedness between the great powers was akin to a real war but the fear of nuclear exchange prevented outright conflict. The USA decided to support western Europe after 1946, when Winston Churchill made his speech at Fulton, Missouri, when he said 'From Stettin in the Baltic to Trieste in the Adriatic, an iron curtain has descended across the continent'. Once Britain pulled out from supporting the pro-west side in the Greek civil war, the USA moved in and after Marshall aid was introduced, was persuaded, partly by the British foreign secretary Ernest Bevin, to participate in a permanent security alliance: the North Atlantic Treaty Organisation (NATO). The Cold War continued throughout the 1950s and 1960s and after the 1962 Cuban missile crisis. In the 1980s US president Ronald Reagan began embarking on an anti-ballistic missile system known as 'Star Wars', designed to destroy incoming missiles from the communist east. The USSR was unable, ultimately, to afford the arms race which resulted from the Cold War and it essentially ended once the USSR collapsed in 1991.

### collective ownership

*See* clause four.

### collective responsibility

A principle of British government that key decisions should be taken only after full discussion in cabinet and that, once taken, all ministers are obliged to support the decision, despite any individual reservations that they may have had. The convention was codified in the document *Questions of Procedure*, which set out ministerial rules of behaviour: 'Decisions reached by the Cabinet or Cabinet Committees are binding on all members of the government'. Anyone breaching this convention will normally be called upon to resign unless there is a special dispensation, as with the Labour cabinet over the question of continued membership of the European Economic Community in 1975, when ministers were allowed publicly to oppose continued membership.

## collectivism
The assertion of the good of society as
a whole, as opposed to the good of the
individual. It is usually associated with the
idea of equality within that society. Further,
it is often associated with state intervention
on behalf of the greater whole and, related
to this, with bureaucracy and inefficiency.
In Britain Labour has been the natural
home of collectivist ideas, although in
the decades before and after the Second
World War both the Liberals and moderate
Conservatives have embodied elements of it
in their own philosophies.

## Combat 18
www.isd.org.uk
Hitler-revering far-right grouping espousing neo-Nazi ideas. Combat 18 is named
after the alphabet positions of Adolf Hitler's
initials. According to their website the
group used to be 'a brigade of fearless storm
troopers' which provided security at meetings
of the British National Party (BNP), but
when the BNP leadership decided to 'play
the game of democracy' Combat 18 were
'promptly given the boot'. The group openly
accepts violence as a policy (or 'constructive Aryan militancy' as their website has
it). The group was active in the north-west
towns of Oldham and Burnley when race
problems caused trouble in recent years.

## commercial radio and television
Before 1973 radio broadcasting was the
preserve of the BBC, although large
numbers of young people tuned in to listen
to pop music broadcast from illegal pirate
radio stations such as Radio Caroline.
However, in 1973 the Conservative government allowed applications for commercial
franchises. They now operate in most
parts of the country, financed by advertising. As far as television was concerned
the BBC monopoly was broken in 1955,
when commercial television was introduced
with over a dozen companies operating all
over the country. The system was policed
by the Independent Television Authority
(superseded by the Independent Television
Commission in 1990), the chair of which

was appointed by the government. In 1982
Channel 4 was launched and in spring
1997 Channel 5. Cable television and
satellite stations also provide a variety of
different channels for the viewer.

*See also* Broadcasting Act 1990;
Independent Television Commission; Office
of Communications.

## Commission for Local Democracy
Independent think tank on local government. In 1995 it judged 'the present system
of local government in Britain as seriously
inadequate to meet the requirements of a
mature democracy'.

## Commission for Racial Equality
www.cre.gov.uk
Set up in 1976 to encourage racial equality
and investigate racial discrimination in
employment and other areas in Britain (a
similar body for Northern Ireland was set
up in 1997). It supports the work of 84
equality councils across the country.

## Committee of the Whole House
The House of Commons meets as a whole
in such a 'committee' when a matter of
particular importance is being considered.
For several centuries any bills concerning
taxation or expenditure were so treated. In
1993 the contentious Maastricht bill was
considered in this fashion.

## Committee of Ways and Means
A Committee of the Whole House, when
the House meets as such to discuss the
budget, presided over by the chairman of
ways and means (i.e. the deputy speaker).
The Committee was abolished in 1967, but
supply is still raised on ways and means
resolutions and it is still the chairman of
ways and means who chairs the budget
debate.

## Committee on Standards in Public Life
www.public-standards.gov.uk
Constituted as a standing body with its
members appointed for up to three years,
successively chaired to date by Lord Nolan,

Lord Neill, Sir Nigel Wicks and Sir Alistair Graham. The work of the committee covers MPs and ministers, civil servants and members of key executive agencies, as well as party funding, for example.

*See also* Neill committee; Nolan committee; parliamentary commissioner for standards; Standards and Privileges Committee.

### committee stage
*See* act of parliament; standing committee.

### Common Agricultural Policy (CAP)
Possibly the most contentious of all European Union (EU) policies. The two key undertakings behind the CAP were the agreement to guarantee prices for agricultural commodities and the guarantee that all surpluses would be bought by the European Community. This was an open invitation to farmers to produce more than was needed, to receive the benefits of a captive market; it also subsidised inefficient production methods. The results included the infamous butter 'mountains' and wine 'lakes'. Two-thirds of the Community budget was spent on the CAP in the 1980s, which almost resulted in bankruptcy. In 1986 a five-year reform programme was introduced whereby farmers were asked to limit production and were compensated for land 'set aside'. By 1992 the proportion of the budget spent on the CAP had been reduced to 55 per cent. In January 2003 Tony Blair rowed with Jacques Chirac when it became known to him that France and Germany had collaborated on changes to the CAP without informing Britain. The addition of 10 more countries to the EU in May 2004 – some of them relatively poor and dependent on agriculture – will have implications for the future of the CAP.

### common law
Derived from court decisions rather than statute, this type of law has been developed by judges from 'custom and precedent'. Much of it developed after the Norman conquest and is based on legal interpretations of local customs to create a law 'common' to all the kingdom.

### Common Market
*See* European Union.

### Commoners' Register
In Bristol a pensions consultant, John Oliver, runs a Commoners' Register, to which he invites members of the House of Lords to declare they do not wish to be known by their titles. The first member was Lord Noel Annan in the early 1990s and he now has 120 members signed up; they include Roy Hattersley, former Labour cabinet minister, David Steel and Shirley Williams. The *Guardian* on 27 April 2001 gave the Register its blessing and announced its policy henceforward was not to use titles in its letter page.

### Commons
*See* House of Commons.

### Commonwealth (British)
www.thecommonwealth.org
The organisation which emerged from the chequered history of the British Empire. Most of the former colonies are members. In 1926, at the Imperial Conference, the 'white' dominions were established as independent states, although with 'common allegiance to the Crown and freely associated as members of the British Commonwealth of Nations'. The Statute of Westminster in 1931 gave legal force to this independent status. After the Second World War most of the countries achieving independence from Britain joined the Commonwealth so that in 1996 there were 53 member states and a total population of 1,500 million. The queen is head of state in 16 countries, while 32 are republics and 5 have their own monarchs. Australia has been ambivalent for some time about the queen being head of state and seeks to make alternative arrangements. Burma withdrew in 1947, the Republic of Ireland in 1949 and Fiji in 1987 (it now seeks readmission). Pakistan left in 1972 but rejoined in 1989. South Africa left in 1961 over disputes

surrounding its racist internal policies; it was readmitted in 1995. Nigeria was suspended in 1995 because of its abuse of human rights but surprisingly in 1997 Mozambique was adopted as the 54th member even though its former colonial country was Portugal.

High commissioners represent Commonwealth members in London and the organisation meets once every two years via the Commonwealth Secretariat, which was founded in London in 1960 and is currently headed by Don McKinnon.

See also Empire (British).

## communication
See political communications.

## Communist Party of Great Britain (CPGB)
www.cpgb.org.uk
Founded in 1920 by a combination of left-wing socialist groups but largely the Socialist Party of Great Britain. From the outset it followed the teachings and became a slavish supporter of international communism based in Moscow. As such it was seen as alien to the British tradition and attempts to affiliate to the Labour Party were rejected. The party attracted little electoral support and in 1932 had only 6,000 members. However, the identification of the USSR as an emergent utopia encouraged membership and CPGB members infiltrated other organisations (for example the Popular Front, the National Unemployed Workers Movement) in order to capture them for their movement. Once the USSR joined the Second World War there was widespread enthusiasm for the party and membership exceeded 40,000, but after the war Stalin's incursions into eastern Europe and the start of the Cold War returned the party to the periphery, with little influence except in certain trade unions. During the 1970s the party split as the more independent 'Eurocommunism' became popular. In 1991, in the wake of the USSR's collapse, the party declined to a few thousand members, dissolved and renamed itself the Democratic Left, though retaining the *Morning Star* as its

newspaper. One splinter group named the Communist Party of Britain claimed continuity with the original CPGB.

## communitarianism
A social philosophy which can be traced back to the ideas of the German philosopher G. W. F. Hegel and the work of T. H. Green, among others. It argues that individuals achieve their identities only through the communities that raise and nurture them; in return these individuals have an obligation to support and contribute towards their communities.

## community charge (poll tax)
Form of taxation to raise revenue for local government. In the wake of the Hundred Years War in 1377 parliament levied a flat charge per head of 4 pence for everyone aged over 14 – a poll tax. When a poll tax was introduced in 1380, it triggered the Peasants' Revolt, and the device lay unused until a Conservative government exhumed it in the late 1980s, though the official name given to it at the time was the community charge. Margaret Thatcher came into power looking for an alternative to the rates system, which was paid by only a proportion of householders. Her answer was the community charge, which she believed was fair in that: it was a flat charge on every elector; it gave an incentive to all voters to keep the charge as low as possible; and it increased the accountability of local government to voters. It was introduced in Scotland in 1988 and in England and Wales in 1989. However, it was deemed unfair by many because: it taxed a duke as much as a labourer; it was expensive to collect and was easily evaded; and central government still determined much of local spending, thus eroding the idea of accountability. It was dubbed the 'poll tax' as it was a per capita charge and, though the government tried, it never shook the popular derisive name for the ill-fated local tax. Opposition was intense and in April 1990 there were riots in central London against the tax. Some commentators assert it was the major reason why Margaret Thatcher

fell from power in November 1990. Despite
the ostensible issue of Europe, too many
Conservative MPs calculated she had lost
an unacceptable degree of popular support
over her stubborn insistence on pushing
through the poll tax. The incoming John
Major appointed Thatcher's long-term
opponent Michael Heseltine to be in
charge of a replacement and he introduced
the council tax, a means of raising finance
not dissimilar to the old rates but this time
based on houses according to bands of
value so that owners of larger houses paid
more than those living in smaller ones.

See also council tax.

### community politics

The concentration upon 'grass roots' issues
like pavements, litter and dog fouling,
adopted by the Liberal Party in the 1970s
as its way of raising the political awareness
of people, and thus winning acceptance at
local level. The Liberal Democrats adopted
the concept when the Liberals fused with
the Social Democratic Party in 1988.

### Competition Commission

www.competition-commission.org.uk
Independent public body set up in April
1999 by the Competition Act 1998. It
replaced the Monopolies and Mergers
Commission, which had been set up in 1973
under the Fair Trading Act by government
to investigate and report on possible monopolies following from mergers and takeovers,
as well as the transfer of newspaper assets.
The Competition Commission similarly
inquires into those matters referred to it by
other competition authorities concerning
monopolies, mergers and the regulation of
utility companies. Tribunals hear appeals
against the decisions of the director general
of fair trading and the regulators of utilities. On 18 June 2001 chancellor Gordon
Brown announced that one of his main
objectives during Labour's second term was
to reduce the productivity gap between the
USA and Britain. He announced plans
to make price fixing a criminal offence via
the Competition Commission – this would
bring Britain into line with US practice.

The Consumers Association welcomed this
measure but the Confederation of British
Industry (CBI) was less impressed and felt
it could backfire and place British firms at
a disadvantage compared with European
rivals. The Office of Fair Trading also
undertakes investigations into price fixing,
and Volvo, P&O Ferries and Tate and
Lyle have all been found guilty of doing so.

See also Office of Fair Trading.

### competitiveness

Ability to compete in the international
economy. In April 1998 the *World
Competitiveness Yearbook*, produced by
the Institute for Management Development
based in Switzerland, calculated Britain
was declining on this crucial index. In 1997
Britain had been shown to have leapt from
19th to 11th place, but in 1998 had fallen
back to 12th, one place behind Ireland. The
USA was top of the index, followed by
Singapore and Hong Kong. The *Yearbook*
judged that the change of government in
1997 did not appear to have altered the
generally favourable conditions caused, as
in the USA, by privatisation, deregulation,
flexibility in the labour market and massive
investment. The high value of the pound,
however, was seen as a potential problem.

See also productivity.

### comprehensive school

The model of education adopted by Labour,
under the influence of Anthony Crosland, to
counteract the socially adverse effects of elitism in education resulting from fee-paying
'public schools' and the selective grammar
schools. During the 1970s Labour did its
best to remove grammar schools although
Harold Wilson, an ex-grammar school pupil
himself, had earlier claimed that 'it would
be over my dead body'. The public schools
were left untouched. Comprehensive schools
are generally thought to have been a failure
in terms of making education more egalitar-
ian, as the children of middle-class families
still dominate those who go on to higher
education. Moreover, as schools recruited
from geographical catchment areas, those
in rundown working-class districts tended

to be of poor quality, dubbed 'sink schools', and those in middle-class areas much more successful. The substitution of comprehensive for grammar schools, therefore, according to their critics, denied the bright working-class child the chance of 'escaping' from an unsupportive culture.

*See also* education policy; 11 plus test; grammar school; public school.

## comprehensive spending review (CSR)

A 'rolling programme' whereby a three-year expenditure plan is updated each year. The 2004 review continued the pattern of generous spending on public services (figures per annum increases for three years): 7.1 per cent on health; 4 per cent on education; about 4 per cent to the Home Office in an effort to cut crime by 15 per cent 2004–07; 10 per cent for the security services to prosecute the war on terror; less than 2 per cent for defence, which will face effective cuts after savings targets are met; and 9 per cent for overseas aid, to bring Britain's spending up to the United Nations' recommended level of 0.7 per cent of gross domestic product. In addition chancellor Gordon Brown announced plans, in accordance with the Gershon report, to cut up to 84,000 civil service posts and up to 20,000 extra in local government and devolved assembly jobs. Chief casualty among the departments was Work and Pensions, which was to lose 40,000 jobs; 15,000 were to go from defence and 17,000 from the Inland Revenue. Unions condemned the wholesale destruction of employment while the opposition ridiculed the chances of the cuts ever happening. David Walker in the *Guardian* (13 July 2004) pointed out that, in parallel with the cuts, Brown was planning to create an extra 350,000 public sector jobs, to produce a net increase. Most commentators agreed the review was an attempt by Brown to set the terms of the debate or otherwise 'create the weather' for the probable 12 months or so left before the next general election.

## comptroller and auditor general

*See* National Audit Office.

## compulsory competitive tendering (CCT)

Part of the Conservative 'market testing' approach to government whereby specific functions should be tested against the kind of competitive bids outside agencies can offer, uncushioned by monopoly provision and strongly protective public sector unions. CCT was introduced during the Thatcher regime, for refuse collection and hospital catering. However, the 1991 white paper *Competing for Quality* asserted that 'Public services will increasingly move to a culture where relationships are contractual rather than bureaucratic'. By 1995 it was claimed by government that some 30,000 staff had been reduced in this way and £750,000,000 saved. New Labour replaced CCT with 'best value' in the provision of local government services.

*See also* best value; market testing.

## Confederation of British Industry (CBI)

www.cbi.org.uk

Formed out of three employers' bodies in 1965 as the 'peak' organisation of business interests. The CBI seeks to defend and represent its 15,000 members' interests. It employs over 400 staff and offers members a range of services. It holds an annual conference and has regular access to government. In 1971 a number of smaller firms withdrew to form the Smaller Business Association and the tension between the large companies, which dominate, and the smaller ones still underlies the CBI and inhibits its effectiveness as a lobbying instrument. After 1979 it had less influence with government as Margaret Thatcher tended to see it as part of the 'consensual culture' she opposed. Tensions surfaced when director general Sir Terence Beckett promised a 'bare knuckle fight' with her government in 1983 over the sharp decline in manufacturing industry (after meeting her he emerged chastened and she unmoved). Technically apolitical, the CBI has many more links with the Conservatives than with Labour, although Tony Blair has done much to lean towards the business lobby.

## congestion charge (for Londoners)

A fee charged to motorists entering the central area of the capital. It was introduced, at £5, in February 2003 by London mayor Ken Livingstone. The aim was to reduce traffic flow by 15 per cent and ease conditions which often approached gridlock. Exemptions for certain groups – minicabs, taxis, school buses, motorbikes – proved controversial as others, especially public sector workers, made the case for similar treatment. The income was to be used for improving public transport. The scheme is policed electronically and fines for non-payment are set at £80. By the summer of 2004 the charge was deemed such a success – with an 18 per cent reduction in traffic flow – that even the Conservatives had ceased to oppose it. Livingstone rode on its success on 10 June 2004 to re-election as mayor of London.

## consensus

See postwar consensus.

## conservatism

This tradition of political thought, at least as it is understood in Britain, can be traced back to Edmund Burke's *Reflections on the Revolution in France* (1790). While there are various strands of conservative thinking, and guises in which it presents itself, it is possible to identify some essential features:

1  a reluctance to theorise or engage in social engineering or attempts to change human nature;
2  an acceptance of human imperfectibility and that, contrary to liberal notions, there are limits to human reason and the degree of progress possible in society;
3  an acceptance of market forces as a natural consequence of human behaviour (but otherwise conservatism has no distinctive economic theory);
4  an acceptance of the inevitability of social inequality and the organic nature of human society;
5  a belief in the need for leadership and the maintenance of law and order through the established institutions of church, family and political authority;

6  a suspicion of radical change, or change for its own sake;
7  a belief in a community of faith, often interpreted as a commitment to the established church, that is, the Church of England.

*See also* Conservative Party.

## Conservative Future

www.conservativefuture.com
Youth organisation of the Conservative Party. It claims 10,000 members, with an upper age limit of 30. It has an elected executive based on the party's 43 regions, each with a chairperson, and separate university branches. The Federation of Conservative Students was too libertarian and poorly behaved. Norman Tebbit wound it up in 1987.

## Conservative Party

www.tory.org.uk
Arguably the traditional party of government in Britain, as it governed for two-thirds of the 20th century; it was out of office for only 17 years between 1945 and 1997. The political scientist Samuel Beer argues that its roots can be traced back to the early Tudor period. There was certainly a Tory grouping of aristocrats in the 17th and 18th centuries who supported the monarchy, Empire and Church, as well as aristocratic privileges and agricultural interests. In the wake of the Great Reform Act of 1832, which established a new expanded franchise, the Tories quickly took advantage of the new environment and, under Robert Peel, organised the embryo of the modern party by registering voters and developing a programme based on his Tamworth manifesto. Benjamin Disraeli contributed a vital element to modern Conservatism with his vision of a united nation based on an alliance between the aristocracy and the working class. As the franchise extended, the party succeeded in winning the support of a significant portion of the new voters. Initially the party tended to speak for the landed interests but soon came to represent business, as the Liberals began to favour more interventionist policies

to restrain the excesses of capitalism and Labour to advocate the imposition of socialism. The extension of the franchise in 1867 caused the formation of the National Union of Conservative and Constitutional Associations in the same year.

In the 20th century the Conservatives were influenced by the emergent economic ideas of the Liberal John Maynard Keynes, and after the Second World War subscribed to a consensus on the mixed economy and the welfare state. However, the relative economic decline of Britain in the 1960s and 1970s produced a strong reaction against consensus politics and under the influence of Enoch Powell, Keith Joseph and Margaret Thatcher the party rediscovered classical liberal thinking on economics, as elaborated by the Chicago School of Economics. Under the leadership of the charismatic Margaret Thatcher, the party won three elections, in 1979, 1983 and 1987, and, after her downfall in 1990, another under John Major, in 1992. However, when Tony Blair repositioned New Labour in the centre-ground, and with the Conservatives now divided over Europe and weakened by growing evidence of 'sleaze', the party's credibility collapsed and it crashed to defeat in the 1997 election.

In its wake, the youthful William Hague was elected leader and set about reforming its internal structure to compete more effectively with the remodelled New Labour machine. A further problem was the Conservative Party's large decline in membership since the 1950s; in addition, the membership had a markedly high average age, of over 60. Hague attempted to emulate Blair by reforming his party, which he did by unifying the parliamentary party with the wider one in the country and establishing a controlling board (see below). He also sought to defuse the debate over Europe in the autumn of 1998 by issuing a questionnaire to the party's members asking them to say whether they agreed that the single currency should not be introduced for at least 10 years. He won the vote handsomely, but the debate continued (not without acrimony) at the

party conference of that year. In 1999, Hague sought to move his party away from his initial 'caring Conservatism' direction and towards the right. In the spring of 2000 this appeared to be meeting with some success, as the Conservatives adopted populist policies opposing the arrival of asylum seekers and supporting the rights of householders to defend their property from intruders. However, Hague's poll position failed to improve and he entered the June 2001 election on a somewhat incoherent right-wing platform, for example advocating policies to 'save the pound' (i.e. opposing Britain joining the single European currency), to address the problem of bogus asylum seekers and to make cuts in planned Labour spending while still increasing public services spending. Faced with Labour's emphasis on public services the party crashed to its second successive defeat, mustering only 166 seats – one more than four years earlier. Hague resigned and plunged the party into an unseemly fight to elect a new leader. After a long process, Ken Clarke and Iain Duncan Smith emerged as the two short-listed for the vote by over 300,000 party members in August 2001, with the latter winning the ballot of members a month later.

Ironically, Duncan Smith swung his party towards the very policies he was seen as opposing at his party's 2002 spring conference. Now it seemed his party favoured a shift towards public services and the 'vulnerable' in society. On 30 April 2003 a report by the think tank Conservatives for Change concluded the party lacked a sense of identity and pointed out that its average poll figure between 2001 and 2003 was 30.4 per cent. Discontent festered throughout the year and came to a head with the party's third place in the Brent East by-election. Duncan Smith's speech at the Blackpool conference was consequently billed as 'career defining' but, despite assiduous coaching and the assistance of young aides, who prompted 19 standing ovations, the speech was generally seen as a failure. Once it was suggested that his wife, Betsy, had been paid improperly for acting as her husband's secretary, letters requesting a vote of confidence in the leader began to reach Sir Michael Spicer, chair of the 1922 Committee. By 27 October the required 25 letters from MPs – representing 15 per cent of the parliamentary party – had been received and the next day the vote took place. Duncan Smith polled a creditable 75 votes but there were 90 against. Possible candidates like David Davis, Michael Ancram and Theresa May stood down to allow Michael Howard a free run at the top job. The 'coronation' took place on 6 November, when Howard pledged to continue with the social justice thrust of the previous leader's policies, although zero tolerance on crime and opposition to the European Union were also stressed.

Membership of the party fell from around 1,000,000 in the 1950s to a third of that by 2001, but in August 2004, at 320,000, it still exceeded that of Labour, with, it was claimed, a membership surge in progress.

In terms of voting intentions, a poll in July 2004 showed the Conservatives level with the Liberal Democrats, behind Labour.

> The party that most willingly embraced economic change most strongly resists the social change that inevitably follows. (*The Economist*, 21 July 2001, on Tory inability to accept Michael Portillo's gay past)

*See also* Conservative Party annual conference; Conservative Party leadership contests; 1922 Committee; Tory.

## Conservative Party annual conference

An annual event of some four days, held usually at a seaside location. Conference involves up to 9,000 'representatives' – they are not elected delegates. It is not organised as a policy-making event (unlike for the Labour Party), at least in theory, but is more a rally of the faithful and a morale-boosting activity for party workers. Arthur Balfour, Conservative prime minister at the start of the 20th century, famously said he would sooner take advice from his valet and this indifference was reflected until 1965, as the leader rarely attended until the final afternoon. However, the political writer Richard Kelly questioned the view that the conference was of marginal importance and suggested that the gathering is best understood within the context of the 60 or so regional and sectional conferences which occur during the year. He maintained that grass-roots concerns 'bubble up' from these conferences, creating a 'mood' which informs policy makers. For example, in the 1980s trade union reform was a powerful theme in Conservative trade unionist conferences, as was the reform of married women's taxation in Conservative women's conferences. In both cases action eventually flowed from this articulation at conferences.

## Conservative Party leadership contest

Originally new leaders used to 'emerge' from a huddle of senior party figures but following the 'emergence' of Lord Home in 1963 this was held to be undemocratic and a new system was introduced whereby annual challenges were made possible. New leaders were to be chosen via a series of ballots, in the first of which a candidate required 65 per cent of the vote (i.e. Conservative MPs) to obtain victory. Edward Heath was the first leader to be chosen via this procedure. Margaret Thatcher missed the required percentage by a mere four votes in 1990, when she was deposed, and when William Hague became leader he (helped by Lord Parkinson) changed the system yet again to make it more democratic. The parliamentary party now votes on declared candidates – the candidate with the lowest number of votes dropping out until only two remain, at which time the national membership of the party is enabled to vote to select the new leader. Hague resigned in June 2001 and five candidates fought for the parliamentary party's choice. Michael Portillo was the shock casualty after the second ballot, leaving Kenneth Clarke and Iain Duncan Smith to fight for the votes of party members. In September 2001 the latter, a Eurosceptic right-winger, triumphed over the Europhile moderate Clarke.

In 2003 the challenge element in the rules was activated against Duncan Smith. This required 15 per cent of Conservative MPs to write to the chair of the 1922 Committee, Sir Michael Spicer, to trigger a vote of confidence. By 26 October 2003 this had occurred, and Duncan Smith was then voted out by 90 votes to 75. The problem with the democratic Hague system was that it enabled a leader to be selected by members whom only a minority of MPs supported. Moreover, the ageing membership was biased against any candidate embracing the centrist or centre left ideas needed to win elections. It was therefore of interest that possible candidates stood down to enable Michael Howard to have a free run at the leadership, and the rank and file membership was not allowed any input into the process. Howard was officially 'crowned' on 6 November 2003.

## Conservative Party reforms, 1998

In 1998 William Hague introduced more far-reaching reforms of his party than any British party has adopted since the 19th century. These included:

1 The party became a single entity – for the first time the parliamentary party, the professional and voluntary parties were unified, and a board was established to manage it.
2 The National Conservative Convention now meets twice a year to link members with leadership.
3 The Conservative Policy Forum was established, through which members can influence policy.
4 A centrally held national membership list was drawn up, which for the first time enables the leadership to know who is in the party and how many members there are.
5 The Ethics and Integrity Committee was established. It was set up to prevent situations like that involving Neil Hamilton and the cash for questions scandal recurring. It expelled Lord Archer from the party for five years.
6 The leadership election rules were changed to enable members to vote on

a shortlist of two, decided upon by the parliamentary party.
7 The Young Conservatives were wound up.
8 Foreign donations were banned.

## Conservative Way Forward

www.conwayfor.org

Established in 1991 by Thatcherites to keep alive the flame of the departed but still revered leader. It was not dissimilar to the No Turning Back Group. Its first chair was Cecil Parkinson and other members included such luminaries as Norman Tebbit and Keith Joseph.

## Conservatives for Change (Cchange)

www.cchange.org.uk

Conservative think tank set up in 2002. Conservatives for Change argues that the 'ability to adapt to an evolving society has been the key to Tory success for more than two hundred years'. Its aim is to modernise the party and ensure its policies are in line with the realities and complexities of modern Britain.

## Consignia

*See* Royal Mail.

## constituency

The name given to electoral registration and voting districts in Britain. In 1997 there were 659 constituencies. The Boundary Commission redraws boundaries every 10–15 years to take account of population changes; it tries to achieve a constituency size of around 65,000. Constituency boundaries will be substantially altered if Britain adopts a system of proportional representation for parliamentary elections, a number of versions of which require the introduction of multi-member constituencies.

## constitution

*See* British constitution.

## constitutional approach to politics

The approach to the study of politics which concentrates on the formal institutions of parliament, the cabinet, ministers and departments of state. This legalistic approach was dominant in Britain until the 1960s, when it was judged to be too dry and failed properly to reflect the nature of political processes. Instead, new approaches have been developed, which focus on issues, political behaviour, psephology and political psychology, for example.

### constitutional checks and balances
See separation of powers.

### Constitutional Commission
The title for the Conservatives' unofficial commission on reforming the House of Lords. On 17 September 1998 it suggested the voting rights of hereditary peers should not be abolished until after the next election. It also suggested the upper chamber could become more effective as a scrutiniser of legislation, giving up its legislative rights in exchange for the enhancement of such a role. Its chair was Lord Mackay, the former Conservative lord chancellor. Most of these suggestions were rendered irrelevant by the ending of the hereditary element by Labour in 2000 and its winning of the 2001 election by a huge majority. The commission was one of three set up by the shadow cabinet in order to contribute to the debate and was disbanded after reporting.

### constitutional law
Britain is unusual in the sense that it does not have a special body of statutes governing state and citizen, sometimes referred to as constitutional or fundamental law. The constitution is the result of the ordinary law of the land as laid down by parliament, the courts and more recently (and controversially) the European Union. Since New Labour entered office, a draft constitution for the UK has been developed by reformers, although it is difficult to see a full-blown written constitution emerging in the near future.
See also British constitution.

### constitutional monarchy
See monarchy.

### constitutional reform
Like any long-standing institution, the British government has been resistant to reform. In 1828 the Duke of Wellington denied it required any reform, as it was already perfect. Traditional Conservatives argue that an organic constitution adjusts 'naturally' to changing social and political conditions. Many of a more radical frame of mind disagree and a constant pressure for change has characterised British government over the last two centuries. Towards the end of the 20th century Labour allied itself with the Liberal Democrats and the campaigning Charter 88 organisation. Initially the raft of proposed reforms, like devolution and change to the House of Lords, were opposed by the Conservatives, but as the measures passed into fact they too began to accept their validity.

### constitutionalism
One of the early elements of 18th-century liberal thinking which, while supporting the need for government, was also mindful of the danger it might pose to liberty through a concentration of power. To guard against this eventuality liberal philosophers therefore argued for constitutionalism, which includes the following key elements:
1  the diffusion of power into different parts of the state;
2  the creation of checks and balances to ensure no single branch of government becomes over-mighty;
3  the establishment of a codified written constitution, to clarify the powers, rights and duties of each part of government in relation to the citizen.

### Continuity IRA
Dissident republican terrorist group, sometimes linked to the Real IRA. It is said to have support in South Down and Fermanagh in Northern Ireland and to have been responsible for many incidents following the Good Friday Agreement when the IRA agreed to a ceasefire. In February 2003 the group threatened to kill Catholic police officers if Sinn Fein joined a new policing board.
See also Irish Republican Army.

**control freak**
Someone who feels the need to exercise
total control. 'Are you a pluralist or control
freak?' asked Paddy Ashdown of Tony
Blair but the answer has never been made
definitively. The implication in the tag,
attached regularly to Blair, is that despite
outward appearances of giving power away,
he still wants to control things personally.
Moreover, it is often asserted, he seeks
to control Labour MPs through party
headquarters, and for example has issued
pagers to MPs to keep them informed of
policy at the centre and to keep an eye
on what they are up to. Evidence cited in
support of the claim includes the suggestion that he gave power via new assemblies
to Scotland, Wales, Northern Ireland and
London but then sought to nominate the
politicians in charge. Further items on the
charge sheet include neutering the Freedom
of Information Act and trying to prevent
a reformed House of Lords becoming an
elected chamber. Finally, he seemed to turn
his back on reforming the voting system in
the wake of the election when he noted that
proportional representation tends to give
disproportionate power to small parties
(*The Economist*, 9 June 2001).

**convention**
Unwritten rule or understanding based
upon past practice. Britain does not have
a fully written or codified constitution
and therefore large areas of government
practice are governed by convention.
For example, it is a convention that the
monarch will call upon the leader who
can command a majority in the House of
Commons to form a government, although
there is no formal law which embodies such
a procedure.

**core executive**
Term used to describe the apex of the
decision-making pyramid, that involving
the prime minister and cabinet, as well as
a network of related personnel, including
the permanent under-secretaries of the
Whitehall departments, the Cabinet Office
and the Downing Street Policy Unit.

**corporatism**
Traditionally the intermediary role played
by corporations and professional associations, or unions, between the public and
the state. In the postwar period, it has
become a pejorative term used by both left
and right. The right point to the over-cosy
relationship between trade union leaders
and the Labour government of the mid to
late 1970s, while those on the left criticise
the close relationship between corporate
business and government during the periods
of Conservative government in the 1980s.
Such a close conclave between peak organisations and government was thought to be
anti-democratic 'high-level fixing', which
sidelined parliament and thus the electorate.
The term tends not to be used so extensively
these days but most governments seek to use
the approach to some extent in practice.
*See also* tripartism.

**council housing**
Subsidised local authority housing. The
Housing and Town Planning Act 1919
established council housing on a large scale.
During the interwar years over a million
houses were built by local councils for rent,
many on the outskirts of large towns and
cities. After the Second World War even
more effort was channelled into this sector
– over 3 million such houses were built in
the period 1945–85. By 1979 one in three
houses was council owned. However, by
the 1980s council estates became identified with social problems and this, together
with the 1.7 million houses sold under
Margaret Thatcher's 'right to buy' policy
and the growing preference for Britons to
live in their own houses, helped reduce the
public sector in housing to under a quarter
of the total. By 1998 local authorities in the
north were finding it hard to find tenants
for houses which had traditionally been
highly sought after. The sale of council
houses, often the best stock, left 3.4 million
homes of variable quality and many families
preferred to buy a cheap terraced house.
This led to a situation in which councils
were having to advertise for tenants to move
in and occupy a huge redundant housing

POLITICS

stock. However, in the south of England waiting lists persisted. By 2000 virtually no new council houses were being built, as the government put more emphasis on new housing association properties instead.

*See also* right to buy.

## Council of Europe
www.coe.int
European body (though not part of the European Union) concerned with human rights, culture and the environment. It was established in 1949 by a resolution passed at the 1948 Congress of Europe and is based in Strasbourg. Founding members were the UK, France, the Netherlands, Belgium, Luxembourg, Denmark, Sweden Norway, Ireland, Italy and Greece. It now has 45 members. The Council has: a Committee of Ministers (foreign ministers); a parliamentary assembly (comprising 286 members divided into five political groups); and the Congress of Local and Regional Authorities of Europe. The Council has its own secretariat of over 1,000 officials, headed by a secretary general elected by the assembly. The Council cannot make laws but issues conventions or charters or codes. In 1997 the Council had a budget of £136 million. Initially the Council was the main forum for discussion about European integration but its advice was largely ignored by member states and the emergent European Economic Community became the leading force in Europe.

## Council of Ireland
Part of the power-sharing Sunningdale Agreement in 1973. The Council was set up to accommodate the 'Irish dimen-sion' and allowed delegates from the north and south of Ireland to discuss common problems. It collapsed along with the Sunningdale Agreement: yet another false dawn.

*See also* Sunningdale Agreement.

## Council of Ministers
http://ue.eu.int/cms3_fo/index.htm
The main decision-making part of the European Union, comprising ministers from

all member states. It is to be distinguished from the Council of the European Union. It meets over 100 times a year, with relevant ministers attending to deal with the issue under discussion, illustrating how wide the impact of the European Union now is upon the politics of member states. The Committee of Permanent Representatives (COREPER) undertakes most of the preparation for these important meetings. This body, in tandem with the Council, is chaired by the country currently holding the six-monthly presidency. Council decisions are issued in a number of forms, two of the most important being: regulations, which have immediate force as European Union law; and directives, which are binding on members, but national governments have discretion on how to implement policies, an example being the UK's decision to use the simple plurality method of elections for the European parliament until 1999, when the system was changed to the regional list system of proportional representation. Decisions are taken via a qualified majority voting system, whereby members' votes are 'weighted' according to population size. This move away from unanimity has been controversial and has been criticised by the Eurosceptics as undermining the sovereignty of member states.

*See also* qualified majority voting (QMV).

## Council of the European Union
http://ue.eu.int/cms3_fo/index.htm
Body that comprises heads of government. It was set up in 1974. In France's case the president attends. Also included are the foreign ministers and two commissioners. It meets twice a year and has been respon-sible for some of the major initiatives in the development of the European Union, like the European Monetary System and the Maastricht Treaty. However, Council meetings sometimes become a matter more of appearance and media events than of substantive discussion.

## council tax
The replacement for the hated poll tax introduced by John Major's government

in 1991. This represented a return to something approaching the rates, in that it is based on property values. However, unlike the old system there are bands based upon the market value, with a 25 per cent reduction for single-person occupancy. Compared with the poll tax the new system was accepted with minimal dissent. However, steep rises, above inflation, in 2004 caused widespread protests and the government moved to cap spending by some local authorities. In July 2004 proposals were made to reform the council tax by introducing more complex banding that takes more account of property values. On 18 July 2004 the government denied claims that the forthcoming review of the council tax would lead to threefold increases; rather, it would clarify problems and issues for further analysis.

*See also* community charge; rates.

### councillor

Elected member of local government. To qualify to stand for election, candidates must: be over 21; be registered voters; have no undischarged criminal sentence; not be insane; and be either resident in the local authority concerned or own property or work within its borders. They must not be an employee of the authority for which they seek election nor a senior employee of any other local authority. Councillors, in common with MPs, are unrepresentative of the socio-economic profile of the people they represent: 80 per cent of councillors are over 45, a third are retired, over three-quarters are male owner-occupiers and only a quarter are working class.

### Country Land and Business Association

www.cla.org.uk
Organisation (formerly known as the Country Landowners Association) with 50,000 members, which promotes the interests of those who own property and land in England and Wales. This body, founded in 1907, speaks for those closely involved in the rural economy from the owner's point of view.

### Countryside Agency

www.countryside.gov.uk
A body set up in 1999 to extend access and recreational opportunities to people who enjoy the countryside. Its remit extends to issues of conservation and landscape beauty. It advises the government on national parks, areas of outstanding natural beauty and nature trails. It replaced the Countryside Commission, which had originally been set up in 1949 as the National Park Commission.

### Countryside Alliance

www.countryside-alliance.net
A loose coalition of lobby groups concerned with the countryside, some of which hold irreconcilable views. The Alliance opposed the private member's bill on banning fox-hunting and in the spring of 1998 mounted a very successful demonstration in London, when it mustered over 300,000 protestors.

### county

Local government unit in Britain. Counties date back to Saxon times. Since the Local Government Act 1888, they have been run by councils elected every four years. The Local Government Act 1972 drastically reduced the number of counties and rationalised structures in England and Wales. As a result there are 47 'shire' county councils containing 333 district ones, as well as six metropolitan counties with 36 elected district councils. In the mid-1980s, the Conservative government controversially scrapped the metropolitan county councils and transferred their functions to the districts or to joint boards.

*See also* Local Government Act 1972; unitary authority.

### county court

Court that hears most cases arising under civil law within each county. County courts deal with claims for up to £5,000 damages and cases that involve, for example, landlord and tenant disputes, mortgage claims, equity trusts and probate, bankruptcies, undefended divorces and injunctions against domestic violence. Cases are heard by either a judge or a registrar (a junior judge). There are over 340 county courts in England and Wales.

*See also* High Court.

## Court of Appeal

Court that hears appeals from lower-level courts. People dissatisfied with a verdict in a criminal or civil court can apply to the Court of Appeal, which was set up in 1968 and comprises a criminal and civil division. It comprises 16 lord justices of appeal plus a number of ex-officio judges. Appeals are not reruns of trials, as the court listens only to arguments put by lawyers and witnesses are not heard again. Rather the court listens to legal argument with reference to the original trial record. Most appeals are heard by three judges; however, their decisions need not be unanimous. The head of the Civil Division is the Master of the Rolls. The Criminal Division is headed by of the Lord Chief Justice and it hears cases from lower courts and can give judgements on the safety of a decision, quash or confirm the conviction, and vary the sentence.

## Crichel Down case

Case that concerned land taken over by the Ministry of Defence during the Second World War and resold improperly. It is a crucial case in any discussion of ministerial responsibility. The minister of agriculture, Sir Thomas Dugdale, knew nothing about the sale but resigned in 1954 as a result of the supposed rule that ministers are always responsible for the actions of civil servants in their departments. However, subsequent analyses suggest that he was forced to resign through lack of backbench support rather than rigorous adherence to the rules governing resignations and ministerial responsibility.

## crime

Britain is usually held to be a relatively peaceful country but crime levels, as in most developed countries, have rocketed since the Second World War. In 1979, for example, there were 2.5 million notifiable offences but by 1990 the figure had doubled. The

Conservatives pride themselves on being the party of 'law and order'. Senior party members, especially home secretaries, are encouraged by the annual conferences to legislate for harsher sentences, including the reintroduction of capital punishment. But the vast increases in crime during their time in office lost the Conservatives their advantage and the public's disaffection was exploited by Labour, traditionally the party which tended to speak up for the civil rights of the accused and argued for wider social answers to rising crime levels. This position changed when Tony Blair, as shadow home secretary, decided to take a tougher line on crime and coined the slogan 'tough on crime, tough on the causes of crime'. This proved an effective blend of the old approach and a more populist, tougher new one; it was to become part of Blair's repositioning strategy for the party when he became leader.

Despite criticism from the Conservatives and voter unease, crime figures reduced during the first term of Labour rule. British Crime Survey figures (based on interviews with a random sample of 40,000 citizens and hence judged to be more reliable than police figures) issued in July 2004 revealed the longest sustained drop in crime figures since 1898 – a fall of 39 per cent from their 1995 peak. The risk of being a victim of crime fell from 40 per cent in 1995 to 26 per cent in March 2004. Police figures continued to show a slight increase overall but with steep rises in violent crime, apart from murder, which registered a fall. The Home Office confirmed on 21 July a government objective of reducing crime by 15 per cent by 2007.

*See also* Crime and Disorder Act 1998; penal policy; vigilante movement.

## Crime and Disorder Act 1998

Since the late 1970s law and order has become a key issue in British politics. During the 1980s and early 1990s successive Conservative governments passed a raft of legislation which strengthened the powers of the police and courts and allowed the party to claim that it, and not Labour, was the trustee of the nation's tranquillity and the enemy of the criminal. However, rising crime figures during the 1980s and early 1990s gave Tony Blair (then shadow home secretary) the opportunity to develop a new approach to the Labour Party's law and order policies. Once elected to office, Labour's home secretary, Jack Straw, introduced the Crime and Disorder Bill as the centrepiece of the party's law and order policies. Enacted in 1998, it contains the following provisions:

1  fast tracking of persistent young offenders;
2  a final police warning to replace the discredited repeat caution system;
3  new compulsory parenting orders and counselling sessions;
4  reparation orders designed to make the offender pay compensation for damage done to victims;
5  local curfew schemes to keep disorderly youngsters at home;
6  local authorities to set up partnerships with voluntary and statutory agencies to tackle crime prevention;
7  the police given powers to apprehend school truants;
8  antisocial behaviour orders introduced to control disorderly or aggressive people in the local community;
9  compulsory testing and treatment of drug offenders;
10 special orders for sex offenders, including the provision that the police monitor the movements of rapists and similar offenders when released from prison;
11 a new offence of racially aggravated assault introduced to deal with racially motivated violence.

*See also* antisocial behaviour order; crime; Macpherson report.

## criminal law

Applies to a vast area of social and public life, ranging from relatively minor offences such as breaking the speed limit (covered by the Road Traffic Acts) to the taking of life. A crime is an act (or failure to act), defined by statute or common law, to be a public wrong and therefore punishable by the state in a criminal court. To count as a crime a person must commit a wrong (*actus reus*) and have a guilty mind (*mens rea*). Ministers of the crown and MPs are subject to criminal law as private individuals. However, MPs do enjoy parliamentary privilege and ministers are protected for actions carried out as part of their official role.

*See also* parliamentary privilege.

## cronyism

Form of favouritism. An accusation frequently made against New Labour is that it moves friends into top jobs. Tony Blair is reckoned to be the chief culprit, with his former flatmate Charles Falconer given ministerial office; his former boss, Lord Irvine, made lord chancellor; and his tennis partner Lord Levy made an unofficial envoy to the Middle East. Irvine, too, when in office, was accused of the same tendency, with former colleagues given roles as government advisors and senior appointments to the judiciary made from among his friends and those connected to government. Blair's opposition to an elected upper house has drawn the criticism that he wants to fill a whole legislative chamber with 'Tony's cronies'.

## cross-bencher

A member of the House of Lords who decides not to take up the party whip and sits instead on the 'cross-benches'. After the expulsion of most hereditary peers in 1999 the cross-benchers held the balance of power in the upper chamber.

## Crossman reforms

Proposals to reform the House of Lords and set up departmental select committees put forward by Richard Crossman in 1968–69. He suggested a two-tier solution to the problem of the upper chamber, involving 250 voting peers with the remainder participating but not voting. Hereditary peers would be abolished; the Lords' power of delay would be reduced to six months and peers would lose the right to vote from the age of 72. The proposals were defeated by a combination of the left, led by Michael Foot, who thought them too mild, and from the right, led by Enoch Powell, who thought them too extreme.

## crown
*See* monarchy.

## Crown Appointments Commission
Body that appoints archbishops and bishops. It was set up in 1976 by the Callaghan Labour government. A 12-strong committee including representatives of the Synod, the House of Laity and the relevant diocese meets to decide on two names to pass on to the prime minister, who chooses one and recommends it to the queen.

## crown court
A court that hears the more serious criminal cases. Crown courts involve the full majesty of the law and are staffed by a judge and jury, with barristers representing both prosecution and defence. They were set up by the Courts Act 1971. Judges can pass sentences up to the maximum set by parliament and hear appeals against convictions in magistrates' courts. Recently Jack Straw, the home secretary, has supported the idea that jury trial should be abolished for certain types of case, including those which involve complex financial matters, where lay people are generally ill equipped to understand the issues involved.

## crown dependency
*See* Channel Islands; Isle of Man.

## Crown Estate
www.crownestate.co.uk
Body charged with administering royal properties. In 1761 the crown gave up revenues from its estates and an office was established to arrange the sale, purchase and management of the crown estates. In 1927 it became embodied in the Commissioners of the Crown Lands. The Crown Estate was formed in 1956.

## Crown Prosecution Service (CPS)
www.cps.gov.uk
The agency which decides whether or not a case should be pursued in a criminal court. The CPS was set up in 1986 for England and Wales. Before its establishment such decisions were taken by the police and police solicitors alone, an arrangement which attracted criticism as it was thought the police were often biased. The CPS is staffed by 2,000 lawyers – solicitors and barristers – operating in 42 prosecution areas, each with its own chief crown prosecutor. The head of the CPS is the director of public prosecutions. The CPS has attracted more than its fair share of controversy and in 1998 the National Audit Office accused it of being over-bureaucratic, slow and inefficient. Its director, Dame Barbara Mills, resigned before the report was published. In October of the same year it was disclosed that a secret list of police informants had been leaked from the CPS to the criminal underworld, placing the informers' lives at risk.
*See also* director of public prosecutions.

## cube law
'Law' of voting adduced originally by David Butler, one of the first British psephologists. It posits that in a two-party majoritarian voting system a mathematical relationship exists between a party's share of the seats in a legislative chamber and the proportion of the vote it receives. Baldly stated, the 'law' predicts that where parties A and B contest an election and the votes are divided in the ratio of $y:x$, the seats won will reflect the ratio $x^3:y^3$. However, the applicability of the cube law began to decline with the development of a three-party system in the 1970s and 1980s and is now rarely cited.

## cultural governance
Norman Fairclough argues in *New Labour, New Language?* (2000) that part of the government's approach to dealing with social exclusion is to change the culture of public services and those they serve, in particular the attitudes of welfare claimants and the general population. A key element in this process is the use of a new language to encourage a new way of thinking about social welfare and social exclusion,

something which Margaret Thatcher and 'new right' activists did in their enthusiasm for the entrepreneurial culture in the 1980s. He quotes from an official press release: 'The Social Security Secretary stressed that as part of the fight against poverty a radical change of culture-confronting attitudes and long-term dependency is needed.... This is the poverty of expectation that we must tackle by changing attitudes, and making sure that people know what help and opportunities are available to them'.

*See also* ideology; new right; political language.

## curia regis

Name given to the royal court of the Norman monarchs. Originally it embodied all the functions of government: making, interpreting and implementing laws. It declined as the functions of the monarchy became more complex and its duties transferred to other specific bodies. Nevertheless, it is one of the founding 'embryonic' institutions of British government.

## Curry report, 2002

Report of the Policy Commission on the Future of Farming and Food, chaired by Sir Donald Curry. Many factors suggested that farming was in crisis in the early years of the 21st century: farmers earned on average only £5,200 a year and that for working a week which for 60 per cent of farmers was over 66 hours long. The Curry Commission studied food and farming policy in early 2002. It recommended: better cooperation between farmers; a relaxation of competition rules to enable farmers to negotiate collectively with the food industry; encouragement for farmers to sell their food locally; the scrapping of production subsidies by the European Union, as they tend to make production inefficient; and creating higher food prices.

*See also* Common Agricultural Policy.

## Cymru Annibynnol

*See* Welsh Republican Movement.

# D

## D notice

Document sent by the Ministry of Defence's D Notice Committee to journalists to prevent the publishing of information deemed harmful to the national interest. D notices were introduced in 1912 in an atmosphere of concern over the risk of German spies. They have not been used very often since the 1960s.

## *Daily Express*

www.express.co.uk
Daily popular newspaper, founded in 1900 and taken over by Lord Beaverbrook in 1916. For many decades it was the leading popular newspaper; its circulation exceeded 4 million during the 1960s but fell dramatically during the next two decades to just over 1 million. Its political stance used to be loyally right-wing Conservative but when sold to Labour-supporting Lord Hollick it changed camps and became 'Blairite'. United MAI now owns *Express* newspapers after they were sold by Lord Hollick. The group is headed by Richard Desmond, who also has an assortment of pornographic publications in his portfolio, which was the reason why his donation to the Labour Party became controversial. The *Daily Express* has a circulation of 950,000; the *Daily Star* 640,000; the *Sunday Express* 840,000; giving United MAI a share of 14 per cent of the national newspaper circulation.

*See also* Beaverbrook, Max.

## *Daily Herald*

Newspaper that was relaunched in 1964 as the *Sun*. It first appeared in 1911 as a strike sheet for the London print unions. The *Daily Herald* was officially founded in 1912 and owned partly by Odhams Press and the Trades Union Congress (TUC). The TUC sold its 49 per cent holding in 1961 to the International Publishing Corporation (which owned the *Daily*

*Mirror*). Throughout its life the *Herald* supported the labour movement and the policies of the Labour Party; ironically, its successor was bought by Rupert Murdoch in 1969 and turned into a raucously right-wing newspaper, the *Sun*.

*See also Sun*; Murdoch, Rupert.

### Daily Mail

www.dailymail.co.uk
Newspaper founded in 1896. It was one of the new kind of popular newspaper invented by Alfred Harmsworth (Lord Northcliffe), which adapted certain American features of design and presentation. It favoured a right-wing political stance and gave much publicity to the forged Zinoviev letter in 1924. It accordingly criticised left-wing protests against unemployment as communist inspired and sympathised with the anti-Semitism of Nazism in the 1930s. It suffered a decline in the 1960s and 1970s but was overhauled in the early 1980s under David English, who was knighted by Margaret Thatcher for his loyal support. Its editor, Paul Dacre, appointed in 1992, was successful in making it 'the housewife's favourite' and added three-quarters of a million readers within five years. In the run-up to the 1997 election the paper nudged closer to New Labour. However, after a few years it returned to opposing the Labour government and during the second term fiercely attacked many aspects of New Labour, including the prime minister's wife. Tony Blair was said to be influenced by the newspaper as the 'voice of middle-class England'.

*See also* Zinoviev letter; Harmsworth, Alfred.

### Daily Mirror

www.mirror.co.uk
Newspaper founded in 1903. The *Daily Mirror* was owned by Lord Rothermere, brother of Lord Northcliffe. It appeared to be dying in the 1930s, as advertisers did not like its tabloid style, and Lord Rothermere abandoned it, but it was relaunched successfully, aimed at a young

working-class audience. It reached a circulation of 1.5 million by 1939. During the war Herbert Morrison defended its right to be critical of the government but its director, Cecil King, was difficult to silence. After the war, under its famous editor High Cudlipp, the *Daily Mirror* became the classic and dominant paper of the working class and Labour in its sympathies. However, it had to give way to a new and brasher competitor, the *Sun*, which came to prominence in the 1970s and pre-eminence in the 1980s. The *Mirror* has maintained a pro-Labour stance but by 2002 its editor, Piers Morgan, was increasingly critical of Tony Blair and all his works. Morgan was sacked in May 2004 after publishing pictures of Iraqi prisoners being mistreated which later proved to be fake.

### Daily Sport

Newspaper founded in 1992 as a soft porn publication by David Sullivan. Its political stance is irrelevant as it virtually eschews news and politics for sex and trivia; indeed, it scarcely passes muster as a newspaper at all.

### Daily Telegraph

www.telegraph.co.uk
Newspaper founded in 1855. The *Telegraph* was the first of the 'penny' papers to be published in London. It merged with the Conservative *Morning Post* in 1937, and has since offered staunch support to the Conservative Party up to the present day.

### Daily Worker

*See Morning Star.*

### de Chastelain commission

*See* Independent International Commission on Decommissioning.

### death penalty

For many years the punishment for murder in Britain, but the subject of much soul searching whenever it was implemented. In 1965 the Murder (Abolition of Death Penalty) Act replaced the death penalty with a mandatory life sentence. The punishment was retained, at least in principle, for 'treason' and 'piracy with violence', but these, too, were dropped after the passing of the Crime and Disorder Act 1998. In 1999 the home secretary signed the sixth protocol of the European Convention on Human Rights, which ensured the death penalty could not readily be revived.

Traditionally, the parliamentary votes on this subject were free of party control and subject to 'conscience'. In every parliamentary session during the 1980s a vote was held and lost; in 1988 the majority opposing reintroduction was 123, in 1994 even bigger. It seemed Conservative MPs who won support in their constituencies for supporting the death penalty changed their minds when they heard the rational arguments against its reintroduction. These included: there was no increase in Britain's low level of murders, about 650 per annum, in the years after abolition (though closer to 900 by the end of the millennium); it would put more pressure on judges and juries; it would remove the possibility of reversing wrong judgements; it would be a retrogressive step for a civilised society; finally, it would cast a shadow over the criminal justice system, which is one of the central institutions of a civilised society. Nevertheless, many Conservative MPs advocated a return of a punishment routinely applied in the USA. Surveys show that two-thirds of the British people tend to agree.

## debate

The principal means whereby conflicts of ideas or policy are examined in democracies. In Britain they occur in the media, for example newspaper articles and current affairs programmes, but more importantly in the House of Commons. Debates take many forms: a substantive motion allowing a wide-ranging discussion; an adjournment motion at the end of a day's business; and second and third readings or the report stage of the legislative process through which a bill progresses. Many debates are initiated by the opposition, which has some 20 days of parliamentary time at its disposal, or by private members (i.e. MPs),

who have most Fridays devoted to their proposals. Debates are controlled by the speaker, who calls contributors alternately from the parties. Similar procedures are followed in the House of Lords.

Critics claim the quality of debate in the House of Commons has declined since the golden years of the 19th century and the brilliance of more modern orators like Aneurin Bevan and Winston Churchill. Debates, however, are very lively compared with those in some other legislatures, for example in Scandinavia. In the Commons members can speak from where they sit, interruptions are very frequent and the cut and thrust of debate is often supplemented by heckling. This means the speaker of the House has a special responsibility for maintaining order and preventing debates degenerating into chaos. The televising of parliament has done nothing to reduce this tendency, but neither has it led to the predicted excesses by those who opposed its introduction. Televised extracts from Commons debates tend to be well received in the USA, although not as well as the reliably eventful prime minister's questions. Tony Blair has been criticised for not participating in parliamentary debates and seldom turning up to vote, thus demonstrating an alleged contempt for parliament.

*See also* act of parliament.

## decentralisation

The opposite of centralisation, an affliction believed to affect British government with its focus on decision making by London-based institutions. Devolution to Scotland and Wales undertaken by the Labour government after 1997 was one form of decentralisation. Another was the hiving off of routine central government functions to agencies following the Ibbs report. Parallel with this tendency, however, is a continuing drift towards centralisation: a desire by Tony Blair not to 'let go' of power and to seek to control appointments/elections to devolved bodies, for example. Peter Hennessy was sufficiently concerned about this trend in July 1998 to speak of the dangers of 'court government' and a 'command premiership', a view echoed by Andrew Rawnsley in his book *Servants of the People* (2000).

*See also* devolution; Ibbs report.

### decolonisation

The process whereby Britain surrendered its imperial possessions, often reluctantly and in the face of armed nationalist demands. By the 1931 Statute of Westminster, Canada, South Africa, Australia and New Zealand as well as Newfoundland gained formal independence as part of the British Commonwealth. The process of succumbing to armed pressure effectively started in the 1930s when Iraq (1932) and Egypt (1936) gained independence. It continued after the war when India, Pakistan and Burma were given independence by Attlee's Labour government in 1947. During the 1950s the Conservatives strove to hang on to the Empire and fought uprisings in Kenya and Malaya, but the pressures of nationalist movements and the expense of resisting them produced a change in policy. In 1960 Harold Macmillan delivered his 'wind of change' speech in South Africa, which, on the heels of independence for Ghana (1957) and Nigeria (1960), heralded another bout of decolonisation. The Empire was virtually gone by the 1980s, with only a few far-flung possessions left, the major one of which, Hong Kong, was transferred back to China in 1997. In 1982 Britain went to war with Argentina over the Falkland Islands, which remain British, a situation still contested by Argentina. Gibraltar is another colony in dispute, with Spain claiming it, although in January 2002 plans were announced of a possible joint sovereignty agreement over the rock. Only a few islands remain as crown possessions.

*See also* Commonwealth (British); Empire (British); Statute of Westminster.

### decommissioning

Term used to describe disarming by paramilitaries in Northern Ireland. The surrender of its arms by the Irish Republican Army (IRA) was a crucial point in the negotiations of the Good Friday Agreement (1998). In its aftermath, the unionists complained that the IRA was showing no signs of movement on an issue which is crucial to the agreement and in January 2000 the power-sharing executive in Northern Ireland was suspended by the then secretary of state, Peter Mandelson, for the lack of progress. However, the executive had been re-established by the early summer of that year when the IRA agreed to put its arms 'beyond use'. The issue remained, however, and David Trimble, under pressure from within his own Ulster Unionist Party, threatened to resign if the IRA failed to begin meaningful decommissioning by the beginning of July 2001. However, when the IRA offered two acts of disarmament the unionists were not satisfied and demanded the disbandment of the IRA; Tony Blair backed this up in October 2002 by requiring republicans to give up paramilitarism. In October 2002 the government suspended the executive for the fourth time.

### defence forces

*See* armed forces; Ministry of Defence.

### defence policy

The government's direction of the armed forces in promotion and defence of the nation's interests. After the Second World War a key aspect of British defence policy was to maintain a role as a world power. The development of nuclear weapons and the maintenance of overseas commitments were both part of this. Relative economic decline, however, and the costs of colonial commitments made this progressively difficult and defence policy was successively scaled down. In the 1960s Denis Healey decided to withdraw the British presence from east of Suez and British entry into the European Community led to a reordering of defence priorities. During the 1980s defence expenditure was further reduced, though the Falklands War delayed the full implementation of this. During the financial year 1998–99 defence expenditure was £22.2 billion, out of a total government expenditure of £332.5 billion (6.6 per cent). The emphasis of defence policy is now firmly tied to the North Atlantic Treaty Organisation (NATO), in particular to react rapidly to overseas trouble-spots, especially terrorist-inspired problems, with flexible airborne armed forces. British armed forces were sent to Bosnia to assist peacekeeping efforts in November 1992; in 1999 to Kosovo to prevent Serbian persecution of mostly Albanian Kosovars; and in March 2003 to Iraq, where some 10,000 troops supported the US-led action against the Saddam Hussein regime. In July 2004 a series of cuts in the armed forces were announced.

*See also* armed forces; Ministry of Defence.

## deference

Term usually used in two senses in relation to British political culture: 'political deference', meaning respect for government and a willingness to obey the laws of the land; and 'social deference', meaning the preference of some people for a political elite drawn from the upper and middle classes. Both forms have declined, some of the reasons being the revelations of 'sleaze' during the time of the Major government (1990–97), which brought upper-class politicians into disrepute, and the decline of a 'superior' political class in the Conservative Party, which preferred grammar school products like Edward Heath, Margaret Thatcher, John Major and William Hague as leaders, rather than those educated at private schools such as Eton and Harrow.

*See also* political culture; sleaze.

## de-industrialisation

A phenomenon caused by the recessions of the 1980s, when whole tranches of heavy and manufacturing industry, for example shipbuilding, coalmining and textiles, found it difficult to compete against foreign producers. Low levels of productivity and profitability were some of the more important reasons for this decline, together with Britain's poor record for industrial

relations. By the mid-1980s many firms had gone bankrupt, putting hundreds of thousands of workers out of work. Less than one-fifth of employees were now engaged in manufacturing, and vast areas of the Midlands and north were reduced to industrial wastelands. During the 1990s many areas began to revive with the arrival of service and 'sunrise' industries and overseas capital investment, especially from Japan and the USA.

## delegate

A person who is authorised to act on behalf of another or group. The term is most usually associated with delegates who attend party conferences to vote on policies and elections of officials. 'Mandated delegates' to the Labour conference have specific instructions to perform certain tasks or vote a specific way; their degree of autonomy is strictly limited. Representatives at Conservative conferences do not expect to help formulate policy, although they will press their views when given the chance.

*See also* representative.

## delegated legislation

'Secondary' legislation or statutory instrument (SI) that is formed on the authority of 'primary' or 'parent' legislation. Legislation often contains authority for regulations to be made by ministers, agencies and sub-national levels of government. An example would be the Baking and Sausage Making (Christmas and New Year) Regulation 1985. This owed its existence to the Health and Safety at Work Act 1974, and comes under the aegis of the Health and Safety Executive, which has authority over working conditions. There are various methods for introducing delegated legislation but typically a 'commencement order' is laid before parliament, and if there are no objections from either House it becomes law within 40 days. The Statutory Instruments Committee has the job of sifting through the SIs and investigating any which take their interest. Few do. In 1996, 1,832 SIs were passed, half of which were concerned with local government and not subject to parliamentary control. Orders in Council, issued by the Privy Council, and local authority bylaws are other forms of delegated legislation.

*See also* Delegated Powers and Deregulation Scrutiny Committee.

### Delegated Powers and Deregulation Scrutiny Committee
www.parliament.the-stationery-office.co.uk/pa/ld199798/ldselect/lddelder.htm
Permanent committee of the House of Lords that examines delegated legislation in order to determine whether the powers so delegated are justified and necessary. It makes recommendations to parliament accordingly.

*See also* delegated legislation.

### Delors plan, 1989
Plan that advocated economic and monetary union between member states of the European Community, named after Jacques Delors, president of the European Commission 1985–88. The plan envisaged a three-stage process of union: increased coordination through the Exchange Rate Mechanism of economic policies; the establishment of a European Central Bank; and finally the introduction of a single currency. Margaret Thatcher said 'The Delors proposal would not command the support of the British cabinet', although Geoffrey Howe (foreign secretary) and Nigel Lawson (chancellor) did support it. She grudgingly agreed at Madrid in June 1989 to the first stage provided the second and third were left open. John Major eventually took Britain into the Exchange Rate Mechanism in October 1989, a decision which he and others would later come to regret.

*See also* Black Wednesday; Exchange Rate Mechanism.

### demand management
*See* Keynesianism.

### democracy
A term derived from the Greek words *demos* (people) and *kratos* (strength). It originally referred to the method of rule whereby citizens of the Greek city states participated in public affairs, the essential idea being that ultimate sovereignty or authority lies with those sections of the population eligible to vote. In most truly democratic countries this is supplemented by genuine respect for opposition parties, free speech, and regular free elections so that the people have a chance to exercise their ultimate power and possibly change the people who rule them. Britain's democracy has an unusual provenance as the country began with a traditional monarchy but adjusted over time to the demands of an emergent parliament. Almost seamlessly, democratic institutions developed to the extent that the monarch was displaced and replaced by a prime minister as chief executive who dominated the legislature by virtue of leadership of the majority party in that branch of government. 'Democracy' is a word that means far more when it is qualified by another like 'liberal' or 'representative'.

> No word in the vocabulary has been more debased and abused than democracy. (Lord Shawcross, 1977)

*See also* direct democracy; liberal democracy; political participation; representative democracy.

### Democracy Movement
www.democracy-movement.com
Party founded in autumn 1998 from a merger between a fledgling organisation run by Paul Sykes, the Yorkshire millionaire businessman, and the Referendum Movement, a successor to James Goldsmith's Referendum Party. The party campaigns against what it sees as the encroachment of the European Union. In 2001 Sykes rejoined the Conservative Party. The Movement campaigned in the general election of that year but in 2004 was not active in the European elections.

### Democracy Party
Eurosceptic political party launched on 21 November 1998 by Worcester businessman Geoff Southall. Commentators and

other 'sceptics' observed the relatively large number of such organisations and perceived the danger that they might be dividing the potential opposition to a European single currency rather than strengthening it.

## democratic control

Control of the executive by the legislature. One of the basic tenets of democracy is that government works best within the context of scrutiny, control and accountability. This is achieved via an active legislature which scrutinises government and a vigorous media that is not easily manipulated or coerced.

In Britain there is some discussion as to whether parliament exercises sufficient control over an executive which has traditionally been strong, but few question the ability of the House of Commons to deny legislation it finds unacceptable or ultimately (via loss of support in the governing party) to dismiss governments.

## democratic deficit

A lack of democratic control with the consequent danger of power being abused. One example relates to the European Community during the 1980s, when the European parliament had few instruments whereby control could be exerted over the powerful European Commission and Council of Ministers.

## Democratic Left

The successor to the Communist Party of Great Britain, formed in 1991 and committed to democratic pluralism. It was no more successful at the polls than its predecessor.

## democratic pluralism

See pluralism.

## democratic socialism

Term applied to those who pursue a socialist agenda through democratic institutions, such as free elections and parliament. Democratic socialists oppose political violence and the subversion of state institutions for political ends.

## Democratic Unionist Party (DUP)

www.dup.org.uk

Ulster political party formed in 1971 and led by the fiery Reverend Dr Ian Paisley, a militant Protestant. The party, unlike the Ulster Unionist Party (UUP), is hotly opposed to the Anglo-Irish Agreement, the Downing Street Declaration and the Good Friday Agreement as well as Sinn Fein, the Irish Republic, and Catholicism and all its works. It consistently appeals to working-class Protestant voters and in the 1997 UK general election won two seats. Paisley seems to express all that is intractable and uncompromising in Ulster, as epitomised in the slogan 'No Surrender'. He was approaching retirement at the time of writing. He was expected to be replaced by his deputy, Peter Robinson, though his son, Ian Paisley junior, might contest this also.

In elections for the Northern Ireland assembly on 25 June 1998 the DUP won 20 seats. In the 2001 the UUP suffered reversals at the hands of Paisley's party in both the Westminster and local elections. The DUP applies powerful pressure on the UUP to be more critical of the republican side than it would otherwise be. In delayed elections to the assembly in November 2003 the DUP gained 10 seats and eclipsed the leadership of the loyalist community formerly occupied by the weakened UUP. The executive remains suspended since autumn 2002.

See also Ulster Unionist Party; Paisley, Ian.

## democratisation

In general terms, the transition of a state from an authoritarian to a democratic form of rule, such as has taken place in many of the former eastern bloc countries. Democratisation involves political institutions, but also economic and cultural ones. It also requires the development of a self-sustaining civil society. In Britain, the expansion of the franchise between 1832 and 1918 was a clear example of democratisation, where elite participation was transformed into mass democracy.

See also civil society.

## Demos

www.demos.co.uk

Leftward-leaning think tank set up in
1993 to encourage long-term non-partisan
thinking by drawing ideas from outside
the political mainstream (for example from
industrialists, scientists and community
activists). Specifically, it seeks to 'modernise the political culture, to make it more
relevant, more international and more at
ease with the future'. In addition, it aims
to target new forms of governance and
democracy for the 21st century. Its founder,
Geoff Mulgan, joined the Number 10
Policy Unit after 1997 and its report on the
reform of the monarchy in September 1998
attracted considerable publicity and discussion. Demos's senior project officer, David
Ashworth, caused some bewilderment by
changing his name to Perri 6; according to
the *Observer* of the day this was 'to make
himself more interesting'.

## Department for Culture, Media and Sport

www.culture.gov.uk

Began in 1992 as the Department of
National Heritage. This department
has been regarded as having a somewhat
uneasy collection of responsibilities. Its
first minister was the Conservative David
Mellor and under Labour Chris Smith
in 1997 took over the renamed portfolio,
which also included responsibility for the
ill-fated Millennium Dome. After the
2001 election, Labour's Tessa Jowell took
over as culture secretary with increased
responsibility for gambling, licensing,
censorship and horseracing, plus planning
for the Golden Jubilee. The new minister
described her department as the 'ministry
of free time', the title given to its French
equivalent.

## Department for Education and Skills

www.dfes.gov.uk

Used to contain science until 1992 when
it was transferred to the Office of Public
Services and Science, a unit of the Cabinet
Office. Over the years the department
has never run schools and colleges directly
but only indirectly via other agencies like
the inspectorate. Under the Conservatives
a new function was created to deal with
grant-maintained schools. Margaret
Thatcher made appointments to education
from the outside with a view to 'sorting out'
its problems.

## Department for Environment, Food and Rural Affairs

www.defra.gov.uk

Government department created in 2001,
partly to take over the role of Ministry of
Agriculture, Fisheries and Food (MAFF).
MAFF was in charge of the foot-and-
mouth crisis in 2001 and was widely
seen as having handled it ineffectively.
As a result of these perceived failures the
ministry was reformulated in June 2001
with Margaret Becket taking charge of a
new Department for Environment, Food
and Rural Affairs. The Department of the
Environment was created in 1971 from the
merger of the older departments of Housing
and Local Government, and the Ministry
of Works. It was concerned with housing,
town and country planning, pollution, and
management of a large portion of the government's 'estate'. Michael Heseltine gave
the department a high profile when he was
placed at its head in 1979 and introduced
MINIS, a new management information
system.

## Department for Transport

www.dft.gov.uk

Department responsible for transport policy
on road, rail, sea and air. It dates from
1919. The policy core of the department,
the Central Transport Group (CTG), has
had some notable successes like the bridge
at Dartford, the second Severn crossing
and the extension to the Jubilee line of
the London Underground, all privately
financed. The department is responsible
for the country's 2,700 km of motorways
and 7,800 km of trunk roads. Strategic
planning is undertaken by the CTG but
maintenance and construction is undertaken by the Highways Agency. Almost

85 per cent of the department's staff now work in one of its eight executive agencies. In 1997 it was included in deputy prime minister John Prescott's Department of Environment, Transport and the Regions. After the 2001 general election this area of government was reorganised to create a Department of Transport, Local Government and the Regions. It was given additional responsibilities for electoral law and the fire service but lost regional development to the Department for Trade and Industry.

*See also* transport policy.

## Department for Work and Pensions
www.dfwp.gov.uk
Despite the fact that pensions appeared early in the 20th century, central administration was put in place only after the Second World War. Initially there were the Ministry of Pensions, the National Assistance Board and the Ministry of Labour. From 1968 to 1988 these functions were combined with health within the Department for Health and Social Security (DHSS). These were split in 1988, and the Department for Social Security itself became the Department for Work and Pensions in June 2001, with some responsibility for what formerly came under the Department for Education and Employment. It is a small department, as much of its routine work is performed by large executive agencies like the Benefits Agency and the Child Support Agency. The department is, however, the biggest spender of any government department – social security amounted to 28 per cent of government spending in the mid-1990s.

## Department of Health
www.dh.gov.uk
Originally the Department of Health had responsibility for housing programmes and sanitary measures. This connection was lost in the years after the union of health with social security. As well as overseeing the work of the National Health Service, the department also supervises local authority community care, as well as social work

provision. The NHS Policy Board is chaired by the secretary of state for health and lays down overall policy but the Blair government introduced a new regional structure in the summer of 2001 to achieve more decentralisation of responsibility.

## Department of National Heritage
*See* Department for Culture, Media and Sport.

## Department of Trade and Industry (DTI)
www.dti.gov.uk
Originally set up in 1621 as the Board of Trade, the DTI has undergone constant reincarnations and mergers. It dates in its modern form from 1970, when it was given responsibility for fostering the competitiveness of British industry, especially in relation to the European Community. It is also charged with regulating the privatised industries and consumer protection, encouraging technology transfer and reducing red tape. Under Margaret Thatcher the DTI was viewed as an 'intervener' in the economy and therefore was not her favourite department. Michael Heseltine injected spice into the office when appointed in 1992; he insisted on using the old title of 'President of the Board of Trade', a practice continued by Margaret Becket after 1997, but not by Peter Mandelson when he was promoted to the office in July 1998.

## departmental select committee
Parliamentary scrutiny committee which shadows the work of a government department. Departmental select committees are therefore, in principle, instruments of the legislature to scrutinise the executive. During the first half of the 20th century there were only two select committees, the Public Accounts Committee and the Estimates Committee. The former examined whether expenditure had been disbursed legitimately, while the latter examined the legitimacy of future expenditure. In the 1940s and 1950s two more were created, concerned with statutory

POLITICS

instruments and nationalised industries, and in the 1960s the Crossman reforms introduced new ones on science and technology, agriculture, education, race relations, overseas development and Scottish affairs. Their efficacy, however, was limited because of their scarce resources and powers.

In 1979 Norman St John Stevas, as leader of the House of Commons, introduced 12 new committees, which shadowed departmental activities. By the late 1990s there were 16 committees:

1 agriculture;
2 culture, media and sport;
3 defence (with 10 subcommittees);
4 education and employment (also with 10 subcommittees);
5 environment, transport and regional affairs;
6 foreign affairs;
7 health;
8 home affairs;
9 international development;
10 Northern Ireland;
11 science and technology;
12 Scottish affairs;
13 social security;
14 trade and industry;
15 Treasury;
16 Welsh affairs.

Most have a remit to examine the expenditure, administration and policy of the department concerned. Committees decide what to investigate and their ability to interrogate ministers and civil servants in public has made them ideal for television. Their deliberations are consequently now taken seriously, although the government does not necessarily accept all of the recommendations produced by the committees, and has no obligation to act on a report produced by one, although there is an obligation to respond in written form – usually within two months. Critics complain the committees have too few resources and limited powers.

In March 2000, the chairs of the select committees banded together to form the Select Committee on Liaison, which issued *Shifting the Balance*, a report on the balance of power between the executive and legislature. It called for bigger budgets, more staff, more time for debates and acceptance by ministers that MPs should have a role in making laws. However, leader of the House Margaret Beckett and chief whip Ann Taylor gave away nothing. The government whips continued to appoint members to committees. Beckett praised their output – 175 reports in 1998–99 – but refused to let committees follow through policy, as it would involve too many civil servants having to give evidence.

*See also* Crossman reforms; non-departmental select committee.

## dependency culture
Very much a term employed by the 'new right' to describe the alleged passive state of dependency of those on government benefits. According to this thinking, large sections of the population, but especially the so-called 'underclass', have become so dependent on state welfare benefits they have lost the will to find work for themselves or to take responsibility for themselves or their own families.

*See also* entrepreneurial culture; social exclusion.

## dependent territories
Territories for which Britain still remains responsible. They currently comprise: Anguilla, Bermuda, British Virgin Islands, Cayman Islands, Falklands Islands, Gibraltar, Montserrat, Pitcairn Islands, St Helena, South Georgia, South Sandwich Islands and the Turks and Caicos Islands. There are also two dependencies offshore in the form of the Channel Islands and the Isle of Man.

## deposit
*See* candidate for parliamentary election; lost deposit.

## deputy prime minister
Constitutionally there is no such office but prime ministers have found it expedient to invent one and it has now become a regular feature of government. Geoffrey Howe was

elevated to the position following one of Margaret Thatcher's reshuffles; Michael Heseltine was also given the title, plus coordinating powers, in exchange for supporting John Major in his re-election as party leader in July 1995. John Prescott was made Tony Blair's deputy and was given a major department portfolio in recognition of his influence with more traditional Labour voters and his role as deputy leader of the Labour Party. The precise duties of deputy prime ministers vary according to the prime minister. Most deputise for the prime minister at question time, for example, but there is no established department for him or her to lead. In the event of a prime minister dying the deputy would take over until a new party leader was elected.

## deputy speaker

In the 19th century the speaker had no deputies but by the middle of that century it became obvious that assistance was needed and so three were created by election from sitting MPs. The deputy's official title is the chairman of ways and means; the holder is elected at the beginning of each parliament and, like the speaker, does not vote or act in partisan fashion. The budget debate is always presided over by the chairman of ways and means, as is the Commons when sitting as a Committee of the Whole House.

*See also* speaker.

## deregulation

A tenet of right-wing economic thinking based on the premise that the economy functions best when it is left to market forces and free from government intervention. Accordingly, sectors of the economy were deregulated by the Conservatives in the 1980s, for example the operation of buses and the Stock Exchange.

## deregulation order

These originate from the Deregulation and Contracting Out Act 1994, which allows for the repeal of primary legislation which has become burdensome to anyone carrying on a trade or profession. The department concerned has to draft a proposal for a

deregulation order and then consult those affected, after which the government takes appropriate action.

## deselection

The decision of a constituency organisation to reject its sitting MP. If deselected, MPs sit in the House until the end of the parliament, when they can decide whether to stand again – possibly as an independent. In 1980 Labour left-wing activists changed the rules of nomination which required sitting MPs to undergo mandatory reselection within the lifetime of a parliament. In practice, this meant right-wing Labour MPs could be deselected and left-wingers substituted. Nearly a dozen were deselected before the 1983 election, and others who joined the Social Democratic Party would probably have gone the same way had they stayed in the party. In 1987 six more were treated in this way, but by then certain left-wingers had come under pressure too. In 1990 it was decided to limit such inquisitions to occasions when the membership in the constituency decides via a ballot to order the deselection process.

*See also* reselection.

## despatch box

Boxes in each of the houses of parliament placed on the table separating the government and opposition benches. They were originally donated to the House by New Zealand to mark the rebuilding of parliament after the Second World War. Speakers tend to lean on the boxes and, when roused, to thump them with fists to emphasise points. The boxes do not hold items for 'despatch' but instead contain Bibles.

## devolution

The transfer of governmental authority from the centre to the regions. Overcentralisation has long been recognised as a weakness of British government and, in an attempt to assuage nationalist sentiment, the Labour government planned regional assemblies for Scotland and Wales in 1979 but failed to attract sufficient support in the referendums held. Under Margaret Thatcher the issue died for a while but not for the nationalists, who increasingly felt they were ruled by an 'alien' government. Labour promised them devolution and in September 1997 the Scottish referendum returned a two to one majority for a separate assembly, plus endorsement of tax-varying powers. The 'No' campaign in Wales was even less well funded than in Scotland and the result was again a victory for the 'Yes' camp, although only by the narrowest of margins: less than 1 per cent. In 1999 the assemblies were elected and they have been operating ever since, but there are substantial problems regarding funding and authority which still remain to be resolved. The first problem arose in January 2000, when the Scottish parliament voted to abolish tuition fees for Scottish university students. Eventually the coalition Liberal Democrat–Labour administration agreed to rescind this measure.

At the Conservative conference in 1998 William Hague made a speech in which he held out the possibility that England would soon seek a separate parliament if Scotland had its own assembly plus the ability to influence English politics via representation at Westminster. In June 2003 Tony Blair reorganised government responsibility for the residual secretaries of state for Wales and Scotland by subsuming them into the new Department for Constitutional Affairs. However, the spokespeople for Wales and Scotland in the House of Commons were to be the leader of the House, Peter Hain, and the transport secretary, Alistair Darling, and this 'part-time' arrangement was condemned by critics as disrespectful to Scotland and Wales.

Regional government for England became a problem during the second half of the first Blair administration when it became obvious the Celtic assemblies were strengthening the Scottish and Welsh bids for resources. Gordon Brown had appeared to join John Prescott in championing regional assemblies but the queen's speech in June 2001 contained no commitment to such an objective. Eventually

a white paper appeared in June 2003 and Prescott announced plans to hold referendums for regional assemblies in the north-east, the north-west and Yorkshire and Humberside. By late summer 2004 the three referendums had been reduced to one, in the north-east, to be held in November 2004.

*See also* Northern Ireland assembly; Scotland; Scottish parliament; Wales; Welsh assembly.

### dignified/efficient (constitution)

A term first used by Walter Bagehot, who made a distinction between those dignified elements of the British constitution which represent the symbols of power (for example the monarchy, the Privy Council, Her Majesty's state opening of parliament) and the efficient parts, such as Her Majesty's government, which actually has the political muscle to bring about change (for example the prime minister's office and cabinet committees). Commentators regularly suggest new items of the constitution have joined the 'dignified' parts, most notably the cabinet, although some have even added the House of Commons, which has allegedly declined as a result of the large government majorities after the 1997 and 2001 general elections, together with the effects of Tony Blair's more personal, presidential style.

### direct action

A generic term for peaceful political demonstrations or an activity compatible with democratic politics but often pushed to the limits of the law, especially in the case of trade union industrial action (for example the miners' strike in 1984–85). Since the 1990s the main proponents of direct action have been environmentalists, who have taken their lead from the US environmental grouping Earth First! These protests have represented an alliance between local and national activists and middle-class sympathisers. The actions against road building at Twyford Down as well as Manchester Airport's second runway were unusual in that they involved protestors living in trees and tunnels, thereby risking their lives. It seems the embrace of some radical campaigns by middle-class 'respectable' people has clothed the notion of direct action (as opposed to political violence) with a degree of respectability.

## direct democracy

A form of government where the people have direct control over policy making and the institutions of the state. It is a form of rule where representatives are not used, but committees, citizen juries and people's assemblies are instead. Direct democracy first appeared in Athens. The new millennium has witnessed its growth in some restricted respects – for example with the introduction of a type of 'virtual' democracy where telecommunications and computers allow instant or 'real-time' feedback from citizens and consumers. Direct democracy is not really appropriate for a country of Britain's size.

*See also* Athenian democracy.

## Direct.Gov.co.uk

Government website that opened in August 2004. It offers a huge amount of information on a variety of activities (e.g. finding jobs) as well as a massive A–Z facility on British government and links for a myriad of related matters.

## direct rule

The term usually employed to describe the decision in 1972 to replace the elected Stormont government in Northern Ireland and rule directly from Westminster. It was hoped the beginnings of local democratic rule had been initiated in June 1998 when the new Northern Ireland assembly was elected and an executive committee was established under David Trimble as first minister. Direct rule was reinstated following yet another crisis in the autumn of 2002.

*See also* Northern Ireland assembly; Stormont.

## directive (EU)

*See* Council of Ministers.

## director of public prosecutions

The person in charge of the Crown Prosecution Service (CPS), which decides whether an alleged offence justifies a court case. The director of public prosecutions is responsible to the attorney general.

*See also* attorney general; Crown Prosecution Service.

## discrimination

The process whereby certain groups of people, usually minorities, are treated badly and often given unequal legal rights. Centuries ago they were often religious groups but in the modern day they are often distinguished by race and sexual orientation. Advocates of a written constitution believe an incorporated bill of rights would protect such groups more effectively and some protection has been afforded by the incorporation into British law of the European Convention on Human Rights.

*See also* civil rights.

## dissolution of parliament

The act by which the sovereign closes a session of parliament and sets in motion the process for a general election and the start of a new parliament. Dissolutions are nearly always requested by the prime minister, usually before the five-year expiry date set by the Parliament Act 1911. Constitutionally, a prime minister will be obliged to seek a dissolution if his or her party loses a vote of no confidence, or the government has been defeated on the passage of a finance act. Finally, the House of Lords can immediately call for a dissolution if the House of Commons attempts to stay in power longer than five years. It is sometimes thought that the threat of dissolution can be used to counter rebellion within the governing party but in practice it is rarely credible, as few prime ministers would risk losing a general election for the sake of party unity.

*See also* parliament; Parliament Act 1911.

## divine right of kings

The idea that a monarch had a holy right to succeed to the throne. Developed in the middle ages, it was used to reinforce the moral position of monarchs. After the defeat of the Royalists in the Civil War the doctrine faded away in Britain.

## division lobby
Corridor running alongside the debating chamber of the House of Commons, used by MPs in the process of voting. The voting by MPs is sometimes therefore called a 'division'. The House of Commons is unusual in maintaining a physical rather than an electronic means of voting. When it comes to the vote, MPs walk through either the 'ayes' (right-hand) or 'noes' (left-hand) 'lobby' and are counted by 'tellers' as they re-enter at the speaker's end of the chamber. Defenders of the archaic system point out that this is one of the few occasions when backbench members can meet up with ministers and have the possibility to raise urgent matters with them. Most reform proposals have tried to maintain this feature of the House's workings.

## Divisional Court
The part of the High Court which hears appeals. It is divided into:
1  the Queen's Bench, which hears points of law from criminal cases in magistrates' courts;
2  the Chancery, which hears appeals from county courts on bankruptcy matters;
3  the Family Division, which hears domestic and matrimonial cases.

   When sitting as divisional courts, three High Court judges need to preside.

## divorce
The legal severing of a marriage contract. Its constitutional importance lies in the fact that the monarch, as head of the Church of England, has traditionally supported the institution of marriage but its authority was eroded by the decision of Edward VIII to abdicate in order to marry a twice divorced woman. Later, several members of the royal family, including Princesses Margaret and Anne, as well as Prince Andrew and Prince Charles, obtained divorces. The broader social importance

of divorce in Britain is that the divorce rate has continued to rise since the Second World War, aided by easing of the relevant laws, in particular the Divorce Reform Act 1967. Concern regarding the social fabric has been expressed by church leaders, and Conservative politicians, because divorce is associated with the increasing number of single-parent families and the fact that Britain has the highest rate of births outside marriage in the European Union.

## 'dodgy dossiers'
In September 2002 the government published a dossier on Iraq's weapons of mass destruction that reported substantial intelligence information. In February 2003 another dossier was published focusing on the Iraqi regime's concealment of such weapons. Neither dossier was judged convincing at the time – especially when the latter was damagingly revealed to include a plagiarised section of a PhD thesis – but in the wake of the war critical scrutiny intensified. It was alleged by journalists that senior intelligence officers were accusing New Labour's Alastair Campbell, the Downing Street press secretary, of adding his own material to the dossiers to 'sex' them up, that is, to make more compelling the case for a war his master favoured. In the ensuing furious row many observed that the intelligence services had been involved closely and unhealthily in the presentation of political arguments.
   *See also* Campbell, Alastair.

## dominant class
The owners of property and capital. The concept is based upon the social analyses of Karl Marx, who perceived the creation in society of social groups according to their relationship to the means of production. He believed such groups were inevitably in conflict and would continue to be so until the working classes finally overthrew the 'ruling' or 'dominant' class. In Britain such a class would be perceived in the mostly privately educated leaders of the main institutions of the country: the civil service, business, parliament, the church, the military, the

judiciary and so forth. It followed, according to Marx, that the dominant class would permeate society with its own ideas and values.

*See also* dominant values; establishment.

## dominant values

Concept associated with the Marxian belief that the ruling ideas of any era are those of the ruling class. According to this perspective the owners of capital dominate all the key positions in society and infiltrate their values into them and the media. Neo-Marxists like Antonio Gramsci argued that the control of the media was the means whereby the working classes were induced to accept dominant values and submit to a class subservience. Only left-wing members of the Labour Party subscribe to such ideas and they worry that Tony Blair's enthusiasm for business leaders indicates support for or absorption of such dominant values.

## Downing Street Declaration

Declaration made in December 1993 by John Major and Irish prime minister Albert Reynolds on the issue of Ulster. Effectively it expressed agreement between the two governments that there would be no change in the status of the province without majority agreement, something which pleased the Ulster unionists, although it did not remove their suspicions of the Irish republicans.

## Downing Street Press Office

This office controls the prime minister's relationship with the media. Since the Second World War it has become gradually more important, so much so that some believe the power of the premier's press secretary rivals that of senior ministers through access to the prime minister and proximity to crucial discussions. This follows from the close relationship Sir Bernard Ingham established with Margaret Thatcher, when he not only interpreted her mind for the media at his daily press conferences but also advised her on a range of important issues. Alastair Campbell occupied a similar role in relation to Tony Blair and was regarded as one of his closest aides.

*See also* prime minister's department.

# E

## early day motion (EDM)

A motion submitted by an MP for an 'early day' debate in the Commons. The debate rarely occurs but the motion is printed and others may add their names. EDMs therefore are like parliamentary petitions and act as barometers of backbench opinion. Sometimes a large number of names have been thought to have initiated action, such as the Conservative EDM in the 1980s to abolish compulsory membership of student unions. In the 1970s and 1980s some 300–400 EDMs were tabled each year. By the 1990s the annual figure had reached 1,000.

## Ecclestone affair

Allegation of sleaze early after Labour's 1997 election victory. In its 1997 manifesto Labour stated that smoking was the greatest cause of preventable illness and that it would ban tobacco advertising if elected. Health secretary Frank Dobson repeated the pledge in June 1997 but said it was not intended to damage sports that benefited from the backing of the tobacco industry. In November the government stated it would exempt Formula One motor racing from the ban. Then it transpired that Bernie Ecclestone, the billionaire figure behind Formula One in Britain, had visited Tony Blair in October and insisted such a ban would lead to 50,000 full-time jobs and 150,000 part-time jobs being lost. It then became public knowledge that Ecclestone – previously a donor to the Conservatives – had made a £1 million donation to Labour and the spectre of a sleaze arose for Labour, very early into its first term. Eventually Ecclestone was given back his donation, and Blair appeared on television to apologise for his mistake.

*See also* sleaze.

## Ecology Party

*See* Green Party.

## economic and monetary unioin
*See* European economic and monetary union.

## Economic and Social Committee (ESC)
www.ces.eu.int/pages/en/home.asp
Institution of the European Union which considers a wide range of legislation. It was originally set up by the Treaty of Rome to supplement the European assembly (now the European parliament) as a forum for employers, employees and other interests to consult, cooperate and advise on policy. While the assembly has evolved into the European parliament, the ESC remains a purely consultative body. National governments appoint members to the committee via the Council of Ministers.

## economic competition
The idea central to (Thatcherite) neo-liberal economic thinking. It is held that if businesses are ranged against each other in the marketplace, they seek efficiency married to quality, to gain the advantage which will enable them to make profits, maintain employment and reinvest in more modern equipment. At the same time consumers are served well as they receive the best possible product at the lowest possible price. Competition therefore is the central requirement for economic efficiency. The Conservatives maintained that the public monopolies created by nationalisation after 1945 created inefficiency, which led to their annual losses, for which the taxpayer had to pay. They also pointed to those countries in eastern Europe with 'command' economies (based on monopoly production and provision of goods) as proof that the communist project had failed to provide prosperity for their citizens. These countries eventually collapsed from economic failure and corruption in the late 1980s. However, the Conservatives did not always practise their ideology in that privatised industries, including British Telecom and British Gas, were allowed to operate as private monopolies for a while. The privatised water companies still enjoy such a privileged position in the marketplace and it is hard to see how any competition, in any case, could be introduced.
*See also* privatisation.

## economic decline
Term used to describe the British economy's postwar lacklustre performance. In 1939 Britain's economy was second only to that of the USA in terms of gross domestic product (GDP) per capita. After the war Britain began a decline which continued until the late 1980s. Although the economy grew in absolute terms it declined relative to its competitors. The reasons are contentious but agreement tends to centre on six factors.

1 *History*. Competitors had the advantage of the latest technology while world war had exhausted Britain and left it in debt, and the ending of 'imperial preference' removed Britain's cushion from the real economic world.
2 *Geography*. Britain was hit harder by world recessions because its island nature make it more dependent on exports.
3 *Culture*. Class divisions fuelled poor industrial relations, the education system tended to discriminate against vocationally useful subjects like engineering and foreign languages, and the emphasis on home ownership blocked the mobility of the workforce.
4 *Politics*. Labour policies after the war encouraged an unhealthily large public sector. Moreover, all parties criticised the lack of continuity in economic policy making, caused by changes of government.
5 *Finance*. Low industrial investment starved research and development of much needed funds.
6 *Economics*. Britain had low levels of productivity and investment, and endemic inflation, which developed into the so-called 'stagflation' of the mid-1970s. This signalled the breakdown of Keynesian demand management and left a gap in macro-economics that was quickly filled by the new right and monetarism.
*See also* imperial preference.

## economic interest group

Pressure or interest group concerned with the economy that seeks to influence government policy. A range of groups represent and promote the interests of business producers like multinational companies; the 'peak' organisation is the Confederation of British Industry (CBI). The trade unions also represent producer interests, from an employee perspective, their main organisation being the Trades Union Congress (TUC). In recent years governments have attempted to promote the interests of consumers, not so much through formal pressure group involvement in policy making, but through the creation of public sector consumer watchdogs.

## economic management

Government management of the economy. The government is able to manage the economy, if only to a degree, through the following:

1 fiscal measures – adjusting direct and indirect taxation;
2 monetary measures – controlling the money supply by adjusting interest rates;
3 stimulating trade via diplomatic means (for example through the Department of Trade and Industry);
4 providing support and subsidies to economic activity (again via the Department of Trade and Industry, though less so under the Conservative governments of the 1980s);
5 providing a national infrastructure of transport and public services.

The Conservatives have tended to view genuine economic growth as best achieved when industry and markets are left alone by government. Labour, before Tony Blair became the party's leader, favoured nationalisation of the commanding heights of the economy (although it never attempted this in practice) and a policy of Keynesian demand management. Under Blair and Gordon Brown the government has pursued economic policies not dissimilar to those of Margaret Thatcher and John Major, although there are a number of New Labour or 'third way' innovations, such

as an independent Bank of England, the promotion of public and private sector partnerships in the delivery of central and local government services, and a more supportive position on membership of the European single currency.

## economic policy making

Possibly the most important function of modern British government. Economic policy making involves a 'community' of individuals in and around the core executive, some of the most important being: the chancellor, the chancellor's personal advisors, the chief secretary to the Treasury, the senior civil servants at the Treasury, the governor of the Bank of England (charged with setting interest rates since May 1997), the Monetary Policy Committee (charged with advising the Bank on interest rates), and other economic ministers, such as the minister for trade and industry. Since Britain joined the European Economic Community (now the European Union) the 'Europeanisation' of policy making has taken place, where key civil service committees are now meshed into the European Union structure. For example, policy making on regional economic development requires collaboration between national and supranational bodies in London and Brussels. Gordon Brown, appointed chancellor in 1997, has proved a dominant minister who controls policy in a very personal fashion. Some tension was discerned between Brown and Tony Blair after the 2001 victory regarding entry into the euro. Brown was seen as cautious and insistent upon his 'five conditions' being met while Blair was seen as more enthusiastic for entry.

*See also* demand management; Keynesianism; monetarism.

## Economist, The

www.economist.co.uk
Weekly journal of news, comment and analysis. It was founded in 1843. *The Economist* has established a respected position in British politics as an authoritative journal which is widely read by the

POLITICS

elites. It sells well worldwide, especially in the USA. It tends to take an orthodox monetarist line on economic policy but is generally liberal on human rights and always independent in its views. Known to employ brilliant young people from Oxbridge, it is occasionally criticised for being arrogant in its lofty prescriptions for the world.

### economy (British)

The British economy was the first to benefit from the Industrial Revolution and Britain became the 'workshop of the world' in the 19th century. The Empire, too, provided huge benefits in terms of cheap raw materials and closed markets. However, other countries caught up, benefiting from the latest plant and machinery while Britain laboured with out-of-date equipment. The Empire also broke up as countries achieved independence and set up their own indigenous industries. Traditional industries like shipbuilding, steel, coalmining and textiles began to decline rapidly – almost to extinction – during the postwar period. However, new industries based on new technology have emerged, many in the service sector: information technology, advertising, financial services and the assembly of mechanical and electrical goods (financed mostly by overseas investment). In absolute terms Britain is almost three times better off in the early years of the new millennium than in 1945. Inflation has increased prices 20-fold but income has increased 50-fold. In relative terms Britain has fallen from its peak as the USA, Germany and Japan now have bigger economies. But as the fourth biggest economy Britain is still a wealthy country. Its economic problems include:

1  poor competitiveness compared with the USA;
2  poor manufacturing output;
3  a balance-of-trade deficit;
4  a pound which has tended to be overvalued, making exports more difficult to sell.

However, Labour's perceived safe stewardship of the economy helped it to win a second victory in 2001. In 2003 economic output was in decline as the world economy was damaged by plummeting share prices and the war in Iraq. Chancellor Gordon Brown was able to claim throughout the period of his incumbency, however, that the British economy had outperformed those of other member states of the European Union and of many other advanced industrial countries in terms of growth, inflation and employment levels. Brown's prognosis for the British economy in July 2004 was a continuation of steady growth for the foreseeable future.

### Education Act 1944

The act that established the principle of free state education for all children from the age of 5 to 15 (and 16 when deemed practical). It left it to local education authorities to determine their own systems of ensuring that a child's education was appropriate to age, aptitude and ability, which in most cases meant the use of the 11 plus test and selection for secondary school.

### education action zone

*See* education policy.

### education policy

The Labour Party manifesto of 1997 stated: 'Education will be our number one priority, and we will increase the share of national income spent on education as we decrease it on bills of economic and social failure'. The electorate were promised: class sizes reduced to 30 for children under seven years old; nursery places for all four-year-olds; an attack on low standards in schools; increased access to computer technology; the development of lifelong learning through a new University for Industry; and more spending on education. Philosophically, the policy commitments, along with ambitious literacy and numeracy targets, originate from two areas of thinking: the third way, in particular the need to create informed citizens; and 'new growth' theory, which views education as a tool governments need to use to produce skilled, flexible workers who can enable the nation to compete effectively in the global marketplace.

In electoral terms, Labour's education policy is part of a catch-all approach to winning elections. For this reason, Labour has carried forward the tough approach of previous governments regarding poor teachers and failing schools. The government has powers to close down schools and re-open them with a new management team and staff (Fresh Start schools), or establish education action zones, to set up local partnerships (a key New Labour word) of businesses, voluntary groups, parents, local education authorities and other interested parties. The education action zone represents one of the most radical solutions, so far, to the challenge of local service provision and goes beyond the simple public versus private alternative of 'old style' politics, at least according to third way theorists. The tough chief inspector of schools, Chris Woodhead, was retained by Labour for some time, despite intense criticism of him by the teaching unions.

The Conservative approach to education tends to favour the private sector together with selection of pupils by schools. It has argued for 'education vouchers', whereby parents would be allowed a financial entitlement to education, which they could supplement to send their children to private schools should they wish.

## Education Reform Act 1988

One of the most important pieces of education legislation since the 1944 act. The Great Education Reform Bill or 'Gerbil' introduced central government control of learning (the national curriculum); increased parental choice by allowing schools to compete with each other for pupils; allowed some schools to opt out of local authority control and receive their funds from central government (termed grant-maintained schools); and established local management of school budgets and staff. Finally, the act made regular pupil testing via 'SATs' (standard assessment tests) an obligatory part of the education process, along with league tables of performance

to help parents evaluate schools. New Labour has continued with this consumer focus, although the party has abandoned the grant-maintained schools in favour of specialist schools.

## Efficiency Unit

Unit set up by Margaret Thatcher shortly after her 1979 election victory designed to improve management within the civil service. It was headed by Derek (later Lord) Raynor, formerly of Marks and Spencer, who had established his reputation advising the Ministry of Defence (1970–72). Raynor was greatly trusted by Thatcher and he was given a free rein to introduce economies and more efficient procedures and enhance the importance of management in the public sector. Raynor's successor, Sir Robin Ibbs, went on to introduce the far-reaching reform of the civil service, the 'Next Steps' programme.

## egalitarianism

See equality.

## elected mayor

An idea, based on US models, originally proposed by Michael Heseltine and then taken up by New Labour as part of its 'modernising' agenda. In London, a referendum approved the idea and a protracted election campaign led up to a poll in May 2000. Ken Livingstone won the election despite the opposition of Tony Blair. The government hoped the idea would prove popular and renew interest in local politics but many councillors objected to it as it diminished the role of the ordinary member of the council. In referendums held on elected mayors up and down the country in 2001–02, less than a dozen out of over 30 council areas voted to move to such a system.

## elected second chamber

A popular proposal to replace the hereditary House of Lords. Another is the representation of specific sections of society, such as the regions, business and academe. Also popular is the idea of using proportional representation to elect members to what has often been called a new 'Senate' rather than Lords. However, the major problem with such a scheme is that if it is given a real job to do in order to attract high-quality candidates, its authority will challenge the presently all-powerful House of Commons and trigger a constitutional crisis. For this and other reasons Tony Blair made it known in January 2003 that he was against an elected second chamber and preferred an appointed one.

*See also* House of Lords; House of Lords reform.

### election

A means by which representatives (for example MPs, councillors and MEPs) are appointed to political office by the people of Britain. The most important are general elections, whereby governments are selected in the British political system. Elections for parliament occur at least once every five years, and are based on the first past the post (FPTP) system. Elections are held on Thursdays, the (alleged) logic being that this allows the maximum number of days campaigning in the last week of the campaign without extending into the weekend. Voting is from 7 a.m. to 10 p.m. Candidates' names are placed in alphabetical order on the voting slip and each elector must indicate a preference by writing a cross opposite the person chosen. Boxes are then sealed and taken away to be counted. The frequency of local elections depends on the council concerned.

*See also* electoral system.

### election campaign
*See* campaigning.

### election campaign costs
The costs incurred by political parties during election campaigns. In 1997 the cost of holding the election was £52 million to the government; and that was in addition to the £50 million it costs annually to maintain the electoral register. In constituency elections agents are required to show expenditure has been under the £10,000

limit. Given this cap, local candidates can do little more than print out leaflets, although they are entitled to free postage for their election addresses plus free hire of school halls for meetings. Until 2001 there was no legal limit, however, to spending nationally by parties or any obligation to publish their election accounts. Modern parties spend huge amounts on advertising, opinion polling, travel and meetings. In 1997 the Conservatives spent £13 million with the Saatchi agency and Labour £7 million with the BMP agency. Such heavy spending, combined with falling membership receipts, has made parties dependent on big donations; the concern is that such a reliance is traded for political influence. Following the Neill Committee's report on funding for political parties in 1998, a cap for national election spending was imposed by the Political Parties, Elections and Referendums Act 2000. The cap applied to those parties contesting all 659 parliamentary constituencies. Lower limits applied to elections to other bodies, such as the devolved assemblies. Limits were also introduced for referendums of between £0.5 and £5 million for a registered political party. The registered treasurer of a party is required to submit accounts after an election to the Electoral Commission, and these must cover the previous 365 days in the case of Westminster elections or four months before the poll in the case of other elections.

### election court
Court that hears disputes over the validity of the election of an MP or a local councillor. The case is raised via an election petition and is decided by an election court that comprises two High Court judges.

### elective dictatorship
A term first used by Lord Hailsham in 1976 and now part of the lexicon of British politics. Hailsham criticised the British constitution's ability to make the majority (or indeed the largest minority) party, once elected, an effective dictatorship until the next election, even though, like the Labour

government of that time, it might be elected on a minority of the national vote. Once the Conservatives were back in office after 1979, Hailsham lost his enthusiasm for attacking this aspect of the constitution.

### electoral college

Usually associated with the US presidential elections but also an occasional feature of British politics, especially in the Labour Party. In 1981 it was introduced to elect Labour's leader. Trade unions, Labour MPs and party members all have a share of the vote, initially in the proportions 40:30:30 but later changed to one-third each. In May 1999 Labour used an electoral college to elect its candidate – eventually the reluctant Frank Dobson – for London mayor. A similar ploy was used to elect Alun Michael (and keep out the popular choice, Rhodri Morgan) as leader of the Welsh Labour Party in the wake of Ron Davies's enforced resignation.

### Electoral Commission

Set up under terms of Political Parties, Elections and Referendums Act 2000 in November of the same year. Its remit is to 'increase public confidence in the democratic process ... and encourage people to take part by modernising the electoral process'. It also reviews the administration and law of elections, encourages greater participation and oversees the activities of the Boundary Committee for England (formerly the Local Government Commission).

### electoral reform

The alleged injustice of the electoral system has given rise to a powerful movement for reform. Initially it was a mainly Liberal obsession and clearly in that party's interests, but others became convinced of the case for reform in other parties; for example, Labour's Robin Cook and Charter 88 took up the cause in the 1980s and 1990s. Despite the scepticism of Jack Straw, the home secretary, and the agnosticism of Tony Blair, Labour in 1997 set up the Jenkins Commission to recommend a more proportional system; it reported in

the autumn of 1998. It recommended an amended version of the German electoral system, with 500 seats elected by the alternative vote from constituencies and the remainder from a regional list which would provide 'top-up' seats to reflect more properly the proportion of votes cast between the parties. A referendum was to determine whether the Commission's recommendations were to be adopted, as it would be a decision with momentous implications for the political life of the country. However, the experience of proportional representation in the devolved assemblies of Scotland and Wales reduced Labour's enthusiasm for reform and talk of a referendum faded, although the Liberal Democrats continued to press optimistically for it.

*See also* electoral system; Jenkins report.

### electoral register (alternatively 'roll')

A list of names of all those entitled to vote in each constituency. Electoral registers are drawn up by local registration officers (employees of local authorities). To be included a person must be resident in the constituency, be over 18 years old and be a British or Commonwealth subject. Irish nationals can vote if they have lived continuously for three months in the UK. Aliens and those judged insane cannot vote (though the latter may do so in periods of mental lucidity), nor can those found guilty of corrupt electoral practices and certain other categories of prison inmates. Approximately 43.7 million people are eligible to vote in Britain, although not all appear on the electoral register. In the wake of the community charge ('poll tax') it was believed thousands – one estimate in 1992 put it at over a million – neglected to register to vote in order to disguise their presence from the authorities charged with collection of the new tax. Registers used to be updated annually, with checks being sent out in the autumn for publication on 16 February each year. However, this annual procedure has now been changed so that the register is constantly updated on a 'rolling' basis. Failing to register as a voter is an offence punishable by a fine of up to £2000. In

September 2001 Brian Robertson, a retired accountant from Pontefract, launched a High Court challenge to his local authority for selling on details of his name to direct-marketing enterprises, something which most local authorities, it transpired, do as a matter of course. The judge found that the government had breached the European Convention on Human Rights in that the interference with Mr Robertson's private life was disproportionate.

### electoral system
The electoral system in Britain is the first past the post (FPTP) or the single member, simple plurality (SMSP) system. The 659 constituencies drawn up by the Boundary Commission elect one member to the Commons at each general election, which occurs at least once every five years, or in by-elections. The person gaining the most votes is the winner, irrespective of the number of candidates and no matter how small the majority. Britain is the only country in Europe to use this system, and even beyond Europe there are few other examples (India, the USA and Canada). The system is straightforward but it produces extravagant anomalies: parties with thin national support can receive disproportionate numbers of seats. This was shown especially in 1983, when the Alliance won 26 per cent of the votes yet only 3 per cent of the seats. Psephologists have also shown how the system at present works to the advantage of the Labour Party (for example even if both parties polled the same number of votes Labour would still win 79 more seats than the Conservatives). For obvious reasons the two major parties, with some exceptions, favour the existing system.

*See also* electoral reform; first past the post.

### electricity industry
British electricity generation (by the Central Electricity Generating Board) was formerly a public utility. However in 1990 it was divided into four companies and sold off to the private sector. Nuclear power, which then produced one-fifth of the nation's electricity, was kept in public hands in the form of Nuclear Electric. National Power, one of the privatised companies, produces half the country's power, from both fossil fuels and renewable sources. Powergen produces 30 per cent of Britain's electricity. Twelve electricity distribution companies were sold off in 1990, for £5.2 billion. The National Grid was sold off in 1996 for £5 billion.

### 11 plus test
Set up by the Education Act 1944, the examination determined which children would go to grammar, technical or secondary modern schools. Although inspired by good intentions, for example to identify those working-class children who would benefit from an academic secondary education as a preliminary for university entrance, the test resulted in injustices. Virtually all children took the examination, with regional variations, of whom about one-third passed. Studies showed working-class children tended not to pass while middle-class ones did. Moreover, the pass mark was adjusted upwards for girls in certain authorities that needed to ensure a gender balance in schools. The system was deemed to be unfair, especially as the future lives of the school population were decided at such a young age. After Labour was returned to power in 1964 the examination was phased out and comprehensive schools gradually introduced. Despite this, pockets of selection remained, such as Kent, Trafford and Tameside.

*See also* grammar school.

### 11 September 2001 terrorist attacks
*See* 9/11, 2001.

### elite
Small group of people who have influence and power out of all proportion to their number. Vilfredo Pareto and Gaetano Mosca argued in the early 20th century that democracy was a sham, as the many are ruled by the few. In Britain the traditional ruling elite was the aristocracy, mainly comprising large landowners, but the Industrial

Revolution added a new group: prominent industrialists. Moreover, with the expansion of the franchise in the 19th century and the growth of higher education, meritocratic virtues substituted new provenances for the elites of Britain. Thus, the social/educational background of MPs is heavily skewed towards independent school and Oxbridge. For example, in 1992 three-quarters of Conservative MPs were privately educated, 10 per cent at Eton alone, and just under half had been to Oxbridge; the figures for Labour were 15 per cent privately educated and 16 per cent Oxbridge. Even higher percentages of such politicians go on to serve in the cabinets of both parties and similar concentrations of upper-middle-class products, upwards of 50 per cent, go on to dominate all the main centres of power in Britain. These include ambassadors, High Court judges, senior military officers, civil servants and directors of major companies; sometimes these elites are joined together by marriage or blood ties. However, Budge *et al.* (in *The New British Politics*, fourth edition, 2004) question the existence of a consolidated elite; instead they suggest a series of 'fragmented' elites, for example media and opinion formers, who may act independently of political leaders. In December 2002, however, *The Economist* published its list of the 100 most important British decision makers, and this showed that since 1992 the percentage who were educated at public schools had fallen from 66 to 46 and those who were Oxbridge educated from 54 to 35.

Some have questioned the whole notion of elite power. Karl Marx argued that political power is derived wholly from the ownership of the means of production; Robert Dahl, suggested that it is one thing for an elite to have the potential to exercise power but it is another for it to ride rough-shod over opposition to get its own way.

*See also* establishment; power elite; social mobility.

## emergency debate
Debate allowed under standing order number 10 of the Commons. Some two or three emergency debates are allowed each year by the speaker. In applying for one, MPs are given a platform of sorts as they are allowed to make a three-minute speech to present their case for such a debate.

## emergency powers
Special powers available to government in the event of a national emergency, or when the civil authorities are unable to deal with a threat to life, property and civil order. Historically significant are the Defence of the Realm Acts 1914, 1915, and the Emergency Powers Acts 1939, 1940, which were used in time of war and gave sweeping powers to government to act in whatever way the circumstances required, including seizure of private property, billeting of troops and other persons, and detention without trial. Although repealed, the authorities can act under later acts to deal with civil emergencies, the most important example being terrorist violence in Northern Ireland. Between 1973 and 1976, the Prevention of Terrorism (Temporary Provisions) Acts and Northern Ireland (Emergency Provisions) Act provided a legal basis for the military to 'aid the civil power when requested by the latter to do so', and for the government to detain suspects without charge for seven days (later reduced to three days with the agreement of a court of law) and to exclude undesirable persons from the UK. More recently the Official Secrets Act 1989 and the Criminal Justice (Terrorism and Conspiracy) Act 1998 gave further legal powers to the authorities in dealing with emergencies and national security.

*See also* Security Commission; Terrorism Act 2000.

## Empire (British)
The foundations for the British Empire were laid in 100 years from the middle of the 18th century, when India, Australia, Canada, New Zealand, Cape Colony and other territories, including Hong Kong, were colonised. In the second half of the 19th century Britain won more colonies through the so-called 'scramble

for Africa'. Early in the 20th century
the Empire covered over one-fifth of the
world's landmass, nearly 12 billion square
miles, and contained 410 million people.
It used to be said, with pride, that the 'sun
never set' on the British Empire. However,
the acquisition of more territories after
the First World War occurred just when
Britain's economic power was beginning
to wane and nationalist movements were
beginning to flex their muscles. The transfer of power to the Dominions (Canada,
Australia, New Zealand and South
Africa) had been orderly and peaceful,
but otherwise the move to independence
often involved bitter conflicts with the
imperial power struggling to hold back the
unstoppable tide. India and Burma gained
independence in 1947 and decolonisation
followed very quickly during the 1950s
and 1960s. In 1998 Hong Kong was
handed back to China.

*See also* Commonwealth (British).

### Employment Acts 1980, 1982

The basis of the Conservative government's
attack on what it believed to be excessive
union power. These acts, together with
the Trade Union Act 1984, weakened
the closed shop; curtailed industrial action
by outlawing secondary picketing; and
imposed balloting requirements for union
officials and for donations to political parties from trade unions (the political levy).
Further acts followed in 1988 and 1990.
The Labour government elected in 1997
retained many of these, thus signalling a
break with Old Labour and the continuation of the Thatcherite agenda of labour
relations, albeit with some third way fine
tuning.

### employment tribunal

*See* tribunal.

### enabling authority

Description of a local authority. The
'enabling' model of local public service
provision suggests that as many functions as
possible should be contracted out to private
companies, in order to achieve efficiency

and thereby keep local taxes to a minimum.
According to this approach, local government plays a strictly limited role, namely
contracting out functions and ensuring they
are performed correctly and at the lowest
possible cost. The Conservative-controlled
London borough of Wandsworth is often
cited as the classic exemplar of such an
authority. The New Labour government
of 1997 was committed to substituting the
somewhat similar (although allegedly more
bureaucratic) 'best value' approach.

*See also* best value.

### energy

Britain in recent years has had an annual increase of 0.5 per cent in its energy
consumption and faces a future as a net
importer of oil and gas. Cost factors make
this possibility problematic. In 2001 the
percentages of energy sources were: natural
gas, 37 per cent; coal, 33 per cent; nuclear,
22 per cent; imports, 3 per cent; oil, 1 per
cent; hydro-electricity, 1 per cent; renewable sources, 2 per cent. By 2020, it is
estimated the figures will be as follows:
gas, 49 per cent; oil, 38 per cent; coal, 6
per cent; renewable sources 4 per cent;
and nuclear 3 per cent. The supporters of
nuclear power believe it will help fill the
gap but there are both safety and cost concerns. There is a prospect that tide-driven
turbines – more reliable than wind power
and ecologically friendly – could provide
more than enough electricity for Britain if
developed sufficiently.

### English Civil War, 1642–51

Conflict between supporters of the
crown – the Cavaliers – and those of
parliament – the Roundheads – under their
leader Oliver Cromwell. Its provenance lay
in the differences between Charles I and
the so-called Long Parliament. Religious
differences were especially important, as
Archbishop Laud had sought to impose a
common liturgy, which had alienated large
sections of the populace. The king lost
the ensuing battle at Edgehill in 1642; he
then lost at Marston Moor in 1644. The
Roundheads' improved military capacity,

reflected in the New Model Army, was confirmed at Naseby in 1645, where Charles was crushed. In 1647 he surrendered. Charles was beheaded in 1649. Subsequent Cavalier risings in different parts of the country culminated in defeat at Worcester in 1651. Cromwell became Lord Protector from 1653 to his death in 1658. The Civil War helped settle the long-running conflict between the British crown and parliament, in the latter's favour.

## Enron

www.enron.com

US energy conglomerate. In January 2002 the company crashed, ruining the lives of thousands of its workers. It seemed some of its activities had been facilitated by favours granted in exchange for plentiful cash handouts to key people in the US Congress and government. Some critics pointed to the money donated to New Labour and the subsequent change in policy on gas-fired power stations (which was to Enron's advantage). The government denied undue influence, claiming the change was won by argument, not purchased influence. It was also the case that Enron had given money to the Conservative Party when it had been in power.

## entrepreneurial culture

National environment conducive to business. An aspect of Margaret Thatcher's self-appointed mission was to reject the culture of the 'nanny' state in favour of a willingness to invest time and money in launching new money-making projects and individuals standing on their own feet. Most surveys of public attitudes suggested her crusade was not especially successful, as many people still believed that the state had a part to play in health and social welfare provision. These findings were noted by Tony Blair and his political strategists in their attempt to forge a new consensus on the proper balance between public and private provision. The legacy of this crusade lives on, not least in the language of New Labour, and the plethora of words imported from the business world and now part of everyday language, for example: 'partnerships' for long-term human relationships, and 'delivering' as a serviceable synonym for 'providing'.

*See also* paternalism; political language.

## entryism

A strategy, used by fringe parties, of gaining power and influence by invading a mainstream democratic party. This method was used by the far left in the 1970s to infiltrate the Labour Party and take over its constituency organisations. The Militant Tendency, a Trotskyist grouping, was the most notorious user of the tactic, which was facilitated by an exodus of members from the Labour Party in the wake of the Wilson governments of the 1960s and 1970s. Entryism caused major problems to Labour's public image and provoked bitter internal conflicts, for example in the mid-1980s when Militant-controlled Liverpool City Council (led by Derek Hatton) confronted Neil Kinnock, who was committed to rebuilding the party as a mainstream electoral force. Labour's National Executive Committee expelled a number of prominent militants during this decade. Critics, especially from the left, have suggested that 'right-wing entryism' has since taken place in the Labour Party: media professionals and London elites having played a central role in the take-over of the party at national level and the creation of New Labour.

*See also* far left; Hayward report; Militant Tendency; Whitty report.

## Environment Agency

www.environment-agency.gov.uk

All-embracing agency set up in 1996 with a wide range of functions, including: flood defence, water resource management, pollution control, fisheries protection (freshwater), navigation of inland waterways, recreational use of water and land, and conservation of landscape and archaeological heritage. Ever since the 1970s there had been calls for an integrated body to protect the environment; this involved the unification of several disparate bodies, notably the Pollution Inspectorate, the National Rivers Authority and the waste regulatory authorities. The Environment Agency has been active in initiatives to promote waste minimisation in business. It has not been afraid to prosecute even high-profile offenders, including ICI three times in relation to its plant in Runcorn, Cheshire.

### environmental group

Pressure group promoting green issues. Traditionally Britain has a well developed environmental lobby and some estimates place membership of such groups at 4.5 million or 8 per cent of the population. Prominent groups include Friends of the Earth (formed in 1969), Greenpeace (in 1972) and the umbrella organisation Transport 2000 (originating in 1973). As well as these there are bodies like the National Trust and National Heritage. Interest in the environment has burgeoned since the 1970s and has given birth to a new kind of direct action politics. However, the radical potency of the movement has been blunted, to some extent, by mainstream parties, which have developed their own 'light green', consumer-friendly environmental policies.

### Equal Opportunities Commission

www.eoc.org.uk
Founded in 1975 by the then Labour government to implement the Sex Discrimination Act 1975. Its function is: to promote equality of opportunity; to strive to eliminate discrimination; and to review sex discrimination legislation. Many criticise it for being toothless and inactive but, arguably, it has helped to create a culture in which discrimination is regarded as illegitimate.

### equality

A social or political relationship in which no special privilege, benefit or status is bestowed on individuals or groups other than those that are morally or logically justified. Two types of equality can be identified: equality of opportunity and equality in outcomes.

First, equality of opportunity refers to a 'level playing field' of rules and conditions between individuals and groups who are in competition for valued social, economic or political rewards. For example, all candidates should be treated equally in the conduct of an examination and the marking of their papers. The British legal system makes use of the associated principle of even-handed treatment, which dictates that people should all be treated alike, regardless of social (or other) status. However, certain categories of persons, for example the police, ministers of the crown and the sovereign do have powers not enjoyed by the 'ordinary' citizen. As far as ideology is concerned, all mainstream parties accept the principle of equality of opportunity, although socialist movements such as Labour have tended to emphasise the socially and morally damaging effects of unrestrained individual liberty, especially with regard to property rights within a capitalist economic system.

Second, equality in outcomes is achieved by taking into account differences between individuals or groups in order for people to be placed in the same situation. For example, socialists and civil rights campaigners have promoted the idea of positive discrimination or quotas for disadvantaged groups (such as ethnic minorities, women, the poor) in the world of work. In this case the principle of equal opportunity is suspended in order to achieve a fairer outcome.

### established Church

*See* Church of England.

### establishment

A pejorative term for the administrative, professional, business and academic elites who have key positions of influence in the British state. This was first used in recent times, according to historian Peter Hennessy, by journalist Henry Fairlie in his *Spectator* column in September 1955, but more truly entered the language after a well known collection of critical essays edited by the then young historian Hugh Thomas which was entitled *The Establishment*

(1959). It contained chapters by, among others, John Vaizey on the class system; Thomas Balogh on the senior civil service; and Fairlie himself on the 'most powerful voice of the establishment', the BBC. Ironically Vaizey and Thomas ended up with peerages and as disciples of Margaret Thatcher; Hennessy quotes Rose Macauley that 'the moderns of one day become the Establishment of the next'.

## ethical foreign policy
When Robin Cook was made foreign secretary in May 1997 he declared there would henceforth be an 'ethical dimension' to the Foreign Office's mission statement, by placing human rights at the heart of the work of his department. A year later critics rounded on policies which seemed to cast doubt on this mission, citing: his approval of arms sales to Sandline International, a mercenary company which assisted General Kabbah in his illegal attempt to regain office in Sierra Leone; and his approval of 64 arms export licences to Indonesia as well as 86 to Turkey for arms which could be used for internal repression. On the other hand, Cook had achieved a new agreement on landmines, a new code on arms exports, and the establishment of the International Criminal Court; he had also promoted the military action which liberated Kosovo. Neal Ascherson, writing in the *Observer* (2 August 1998), judged that other foreign ministers recognised that 'the British, especially during their presidency of the EU, have shown vigour and at times leadership in forcing a human rights dimension into international agreements and institutions'. However, by January 2000, the 'ethical' theme to Foreign Office statements had been toned down, possibly in response to the doubts of officials. Tony Blair's later active support of the US war on terrorism and Iraq was sometimes presented as an extension of this ethical theme.
*See also* foreign policy.

## ethical socialism
The name given to 19th-century socialist thinkers, for example Robert Owen and William Morris, who condemned capitalism as an evil system and advocated a socialist society in which private enterprise would be abolished and human nature changed for the better. This was a noble vision, if a somewhat vague approach, which offered no answers to several key questions: How free would people be in a socialist society? How would wealth be created? Who would be in charge of the economy? Tony Blair attempted to reintroduce elements of ethical socialism into his approach to social problems, although critics pointed out that he was doing so just as he was burying traditional notions of the doctrine within the party.
*See also* Christian socialism.

## ethnic minority
*See* immigration.

## ethnicity
Refers to social groups who distinguish themselves from others, or are distinguished by others, by differences in cultural behaviour – which may include language and religion – or physical appearance. Sociologists often use this term to describe British citizens who can trace their origins to Commonwealth countries or émigrés fleeing persecution in eastern Europe in the first half of the 20th century. The term 'race' is seldom used as a sociological description owing to its direct association with the discredited eugenics movement and the bogus scientism of the Nazis in the 1930s. In the 1991 census, the ethnic composition of the UK was 94.5 per cent white and 5.5 per cent ethnic minorities. The distribution of ethnic minorities is very uneven, with most being concentrated in the inner cities and very few in rural or semi-rural areas. This has favoured the Labour Party, which is perceived by ethnic voters as close to meeting their economic and social concerns. However, there is evidence that second- and third-generation ethnic Britons are now moving up the class ladder, securing jobs in the professions and adopting middle-class lifestyles. The full impact of this on British politics, and party allegiance in particular,

has yet to become clear. It would seem, however, that all mainstream parties would need to broaden their appeal by increasing membership among ethnic minorities and placing their concerns on the political agenda. In 2003, Labour seemed to have the best opportunity of achieving this – for the reasons stated above and the fact that the Labour government was committed to tackling social exclusion – but the Iraq war lost the party support among muslims. The Conservatives (at least through the legacy of William Hague) are less well placed, as they tend to be associated with harsh immigration controls and a lack of sympathy with ethnic groups, whether deserved or not.

### eugenics

The 'science' of how physical and mental attributes of a population can be improved through policies which improve the 'breeding stock'. It was popular across Europe in the latter part of the 19th and early part of the 20th century. Some British intellectuals flirted with the idea, including Sidney and Beatrice Webb and George Bernard Shaw. However, it is now more widely known for its adoption by the Nazi regime, which sought to engineer a dominant Aryan race and eliminate 'inferior' races.

### euro

Name for the European single currency. European economic and monetary union (EMU) was a dream of Europhiles for many years, although it was not officially mentioned until the Single European Act of 1986. The Delors plan included an intergovernmental conference on EMU and this in turn led to the 1992 Maastricht Treaty, which called for the eventual creation of a single currency. A European Central Bank was set up to supervise the single currency and in January 1999 11 members (later joined by Greece) of the European Union subscribed to the new currency. Britain and three other member states decided to stay out and wait until the conditions were right for them to join. This 'wait and see' policy provided both John Major and Tony Blair with their positions,

although chancellor Gordon Brown insisted on five conditions being met before Britain could join the single currency. In January 2002 euro notes and coins were introduced in the 12 'Euroland' countries and this applied more pressure to the Labour government to declare itself willing to risk a referendum on Britain joining. However, Brown stood firm, despite signs that opinion might be shifting slightly towards entry, with a majority believing it to be in any case inevitable.

*See also* European economic and monetary union; five tests.

### Eurocommunism

Body of thought developed in the 1970s by Italian, French and Spanish communists. Essentially this new approach disengaged communism from the USSR as the sole model of communism and argued that each party needed to adapt to national conditions. It also urged collaboration with other 'progressive' forces to transform society to the left. In Britain the emergence of a Eurocommunist faction helped bring about the demise of the British Communist Party.

### European Atomic Energy Community (Euratom)

Formed by Treaty of Rome (1957) to promote and develop peaceful uses of atomic energy in Europe. In 1967 it merged with the European Coal and Steel Community (ECSC) and the European Economic Community (EEC) to become part of the European Community (EC).

### European Commission

http://europa.eu.int/comm/index _ en.htm The main administrative body of the European Union (EU), sometimes known as 'the College of Commissioners'. It is the most dynamic element of the EU and has responsibility for: proposing legislation and policies; implementing the decisions of the EU Council and parliament; enforcing European law (jointly with the Court of Justice); and representing the EU on the international stage.

Members of the Commission are supposed to uphold the interests of the EU as a whole and not to be bound by loyalty to their own home countries. Its president is often seen as the embodiment of the EU and its most important spokesperson and leader. Usually members of the Commission are distinguished politicians who have a commitment to the idea of Europe. Previously, the bigger countries nominated two each of the then 20 commissioners and the smaller countries one, but since the accession of 10 more members on 1 May 2004 all members nominate only one each. When Bulgaria and Romania join the EU it will have 27 member states, at which point the Council will fix the maximum number of commissioners. This figure will be below 27 and their nationality will be determined by a system of rotation. On 1 November 2004 25 commissioners took up their office under the presidency of the Portuguese Jose Manuel Barroso. Britain's nominated commissioner was Peter Mandelson, who was given the trade portfolio.

## European constitution

Proposed constitution for the European Union (EU). A European convention, chaired by former French president Giscard D'Estaing, was established to draw up a draft constitution for the EU by May 2004, when 10 new members joined. The aim was to reshape and simplify existing treaties. After several years of fairly intense discussion the resultant document was deemed, by most commentators, to favour the larger, more populous countries in the form of decision-making proposed. A charter of fundamental rights was resisted by some British experts on the grounds that this would cut across Britain's unwritten constitution. Similarly, a proposed new foreign minister for the EU was controversial, as it appeared to undermine the sovereign rights of nations to conduct their own relations with others. Defence, too, was problematic, especially the idea favoured by France, Belgium and Germany for a new defence planning staff, to be set up in Tervuren in Belgium.

The British government initially argued that no referendum was necessary on the new constitution as it did not propose to alter the fundamental nature of Britain's relationship to the EU. The Conservatives vigorously disagreed and Michael Howard, once installed as leader in November 2003, threw his weight behind the campaign to hold a referendum, in line with certain other member states. In the spring of 2004 Tony Blair performed a volte face on the issue (and was consequently much criticised by supporters of the EU) and declared a referendum would be held. This made it essential that his position appeared to defend national interests and he insisted his so-called 'red lines' would be protected from excessive EU control.

*See also* red lines.

## European Convention on Human Rights (ECHR)

Convention of the Council of Europe, established in Rome in 1950 and signed by Britain in 1951. It spells out those rights which should be protected – for example the rights to life and freedom of thought and speech – and lays down the procedures for determining infringements. If necessary cases can be referred to the European Court of Human Rights. Since 1998, following a pledge in the 1997 Labour manifesto – the Convention has been incorporated into British domestic law via the Human Rights Act 1998 and has the effect of adding another written element to the British constitution, as well as giving a more political, more interpretive role to senior judges. From October 2000 British courts began to hear cases brought by British citizens under the Convention. Tony Blair's wife, Cherie, was involved in new chambers, Matrix, formed to specialise in human rights cases. In August 2001 several inmates of a detention centre for asylum seekers at Oakhampton took legal action under the new human rights legislation. They claimed their rights had been violated through their physical detention in the centre when they offered no threat to the community. The judge upheld their claim, angering the Home Office and leading to some calls for new legislation to make detention of asylum seekers legal: a difficult measure as it would require the recasting of the ECHR itself and the agreement of all signatories.

*See also* European Court of Human Rights.

## European Council

*See* Council of the European Union.

## European Court of Human Rights

www.echr.coe.int

The court established in Strasbourg by the 1950 European Convention on Human Rights. It hears cases referred to it from the European Commission of Human Rights when a satisfactory resolution has not been found to a case where an individual has complained of a violation of rights by the government of a member state. Court rulings have had far-reaching effects, for example forcing Ireland to drop its constitutional clauses against homosexuals. By the early 1990s Britain had appeared before the court some 200 times and was found guilty of violations in two-thirds of cases. In 1998 the European Convention on Human Rights was incorporated into British domestic law; the major advantage of this for claimants is that is they can now have their cases heard in British courts, thus saving time and not an inconsiderable amount of money.

*See also* European Convention on Human Rights.

## European Court of Justice

http://europa.eu.int/cj/en/index.htm

Deals with alleged breaches of European Union law. It is based in Luxembourg and is formally entitled the Court of Justice of the European Communities (it should not be confused with the European Court of Human Rights at Strasbourg). It ensures that European treaties are observed and their terms are interpreted fairly. It is the highest court in the EU. It comprises one judge from each member state plus one

extra. Cases can be brought before the court by member states or institutions of the EU or by the Commission against non-complying members. Individuals who feel European laws have been breached to their disadvantage can also bring cases against national governments. Most of the court's work, however, arises from requests from member states for clarification of aspects of European Community law. Only the most important cases are heard in plenary sessions of seven judges; mostly panels of three sit in hearings which vary from rulings on treaties to rulings on decisions made by the Commission. Because of the weight of cases, a Court of First Instance has been set up to deal with minor cases.

## European economic and monetary union (EMU)

A key element of the development of the European Union (EU), involving the creation of the single currency for member states. Supporters believe it will deliver prosperity and long-term peace, while opponents point to the erosion of national sovereignty, especially in domestic economic policy making (public expenditure planning and taxation). In particular, they fear it could never serve the heterogeneous needs of so many different economies; for example, some will require high interest rates to control inflationary pressures, whereas others will not need such monetary constraint. Some suggest that the tensions will be such that economic disaster for millions of Europeans will result. EMU was launched in the summer of 1998, when 11 countries joined the scheme; the other four member states of the EU, including Britain, withheld judgement and membership until it had got under way after January 1999. By January 2000 the euro was trading badly on the foreign exchanges and sections of the British political and economic class were signalling at best a cooling of interest in the scheme. However, the currency recovered strongly as the dollar languished in 2002. The prospects for British entry remained unclear by mid-2004.

## European Economic Area (EAA)

Free trade area formed through collaboration between members of the European Free Trade Association (EFTA) and the European Union (EU). It was set up in May 1992 by a treaty signed in Oporto and embraces 18 countries with 380 million inhabitants. The EEA Council meets twice a year at ministerial level; the Joint Committee, comprising senior officials, meets monthly and takes decisions by consensus. The EEA Joint Parliamentary Committee meets twice a year for discussions on general matters with the EEA Joint Consultative Committee performing a similar role.

## European Economic Community (EEC)

One of the three institutions that merged in 1967 to become the European Community and in turn the European Union. After the Second World War a number of idealists, including the two French statesmen Jean Monnet and Robert Schuman, set up the European movement. Monnet believed the problem of national sovereignty would have to be tackled on one 'front' at a time. The strategy began with heavy industry – coal and steel – but Monnet made it clear this was only a 'narrow front' and the ultimate objective was political integration. After the formation of a number of European organisations the core countries of France, Germany, Belgium, Italy, the Netherlands and Luxembourg came together to form the European Economic Community, more popularly known as the Common Market, by signing the Treaty of Rome in 1957. This had the eventual aim of furthering economic efficiency and consumer choice by removing trade tariffs, facilitating the free movement of goods, services, persons and capital, and the necessary harmonisation of the legislation of each member state. Thus economic logic would demand a degree of political union. Britain, which had shown little warmth towards the idea in its early days, changed its mind once the experiment proved economically successful. It tried unsuccessfully to join twice in the 1960s – President de Gaulle vetoed the 'Anglo-Saxon' application – but was admitted in 1973 when the application made by Edward Heath's government was accepted. In 1993 the term EEC was superseded by 'European Union' (EU).

*See also* European Atomic Energy Community; European Union.

## European election

The means whereby membership of the European parliament is determined. Elections take place every five years. There are 626 members. The UK elects 78 MEPs (75 from the mainland, plus 3 from Northern Ireland; the total had been 87 before enlargement of the EU in May 2004). In 1999 the UK managed a turnout of only 24 per cent, compared with an EU average of some 50 per cent. The Conservatives, who fought a Eurosceptical campaign, won the most seats (36 out of 87) based on this pitifully low turnout. On 10 June 2004 postal voting in the European elections helped raise turnout to a still woefully low 37 per cent (compared with an EU-wide average of 45 per cent). At 52 per cent Northern Ireland had the highest turnout, but the south-west only 31 per cent. Both the main parties, competing for the lower total of 75 seats (following the entry of 10 new members in May 2004), lost votes and seats: Conservatives 27 per cent of the vote and 27 seats (down 8) and Labour 23 per cent of the vote and 19 seats (down 6). The Liberal Democrats gained 15 per cent of the vote and 12 seats (down 2) and the Greens gained 2 seats from 6.3 per cent of the vote. The British National Party garnered 5 per cent but no seats. However, the spectacular success of these elections belonged to the United Kingdom Independence Party (UKIP), campaigning on a platform of withdrawal from the EU: it gained 16% of the vote and 12 seats (up 2 from 1999).

## European Free Trade Association (EFTA)

www.efta.int

Set up in January 1960 as a low-tariff agreement to counter the successful European Economic Community. It originally comprised Britain, Denmark, Portugal, Austria, Norway, Sweden and Switzerland. Some countries subsequently left EFTA to become members of the European Union (EU) but other countries later joined EFTA. In 1994 the diminished EFTA and the EU established the European Economic Area as a common market.

## European idea

Enthusiasts for the ideal of a federal Europe originally helped to launch the idea of a united continent from previously warring countries. In a poll taken in 1994, the populations of eight out of the then 12 member states registered a minority of supporters for the federal ideal. In Britain, enthusiasm for all things European tends to be lower than in most member countries, with opposition concentrating in the Conservative Party, where the Eurosceptics caused John Major's government so much trouble. Advocates of the European idea are often accused by 'sceptics' of being a small elite who wield great power from positions of authority within the governing classes of European Union countries and impose their integrationist policies on populations who often object when they learn the facts or are consulted in referendums.

## European Monetary System (EMS)

An arrangement whereby the members of the European Union fixed the exchange rates of their currencies to guard against large fluctuations. It began in 1979 with the aim of countering inflation and encouraging steady economic growth. The main instrument used was the adjustment of interest rates to keep variations within a narrow range, called the Exchange Rate Mechanism. In 1994 the European Monetary Institute was set up as a transitional step towards the European Central Bank (ECB) and a common currency. The ECB was created in 1998 and in 1999 the single currency, the euro, was introduced, though Britain, Denmark and Sweden opted to stay outside the 11-nation 'eurozone', while Greece joined it in 2001.

## European parliament

www.europarl.eu.int

The 'legislature' of the European Union (EU) but for many years seen merely as a 'talking shop', with scant powers in relation to the European Commission and Council of Ministers. However, since the 1980s it has acquired considerable powers and its prestige has grown accordingly. Plenary sessions take place in Strasbourg yet, awkwardly, committee meetings take place in Brussels and nonsensically its secretariat is based in Luxembourg. The parliament used to be a feeble democratic instrument but in the 1970s it gained influence over the Community budget and with the Single European Act in 1987 it gained more legislative power. At Maastricht in 1992 it also gained 'co-decision' powers, which gave it ultimate power to reject legislation altogether. In addition it has the ability to veto the accession of new member states. MEPs sit according to compatible ideological groups, which include: Greens, Socialists, Liberals and the conservative European People's Party (which includes the British Conservatives). Britain initially refused to use proportional representation for elections to the European parliament, unlike the other member states, as the Conservatives in particular felt it would be the thin end of the wedge for similar changes for Westminster elections. However, the change was made when Labour came to power in 1997 and the first elections using proportional representation, based on 11 electoral districts nationwide, were held in 1999. Results in this election reflected a very low turnout – 24 per cent – and some sympathy for the Conservatives' Eurosceptic manifesto: 36 Conservative, 29 Labour, 10 Liberal Democrat, 3 UK Independence Party, 2 Green, 2 Plaid Cymru, 2 SNP, 3 others. Criticism has been aimed at the way in which the regional lists and the order of candidates were drawn up, even though all parties claimed members were consulted as much as possible. In June 2004 the Conservatives won 27 seats, Labour 19, the Liberal Democrats 12, the UK

Independence Party 12, the Scottish National Party 3, the Greens 2 and Plaid Cymru 2.

*See also* European Union decision making; regional party list.

## European rebate to Britain

Money refunded to Britain from its contribution to the European budget. The question of a rebate arose upon the accession to power of Margaret Thatcher in 1979. Her advisors noted that Britain received only a tenth of Community agricultural expenditure, which comprised two-thirds of the total budget, while it contributed a fifth of the Community's revenue. They argued that Britain's contribution was higher than its gross domestic product (ranked seventh in the European Community) merited; indeed, that Britain and Germany were the only net contributors while all the others were recipients. Thatcher refused an initial offer of £350 million, despite Foreign Office advice to settle, and she held out stubbornly for more. She eventually won £2 billion for the years 1981–82 plus a formula for annual rebates. Her stance convinced her that intransigence was the best way to deal with the Community.

In July 2004 it was argued by EU partners that Britain's revived economy now made the rebates unnecessary but Tony Blair emphatically refused to accept this.

## European Regional Development Fund (ERDF)

Set up in 1975 to help poorer areas within the European Community. The ERDF and European Social Fund (ESF) demonstrate that the European institution now fills the gap left by the nation state, since many economically distressed regions across Europe have common interests best served by a supranational organisation. The UK has benefited from regional aid in areas like Northern Ireland and Merseyside. The addition of 10 new EU members in May 2004 means that available funds will have to be spread more thinly, especially as many of the new countries are relatively poor.

## European Social Fund

Used by the European Union to feed resources into social policy programmes connected, for example, with employment training or retraining. Both this and the European Regional Development Fund benefited from the desire in the 1980s to achieve 'cohesion' and to avoid any disadvantage being suffered by member states as a result of the internal market. The funds will be spread more thinly after the accession of 10 new members in May 2004.

## European Union (EU)

http://europa.eu.int

Intergovernmental and supranational organisation that can be traced back to the Treaty of Paris, signed in 1951, when France and Germany established, under the Schuman plan, the European Coal and Steel Community (ECSC). Since then, the organisation has deepened in terms of integration and enlarged in terms of membership. In 1957 the Treaty of Rome established the European Economic Community (EEC) and Euratom and was signed by the then six member states. In 1986, the Single European Act (SEA) put into effect the idea of a Europe open to trade, qualifications, movement of workers and important aspects of regional and social policy. In 1992 the Maastricht Treaty accelerated the processes of integration, though prime minister John Major negotiated an opt-out from the provisions of the Social Chapter. With Maastricht came a formal change of name to reflect more properly the unifying nature of the organisation: European Union. By 1992, the EU had a number of institutions: the European Commission, the Council of Ministers, the European parliament and the European Court of Justice. The stated objective of the EU is to move towards greater economic and political union, but members differ in their enthusiasm for such a goal. Britain was initially kept out of the EEC by General de Gaulle, who was suspicious of Britain's 'special relationship' with the USA, but after his death France withdrew its veto and Britain joined in 1972, premier Edward Heath signing the Treaty of Accession. In 2004 10 new members joined, taking total membership up to 25.

## European Union constitution
*See* European constitution.

## European Union decision making
Complex process involving a number of separate procedures. Very generally the process can be seen to originate in the European Commission, which has always consulted widely before putting forward a policy proposal. The proposal is then forwarded to the Council of Ministers, where it is considered by specialist officials of member states. At the same time it is sent to the European parliament and the Economic and Social Committee, which submit reactions to the Council. The so-called 'co-decision' and 'consultation' reactions are the most frequent. During this phase extensive lobbying takes place before a decision is reached.

*See also* Council of Ministers; European Commission; European parliament.

## Europhile
Person or party enthusiastic about the European idea and the European Union (EU). Early Europhiles included Winston Churchill and Ernest Bevin, though there were limits to their enthusiasm. The most enthusiastic Conservatives after Churchill included Harold Macmillan, Edward Heath (who negotiated Britain's entry in 1972), Michael Heseltine and Kenneth Clarke. On the Labour side Roy Jenkins – a president of the Commission – was prominently pro-Europe as were, of current politicians, Tony Blair, most of his party in the Commons and the cabinet. The Liberal Democrats are the most pro-EU of the mainstream parties; the *Guardian*, *Independent* and *Observer* are the most Europhile of the major newspapers.

## Eurosceptic
A word popularly used to describe a person or party opposed to further economic

or more especially political integration within the European Union (EU). Some believe such integration will erode British sovereignty and lose the country valuable national symbols, like the pound. Others argue for complete withdrawal from the EU. Opposition has existed ever since Britain proposed to join the European Community and used to characterise the approach of Labour's left wing in the late 1960s and early 1970s. However, this faded and by the 1980s the Conservatives became the chief Eurosceptic party. A small group of recalcitrant MPs, led by William Cash (not to mention a group in the Lords led by Norman Tebbit), eventually had the whip withdrawn in 1994 for their open hostility to John Major's attempt to get the Maastricht Treaty through parliament, although it was soon restored. In April and June 1996 two anti-European motions attracted the support of one-third of backbench Conservative MPs. During the 1997 election the split between the Eurosceptics and the leadership, especially over Britain's putative membership of the European single currency, contributed to the party's and leader's difficulties. Divided parties lose elections and the Conservatives were deeply divided over Europe; they subsequently suffered one of their worst defeats in 1997. Leading Eurosceptics included: John Biffen (who saw himself almost as a mentor to the sceptics), Teddy Taylor, Nicholas Budgen, George Gardiner, John Wilkinson, Lord (Woodrow) Wyatt, Lord Beloff, Lord MacAlpine and, of course, Margaret Thatcher. Labour Eurosceptics include Dennis Skinner and Austin Mitchell, though the best known was probably the late Peter Shore and the former MP Tony Benn. There are also many Eurosceptics in the rank and file of both the Labour Party and the Conservative Party. The United Kingdom Independence Party (UKIP) won 16 per cent of the vote in the June 2004 European elections; nearly half of these votes came from former Conservatives but a fifth were drawn from Labour voters. In addition, rich business people are prepared to fund Eurosceptic parties: for example the late James Goldsmith and the Yorkshire businessman Paul Sykes. The British press is characterised by a number of broadsheets and tabloids hostile to the idea of closer integration, most notably the *Sun* and the other Murdoch-owned papers, *The Times* and *Sunday Times*. The *Daily Mail*, the *Express* and the *Daily Telegraph* have been hostile to a greater or lesser degree.

### e-voting

Voting by electronic means. On 17 July 2002 a consultation paper was released on e-voting that suggested it had a bright future. According to the proposals the existing system of ballot papers and voting booths would be scrapped and all voters offered four voting options: online from home or work, by post, by telephone, or at polling stations equipped with online terminals. The proposal was to set up the new system by 2006 and to have the electoral register maintained electronically. A total of £30 million has been allocated to develop e-voting over the years 2002–05. Experiments are due to continue over this period and the hope is that such new accessibility will increase voter turnout and help reverse evidence of voter apathy.

### Exchange Rate Mechanism (ERM)

The part of the European Monetary System of the European Union (EU) which attempted to maintain exchange rates within a narrow band. Nigel Lawson and Geoffrey Howe, the British chancellor and foreign secretary respectively, were in favour of joining but succeeded in persuading Margaret Thatcher only in late 1990 and then at a rate to the Deutschmark of 2.95, which was hard to sustain. In the autumn of 1992 currency speculators targeted the weaker EU currencies in the ERM. Given fears about the future of European integration, there was a huge exodus of currency out of the weaker ones – the lire, pound and franc – into the Deutschmark. Britain was unable to persuade Germany, scarred by unhappy memories of inflation, to reduce interest rates, and on 16

September 1992 (Black Wednesday), Britain became the subject of a concerted attempt by speculators to exploit the weakness of the pound. Two increases in interest rates had no effect, nor did huge sums transferred from Britain's foreign exchange reserves, and the chancellor, Norman Lamont, had to withdraw Britain from the ERM and effectively devalue the pound. The value of the pound fell quickly, aided by sharp cuts in interest rates. Ironically the economy began to recover from recession but the impression of economic incompetence was very damaging to Conservative fortunes and some commentators date their loss in 1997 and subsequent decline to this single catastrophic event.

*See also* Black Wednesday; European Monetary System.

### exclusion
*See* social exclusion.

### executive
Often used to describe the institutions tasked with the job of day-to-day government or the execution of policy. In Britain this would include the cabinet, departments of state, the civil service and other agencies of government. The other two branches of government usually cited are the legislature (law-making bodies) and the judiciary (law enforcement and interpretation).

### executive agency
A generic term for any government body but given specific sense by the Ibbs report in 1988, which led to the so-called 'Next Steps' agencies. These represent the hiving off of certain of the more routine government functions to new organisations, which are given substantial management and financial autonomy under a director, who reports to the permanent secretary of the department involved. The idea is to relieve the workload and responsibility falling upon ministers. Examples include the Driver and Vehicle Licensing Agency, the Training Agency and the Benefits Agency. By the spring of 1997 nearly 80 per cent of all civil servants were employed in some 200

agencies. Tony Blair has fully accepted that the agencies are now part of Britain's system of public administration and has gone further in plans to privatise National Air Traffic Services (NATS) and a number of other public services. However, major concerns have been expressed by many observers at the lack of accountability of the agencies, which are run at arm's length from the minister, away from direct parliamentary scrutiny, a problem graphically illustrated by the sacking of the head of the Prison Service, Derek Lewis, in 1995.

## exit poll

An opinion poll commissioned either by a party or by a media organisation which takes place immediately after people have voted at a polling station. Such polls are said to be more reliable for a number of technical and psychological reasons. However, in the 1992 general election the technique was questioned, along with the polling industry generally, when, together with late campaign polls, exit polls overestimated Labour support and resulted in a gross underestimate of the Conservative vote during the coverage of the event on television. The problem was avoided in revised methods of polling used for the 1997 general election.

## exploitation

In general terms, the unfair extraction of benefit or an advantage taken from another person or group. Although a feature of many societies, though not necessarily of all, the term is closely associated with Karl Marx's analysis of power in a capitalist society based on his studies of 19th-century Britain. He argued that the owners of the production process receive unfairly the value created from the work of their employees (termed surplus labour value) and who thus 'exploit' them. The concept was based on the labour theory of value

first adduced by John Locke, who stated: 'whoever created things from nature by their own labours had joined to it something that is his own, and thereby makes it his Property'. Marx developed this idea that the exchange value of a good was determined by the quantity of labour that had gone into producing it. The worker was entitled to this value but received only enough to continue living. The capitalist extracted the 'surplus value' and the workers were thus 'exploited'. Clause four of the Labour Party constitution, abandoned after Tony Blair became leader in 1994, referred to these arguments when it stated its objective of securing for the 'workers ... the full fruits of their industry'.

## extra-parliamentary party

Political party that is not represented in parliament. There are a number of these in Britain, especially on the far left and far right. The first past the post electoral system discriminates against smaller parties in that those with thin national support find it difficult to win any seats. Being excluded from parliament means effectively being excluded from shaping the political agenda and most extra-parliamentary parties have short, unhappy lives. Some Marxist parties have condemned the parliamentary struggle as a diversion, as part of the mystification used by the ruling class to disguise their dominance. Instead, they urge action on the streets and the mobilisation of the workers for some form of revolution. To date, workers have tended to ignore such injunctions, preferring to earn enough to keep themselves and their families rather than risk everything in a speculative revolutionary process. Modern Marxists argue that this is an important feature of capitalist democracies, where formal or procedural rights, such as the freedom to vote, obscure powerful economic forces, which make 'citizens' prisoners of their material circumstances.

# F

## Fabian Society
www.fabian-society.org.uk
Left of centre membership-based think
tank, founded in 1884 by such socialist intellectuals as Sidney and Beatrice
Webb, George Bernard Shaw and H. G.
Wells. The Fabians followed the cautious
strategies of the Roman general Fabius
Maximus and favoured a gradual, reformist path to socialism. It was a founding
member of the Labour Representation
Committee in 1900 and did much to
encourage development of early policies
via pamphlets, books and discussion events
like summer schools. These roles continue
to the present day; the Society has several
thousand members, including some half
of the Parliamentary Labour Party. Few
would claim, however, that the Fabians now
exert as much influence as they did during
the early days of the labour movement.

*See also* Labour Representation
Committee.

## Factortame case, 1990
A landmark case brought by the Spanish
company Factortame against the British
government that illustrated the impact of
membership of the European Union on
British law. The case originated when
Spanish trawler owners challenged the
British Merchant Shipping Act 1988, which
had sought to prevent 'quota-hopping', on
the grounds that it was contrary to European
law regarding the registration of shipping.
Eventually the European Court of Justice
found for the trawler owners, and this
emphasised the superiority of European law
over domestic law and the fact that Britain
was no longer supreme as it once was over its
own laws: a higher European authority had
proved it could overrule statute law.

## Falklands War
The Falkland Islands (area 12,173 square
miles, population 2,120) in the South
Atlantic were invaded on 2 April 1982
by the right-wing military government
of Argentina. The Falklands had been
claimed for Britain in 1690 and became a
colony in 1833. Sheep farming is the main
occupation and the islands were known as a
telecommunications relay station. Once they
were occupied by Argentina, Margaret
Thatcher's government sent a task force to
recapture them. Shuttle diplomacy by the
US secretary of state and intervention by
the United Nations failed to prevent a short
but vicious conflict in which several ships
were sunk on both sides, the most controversial being the British sinking of the
*General Belgrano*, an Argentinean battle
cruiser which was heading away from the
battle zone when torpedoed. The war and
the fortunes of the task force on these in-
hospitable islands transfixed public opinion.
Thatcher, then unpopular at home, won
plaudits for her coolness of nerve and determination to repel the enemy. Argentinean
forces on the islands surrendered on 14
June. The war succeeded in strengthening
the political position of Thatcher's government and she gained a huge win in the
1983 general election, albeit over a divided
opposition. The Argentinean government
fell and was replaced by a democratically
elected one. The islands continue to be
occupied by a British force and agreement over their future is still to be reached
between the two countries.

*See also General Belgrano.*

## family
Families have long been a concern to
governments. Margaret Thatcher famously
said 'there is no such thing as society.
There are individual men and women,
and there are families'. John Major sought
to strengthen social stability by taking the
country 'back to basics' but the campaign
was derailed when the press decided to
apply 'family values' to Conservative politicians and revealed some of them to be
more than occasionally adulterous and hypocritical. The Blair government revealed
its belief in the family with a report in
October 1998 that proposed to bolster and

strengthen this basic building block of society. The government was clearly concerned by statistics which suggested the traditional family was in decline. For example, studies show: by 2010 the traditional nuclear family will be in the minority and half of all marriages will end in divorce; 3 per cent of couples who married in the early 1960s divorced within three years whereas in 1998 the figure was 12 per cent; a quarter of children were born out of wedlock in the late 1990s. However, a survey in the *Observer* (25 October 1998) revealed that a majority of respondents felt: unhappy parents should not stay together for the sake of their children; single parents could take care of children as effectively as married parents; and that it was none of the government's business how people conduct their lives as long as they stay within the law. It also revealed over half of respondents could be classified as 'broadly permissive' while only 16 per cent could be classed as 'traditional', with more youthful people in the former category and more older people in the latter.

### far left

Parties centring on Marxist or Trotskyist ideas. There are several such parties in Britain. In both cases emphasis is placed upon a 'vanguard party' of hardened revolutionaries who will lead the masses when the time is right and resist the inevitable counter-revolution of capitalism. Trotsky was a renegade communist to followers of the orthodox Moscow line but his vision of worldwide revolution was attractive to western activists on the left, and a number of factions supported his views. The originally Moscow-leaning Communist Party of Great Britain folded in 1991 to become the more pluralist and gradualist Democratic Left. The Revolutionary Socialist League spawned a number of followers, among them Militant Tendency, formed under the influence of Pat Taafe and Ted Grant on Merseyside. Militant used entryism to influence the Labour Party but this tactic was rebuffed by Labour in the 1980s and the influence of the far left declined once Tony

Blair became Labour's electoral saviour after 1994. Other left-wing parties include the Socialist Workers Party, the Workers' Revolutionary Party and a host of others, almost all with small memberships and minimal electoral support.

### far right

Parties centring on fascist and racist ideas. The British Union of Fascists was established by Oswald Mosley in the 1930s. His violent rallies in the East End of London were curbed by legislation and Mosley was interned during the war in case he aided the enemy. After the war he attempted to revive his party but to no avail. In the late 1960s the National Front emerged from a coalescence of right-wing groups and fought some elections with scant success. After 1979 Margaret Thatcher's tough line on immigration tended to attract back right-wing members for mainstream Conservatism and the National Front's fortunes slumped yet again. The British National Party (BNP) is the closest to a successor in recent years. In 1993 the BNP won a council seat in Tower Hamlets and in 2001 two BNP candidates polled over 10 per cent in the two Oldham constituencies. The BNP also won a council seat in early 2003 near Halifax. Combat 18 overtly uses violence and infiltration to achieve an impact; it targets football hooligans for recruitment and support. Although small in number, far-right groups contribute to the shaping of the political agenda by exploiting popular concerns of the day, for example capital punishment, child abuse, or alleged bogus asylum seekers. A recent development has been a change in language, evident in groups' websites, where a more reasonable, quasi-intellectual tone of expression has replaced the crude and overtly offensive 'rants' of former years, but which nevertheless promote a thesis of 'white tribe' separateness.

### fascism

Right-wing ideology based on authoritarian nationalism. The term, based on the

Latin symbol of the state, a bundle of rods or *fasces*, was usurped by Mussolini's movement, which came to power in Italy in 1922. Subsequently it has been used as a generic term for similar ideologies. Fascism is based on: xenophobic nationalism; worship of a unified state; a revered and charismatic leader; a fundamentalist vision of society; a struggle to achieve these objectives both domestically and internationally; and a hostility to social pluralism and liberal democracy. These ideas were put into practice in Mussolini's Italy, and influenced, along with other factors, the development of National Socialism or Nazism in Germany. However, Italian fascism lacked the highly systematised and terrorist elements of German National Socialism, and did not have the latter's single-minded obsession with racial purity. Generally speaking, British people have tended to steer away from extremist nationalistic ideologies, especially any containing overt hatred of others, despite a recognisable xenophobic tendency which surfaces periodically, as in the growth of Mosley's British Union of Fascists in the 1930s, support for the National Front in the 1970s, and Enoch Powell's ideas.

## fat cat

Derisory name given to executives of big companies who receive large salaries. It became an even more live issue in the autumn of 2001 when Lord Simpson, the head of Marconi, received a £2 million payoff after presiding over a catastrophic slump in share prices, from £20.50 per share to a mere 29 pence: effectively a loss of 98 per cent of the multinational's value. The company had to lay off 10,000 employees. This followed the award of £1.3 million to Gerald Corbett, former head of Railtrack, who failed to turn the ailing service around but who nevertheless benefited hugely and went on to another lucrative job with Woolworths. Such rewards were hard to justify at any time (the usual argument is that huge salaries are necessary to prevent able managers from being 'poached' by US companies) but even more so when the

recipients have clearly failed to make their companies more profitable. Patricia Hewitt at the Department of Trade and Industry introduced measures to enable shareholders to vote down pay increases more easily and to make companies more accountable to shareholders generally (*Observer*, 9 September 2001).

## father of the House

Title given to the MP who has served for the longest unbroken period. The title came to be used in the 19th century and holders have included former prime ministers like Winston Churchill and Edward Heath. Duties are minimal and seem to be limited to chairing the election of a new speaker. The holder of the title in 2004 was Tam Dalyell, veteran MP for Linlithgow and an MP since 1962.

## fatwa

The binding legal decision of a Shiite Islamic court. Unlike the nations of the European Union, North America and other secular states, Islamic fundamentalist countries such as Iran fuse state law with religious or ecclesiastical law. An example of this is the fatwa. In February 1989, the author Salman Rushdie was accused of blasphemy against the prophet Mohammed in his book *The Satanic Verses*. Demonstrations by British Muslims took place in many cities. However, a more sinister turn of events took place when a court in Iran issued the fatwa against Rushdie and offered a reward for the 'execution' of the author. He went into hiding under the protection of armed officers, though he emerged from 'exile' as the threat receded; it was formally withdrawn in 2000. However, despite changes in the domestic politics of Iran and a thawing in British relations with that country it will be some time before Rushdie can be assured of his personal security from freelance assassination squads. The significance of the case is to point up the political linkages between 'sovereign' states and the different interpretations of freedom of expression within a democratic multicultural society.

## federalism

An arrangement whereby power is constitutionally divided between a central government and other constituent units. The USA is often taken as the example whereby states retain authority over discrete, mostly local functions while the federal government takes care of country-wide ones: for example defence, economic management and diplomatic relations. In the UK there are two aspects to this debate. First, there are those who advocate a federal structure, with Scotland and Wales and Northern Ireland, though not usually the English regions, having legislatures and powers analogous to American states. Second, there are those who urge a similar constitutional setting for Europe, with increased integration towards such an ideal. Supporters of the latter vision are more likely to be found among the ranks of the Liberal Democrats than in the Labour Party, and less likely still among the Conservatives, who may be more generally characterised by a visceral hostility to a concept which would dilute and deny national sovereignty.

## Federation of Young Conservatives

*See* Conservative Future.

## feminism

A set of perspectives on the damaging effects of patriarchy in modern politics and society. It contains strands of thought which range from broadly social reformist measures to Marxist and radical feminist solutions to patriarchy. Britain was influenced strongly by the feminist movement of the 1960s and 1970s in response to the subordinate roles performed by women in many walks of life, including work, central and local government and the law. Since then significant strides have been made, particularly with the provision of equal opportunities legislation for pay and conditions at work. There has also been greater representation at many levels within public and private sector organisations. For example, 106 women Labour MPs were elected in 1997 and several were given

government office by Tony Blair, including Margaret Beckett (Board of Trade) and Harriet Harman (Social Security). In their book *Contemporary Feminist Politics* (1993), Joni Lovenduski and Vicky Randall discerned a falling off of activism during the Conservative years of the 1980s and a 'deradicalisation' as activists retired or died. Even though huge tasks remain, the authors argue, allied with this decline has been a greater permeation of feminist ideas within most important areas of society but especially: political representation; work; health and reproductive rights; motherhood and childcare; and male violence. One of the earliest feminist writers was Mary Wollstonecraft, who wrote arguably the first feminist tract, *Vindication of the Rights of Women* (1792); a more recent contributor has been the Australian academic and media personality Germaine Greer, whose most celebrated work is *The Female Eunuch* (1970).

## feudalism

A medieval system of land tenure whereby tenants paid rent in terms of services and received protection in return. Feudalism is believed to have started in France and to have been imported to Britain by the Normans. Pledges of allegiance were made by both sides (tenant and landowner) and upwards ultimately to the monarch. In the modern day the term is used to describe any aspect of government or society which harkens back to medieval times and so, for example, may be used to describe working-class deference and the House of Lords.

## filibuster

An American term, used also in Britain, for an attempt by a politician to oppose a measure by talking on it at excessive length. In the Commons this takes the form of a concerted effort by an opposition, hotly opposed to a measure, to pressure the restricted legislative timetable and thereby prevent its passing. It is also used in debates on private members' bills, where a strict time limit is enforced. The government can respond by setting its own

POLITICS

limits to debate in the form of a guillotine motion.

*See also* guillotine motion.

## Finance Act
*See* budget.

## Financial Management Initiative (FMI)
A series of efficiency drives in central government departments. It was launched in 1982, in the wake of the Number 10's Efficiency Unit. The FMI has been led mostly by business people. The essence of the changes it has promulgated are: a delegation of budgets; the setting up of effective information systems; and account-able management – managers are allowed freedom within set limits as long as they meet resource and performance targets. The evaluation of FMI changes in 1988 led to the report by Sir Robin Ibbs which set up the Next Steps reforms leading to executive agencies.

*See also* Efficiency Unit; executive agency; Ibbs report.

## financial market
Margaret Thatcher once said 'you cannot buck the markets', meaning the laws of supply and demand throughout the world would ultimately determine economic choices, and success or failure. What the national and global markets will or not accept circumscribes much of economic policy. An illustration of market power overruling government policy was Black Wednesday, when speculators drove Britain out of the Exchange Rate Mechanism, causing huge losses to the Bank of England and huge gains for speculators such as George Soros.

## *Financial Times*
http://news.ft.com/home/uk
Newspaper founded in 1888 and control-led by the Pearson Group since 1957. The 'FT', as it is sometimes called, pursues an independent line dictated more by financial than by political considerations. It usually backs the Conservatives, but surprisingly advised readers to vote Labour in 1992 and then, less surprisingly, advised them similarly in 1997 and 2001.

## First Division Association (FDA)
www.fda.org.uk
The professional association, or effectively trade union, of the administrative class of the civil service, which is consulted over pay as well as terms and conditions of service. The FDA has over 7,000 members, includ-ing most of the permanent secretaries.

## first lord of the Treasury
The formal title of the prime minister. In the 17th century the first lord was in charge of the commissioners who ran the nation's finances on behalf of the monarch. Given the relative unavailability of Queen Anne and then George I, the first lord became the person virtually in charge of government. Robert Walpole was the first politician to realise fully the potential of the office and became the first prime minister as a result. The term 'prime minister' was originally used in a satirical or derisive sense until it entered mainstream usage. Once prime minister, the first lord tended not to attend meetings of the Treasury com-missioners and it was the chancellor of the exchequer who substituted, thus creating the second most important political position in government.

*See also* prime minister; Walpole, Robert.

## first minister
The name given to the head of the execu-tive committee set up after the elections to the Northern Ireland assembly, Welsh assembly and the Scottish executive; effectively prime minister of the province. David Trimble, head of the Ulster Unionist Party, was the first incumbent, with Seamus Mallon of the Social Democratic and Labour Party as his deputy. He was under great pressure in 2001 to resign or to threaten to do so unless the IRA agreed to disarm. He resumed his office when the IRA agreed to compromise on the issue. In Scotland the first first minister was Donald

Dewar. In Wales, Rhodri Morgan is the
first minister.

## first past the post

Popular name given to the voting system
used in Britain and the USA. According
to this the candidate receiving the most
votes is elected, whatever proportion of the
popular vote the candidate receives. This
has led to many candidates (over half)
being returned on less than 50 per cent
of votes cast. The system is also criticised
for penalising small parties with thin
national support; for example, the Alliance
in 1983 won 26 per cent of the vote but
received only 3.5 per cent of the seats. It
can produce other anomalies; for instance,
in the 2001 general election Labour won
a majority of 167 or 63 per cent of the
seats on 42 per cent of the votes, while the
Conservatives won 25 per cent of the seats
on 33 per cent of votes cast. A commission
chaired by Lord (Roy) Jenkins reported in
1998 and advised the adoption of a modified version of the German electoral system.
   See also Alliance; Jenkins report.

## fiscal policy

See taxation.

## five tests (for Britain's membership
of the euro)

The conditions which have to be met before
Britain can safely join the European single
currency, the euro, as set out by chancellor
Gordon Brown in October 1997.

1  Is our business cycle compatible with
   that of the euro zone so that Britain
   can live comfortably with European
   interest rates? This is probably the most
   important test. Despite an apparent
   convergence in recent years the British
   economy is qualitatively different to that
   of the rest of Europe in some respects,
   such as the proportion of the population
   who have mortgages and are thus sensitive to changes in interest rates. Further,
   some people worry that a 'one size fits
   all' single interest rate across Europe
   would not always be the optimal one for
   Britain.

2  Would there be sufficient flexibility to
   deal with problems as they emerge? For
   example, interest rates which are too
   high could inhibit growth and
   wage cuts would have to replace the
   device of adjusting the exchange rate,
   which has made exports cheaper in the
   past.

3  Would entry have an adverse effect on
   the competitive position of Britain's
   financial services industry? Finance is a
   major sector of the British economy.

4  Would entry create better conditions for
   inward investment in Britain? Britain
   has been the prime destination for
   foreign capital investment in Europe for
   a number of years.

5  Will joining help promote higher
   economic growth, stability and employment? If the other four tests are met then
   this final one would automatically be met
   also.

Critics maintain that these five tests are
so vague that Brown can interpret them
more or less as he pleases, thus retaining
control over the nation's economic future
and the key to the most important political
decision the nation faces.

   See also euro; European economic and
monetary union.

## floating voter

One of the unaligned group of voters who
determine the outcome of elections by
shifting their support to the party which
wins their approval. It was at one time
believed that it was this group in British
politics which decided general elections.
The argument ran that the two main parties drew on class constituencies and that
it was those detached from regular class
fidelities who could prove decisive. Many
floating voters were attracted by the policies
of the Liberal Party, but in more modern
elections class attachments have weakened
and psephologists have discerned a greater
volatility. In other words, a huge segment
of the electorate is now 'floating' at election
time; they are open to persuasion as to how
they will vote.

   See also partisan dealignment.

## focus group

An import from the world of marketing and advertising. Focus groups are sometimes used as an alternative, or in addition, to opinion polls as indices of opinion. They comprise small collections of socially representative people (usually 8–12 or so) who are questioned in depth on particular subjects. Focus groups can be ad hoc or part of a series addressing a number of topics. Following the failure of polls to predict the 1992 Conservative victory, Labour placed more faith in focus groups. Philip Gould, a former marketing expert and one of Tony Blair's close advisors, was the man who championed the use of focus groups and who had observed their use in the USA. In late 1997 it was said that the monarchy had assembled a focus group to help it keep abreast of public opinion. In the summer of 2000 focus groups became the subject of attack as the impression grew that the Blair government used this technique to respond to public opinion rather than to lead it. Ironically, the complaint in 2003 was that he had ignored public opinion and gone ahead with the Iraq war, notwithstanding widespread opposition.

*See also* opinion poll.

## Food Standards Agency (FSA)

www.food.gov.uk
Government body set up in April 2000 in the wake of the BSE crisis to 'protect people's health and the interests of consumers in relation to food'. It is based in London but also has offices in Scotland, Wales and Northern Ireland. The Agency can commission research and make its recommendations public. The FSA employs 2,200 staff throughout the UK, most in the Meat Hygiene Service, an executive agency of the FSA.

## foot-and-mouth disease

Contagious disease affecting sheep, pigs and cows. Outbreaks of foot-and-mouth disease in February 2001 soon spread from Heddon on the Wall in Northumberland to most parts of Britain, facilitated by the rapid and widespread movements of sheep and cattle around the country. By April the number of outbreaks had risen to over 40 a day and the customary solution of slaughtering infected animals followed by their incineration caused great anguish to farmers and to the country as a whole. The tourist industry was also heavily hit by the closures enforced by the Ministry of Agriculture, Fisheries and Food (MAFF) under minister Nick Brown. Some critics pointed out that the value to the national economy of meat exports was only £0.5 billion annually, while tourism earns over £12 billion. Others argued that vaccination rather than slaughter is a better solution to the disease on economic as well as moral grounds. As the number of outbreaks continued to rise during April Tony Blair decided to postpone the next general election, widely expected on 3 May, to June. By this time outbreaks had fallen to single figures per day – on 15 May there were no outbreaks reported, for the first time since the problem arose – but the disease was not beaten and continued to afflict the farming community for several months afterwards.

Some 2,030 cases of the disease occurred – making it worse than the last such crisis in Britain, in 1967–68 – and some 6 million animals were slaughtered then incinerated, representing 10 per cent of Britain's livestock. Some calculations put the total cost of the crisis in excess of £20 billion and 60,000 jobs were lost as a result of the outbreak.

The reputation of MAFF was destroyed by the outbreak and its poor response to it. Nick Brown paid with his job in the post-election reshuffle, when he was demoted out of the cabinet and the ministry itself was merged into the new Department for Environment, Food and Rural Affairs, under Margaret Beckett. MAFF was criticised for its assumption – reinforced by the National Farmers' Union – that agriculture is the backbone of the rural economy when in fact tourism is much more important in the present day; in consequence tourism was neglected and food production was given priority, causing bigger losses than should have been the case. A report by the Council for the Protection of Rural England declared on 24 September 2001 that the 'cure was worse than the disease'.

## Foreign and Commonwealth Office (FCO)

www.fco.gov.uk

Government department headed by the foreign secretary, and whose purpose is to enhance the security and prosperity of the country and its citizens overseas, by providing them with a consular service. It was formed in 1782, when it was decided to deal with political matters for home and abroad separately. Despite Britain's reduced international role, the FCO is still of key importance and, in the view of former foreign secretary Douglas Hurd, enables the country to 'punch above its weight'. Some 215 overseas posts are funded by the FCO and funds for the overseas service of the BBC also come out of its budget. Most effort is focused on the European Union, NATO and the United Nations, and much more emphasis is now placed on promoting British exports and attracting inward investment. Altogether the FCO employs 9,700 civil servants.

## foreign policy

Traditionally British foreign policy entails three interlocking circles, namely Europe, North America and the Commonwealth. Until the 1950s the Empire still exerted an influence and the wartime alliance with the USA was a powerful cultural and historical bond. But the economic success of the European Community encouraged politicians to overcome their sense of superiority to the Continent and in 1972 the die was cast and – despite rearguard actions by Eurosceptics – Britain has become ever more deeply involved in the European Union, both economically and politically. On becoming foreign secretary in 1997, Robin Cook announced that Britain would henceforth pursue an ethical foreign policy, although three years into government the term 'ethical' was quietly dropped from public statements.

*See also* ethical foreign policy.

## foreign secretary

The minister responsible for Britain's diplomatic relations with the rest of the world. This post is especially high profile, both internationally and domestically, with the post holder usually being a senior politician and a possible candidate for the prime minister's job. Many distinguished politicians have held this office, from Lord Castlereagh and Viscount Palmerston to Ernest Bevin, Anthony Eden and Lord Carrington. In recent times both James Callaghan and John Major went on to Number 10 following a period as foreign secretary. On coming to power in 1997 Tony Blair appointed Robin Cook as foreign secretary, who attempted to pursue an 'ethical foreign policy' with mixed results; in 2001 Jack Straw took over.

*See also* ethical foreign policy; foreign policy.

## foreign trade

Trade patterns have changed radically over the past 50 years with Commonwealth trade declining and European trade growing vigorously. In 1996 Britain's trade with Asia represented 19 per cent of all its overseas trade; Australasia, 2 per cent; Europe, 55 per cent; USA, 20 per cent; and Africa, 3 per cent. The emphasis of modern trade on Europe is illustrated by the fact that Britain has more trade with Germany than with the USA.

## foundation hospital

Hospital run by a board representative of the local community, with the right to opt out of government guidelines and to set its own clinical and financial priorities, and possibly set its own pay levels. At the 2002 Labour Party conference in Blackpool Tony Blair argued that 'foundation hospitals would put power in the hands of patients and NHS staff'. The idea is to let good hospitals develop but many fear such a move will create a 'two tier' hospital service. Old Labour voices, like that of former health minister Frank Dobson, were hotly raised in opposition and chancellor Gordon Brown was said to oppose it as it would give the National Health Service a blank cheque to spend more money. The Conservatives support the idea, which made it even more difficult for Blair to sell it to his own party. In July 2003 the necessary legislation was passed with a majority of only 35.

### 14-day rule

Rule in force after the Second World War which forbade the mention on television of anything of topical political interest that was likely to be discussed in parliament during the next 14 days. This stemmed from suspicion by the political class of this new medium with such a massive potential for influencing people. Winston Churchill, for example, saw the BBC as a 'red conspiracy' and supported the rule. It was broken by Granada Television, which covered the Rochdale by-election in 1957 in defiance of the rule and suffered no repercussions. After that breach the rule was ignored.

### foxhunting

*See* hunting.

### franchise

The right or eligibility to vote. Political scientists also use the term as an indicator of political modernisation. Thus, at the start of the 19th century Britain was a kind of 'elite democracy' with a tiny electorate, where the right to vote was determined by property ownership and being male. Furthermore, before the Great Reform Act of 1832 the franchise was a patchwork affair with some constituencies returning MPs on the basis of a handful of voters or, as in the case of Old Sarum, no voters at all. The Reform Acts in the 19th century widened the franchise successively in 1867 and 1884, until women were given the right to vote on a limited basis in 1918 and then generally in 1928. In 1969 people aged 18 and over were granted the vote. Britain had become a mass democracy.

*See also* Reform Act.

### free vote

Parliamentary vote for which the whip is removed to allow MPs to vote freely on matters of personal conscience or inclination. The most well known example concerns capital punishment, but others have been allowed, for example on fox-hunting in the autumn of 1997.

### Free Wales Army (FWA)

Tiny militant faction active in the late 1960s. The FWA was founded by 'Cayo' Evans, a public school boy and former serving soldier. It was dedicated to freeing Wales from 'English rule' and provided a colourful but unimportant accompaniment to events in Wales. Evans died in 1995 but earned the compliments of a biography and a Cardiff pub in his name.

> The only thing the English understand, boy, is ... bullets! (Cayo Evans to author, 1969)

### freedom

Alternatively known as liberty and having two important senses. Negative freedom, championed by thinkers such as Adam Smith and John Stuart Mill, and in this century Friedrich Hayek and Robert Nozick, is interpreted as the absence of interference from others. However, political philosophers have pointed to the fact that capacity or resources are important prerequisites for exercising freedom and this leads to the second sense of freedom: positive freedom. This is the capacity to do things to improve one's lot, and in this sense T. H. Green argued in the 19th century that anyone prevented from realising personal potential, perhaps due to poverty, was not a free person. This dichotomy of meaning has characterised the two main parties in Britain, with the Conservatives championing negative freedom as the only legitimate form and Labour the positive variety.

*See also* equality; libertarianism.

### freedom of information

The open and unrestricted access of the public to information held by government and its agencies. This applies not only to the workings of government and policies pursued under particular administrations, but also to information which government may have on individual citizens. In the USA there is a Freedom of Information Act which enables the public and journalists to examine government papers. In Britain there is a culture of secrecy, sustained by the Official Secrets Act, which many argue acts as a cloak for what governments do not want the public to know. Conservatives tend to ignore calls for more information and argue that government needs secrecy in order to function efficiently. In opposition in the 1980s and 1990s Labour argued strongly for a Freedom of Information Act and it was a regular feature in the party's manifestos. However, in office Labour's freedom of information measures (the Data Protection Act 1998 and Freedom of Information Act 2000), introduced by Jack Straw when home secretary, were much criticised for being half-hearted and arguably restrictive.

*See also* Freedom of Information Act; freedom of speech; Official Secrets Act.

### Freedom of Information Act 2000

The promise of such an act along US lines appeared in Labour Party general election manifestos but the promised legislation has not been forthcoming. The original minister charged with piloting the measure through, David Clark, was replaced by the home secretary, Jack Straw, in 1998, but he was a sceptic on freedom of information. The Select Committee on Administration, chaired by a Labour MP, tried to insist that the measure appeared in the queen's speech for 1998–99 but was unable to secure this. Large exemptions were agreed during 1997 to such a bill, should it ever begin its journey through parliament, including: the police, immigration and security services, privatised utilities and civil service policy advice to ministers. The act was passed in 2000 but in October 2001 the *Guardian* reported that Tony Blair was keen to delay the implementation of the act until 2004, shortly before the next election. Straw supported such a move but Lord Irvine, the lord chancellor, favoured an earlier, phased

introduction. Some weeks later the paper announced that Blair had won his argument and that the new legislation would not come into effect until January 2005. Lord McNally of the Liberal Democrats described this as a 'betrayal of the agreement we negotiated with the government with the aim of getting the act passed and implemented rapidly'. Labour MP Mark Fisher said there was 'no reason why this should be delayed for so long after parliament has examined it at such length'. The information commissioner, Elizabeth France, sided with Lord Irvine's objections.

### freedom of speech

The liberal thinker John Stuart Mill argued that freedom of expression and its concomitant, freedom of thought, are important qualities of a free person. Moreover, freedom of speech and the free interchange of ideas have long been perceived as a key liberty in the British political system, and a basic condition for democratic government. However, there are limits laid down regarding what can be said about people (for example the libel laws and laws against incitement to racial hatred). The Official Secrets Act in its various guises makes it a criminal offence for a person to communicate classified information to an unauthorised person.

*See also* freedom of information; Freedom of Information Act; Official Secrets Act.

### Friends of the Earth (FOE)

www.foe.co.uk

Environmental pressure group founded in the USA in 1969 and in the UK in 1971. It has 250 groups in the UK, which target environmental issues at central and local government level, and support various other groups and occasionally direct action concerning motorways and similar developments. It is now a respected group which government regularly consults. Along with the Green Party it played a significant role in drafting the Road Traffic Reduction Act 1997. In 2001 FOE membership was just over 110,000.

## fuel protest, September 2000

Action by consumers which plunged the
country into near paralysis. With fuel costs
and taxes continually going up, British
consumers copied French road hauliers and
used direct action to advance their protest.
Farmers for Action, with links to North
Wales, were joined by taxi drivers, lorry
drivers, fishermen and others in blockading
petrol refineries and thus preventing the
distribution of fuel nationwide. Panic buying soon emptied the petrol stations and the
nation ground to a halt. Polls showed that
a huge majority supported the protestors
and that the Conservatives had taken a
lead over Labour. After some undignified
manoeuvring the government conceded
some ground on fuel tax despite its harmful
environmental side-effects and the protest
fell away.

## full employment

A notion introduced as an achievable
objective by the Beveridge report during
the Second World War. Buttressed by
Keynesian economic theory, this objective
was pursued by both major parties during
the 1950s and 1960s. It was also the
official policy of the Labour Party as late
as 1983. This changed in the late 1980s as
full employment no longer seemed achievable, as government spending was held to
create inflation and undermine competitiveness. Under Neil Kinnock the Labour
Party eventually adopted a position similar
to that of the Conservatives in seeking
merely to minimise unemployment, though
when in office under Tony Blair New
Labour showed considerable vigour in pursuing its New Deal programme, designed
to get people off benefit and into work.
Given the numbers of people who cannot
work for various reasons an unemployment
rate of 5 per cent, which was the level in
the summer of 2004, effectively represented
'full employment'.

*See also* New Deal.

## Fulton report, 1968

A report on the recruitment and structure
of the civil service. It made a number of
criticisms of British public administration, which had not changed since the
Northcotte–Trevelyan reforms of the 19th
century. In particular, it pointed to the
fact that senior civil servants came from
a narrow and unrepresentative social
background, their education reflected
an Oxbridge elitism, there were too few
representatives from other walks of life such
as business and the law, and there was a
somewhat amateurish faith in the generalist
all-rounder instead of the trained specialist
(as would be found in France). The report
made a number of recommendations, some
of which were implemented, for example the
establishment of the Civil Service College.
However, the report is more remembered
for what it did not do, rather than the
changes it introduced, as many of its suggested reforms were blocked by civil service
mandarins.

*See also* civil service; executive agency;
Northcotte–Trevelyan report.

## functional representation

The idea that groups in society can be
represented in legislative chambers as well
as by constituency members. There is a
long tradition of individual representation
in the British political system, with MPs
being elected by individual members of a
constituency. However, some reformers
have argued that the British political system does little to represent specific groups
in society and they suggest a reformed
House of Lords might rectify this if it
comprised elected representatives of groups
in society, such as academics, doctors, business people, lawyers and so forth. Others
argue pressure group activity serves this
purpose, although these groups lack the
formal status which functional representation would provide.

POLITICS

# G

## Gallup
www.gallup.com
Polling organisation established by George Gallup in the USA in 1935. There is now a branch in Britain. Gallup polls initially appeared in the *News Chronicle*, but since the 1960s the *Daily* and *Sunday Telegraph* have become their regular home, where Professor Anthony King used to provide academic analysis of them.

*See also* opinion poll.

## gang of four
The pejorative/ironic term given to the original group of Labour Party defectors who established the Social Democratic Party (SDP) in 1981. Shirley Williams, David Owen and Bill Rodgers were soon joined by Roy Jenkins, making the group congruent with the Chinese 'gang of four' who briefly led the country in the 1970s after the death of Mao Tse-tung.

*See also* Social Democratic Party.

## garbage-gate
The derisive term used by Tony Blair to refer to the furore surrounding the revelation that he had signed a letter supporting the attempt of an Indian billionaire, Lakshmi Mittal, to buy Sidex, a Romanian state-owned steel company. The outcry was occasioned by the facts that Mittal had donated £125,000 to the Labour Party, his company, LNM, was not British, and he proved to be a lobbying champion of measures in the USA which disadvantaged the British steel industry. On its own the issue was not especially important but, ranked together with the Ecclestone affair and the alleged ability of Rupert Murdoch to influence in Number 10, it seemed to be part of a pattern of 'cash for influence'.

## G8
An intergovernmental organisation comprising the eight richest industrial nations: Italy, Canada, the USA, Britain, Germany, France, Japan and, from July 2001 (before which it met as G7), Russia. Since the 1950s they have met once a year to discuss questions of international finance. British ministers regard membership as an important symbol of Britain's continuing status as a major economic and political power, a fact borne out by the G7's involvement, along with Russia, in the attempt to end the 1998 Kosovo crisis in the former Yugoslavia. In July 2001 the group met in Genoa and the growing international opposition to globalisation resulted in major riots which left one demonstrator dead and much property damaged.

## gender gap
Difference in the percentage of women voting for a party as compared with men. For the Labour Party it was around 17 per cent in the 1950s but has reduced gradually since then, so that by 1997 it had virtually disappeared. Some polls in 2001, however, showed that women were less likely than men to be satisfied with the Labour government. This was possible because, in the view of some, 'women's issues' had languished and 'Blair's babes' – the 106 female Labour MPs elected in 1997 – failed to make much of an impression.

## *General Belgrano*
The name of a battle cruiser of the Argentinean navy that was torpedoed and sunk by the submarine HMS *Conqueror* on 3 May 1982 in the Falklands War. The sinking caused much debate, as the loss of life was heavy and evidence suggested the ship had been heading away from the 'exclusion zone' and not towards it, as claimed by the government at the time. Margaret Thatcher was at the peak of her power and the allegation that the ship had been sunk for political reasons, namely to pre-empt the possibility of peace negotiations, attracted much attention. Her defence of the decision to sink the ship was that the *General Belgrano* was a threat to British ships and service personnel. The issue gained further notoriety

when a Ministry of Defence official, Clive Ponting, leaked secret material to the Labour MP Tam Dalyell. In the summer of 2004 support for Thatcher's decision arrived from an unlikely source: the former captain of the *Belgrano* claimed he would have done the same thing if had he been the *Conqueror*'s captain.

## General and Municipal Workers' Union

*See* GMB.

## general election

The Septennial Act 1716 increased the life of parliaments from three to seven years. This move was designed to bolster the power of the Whigs but historians judge it had more effect in underpinning the stability of the House of Commons. The Chartists' demands in the mid-19th century included one for annual parliaments, but few others seriously wanted this, as it would be likely to introduce too much instability. The Parliament Act 1911 reduced the maximum term to five years. However, critics of the system focus on the right of the prime minister to choose the election date. This hands to him or her the advantage of waiting for an opportune time to call an election, perhaps when the economy is growing and creating a 'feel good factor' or until the opinion polls are sufficiently favourable. In recent times prime ministers have tended to go to the polls after four rather than five years, to avoid being boxed in by unpredictable events as the deadline approaches. The last general election (at the time of writing) was held on 7 June 2001, after Tony Blair's preferred date, 3 May, was deemed unsuitable because of the intensity of foot-and-mouth disease, which was ravaging the countryside. The campaign was relatively short (four weeks) but failed to engage the public to any significant degree. Blair ran on his record and the promise to improve public services. William Hague for the Conservatives hoped hostility to Europe would deliver seats but he was disappointed. The result was a second landslide for Labour: 413 (down 6) to 166 (up 1) for the Conservatives with the Liberal Democrats on 52 (up 6). Labour gained only 10.7 million votes (41 per cent), fewer votes than any winning party since 1929. The turnout was a mere 59.2 per cent.

*See also* apathy.

## general management committee (GMC)

The decision-making body of each Labour constituency party. It used to select candidates in most instances (a shortlist for such candidates was drawn up and the GMC would make the final decision). However, infiltration of GMCs by Militant Tendency supporters in the 1970s and 1980s led to changes. Now open meetings for selection are held and the selection is according to votes by all constituency members following presentations by each aspirant candidate.

## General Medical Council (GMC)

www.gmc-uk.org

The professional body which regulates entry to and conduct of the British medical profession. Traditionally doctors, and in particular hospital consultants, who can earn over £120,000 per year, have enjoyed a social esteem and autonomy unrivalled by any other profession. However, in recent years there has been increasing media attention on medical errors and the failure of the GMC to act decisively to deal with medical incompetence. Politicians have locked on to this public concern as a way of tightening control over the profession and the British Medical Association and General Medical Council have reacted by trying to tighten up supervision and disciplinary procedures, in an attempt to avoid state control.

## General Strike, 1926

Strike that took place between 3 and 13 May 1926, called by the Trades Union Congress (TUC) in an attempt to support coalminers already on strike against pay cuts. It was not strictly 'general' as only key industries were targeted, like railways, docks and the power industries, but with over 2 million men on strike it worried the government considerably once in progress. Considering this was the closest Britain came to a left-wing revolution in the inter-war years, the strikers and the authorities were remarkably civil to each other. The government under Stanley Baldwin kept basic services going throughout the 10 days and the TUC eventually called off the action, thus reinforcing the moderate trade unions and relegating a workers-led revolution in Britain to a very remote possibility from then on.

### genetically modified (GM) food
This debate took off in the late 1990s when there was public opposition to the introduction of GM crops, something which had not raised much comment in the USA when they had been introduced there on a commercial basis. The government was generally in favour of GM food, as it predicted large financial and other advantages, but environmental pressure groups were hotly opposed and sabotaged crop trials in various parts of Britain. Opinion polls showed public concern and opposition, and their stance seemed vindicated by the October 2003 results of three major trials of GM crops, begun in 1998, which revealed that in two cases damage to wildlife had been recorded, with long-term effects on the bee, butterfly and bird populations. The case against GM foods seemed to have been proved but the government refused to confirm that this was so.

### gerrymandering
The drawing of constituency boundaries in such a way that one party benefits. The name originates with that of a governor of Massachusetts in the early 19th century who was guilty of such practices. In Britain the Boundary Commissions are supposed to eliminate the risk of such outcomes but in Protestant-dominated Northern Ireland gerrymandering became an established part of the political culture. The practice spread to mainland Britain in the 1980s, and both major parties have been accused of gerrymandering. Labour has been accused

of the practice in Newcastle, Liverpool and, in Scotland, Monklands. However, the most notorious case was in Westminster, where the council was accused of a kind of gerrymandering by seeking to sell its council properties only to more affluent, Conservative-voting buyers. The Audit Office report of 1996 named both councillors and officials, including the leader of the council, Tesco heiress Dame Shirley Porter, who was later cleared on appeal but this appeal was itself overturned in 2001 and she was forced to settle by paying over £12 million in 2004.
See also homes for votes scandal.

### Gershon report, 2004
Report proposing reform of the civil service by Sir Peter Gershon, a former senior executive with BAE who became head of the Office of Government Commerce. His recommendations amounted to a virtual revolution in Whitehall – cutting bureaucracy and 'back office' functions, to save a total of £14.5 billion by 2007. His suggestions included: central procurement agencies to replace the myriad buying arrangements; shared human resources services; centralised information technology for groups of departments; reformulated retail networks; and the use of insurance companies and banks as collecting agencies for taxes and fines. Overall, his programme planned huge savings, but at the cost of 80,000 jobs. Oliver Letwin, the shadow chancellor, tried to exploit the report, which was leaked at the same time as his spending proposals, by suggesting that a 'consensus' already existed between the parties over cuts in the bureaucracy. However, while the government wished to plough back savings into spending, Letwin proposed to use them for tax cuts. In his statement on future spending in July 2004, chancellor Gordon Brown drew upon the report when he proposed savings involving the abolition of over 80,000 civil service jobs.

### Gibraltar
A British dependency on southern tip of Spain, with a population of 30,000 (area

2.5 square miles). The Moors ceded the rock to Spain in 1462 but the English admiral George Rooke captured it from Spain in 1704 and the Treaty of Utrecht made it a British possession in 1713. Inhabitants strongly wish to remain British but Spain is keen to regain this promontory. The British military garrison was halved in 1989 and removed in 1991, though air and naval units remained. Talks in late 2001 indicated a joint sovereignty arrangement had been negotiated by Jack Straw with his Spanish counterpart but the Gibaltarians were stoutly opposed and began a vigorous campaign, including a referendum, which it overwhelmingly won to frustrate the plan.

## Glasgow University Media Group
www.gla.ac.uk/departments/sociology/media.html
Research-based grouping of academics within the sociology department of Glasgow University. These media researchers (for example Greg Philo) argue that broadcast news on television is characterised by systematic, if unconscious, bias against trade unions and their activists. Thus in industrial relations disputes, union representatives tend to be presented as scruffy, somewhat irresponsible men on picket lines while the management are seen pronouncing reassuringly from behind desks and wearing suits. The Group's work on the Falklands War suggests that television and press journalists uncritically recycled Ministry of Defence propaganda on the bombing of the Port Stanley airfield, and reported it as objective fact. The Group's methods of analysis have received much criticism. However, it has stimulated useful discussion and opened up an important area of debate on the supposed objectivity of news broadcasting.

## globalisation
A term that refers to the many ways in which countries are connected by transactions beyond the nation state boundary, for example new communications technology; growth of trade (increased at least 10-fold since 1913); the foreign exchange markets;

and multinational companies (for example Microsoft). Britain has seen globalisation affect it in many ways, for example: the speed at which the financial world turned against the pound on Black Wednesday in September 1992; the need to keep workforce levels to a minimum in order to compete; the 'outsourcing' of call centres to cheaper providers in the developing world; and the worldwide television audience which watched the funeral of Diana Princess of Wales in 1997.

> Tony Blair embraces globalisation with almost evangelical zeal, as opportunity rather than threat. (Blairite Labour MP Tony Wright)

## Glorious Revolution, 1688–89
Name given for the events leading to the removal of James II from the throne and the installation of his daughter Mary and her husband William of Orange. James's injudicious rule had led seven prominent statesmen to invite William to invade Britain. When he did so, James disappeared to France. William and Mary both accepted the Bill of Rights in February 1689 and were then declared sovereigns. The document stated that parliaments must be held regularly and must be free, and that there should be freedom of speech and other safeguards. It is usually held to be the point at which the British crown accepted the supremacy of parliament and began its journey towards a respected but ceremonial role in the constitution.
  *See also* Bill of Rights; British constitution.

## GMB
www.gmb.org.uk
Union originating in 1889 as the General and Municipal Workers' Union with the legendary trade unionist Will Thorne. It joined with two other unions in 1924 to provide one of the biggest unions in the postwar period. In 1982 it merged with the Amalgamated Society of Boilermakers, Shipwrights, Blacksmiths and Structural Workers to form the General, Municipal,

Boilermakers and Allied Trade Union.
In 1989 it became simply the GMB. Its
membership, mainly distributive industries
and local government personnel, fell drastically after 1979 but it still boasted 700,000
members in 2003. The union has tended
to be on the centre or right of the political
spectrum and generally supportive of the
Labour leadership. On 8 July 2004 the
union's general secretary, Kevin Curran,
met with MPs sponsored by the union. The
latter criticised the union's policy of withholding financial support from those MPs
'loyal to GMB policies and values'. Curran
warned in a *Guardian* article (9 July 2004)
that total disaffiliation of the union from
Labour remained a 'real option'.

### golden triangle
Term used by Peter Hennessy and others
to describe the select group of cabinet
secretary, prime minister's principal private
secretary and the queen's private secretary,
who sit at the 'heart of the constitution'
when problems arise and decisions need to
be taken.

### Good Friday Agreement, 1998
The peace negotiations in Northern Ireland
initiated by John Major but which reached
a climax at Easter 1998, under Tony Blair.
To avert an impasse, Blair flew to Stormont
on 10 April along with Irish premier Bertie
Aherne. After 36 hours of non-stop negotiations the agreement was announced with
the following provisions:
1   a recognition that a majority of the
    people of Northern Ireland at present
    wished to remain part of the UK;
2   amendment of articles 2 and 3 of the
    Irish constitution, to remove its territorial
    claims over Northern Ireland;
3   a 108-member assembly elected by
    single transferable vote;
4   a Northern Ireland executive;
5   a North–South Ministerial Council
    designed to foster consultation, co-
    operation and action within the island of
    Ireland;
6   a British–Irish Council, incorporating
    the British and Irish governments and

representatives of the devolved assemblies of Northern Ireland, Scotland and
Wales;
7   a British–Irish intergovernmental confer-
    ence, which would facilitate cooperation
    on non-devolved matters;
8   the secretary of state for Northern
    Ireland would remain responsible for
    matters not devolved to the assembly.

The agreement was initially implemented
in the autumn of 1999 but it failed to become fully operational through lack of trust
between the two sides and the refusal of the
more militant unionists to accept it.
*See also* Northern Ireland.

### governance
The exercise of power and authority in
governing. It is a term that is increasingly
used in political debate. Questions relating
to power and authority can no longer be
answered by reference to the British state
and its formal institutions alone, but must
include consideration of non-state institutions and agencies. In modern Britain,
power is increasingly shared between state,
community, business and voluntary groups.
Moreover, in the age of globalisation the
institutions of the British nation state can no
longer be assured of control or influence over
the people but must share power with international market forces and global media.
*See also* cultural governance; government; ideology; political language.

### government
The authoritative decision-making arrangements of the state at central and local level
(distinct from governance). Its provenance
includes the whole machinery of administration, including the civil service and other
official agencies. It is also used to describe
the particular party controlling the administration of the state at any given time.

### Government Communications Headquarters (GCHQ)
www.gchq.gov.uk
Establishment, based at Cheltenham,
responsible for the gathering and analysis of
intelligence signals from British 'listening'

stations across the world. A civil service strike in 1981 interrupted the flow of information and angered the US intelligence service, with which information was pooled. The director of the agency recommended de-unionisation, but the Permanent Secretaries Intelligence Steering Committee advised against it. When Frank Cooper (permanent secretary at the Ministry of Defence) and Douglas Wass (permanent secretary at the Treasury) retired, however, Margaret Thatcher proceeded to ban the unions, even though a no-strike agreement seemed achievable. Trade union rights were restored under Tony Blair's incoming Labour government after 1997.

## Government of Ireland Act 1920

A landmark in the development of the 'troubles' in Northern Ireland. The act attempted to strike a compromise between the competing claims of Protestants and Catholics by splitting Ireland (then a constituent state of the UK) in two. A 26-county, predominantly Catholic, state was carved out in the south and ruled by a devolved Dublin parliament – the region did not become an independent state until 1949. The remaining six counties, predominantly Protestant, though with substantial Catholic minorities, became the new administrative unit of Northern Ireland, and still remain part of the UK.

*See also* Good Friday Agreement; Irish Republican Army (IRA); Ireland; paramilitary.

## grammar school

Type of school established by the (Butler) Education Act 1944. Grammars were selective which pursued an academic curriculum for the fortunate one-third or so of pupils who passed the 11 plus test. Their products often went on to do well at university and in later life. However, many educationalists and other observers, including many in the Labour Party, felt that the problems of the 11 plus test and the domination of the grammar schools by the middle classes were undermining the principle of parity of esteem which the 1944 Act had tried to establish.

From the mid-1960s, many local authorities started to replace the grammars with comprehensive schools. The Conservative government of Edward Health (1970–74) continued the process, with, ironically, Margaret Thatcher as education secretary. However, some grammars survived in a few education authorities (for example Kent and Tameside) or were converted to grant-maintained schools. The New Labour government elected in 1997 decided not to pursue the full abolition of grammar schools, but introduced the option of parental ballots to decide each school's future.

*See also* comprehensive school; 11 plus test; grant-maintained school.

## grant-maintained school

Term used to refer to a school, usually a grammar, which received a grant to supplement its funding from local authority sources. Grant-maintained schools mostly became independent in the 1970s (the Manchester Grammar School, for example). The term took on a new meaning in the 1980s when Conservative education ministers freed certain schools from local authority control and funded them directly from the centre. It was generally recognised that such schools tended to be better funded than if they had not applied for such status. The most famous example of such a school was the Oratory in London, where Tony Blair sent his son Euan, despite opposition from the left of the party and unease from the rest.

## Grassroots Alliance

Contested the elections to the Labour Party's National Executive Committee in autumn 1998. Former party leader Neil Kinnock lambasted these 'Trotskyists, sectarians and other selfish parasites' (*Guardian*, 18 September 1998). However, four of the six members of the Grassroots Alliance were elected in September 1998, including Liz Davies, who had been banned as a candidate in 1997 for allegedly Trotskyite political views – allegations she dismissed as rubbish and a smear by the leadership to stifle criticism.

*See also* Militant Tendency.

## great and the good

A somewhat ironic term to describe the list of worthy people whom the government and key opinion formers think fit to chair or sit on public bodies. The list is slightly mysterious but was kept by the Treasury when it was responsible for the civil service as a whole. Politicians have been sufficiently frank to admit that the membership of royal commissions is often 'rigged' through the appointment of people who will come up with the recommendations the government thinks are appropriate. Peter Hennessy in his book *Whitehall* (1991) reported a 1954 minute on discussions relating to membership of the Independent Television Authority, which classically states: 'The qualities required in the chairman and members [are] tact and sound judgement rather than energy and administrative ability'.

*See also* establishment.

## Great Reform Act 1832

Usually seen as the Act which marked the death of the old political system, when the aristocracy could influence the composition of the House of Commons. It was passed as a result of widespread political unrest. The act was passed only because William IV was willing to create enough peers to vote it through the House of Lords. It removed 56 'rotten' and 'pocket' boroughs, redistributed 143 seats to under-represented county and urban areas, and extended the franchise to include a wider range of property holders (to borough householders paying an annual rent of £10 and to leaseholders paying £50 a year). The act increased the electorate from 435,000 to 652,000. Effectively it enfranchised the middle class but still excluded the working class, who refused to be forgotten. Pressure from the working class and from radical reformers helped bring about the Reform Acts of 1867 and 1884 and led the way to the development of the mass democracy of the 20th century.

## Greater London Authority (GLA)

www.london.gov.uk/gla
Set up by Labour in 1998 to accompany the elected mayoral elections of summer 2000. The white paper *New Leadership for London* stated that the GLA 'will be a unique category of local government in which there will be an explicit separation of powers between the executive, the Mayor, and the legislature, the assembly'. The idea, based on the elected mayor schemes of the USA, involves a 25-member GLA having scrutiny and investigatory powers, but not substantial executive-checking ones, though it is able to amend a budget prepared by the London mayor. The budget covers police, fire service, public transport coordination, strategic planning and economic and industrial development. The GLA has taken over control of the Metropolitan Police, formerly the responsibility of the home secretary.

The GLA is elected for four-year terms; 4 per cent of the vote is needed to save a candidate's deposit. An adapted additional member system (AMS) is used, with 14 constituency members from the boroughs (average electorate 350,000) and 11 from London-wide party lists. The nomination process for mayor took place in late 1999 and early 2000, with acrimony between Ken Livingstone and Frank Dobson on the Labour side and scandal surrounding the Conservative candidate bid of Jeffrey Archer. Although Labour took 50 per cent of the vote in the 1997 general election, it struggled in the mid-term GLA election, especially after the debacle of the most popular candidate, Ken Livingstone, standing as an independent against Labour's official candidate Frank Dobson. The latter had been 'steered' towards the election by Tony Blair, who was opposed to Ken Livingstone standing as the official Labour candidate despite his popularity, because, allegedly, he was associated with the 'loony left' days of the defunct Greater London Council.

In the June 2004 election, Labour won seven seats, the Conservatives nine, the Liberal Democrats five, the Greens two and the United Kingdom Independence Party two. George Galloway's Respect party did not win a seat but polled commendably well.

## Greater London Council (GLC)

The body that replaced the London County Council in 1965. When it became the centre of left-wing activism, especially during the tenure of Ken Livingstone as leader in the early 1980s, the Conservatives reacted by abolishing it in 1986 and the Inner London Education Authority by placing the powers released in the boroughs and various joint boards. After the Labour victory in 1997, Labour introduced an elected mayor and a small council called the Greater London Authority.

## green paper

Statement of proposed policy by government. This type of statement is usually consultative and aims to elicit comment from interested parties so that a more definite statement in the form of a white paper can be produced.

## Green Party

www.greenparty.org.uk
This began life as an environmental pressure group in 1973, became the Ecology Party in 1975 and changed its name to the Green Party in 1985, in line with Continental groupings. In the 1983 general election the party's 108 candidates polled only 1 per cent of the vote, but in 1989 it gained some of the protest votes which had previously gone to the Alliance and registered an astonishing 15 per cent in the European elections. However, its amateurish approach to politics and the greater 'green' emphasis of the main parties has seen its support collapse back to its 1983 levels. The claim of one of its spokespeople, David Icke, in 1991 that he was 'an aspect of the godhead' damaged the party's credibility. In 1997 the Greens contested only 80 seats. However, membership of the party grew from 3,500 in 1996 to 5,000 in 2002. In the 2001 general election the Greens won an average of 2.45 per cent in the 145 constituencies it contested. Brighton Pavilion, however, saw it poll a respectable 9.3 per cent and in Bradford West the party received more votes than the Liberal Democrats. In June

2004 the Green showing of 6.3 per cent in the European elections marked a slight improvement and in the local elections it won nine extra seats plus 2 per cent of the vote for the London assembly.

## green thinking

An umbrella term for a constellation of different environmental perspectives, which share a commitment to 'reintegrating' humans back into the natural ecosystem, and to protect the natural environment for future generations. Its basic standpoint is that the world's resources are finite and the planet should be preserved for future generations. Green thinking can range from 'light green' or consumer-friendly environmentalism, where the market is used to internalise the costs of pollution for example, while at the same time maintaining high-technology economic growth, through to 'dark green', where there is a fundamental rejection of economic growth and modern industrialism and a wish to return to a form of small-scale cooperatives. All major parties have recognised the potency of these ideas and sought to embody their less radical elements into mainstream political programmes. Extremist parties, in particular those on the far right, use environmental messages to 'hook' on to the concerns of potential supporters.

## Greenham Common

US airbase which became the scene for a long-running women's demonstration against Cruise missiles (carrying nuclear warheads). In September 1981 a march by Women for Life on Earth reached Greenham Common to protest at NATO's decision to site Cruise missiles at the base. In March the following year 250 women blockaded the base and arrests were made. In November 1983 some 70,000 members of the Campaign for Nuclear Disarmament linked arms to create a 14-mile demonstration against the missiles. By this time a camp had been set up by a number of women, who gave that as their postal address. In 1987 Ronald Regan and Mikhail Gorbachev signed the Intermediate Nuclear

POLITICS

Forces (INF) Treaty and Cruise missiles began to be withdrawn. By 1992 US forces had left the base but the camp remained in existence until the millennium had passed.

## Greenpeace
www.greenpeace.org.uk
The world's largest environmental pressure group. Greenpeace was founded in 1971 by a small group of US campaigners concerned about the environment. Since then its membership has increased to 4.5 million people from 158 different countries. In Britain its membership was just under 20,000 in 2002. In addition to normal pressure group methods such as lobbying decision makers, it also uses high-profile techniques, sometimes involving its own ocean-going vessels, to protest against nuclear tests, nuclear power, commercial whaling and sealing. Its most active campaigners risk their lives in pursuit of a cleaner world, not only through accidents at sea, but through human malice, as demonstrated by the sinking of the Greenpeace vessel *Rainbow Warrior* by agents of the French government in 1985.

## grey power
The political power of those aged over 65 years. This constituency has long been recognised but is growing as a result of demographic changes. The over-65s constitute one-fifth of the electorate but one-quarter of the vote as they are much more likely to turn out. They tend to be poorer, perceive themselves as poorer and thus care more about welfare issues. In 1997, 38 per cent voted Labour and 29 per cent Conservative but by 2001 polls showed the gap was much smaller, possibly influenced by the chancellor's award of a mere 75 pence per week pension increase in 2000 – something for which he subsequently apologised.

*See also* ageing population.

## gross domestic product (GDP)
The value of all goods and services produced within a country. Usually the figure given is for the year as a whole but it is

often given per capita. In 2001 the GDP of the UK was $1,424.1 billion – the fourth largest in the world – and per capita it was $25,400 – 18th in the world.

## gross national product (GNP)
This is measured as GDP plus the total value of goods and services produced by companies owned by a country (income from abroad minus income earned by foreign investors).

## *Guardian*
www.guardian.co.uk
Originally the *Manchester Guardian* when it was founded in 1821 and the mouthpiece of Manchester radical liberalism. It is now owned by the independent Scott Trust. Its editors have included some distinguished journalists, such as C. P. Scott and A. P. Wadsworth. It traditionally took a liberal line and still does. It tends to support a pro-Labour line when the party is in opposition but is often less supportive when Labour is in power.

## Guildford Four
Infamous case of a miscarriage of injustice relating to alleged Irish republican terrorists. In 1975, four Irish people, Gerard Conlon, Carole Richardson, Patrick Armstrong and Paul Hill, were found guilty of placing bombs in Guildford and Woolwich public houses. They served 14 years in prison but after a hard-fought campaign on their behalf from supporters, and procrastination on the part of the authorities, their convictions were found to be unsafe and they were released in 1989.

*See also* Birmingham Six.

## guillotine motion
A procedural device used in the House of Commons. More formally called an 'allocation of time motion', this is a device which speeds up the passage of contentious legislation. It was introduced in the 1880s to prevent Irish MPs from obstructing legislation. A strict time limit is placed upon the debate of any clause and when it expires a vote is taken. This device

effectively counters the filibuster technique used by politicians opposed to a measure, but is introduced only after a considerable time has already been spent discussing a measure. Debate can also be curtailed by an informal agreement between the party whips or by a programming motion, which amounts to an agreed timetable for a measure.

*See also* filibuster; programming motion.

# H

## habeas corpus

An ancient constitutional rule, dating back to Edward I, whereby a person cannot be detained without due cause. The Habeas Corpus Act 1679 laid down that a prisoner must be brought before a court without delay. This rule is the citizen's guarantee against arbitrary arrest and detention, hallmarks of a civilised society which adheres to the rule of law. In practice it takes the form of a writ challenging the validity of someone's detention, issued by the Divisional Court of the Queen's Bench Division. Parliament has suspended the act in times of emergency, as in 1715, 1794 and 1817. There was much controversy about the Terrorism Act 2001, which allowed terrorist suspects to be held without trial for an indefinite period.

## half-hour adjournment

Most well known form of Commons adjournment debate. It takes the form of a motion tabled at the end of the day's proceedings when an MP, selected by ballot, can use it to air any issue he or she chooses. Competition is fierce as the debate is for 30 minutes. The final adjournment debate before recess is longer and the motion is chosen by the government.

*See also* adjournment debate; early day motion; private notice question.

## *Hansard*

www.parliament.the-stationery-office.co.uk/
pa/cm/cmhansrd.htm (Commons)
www.parliament.the-stationery-office.co.uk/
pa/ld/ldhansrd.htm (Lords)

The official record of parliamentary proceedings. It includes all speeches, questions asked and answered and statements made in both houses of parliament. It started life in 1803 as a set of informal notes taken by William Cobbet. Luke Hansard succeeded him and, using a team of skilled shorthand writers, he produced a verbatim account which could be published. His family continued to be associated with the work until late into the 19th century, when the government took over the job. In 1943 the name *Hansard's Parliamentary Debates* was restored to the title page. Each reporter works only for a short time as such intensive shorthand is exhausting. Members can review their speeches before final publication in *Hansard* to amend simple errors and grammar is almost always corrected by the official record takers.

## Harris Research Centre (HRC)

www.harrisinteractive.com

An opinion polling organisation. HRC was set up by the *Daily Express* and Louis Harris, an American pollster. It took over the ORC polling organisation in 1983. It continues polling for the Conservatives and publishes its findings in the *Observer* and via several television current affairs programmes.

## Hayward report, 1982

Labour Party report into the Militant Tendency. Hayward exposed the determined entryist tactics of the organisation and persuaded the leadership to take decisive action. It advised the compilation of a 'register of recognised groups allowed to operate within the party'. In practice, however, this proposal had little effect and it was left to the Whitty report (1985) to initiate tougher and more effective action.

*See also* entryism; Hayward report; Militant Tendency; Whitty report.

## head of state

The personification of a nation state and its people. Heads of state may be purely symbolic or ceremonial, carrying out duties at home and abroad. They may also be functional, as head of a government.

The British head of state, Her Majesty Elizabeth II, is a hereditary monarch and was crowned at Westminster Abbey in 1953. She has a wide range of official and ceremonial duties, including the state opening of parliament, the queen's speech, giving the royal assent to parliamentary bills, dissolving parliament, and appointing a prime minister. In theory she could exert political power in the event of a hung parliament through her ability to invite a likely person to form a government. However, in practice few constitutional experts believe she could intervene decisively in the political process as she acts on the 'advice' of her ministers.

## Health and Safety Commission

www.hse.gov.uk/aboutus/hsc
Body responsible for overseeing the Health and Safety Executive (HSE). The Commission has the power to delegate any part of the HSE's functions but cannot direct the HSE to interpret the Health and Safety at Work Act 1974, which established the HSC and HSE.

## Health and Safety Executive (HSE)

www.hse.gov.uk
Body responsible for the protection of health, safety and the welfare of employees and for safeguarding those who may be exposed to risks from industrial activities. It was set up by the Health and Safety at Work Act 1974.

## hegemony

Antonio Gramsci's term for the values of the ruling capitalist class which condition the thinking of all other groups and institutions. In so doing, the system is perceived as 'natural' and appeals to common-sense assumptions and therefore exercises a persuasive power over its victims which brute force could never do. Some commen-tators believed Margaret Thatcher's period in office during the 1980s demonstrated such control, although others dispute this. A second meaning is associated with the worldwide influence of Britain during the 19th century and the USA since 1945.

## Herbert report, 1960

Report on the local government of London that led to the replacement of the London County Council by the Greater London Council, which itself was abolished in 1986 by Margaret Thatcher's government.

*See also* Greater London Authority; Greater London Council.

## hereditary peerage

A title conferred originally by the mon-arch and then handed down through the generations via inheritance. Because the aristocracy were major owners of prop-erty they tended, naturally, to support the Conservatives and so the House of Lords represented a stronghold of Conservative political power until 1998, when all but 92 hereditary peers were abolished by the Labour government. Some peerages (mostly life but also some hereditary ones) were created by Labour prime ministers and there were Liberal peers as well as cross-benchers with no party affiliation, but the Conservative dominance was never broken. In the 1950s Lord Stansgate, or Anthony Wedgwood Benn as he was then called (later Tony Benn), sought to disclaim his title in order to sit in the Commons; the eventual result of his efforts was the passing of the Peerages Act 1963, which made this possible. Following the House of Lords Act 1999, hereditary peers were able to sit in the House of Commons (for example Douglas Hogg, Viscount Hailsham).

The order of seniority among such peers is: duke, marquess, earl, viscount and baron.

*See also* House of Lords reform.

## High Court

Court that hears all the more important civil cases and some criminal appeals. In the hierarchy of courts, the High Court occurs between the Court of Appeal and the crown and county courts. It has three divisions:

1 Chancery hears contract cases, tort claims and claims for the recovery of land. Seventeen judges work in this division, which has a vice chancellor at its head. It deals with huge sums of money and such cases as the aftermath of Robert Maxwell's death or the Lloyds insurance crisis in the late 1990s.

2 Queen's Bench hears equity matters such as mortgage repossessions. It has 69 judges and deals with cases too complex for county courts or which involve large sums of money. The division also includes a commercial court and an admiralty one dealing with shipping cases. The Divisional Court of the Queen's Bench can issue writs of habeus corpus regarding unlawful imprisonment. It is also the destination for appeals against government actions which may have exceeded statutory authority. The court dealing with such cases is called the Administrative Court.

3 The Family Division hears disputes over adoptions and defended divorces, for example; it also dealt with Diane Blood's request to receive insemination from her dead husband's sperm. This division has 16 judges.

## high Tory

Originally a group of Tories in the early 18th century who were devoted to the Church of England and who opposed most constitutional changes, including union with Scotland. Today it is used as a term to describe old-fashioned Conservatives who are sceptical about any radical reform. For example, high Tories see the constitution as an organic thing which is best left alone to develop 'naturally' over time. They tend to be against reform, almost on principle. Thus, Douglas Hurd while foreign secretary (1989–95) cautioned against pushing the tide of reform too far and too fast in the Thatcherite revolution.

## Hillsborough Agreement, 1985

Treaty between Britain and Ireland signed in November 1985 which allowed the latter a consultative role in the government of Northern Ireland in exchange for a pledge that the province would remain part of the UK as long as a majority of its population wished it. In the short term the agreement caused bitterness on the part of unionists and did not stimulate the round-table negotiations the two governments desired. However, in a historical context, it marked a degree of collaboration between London and Dublin which foreshadowed the more successful talks of the mid-to-late 1990s.

## Hinduja brothers

Three wealthy Indian businessmen who were accused of various improprieties in their own country and who donated £1 million to the struggling Millennium Dome. When a citizenship application for one of the bothers was dealt with much more quickly (in six months) than normal, accusations were made of improper favours being granted in exchange for the brothers' donation to a New Labour project. Peter Mandelson was the minister (without portfolio) in charge of the Dome when the donation was made and it was alleged that he rang up the Home Office to apply pressure on behalf of his Dome 'sponsor' in 2001, when he was secretary of state for Northern Ireland. A small group of ministers, including Derry Irvine, Tony Blair and Jack Straw, eventually asked Mandelson to resign in January 2001, and he did so, albeit reluctantly. The Hammond report into the matter appeared to clear Mandelson.

*See also* Mandelson, Peter.

## Holyrood

The seat of the Scottish parliament since 1997. Controversy broke out regarding the new site for the parliament building when the original cost of £40 million rose to £195 million by 2001. Removal of the spending cap in that year opened the prospect of the cost rising well over the £200 million mark. Some critics claimed the new building was becoming Scotland's 'Dome'. By the spring of 2004 predicted costs had been 'held' to £431 million. In

September 2004 it finally opened for use by the Scottish parliament.

## Home Affairs Committee
*See* departmental select committee.

## Home Office
www.homeoffice.gov.uk
Government department responsible for home affairs. It was formed in 1782, when it was decided to deal with political matters for home and abroad separately. Something of a 'catch-all' department, it covers a vast area of public policy including: passports, immigration and race relations, broadcasting, prisons, sentencing policy, betting, gaming and liquor licensing, administration of justice and the police. The department is usually recognised as fourth in the ministerial hierarchy, after Downing Street, the Treasury and the Foreign Office. In common with other government departments, the Home Office now has its own mission statement and corps of special advisors who deal with marketing and public relations issues.

## Home Policy Committee
One of key the committees of Labour's National Executive Committee (NEC) in the 1980s. In the late 1970s and early 1980s Tony Benn was its chair and did much to move official policy to the left, with arguably disastrous electoral consequences for the party. After 1983 Neil Kinnock as party leader concentrated on strengthening his position on the NEC and Benn's power waned. After Labour's 1987 general election defeat Kinnock authorised a comprehensive review of policy to be undertaken not by the Home Policy Committee but by seven other policy groups. The reports of these groups moved the party decisively to the centre and right and paved the way for Tony Blair to accelerate the move after 1994.

## home secretary
The cabinet minister in charge of the Home Office, a key spokesperson on law and order issues and a major 'player' in the race for the prime minister's job. The home secretary also used to be directly responsible for the Metropolitan Police Force (now rechristened 'Service') but this responsibility has now passed to the Greater London Authority. Notable recent Conservative holders of the office have included William Whitelaw, Douglas Hurd and Kenneth Clarke. Under New Labour, Jack Straw took a robust and proactive line on racism in society and public bodies, in particular the police force. However, in common with previous incumbents, he steadfastly refused to consider the decriminalisation of so-called 'soft drugs' such as cannabis. His successor David Blunkett, however, did relax the laws on cannabis to a small degree.

## homelessness
The most visible symptom of poverty. Homelessness was especially visible in the big cities during the 1980s, often in the form of young people (16–17-year-olds had had their right to state benefits withdrawn) sleeping in shop doorways or in 'cardboard cities' under railway arches. In theory local authorities have a duty to house anyone without shelter. However, partly because of the decline of council house stock (a result of the right to buy policy of the early 1980s) local authorities have not been able to house everyone. Shelter's figures show a subsequent decline in the number of homeless people, from 223,860 in 1991, to 179,610 in 1996 and 172,760 in 2000. On 3 August 2001 the government's Rough Sleepers Unit, headed by Louise Casey, reported a drop in homelessness. According to its report there were 703 people sleeping rough in England each night, down from 1,180 in 2000. In London, too, the number had nearly halved: down from 621 to 357.
*See also* council housing; Shelter.

## 'homes for votes' scandal
Scandal involving Westminster council. The district auditor John Magill investigated the accounts of the council in 1994 and revealed that housing had been

preferentially sold to people deemed likely to vote Conservative. The council – especially its leader, Dame Shirley Porter – was condemned by the report and she was ordered to repay some £35 million. Those accused vehemently denied the charges and Porter was cleared on appeal in May 1999. However, in December 2001 the House of Lords reimposed a £26.5 million surcharge. In August 2002 the council won a High Court judgement to help it recover the sum but Porter claimed that her net assets were now only £300,000 rather than the estimated £70 million she was reputed to be worth. In April 2004 a £12.3 million settlement was reached between the council and Dame Shirley.

## homosexuality
In medieval times, ecclesiastical or Church law designated homosexual acts as a sin, though not too serious a crime. The first law against homosexuality was passed in 1534. In 1885 buggery was made a criminal offence, even if performed in private between consenting adults. The most famous person convicted for homosexual activity was Oscar Wilde, in 1895, who was given two years in Reading prison. In that same year homosexual importuning was made illegal; however, attempts to extend the law to lesbianism in 1921 failed. In 1957 the Wolfenden report recommended repeal of laws pertaining to homosexuality and in 1967 homosexual acts between consenting males over 18 were no longer a criminal offence in England and Wales. However, Scotland, the Republic of Ireland and Northern Ireland had to wait much later for decriminalisation. In 2000, the Labour government embarked on repealing section 28, which had made it an offence for local authorities to 'promote' (the precise meaning of which is unclear) homosexuality, for example in schools. These changes reflect a more tolerant moral climate towards alternative sexual orientation in Britain.

*See also* section 28; Wolfenden report.

## honourable
*See* parliamentary terms of address.

## Honours Scrutiny Committee
Committee of parliament which checks whether nominees for honours are a security risk or have a criminal record. It allegedly was responsible for turning down Margaret Thatcher's attempt to elevate Jeffrey Archer in 1990. In 2000 the Neill Committee on Standards in Public Life recommended the committee be given responsibility for checking whether honours were connected to political donations.

## honours system
The system whereby the crown, advised by the government, hands out peerages, knighthoods and sundry medals to those thought deserving of such honours. Opponents claim this is a feudal relic which should be abolished as it adds even more power to the incumbent of Number 10 Downing Street. Defenders say it is a means of rewarding citizens for outstanding services to the life of the nation. It comprises a whole hierarchy of awards, from the MBE, CBE and OBE to knighthoods and peerages. Life peers are entitled to sit in the Lords. There have been accusations that governments have been prepared to give honours in exchange for contributions to party funds and there is some evidence to support this, despite the filtering work of the Honours Scrutiny Committee. The Labour government introduced in January 2001 a new category of honour called 'people's peers', whereby individuals could nominate themselves or others. The first such list was much mocked, as it included a number of professors and successful business people.

In February 2004 the Commons Public Administration Committee, chaired by Dr Tony Wright MP, announced it would hold an inquiry into reform of the honours system, declaring reform was a matter of 'when, not if'. This followed revelations in December 2003 of a system which was: too secretive; dominated by civil servants; and characterised by a surprising number of people who chose to refuse acceptance of any proffered honour. In July 2004 the committee urged a drastic reduction in the honours given; for example, dames and knights should go as well as the Order of Bath, and the name 'Empire' should be changed to 'Excellence'.

> Members of the civil service orders rise from CMG (known sometimes in Whitehall as Call Me God) to the KCMG (Kindly Call Me God) to – for a select few governors and super ambassadors – the GCMG (God Calls Me God). (Anthony Sampson, *Anatomy of Britain*, 1962)

*See also* Commoners' Register.

## House of Commons

www.parliament.uk/about_commons/about_commons.cfm

The so-called 'lower' chamber of parliament – the Lords is the 'upper' – and effectively the forum for democratic government of the country. This can be traced back to the gathering of representatives from local communities. In 1295 Edward I summoned two knights from each of the shires, two citizens to represent each of the cities and two others to represent each of the boroughs. This assembly came to be known as the Commons and in time sat separately from the House of Lords. Over time it was the Commons which agreed to grant taxation to the monarch and its support was also sought in respect of certain royal policies. In exchange for such support the crown agreed to redress grievances from the citizenry and from this foothold the Commons came to exert its right to help formulate new laws. In 1547 the Commons were allowed a permanent location in the chapel of St Stephen in Westminster. During the English Civil War the Commons became the seat of rebellion against the crown and by the end of the 17th century its importance was entrenched by the Glorious Revolution (1688–89). The decision to invite Mary and William of Orange to accede to the throne in place of James II was made on certain conditions. Parliament was to entrench its control over the supply of finance to the crown and to insist the crown could govern only with the 'consent' of parliament. The 1694

Triennial Act removed the crown's ability to extend the life of supportive parliaments indefinitely. The Lords, however, still held the important national debates and extensive patronage enabled the aristocracy to dominate membership of the lower chamber. However, the Great Reform Act 1832 ended such control and elections to the Commons came to provide the legitimate government. The right to vote was extended in 1867 and 1884 and the number of MPs rose to 707 in 1918, though fell to 619 in 1920 after the creation of the Irish Free State. In 1997 there were 659 MPs elected, all representing single-member constituencies. The Parliament Act 1911 marked the end of the hegemony of the Lords and the beginning of the modern era in which the election of candidates to the Commons determines the party which is to form the government of the day. In 1997 the Commons cost a total of £202 million to run.

*See also* Westminster Hall.

## House of Commons reform

Reform of the Commons was a concern of many MPs and activists before New Labour came to power in 1997 – the chief complaint being that the legislature was too weak in relation to the executive. Labour has not greatly changed that imbalance but did introduce a number of reforms after 1997, including the dropping of the use of a top hat for points of order (a member had to place the top hat on his head to indicate he had a point of order to make) and the speaker's wig, extra debates in Westminster Hall, more pre-legislation consultation, Thursday morning sittings, early finishes on Thursday evening, fewer Friday sittings and better staff and facilities. In the autumn of 1998 the Jenkins commission reported on the reform of the voting system which elects MPs to the Commons but, at the time of writing, no action has been taken as a result.

In the summer of 2000 the chairs of select committees wrote a report recommending more power to the legislature but the then leader of theHouse, Margaret Beckett, was unimpressed. After June 2001 the same group of MPs hoped to convince the new leader of the House, Robin Cook, that such a shift of power was necessary in a chamber with such a massive government majority and a premier who tended to ignore it. On 21 June 2001 Robin Cook gave heart to reformers by promising to bring parliament's procedures into the 21st century and act as an effective democratic check on the executive. He introduced a raft of reforms in the autumn of 2002, including an earlier finishing time for debates, but critics insisted he had done little to improve the overall balance between the government and the legislature.

> Being an MP feeds the vanity and starves the self respect. (Mathew Parris, 1997)

> The earlier parliament can get in on the act of drafting bills, the better the chance of MPs of influencing the shape of bills. (Robin Cook, 7 January 2002)

## House of Lords

The upper chamber of parliament. Originally the Lords comprised those senior nobles, usually substantial landowners and clergy, who advised the monarch. Despite the fact that the representatives of local communities (the Commons) became powerful through their control of granting taxation revenues to the monarch, the Lords provided the most important personnel of government right up until the late 19th century. However, the changing balance of economic power from the landed aristocracy to industrial middle class was slowly becoming reflected in the highest circles and at the end of the first decade of the 20th century a great conflict occurred in which there could be only one winner. David Lloyd George's people's budget of 1909 contained social reforms and dared the Lords to refuse a money bill – something which by convention it had always passed. Eventually it was passed but the reforming government of Herbert Asquith was determined to curb the undemocratic upper chamber. The Parliament Act 1911 restricted its powers to delaying money bills by one month and two years for other pub-

lic bills; the Parliament Act 1949 reduced the latter to one year. The Labour Party initially resolved to abolish the chamber but then softened its position to one of reform as it basically accepted that the Lords' functions of debating, amending and revising were worthwhile and necessary.

In March 2003 the Lords had 678 members, of whom 569 were life peers. This broke down politically to: 213 Conservatives (164 life); 188 Labour (184 life); 178 cross-benchers (146 life); 65 Liberal Democrats (60 life); 26 archbishops and bishops; and 8 others (7 life).

> I went to the House of Lords because I had nowhere else to go. (Emmanuel Shinwell, 1977)

> A big cat detained for a period in a poodle parlour, sharpening her claws on the velvet. (Matthew Parris on Lady Thatcher in the Lords, 1993)

## House of Lords Appointments Commission (HLAP)

www.houseoflordsappointmentscommission. gov.uk

Non-departmental public body, set up in May 2000, sponsored by the prime minister. It recommends appointments of all non-party political life peers and vets all nominations for the chamber. This new body took on a role previously undertaken by the prime minister, who now informs the Commission of the number of nominations required for non-party political peers. The premier then puts the Commission's recommendations to the queen in the same way as nominations made by political parties. In addition, the Commission vets nominations to the Lords 'to ensure the highest standards of propriety'. The government's consultation paper on reforming the Lords, published September 2003, envisaged a statutory appointments commission to take over the work of the HLAP.

## House of Lords reform

This has been a source of much debate and conflict since Labour announced it would reform the chamber in its 1997 manifesto.

Some reformers even argue that the upper chamber is redundant and that only one is necessary for good government, as shown by Sweden, which has abandoned its second chamber. The hereditary peers were virtually abolished in 1999, although 92 were retained as part of a compromise until the nature of the new chamber had been resolved. Then the Wakeham royal commission proposed a new chamber, for which 20 per cent of the members would be elected. The resultant white paper built on these proposals but they were savaged by party critics and a joint Lords–Commons committee proposed a number of options for reform, which were debated in February 2003. Tony Blair, together with the Lords themselves, favoured an all-appointed House but all the options for a new House were voted down. In September 2003 Lord Falconer, the lord chancellor, announced the imminent abolition of the residual 92 hereditary peers and declared the House would be filled by appointment, an outcome which was denounced as contrary to the 2001 manifesto and to a specific vote in January 2003.

See also Wakeham report.

### houses of parliament

Also known as the Palace of Westminster. Most of the medieval royal palace was burnt down in 1834, but it was rebuilt over two decades (1840–60) by Charles Barry and A. W. Pugin in a distinctive Gothic style. In 1940 the debating chamber was burnt down following an attack by incendiary bombs during the Blitz. It was rebuilt in its original form by G. G. Scott and opened in 1950. The palace is often perceived as the foremost symbol of British democracy and is one of the best-known buildings in the world.

### housing association

An association of tenants independent of a local authority. Housing associations were encouraged by the Conservative governments of the 1980s and increased their share of dwellings from 1 per cent in 1979 to 4 per cent in 1995.

See also housing policy.

### housing policy

This effectively began after the First World War, when the government decided to subsidise local authority housing with contributions from local government and tenant rents. In 1972 a rent rebate was introduced to give means-tested assistance to some tenants. By 1980 councils owned 32 per cent of all dwellings. Margaret Thatcher's government was in favour of helping people to buy their own homes. In 1980 the right to buy policy enabled tenants to buy their own council houses at a discount. In 1982 housing benefit was introduced by local authorities. During the 1980s housing subsidies were drastically slashed and housing was subject to more cuts than any other form of public spending. By the end of the decade over 65 per cent of people owned their own homes and only 18 per cent of the population resided in council housing. John Major's government reduced the proportion of mortgage interest payments eligible for tax relief, a process completed by Labour chancellor Gordon Brown.

The 2001 queen's speech revealed that two new reforms were in the pipeline. First, conveyancing would be brought up to date – a practice hitherto based on an 1875 Act. New procedures would be based on electronic methods, to speed up the process of house purchase. Measures to reform leasehold tenure were also unveiled; these were aimed at ending the activities of unscrupulous landlords and giving tenants a say in the management of the property they rent.

The Guardian (21 June 2001) reported that council housing appeared to be in terminal decline as a local authority responsibility. In 1988 the Conservatives gave permission for councils to sell off all of their council house stock but in recent years it has been Labour and Liberal Democrat councils which have taken advantage of the measure. Mostly the houses are sold to housing associations, as they are subject to fewer financial constraints than are local authorities. By 2015, the Guardian calculated, there would be 5 million houses owned by housing associations and only a handful of council houses left.

In March 2002 the Joseph Rowntree Foundation produced a report which predicted that Britain needed to build 4 million houses by 2012 if house price inflation was to be curtailed. The report was concerned that large numbers of public sector workers could no longer afford to buy homes.

In his comprehensive spending review in July 2004 chancellor Gordon Brown announced a 4.1 per cent increase in spending on housing for the three years from 2005. In money terms this amounted to a pledge of £1.3 billion, enough to build an extra 10,000 homes a year for renting by 2008.

## human rights
Basic entitlements which a human being can expect to receive from the state and power holders, such as the rights to life and freedom from unlawful imprisonment and torture. More recently claims have been made to include such entitlements as economic and social resources as a basic human right. All civilised societies claim to respect human rights. Britain, a signatory of the United Nations' Universal Declaration of Human Rights (1948) and the European Convention on Human Rights (1950), generally has a good record on humanitarian treatment of its citizens as well as aliens, although Britain has a poor record in terms of judgements in the European Court of Human Rights. In October 2000, the European Convention was incorporated into British law by the Human Rights Act 1998, thus fulfilling a pledge made by New Labour in its election manifesto of 1997.

## hung parliament
A situation when no single party commands an overall majority in the House of Commons. The end result is most likely to be the formation of a coalition or minority government, at least in the short term, until a new election is called by the prime minister. Precisely whom the monarch should invite to form a government is the subject of debate, though in the first instance it would almost certainly be the leader of the largest party in the Commons. If no pact could be established to create a working majority the monarch would be advised to dissolve parliament and call another election.

See also head of state; Lib–Lab pact.

## hunting
Labour promised to ban hunting with dogs in its 1997 manifesto but was influenced by the outcry this caused in the countryside, as expressed by the Countryside Alliance, which mobilised marches in London and other demonstrations. In September 2004 Tony Balir fulfilled his 2000 promise to push a hunting ban through. This sop to his party was not won without violent demonstrations outside and within the Commons. The ban is due to come into effect in July 2006; in Scotland it is alrady banned.

## hustings
Place of electoral debate. Before the Ballot Act 1872, parliamentary candidates would be nominated at open public meetings, and would make speeches to the electorate from a platform. The term is still used to describe the debates during election campaigns, although live public meetings have, since the 1960s, tended to die out as elections have increasingly been fought via the media. As a result of this many politicians have not troubled to acquire the art of public oratory, and now rely upon the professional speech writer and media advisor or spin doctor to burnish their performance.

## Hutton report, 2004
www.the-hutton-inquiry.org.uk
*Report of the Inquiry into the Circumstances Surrounding the Death of Dr David Kelly.*
The inquiry was set up in July 2003, under Lord Justice Hutton, to investigate the circumstances of the death of Dr David Kelly, a Ministry of Defence (MoD) weapons advisor who committed suicide after it became known he had spoken to BBC reporter Andrew Gilligan earlier in the year. Gilligan had claimed, in a May 2003 report on the *Today* programme on Radio

POLITICS

4, that a 'senior intelligence source' had told him that the September dossier (on Iraq's weapons of mass destruction) had 'sexed up' the material provided by the security services. The name of Alastair Campbell, the Downing Street press secretary, was specifically mentioned. The resulting row between the government and the media was volcanic. The key questions which witnesses were pressed upon were:

1 The decision by the MoD to make Kelly's name public. It transpired that senior civil servants and ministers, including Tony Blair and Geoff Hoon, were involved in the decision and the methodology whereby the MoD virtually encouraged the press to identify him.

2 Whether the claim that Iraq could mount an attack with weapons of mass destruction in 45 minutes was correct or a wilful exaggeration. Evidence revealed that the claim referred only to 'battlefield' and not long-range weapons.

3 Whether staff in Blair's office manipulated intelligence material to help persuade a doubting country that war was justified. It seemed clear, from evidence submitted to the inquiry, that some elaboration of the dossier did take place at the behest of Number 10.

Lord Hutton announced the conclusions of his report on 28 January 2004. He astonished the political class by finding almost wholly for the government and clearing politicians (Blair, Hoon), senior civil servants (Sir David Omand, Sir Kevin Tebbit) and senior intelligence staff (John Scarlett). It was the BBC which bore the brunt of the criticism: he found fault with its editorial control of Andrew Gilligan and with its governors for backing a flawed story without checking the facts. The next day the BBC chairman, Gavyn Davies, the director general, Greg Dyke, and Gilligan himself all resigned. Press and public reactions were generally adverse, with loud accusations of a 'whitewash' by an establishment figure; one poll suggested the public did not believe Hutton had achieved the right balance.

*See also* weapons of mass destruction (WMD).

## hybrid bill

Bill with the characteristics of both a private and public bill; that is, while it may be of general interest it may also have significance for certain individuals or organisations. The procedure to be followed in respect of such bills includes elements of the procedures for both public and private. Backbenchers may introduce bills which come to be judged as hybrid, but this is rare – the most recent example being the Channel Tunnel Rail Link Act 1996.

## hypothecated tax

A tax raised by a particular means for a specific purpose. The Liberal Democrats regularly declare such 'ring-fencing' in their manifestos (for example a penny on income tax for education). Other parties have considered the idea but, despite some evidence that the public favours it, the Treasury resists any weakening of its control over how the general tax take should be disbursed.

# I

## Ibbs report, 1988

*Improving Management in Government: The Next Steps*, by Sir Robin Ibbs. The report recommended the separation of the routine from the policy-advising functions of the civil service. This meant in practice the hiving off of routine government functions into executive agencies – good examples of which are the Benefits Agency and the Driver and Vehicle Licensing Agency, at Swansea. Some 70 per cent of civil servants now work in such agencies.

*See also* executive agency.

## ICM

www.icmresearch.co.uk

Polling organisation which began life as Marplan and whose polls were usually reported in the *Guardian*. In 1989 the chief researcher left Marplan and set up ICM. The *Guardian* is still its regular customer for political polls.

## identity card
A means of identifying every citizen in a country. Home secretary David Blunkett announced a consultation exercise on compulsory identity cards on 5 February 2002. The idea was to make them 'entitlement cards', which would help to prevent fraudulent use of public services and the police to combat terrorism and credit card fraud, for example. Opponents claimed it would cost over £1 billion and would violate civil liberties. Blunkett made clear, however, that the police would not be able to demand sight of the card and not having one would not be an offence. In July 2002 over 100 MPs plus a battery of pressure groups declared their opposition to the scheme. Peter Lilley, former social security secretary, condemned the idea as unworkable and an affront to civil liberty. In September 2003, however, Blunkett insisted the plan was worth introducing despite the cost and the scathing opposition of civil libertarians. After a battle in cabinet Blunkett overcame opposition from chancellor Gordon Brown to the idea in November 2003 but the plan now was to introduce the scheme gradually, in the following stages: a six-month pilot of the new face and fingerprint 'biometric' security features involving 10,000 volunteers; legislation to authorise identity cards by 2004; introduction of a biometric 'credit card' passport in 2006; full identity cards to be introduced by 2007; and a final decision to proceed with a compulsory scheme in 2013. A draft bill on identity cards was introduced on 23 June 2004. On 29 July 2004 the Home Affairs Select Committee gave qualified backing to the scheme.

## ideology
One of the most hotly debated and used terms in politics. Generally speaking there are two meanings: a 'relaxed' definition, which sees ideologies as necessary intellectual constructs by which people make sense of the world around them; and a 'restricted' definition, which argues that a ruling group sustains its position and privileges in society not by force alone, but through a set of ideas which have great intellectual and psychological force upon individuals and groups within society. An example of the latter usage is the Marxist analysis of liberal democracy (sometimes called capitalist democracy), which argues that people have formal political power through the vote but that real power is located deep down in the economic relations of capitalist society – governments may come and go but the economic order remains largely unchanged. In the British context this would translate into a view that asserts the establishment is always in control and the general lack of difference between the agendas of the two main parties in the early years of the new millennium might be seen as further reinforcement for such a view.

British politics has always tended to be non-ideological, in the sense that parties avoid extreme beliefs and values, but there have been coherent sets of political ideas informing political parties since the 18th and 19th centuries: conservatism, socialism and liberalism. Marxism and fascism never made much headway, though 'green thinking' won converts towards the end of the 20th century. The British tradition is essentially pragmatic within the context of a system which reflects, and is underpinned by, liberal assumptions. Some political scientists argue that British political culture is rather non-intellectual compared with, say, the French, and indeed suspicious of grand systems of thought such as Marxism. After the Second World War, sharp disagreements in ideology tended to diminish as the postwar consensus on the Keynesian mixed economy and welfare state became established. But the relative economic decline during the 1960s and the appearance of stagflation in the 1970s caused the fracture of the cross-party agreements and ideology re-emerged in the form of the new right in the Conservative Party led by Margaret Thatcher and Keith Joseph. She championed classical liberal ideas on the economy and favoured a minimal role for the government, at least in terms of the economy and social provision. Labour experienced a similar radicalisation but left-wards, the party producing one of the most socialist manifestos in its postwar history for the 1983 general election. However, the rout of the party at the polls gave credence to Gerald Kaufman's quip that the mani-festo was the 'longest suicide note in history'.

After this debacle, the Labour Party was reconstructed, first by Neil Kinnock, then John Smith and latterly by Tony Blair, the result being the repositioning of Labour into a centrist position which is closer to Thatcherism than socialism in a number of key respects, especially: an anti-inflationary economic strategy, a tough line on crime and the acceptance of privatisation in the public services. Since its landslide vic-tory in 1997, Labour has continued the macro-economic policies of Margaret Thatcher and John Major in a number of ways, though chancellor Gordon Brown did substantially increase public spending. Political scientists are divided, however, on whether the party is developing an authentic ideological position, namely the 'third way'. Some argue that the position is essentially Thatcher(ite) with a socialist 'spin' via distinctive New Labour language. Others argue it responds to events and reacts to focus groups in particular, as part of a strategy of maintaining popularity at all costs. Indeed, Robert Worcester, chairman of MORI and former advisor to Harold Wilson, has suggested that political parties in 2001 are mainly concerned with win-ning elections, rather than developing any distinctive ideological position, an argument reinforced by students of political marketing like Jennifer Lees-Marchment.

See also postwar consensus; hegemony.

## image

The perceptions of party, leader and policies formed in the minds of voters and opinion formers. In this political sense, at least, appearances make reality and in the media-dominated world of modern politics the presentation of ideas is as important as content, if not more so. One expert

commentator (B. Bruce, *Images of Power*, 1992) has reported that 'the impact we make on others [on the television] depends on … how we look and behave (55 per cent); how we speak (38 per cent); and what we say (only 7 per cent)'. Despite the media skills of Harold Macmillan and Harold Wilson, not to mention James Callaghan, Margaret Thatcher was the first modern British politician fully to embrace the implications of the media for politics. Her advisor, Gordon Reece, encouraged her to take great care with her image: her appearance was transformed from frumpy housewife to warrior queen, and her voice was lowered to avoid its disconcerting ten-dency to be shrill. In addition, her speeches were studded with sound bites to catch the attention of the news bulletins. Under the tutelage of spin doctors like Peter Mandelson and Alastair Campbell, the Labour leadership followed suit and soon bettered the Conservatives at projecting the image of New Labour under the attractive televisual image of Tony Blair. It is widely believed the political career of Robin Cook would have flourished more had he been born with a face which looked attractive on television – a sad comment on our times.

See also campaigning; political market-ing; spin; spin doctor.

## immigration

The movement of people into the country for residence, for whatever reason but often to seek asylum or refuge or for economic betterment. Before 1945 immigration con-trols were minimal and waves of refugees from overseas regularly arrived, including Jews, socialists and other political creeds. They were all attracted by the reputation Britain had built up as a welcoming refuge for such persecuted groups. Around the Second World War migrant Jews and Poles were assimilated with relative ease. Shortly thereafter, the government encouraged economic migration from Commonwealth countries to meet shortages in service industries like the National Health Service and London Transport. It did this by introducing the British Nationality Act

1948, which gave British citizenship to all Commonwealth citizens and so provided the legal basis for the influx of workers, initially from the Caribbean. Later India and Pakistan were the source of thousands of emigrants, who generally found employment in low-paid, traditional sectors like textiles. Many immigrants lived in inner-city areas of the big conurbations like London, Manchester, Leeds and Bradford.

By the 1960s some problems integrating the newcomers into British culture were being experienced and the government decided to place curbs on future immigration. The Commonwealth Immigration Act 1962 was consequently passed. It limited entry to holders of passports issued in Britain itself and required immigrants to hold 'work vouchers'. The Race Relations Act 1965 outlawed discrimination on the grounds of race. The Race Relations Act 1976 set up the Commission for Racial Equality. From 1968 immigration became a volatile political issue after Enoch Powell, a Conservative front-bench figure, forecast 'rivers of blood' if immigration were not drastically reduced (he later called for it to be ended). In 1978 Margaret Thatcher expressed her opposition to unlimited immigration by saying Britain did not wish to be 'swamped' by new cultures. This confirmed her party as the main opponent of immigration, apart from the overtly racist far-right parties. The British Nationality Act 1981 and the Immigration Act 1988 sought to restrict immigration.

There are often suggestions that poorer white people in immigrant areas feel that immigrants and asylum seekers receive too many favours and hand-outs. Some commentators argue that Britain has been hypocritical over immigration, encouraging it in the 1950s when cheap labour was required but closing the door in the 1970s once economic problems had put a squeeze on employment. However, population projections suggest more rather than less immigration will be needed again, as a result of the declining birth rate.

*See also* asylum seeker; Commission for Racial Equality; imperialism.

## impeachment
Form of criminal trial initiated by the House of Commons with the Lords acting as judge. It emerged in the 14th century but then fell into disuse until the 17th century, when the Indian administrator Warren Hastings was impeached; his trial lasted seven years, after which he was found innocent but was financially ruined. Its last employment in Britain was in 1848 but in August 2004 Adam Price MP (Plaid Cymru) attempted to impeach Tony Blair for misleading the country into war in Iraq. The process requires an MP to make the accusation and present the case to the House. If a majority agrees, a committee draws up articles of impeachment and then the case is heard before the Lords.

## imperial preference
A system of defensive tariffs designed to advantage the British Empire. The author of the idea was Joseph Chamberlain and the aim was to offset Britain's relative economic decline. The national government adopted the policy in 1931; the Ottowa Conference in 1932 added the Dominions; crown colonies were included in 1933. The postwar preference for Commonwealth goods was gradually phased out over time, and ended when Britain entered the European Community in 1973.

## imperialism
The policy of developing an empire, which Britain did partly for economic reasons and partly for the glory. Britain began building its empire in the 16th century; the process gathered pace through to the 19th century and then declined in the 20th. Some historians argue that the empire was acquired almost accidentally; for example, once the Suez Canal had been bought by Disraeli it followed that the countries bordering it needed to be friendly to Britain, hence the need to extend British influence in Northern Africa and the Middle East. The imperialist idea was sustained and overlaid by a belief (or at least assertion) that Britain was fulfilling a mission to civilise and improve backward peoples.

This nourished a defensive attitude towards colonial subjects, perhaps accompanied by a feeling of superiority. A nostalgic atavism regarding the empire helps to explain some of the hostility of the Conservative Party towards the Europe Union. The availability of cheap labour in the empire led to waves of immigration, which was often encouraged by British governments in the 1950s and 1960s to meet Britain's labour shortages, a situation sharply curtailed by Immigration Acts when economic problems emerged in the early 1970s and Britain no longer needed its imperial mobile labour force.

A related term, 'cultural imperialism', developed in the 1960s and 1970s and is used to describe the impact of a dominant western culture, usually associated with the USA, on other countries. This is manifested in music, film, clothes and language. In Britain and many other countries, both inside and outside Europe, the baseball cap and Coca-Cola have become icons of a US-inspired style.

## Improvement and Development Agency
www.idea.gov.uk
Agency devoted to improving the delivery of public services by local government. It was set up in 1999 with the aims of: offering practical solutions to performance problems; developing innovative approaches (for example e-government) to ensure internal knowledge transfer; and acting on behalf of local government as a whole.

## *In Place of Strife*
Title of a white paper on industrial relations written by Barbara Castle in 1968. At the time, Britain's economy was being damaged by a wave of unofficial strikes and the white paper was an attempt to bring some order to the apparent anarchy. It ignored the voluntary regulation urged by the 1968 Donovan report on labour relations and instead advocated legal sanctions. There was to be a 28-day 'cooling off' period before strikes could legally take place. Workers who ignored this condition

could be prosecuted, fined or imprisoned. In addition, it proposed government-imposed strike ballots and settlements to inter-union disputes. British unions, at that time, opposed government or legal interference in their concerns as an article of faith and the bulk of them angrily rejected these ideas. In the early months of 1969, Castle was supported by her prime minister, Harold Wilson, and the chancellor, Roy Jenkins, but was opposed most notably by the home secretary, James Callaghan, plus a majority of the parliamentary party, not to mention the incensed ranks of the trade unions. The proposals fell and along with them the prospects both for Castle's long-term political success and for trouble-free industrial relations during the coming decade.

## incentive
The key to right-wing ideas about the economy and founded on an assumption about human nature. Conservatives have always argued that human beings are motivated by the anticipation of personal gain and that this is no bad thing, as it creates enterprise, employment and wealth in society. They have opposed the gradual equalisation of incomes favoured by Labour with its redistributive welfare programmes and have argued that workers need to be given the opportunity to become rich, as restrictions only inhibit the working of the market and reduce efficiency and prosperity. Consequently they have argued for increased incentives for high earners through a reduction of taxation levels; they delivered this during the 1980s, especially through the reduction of the top rate of income tax to 40 per cent.

## income tax
First introduced in 1799 at two shillings in the pound to help finance William Pitt's war against Revolutionary France. The measure was briefly repealed in 1802, was then reintroduced from 1803 to 1816 and then abolished, with all records destroyed, until Robert Peel reintroduced it again in 1842. Robert Peel reimposed it to

compensate for cuts in customs duties and by the end of the century it was a reluctantly accepted feature of life and a major source of government funding. David Lloyd George recognised the need for allowances for pensioners and, at the other end of the scale, introduced a 'surtax' on the very rich. Since the Second World War (during which the standard rate was over 50 per cent of earnings) manifold allowances were introduced to take account of people's needs and government health and welfare priorities. By the 1970s income tax was thought to be too high by the Conservative Party and Margaret Thatcher resolved to bring it down to provide incentives for people in work. In 1987 chancellor Nigel Lawson reduced the top rate from over 80 pence in the pound to 40 per cent. The incoming Labour government in 1997 retained income tax at this level and relied on indirect taxes to raise more revenue. After 2001 Tony Blair still opposed any increase in income tax on the grounds that it would be unacceptable to 'middle England'. This appears to contradict Labour's preference for progressive taxation (taxing the rich proportionately more) but is to some extent offset by chancellor Gordon Brown's redistributive budgets since 1997. Britain's levels of income tax are lower than those of most of its European neighbours, where the typical upper rate is 50 per cent.

*See also* indirect taxation.

## incomes policy
Government regulation of wage increases across the whole economy. John Maynard Keynes argued for full employment, although he was aware that in a free market workers have the power, through free collective bargaining, to negotiate higher wages, which are then passed on to the market in higher prices, which then stimulate further demands for wage increases – in other words a price spiral or inflation. Governments after the war tried all kinds of incomes policies to deal with this problem, for example pay freezes and pay norms, but they all, eventually, broke down. In the 1970s the collapse of

the Conservative prices and incomes policy was disastrous and set off an inflationary price spiral which Labour, in power after February 1974, initially could not control. After inflation reached 30 per cent per annum the Social Contract was agreed between unions and the government, which gave the unions a say in certain areas of policy in exchange for a pay norm for the year. This approach brought inflation down to single figures, but in 1979 the Trades Union Congress refused to accept a 5 per cent norm and there was an outbreak of strikes by the lower paid, resulting in the so-called 'winter of discontent'. This eventually helped bring down the Labour government of James Callaghan, and the incoming prime minister, Margaret Thatcher, emphatically rejected an incomes policy. Instead she insisted on tight control of the money supply via interest rates to reduce inflation. This was intended to demonstrate to the unions that there was no money available, and thus inhibit wage demands, but in practice it pushed up the value of the pound and made business more difficult. The resulting unemployment, which exceeded 3 million, was one of the reasons why wage claims reduced and inflation came down.

## incrementalism
The theory that decisions are made by governments through minor adjustments to existing policy. Charles Lindblom suggests that policy makers are not so much rational in their choices but rather build on the status quo and then 'muddle through', making incremental adjustments where appropriate. The theory may be useful in explaining British policy making, which is notorious for 'muddling through'. For example, the policy of privatisation in the 1980s was not prepared by the Conservatives in opposition and did not appear in their 1979 manifesto. Instead it was adopted incrementally and, once it became popular with the electorate, was developed and extended to become possibly the Conservatives' major policy platform by the end of the decade. In keeping with

this theory, the New Labour government of Tony Blair, elected in 1997, has not reversed significantly any of the privatisations; indeed, Labour has built upon them with further sales of public utilities such as the National Air Traffic Services (2001). However, one of the problems of the theory is that it fails properly to explain sharp and radical changes in policy, perhaps as evidenced by the abandonment of demand-side Keynesianism in the 1970s and the adoption of a monetarist-inspired approach to the economy from the late 1970s. Another example might be the railways, which were privatised in the mid-1990s but, in view of their failure, effectively taken back into government hands by 2002.

## Independent Broadcasting Authority (IBA)

Set up by statute in 1954 to regulate the 15 independent broadcasting companies. The chair was appointed by the prime minister but the source of revenue from advertising made independent television freer from government pressure. It oversaw the setting up Channel 4 in 1982 and approved satellite broadcasting some years later. The IBA was replaced by the Independent Television Commission under the Broadcasting Act 1990 (itself replaced by Ofcom in 2003).

*See also* Broadcasting Act 1990; Independent Television Commission.

## Independent International Commission on Decommissioning

Set up in 1995 to assist the disarming of the paramilitaries in Northern Ireland. The Commission has been headed since its inception by the Canadian General John de Chastelain. The general's patience was sorely tried for several years until May 2000, when the IRA offered to give up its weapons. Two arms inspectors, Marti Ahtisaari and Cyril Ramaphosa, visited a number of arms dumps and declared the arms could not be used without their knowledge. However, the IRA has fought shy of actually destroying its caches of arms and ammunition and the Commission's work remains to be completed.

## Independent Labour Party

Founded in 1893 (i.e. before the Labour Party) by Keir Hardie as a vehicle for working-class representation in parliament. It was one of the organisations affiliated to the Labour Representation Committee in 1900 and thus was instrumental in the setting up of the modern Labour Party. For the next 46 years it ran alongside Labour, usually as a left-wing gadfly under the leadership of the likes of Fenner Brockway and James Maxton. When the latter died in 1946 the influence of the three-man party was at an end, although it still exists in a kind of twilight world of the utopian socialist political fringe, with a diminishing band of elderly members.

## independent MP

An MP with no party affiliation. Entry into the Commons is now mainly dependent on membership of a party, but there were more independent MPs in the past: some two dozen represented university seats; nearly a dozen were elected as a result of wartime exigencies; nearly another two dozen were maverick Conservatives (including Oswald Mosley 1922 and 1923); 10 were dissident Liberals; 8 dissident Labour (including D. N. Pritt in 1945 and S. O. Davies in 1970); and six were elected by virtue of support from the left (including Vernon Bartlett).

Few independent candidates can now secure a seat without the support of a political party. Recent examples include Martin Bell, the former BBC foreign correspondent who took the Cheshire seat of Tatton from the Conservative MP Neil Hamilton (who had become engulfed in accusations of sleaze in the run-up to the general election of 1997) and, in the 2001 general election, a retired consultant, Richard Taylor, who was sensationally returned for Wyre Forest on a campaign against the removal of emergency treatment facilities from Kidderminster Hospital. Following his ejection from the Labour Party in October 2003, George Galloway became an independent MP, though he also stood (unsuccessfully) as a candidate for the

European parliament in the June 2004 elections for the anti-Iraq war Respect party.

## Independent Police Complaints Commission (IPCC)

www.ipcc.gov.uk

Fifteen-strong independent commission, set up in April 2004, tasked with initiating, carrying out and monitoring complaints against misconduct by the police. Complaints can be made by individuals in police stations or direct to chief constables or via third parties like MPs, solicitors or the Citizens' Advice Bureau.

## independent school

Any privately funded school. The private sector, including most boarding schools, accounts for about 7 per cent of all children in education. The more established and exclusive, not to mention expensive, private schools are confusingly called 'public schools'. School fees vary widely but usually exceed £10,000 per pupil per annum.

*See also* assisted places scheme; public school.

## Independent Television Commission (ITC)

Established in 1990 as the successor organisation to the Independent Broadcasting Authority but itself subsumed within Ofcom (the Office of Communications) in December 2003. The ITC was an attempt to introduce market forces into the cosy world of independent television. In 1990 it decided on applications for the new franchises. The ITC was charged with selecting companies on the basis of who would pay the largest annual fee to the government each year, subject to a quality threshold. As a result of the auction Thames TV, TVAM, TVS and TSW lost their franchises and were replaced by new contractors. The Commission also had a quality remit and in the early 1990s reprimanded Carlton Television for the standard of its programming. It also laid down regulations on questions of decency

in advertising and programming. In 1997 it oversaw the introduction of Channel 5 broadcasting.

*See also* Broadcasting Act 1990; Independent Broadcasting Authority; Office of Communications.

## indirect taxation

Taxes upon spending on retail products and services. When most people think of tax they think of direct taxation: the proportion of total income deducted at source by their employer and sent straight to the Inland Revenue. However, taxes upon retail products such as alcoholic beverages, tobacco and petroleum produce huge amounts of money for the Treasury. Value added tax (VAT) amounted to about £50 billion in the late 1990s.

Conservative economists tend to favour indirect taxes, as a consumer can choose not to pay the tax by not buying that particular product. This was one of the reasons why Geoffrey Howe increased VAT substantially, in contradiction to pre-election statements, soon after the Conservatives came to power in 1979. However, consumers will continue to buy certain types of product irrespective of price increases, for example petrol, which is a necessity for motorists in rural areas, ill served by public transport. In 1999/2000, Conservative politicians, among others, started to use the term 'stealth taxes' to describe the increased level of indirect taxation under New Labour.

## industrial democracy

The view that workers should have active participation in the running of their work organisations. Apart from a number of minor and isolated examples, full industrial democracy is unknown in Britain, and even under Labour the nationalised industries did not develop democratic structures for workplace management in anything like the way they did in countries such as postwar Germany. Under New Labour no radical changes have been introduced to the management of private or public organisations.

## industrial relations

Relations between workers and employers. In Britain these have traditionally been fraught because of an 'us and them' set of attitudes based on class antagonisms. Moreover, compared with other European Union countries there is no strong framework of law to regulate this area in Britain. Indeed, traditionally unions enjoyed legal immunities, though not rights, protecting them from being sued for industrial action. Free collective bargaining was extensively practised, with no central machinery for national wage bargaining. Governments have tried with varying degrees of success to introduce a framework for industrial relations: Harold Wilson's *In Place of Strife* was destroyed by union and Labour opposition inside cabinet; Edward Heath's statutory approach (including an industrial relations court) came to nothing and ended with his election defeat in 1974; and James Callaghan's Social Contract was destroyed by the 'winter of discontent' of 1978–79. Riding on public dissatisfaction with Labour's closeness to the unions, Margaret Thatcher won the 1979 general election, and passed legislation curtailing union power and letting market forces decide wages and employee–employer relations. The miners' strike of 1984–85 was a watershed in that it marked the breaking of the industrial muscle of organised labour; power now passed away from the unions and to the employers, and unemployment further weakened the unions through its ability to reduce the willingness of workers to take industrial action. Consequently the number of days lost through strike action fell to record low levels in the 1980s and 1990s. The New Labour government has not repealed Conservative trade union legislation; however, it has passed legislation to make employers recognise trade unions if more than half the employees want one. The government has also signed the Social Chapter, which grants workers certain basic rights and regulates working times.

*See also In Place of Strife*; Industrial Relations Act 1971; Information and Consultation Directive; Social Chapter; Social Contract.

## Industrial Relations Act 1971

An ill-fated piece of legislation intended to solve intractable industrial relations disputes in Britain. It was introduced by the Heath government. It provided a framework of law for unions and established a national industrial relations court. Its legal terms allowed for compulsory recognition of unions, a registration system for unions, legally binding contracts between unions and employers, strike ballots, and cooling off periods during a dispute. The Trades Union Congress condemned the act and unions simply refused to register. Lord Donaldson's Industrial Relations Court was little used and many questioned whether the law could adjudicate over wages and conditions of work. The Wilson government of 1974 repealed the act.

## Industrial Revolution

A term applied to the period 1750–1850 and usually associated with Arnold Toynbee's lectures in the 1880s. Historians still debate the precise causes but the symptoms began with a move of labour away from the land, as it underwent enclosure and a drive for agricultural efficiency, into the towns. Combined with this a series of inventions, for example Arkwright's 'spinning jenny' and Crompton's 'mule', made textile manufacturing more efficient and profitable. Moreover, the availability of accumulated capital in the hands of merchants and aristocrats enabled these inventions and others, such as the steam engine, to be disseminated throughout the British economy. Other important factors include the availability of economic markets for textiles and the rapidly improving infrastructure of roads and canals. There is no single or even multiple group of reasons to explain the Industrial Revolution, except perhaps for the fact that all these factors happened simultaneously and interacted. The effect of this economic revolution was to move the balance of economic, and hence political, power from the landed gentry to the industrialist middle classes. The creation of a huge urban proletariat also provided concentrated masses of population, who responded to calls for greater democracy which followed from the French and American Revolutions.

By 2000 many economic historians spoke of a post-industrial age, where, in the west, manufacturing has given way to new 'sunrise' industries in the service sector – computers and telecommunications being two of the most important.

## industrialism

A term used by Jonathan Porritt in *Seeing Green* (1984) to describe the consensus between the major parties on the need for economic growth. The ecologist sees such development as injurious to humankind's interests in that it encourages the over-consumption of resources. 'Industrialism' continues unabated in the 2000s, with pollution and environmental destruction. Green thinking, in all its guises, urges the adoption of an alternative set of policies, including sustainable economic growth, with low-energy, low-consumption strategies and the decentralisation of decision making.

*See also* Green Party; green thinking.

## inequality (economic)

When the share of national income earned by the richest 20 per cent of the population is divided by that of the poorest 20 per cent, an index of inequality is achieved: the higher the figure, the greater the inequality. According to this, Britain, in 1996, managed a figure of 9.6, higher than the USA (8.9), Germany (5.8), Denmark (7.1) and Sweden (4.5). In 1997, 24 per cent of all workers in Britain earned less than £4 per hour and 8 per cent less than £3. Compared with other countries Britain was second only to New Zealand in the growth of economic inequality during the period 1977–90. Some have suggested that one of the results of this development has been the growth in Britain of an underclass. Figures from the Department of Social Security's Family Expenditure Survey (15 October 1998) revealed that the proportion of people living on less than half the average income, a widely accepted

measure of poverty, had increased to 24 per cent. During the Thatcher administrations numbers below the line tripled but these fell back after John Major came to power. The gulf began to reopen, however, after 1995, despite the improvement in the nation's economic performance. From 1979 to 1997 average incomes grew 44 per cent in real terms after allowing for housing costs. However, the top tenth of earners gained a 70 per cent increase, while the poorest tenth suffered a drop in real income by 9 per cent. Debate exists over absolute poverty and relative poverty: the Conservatives stress that, in absolute terms, poverty as known in the 19th century has been abolished. However, those on the left, and many sociologists who specialise in this area, point out that relative poverty is the more realistic index, since it draws attention to people being excluded from participation in activities which many in society enjoy, for example going on an annual holiday, or having a balanced and varied diet.

*See also* poverty; social exclusion.

## inequality (gender)

Differences of wealth and opportunity which disadvantage women. Reports in February 2000 and January 2001 from the London School of Economics claimed that women in Britain earned on average £250,000 less than men during their lifetimes. This is because women tend to be concentrated in low-paid jobs and because they are often paid less than men for doing the same work. Women working full-time earned 84 per cent of male earnings for the same jobs while part-timers earned only 58 per cent. The Equal Opportunities Commission reported also that women are routinely denied access to bonus payments and pension schemes.

## inflation

Defined by most economists as continuous rises in prices across the whole economy over a relatively short period. In addition to economic problems such as uncertainly for business and investors, inflation can, as the German Weimar Republic demonstrated,

erode democratic institutions and lead
to extremist politics. In Britain after the
Second World War inflation was generally
low but the growth of union power in the
1970s, the maintenance of full employment
and the oil price rises of the early 1970s
created pressures which pushed up wages
as well as prices. The result was a rate
of inflation which exceeded 25 per cent
per annum in 1975. The Social Contract
agreement between government and the
unions brought this down to below 10 per
cent by 1978 but by then faith in Labour
had evaporated and the Conservatives came
into power in 1979. Margaret Thatcher
attacked inflation through confronting the
unions and the imposition of high interest
rates but it still hit double figures in 1980
and 1990 and ran ahead of that of other
European economies. Since the early
1990s it has levelled out at below 4 per cent
per annum. The credibility of a government rests on the electorate perceiving it
as a sound economic manager and thus it
is no surprise that New Labour has been
assiduous in fostering an image of a sound
manager of the nation's finances, with
Gordon Brown being characterised as the
'Iron chancellor'. Indeed, his stewardship
of the economy – aided by the Monetary
Policy Committee's control of the inflation
via interest rates – has produced for Britain
the lowest inflation rate in the European
Union, at around 2 per cent per annum.

## Information and Consultation Directive, 2001

A directive issued by the European Union.
Writing in the *Observer* (17 June 2001)
Will Hutton described the introduction of
this directive as an 'earthquake'. It means
that British employers now have to consult
workers, not just on redundancies but on
'every strategic and financial development of
their organisations'. Similar attempts to introduce consultation were rejected by union
leaders in the 1970s as a 'sell-out' to capitalism. Hutton reflected that the unions had
lost their 'negative, oppositional power; what
they have won is integrated positive power'.
The Confederation of British Industry

proved wary of the directive and criticised
it, though its own survey in summer 2001
of 673 firms revealed that 40 per cent had
adopted some form of consultation already.

## information commissioner

www.informationcommissioner.gov.uk
Official set up by the Freedom of
Information Act 2000. The post incor-
porates that of the role of the previous data
protection registrar, namely to 'promote
good information handling and enforcing Data Protection and Freedom of
Information legislation'. On 16 August
2004 information commissioner Richard
Thomas warned that three developments
threatened to nudge Britain a little too
far towards a 'Big Brother' state – the
dystopian view of a wholly controlled society envisaged in Orwell's novel *Nineteen
Eighty-Four*. They were: David Blunkett's
identity card proposal; a separate population register planned by the Office for
National Statistics; and the proposals for
a database of all children from birth to age
18.

> [The proposals] enable the government to
> build up quite a comprehensive picture about
> many of your activities. My job is to make
> sure no more is collected than necessary for
> any particular purpose. (Richard Thomas)

## Inland Revenue

www.inlandrevenue.gov.uk
The government department which collects
and controls income tax, together with other
direct taxes, like fuel excise duties, capital
gains and corporation tax. Its Valuation
Agency assesses property for council tax
valuation purposes. In 1998–99 it collected
£84.3 billion in income tax and £30.0 billion in corporation tax.

## 'inner' cabinet

A small group of ministerial colleagues who
offer the prime minister advice. Every premier, records show, since Robert Walpole
has developed one. After 1945, Clement
Attlee relied on Ernest Bevin, Herbert
Morrison and Stafford Cripps. Margaret

Thatcher in the early 1980s looked to John Biffen, John Nott, Geoffrey Howe and Keith Joseph. Tony Blair, unsurprisingly, includes Gordon Brown and John Prescott in his inner cabinet.

## inner city

Urban residential area close to the centre and often characterised by poverty and crime. In the early years of the Industrial Revolution much economic activity grew close to centres of settlement, especially in the northern industrial areas of England. As the economy grew, factories moved further afield from what had become cities, with the original centres taking on administrative and shopping functions. The cheap housing originally used by industrial workers became run down and occupied by lower income earners and immigrant groups. Consequently these areas developed problems caused by poverty, poor housing and racial tension. In the 1980s unemployment exacerbated such problems and riots broke out in major cities like Manchester, Liverpool and Leeds, as well as London. After her 1987 election victory Margaret Thatcher declared she would solve the problems of the inner cities, but they were only marginally ameliorated and remained a problem well into the new millennium, despite strenuous attempts at urban regeneration by local authorities and central government, even with European Union funds.

## inquiry

Investigation undertaken under the aegis of government. Tony Blair's New Labour government seemed to specialise in inquiries into virtually everything. Such activities are useful to politicians in that: they can genuinely identify good policy options; they can buy time; and they can take the heat out of an issue by providing the appearance of action plus the excuse not to comment while the inquiry is doing its work. The Saville inquiry into Bloody Sunday was drawn out and hugely expensive and Blair's government preferred shorter, more focused inquiries, like those chaired by Hutton

and Macpherson. However, such initiatives carry risks: reports can criticise, like Macpherson's claim that the police were guilty of 'institutional racism', something about which the government could do little. In February 2004 the Public Administration Committee decided to make a study of inquiries, so numerous had they become. One possible reason was that the Hutton inquiry had been able to obtain many more documents than the Foreign Affairs Select Committee, which actually had superior legal powers.

*See also* royal commission; select committee.

## insider group

A term invented by Wyn Grant of Warwick University to describe pressure group proximity to government decision making. Insider groups have been drawn into the process of government itself and a classic example is the link established during the Second World War between the National Farmers' Union and the Ministry of Agriculture, Fisheries and Food.

*See also* outsider group; pressure group.

## Institute for Public Policy Research (IPPR)
www.ippr.org.uk
A think tank founded in 1986 by 'leading figures in the academic, business and trade union community to provide an alternative to free market think-tanks'. It has produced blueprints for New Labour policy but has also trodden on previously forbidden ground, for example by suggesting in 1992 that universal welfare benefits might be profitably replaced with targeted ones. Its one-time director was Patricia Hewitt, a former advisor to Neil Kinnock and later a government minister.

## Institute of Directors
www.iod.co.uk
A right-wing think tank with campaigning tendencies. It opposed prices and incomes restraints when the Confederation of British Industry (CBI) was prepared to accept them. It enthusiastically supported

POLITICS

Conservative policies of privatisation, reducing public spending and freeing up economic markets. In fact it still holds true to a Thatcherite set of economic policies, although the influence of all think tanks declined towards the end of the Conservative period of rule, largely because most of their aims had been achieved and partly because of spectacular failures like the poll tax, which originated in think tank deliberations.

### Institute of Economic Affairs (IEA)
www.iea.org.uk
Set up in 1955 to advance then unfashionable right-wing economic ideas. It was a bitter critic of the public sector, which it saw as the child of vote-courting politicians and sectional interests. The IEA was especially important in giving a wider audience to the ideas of Friedrich von Hayek and Milton Friedman. It argued that the role of government should be limited to providing essential services like defence and clean air; all else can be provided by market forces. Some of its more controversial policies included the wholesale privatisation of health and education.

### institutionalised racism
*See* Macpherson report.

### Intelligence and Security Committee
www.cabinet-office.gov.uk/intelligence
Body established by the Intelligence Services Act 1994 to examine the 'expenditure, administration and policy of the Security Service, SIS and GCHQ'. The Committee comprises nine members drawn from both houses. They are appointed by the prime minister in association with the leader of the opposition. It reports annually to the prime minister, who then lays the report before parliament. In May 2003 the Committee was tasked with investigating the intelligence on which Tony Blair based his case to make war on Iraq. Critics complained the Committee was too much in the gift of the prime minister and therefore not sufficiently independent.
*See also* security services.

### intelligence services
*See* security services.

### intelligence services commissioner
Official tasked with authorising intrusive surveillance and interference with property. The post was established under section 59(1) of the Regulation of Investigatory Powers Act 2000. The commissioner – a person who has held high judicial office – has the job of ensuring warrants issued by the secretary of state to undertake intrusive surveillance are done so on a proper basis. The commissioner submits a report to the prime minister once a year, which is also laid before parliament. Lord Robin Justice Brown was reappointed from April 2003 for a further three-year term.

### interest group
*See* pressure group.

### interest rate
A key instrument in economic management since the interest rate influences the speed of economic growth and the rate of inflation. Businesses rely on borrowing money to install new machinery, set up new enterprises and to survive downturns in economic activity. Most economists accept that increasing interest rates tend to reduce inflation through reducing the amount of money in circulation, as they make borrowing more expensive. However, sharp increases also push businesses into debt and sometimes bankruptcy. This happened on a massive scale in the early 1980s, when the Conservative government pushed up rates to counteract inflation. One of the side-effects of high rates is that the pound becomes more attractive to foreign investors. This in turn pushes up the exchange rate of sterling with the result that exports become more expensive to overseas buyers, making British goods less competitive. High interest rates also caused a deep recession in the early 1990s when chancellor Norman Lamont used them to bring down inflation and maintain sterling's exchange rate in the European Monetary System (EMS); this was successful eventually in quelling inflation but only

at a high economic cost in terms of business failures and mortgage repossessions. When Labour won its 1997 victory one of the first actions of chancellor Gordon Brown was to give control over interest rates to the Monetary Policy Committee (MPC) of the Bank of England in the hope that purely economic criteria would be applied, thus ensuring long-term low inflation. Brown has been successful, through such devices, in keeping the British rate of inflation either under or close to 2.5 per cent since 1997. The correct interest rate for the British economy is a crucial factor in relation to the debate over the country's joining the single European currency.

*See also* euro; European Monetary System; inflation; Monetary Policy Committee.

## International Monetary Fund (IMF)
www.imf.org
Established by the 1944 Bretton Woods agreement as part of the United Nations. It aims to facilitate world trade and payments between nations. The IMF also provides standby loans for members who face problems with a balance of payments deficit but they usually have to implement remedial measures as the quid pro quo. In 1976 chancellor Denis Healey was forced to seek a substantial loan from the IMF to tide the country through a bad economic period; he had to accept conditions including cuts in public expenditure, limits on incomes and monetary growth. Economists point to this date as one of the first uses of monetarism.

## internationalism
A view of international politics which claims its major problems can be solved through cooperative action by states. Radical Liberals like J. A. Hobson, Norman Angel, E. D. Morel, H. N. Brailsford and Charles Trevelyan elaborated a critique of the international system in the early part of the 20th century which focused on secret diplomacy, imperialist competition for markets, balance-of-power policies and the arms trade. The antidote offered to such shortcomings

was often couched in terms of strong international institutions. Such ideas helped to form the League of Nations in 1919 but it was seen as feeble indeed by the mid-1930s and it failed to prevent the rise of Hitler. The United Nations, which was formed in 1945, was a more carefully constructed body but has been only marginally more successful than its predecessor. However, many commentators on international affairs still insist that the only hope for the world is through greater cooperation by all states.

## Internet
A worldwide network of computers linked together. Its origins lay in the US defence community's need for computers to talk to each other. Since then the system has expanded and in the past decade has become of increasing importance as a source of information and exchange, not least because it has no central source or controlling authority, although service providers are legally liable for breaches of criminal or civil law. British political parties have not been slow to try to exploit the 'net' for communicating with members of the public and supporters; a special feature of Labour's website is the opportunity for party members to give their opinion on developments in policy making. As part of its programme of modernising government, government departments and Number 10 have their own web pages, which provide information for the general public and students of politics.

*See also* mass media; virtual politics.

## internment
During the Second World War some foreign nationals, not to mention the British fascist leader Sir Oswald Mosley, suspected of loyalty to Germany, were held in internment camps. The device was used again in the early 1970s in Northern Ireland when IRA suspects were held without trial, but the backlash against it in the nationalist community was such that it was deemed to have been unsuccessful. In the wake of the Good Friday Agreement, a bomb explosion in Omagh in August 1998 awakened calls for internment to be reintroduced.

## inward investment

Capital investment by overseas companies. Attracting such investment from the likes of Japan and the USA has been a policy successfully pursued by both Conservative and Labour governments over the last three decades. Such activity benefits employment substantially and also has the effect of improving the productivity of business elsewhere, as foreign-owned firms produce 40 per cent more per worker than native businesses. According to *The Economist* (14 July 2001) inward investment was not damaged by Britain's absence from the euro: for the two years after the currency's creation in 1999, inward investment was buoyant, at £86 billion in 2000, and the stock of inward investment was worth about a fifth of gross domestic product. In 2001, moreover, it leapt to more than a third. In July 2003 Patricia Hewitt, the trade and industry secretary, announced that during 2002–03 709 new projects had resulted from inward investment and 34,000 new jobs.

## Ireland

England's first involvement with Ireland began in 1171, when Henry II invaded the island. Thereafter it became a country substantially owned by absentee landlords living in England. English settlement occurred in the prosperous parts of the country and the Irish were forced to live in the less fertile regions, such as upland and bog areas. For centuries Ireland remained a land simmering with conflict and rebellion and became more so after the plantation policies in which Catholic Irish tenants were replaced with those of English or Scottish descent, usually Protestant. Disaffected Gaelic leadership threw in their lot with the enemies of England and this led to several invasions and repressive measures. There was a rebellion in 1641, savagely put down by Oliver Cromwell, especially at Drogheda and Wexford, where thousands were put to the sword. Catholic landowners were dispossessed and expelled and excluded from sitting in the Irish parliament. In 1800 the Act of Union was passed, which united the Britain and Ireland from January 1801. In the 19th century the decision of Irish MPs sitting in the Commons to campaign for Home Rule dominated much domestic debate. Gladstone decided to give Home Rule to Ireland but the plan was never implemented and the First World War intervened. After the war the Protestant minority demanded and received six northern counties as their own homeland, thus creating the still ongoing problem of Northern Ireland, while the 26 southern counties achieved independence. In 1949 Ireland became a republic and left the Commonwealth.

*See also* Northern Ireland.

## Irish National Liberation Army (INLA)

Militant nationalist paramilitary organisation. In 1975 after the IRA declared a cease-fire a third of the membership of the official IRA broke away to form the INLA. Its first high-profile victim was Airey Neave in 1979. The splinter group proved vulnerable to internal disputes and several members died in bloody reprisal killings. In 1980 it killed 17 people in Derry in the Drop In Well disco; in 1981 three INLA prisoners were among the 10 who starved themselves to death in the Maze Prison; in 1982 it killed more people than the IRA itself; in 1995 its former chief, Hugh Turney, declared a cease-fire from the dock of a Dublin court; in December 1997 its members shot Billy Wright, leader of the Loyalist Volunteer Force, inside the Maze; finally, in August 1998 the INLA declared a cease-fire in recognition of the changed situation in the province as evidenced by the referendum in favour of peace.

*See also* Irish Republican Army.

## Irish Republican Army (IRA)

Militant nationalist paramilitary organisation. The IRA is a body of the political party Sinn Fein, both of which are dedicated to a united Ireland and were long prepared to use violence to achieve this. Founded in 1919 by Michael Collins, it prosecuted a successful war against the occupying power in 1919–21. It took a back seat for several decades and was militarily inactive between 1962 and 1969, although it did pursue a programme of Marxist-inspired social agitation. The more radical Provisional IRA split away from the Official IRA in 1970 and henceforth pursued an aggressive military campaign against the Royal Ulster Constabulary (RUC) and the British army; it also engaged in some 'policing' of Catholic areas. Violence reached a climax in 1972 with a brutal campaign of bombing on the British mainland. In the 1980s violence declined and but there was another mainland campaign in London and Manchester in the mid-1990s. The IRA and Sinn Fein agreed the Good Friday Agreement in April 1998. The IRA remained, however, and insisted on retaining its weapons, albeit 'putting them beyond use' in arms dumps that were subject to inspection by the de Chastelain commission (the Independent International Commission on Decommissioning).

See also Irish National Liberation Army; Provisional IRA; Real IRA;

## iron law of oligarchy

A theory developed by the German sociologist Robert Michels, who argued that socialist political parties would be controlled by a small powerful elite who were dedicated to retaining power despite the existence of democratic structures and claims of internal democracy. Although based upon the self-evident truths of classical elite theory, the 'law' raises questions about the degree of internal party democracy which has existed in various periods of Labour Party history.

## Islamic Party of Britain

www.islamicparty.com
Founded by David Musa Pidcock in 1989 to help campaign against Salman Rushdie's novel *Satanic Verses*. It also campaigned for state funding for Muslim schools. The

party fielded four candidates in the 1992 election; however, it mustered a mere 1,085 votes.

## Isle of Man

Crown dependency off the coast of north-western England. It remained Norwegian until 1266, then was Scottish until it was ceded to Britain in 1765. It has a legislative council, a lieutenant governor and the representative House of Keys, which together make up the Court of Tynwald. It passes laws subject to the royal assent. Westminster laws affect it only if specifically so stated in the statute.

## issue voting

Voting for candidates on the basis of their stance on particular issues. In the postwar period, British voters traditionally reflected class loyalties, but from the 1960s onwards psephologists noted that the degree of class loyalty was declining and that people were voting more and more on the basis of key issues. The rise of issue voting is associated with a number of developments, including the fragmentation of the electorate into 'market segments' based on housing tenure and consumption patterns, the growing impact of the mass media on voters' decision making and the decline of the ideological or class party. Furthermore, the political scientist Ivor Crewe delineates 'salience' – the extent to which people are aware of an issue – and 'party preferred' in terms of policies on that issue.

Issues vary according to elections; in October 1974 it was mainly prices but in 1983 it was unemployment. Defence has seldom been a key issue but was in the post-Falklands 1983 election. In August 2004 the *Guardian*'s ICM poll showed that, of the 10 most important issues facing voters, health and education were close to the top, while Iraq and the European Union were 8th and 10th, respectively.

See also catch-all party; political marketing.

POLITICS

# J

## Jenkins report, 1998

Report of the Independent Commission on
Voting Reform. Lord Jenkins of Hillhead
was asked by Tony Blair to chair the
Commission, to find an alternative which
achieved proportionality, stability, extension of voter choice and maintained the link
between MP and constituency. Studies
calculated that there were long periods
when the voting system worked strongly
against one side or the other. Between 1945
and 1970, it worked for the Conservatives:
Labour piled up votes in safe constituencies but failed to muster enough votes in the
decisive marginal constituencies. However,
the bias moved in favour of Labour, with
a vengeance, in the 1990s. In 1992 the
Conservatives received a similar percentage
of the vote to Labour in 1997, yet enjoyed a
majority of only 21 compared with Labour's
179. Indeed, if the two parties had received
an equal number of votes in 1992, Labour
would have had a majority of over 80.
Jenkins explained the reasons for this bias:
Labour benefited from the over-representa-
tion of seats in Scotland and Wales; the
Liberal Democrat electors voted tactically
to keep the Tories out; some constituencies were unequally populated in England
and the Boundary Commission always
runs a few years behind such shifts; and
Labour wins a high proportion of low-poll-
ing inner-city seats, which gives it a higher
ratio of seats to votes than the Tories. An
alternative voting system would have much
to offer the Tories, but they prefer to stick
with the existing system of first past the
post. Jenkins recommended the alternative
vote (AV) 'top-up' – a system combining
the German additional member system with
the existing first past the post system. The
Commission suggested that 85–90 per cent
of seats should be elected in single-member
constituencies via the alternative vote and
the rest to act as top-up seats drawn from
80 special constituencies, to be used to
make the overall result more proportional.
Initially it seemed a referendum would be
held to discover whether the country wanted
to change its voting system and the Liberal
Democrats became optimistic of finally
gaining a regular place in government. But
Labour's landslide in 1997 convinced many
MPs they could continue to win majorities,
and experience of coalition government in
Scotland and Wales highlighted some of
the problems which proportional representation can usher in.

## jerrymandering
*See* gerrymandering.

## 'joined up' government
Phrase introduced by the New Labour government after 1997 to describe governing in
a way which showed regard and awareness
for what was being done by other parts of
the government machine. Naturally, New
Labour has argued that it achieved this
ideal in practice.

## Joint Intelligence Committee (JIC)
The committee which coordinates intelligence from Government Communications
Headquarters (GCHQ) and other
agencies, such as MI5. It decides what
the national requirements of the intelligence services are and then sets about
meeting them via the agencies concerned;
this work also involves liaison with foreign
intelligence services, for example the US
Central Intelligence Agency (CIA). The
person who takes the lead on this is the
intelligence coordinator. The JIC and
its head were forced out of the shadows
of national life in the summer of 2003
when the Hutton inquiry summoned John
Scarlett to give evidence on the circumstances leading to the death of Dr David
Kelly. The role of the JIC in the production
of the intelligence-based dossier on Iraq's
weapons of mass destruction published in
September 2002 was investigated in detail.
Hutton's report cleared Scarlett but some
suspicions remained that he had been over-
accommodating of the political priorities of
Number 10. Significantly, in the wake of

the Hutton report, another inquiry – this time into the intelligence services themselves – was set in train under the chairmanship of the former cabinet secretary Lord (Robin) Butler.

## joint select committee

Set up by the two houses of parliament on particular subjects. For instance, in July 2002 a joint committee was appointed to consider the future of the House of Lords. Members of a joint committee are usually chosen in equal numbers by the respective houses.

## Jopling report, 1992

Report (*Sittings in the House*) of a committee chaired by a former Conservative cabinet member. It recommended for the Commons a reduction of late-night and Friday sessions and that morning sessions take place on Wednesdays. These changes were introduced in 1994 and, according to political scientist Philip Norton, 'provided a somewhat more rational timetable for plenary sessions and reduced pressure on the floor'.

## judge

There are more than 11,000 full-time and 2,000 part-time judges, with the lord chancellor being the most senior judge of all. The hierarchy from this office downwards entails: Lord of Appeal in Ordinary (House of Lords); Lord Justice of Appeal (Court of Appeal); High Court judge (High Court); circuit judge (crown or county court); recorder (crown court). Judges are drawn almost exclusively from the ranks of barristers of at least 10 years' standing, though more recently solicitors can also become High Court judges. Appointments are advertised publicly and made by the lord chancellor from the relatively small pool of senior barristers. Information on likely candidates is stored in the Lord Chancellor's Department. Lord Irvine defended this subjective system as 'unrivalled in its breadth and thoroughness', but it has its critics and the selection system is changing.

The distinguished law professor J. A. G. Griffith alleged that judges were drawn

from an overly exclusive social background and were predominantly male and elderly (judges do not have to retire until aged 70). In 1998 only 8 out of 143 senior judges were female and only one was not white. Over 80 per cent went to public school and a majority went to Oxford or Cambridge. Critics claim judges are out of touch with the rest of society and their occasional ignorance, when expressed in court, causes them to lose public respect. Defenders of the present system dismiss this critique as a caricature. They argue the best legal brains tend to rise to the top and should take up senior places irrespective of background; they argue a public school Oxbridge background in no way precludes the ability to reach independent and balanced judgements.

In December 1999 Sir Leonard Peach reported on his Independent Scrutiny of Appointment Processes for Judges and QCs. He recommended the introduction of a commissioner for judicial appointments to advise on appointments and audit the process. This was set up in 2001 with a brief to handle complaints arising from judicial appointments. A Judicial Appointments Commission (similarly named but different) was proposed in the Constitutional Reform Bill being considered by the Lords in the summer of 2004. The Commission would comprise: five judges, two professional lawyers, six lay people, one tribunal member and one magistrate. This body, it is envisaged, will recommend names for appointment as judges to the secretary of state for constitutional affairs.

On 1 July 2004 the new Commission for Judicial Appointments reported on its first ever investigation of senior judicial appointments made under the old system during 2003. It found 'substantial inequalities in the treatment of the candidates' with a 'substantial inbuilt bias' in favour of QCs and against solicitors and circuit judges seeking promotion to the High Court bench.

## judicial review

The ability of judges to call government and other statutory authorities to account if they exceed their statutory powers. This is also sometimes called 'judicial activism'. The cases are heard by the Administrative Court of the Divisional Court of the Queen's Bench Division. During the 1970s there were four cases where the courts found Labour ministers had exceeded their powers. Equally, they found against several Conservative ministers in the 1980s and early 1990s, especially Michael Howard as home secretary (1993–97). This willingness has encouraged individuals to apply for judicial review; in the early 1980s there were 500 a year but by 1990 there were 2,000 and by 1994 there were 3,208. Increasingly the courts have taken on an assertive role in relation to the executive, insisting on interpreting the law in a way which defends the rights of the individual and enhances the role of the judiciary. The government can, if it so wishes, overrule the courts by changing the law but there are penalties attached to this course of action, not least the signal that it is 'moving the goalposts'. In most cases it accepts the judgement with the best grace it can muster.

**judiciary**
Perhaps a neglected aspect of British government in that it has always been seen as subordinate to parliament. Judges are currently appointed by the lord chancellor, a political appointee, as the head of the judiciary (though the situation is due to change), and parliament has sovereign authority in terms of what it may pass into law. However, the judiciary has a degree of independence in terms of security of tenure in appointments and judicial review. This has opened a new area in which the courts find themselves 'checking' the executive and providing new interpretations of the law, although to nothing like the extent which is possible in the constitutionally entrenched Supreme Court of the United States. The embodiment of the European Convention on Human Rights into British law in October 2000 was a major development, because although judges cannot strike down parliamentary statutes, senior British judges now have a power of legal interpretation hitherto unknown in the

British political system. The legal hierarchy begins with the magistrates at the bottom, then up to the county and crown courts, followed by the High Court with its three divisions of Family, Chancery and Queen's Bench. From there the next tier up is the Court of Appeal with its Criminal and Civil Divisions, topped off by the House of Lords Appellate Committee.

In June 2003 Tony Blair in a cabinet reshuffle dropped his former mentor Lord Irvine as lord chancellor and replaced him with a former flatmate, Lord Falconer, as secretary of state for constitutional affairs in charge of the old Lord Chancellor's Department and also the residual responsibilities of the Welsh and Scottish secretaries. Falconer was to hold his new title along with the lord chancellorship until the latter was phased out. So the 1,400-year history of the lord chancellor's office was effectively ended. While there was much criticism of this changing of the constitution through a reshuffle, few contested that the office, with its foot in the legislature, via the Lords, and the executive, via the cabinet, was an anomaly in need of removal.

See also judge; judicial review.

**jury**
Introduced by the Normans as a means of determining the guilt or innocence of the accused. The jury was developed, mainly in English-speaking countries, into a panel of usually 12 citizens chosen at random from the electoral register. In an English or Welsh court a jury can reach a verdict by a 10–2 majority. In Scotland a jury has 15 members and can return a verdict of 'not proven'. In the late 1990s moves began to be made to reduce the option of a jury trial for certain types of crime. Such a measure was proposed in the Auld report into the criminal justice system in 2001. However, many senior judicial figures spoke out against this proposal and eventually it was dropped in January 2002, though it was reintroduced for certain categories of criminal charge by the Criminal Justice Act 2003.

See also Auld report.

## Justice and Home Affairs
One of the three 'pillars' of the European Union (EU). It covers such areas as asylum, immigration, drug addiction, international fraud and terrorism. The other two 'pillars' of the EU are the European Community and the Common Foreign and Security Policy.

## justice of the peace (JP)
*See* magistrates' court.

## Keep Left
Group on the left wing of the Parliamentary Labour Party which formed in 1947, led by Michael Foot, Richard Crossman and Ian Mikardo. It urged a more independent foreign policy from the USA and favoured an alternative approach based on social democracy rather than US capitalism or Soviet communism. Elements of this group and its near successor, Keeping Left, went on to support Aneurin Bevan's unsuccessful bid for the party's leadership in the 1950s.

## Keynesianism
Theory of macro-economics developed by the British economist John Maynard Keynes and set out in *The General Theory of Employment, Interest and Money* (1936). This overthrew economic orthodoxy by arguing that, when the economy was in recession, the government ought to spend or invest money to stimulate the economy and boost demand. Similarly it suggested that governments should use the instruments of taxation (fiscal policy) and interest rates (monetary policy) to manipulate demand within the economy to sustain growth and deter recession. In one of his most memorable phrases he called for a 'comprehensive socialisation of investment' as a prerequisite

for full employment. However, he was no socialist, since he argued that full employment could be achieved by a partnership between the public and the private sector, a phrase echoed in the language of the New Labour government elected in 1997.

## Kilmuir guidelines
Advice to judges issued in 1955 by Lord Kilmuir that they should not make any overt political or partisan comment in recognition of their sensitive position as members of the judiciary. Kilmuir was a distinguished Conservative lord chancellor. The guidelines were relaxed in 1970 but reimposed by Lord Hailsham as the lord chancellor in 1980, as he felt politicians and judges should stick to their own spheres. In recent years, some judges (notably Judge Pickles of the northern circuit) have become short-term celebrities by airing their views in the media.

## kitchen cabinet
Name popularly given to the small group of advisors based in 10 Downing Street. It originated with the advisors to Harold Wilson in the 1960s, most notably Joe Haines (press secretary) and Marcia Williams (personal secretary). Today it is usually considered to include the press secretary, the chief of staff and in addition, possibly, the Policy Unit, which can include over a dozen advisors (nearly 30 special advisors are based in Number 10). By this definition, Tony Blair's corps of unelected advisors requires somewhat more accommodation than is afforded by the normal-sized kitchen.
*See also* cabinet; 'inner cabinet'.

## Kosovo crisis, 1999–2000
Balkan war in which Britain became a prominent player through its NATO role. Kosovo is the southern section of the Yugoslavia Federation and includes a majority of people with Albanian origins. This majority was keen to win independence from the Federation and the Kosovo Liberation Army (KLA) had sprung up by 1999. Slobodan Milosevic used the

POLITICS

KLA as an excuse to use Serbian forces to quell Kosovo, a region with special resonance to most Serbians. Regular army units were augmented by irregulars, some of whom had seen service in Bosnia. Atrocities soon began to happen as the Kosovan Albanians were driven from their homes. British politicians began to call for NATO troops to defend the Kosovans. Eventually a NATO force was assembled and air strikes began to be made against Serb targets in Kosovo and Serbia. The conflict seemed to be interminable but when Russia withdrew support for Milosevic he was persuaded to back down. Tony Blair, Robin Cook (foreign secretary) and George Robertson (secretary of state for defence), the British politicians most involved, received considerable credit for their resolution during a conflict which seemed not to advance significant British interests.

**Kyoto Protocol, 1997**
Agreement reached by industrialised nations to reduce emissions of carbon dioxide to below 1990 levels by the year 2012. Britain was one of the prime movers in this agreement, via John Prescott. He was less successful at making the agreement stick when another summit on global warming, convened by the European Union at The Hague in 2000, foundered on US reluctance to be bound by Kyoto. George W. Bush refused to accept the phenomenon of global warming while campaigning for the presidency but in 2001 reversed his position when scientific reports proved it beyond any doubt. Critics argue he was merely defending the interests of the oil industry. When visiting Britain in July 2001 he argued that the USA could not support any agreement which harmed its economy and threatened employment. In July 2001 an attempt was made to save Kyoto at a meeting in Bonn convened by the United Nations. After several days of non-stop negotiating, an agreement was reached which was legally binding. Despite rejection by the USA, the Kyoto Protocol had been resuscitated and endorsed by many of the world's nations. The Bonn agreement was a triumph for the

European Union and a slap in the face for the USA, whose delegate was booed as she read out a statement. Michael Meacher for Britain hailed a 'historic day'.

The protocol needed to be ratified by 55 nations – together accounting for 55 per cent of the world's carbon dioxide emissions – to come into force. Without the participation of the USA this target is impossible to reach. Britain has 1 per cent of the world's population but produces 2.3 per cent of its carbon dioxide emissions. The USA has 4 per cent of world population yet produces 36 per cent of its emissions (*The Times*, 23 July 2001).

# L

**Labour Coordinating Committee**
A left-wing group which led the party's move to the left in the 1970s, and created, along with other factors, the conditions for the intra-party conflict of the early 1980s. However, in the mid-1980s the grouping helped Neil Kinnock start the process of moving the party into the centre and ceased to be such an important player in left-wing politics.

**'Labour isn't working'**
Slogan on a billboard poster designed in August 1978 by Saatchi and Saatchi, depicting a dole queue. It was later used in the 1979 election campaign to communicate the idea that the Labour government of 1974–79 was responsible for rising unemployment. Its significance lies in the fact that it is an early example of the Conservatives' use of commercially inspired techniques of election campaigning.

**labour movement**
Groups of the skilled and unskilled working class, who since the 19th century have advanced their economic, social and

political interests through trade union organisation. The principal vehicle for political action has been through the Labour Representation Committee (1900) and the Labour Party (1906) and as such the movement has been committed to a non-violent, social reformist approach to change, rather than the revolutionary one seen at times elsewhere in Europe. The movement has undergone significant change in recent years, including a decline in trade union membership since 1979 and the fragmentation of the working class, most notably the development of, according to political scientist Ivor Crewe, a new working class, who work in the private sector, are non-union members, live in the south of England and who do not have a 'natural' loyalty to the Labour Party. Under Tony Blair, New Labour has distanced itself from the trade unions, and thus the labour movement, but many institutional and emotional connections remain, notwithstanding.

## Labour Party
www.labour.org.uk
Formed in 1906, when the Labour Representation Committee was renamed. The party was given a constitution in 1918, drafted by Sidney Webb, which committed it to socialism via nationalisation. An electoral pact with the Liberals in 1903 gave the embryonic party 29 seats in 1906. In 1918 it gained 63 seats and in 1923 191 seats, when Ramsay MacDonald formed a 10-month minority government. In 1929 MacDonald was returned again as a minority leader but he was unable to find a solution to the acute economic depression and when he made a deal with the Conservatives his party split and he became prime minister in a national government; the majority of the remaining Labour MPs went into opposition. In the ensuing 1931 general election Labour won only 52 seats, and remained in opposition for a decade, when it supported opposition to fascism in Spain and Germany. George Lansbury was leader until 1935 but Clement Attlee took over soon afterwards. During the Second World War Labour

and the Conservatives formed the national government led by Winston Churchill and Clement Attlee. In 1945 Labour won by a landslide of 393 to 213 and implemented a programme of nationalisation of the main utilities and the development of social services, including the National Health Service in 1948. The government faced shortages and introduced austerity measures to combat them but the nation's enthusiasm for socialism waned and Labour scraped home by a thin margin in 1950. By 1951 the leadership was exhausted and the election in 1951 saw the party defeated, although it obtained its highest ever number of votes, at 13.9 million. Thirteen years of opposition followed, during which the party suffered internal conflicts over defence, with Aneurin Bevan mounting a divisive challenge to the leadership of Hugh Gaitskell. In 1964 Harold Wilson won a narrow general election victory over Alec Douglas-Home and in 1966 a much larger one over Edward Heath – by over 100 seats. During this period the Labour government was dogged by economic problems of devaluation, balance of payments and strikes. Left-wing dissenters harried it over its support for US involvement in Vietnam and prevented reform of the unions taking place in the later part of the decade. In 1970 Heath won a surprise victory. In opposition Wilson adopted a cooler position over Britain's membership of the European Economic Community and Europe as a whole, which he reversed once back in office in 1974. However, in 1976 he resigned as prime minister and James Callaghan took over. Despite his assured leadership the country was forced to borrow heavily from the International Monetary Fund and reduced inflation only via wage deals with the unions and huge cuts in public spending. When the unions refused to accept a 5 per cent pay norm in 1978 the stage was set for the 'winter of discontent', which destroyed Labour's credibility and opened the door for 18 years of Conservative rule. Margaret Thatcher won in 1979 and then again in 1983, arguably with the help of the successful Falklands

War. Michael Foot was elected leader in 1980 and presided over one of the party's gravest electoral defeats in 1983, when it was lucky not to have been beaten into third place behind the Alliance. In 1983 Neil Kinnock became leader and is credited with starting the party's slow climb back to electability. He introduced, via Peter Mandelson and Philip Gould, significant innovations in election campaigning, which made the party once more electorally credible. Although the party lost in 1987 and 1992, the shift to the centre, initiated by Kinnock, was decisive in advancing the cause of the 'modernisers'. John Smith became leader after 1994 and introduced the one member one vote system (OMOV) into party elections, partially replacing the trade union block vote. After his untimely death in 1994, he was succeeded by Tony Blair, who made a major step to electoral success by persuading the party to abandon clause four. He was also successful in repositioning the party as New Labour, in order to widen its electoral appeal to include middle-class and skilled working-class voters. He is arguably one of the most effective Labour leaders since Attlee and, along with Peter Mandelson, engineered the landslide victory of 1997. With Mandelson lost through various misadventures Blair succeeded in winning another landslide victory in 2001: Labour 413 seats (42 per cent of the vote); Conservatives 166 seats (33 per cent of the vote); Liberal Democrats 52 seats (19 per cent of the vote). However, the gloss was taken off the victory by a record low turnout of only 59 per cent, and a mere one in four of the electorate actually voted for New Labour. Blair's priority for a second term was to revitalise the public services and deliver on election promises before the next election, due before 2006.

On 10 July 2001 a new chair of the Parliamentary Labour Party was elected. Previously it had been Clive Soley, who was widely seen as being a bit too supportive of the Blair government. Jean Curston, Bristol East's MP, was elected in preference to Tony Lloyd, who was seen as a

more anti-leadership candidate, especially over public–private partnerships.

Labour's membership soared to over 400,000 after Blair became leader in 1994 but this soon slumped and was 270,000 in 2003; by 2004 the figure had declined to 208,000 and, if those yet to renew membership were excluded, only 190,000.

The party's 28-strong National Executive Committee (NEC) is elected by conference – the unions having the biggest say – and runs the party from day to day. Under Tony Blair the NEC has not been a potent source of policy initiatives – as it had during the 1970s and early 1980s.

*See also* Labour Representation Committee; National Executive Committee; Parliamentary Labour Party.

**Labour Party leadership contest**
Whether in opposition or the party of government, a challenger needs to command 20 per cent of the votes of the Parliamentary Labour Party (PLP) and the contest needs to be approved by two-thirds of the annual conference. Once approved, the electoral college is activated, in which trade unions (political levy payers only), constituency parties and the PLP vote separately and have one-third of the vote each. If no candidate receives more than half of the accumulated votes on the first ballot a second is held, with the second preferences being redistributed.

**Labour Party shadow cabinet election**
Elections by the Parliamentary Labour Party (PLP) of those people it would like to see in the shadow cabinet. When in opposition the PLP elects a shadow cabinet. Each member casts 18 votes; since 1992 four of these must be for women candidates. These elections have become something of a popularity contest for Labour MPs. The leader, deputy leader, chief whip and chair of the party select the shadow cabinet from those elected. Since 1980 the leader is obliged, after a general election victory, to form the first cabinet from those who served in the preceding

shadow cabinet, but the leader is not bound in any way in subsequent reshuffles.

## Labour Representation Committee (LRC)

The committee out of which the Labour Party emerged. It was established following a conference in 1900 of trade unionists and socialist societies, including the Independent Labour Party, the Marxist Social Democratic Federation and the Fabian Society. The conference decided to sponsor candidates for election and the LRC won two seats in 1900. In 1906 the LRC was renamed the Labour Party but it did not receive a proper constitution until 1918.

## laissez faire economics

*See* classical liberalism.

## law and order

*See* crime.

## law lord

Type of life peer. They are the lords of appeal in ordinary who sit in the House of Lords. They are limited to a maximum of 12 in number, must have at least two years' high judicial office and are appointed by the queen on the advice of the prime minister. They refrain from participating in party political debate, other than debates which pertain expressly to matters of legal reform or the administration of justice.

*See also* Appellate Committee of the House of Lords.

## Law Society

www.lawsociety.org.uk

Professional body which ensures solicitors do their jobs properly. It provides training for solicitors; anyone wishing to join the profession must receive the required training and education. They are then 'admitted to the rolls' and allowed to practise. For this they need a 'practising certificate' issued by the Society. In 2002 there were 90,000 solicitors holding such certificates. The Society also lays down rules regarding the management of clients' money and assets. It also has disciplinary powers and investigates complaints against members.

## Layfield report, 1976

Report of a committee set up in response to a perceived crisis in local government finance in 1974. It criticised the lack of responsibility for spending levels and urged greater accountability, at either central or local level. The majority of the committee favoured more local fund-raising instruments, especially local income tax. The Labour government of the time was unimpressed and decided to continue with the status quo, although it signalled it favoured 'greater central control over local government spending', something which the Thatcher government provided in abundance during the following decade.

## leader of the House of Commons

Cabinet post concerned with the parliamentary timetable and the management of government legislative business. In addition, the incumbent is in charge of the select committee network and any reforms of the House of Commons. The post is not of key importance but usually requires a senior politician who is familiar with the ways of the House. John Biffen was a respected holder of the office and it became the consolation prize for Robin Cook when he was sacked as foreign secretary in June 2001. He declared he was in favour of strengthening the House in relation to the executive; some refused to believe this would ever happen, so great is the government's desire to move business smoothly through the legislative process. In February 2003 he suffered a rebuff when his hopes of reforming the Lords to become at least partially elected was contradicted by Tony Blair and all the options were voted down. The government also has a leader of the House of Lords, often a cabinet post as well.

*See also* House of Lords reform; lord president of the Council.

## leadership

A role or office in organisations, political or otherwise, associated with the exercise of authority. Max Weber, the German political economist, pointed to the legitimate basis of leadership, namely charismatic, traditional and legal rational authority. The procedures for selecting a party leader in the British system of government have varied over time and between parties. However, in the new millennium all mainstream parties operate, in various forms, a system of internal party democracy for the selection of leaders. In terms of leadership style, British party leaders have been, with a few exceptions, safe and cautious: for the Conservatives Stanley Baldwin and Arthur Balfour; for Labour Clement Attlee, Harold Wilson and James Callaghan. There have been charismatic premiers, however, like the war leaderships of David Lloyd George and Winston Churchill and the dynamic reformer Margaret Thatcher. On the Labour side, too, there have been charismatic leaders such as Ramsey MacDonald and latterly Tony Blair; the former, however, proved unreliable and a 'traitor' to the party, though the latter, so far, has proved highly successful, despite accusations of betrayal by some party activists.

Philip Norton distinguishes a number of different types of premier: innovators (Churchill, Heath, Thatcher); reformers (Campbell-Bannerman, Asquith, Attlee); egoists (Lloyd George, MacDonald, Eden, Wilson); and balancers (Bonar Law, Douglas-Home).

> I learned that a great leader is a man who has the ability to get other people to do what they don't want to do and like it. (Harry S. Truman, US president)

See also authority.

### leadership team (Conservative Party)
Title given to Michael Howard's shadow cabinet, selected on 11 November 2003. He decided to reduce the shadow cabinet from 22 members to a mere 12, to increase focus and improve the degree to which his main players would be recognised. Some members, like Tim Yeo, were given

wide-ranging jobs, in his case covering the whole of the public services; deputies were appointed to cover individual ministries. Howard sought to cover all sections of the party – including the Europhiles and modernisers – in his team, though the reduced number of the main portfolios must have bruised a few egos. Howard showed additional skill in keeping former leaders onside by setting up an advisory group comprising John Major, William Hague and Iain Duncan Smith, plus the talented Europhile Ken Clarke. The idea was to call upon their expertise and experience and occasionally to ask them to speak for the party from the front bench.

### leak
Release of information via informal channels (usually illicit). Leaks are a familiar characteristic of modern government. They are sometimes unofficial and deliberate, for example Clive Ponting's leaking of confidential material on the sinking of the General Belgrano to a Labour MP, or officially sanctioned, like the leaks of intended budget measures designed to test public reaction before final decisions are made. Because of the tradition of secrecy in British government, leaks have a news value they would not otherwise have. Every effort is made to trace the source of leaks within departments; they often come from officials opposed to the measures concerned. The price paid by the source of the leak may be the loss of his/her job or, worse still, prosecution under the Official Secrets Act. Some ministers deny that something they have told a journalist constitutes a leak: James Callaghan once said to a questioner, 'You leak, I brief'.

> I don't want a leak inquiry. I want to find out who did it. (Jim Hacker in the Yes, Prime Minister series, when told the civil service would spare no effort to discover the source of a leak in his department)

### left–right continuum
The traditional classification of political stance. It derives from the seating arrange-

ments in the French Estates-General in 1789, where the popular movements sat to the left of the king and the aristocrats on his right. Left-wingers in Britain, typically socialists in the Labour Party, have come to represent the values of equality, collectivism and collective or social ownership (formerly called nationalisation), while the Conservative right has been characterised by freedom, individualism and free enterprise. Centre parties like the Liberals have adopted various syntheses of both left and right. However, a more sophisticated way of mapping ideological positions can be found by using, in addition, the authoritarian/libertarian continuum, as is done by the Blundell–Gosschalk classification. New Labour sought to transcend the left–right dichotomy by asserting the third way: a so-called synthesis of the socialist and Conservative traditions.

*See also* Blundell–Gosschalk classification; third way.

## legislative process

How a bill becomes an act. A governing party has the lion's share of parliamentary time to pass public bills, which are the principal means of implementing manifesto pledges. Each year civil servants and senior ministers decide on the legislative programme, as announced in the queen's speech. A drafting and consultation process then follows, where the sponsoring department and minister issue a green paper and sometimes a white paper. The final form of the bill is then introduced in either of the houses of parliament.

If all the stages are complete the bill goes to the queen for the royal assent and then becomes law.

*See also* act of parliament.

## legislature

The law-making assembly of a political system. In the case of Britain, the legislature developed from the councils of nobles assembled to advise the monarch and to provide the revenue to run the monarch's court and conduct wars. Over a period of a thousand years these assemblies used

their control of finance to accumulate the right to pass and scrutinise new legislation. Eventually the monarch tried to rule without their help and the 17th-century Civil War resulted, after which parliament was in the ascendant and the monarchy became purely constitutional, presiding over a system of an elected Commons and a cabinet led by a prime minister. Once political parties developed in the 19th century the leader of the biggest party elected at a general election generally became the person invited by the monarch to become prime minister. Parliament comprises the monarch, the Commons and the Lords. Britain has an unbalanced bicameral legislature, meaning there are two chambers of unequal power: the House of Commons and the (reformed) House of Lords.

## legitimacy

The justified exercise of power or authority. A political regime is unlikely to last long without some form of justification and acceptance by citizens: might must be turned into right. British government has traditionally been perceived as having high legitimacy, through its longevity and sequential solving of great political questions like relations between the church and state, the crown and state, and the extension of the suffrage. It is also suggested that the ceremony and salience of the monarchy as a symbol helps the British people to feel comfortably part of a unified political entity.

*See also* authority; political culture.

## Levellers

Reformist grouping at the time of Civil War. The name, as so often, began as a term of abuse but stuck. John Lilburne and others wrote pamphlets advocating wide-ranging reforms to the franchise and government. Initially they received support from the ranks of the army but senior officers eventually opposed them and they were repressed after mutinies in 1649. The movement then faded away but is still invoked by modern-day radicals like Tony Benn.

## Liaison Select Committee

www.parliament.uk/commons/
selcom/liahome.htm
Committee established in 1980 and
comprising, for the most part, chairs of the
other select committees. Its prime function
is to coordinate the work of select committees, which were also established in 1980.
Chairs are shared between parties. There
is no formal requirement for the chair of the
committee to come from the government
side, although in practice this has always
been the case.

The Liaison Select Committee leapt
into the public spotlight on 16 July 2002
when the prime minister, after initially
refusing, agreed to give evidence to the
gathering. In the event, most commentators
thought the experiment a success. Tony
Blair spent two and a half hours answer-
ing questions and was certainly more
forthcoming than he was able to be during
prime minister's questions. He agreed New
Labour had become too involved with
'spin' and attributed it to the years spent in
opposition, when it was easy to 'believe the
announcement is the reality'. He answered
questions on Iraq, parliament and his own
battery of special advisors. It seems this
inquisition is likely to become a regular
part of British politics and part of Blair's
attempt to connect more directly to his
critics and become more accountable.

> He has discovered that he is his own best
> spin doctor. (Simon Jenkins on the extended
> questioning session, *The Times*, 17 July
> 2002)

## Lib—Lab pact, 1977—78

The Labour government under James
Callaghan lost its thin overall majority in
1977 and, in order to stay in office, when
faced with a vote of confidence on 23
March, made a deal with David Steel's
Liberals. The pact was renewed in the
autumn of 1977. In practice this did not
mean Liberals sitting in the cabinet but
merely some nominal consultation with a
named Liberal for each important function
of government; for example, Denis Healey

consulted with John Pardoe over economic
policy. Steel formally ended the pact in
June 1978, judging it to be a vote loser in
the run-up to the by then imminent general
election.

## liberal democracy

Form of democracy (and there are others)
developed in Britain during the 18th and
19th centuries, and in many other parts
of the economically developed world,
including North America and western
Europe. It is essentially an amalgam of
liberalism with a number of crucial political
and individual rights and characteristics,
including:
1  there is freedom of speech, within the
   law;
2  there is freedom of the press, within the
   law;
3  there is freedom of thought and religion;
4  overall political authority lies with the
   electorate, who vote in periodic free
   elections;
5  elected representatives exercise authority and have the ability to remove the
   government;
6  there is respect for human rights and
   dissenting minority political rights;
7  there are economic freedoms, associated
   with free market capitalism.

Since the collapse of the Soviet Union
and its satellites in eastern Europe in
the late 1980s and early 1990s, liberal
democracy has extended its reach, with
varying degrees of success. For this reason,
Francis Fukuyama, the US political
philosopher, argued that western liberal
democracy has in effect 'won' the battle
of ideas and that we face the 'end of
history', whereby liberal democracy will
preside indefinitely – a challenging thesis
which has provoked much discussion
but little agreement. However, the fierce
demonstrations mounted by those opposing
corporate capitalism at various world
and European summits over the past
decade, together with the challenge to the
west mounted by militant Islam, suggest
Fukuyama's predictions may be overly
complacent and naive.

## Liberal Democrat Youth and Students

www.ldys.org.uk
Youth organisation of Liberal Democrats. It claims 17,000 members, with an upper age limit of 30. Its executive is elected and it has local and university branches.

## Liberal Democrats

www.libdems.org.uk
Formed out of a merger between the Liberal Party and the breakaway Social Democratic Party in 1988. The 1987 election campaign had revealed the problems of an 'alliance' with two leaders, David Steel and David Owen, and it seemed logical to formalise what had in any case taken place on the local level between activists in the two political groupings. However, despite his party's acceptance of the merger and the launch of the Social and Liberal Democratic Party (SLD), Owen insisted on leading a small rump party into the political wilderness. In the 1990 Bootle by-election, it famously came seventh, behind Screaming Lord Sutch's Monster Raving Loony Party and was wound up shortly afterwards. When Steel stood down Paddy Ashdown took over as leader in March 1988, defeating Alan Beith in the leadership election, with 72 per cent of the vote. In 1990 the party became known as the 'Liberal Democrats' after an all-member ballot agreed and the fuller title was dropped.

The party has a federal structure with autonomy given to regions for the selection of candidates and for conference and policy committees. In theory the two annual conferences have the power to make party policy but in practice the leadership has the decisive say. In the 1997 general election the party increased its representation from 20 to 46 MPs. Ashdown steered a course of 'constructive opposition' to Tony Blair's government, advocating more spending on welfare services, a more ethical foreign policy and constitutional reform, especially of the voting system. Ashdown was given a seat on a cabinet committee on constitutional reform. After Ashdown's resignation, Charles Kennedy was elected leader in 1999. He indicated he was going to eschew a drift to the left but he entered the 2001 election campaign committed to specified tax increases and increased spending on public services. His laid-back style worked and stilled criticism that he was lazy and lacking in leadership qualities. The Liberal Democrats increased their share of the vote to 19 per cent in 2001 and their number of seats to 52. However, the prize of a new voting system still eludes them and is dependent on the massive majority of Labour. On 30 June 2001 the *Observer* carried a report that the Transport and General Workers' Union was considering backing the party because of the New Labour government's plans to increase the involvement of the private sector in the public services. In the autumn of 2001 dissident Labour MP Paul Marsden joined the Liberal Democrats after extended disputes with his party's whips; this increased the party's membership in the Commons to 53. Early in 2003 some polls showed the party closing on the Conservatives as Kennedy voiced widespread criticism of Blair's support for the US military action against Iraq. Soon after the war, when it seemed to have been justified, the party showed some decline in the polls but when occupation proved problematic and opinion shifted against the rationale for the war – and Charles Kennedy took a more aggressive line against New Labour – the Liberal Democrats began to pick up support, most notably demonstrated in the stunning by-election victory at Brent East on 18 September 2003. Soon afterwards a *Guardian* ICM poll showed the party on 28 per cent and nudging the Conservatives as the most popular opposition party. In July 2004 the party won the Leicester South by-election on a 20 per cent swing and narrowly failed to win the Birmingham Hodge Hill one despite a 27 per cent swing.

### liberal elite

Group of people in society regarded as espousing and representing progressive views. In the summer of 2000 the Centre for Policy Studies published a pamphlet called *The Great and the Good: The Rise of the New Class*. It argued that Tony Blair has brought about the rise of a new 'establishment' or liberal elite, which includes the likes of David Putnam, Greg Dyke and Helena Kennedy. Allegedly they all believe in social engineering, state regulation and political correctness. In support it pointed out that Blair had ennobled 176 peers in just over three years compared with Thatcher's 216 over 11.

## Liberal National Party

Formed when 23 Liberal MPs led by Lord Simon split from their party to join the national government in 1931. However, in 1932 supporters of Herbert Samuel left in opposition to the protectionist policies of the government. Supporters of Lord Simon won 33 seats in 1935. By 1945, however, they could only muster 13 seats. In 1948 they changed their name to the National Liberal Party, a label abandoned finally in 1966.

## Liberal Party

Party that emerged from an amalgam of the Whigs, Radicals and supporters of Robert Peel in the middle of the 19th century. It advocated laissez faire economics, international trade, political freedom and constitutional reform. After the Reform Act 1867 the party appealed effectively to the enlarged electorate and held office in 1868–74, 1880–85, 1886, 1892–95 and 1905–16. Gladstone dominated the middle of the century with his preference for gradual reform and free trade but his decision to support Irish Home Rule split the party and kept it out of office until 1906, when Henry Campbell-Bannerman won a massive landslide. His reforming administration effectively represented working-class interests and social and trade union reform resulted in a programme reflecting a more interventionist role by the state. Herbert Asquith, prime minister from 1908, gave his dynamic colleague David Lloyd George a role in government which led to his wartime premiership and provided a launching pad for the coup which the Welshman

made, with Conservative support, to become prime minister himself. However, in the process the party was yet again split, with a large group remaining loyal to Asquith. This division helped Labour to become the natural opposition party and marked the end of the Liberals' possession of political power in the 20th century. In 1924 the party gained only 40 seats and in 1929, 59; a small group around Lord Simon thereafter became indistinguishable from the Conservatives. In 1935 the reduced party gained 20 seats and this figure dropped to 12 in 1945; in 1951, 1955 and 1959 the party won only 6 seats.

Jo Grimond stimulated a revival in the 1950s but even though Liberal votes increased the party failed to make the threshold required in a first past the post system. Reform of the voting system became probably the chief objective of the party after 1945, as the vote it received was never proportionally represented in parliamentary seats. It also sustained its tradition of internationalism by championing the cause of European integration, a platform which the Liberal Democrats fully absorbed. Jeremy Thorpe was an effective leader but the scandal which engulfed him damaged his party and it was left to David Steel to pick up the pieces and lead the party into the Lib–Lab pact in 1977. After the Alliance with the Social Democratic Party, the Liberals merged in 1988 to form the Social and Liberal Democrat Party, the forerunner of the Liberal Democrats.

## Liberal Unionists

Party created in 1886 when the Liberal Party split over Home Rule for Ireland. The Liberal Unionists, led by Joseph Chamberlain, opposed Home Rule. In the 1895 election 70 Liberal Unionists were elected; they became absorbed into the Conservative Party and went on to constitute its liberal, social reforming wing.

## liberalism

Essentially, a belief in the freedom of the individual and human improvement. It is one of the major traditions of political thought in Britain, along with conservatism, socialism and Marxism. It is associated with the social and economic forces of the industrial revolution and the intellectual speculations of the Enlightenment, although traces of liberal thinking are present in John Lilburne's tracts and his Levellers during the time of the English Civil War. Prominent thinkers from this tradition include John Locke, Tom Paine, John Stuart Mill, Jeremy Bentham and the political economist Adam Smith. In British political history 'liberalism' is the doctrine of the Liberal Party and initially comprised a commitment to: individual rights, laissez faire economics, minimal government, representative government, a utilitarian approach to legislation and peace through trade. By the end of the 19th century the party's appeal to the newly enfranchised working class led it to embark on a path towards emphasising a more paternalistic, protective approach, by which the brutal excesses of capitalism were to be curbed. Moreover, the state was looked upon as a necessary agent for social reform, taking on responsibility for the welfare of the poor and old in order to reduce inequality in society. Later the Liberal economists William Beveridge and John Maynard Keynes elaborated the more interventionist approach which was adopted by Labour as its own. The 1970s witnessed a renewed interest in classical liberal ideas of the free market, which the new right took up and which were personified by Margaret Thatcher, who was sometimes described as a 'classical liberal'. Liberalism has thus been one of the most powerful political doctrines of the last 200 years.

*See also* classical liberalism; communitarianism; new right.

## libertarianism

In modern usage, the rights of the individual, unencumbered by moral, legal or political restraint. In essence individual liberties come before obligations to the state. However, there are different forms of libertarianism. One school, associated with the political philosopher Robert Nozick,

argues that the rights of the individual should never be abrogated and that the state should act only to promote individual liberty, including economic freedoms. The economist Friedrich von Hayek moves beyond the individual to assert that the free market is beneficial to all and that the interventionist state can only be inefficient and a threat to the general good. Another stream of libertarian thought retains the state, but shrinks it to a minimum, whereby it provides only territorial defence against invasion, sound currency and a bare body of civil and criminal law. The new right was influenced by some, though not all, of these ideas, and Margaret Thatcher went as far as to say that she wanted to 'roll back the state' and that there was 'no such thing as "society", only individual men, women and families'. The value of libertarianism to an understanding of modern British politics lies in its ability to throw into sharp relief the interdependent nature of modern social and political organisation, a phenomenon underlined by globalisation.

*See also* limited government.

## liberty
*See* freedom.

## Liberty
www.liberty-human-rights.org.uk
The new name for the National Council for Civil Liberties. This was founded in 1934 by Ronald Kidd, who had been deeply affected by the police's use of agent provocateurs, or police agitators, during the 'hunger marches' of 1932. His solution was to encourage reliable people to attend public events and be independent witnesses to complaints of police misbehaviour. His activities widened to include other threats to civil liberties, such as the rise of fascism and government censorship. Liberty is committed to the defence and extension of civil liberties in Britain and to the rights and liberties recognised by international law. Sister organisations are the Scottish Council of Civil Liberties and Northern Ireland's Committee for the Administration of Justice.

POLITICS

## life peerage

Introduced by the Life Peerages Act 1958 which allowed the creation of non-hereditary members of the House of Lords, including women for the first time. After the Act it was still possible to create hereditary peers, although this was not used again after 1964 until Margaret Thatcher so ennobled Harold Macmillan, Willie Whitelaw and George Thomas in 1983. Life peers have since constituted the most active element in the Lords and have been responsible for a renaissance in its activity and effectiveness. In 1999 Labour ended the hereditary element in the Lords except for 92 survivors, who would go once the reforms were complete. But Labour gave no indication of any overall reform of the chamber. Some critics observed that if only the 'lifers' remain, then the chamber will quickly become a giant quango, appointed by the prime minister and comprising, in the argot of the tabloids, 'Tony's cronies'.

*See also* House of Lords reform.

## limited government

A crucial element of early liberal ideology and libertarian thinking, that government should be limited to the bare necessities of maintaining national security and a sound currency. The corollary of the idea is that citizens should be allowed to live their lives unimpeded by government as far as possible. Conservative theorists of the new right adopted the idea in reaction to the postwar consensus. However, despite Margaret Thatcher's often quoted wish to roll back the state and to promote economic deregulation, she presided over a substantial increase in central government power. This included: restrictions on local government finance, the introduction of a national curriculum in schools, increased powers for the police and the abolition of trade unions at Government Communications Headquarters (GCHQ).

*See also* consensus; libertarianism; new right.

## lobby

Organisations that seek to influence government in the interests of the specific groups they represent. It derives from the name given to the area close to a legislative chamber where it is possible to gain access to members. The term is more American but in Britain it is also used, as are 'lobbying' or 'lobbyist', although 'pressure groups' or 'interest groups' are more frequent. This said, in recent years there has been a growth in companies and consultancies that offer professional services to those companies and groups which wish to gain access to key people in and around government. One of them, associated with the former MP Ian Greer, was involved in the 'cash for questions' scandal.

## lobby system

The system that governs journalists' access to politicians in Westminster. In Victorian times William Gladstone used to commune with selected journalists and give them privileged information about his plans and thoughts. During the 20th century this practice became formalised, the numbers grew and aspirant members of the parliamentary lobby had to apply. Some 200 attend the twice-daily briefings from Downing Street and the Commons. They can also roam the corridors of Westminster and have access to most areas except for the floor of the chamber itself. The idea is that they receive information in briefings they would not otherwise learn but in exchange do not reveal the origin of their source. This led to code words being used like 'sources close to the prime minister' (the prime minister's press secretary) and the meetings and even meeting places were kept secret, unlike the on-the-record televised briefings used in Washington, DC. In the late 1980s the *Independent*, the *Guardian* and the *Scotsman* withdrew from the lobby for a while, arguing that it enabled government to control the agenda of discussion, to favour one section of the press over another, and to use the briefings to fly kites or rubbish other members of the government or otherwise manipulate the news agenda. In 1997 Alastair Campbell, Tony Blair's press secretary, decided to allow himself to be identified in stories as the 'prime minister's spokesman' in an attempt to make the system less secretive. As the 2001 general election approached Campbell withdrew from daily briefings to occupy a more strategic role. In May 2002 certain changes were made whereby morning lobby briefings would be open to all journalists and, when ministers attend, are both on the record and on camera. Edited versions of the briefings also now appear on the Number 10 website. On 20 June 2002 a lobby briefing was televised for the first time. Michael White, political editor of the *Guardian*, predicted that few briefings would be televised, as they were so 'boring'.

## local government

A form of devolution whereby decisions about local services are placed nearest to the people who use them. The Municipal Corporations Act 1835 established rules for the election of councillors, their duties and the powers of councils. As the life of industrial Britain became more complex, local government took on additional duties in terms of education, health and planning, to the extent that more uniform and stronger structures were required. The Local Government Act 1888 established the procedures for elected county authorities, and in 1894 legislation created urban and rural district councils within those counties. This system survived into the next century but was found inadequate and many functions like health were lost to other bodies. The Local Government Act 1972 reformed the system quite drastically but further change was still to come. This included the abolition of the Greater London Council and other metropolitan counties in 1986 and the creation of unitary authorities in the early 1990s. This was achieved in Scotland and Wales, but only partly in England, for example York and the Isle of Wight. More significant have been the local government reforms since 1997 and devolution in Scotland and Wales.

In the local elections held on 1 May 2003, the Conservatives won back a big slice of control of English local government, with well over 500 gains. The Liberal

Democrats also did well, with 150 gains, and Labour suffered over 700 losses. In the 2004 elections the usual mid-term swing against the government – this time aided by opposition to the Iraq war – produced 232 more seats for the Conservatives and 151 more for the Liberal Democrats, while Labour lost 468. This left Labour controlling only 39 councils compared with the Conservatives' 50, the Liberal Democrat's 9 plus 65 without overall control. Turnout was up, to average 40 per cent, partly as a result of the experiment with postal voting in three regions.

*See also* London government; regional government.

## Local Government Act 1972

Introduced two tiers of government: county and district. It also introduced 6 metropolitan counties, 36 metropolitan districts, 53 shire counties and 369 shire districts, all performing different functions. The act took effect in 1974. To counteract the increased remoteness of local government, parish councils were retained but had little practical role. New shire counties were created in Avon, Cleveland and Humberside, while old counties such as Rutland disappeared. New names, such as 'West Yorkshire', were introduced to replace the age-old West Riding of Yorkshire. Many of these changes provoked anger and resentment among local people, which lives on today.

## Local Government Act 1988, section 28

*See* section 28.

## Local Government Association

www.lga.gov.uk

Voluntary lobbying organisation that represents the interests of local government. It was formed in 1997 and represents some 500 local authorities – that is, virtually all – which cover some 50 million people and annually spend £78 billion. It is located near the centre of London within easy access of decision-making centres. Strategic objectives for 2001–06 include redressing the balance between the centre and local

POLITICS

authorities, increasing the powers and flexibility of local authorities and improving their financial situation.

## local government finance

The money raised by local authorities through local taxation (principally the council tax and uniform business rate); central government grants (principally the revenue support grant and other specific grants); fees and charges for services (for example rents); and borrowing from banks and the like. Capital can also be obtained from the European Union, the National Lottery, the Private Finance Initiative and the sale of assets. Funds are also available from the Department of the Environment for specific projects in transport, education and other areas. Local government spends large sums of money (£46.4 billion in 1997/98). It is subordinate to central government and can act only within statutes passed at Westminster and this constitutional fact has determined the development of local government finance during the 1980s. In 1980, 1982 and 1984 Conservative governments passed a raft of legislation to control spending by local authorities. The measures included rate capping, grant-related expenditure assessments, compulsory competitive tendering, the introduction of the poll tax or community charge, the sale of council houses and the introduction of standard spending assessments. Supplementary rates were made illegal in 1981 when the High Court ruled that the Greater London Council (GLC) had acted ultra vires, or beyond its powers, in using an additional rate to subsidise London Transport buses and tubes. The abolition of the GLC and the metropolitan counties in 1986 further reduced the financial independence of local government. Despite further changes since 1997, the local authorities appear to have insufficient money to fund the services which many supporters of local government call for.

## local government reform since 1997

Since 1997 the Labour government's approach to local government has been characterised by a change of emphasis, and some innovation, rather than wholesale reform, a theme very much in line with the party's eclectic policy making. Significant innovations include:

1  democratisation of councils, for example by means of directly elected mayors;
2  councils to hold local referendums and introduce innovations in polling to increase participation rates;
3  crude council tax capping to end, though with reserve powers left with central government;
4  beacon councils to be established, which set standards of excellence for service delivery;
5  more consultation with local people and businesses on service provision;
6  compulsory competitive tendering replaced by 'best value'.

However, continuity with the Thatcher and Major years is maintained by the retention of the national business rate, although with some latitude for variation, and by the emphasis on efficiency, economy and effectiveness (the three 'E's) in the delivery of services. Overall, the Labour government has moved some way towards recognising the value of local government, albeit with continued centralisation from Westminster.

## local taxation

*See* community charge; council tax; local government finance.

## London government

The Local Government Act 1888 created the London County Council but this was replaced by the Greater London Council in 1965, which looked after city-wide functions like transport and planning which the 32 boroughs could not easily deal with. When Margaret Thatcher came to power she immediately encountered conflict from Labour-controlled city governments, especially in London, where Ken Livingstone led a high-profile left-wing administration. While her abolition of other metropolitan counties caused no outcry, the loss of an area-wide council for the nation's capital provoked heated criticism and not just from Labour. Back in power Labour introduced plans for an elected mayor for the capital. The first elections took place in May 2000, amid controversy over nominations and candidates in both major parties. Ken Livingstone, despite standing as an independent (Tony Blair had effectively vetoed his official candidature), won, leaving Frank Dobson, the official Labour candidate, humiliated and Tony Blair tainted with accusations of 'control freakery'. Labour's National Executive Committee voted to allow Livingstone back into the party in January 2004; he went on to be easily re-elected as London mayor in June of the same year.

## London Underground

During Ken Livingstone's campaign for the mayoralty of London in 2000 he made great issue of the future of the Underground. The government favoured a public–private partnership involving three companies to run the services – tracks, stations and signalling – on franchises. Livingstone disagreed and favoured raising the necessary billions of pounds via a public bonds route. Deadlock ensued once 'Red Ken' was in office, with the government – especially chancellor Gordon Brown – refusing to back down. Bob Kiley, a former CIA agent who solved New York's subway problems, was brought in by Livingstone to apply similar magic. He condemned Brown's plan as 'fatally flawed', the chief problem relating to fragmentation caused by the three companies, which would, he claimed, endanger the safety of London's 3 million daily passengers. Still the deadlock continued but increasingly London MPs (not to mention the Health and Safety Commission plus most of the media outlets) seemed to come out in favour of Kiley's plan. The dispute went to court during the summer of 2001. On 17 July Kiley was sacked by secretary of state Stephen Byers as chair of London Transport – allegedly on the insistence of Tony Blair, under pressure from Brown – on the grounds that he had 'issued instructions to senior management to halt

negotiations with private firms [identified as the providers of a new-style London Underground]. This is unacceptable. Mr Kiley took no notice of board policy and was acting unilaterally.' Kiley remained as transport commissioner for Greater London. In his book *The Rivals* (2001) James Naughtie cites this issue as demonstrating vividly the reluctance of Tony Blair to overrule his chancellor on a financial issue on which he had made up his mind.

## Lonrho affair, 1973

Scandal involving excessive payments to Duncan Sandys, chair of the African mining company Lonrho. This company had been built up by the dynamic but controversial Tiny Rowland in the 1960s as a huge African enterprise. The scandal erupted at a time when prime minister Edward Heath was trying to 'create a national mood of restraint'. A group of directors was seeking to dislodge Rowland and during the course of the struggle it emerged that the chairman of the company, Duncan Sandys, a former cabinet colleague of Heath, had received $10,000, deposited in a Cayman Island account, apparently to avoid tax payments. Heath decided this was indefensible and denounced it as 'the unpleasant and unacceptable face of capitalism'. He denied, however, that the 'whole of British industry consists of practices of this kind'.

## lord advocate

www.crownoffice.gov.uk/who/office_of_lord_advocate.htm
Government's principal law officer in Scotland, in charge of public prosecutions and who pleads in all cases that concern the crown. The lord advocate is the head of the system of public prosecutions and is aided by a solicitor general and by 'advocates depute'. The office was established early in the 16th century; the office holder is allowed to wear a hat in court. The officer oversees three offices:
1 the Lord Advocate's Department, which assists, among other things, in the drafting of Scottish legislation;
2 the Crown Office in Edinburgh, which

deals with the administration of criminal law in Scotland;

3 the Scottish Courts Administration, which deals with civil law in Scotland.

## lord chancellor

Formerly the oldest public office, dating back, as it did, 1,400 years. It used to be cited as a constitutional anomaly, in that its holder was at once a member of: the judiciary, as its head; the executive, by virtue of being in the cabinet; and the legislature, by virtue of being a member of the House of Lords. The lord chancellor also acted as the speaker of the Lords (and so sat on the woolsack). Lord Irvine of Lairg was lord chancellor to Tony Blair for six years and was a staunch defender of the powers of his ancient office. However, he was forced to retire in June 2003 as the office was reformed into the Department for Constitutional Affairs, with an additional responsibility for the residual duties of the Scottish and Welsh secretaries. Lord Falconer was appointed as lord chancellor until the title could be changed by legislation. The Judicial Appointments Commission was also set up to appoint judges. Blair was criticised for lack of consultation, though few argued with the sense of separating the judiciary more clearly from politics.

## Lord Chancellor's Department

In charge of the administration of the courts but also tasked in June 2003 with the residual responsibilities of the Welsh and Scottish secretaries via the part-time attentions of the leader of the House and transport secretary, who took on these additional duties. This untidy arrangement was hotly criticised by judicial figures and others at the time. This criticism bore fruit in the spring of 2003, when the office was to be phased out in favour of a secretary of state for constitutional affairs. This arrangement was in turn criticised by the judiciary for lack of prior consultation. In response the government proceeded with its reforms at a slower pace. The measure was defeated in the House of Lords in July 2004.

## lord president of the Council

The person charged with running the Privy Council and its office but the job is merely ceremonial. The office holder is usually the leader of the House and also a senior cabinet minister who chairs committees and reports back to cabinet.

## lord privy seal

In the middle ages the officer who took charge of the privy seal but now, as with so many ancient posts, one of those 'dignified' constitutional roles which sound grand but have virtually no power. The office is now often given to a senior politician, known to have good judgement, who chairs important cabinet committees. Occasionally the office is given to someone with a specific and important job to perform, like Edward Heath in 1960–63 when negotiating Britain's entry into the European Community.

## lost deposit

Each candidate in an election has to deposit a certain sum which is lost unless a certain proportion of the vote is mustered. Originally the Representation of the People Act set the deposit at £150 but this soon became outdated through inflation and failed to deter a plethora of joke candidates. In 1985 the sum was increased to £500 but the limit required was lowered from one-eighth to one-twentieth of the poll.

## Low Pay Commission

www.lowpay.gov.uk
Independent agency set up by the National Minimum Wage Act 1998 to advise the government on the minimum wage. The Department of Trade and Industry is responsible for the operation of the minimum wage.

## Loyalist Volunteer Force (LVF)

Formed in 1996 from renegade elements of the Ulster Volunteer Force (UVF). This sect is opposed to the Northern Ireland peace process. Billy Wright was an early leader before being shot dead in Maze Prison by the Irish National Liberation Army (INLA) in 1997. It has around 500 members.

# M

## Maastricht Treaty, 1992

The Treaty on European Union. A meeting of the European Council that took place at Maastricht in the Netherlands on 11 December 1991 agreed amendments to the founding treaties of the European Union (EU) necessary to achieve economic and political union. European ministers met again in February 1992 at the same place to sign what became known as the Treaty on European Union, which came into force on 1 January 1994, at which point the European Community became the European Union (EU). The treaty's main aim was to register, according to Article A, a 'new stage in the process of creating an ever closer union among the peoples of Europe'. Accordingly it provided, among other things, for extended majority voting rather than unanimity in the Council of Ministers and gave increased power to the European parliament. John Major, negotiating on behalf of Britain, insisted on the addition of two protocols which removed the requirement for Britain to move towards economic and monetary union and to accept the Social Chapter, which commits members to improve employment and working conditions. Initially the agreement was received calmly but when Denmark rejected the treaty in June 1992 internal opposition within the governing Conservative Party began to grow, encouraged by France's wafer thin referendum endorsement (a 2 per cent margin) in September. In December 1992, at Edinburgh, Maastricht was formally endorsed but Major was able to extract more concessions, especially on 'subsidiarity', which is the notion of decision making being made at more local levels wherever possible, and which was designed to assuage fears of a drift towards federalism or a European 'super-state'. A rider to Article A was therefore added: 'in which decisions are taken as closely as possible to the citizen'. Even this addition was deemed insufficient by Conservative 'Eurosceptics' and the treaty took over 200 hours of passionate Commons debate and a government defeat before being ratified on 2 August 1993. The German chancellor Helmut Kohl alerted Eurosceptics to the implications of the treaty when he described it as the 'foundation-stone for the completion of the European Union … the United States of Europe'.

## Macpherson report, 1999

Report of an inquiry by Sir William Macpherson into the murder of a black student, Stephen Lawrence, and the failure of the Metropolitan Police to conduct the case properly and secure convictions. In particular, the police were condemned for failing to recognise that the crime was racially motivated and for their treatment of the Lawrence family plus his friend, Dwayne Brooks, who survived the attack. However, the inquiry went further and revealed that racism was not just a problem for individual police officers, but also for the culture of the Metropolitan Police and other public service organisations. Macpherson used the term 'institutionalised racism' to describe the collective failure of an organisation to provide appropriate and professional service to people because of their colour, culture or ethnic origin. It can be seen or detected in processes, attitudes and behaviour which amount to discrimination through unwitting prejudice, ignorance, thoughtlessness and racist stereotyping, which disadvantage minority ethnic people. The report proposed a raft of recommendations, including the following:

1 All public service organisations should assess whether they are acting fairly, that they are meeting the needs of the communities they serve, and that professional standards are maintained in every situation.

2 Management structures and procedures should be in place that give effect to these tests.

3 The Race Relations Act 1976 should be amended to make it unlawful for the

police to discriminate on racial grounds in the exercise of law enforcement.

4 Independent investigations should take place of serious complaints against the police.

5 Racially aggravated offences should receive stiffer sentences.

6 There should be increased recruitment of ethnic minority police officers, with targets established and monitoring of performance in this respect.

**magic circle**

Name given to describe the informal system of appointing Conservative leaders up to 1965, when Edward Heath became the first to be openly elected. Leaders emerged after extended internal soundings made by leading members of the party. The last leader to emerge in this way was Alec Douglas-Home in 1963.

**magistrates' court**

The most junior court in the country, yet the 650 of them hear the vast majority of cases brought forward – over 95 per cent. Most magistrates, or justices of the peace (JPs) to use the traditional title, apart for the 'stipendiary' ones in the big cities, are voluntary unpaid judges recruited from local people of good standing. They can hear both civil and criminal cases, although the latter provide the bulk. All criminal prosecutions must begin in a magistrates' court. On the civil side, magistrates have extensive powers to make maintenance, affiliation and adoption orders and to set restrictions on violent husbands' access to their families, for example. They also deal with juveniles, liquor laws and applications for betting licences. Magistrates receive some training but the source of much legal knowledge is the clerk to the court, by profession an experienced solicitor or barrister and often the real source of the decisions made by lay magistrates.

*See also* crown court; judiciary.

**Magna Carta**

The fundamental statement of British liberties, signed by King John at Runnymede in June 1215. It arose from the acute discontent of the king's barons with his heavy tax burden and was the product of there not being an adult member of the royal family to foment a rebellion, John being the last of the Plantagenet line. Consequently the barons had to lead their own revolt behind a charter of reform. John decided to accept the charter when the rebels seized London. This did not stop the fighting, however, and modified charters were issued in 1217 and 1225, the latter text, with 63 chapters, being the one lying on the statute book as the most basic of British laws. The best-known clauses guarantee the citizen freedom from illegal interference with person or property and justice to everyone. The king was forbidden from raising certain taxes without the consent of the 'common council' of the realm. The original charter was to be enforced by a council of 25 barons, who threatened war if the king went back on his promises. The four remaining copies of the charter are in Salisbury and Lincoln Cathedrals and the British Library (two copies).

**Mainstream**

Centre-left umbrella body for individuals and groupings in the Conservative Party. It has been led by former ministers, such as David Curry, Ian Taylor and Stephen Dorrell.

**maladministration**

*See* ombudsman.

**Managerial, Scientific and Financial Union**

*See* Amicus.

**Manchester radicals**

Mid-19th-century advocates of laissez faire economics, including Richard Cobden and John Bright. Regarded as extreme in their day, their ideas came to influence Thatcherism over a century later.

**mandate**

The endorsement of policy proposals by victory in an election. There are intriguing questions on the use of the term: is the mandate a general authority to govern in the best interests of the people, or a specific instruction from the electorate on each and every promise made in a party's manifesto, or is it both? There are no definitive answers to this question; history is a better guide. Some within the Labour Party, especially in the early part of the 20th century, interpreted it as a duty to fulfil promises given and therefore believed it was incumbent on all elected representatives to do this.

As a verb, again in the Labour Party, it indicates a duty to behave in a certain way, as when a union delegation is 'mandated' by the union's conference to vote a particular way at the Labour Party conference.

Another usage views the mandate as a rod with which to beat the House of Lords: an unelected chamber has no right to reject legislation promised in a party's manifesto and passed by elected representatives in the House of Commons. This argument, the Salisbury doctrine, was used by Margaret Thatcher a number of times in conflicts with the upper chamber in 1985.

*See also* manifesto.

## manifesto

The programme of government presented by parties to voters at election time. The first was the Tamworth manifesto in 1835, which Robert Peel drew up in response to the Great Reform Act of 1832. In theory, Labour's manifesto is endorsed by the party conference and a two-thirds majority vote on a proposal guarantees its inclusion. Once elected into office the Parliamentary Labour Party is 'mandated' to carry it out. In an age of television politics very few ordinary voters actually read the manifesto document; nevertheless, it is still important because it contains a party's programme for government. It is also an anchor point for a party's campaign, politicians referring to it or defending it from attack. The style of the document has changed from the dull 'wordy' tracts of the 1950s to the glossy, picture-rich policy statements headed up with catchy titles of today. For example, in 1997 the Labour Party's manifesto had a

picture of Tony Blair on the front cover, with the words 'New Labour: Because Britain Deserves Better'.

*See also* mandate; Tamworth manifesto.

## Manor of Northstead
*See* Chiltern Hundreds.

## marching season
*See* Orange Order.

## marginal seat
A parliamentary constituency where the margin of victory between the winner and runner-up is close, often no more than a few percentage points difference. As distinct from 'safe seats', where large majorities, sometimes of 40 or 50 per cent, are secured by winners, the outcomes in marginal seats are difficult to predict. Factors which swing the balance may include tactical or negative voting, the impact of national issues, party or leader image, the personality or reputation of the candidate and the effectiveness of the local campaign. For these reasons, marginal seats often hold the key to victory in general elections and parties will therefore target their campaigning there. That said, in 1997, many safe seats, occupied by senior members of the government, fell to Labour in a surge of anti-Tory sentiment, altering the electoral map of Britain. In the 2001 general election the Conservatives did not generally perform well in the marginal seats, where often Labour managed to improve on its small 1997 majority. One of the reasons was a continuous monitoring of voter opinions by Labour in these seats, whereby 'tailored' approaches could be made to the 1,000 or so voters who would decide the contest.

## market
The mechanism in society whereby supply meets demand. In the process society is changed profoundly and so markets are politically significant. In a free market goods are offered to the public at prices which the producer thinks they are worth and which the public are prepared to pay. If they are successful business flourishes,

people are employed and profits are used for purchasing and reinvestment. However, if they are not a success, business failure follows, with unemployment and possibly misery until success in a new market can be achieved. In this way people come to be rich or poor, employers or employees and their chances in life, not to mention those of their families, are influenced accordingly. In Britain a market economy was established in the 19th century but the excesses of poverty were criticised and so socialism through the Labour Party became a popular option. After 1945 the economy was affected by nationalisation, whereby 20 per cent of it was taken into public ownership. In the 1970s the government intervened in the economy in many ways and provoked the neo-liberal reaction of Thatcherism, which led to privatisation in the 1980s and a determination to allow the market to proceed unfettered by government action so far as possible. New Labour, when it came to power in 1997, accepted this view of the market and has more or less adopted the Conservative attitude towards it.

## market testing

A process of competitive tendering. Market testing was inspired by the privatisation policies of the 1980s and the success (in terms of cost savings) of compulsory competitive tendering (CCT) in local government and the National Health Service. John Major went further and the 1991 white paper *Competing for Quality* proposed the market testing of a number of central government functions, including secretarial, accountancy, statistical and information technology services. The aim was to allow competitive bids from the private sector to undertake the same work and to award a contract to those that could deliver quality and efficiency of service. Certainly the tendering process identified true costs and sharpened up operational practices, but the approach was criticised by some as bureaucratic, costly and inimical to the public service ethic of the civil service. By 1996, Major's government claimed to have saved £720 million per year and to have

shed some 30,000 posts. The scheme was replaced in 1997 by 'best value', where there was increased emphasis on service quality and the dropping of the need to have a compulsory tendering process.

*See also* best value; compulsory competitive tendering.

## Marshall aid

The US funds given as part of the Marshall plan or European Recovery Program. This was passed by the US Congress, not without doubts, in 1948. Its impulse was to bolster a weakened Europe against the threat of communism from the east. Secretary of state George Marshall was the author of the plan, which invited European countries to articulate their requirements for recovery. British foreign secretary Ernest Bevin was quick to react to the offer and helped to make it a reality for the whole of Europe. The Soviet Union refused to participate and tried to subvert the plan. The Organisation for European Economic Cooperation was set up to administer the plan. Between 1948 and 1951 over $13.5 billion was disbursed via the plan, which is considered in the light of history to have been farsighted and highly successful.

## Marxism

One of the most significant political and intellectual movements of the 19th and 20th centuries, and named after the scholar and radical Karl Marx. Marx believed he had discovered the true motor of history in the relationship of people to the changing means of wealth production. He argued that those who controlled the means of production always became the dominant class of people in any society and went on to permeate that society with the ideas and values which underpinned their supremacy. He analysed history along these lines, declaring that, in the modern industrial era, 'bourgeois' owners of capital were the ruling class and the proletarian masses the subordinate one. The latter were exploited by the capitalist class to produce wealth, which only the ruling minority truly enjoyed. He predicted that the constant search by capitalists for bigger profits and lower prices to beat the competition would push down wages and create increasing poverty for the proletariat. Eventually the masses would rise up and throw off the controls of the dominant bourgeoisie and would go on, after a period of dictatorial control, to eliminate capitalism, and to introduce a socialist society in which ownership of property would be collective and not private. Once common ownership was introduced the benefits of social justice and equality would work their way through the economy and society and create a human fellowship based on trust and cooperation. Eventually, he predicted, the state would 'wither away' as an international commonwealth of communists came into being.

Marx did not have any doubts about his analysis and his predictions, which, he claimed, were based on the 'scientific' study of society and therefore inevitable. Lenin, a Russian intellectual and radical, reinterpreted Marx's original formulations and applied them to Russia in the revolution of 1917, but any hopes of a socialist utopia soon withered as Stalin took total and murderous control. Similar regimes were set up after 1945 as the USSR assumed a hegemony over eastern European countries. All of the world's communist regimes, except China, North Korea and Cuba, collapsed in the late 1980s and early 1990s and were replaced by regimes sympathetic to capitalism if not always to liberal democracy. It is historical fact that Marxism as a political programme was a gigantic and costly failure for many of the people who lived in communist countries; it failed to protect minimum human rights and produced precious little material prosperity either. Britain tended to be immune to any substantial Marxist influence, albeit the country had a tiny Communist Party and a few sympathetic trade unions, as well as Militants (following a Trotskyist version of Marxism) in the Labour Party, who were in any case by and large expelled in the late 1980s. This having been said, Marxism was and remains a formidable system of intellectual thought, which is still used by social scientists as a form of analysis, and is respected even by some of those hostile to its revolutionary prescriptions. There is some truth in the quip that 'Marx was right about what was wrong but wrong about what was right'.

See also capitalism; Marx, Karl.

## mass media

Defined by Dennis McQuail (a political scientist) as: 'The organised means for communicating openly and at a distance to many receivers within a relatively short space of time', and usually taken to mean the press, broadcasting (especially television), advertising, books and periodicals, cinema and, more recently, the Internet. In Britain there are 10 daily newspapers and nine Sundays. The BBC runs five national radio channels and two television ones, as well as digital radio and television channels. Independent television came into being in the 1950s and now runs three channels. Satellite television arrived in the 1990s and after a shaky start became successful. There is also a plethora of cable companies. Most people now derive their political information from television and tend to trust in its impartiality. On average people watch well over 20 hours of television a week and a fair proportion – some 20 per cent – covers news and current affairs. Since 1959 all elections have become television events, with voters forming their opinions about politicians by seeing them interviewed or otherwise speaking on television. Since Richard Nixon's 'Checkers' speech in 1952, in which his crude sentimental appeal to voters to trust him proved spectacularly successful, and the same man's failure to best John Kennedy in the 1960 presidential debate, politicians have realised the image projected is vital, hence the importance of media advisors and 'spin doctors' such as Peter Mandelson and Alastair Campbell. Indeed, most political commentators argue that the mass media, and television in particular, have turned attention away from the content of a message and towards its presentation. In the run-up to the 2001 general election New Labour came in for much criticism for relying too much on 'spin' and presentation. Certainly Labour had tended to continue in government the focused management of the media which had characterised its recent years in opposition.

*See also* political marketing; spin; spin doctor.

### Master of the Rolls

Originally the person who looked after the parchment records for the lord chancellor. In the 18th century the Master of the Rolls became the second judge in the court of Chancery and in 1881 a member of the Court of Appeal. The office holder presides in the Civil Division of this court and has special responsibility for solicitors. The Master of the Rolls is one of the most important judges in the land and can influence the legal climate of the times on a wide range of issues. Legal records are now kept in the Public Record Office.

### Matrix Churchill case, 1992

This originated when three businessmen were prosecuted for selling arms to the Middle East which ended up in Iraq, contrary to government guidelines. In court a government minister, Alan Clark, testified that the businessmen had been informally told their planned sale was acceptable. The huge row which resulted led to the Scott report into the affair and the identification of some officials and ministers who had acted less than properly. William Waldegrave was found to have misled the Commons over the government's policy in this area and wrongly advised ministers to sign public immunity certificates, which had the effect of allowing the government to withhold documents which the defence would have used to demonstrate that the businessmen were merely following the informal guidance given by government.

*See also* Scott report.

### May Day

1 May and the most important holiday for workers on the continent of Europe. It has also been a day of demonstrations and celebrations by trade unionists in Britain.

Under New Labour, enthusiasm for such activities has declined. In recent years May Day has become an occasion of anti-capitalist demonstration.

### mayor

A formal title given to the non-executive head of a district council granted borough status. In some cases, usually big cities, the chair of the council may be called lord mayor. In terms of power, the mayor is little more than a figurehead, opening fetes and presiding over council meetings, though the dignity of the office and the accompanying mayoral chain makes it an honour sought after by many councillors. The Labour government of 1997 proposed a US-style elected mayor for London and, by implication, for other cities.

*See also* elected mayor.

### Maze Prison

Symbolised the intractable conflicts of Northern Ireland. The prison, sited on a disused RAF airfield at Long Kesh, began as a prisoner of war camp in 1941. In the early 1970s it was used to intern IRA suspects without trial, who organised themselves along the lines of prisoners of war. In 1978 eight H blocks were opened at the site for the detention of paramilitaries and the prison was renamed the Maze. In 1981 Bobby Sands and nine others starved themselves to death. In 1998 Mo Mowlam, then Northern Ireland secretary, visited the Maze to assist the peace process. The prison closed in 2000.

### means-testing

An assessment of wealth to determine a person's eligibility for a benefit, usually a state one. In the 1930s the poor were means-tested as a condition of benefit and sometimes had to sell items of a sparse household to qualify. Consequently the approach was discredited until more recent years, when universal benefits were judged to advantage the wealthy, who did not need them. The alternative to means-testing – targeting payments or benefits – has received considerable attention since

Labour came to power in 1997 and has been applied in some areas, for example student loans.

## Mebyon Kernow

Established in 1951, this small party celebrates Cornish language and culture and calls for home rule for Cornwall. In the 1970s the party won council seats and averaged 15 per cent in local elections. Its call for a separate seat for the county in European elections won it over 10,000 votes in 1980. However, in elections for Westminster candidates have mustered only a few hundred votes.

## media bias

While newspapers openly display their political opinions, which is a legacy of the development of the press in Britain, broadcast media are required by law to maintain a political balance in their coverage of party political issues. However, politicians from Winston Churchill, Harold Wilson and Edward Heath to Margaret Thatcher and Tony Blair have accused the BBC of bias. On occasion politicians threaten, usually vaguely, to alter the basis of the Corporation's funding or attack particular programmes which they allege display the bias, for example (and especially) Radio Four's *Today* programme. After 1945 the press was usually pro-Conservative in its sympathies, but this changed in 1997 when many publications, most notably the *Sun*, owned by Rupert Murdoch, changed sides. Until this time Labour used to regard the press as hostile and the radio and television as 'our' media. Marxists and neo-Marxists like Antonio Gramsci assert that ruling-class values underpin most media output, which helps to indoctrinate the masses and blunt their ability to question such values. Others, like the Glasgow University Media Group, have suggested that working-class activists or striking trade unionists are generally represented as 'irresponsible extremists', whereas management or other authority figures are portrayed in a flatteringly 'responsible' light, thus legitimising an establishment agenda.

## media cross-ownership

This is an issue which focuses largely on the role of media magnate Rupert Murdoch, who owns four daily newspapers in Britain as well as the television satellite broadcaster Sky. Rules were established to prevent newspaper proprietors also owning more than 20 per cent of a terrestrial television company. The Communications Bill published in May 2002 offered a number of changes. These included the possible merging of all independent television companies and it allowed Murdoch, in theory at least, to make a bid for Channel 5. Broadcasters were surprised at the latter measure and most concluded a deal had been done by the Australian-American with the Blair government. Certain key regulations remained, however, for example that national newspaper groups are not allowed to own a television company and regional newspapers may not own a local television licence.

## Meibion Glyndyr (Sons of Glyndyr)

Militant Welsh faction which objected to the English 'invasion' of Wales for holiday homes as this, it was claimed, caused high house prices for local people. Some 300 holiday homes were firebombed between 1974 and 1994. In 1989 the organisation declared 'every white settler is a target'. The group also placed incendiary bombs in estate agents' offices in London, Liverpool and Sutton Coldfield. In 1990 the Welsh poet R. S. Thomas called for a campaign to deface English-owned homes; in 1993 Sion Aubrey Roberts was jailed for three years for sending letter bombs to Conservative politicians.

> Dal dy dir. [Stand your ground.] (Slogan of Cymuned, a Welsh pressure group dedicated to the defence of Welsh culture and language)

*See also* Free Wales Army.

## member of parliament (MP)

Any member of either of the houses of parliament (though in the public mind usually the Commons). MPs used to be unpaid and drawn substantially from the landed gentry; however, after 1911 they started to receive salaries and expenses. In April 2004 MPs received £54,485 per annum plus between £66,000 and £78,000 staff allowance. Cabinet ministers received £135,000 and Tony Blair £171,554. There are 659 MPs, though with the evolution of regional assemblies there is pressure to cut this number down to 500 or so. Fabian author Greg Power argues that MPs waste too much time on constituency problems and suggests that an ombudsman could take care of such matters, while MPs concentrate on holding the executive to account. He also argues for a proper career path for MPs to rival the lure of ministerial office, something which effectively neutralises up to a third of them, and often the brightest, as effective parliamentarians. Since the Second World War the House of Commons has become increasingly middle class. In 1951, 24 per cent of Conservative MPs had been to Eton, 65 per cent to university and 52 per cent (of the total) to Oxbridge, while the figures for Labour were 1 per cent to Eton, 41 per cent to university and 19 per cent to Oxbridge. By 1992 this had changed to 10 per cent to Eton, 73 per cent to university and 45 per cent to Oxbridge for the Conservatives, and for Labour it was 1 per cent to Eton once again, 61 per cent to university and 16 per cent to Oxbridge.

### meritocracy

The idea that a ruling elite should be selected on the basis of ability rather than social origins. Often this is thought to be a concept favoured by those liberals working for a fairer society. However, Michael Young showed in *The Rise of the Meritocracy* (1958) that it can be just as harmful as a hereditary elite. New Labour under Tony Blair enthusiastically talked of making Britain a meritocracy, where opportunities existed for all who had the talent to succeed. However, Young's book had been a warning rather than a blueprint. As he wrote in the *Guardian* (29 June 2001), he was arguing that while it is

sensible to give jobs to people on merit, it is the opposite 'when those who are judged to have merit harden into a new social class without room in it for others'. A free market in ability, in other words, can produce just as exclusive an elite as one based on birth or the accumulation of money. He pointed out that education had served to select a new kind of ruling elite based on ability, something which, like aristocratic credentials, is given by birth. These academically able children – predominantly born into the meritocratic class – are selected to shine at a young age while the rest are relegated to the bottom streams 'at the age of seven or before'. This large excluded group are destined to feel failures, to feel disconnected and to lapse into demoralised apathy, even failing to vote. The result is that the masses become disenfranchised as their potential leaders are sucked into the meritocracy. Young points out that the giants of Clement Attlee's cabinet were working-class men like Ernest Bevin, Herbert Morrison and Aneurin Bevan. In contrast, Blair's cabinet members are all products of the educational meritocracy. The result, predicted Young's prescient book, is a polarised society which is becoming more so, even to the extent of selection being reconsidered for education. Lord Hattersley reasserted Young's thesis in articles in the *Guardian* during 2001 and attracted some support in the party for his more traditional line of argument.

### metropolitan county

Set up by the Local Government Act 1972. These were urban 'super counties' with near regional functions regarding planning and transport. As well as Greater London (set up by an earlier act) there were Tyne and Wear, the West Midlands, West and South Yorkshire, Greater Manchester and Merseyside. In the 1980s they were all Labour controlled and Margaret Thatcher decided to abolish them in 1986. Labour warned that a huge outcry would result but there was none, although there were complaints from sections of the political class and media. The counties passed away largely unlamented and unnoticed.

## middle class

According to the British Market Research Association's six-category scheme, the middle classes are A (3 per cent of households) and B (16 per cent) and C1 (26 per cent) – the working class being C2 (26 per cent), D (17 per cent) and E (13 per cent). John Goldthorpe's alternative seven-point classification, of which the first four would qualify as middle class, runs through: higher salariat (12 per cent); lower salariat (16 per cent); routine clerical (24 per cent); petty bourgeoisie (7 per cent); foremen and technicians (5 per cent); skilled manual (11 per cent); unskilled manual (25 per cent). As traditional industries died out new ones, in the service sector for example, developed which tended to employ more educated middle-class people. In 1914, 80 per cent of Britain's population was working class; by the 1980s, less than 50 per cent could be so described. The middle class has therefore swollen and become dominant, with consequent changes in aspirations and ways of life; for example, one in three children in the 1990s proceeded to university, compared with only one in 20 in 1960. Significantly, the leader of the 'working class' party, Tony Blair, has classic middle-class qualifications, and more importantly values, of the kind usually associated with Conservative leaders. And while the Conservatives were able to claim four-fifths of middle-class votes in the 1960s, by the 1990s their share had fallen to three-fifths; similarly, Labour received a diminishing share of a shrinking working-class vote until the landslide victory in 1997 reversed the trend, when some of the largest swings to the party were from the lower middle classes, or C1 groups, a result assiduously pursued by Blair via his appeal to 'middle England'. Significantly there was a drift away from Labour among working-class voters in the 2001 general election but a drift towards Labour among the middle-classes, which suggests Blair's appeal is more attractive to the latter than the former.

See also class.

## middle England

Term used to denote the group of middle-class voters who can allegedly swing elections. Certainly the Labour Party needed to woo this section of the populace as the size of its traditional working-class constituency shrank along with manual occupations.

## MI5

See security services.

## Militant

See Militant Tendency.

## Militant Labour Party

Set up by Peter Taafe in 1993 in the wake of the Labour Party's successful campaign to expel members of the Militant Tendency, an extremist Trotskyite organisation that tried to infiltrate the party and influence its policy towards revolutionary goals.

## Militant Tendency (Revolutionary Socialist League)

One of the most prominent Trotskyist political groupings in Britain since the Second World War. In political terms, militancy refers to aggressive, combative action, sometimes direct action, in pursuit of political or ideological objectives. A militant would see politics as warfare, a struggle against opposites, whether these are from the left or right. The Militant Tendency was led by the South African Ted Grant, formerly of the Militant Labour League and the Revolutionary Communist Party before the two merged to form the Revolutionary Socialist League. Grant teamed up with Peter Taafe from Liverpool to set up the Militant newspaper and the League adopted the policy of 'entryism' to infiltrate the Labour Party. The League therefore took a covert role and members of Militant were in theory only supporters of a 'Tendency' or a newspaper and not a party within a party, which would have been against Labour Party rules. However, this 'nonexistent' organisation succeeded in taking over Liverpool council, with its member Derek Hatton becoming deputy leader and

POLITICS

someone with a national profile. After 1983 Militant boasted two MPs: Terry Fields, a fireman from Liverpool, and Dave Nellist, who represented a Coventry Labour seat. Although numbering only some 5,000 members, its impact on Labour's public image was significant, as it provided ammunition for Labour's enemies in parliament and the press. The crunch came when Militant ran Leslie Mahood against Peter Kilfoyle in the Walton by-election following the death of Eric Heffer; Kilfoyle easily won and those who supported the Militant candidate revealed themselves as supporters of a party hostile to Labour and were therefore vulnerable to expulsion. Labour leader Neil Kinnock also won a huge moral victory at the 1985 conference by bitterly attacking Militant and its extremist policies, which in Liverpool had nearly brought the city to bankruptcy. Towards the end of the 1980s Militant suffered expulsions from Labour and lost support. In 1993 it re-emerged as the Militant Labour Party, a separate party with scant support. Its policies included nationalisation of the top 200 companies; extension of state control to the whole of the economy; workers' control; and the nationalisation of the media. Remnants of Militant joined the Socialist Alliance, an umbrella grouping on the left which fought some seats in the 2001 general election with no success.

*See also* entryism; Hayward report; Whitty report.

**military**
*See* Ministry of Defence.

**Millbank Tower**
Former headquarters of the Labour Party and, for mordant critics of the party's modernisation, the nerve centre for Labour's media machine. These smart offices were occupied for the 1997 election after the less salubrious accommodation of Walworth Road was left behind. Its high-tech resources and the proactive style of its staff became associated with the party's alleged 'control freak' tendencies, whereby MPs, members of the National Executive

Committee and even ordinary members were coerced into toeing the New Labour line. On 20 March 2002 it was announced Labour would be moving again, this time to modern offices in Old Queen Street, behind the houses of parliament, at a cost estimated at £6 million. This is Labour's fifth home in 102 years.

*See also* on message.

**Millennium Dome**
Conceived by John Major's Conservative government in 1996 as a celebration of the forthcoming millennium celebrations, it was supported by Tony Blair's incoming Labour administration in 1997. Some suggested Blair saw the project as a symbol of a new 'inclusive' Britain. Richard Rogers, the architect, designed the building, which cost £750 million to erect. However, controversy developed early on, when the creative director resigned in January 1998 and the opening night was a disaster in that 3,000 guests were stuck in queues for hours, including journalists and other influential people. In February 2000 the chief executive was replaced by Pierre-Yves Gerbeau, recruited from Disneyland in Paris. Despite his colourful efforts, he failed to bring in the planned millions of visitors and the Dome was forced to go cap in hand for more money, first £29 million in May 2000, then £43 million in August and another £47 million in September, when it acquired yet another new management team. The Japanese company Nomura considered buying the Dome in August 2000, planning to turn it into a theme park. Few supporters of the Dome remained and when Nomura pulled out during the latter part of the year the matter became even more of an embarrassment to the Blair government, both as a commercial venture and as a symbol of its 'big tent' inclusive philosophy. Responsibility for the debacle shifted ministerially around the Labour cabinet, ending up with Lord Falconer, who, despite frequent calls from the opposition, refused to resign following the Dome's failure.

In May 2002 the Dome was finally disposed of: it was given, for no charge, to a business syndicate, which planned to convert it into an entertainment complex. In exchange the government was to receive a share of the profits.

> I'm sorry, with the benefit of hindsight, we should have thrown in the towel. (Peter Mandelson, once minister in charge, on the Dome to GQ *Magazine*, July 2002)

*See also* Hinduja brothers.

## miners' strike, 1984–85

A watershed event of the 1980s which confirmed Margaret Thatcher's political dominance and broke the power of unions to determine political events. The miners' strikes of 1972 and 1974 are widely understood to have brought down the Heath government in 1974. In 1981 Joe Gormley, the President of the National Union of Mineworkers (NUM), won his confrontation with the government, but only because it felt unable to sustain a fight. In 1984 the situation was different. The union was now led by Arthur Scargill, an avowed revolutionary and charismatic leader who was convinced the miners could lead a political rising against the Conservatives. He was a clever tactician and skilful with the media but a poor long-term strategist and was too convinced that he knew best. Ostensibly the dispute focused on the proposed closure of pits but Scargill had his own agenda. The stocks of coal available to power stations was plentiful and sufficient to last out the winter of 1984–85, at which time miners had already been without pay for six months. The Coal Board was led by someone unafraid of Scargill and unaffected by recent political history, Ian McGregor. The police took a much more militant approach to the strikers than had been taken in 1972. The cabinet remained united and Thatcher instructed McGregor not to settle. The Labour Party was noncommittal throughout. Scargill was possibly unnerved by two previous members' ballots which had refused to endorse strike action and declared a strike without any such reinforcement, now legally a requirement under the Employment Act 1982.

The courts were able to declare the action illegal and sequester union assets, to the detriment of the union's ability to continue the struggle. Finally and decisively, the Midlands miners decided to go back to work and defy the NUM; they also set up their own breakaway union, the Union for Democratic Mineworkers. The NUM decided to go back to work at the delegate conference of 5 March 1985, a year after the miners had first gone out. It had been a defeat of massive proportions, leaving a residue of bitterness and weakening the trade union movement for a decade or more. Subsequent events proved Scargill's predictions regarding the closure of pits to be more than justified. The number of miners now working in Britain is a small fraction of what is was (over a million) in 1945.

*See also* Scargill, Arthur.

## miners' strikes, 1972 and 1974

Miners' strikes which weakened and finally helped destroy Edward Heath's Conservative government elected in 1970. The first centred on pay and began in January 1972. By February a state of emergency had been announced when coal supplies were low enough to threaten industrial production. The young Yorkshire miners' leader Arthur Scargill closed Saltley Power Station in Birmingham through the use of 'flying pickets', who outnumbered police 7,000–500. The Wilberforce report soon recommended a massive pay increase, which made a mockery of Heath's attempted industrial relations strategy.

The 1974 miners' pay claim and resultant strike occurred in the shadow of the massive increases in oil prices prompted by the Organization of Petroleum Exporting Countries. Given the support for the miners by other unions together with the residual sympathy the miners were always able to provoke, the strike hit hard. In January 1974 Heath called a three-day week to conserve coal supplies. He then called an election with the theme of 'Who Governs Britain?' in a direct challenge to the unions' power. Sadly for Heath the voters were not ready to oppose union power and he was forced to give way to Wilson's third term of government.

*See also* three-day week.

## minimum wage

Part of Labour's 1997 general election manifesto. The minimum wage was introduced after 1997 at £3.60 per hour; employers paying below that amount would be liable to legal action. A lower level was set for 18–21-year-olds. Contrary to warnings from the Conservatives and the Confederation of British Industry, its introduction had minimal impact on employment levels, as it was widely believed to have been set sufficiently low. The new measure had the effect of improving the pay of 1.7 million workers. In October 2000 the rate was increased to £3.70 but the Trades Union Congress (TUC) campaigned for a flat rate of £5.00. The government's Low Pay Commission makes recommendations regarding the appropriate rate. John Monks, secretary general of the TUC, described the minimum wage as 'one of the government's greatest achievements' in August 2000. In October 2001 it was increased from £3.70 to £4.10 and the lower rate for younger workers (18–21) from £3.20 to £3.50 per hour, rising to £3.60 by October 2002. It was estimated by the government that, as a result of the minimum wage, over 1 million people – mostly women – enjoyed an average increase in their wages of over 15 per cent. In the 2004 budget the minimum wage was increased to £4.85 per hour for workers over 22 and £4.10 for those aged 18–21. Fears that the new measure would cause widespread unemployment proved groundless and the Conservatives dropped their opposition to the measure.

## MINIS

Management Information System for Ministers, invented by Michael Heseltine while he was secretary of state for the environment. In essence, according Michael Crick, it was 'knowing about whom in

his [Heseltine's] department did what, and at what cost' (*Michael Heseltine: A Biography*, 1997, p. 206). The idea was that the minister could then make judgements about those activities that were worthwhile and those that were not. He claimed this would make officials more cost-conscious and help to keep bureaucratic growth in check. Each of the Department of the Environment's 65 directorates produced a long report on their activities in 1980, setting its priorities, expenditure and staff costs. The process became a rolling annual one, with the minister passing responsibility over to officials after the first year. At first civil servants resisted the system as unjustifiably intrusive but eventually came to accept it as useful.

## minister

Person appointed to government by the prime minister on behalf of the queen. Ministers represent the 'front line' of democratic control of the government machine on behalf of voters; they provide the connection with the voter in that they are drawn from the largest party elected at a general election. That said, it is not necessary for a minister to be a member of either house (a notable example was Patrick Gordon Walker). It is a convention that they do so, though the solicitor general for Scotland has variously not been an MP or peer. In theory ministers lay down the policy their department will pursue but in practice much of it will have been decided in opposition and much of this will be modified and interpreted by civil service advisors.

The most junior ministerial rank is that of parliamentary private secretary, a kind of parliamentary 'bag carrier' but nevertheless part of the team and, if promise is shown, likely to progress further. Next comes the parliamentary under-secretary, a junior minister who will speak for the department in the house and help usher through bills. The minister of state comes next, a middle-ranking position, followed by ministers who are heads of department but not in the cabinet. Finally come full cabinet ministers, usually known as secretaries of state.

It is possible for a minister to be head of a department but not to be given a place in the cabinet, and some ministers attend cabinet though not as members, the main one being the chief whip (a class of minister), though others occasionally do, like John Reid, who in 1998 was transport minister.

> You can read. It is a great happiness. I totally neglected it while I was in business, which has been the whole of my life, and to such a degree that I cannot now read a page – a warning to all Ministers. (Robert Walpole, the first prime minister, on seeing Henry Fox, Lord Holland, reading in a library at Houghton)

## ministerial code of conduct

A substantial publication produced by the Cabinet Office. It was originally drawn up in 1945 but was kept confidential until 1992. Its purpose is to provide guidance and regulation of relationships between ministers, the prime minister and government departments. It was reissued in 1997 under the title 'A Code of Conduct and Guidance on Procedures for Ministers'. The code is advisory and there are no stated sanctions, but under Tony Blair it has been seen as part of New Labour's concern to control ministers from the centre. The newly written paragraph 88 in particular was cited in support of this argument: it insists all new policy initiatives and proposed public interviews with ministers be cleared first with the Number 10 Press Office.

*See also* code of conduct for MPs.

## ministerial resignation

Reasons for ministerial resignations include the following:

1 they feel unable to support government policy (for example Aneurin Bevan and Harold Wilson over cuts to the National Health Service in 1951, Michael Heseltine over Westland);
2 they are asked to do so by a prime minister who wishes to dispense with their services (for example David Mellor after the scandal involving his affair with the actress Antonia de Sancha);
3 they wish to run for the leadership (for example John Redwood in July 1995; it was also suggested this was Bevan's true motive when he resigned);
4 they feel they have to take responsibility for policy failure (for example Lord Carrington over the invasion of the Falklands Islands in 1982);
5 they are subject to intense public criticism (for example Nicholas Ridley after his anti-German comments in 1990);
6 like Estelle Morris in October 2002, they feel they are not 'as effective' as they should be.

Alan Milburn resigned as health minister in June 2003 because he wanted to spend more time with his young family. Ministerial sackings are sometimes formally described as resignations, for example the departure of Peter Mandelson after his apparent lapse involving the Hinduja brothers. John Major's governments 1990–97 witnessed 12 altogether: four resignations as a result of sex scandals; three as a result of financial scandals; four from principle; and one because of public criticism.

*See also* ministerial responsibility.

## ministerial responsibility

A constitutional principle that ministers are responsible to parliament, effectively the House of Commons, for what they and their departments do. In the 18th century ministers were still responsible to the monarch but as power shifted to parliament their accountability shifted accordingly. Ministers now became responsible to parliament individually and collectively, and would be required to resign if a policy or ministerial action proved impossible for the cabinet to support. Ministers also resign occasionally from a sense of honour, as in the case of Lord Carrington over the Argentine attack on the Falklands Islands, although few of his colleagues felt he was personally responsible. He went after Conservative MPs saw fit to criticise his department as culpable; he believed it not to be, but felt could not carry on without the confidence of his party.

*See also* collective responsibility.

## Ministry of Agriculture, Fisheries and Food (MAFF)

Name given to the ministry in charge of agriculture 1903–2001. Once the principal source of wealth in Britain, agriculture now employs less than 3 per cent of the workforce. However, its political importance should not be underestimated. The Board of Agriculture was established in 1793 to stimulate agricultural improvement. In 1893 a ministry was set up and it embodied fisheries from 1903. In 1955 it absorbed food to become the Ministry of Agriculture, Fisheries and Food (MAFF). The National Farmers' Union worked closely with the ministry and was regarded as exerting a less than healthy influence over its policy formation by some. MAFF was a cabinet ministry but was not regarded as being in the first rank of importance, although occasionally it became so for political reasons. In theory it was responsible for public consumption of food and those who produced it. The conflict was exposed during crises such as that which occurred over BSE (bovine spongiform encephalitis), where it was unclear whether MAFF's principal concern was with the consumers or the farmers. The Phillips report into the handling of the BSE crisis was highly critical of the ministry. MAFF negotiated with Brussels over payments under the Common Agricultural Policy (CAP) of the European Union. It also: looked after the countryside and the coast; licensed veterinary products; registered pesticides; and undertook necessary scientific research. MAFF was in charge of the foot-and-mouth crisis in 2001 and again was widely seen as having handled it ineffectively. As a result it was subsumed within the new Department for Environment, Food and Rural Affairs in 2001.

See also bovine spongiform encephalopathy; Curry report; Department for Environment, Food and Rural Affairs; foot-and-mouth disease; Phillips report.

## Ministry of Defence (MoD)

www.mod.uk

Ministry in charge of armed forces. The three armed services used to boast a ministry each – the Admiralty, War Office and Air Ministry – but they were brought under one umbrella in 1964. Initially it had coordination responsibilities only but in 1964 the MoD was established as a ministry in its own right and was later led by Denis Healey, the powerful Labour politician. According to the annual defence white paper the MoD's mission is to 'provide, by the most effective means, armed forces of appropriate capacity, readiness and sustainability to implement our defence strategy through national, NATO, UN, WEU and other allied operations as necessary'. Since the amalgamation of the three services in the unified ministry the armed forces are treated more as a single unit than a tripartite one.

See also armed forces; defence policy.

## minority government

A government that takes office or continues in office without the absolute majority needed to vote its measures through. This has happened in the case of Labour governments in 1924 and 1929–31. In February 1974 Labour formed a government despite being in an overall minority, something which was corrected in the October 1974 general election, when Labour managed a majority of three. However, this thin advantage did not last and from 1976 to 1978 the Liberals supported Labour: the so-called Lib–Lab pact. After the elections to the Welsh assembly in 1999 Labour failed to win a majority but decided to rule as a minority administration based on the calculation that the Liberal Democrats and Plaid Cymru had no reason to bring it down when the assembly was still in its early stages. Soon after Labour entered a coalition with the Liberal Democrats, thus matching the arrangement in the Scottish parliament.

## MI6

See security services.

## mission statement

Strictly speaking, the purposes and scope of an organisation's activity. The term, usually associated with commercial organisations, has now spread to hitherto non-business operations such as charities, educational institutions and most recently central government departments. Mission statements have been introduced into many government departments, an example being the Home Office, whose mission is 'Building a Safe, Just and Tolerant Society'.

*See also* political marketing.

## mixed economy

A concept which effectively entered the language after 1945, when the Labour government nationalised 20 per cent of the economy. This produced a substantial public as well as private sector – hence a 'mixed' economy. Left-wing members of the Labour Party called for a bigger public sector from the 1950s onwards, while those on the revisionist right believed the private sector was now 'tamed' and functioning in a more or less responsible fashion. The debate continued through the 1960s and 1970s but the size of the public sector shrunk drastically in the 1980s, when Margaret Thatcher pursued her privatisation policies. The Labour government under Tony Blair seems happy with the 'mix' in the national economy inherited from John Major and indeed took a pragmatic approach to further privatisations if they seemed to offer the best means of delivering a service.

## modernisation

Name given to the changes wrought in the Labour Party after its disastrous defeat in the 1983 general election. Neil Kinnock as Labour leader thereafter urged his party to rethink its structure, decision making and its policies, especially on Europe, unilateralism, nationalisation, the free enterprise economy and the unions. John Smith, Kinnock's successor, advanced the process still further, with reforms of the party's links with the unions and democratisation of the annual party conference. But the biggest changes were introduced by Tony Blair and Gordon Brown, assisted by 'modernisers' like Peter Mandelson (who had been appointed the party's communications director by

Kinnock). They moved Labour policy both in opposition and government to be far more friendly to business and less radical in most policy areas except constitutional reform. For example, Blair's abolition of clause four removed the damaging fiction that Labour wished to impose state control over the whole of the economy. Part of the process was designed for political purposes – to demonstrate within the party what could be done nationally, that is, a modernised party would be a model for a modernised monarchy, business world, or indeed the whole country. The constitutional changes introduced in the early years of the Labour government after 1997, such as devolution, elected mayors and the reform of the House of Lords, were all part of this modernising agenda. The term has now assumed the status of an article of faith for those committed to the 'project' of reinvigorating British society and institutions. The term surfaced in Labour's plans for changes in central government, as announced in the white paper *Modernising Government*, published in March 1999. This signalled a drive not only for efficient, integrated or 'joined up' government, but also open and citizen-focused administration.

## Modernisation Committee

Select committee considering how the House of Commons might be modernised. This 15-member committee was set up in June 1997 by a standing order of the House, which was renewed in 2001. Its terms of reference tasked the committee to 'consider how the practice and procedures of the House should be modernised, and to make recommendations thereon'. The committee has produced a number of reports and under the chairmanship of Robin Cook introduced substantial changes which became operative in January 2004.

## monarchy

www.royal.gov.uk

A traditional form of government which held sway for over a thousand years since Britain emerged from the struggles among the seven kingdoms comprising Anglo-

Saxon England. Early monarchs wielded supreme power but the monarch is strictly limited in the modern day to performing ceremonial functions, like opening parliament and meeting delegates from abroad. The monarch is, in theory, the supreme head of the country and can reject legislation but in practice the queen follows the instructions of the prime minister of the day. Some constitutional experts argue that the monarch's residual right to choose the prime minister when there is no clear winner after a general election is important and could be vital if, for example, the voting system were to be changed to one of proportional representation, when coalition government would become much more likely. Other experts disagree and argue that any such intervention would precipitate action to abolish these remaining powers. The scandalous events surrounding the British monarchy during the 1980s and 1990s diminished its popularity but polls show the public still felt the country needs a monarch and a majority believed Prince Charles had done a good job of bringing up his two sons following the death of their mother in 1997. According to commentators, as the new millennium approached, the monarchy was ripe for 'modernising' reform. In 1994 the queen had met some of her critics by agreeing to pay tax on her private income. By early 2000 cuts in the civil list were predicted and the monarchy was urged to save money, as it proved it could do in respect of travel costs in the year 2000. In February 2002 Kevin McNamara moved a 10-minute rule bill to repeal the law which bans Catholics from succession to the throne. The Act of Settlement in 1688 enshrined this measure following the replacement of Catholic James II by William and Mary.

> Monarchy is something kept behind a curtain about which there is a great deal of hustle and fuss, and a wonderful air of seeming solemnity. But when by accident the curtain happens to be opened and the company see what it is, they burst into laughter. (Tom Paine)

*See also* civil list.

## Monday Club

www.conservativeuk.com

Conservative group set up in 1962 in the wake of Harold Macmillan's 'wind of change' speech, which anticipated the country's withdrawal from its imperial possessions. It concerns itself with defence and foreign affairs and immigration and takes a militant right-wing stance, to the extent it has attracted accusations of being suspiciously close to neo-fascist groupings. The organisation comprises 'members and supporters of the Conservative Party and Conservative Associations' but is usually best known via its MP members, who have included, over the years, George Gardiner, Harvey Proctor and Neil Hamilton.

## monetarism

The theory that the supply of money circulating in the economy has a direct relationship to price levels. The theory leads to the assertion that excessive money supply causes inflation. It was articulated in the 1970s by Milton Friedman and the Chicago School of economists and influenced the Labour chancellor Denis Healey as well as the more ideologically sympathetic Conservatives, including Keith Joseph, Geoffrey Howe, Nigel Lawson and Margaret Thatcher. The Conservatives applied their brand of monetarism in the 1980s and their medium-term financial statement (MTFS) was designed as a way of limiting future money supply. Although the MTFS was never a good guide to rates of inflation or public spending, and the targets were regularly overshot, the basic tenets of monetarism have not been rejected; rather they have been absorbed into Treasury thinking.

*See also* Chicago School of Economics; new right.

## Monetary Policy Committee (MPC) (of the Bank of England)

The body, set up in 1997, that sets the rate of interest for the British economy. The ability to set interest rates is possibly one of the most powerful tools a government possesses in controlling the national economy. Traditionally the Bank of England did this on the instructions of the chancellor. Many criticised the 'politicisation' of the process by which interest rates were raised or lowered according to political rather than economic criteria, the cost being to the long-term health of the national economy. To counter this and mark a break with the past Gordon Brown, the Labour chancellor, announced in early May 1997 that he would be giving the Bank of England the power to set interest rates independently. The Monetary Policy Committee of the Bank was given responsibility to set interest rates in order to achieve price stability, as defined by the 2.0 per cent government inflation target. This was a momentous change to the role of the Bank and required legislation which amended the Bank of England Act 1946, a decision strongly influenced by Ed Balls, the chancellor's economic advisor.

The MPC is composed of the governor of the Bank, the two deputy governors, the Bank's chief economist and executive director for market operations, and four external members appointed by the chancellor. It meets once a month, when decisions are made on the basis of one person one vote (however, the governor has a deciding vote if there is no majority). In keeping with the principle of open government espoused by New Labour, minutes of the meetings are published, and the MPC is accountable to the House of Commons through the Treasury Committee. Brown signalled that British monetary policy would be attuned to the needs of the national economy and aligned Britain with the independent central banks of many other countries.

**money bill**

An item of legislation which concerns taxation or public expenditure. The Parliament Act 1911 provided that money bills passed by the Commons become law if not passed without amendment by the Lords within one month. Nonetheless, the Lords can and

sometimes does debate money bills, as it is always possible that the government may be influenced. There is normally a short debate on second reading of the Finance Bill, for instance. Few bills are certified as money bills because they have to deal exclusively with money – if a bill has any non-supply provisions, then it cannot be so certified.

**money supply**

See monetarism.

**Monopolies and Mergers Commission**

See Competition Commission.

**Monster Raving Loony Party**

www.omrlp.com

Set up in the 1960s by ('Screaming') 'Lord' David Sutch, a pop singer. It proposed a nonsensical set of policies, to re-place Commander Bill Boackes, who used to turn up at the counts in his wellington boots and scruffy overcoat, as the regular by-election 'joke' candidate. It fought over 40 such contests and never saved its deposit but once, in 1994, mustered 4.8 per cent of the vote. In 1989 it polled more than David Owen's rump Social Democratic Party at the Bootle by-election, an event that was rumoured to have persuaded Owen to wind up the organisation. It once had a council-lor sitting under its banner in the West Country. 'Lord' Sutch died in 1998 but his party fought the 2001 general election, when it won some 6,000 votes in total; it promised smaller class sizes through the device of asking the children to stand closer together.

See also Sutch, David.

**Mont Pelerin Society**

www.montpelerin.org

International conference formed imme-diately after the war in which academics and politicians met to discuss the ideas of Friedrich von Hayek and Milton Friedman. It provided the inspiration for the forma-tion in 1957 of the Institute of Economic Affairs, which did so much to introduce free enterprise and monetarist thinking into the Conservative Party.

## Moore's email, 2001

Email sent to departmental press staff in the immediate wake of the 11 September 2001 terrorist attacks in the USA in which Jo Moore suggested this was an opportune moment to 'bury' sensitive announcements, for example on councillors' expenses. Jo Moore was an advisor to transport secretary Stephen Byers and her email caused outrage. Jonathan Freedland in the *Guardian* wrote that the message 'will remain forever the set text of the spin doctor's craft' and will be cited as 'evidence of New Labour cynicism for years to come'.

The case was further complicated when it emerged she was in conflict with the head of communications at the ministry, Martin Sixsmith. Jo Moore hung on for several months but was forced to resign in February 2002 when it was alleged she had issued a similar message regarding Princess Margaret's funeral. Sixsmith's departure was more turbulent, as his resignation was originally announced by Sir Richard Mottram, the permanent secretary to the department, but Sixsmith then denied that he had resigned and a public row broke out in which Byers' veracity was prominently questioned. The whole saga placed the 'culture of spin' in New Labour in the spotlight and reflected very badly on the government.

## MORI (Market and Opinion Research International)

www.mori.com
Polling and market research organisation founded by the political scientist Robert Worcester. MORI used to provide private polls for the Labour Party and is one of the most respected names in British market research. It now publishes its surveys in *The Times*, *Sunday Times*, *Daily Express*, *Daily Star* and *The Economist*, among others. It also conducted the research work for the government's People's Panel, which is freely available on the Internet.

## *Morning Star*

www.morningstaronline.co.uk
Newspaper founded in 1930 as the *Daily Worker* by the Communist Party of Great Britain and an assiduous follower of the line set by Moscow, even during the Molotov–Ribbentrop Pact in 1939. For a while in the early part of the Second World War it was suppressed, as the Soviet Union's neutrality at that time was felt to be friendly to Hitler. Once Hitler attacked the Soviet Union in 1941 the ban was lifted and the newspaper became part of the war effort. In 1966 the paper changed its name to the *Morning Star*. Circulation figures for the publication were regularly boosted by the extra copies bought by the Soviet Union. The paper is no longer connected to the Communist Party but its editor, John Haylett, claims its 'credo is based on the nonsectarian approach of Britain's Road to Socialism, the programme of the Communist Party of Britain which was set up in 1988 as the re-establishment of the party founded as the Communist Party of Great Britain (CPGB) in 1920'.

## motion

The device used to initiate a debate in either house. A motion to 'take note' is often used to debate something specific like a report of a select committee. A motion 'calling for papers' is often used by backbenchers to direct attention to something they feel strongly about. At the end of the debate convention demands that the backbencher withdraws the motion.

## MP

*See* member of parliament.

## multiculturalism

The assumption that people from different ethnic backgrounds can live side by side, accepting diversity and respecting other cultures. However, the riots in Oldham, Burnley and Bradford in 2001 revealed ethnic communities which were isolated and polarised, living 'parallel lives'. The Cantle report called for proactive measures to encourage social cohesion, including the need for better training in English and the confronting of practices at variance with British values, like forced marriages.

*See also* Cantle report.

## multilateralism

Consensus-based approach to problem solving in international relations. Elements of multilateralism can be discerned in the 19th century but received institutional expression in the form of the League of Nations in 1918 and the United Nations in 1945, the Bretton Woods agreement in 1945 and many agreements since. Regional organisations like the European Union have undermined some of the consensus and the determination of US president George W. Bush to disown agreements like the Kyoto Protocol on global warming was a major setback to those who view this approach as the only hope for the world.

## multi-party system

*See* party system.

## Munich agreement, 30 September 1938

Signed by Neville Chamberlain, Mussolini (for Italy), Hitler (for Germany) and Daladier (for France). The German dictator had threatened to go to war in support of German-speaking Nazi supporters in the Sudetenland, part of Czechoslovakia. Chamberlain, who feared another world war, agreed to the transfer of the territory; the Czechs were neither present nor consulted. He returned home to announce 'peace in our time' to a relieved nation. Hitler marched in on 5 October and in March 1939 occupied the rest of the country. In retrospect Munich is seen as a betrayal and invitation to Hitler to continue until war was inevitable,

but some argue 'appeasement' enabled Britain to prepare more effectively for the imminent war.

## Municipal Corporations Act 1835

First attempt to reform local government in towns and cities in response to the vast economic and social changes of the Industrial Revolution. The act established councils elected by ratepayers and indirectly elected aldermen and mayors.

## Muslim community

There were 1.8 million Muslims in Britain in 2002, over 80 per cent of whom voted Labour in 1997. However, signs emerged by 2001 that Muslims were quite prepared to vote for another party if their candidate was also Muslim. In the 1997 general election the Labour majority in Bradford West was slashed after Labour adopted a Sikh candidate, Marsha Singh; the Conservatives fielded a Muslim candidate, Mohammed Riaz, who clearly persuaded substantial numbers of former Labour-voting Muslims to switch sides. However, Labour's share of the vote increased in the 2001 general election in that constituency. In seven constituencies – in the north and the Midlands as well as London – the Muslim vote exceeds Labour majorities, so is clearly important.

Since 11 September 2001 Britain has awoken to the threat posed by militant Muslim groups, including Al-Muhajiroun, Hizb-ut-Tahrir and Supporters of Sharia, as well as individuals like Asif Mohammed Hanif, who became a suicide bomber in Tel Aviv in April 2003.In July 2004 Muslim disaffection caused by the Iraq war helped create massive swings against the government in two by-elections in Leicester and Birmingham.

POLITICS

# N

**nanny state**
*See* paternalism.

**'Napoleonic system'**
Phrase famously used in 1997 by Jonathan Powell, Tony Blair's chief of staff, to describe the way in which the 'feudal barons' of Whitehall would be bent to the government's will. Andrew Rawnsley in the *Observer* (18 February 2001) judged that this had not happened: 'The Civil Service has frustrated the PM subtly and sinu-ously'. He went on to argue that the civil service had managed to defend both the status quo and its own failings remarkably successfully.

**nation state**
The main unit of political and social organ-isation, and an organising concept in the study of history and international relations (a branch of political science). Nation states are characterised by territorial sovereignty and the sharing of features of history, language and cultural identity. The idea of a nation also has ideological uses, for example in the building of political movements such as nationalism. However, very few states exhibit all the characteristics stated above, in par-ticular the quality of having a single cultural and linguistic identity.

The United Kingdom is by definition a state which originated from the separate political units of England, Scotland, Wales and (Northern) Ireland. However, these 'provinces' still retain strong cultural and, in the case of Wales, linguistic traditions, which symbolically challenge the idea of a United Kingdom. The force of this challenge is evidenced by the devolution measures introduced by Labour after 1997 to satisfy nationalist sentiment. The 'troubles' in Northern Ireland go beyond symbolic representations and bear wit-ness to the fact that not all inhabitants of the United Kingdom consent to be part of that state. Moreover, the development of a British multicultural society further emphasises the mythical elements of a single British nation. This having been said, the concept is still important in the Conservative Party, as nationhood constitutes a central element in the party's traditions. The idea of a nation state also has value to those who claim that British sovereignty is threatened by supranational organisations such as the European Union.
*See also* devolution; sovereignty.

**National Air Traffic Services (NATS)**
www.nats.co.uk
The body that provides air traffic control services over UK airspace. During the run-up to the 1997 general election future Treasury minister Andrew Smith declared that 'our skies are not for sale' and criticised Conservative plans to privatise NATS. However, once in power Labour decided on a part privatisation of the system, al-legedly in order to facilitate much-needed private investment. There was a great deal of criticism from within the party, especially as the privatisation of the railways was unravelling during this time. However, the measure was pushed through in 2000 in the form of a sale of a 51 per cent stake for £750 million to a consortium of seven airlines, led by British Airways, Virgin Atlantic and EasyJet. Some thought this price excessive given the volatile state of the industry and the beginnings of recession in the US economy. Financial targets set by the new consortium – involving stringent cost and staff savings – were regarded as tough and on top of that came the reluc-tance of people to fly in such great numbers following the terrorist attacks in the USA on 11 September 2001. By February 2002 NATS was in difficulties and required more funding as well as a possible increase in its charges. In March 2002 the govern-ment fed in £30 billion of a planned £60 billion worth of aid. Two months later NATS suffered from computer break-downs but after that has functioned without noticeable public complaint.

## National Archives
www.nationalarchives.gov.uk
The Public Record Office merged with
the Historical Manuscripts Commission in
April 2003 to form the National Archives.
This body, based in Kew, west London,
looks after the records of central government and the law courts and makes them
available to the public.

## National Asset Register
A 900-page modern-day Domesday
Book compiled by the Treasury in 2001,
designed to inform government of what the
state owns and to sell off anything which
is superfluous to requirements. Number 10
Downing Street was priced at £20 million;
a Trident submarine at £800 million; and
the British Library at £400 million.

## National Association of Schoolmasters and Union of Women Teachers (NASUWT)
A rival to the National Union of Teachers.
The union has over 200,000 members. It is
not linked to any political party.

## National Audit Office (NAO)
www.nao.org.uk
Originates from the office of the comptrol-
ler and auditor general (who now heads the
NAO), which was established in 1866 to
ensure money raised through taxation is
used for the purpose parliament intended.
The staff has grown to around 800 and the
NAO focuses its investigations on value for
money and efficiency in the public services.
The auditor general is responsible to the
Public Accounts Commission (PAC, not
to be confused with the Public Accounts
Committee), which comprises nine senior
MPs and was set up in 1984. In 1987–88
the NAO made 174 recommendations to
achieve value for money; the PAC accepted
161 of them and passed them on to the
government, which accepted 153. The
comptroller and auditor general is forbidden
from commenting on policy but inevitably
the reports have clear policy implications.
The NAO provides reports on all government spending, although shares government

auditing with the Audit Commission and
other agencies of public audit. Some NAO
reports are not published and decisions to
publish in sensitive areas can be controversial. In the *Guardian* (20 July 2001) David
Walker commented that, for all the excellence of the job it does, savings from NAO
activities amounted to a relatively miniscule
£400 million in 2000–01, compared with
a total public spending figure of over £600
billion.
  *See also* audit; Audit Commission.

## national debt
Sum of the funds which government bor-
rows at home (internal debt) and from
creditors abroad (external debt). The debt
originated in 1692 to fund the war with
France and was more formally established
in 1694, when the Bank of England was
set up, partly in order to deal with it.
Robert Walpole set up a sinking fund in
1717 to allocate money for the repayment
of the debt but it was eventually hijacked
by other spending objectives and external
events like the Napoleonic Wars.
  The national debt rose from £33 billion
in 1971 to £113 billion in 1981, though
inflation was responsible for an element of
this increase. In 2000 the national debt was
£350 billion or about £5,900 per person.
The higher the level of debt a government
faces, the higher its interest charges and the
less it can spend on, for example, public
services. The Blair governments have been
keen to repay elements of the debt to reduce
the associated interest payments.

## National Economic Development Council (NEDC)
Set up in 1962 by the Macmillan government to advise government on economic
policy. Its members were drawn from business, government and the unions. There
were a number of smaller 'Neddy' committees that dealt with specific areas. The
Conservative governments after 1979 did
not support this approach to economic
policy making as it smacked too much of
'corporatism' and intervention in market
forces. The body limped through the

Thatcher years but John Major finally abolished it in 1992.

### National Enterprise Board
Set up in 1975 to promote economic efficiency. The board invested in a number of enterprises including the ill-fated British Leyland. In 1981 it merged with the National Research and Development Corporation.

### National Executive Committee (NEC) (Labour Party)
The body which runs the Labour Party's organisation. The unions once dominated this governing committee of the party, but changes in the 1990s reduced union influence. Now its 32 members are as follows: the leader, deputy leader and treasurer (all elected by conference); 12 trade union members (elected at the annual conference), 6 constituency party members (elected by all members of the party – not MPs); 3 government ministers (chosen by cabinet); 3 MPs or MEPs (elected by conference); 2 Labour councillors (elected by the Association of Labour Councillors); 1 Young Labour representative (elected by the youth conference); 1 representative of the socialist societies (elected at the annual conference); and the leader of the European Parliamentary Labour Party (elected by Labour MEPs). The NEC used to be influential in the days when Tony Benn chaired its Home Policy Committee but since Neil Kinnock and Tony Blair wrestled control of policy back to the leadership the body has been relatively peripheral.

### National Farmers' Union (NFU)
www.nfu.org.uk
Represents farmers and growers in Britain. It was founded in 1904 by nine Lincolnshire countrymen. Farming was so important during the Second World War that the NFU managed to win statutory rights of consultation with the Agriculture Act 1947. From being a key 'insider' group with the Ministry of Agriculture, Fisheries and Food (MAFF) it extended its lobbying activities to take on the European Community after 1973.

### National Front (NF)
www.natfront.com
Right-wing neo-fascist political party founded 1967 out of the League of Empire Loyalists, the British National Party, former members of the White Defence League and sundry ex-Mosleyites. It fought 10 seats in the February 1974 general election and 92 in the October 1974 one. During the 1970s it was rumoured that the NF was close to the Monday Club, especially over the issue of immigration. Ostensibly the NF opposed immigration and the alleged flexibility of the law that allowed New Commonwealth citizens to enter the country and to find work. Its beliefs, however, are more accurately described as neo-fascist: anti-Semitic, imperialist and racist. It stimulated the formation of the Anti-Nazi League. In 1979 the NF's vote collapsed, possibly as a result of the Conservatives taking a much tougher line on immigration, and the grouping spawned several smaller units, including the British National Party, which won a council seat in 1993 in the East End of London and various other council seats in the north-west in 2002–03. In June 2001, 11 NF members drawn from all over the country were convicted of taunting Asians in Oldham during the general election campaign. NF members had travelled up to support two candidatures of the British National Party in Oldham.

> The National Assistance Board pays the blacks for the coffee coloured monstrosities they father.... Material rewards are given to semi-savages to mate with the women of one of the leading civilised nations of the world. (Colin Jordan, when leader of the White Defence League, a forerunner of the NF, 1958)

> In our democratic society the Jew is like a poisonous maggot feeding off the body in an advanced state of decay. (John Tyndall, later of the NF, 1962)

*See also* British National Party; Monday Club.

## national government

Name given to the administrations governing from August 1930 to May 1940. The first was led by Ramsay MacDonald following the ending of the Labour government. MacDonald split his party by joining the Conservatives; Labour and Liberals formed the opposition. In October 1930 the general election saw the government returned with 554 Conservative seats to 54 Labour. In June 1935 Stanley Baldwin replaced MacDonald as prime minister, in a government which was essentially Conservative. He went on to win an election victory over Labour later in the year. Neville Chamberlain replaced Baldwin in 1937 and his government survived until May 1940, when Winston Churchill's wartime coalition came into being. It is often forgotten that this government's mandate dated back to 1935 and was not succeeded until 1945.

## National Health Service (NHS)

www.nhs.uk

Set up by the National Health Service Act 1946. The service, fully funded out of taxation, began in July 1948, and provided free medical, dental and optical treatment to citizens irrespective of income or status. After a few years of operation partial charges were introduced for spectacles and later dental treatment and medical prescriptions. Its founder, Aneurin Bevan, hoped the service would eventually cost less as the nation became healthier but an ageing population and more expensive treatments ensured this was a fallacy. Throughout its history the NHS has been short of funding but its popularity has ensured that all Conservative governments have sustained it as much as they felt able. In this respect Margaret Thatcher declared 'the NHS is safe in our hands', although internal reforms were introduced in the early 1990s to separate consumers from providers via an 'internal market'. Labour chancellor Gordon Brown announced substantial extra funding in July 1998. In the summer of 2000 still more funding was pledged – an average 6 per cent annual

increase for the next five years – along with Tony Blair's announcement of a comprehensive modernisation of the service. More funds for the NHS was a main theme in the 2001 election campaign for Labour but was neglected by the Conservatives. In July 2001 former Labour leader and then vice president of the European Commission Neil Kinnock suggested the NHS required more money, raised through taxation but 'ring fenced' and used specifically for the health service. This contrasted with the public–private strategy favoured by Blair and chimed in with the hypothecation of taxes as advocated by the Liberal Democrats.

In his 2002 budget Gordon Brown announced increases in taxation to fund even more spending on the NHS. However, a survey in May of that year revealed that only a small minority believed the government would fulfil its pledges regarding the promised increased numbers of nurses and doctors as well as the reduction of waiting times for operations to a maximum of six months. However, the survey also showed that three out of four patients were either 'very satisfied' or 'quite satisfied' with their last visit to a general practitioner or local hospital.

## National Labour Party

Formed in 1931 by the few supporters of Ramsay MacDonald's national government. In the 1931 election 13 of its 20 candidates were elected and in 1935 8 of its 20 candidates. Just before 1945 the party wound itself up.

## National Lottery

www.national-lottery.co.uk

A government-approved national lottery which makes a profit for its private operator and contributes a proportion to sport, arts and charities. John Major's government passed the National Lottery Act 1993 and set up Oflot (now the National Lottery Commission) to regulate it. It began in 1994. The company operating it is Camelot, though in the autumn of 2000 a rival company, the People's Lottery, chaired by Richard Branson, was awarded the new operating licence only for this to be rescinded and Camelot to regain its original role. Its average weekly sales are around £90 million; total sales between May 1999 to May 2004 were £22.4 billion.

### National Lottery Commission
www.natlotcomm.gov.uk
Body which in 1999 took over from Oflot (set up in 1993) the issuing of licences for the company running the lottery and the responsibility for monitoring its progress. The Commission re-awarded the licence to the company Camelot in 1999, to run until January 2009.

### National Policy Forum
Policy-making body of the Labour Party. Set up in the middle of the 1990s, the Forum is made up of 180 activists, trade unionists, MPs and senior ministers. It meets in private – thus avoiding the public conference rows of the past – and (so it is claimed) makes party policy. The Forum debates new policy and, if approved, it becomes party policy. Critics claim it has usurped the role of conference but others claim the Forum is itself a 'farce'; writing in the *Guardian* (11 July 2004) Roy Hattersley claimed education policy, about to be debated in the Forum, had already been decided: 'conceived in the back rooms of Downing St', then 'imposed' on Charles Clarke at a meeting with the prime minister and finally 'announced' to the Commons on 8 July.

### national service
Conscription of civilians into armed forces or industry from 1947 to 1962. The perceived threat of the USSR after the war led to the retention of conscription after the Second World War. National service applied to men aged 18. It was initially two years' military training but was then reduced to 18 months. It has long been thought subsequently by some that this experience of military discipline was good for those involved and ought to be reintroduced.

### National Socialism
*See* fascism.

### National Union of Journalists (NUJ)
www.nuj.org.uk
Founded in 1907, it represents some 30,000 people working in print, television or radio journalism. It has no political affiliation.

### National Union of Rail, Maritime and Transport Workers (RMT)
www.rmt.org.uk
A merger between the Seamen's Union and the Railway Workers' Union (both dating back to the 19th century) in 1990 established this 70,000-strong union, the general secretary of which, for many years, was the gravel-voiced Scotsman Jimmy Knapp.

### National Union of Teachers (NUT)
www.teachers.org.uk
Founded in 1870 to represent the interests of teachers, by the 1980s it had lost members to its less militant rivals. It orchestrated opposition to the introduction to school testing in the early 1990s. It had 179,000 members in 1995.

### nationalisation
The policy of taking whole enterprises into public ownership adopted by the Labour Party, especially after the Second World War. The original idea, based upon the party's clause four, was to end private ownership, believed by Karl Marx to be the basis of capitalism's evils. However, it was also thought that nationalised industries would be more efficient than privately owned ones. The major public utilities like gas, electricity and water were nationalised by the postwar Labour government as well as the coal industry; nationalised industries then made up 20 per cent of the economy. In some cases during the 1970s ailing industries were taken over by the government to prevent their collapse, as in the case of part of Rolls-Royce in 1970. The policy was perceived to have failed as early as the 1950s in terms of efficiency and even the Labour Party leadership sought to distance

itself from it. The left wing, however, remained true to the old ideal and refused to
believe the policy had not been successful,
despite the billions of pounds which were
required by government to subsidise these
loss-making enterprises. The Conservative
governments after 1979 introduced 'privatisation' to reverse nationalisation in most
areas. The Labour Party urged more state
control in its 1983 manifesto but after its
catastrophic loss began to abandon the
idea and Tony Blair had few problems in
changing clause four; this was endorsed by
a large majority at a special conference in
1994. Only the more eccentric parts of the
mainstream left now advocate the policy,
though the railways were effectively taken
back under government control in 2004.
State control, however, does remain part of
the programmes of numerous far-left minor
parties.

## nationalism

A love of one's nation that is distinguished
from patriotism by elevating its virtues
above those of others. The 19th century is
often seen as the 'age of nationalism' when
a variety of ethnic minorities, citing the
principles of the French Revolution, asserted their right to run their own affairs. In
some cases this applied to minorities within
large political structures like the Austro-
Hungarian Empire or to ethnic majorities
covering large geographical areas, as in the
case of Germany and Italy. More nation
building occurred after the First World
War, such as Czechoslovakia being formed
out of the Austro-Hungarian Empire in
1918, and after the Second World War
many colonies of the British Empire
spawned nationalist movements, which
demanded self-rule. Nationalist parties also
asserted themselves in Wales and Scotland
after the war and gained representation in
the Commons. To some extent the policy
of devolution was designed to assuage
nationalist sentiment in the UK but it is
arguable whether it merely encouraged
the movements to set their sights higher.
In Britain nationalism is seldom expressed
openly except during international sporting
events, notably cricket and football, where
a form of sublimated patriotism may exist,
but it runs deep nevertheless, as was evidenced during the Falklands War. It is also
expressed indirectly through racism – and
the National Front and the British National
Party seek to make political capital out of
fusing the two.

*See also* nation state.

## nationalist party

*See* Plaid Cymru; Scottish National Party.

## NATO

*See* North Atlantic Treaty Organisation.

## Natural Law Party

Party, founded in April 1992 by Geoffrey
Clements, that sought to advance the meditation ideas of Marahishi Mahesh Yogi
– that regular meditation can end world
conflict and that 'yogic flying' has the same
effect. Television coverage of such 'flying'
has proved singularly unconvincing as
exponents, from their determined lotus positions, strive mightily to become airborne. It
fielded 310 candidates in the 1992 general
election but failed to save a single deposit.
The party ended in January 2001.

## negative voting

*See* tactical voting.

## Neighbourhood Watch

Scheme set up in the 1980s to help deter
theft from a neighbourhood. Neighbours
get together, usually with a representative
from the police, and agree to keep an eye
on each other's property, and to alert the
police if anything suspicious occurs. Some
40,000 schemes were established by the
end of the decade and to a certain extent
they have been successful.

## Neill committee

The Committee on Standards in Public
Life under its second chair, Lord (Patrick)
Neill (of Bladen). Under its first chair,
Lord Nolan, John Major had specifically
excluded from the remit of the committee
the subject of party finance. This, however,

was taken up by Neill, who produced his report in October 1998. It made over 100 recommendations but the main ones were:

1 full disclosure of donations of more than £5,000 nationally and £1,000 locally;
2 a maximum of £20 million for each party's election expenditure;
3 'blind' trusts (when donors do not make their names public) to be abolished;
4 donations by people living abroad who are not British citizens to be banned;
5 no anonymous donations above £50;
6 a powerful parliamentary commissioner for standards to oversee party funding.

*See also* Committee on Standards in Public Life; Nolan committee; parliamentary commissioner for standards.

### neo-liberalism
*See* new right.

### Network Rail
www.networkrail.co.uk
Non-profit-making company that maintains the railways. Railways were nationalised after the Second World War and public dissatisfaction with British Rail had been a feature of Britain ever since. Many hoped privatisation in the early 1990s might improve things. However, the service was so under-funded it had to receive substantial public injections of cash – over £1.5 billion – before the transition was possible and in the event was somewhat rushed. In 1996 Railtrack, which owned the infrastructure, was sold off separately for £1.8 billion and companies were awarded 25 franchises to provide services. The Public Accounts Committee in August 1998 condemned the failure to insert 'claw-back' provisions to prevent easy profits. The Strategic Rail Authority was set up as the body to run the industry.

The privatised rail service was much criticised, not least for its over-fragmentation. The public complained even more bitterly about punctuality and regularity of service after privatisation than they did when the industry was in public hands, the most notorious offender being Virgin, which runs the West Coast Line.

Furthermore, the Health and Safety Executive in March 1998 argued that many parts of the network were unsafe. During the autumn of 1999 there were a number of railway accidents, most notably at Hatfield, where four passengers were killed, and Ladbroke Grove (Paddington), where 31 were killed. As a result, the network was forced to undergo repairs and delays became a national scandal. By the summer of 2001 repairs were virtually complete but the shares of Railtrack had plummeted in value. Many urged the renationalisation of the railways but the New Labour government signalled it was disinclined to do so. *The Economist*, on 9 June 2001, published a poll which showed that 70 per cent of the public favoured renationalisation of the railways with only a tiny percentage opposed.

On 19 June 2001 Lord Cullen published his report into the Paddington rail disaster. He condemned the industry for 'institutional paralysis'. He criticised Railtrack especially for its 'lamentable' failure to check faulty red signal lights. He also reserved harsh words for the railways inspectorate, which he said lacked resources, was too slack and placed too much faith in Railtrack. In all he made 88 recommendations, which he asked for the Health and Safety Executive to implement during the following two years.

In 2001 Stephen Byers was made transport secretary but his 10-year plan to revive transport was defeated by events. In the autumn of 2001 Railtrack applied to the government for another injection of cash – some £3.3 billion – but Byers refused. Railtrack shares continued to slide, which elicited complaints from those employees who had invested in their own company with retirement in mind. Byers declared the company effectively bankrupt and replaced it with a non-profit-making company, Network Rail, as a preliminary to further restructuring but, in early 2002, many believed renationalisation was effectively taking place. In January of that year Tony Blair, occupied with foreign affairs, asked former BBC head John (Lord) Birt to prepare a report on Britain's transport system. This move was widely perceived as a snub to Byers, who was sacked shortly afterwards and replaced by Alistair Darling.

The Strategic Rail Authority, which Byers set up in 2001 to oversee a 10-year plan for the railways, lasted less than four years. On 15 July 2004 Alistair Darling announced its demise, with most of its functions passing to Network Rail and to the Department of Transport. With punctuality still lagging behind targets and money still being poured in, the railway system faces a tough battle to achieve quality and credibility.

## New Deal
A New Labour programme designed to move unemployed people from benefits into work. It used a windfall tax on the privatised utilities to help 460,000 young and 165,000 long-term unemployed people into jobs. In December 2003 chancellor Gordon Brown announced that the windfall tax would henceforward be used to contribute to enhance skills of the unemployed. The pilot schemes funded employers – usually small companies – to allow workers time off to upgrade their skills in such areas as literacy and numeracy. The scheme was to be extended to cover a third of the country and 80,000 employees, most of whom had left school early with no qualifications. The chancellor also announced that all claimants on job-seekers' allowance would be forced to attend a skills course or lose their benefit. Lone parents, of whom 225,000 had found jobs under the New Deal, would also be forced to attend work-focused interviews and courses.

## New Labour
Name given to the Labour Party by Tony Blair and his media-savvy team after 15 years of opposition (from 1979 to 1994). Blair was seeking to present a party free of vote-losing ideological baggage and associations, and so the prefix 'new' was widely used, to rebrand a party that had shifted to the centre-ground. Given the ridicule

heaped on the name it did quite well to survive into the new millennium.

## new left
Political movement developed in reaction to the disillusion felt in the 1950s at the behaviour of the Soviet Union, especially Khrushchev's revelations about the brutality of Stalinism at the Twentieth Congress of its Communist Party in 1956 and the invasion of Hungary. Elements of the new movements in left wing thought included Maoism, the Cuban revolution of 1959 and the anti-colonial movements in Asia and Africa. In the 1960s groups of women, black-power militants and anti-Vietnam War activists claimed to represent the interests of the proletariat and took to the streets. The high point was the May events in Paris in 1968 but the intellectual influence of new-left gurus like Herbert Marcuse and Antonio Gramsci, who were concerned with alienation and cultural transformation, continued into the 1970s and 1980s.

## new liberalism
Brand of liberalism, sometimes referred to as reconstructed liberalism, that emerged at the end of the 19th century under the influence of writers such as T. H. Green and L. T. Hobhouse. In contrast to laissez faire or classical liberals, Green believed the state had an obligation to intervene in order to improve the living conditions of the less fortunate, such as the working class, the old and children. Later liberal thinkers like John Maynard Keynes and William Beveridge took Green's ideas forward and developed interventionist policies on the economy and social insurance.

## New Politics Network (NPW)
www.new-politics.net
Think tank which campaigns on democratic renewal and popular participation. Founded in 1999 following the winding up of the Democratic Left, the NPW was formed from the ashes of the Communist Party of Great Britain. It now carefully

eschews any current political bias and seeks to 'encourage cooperation and the sharing of best practice between people and organisations involved in the modernisation of politics'. The NPW emphasises its independent status and willingness to work with people across the political spectrum.

### new right

Term applied to the political economy associated with the classical economic liberalism of Adam Smith, and thus sometimes called neo-liberalism. Its ideas emerged during the late 1970s from the Chicago School of economists, who advocated the rigorous application of market forces and the withdrawal of the state from its interventionist stance adopted since the end of the Second World War. In particular, it argued for the denationalisation of state-run industries, letting 'lame-duck' companies fail and the application of monetarist economic policy. It also advocated the curtailing of trade union power, as it acted as a block on the operation of market forces, and the reduction of the welfare state, which, the new right argued, had a debilitating effect on individual responsibility and wealth creation. Deregulation was to take place in the operation of industry and flexibility in labour markets was to be encouraged. There was also an acceptance of capital mobility, not only within economies but also on a global scale. The movement came to influence Ronald Reagan and the Republicans in the USA and crossed the Atlantic where, in Britain, it was promoted by think tanks such as the Institute of Economic Affairs, the Adam Smith Institute and the Centre for Policy Studies. Also influential were individual politicians like John Biffen, Keith Joseph, Nigel Lawson and, inevitably, Margaret Thatcher. She blended these liberal elements with her belief in strong political authority plus a traditional Conservative line on law and order. She often referred to herself as a 'neo-liberal' Conservative.

*See also* Chicago School of Economics; monetarism.

### *New Statesman*
www.newstatesman.com
Weekly journal of comment and analysis founded in 1913. It was always close to Fabian Society positions, independent but sympathetic to radical liberal policy on international questions and Labour Party policy on domestic issues. Kingsley Martin was its long-serving editor from 1931 and other notable editors included Richard Crossman and Anthony Howard. It teetered on the brink of collapse in the late 1980s but was saved by a rich benefactor.

### news
In a literal sense, that which is new, unexpected or different. In relation to mass media, it refers to the reporting of newsworthy events, understood by journalists as a story which is interesting to themselves or their audiences. This has led students of the media to argue the news is a wholly artificial construction based upon a number of professional values, which compresses complex events and ideas into a certain form and size. Furthermore, the Glasgow University Media Group has suggested that news creation includes a wide range of mainstream assumptions about social reality which often exclude more radical interpretations. In the world of politics the news is the means whereby the political system is driven forwards and therefore a controversial aspect of the media among political parties. On average British people watch well over 20 hours of television per week, 20 per cent of which is current affairs and news. How politicians appear on news broadcasts has become of key importance ever since the primacy of image in politics became fully appreciated. The news has also become the target of regular 'sound bites', which are short, self-contained messages, carefully crafted to be both memorable and sufficiently brief to fit easily into a news bulletin. Both the BBC and Independent Television News are required to be unbiased but they regularly are accused of bias by politicians and their spin doctors.

*See also* Glasgow University Media Group; image; political marketing; sound bite; spin; spin doctor.

## news values

Criteria employed by editors in the print
and broadcast media in the selection of
stories. Experience suggests that these
values lead to the selection not of things
like policy briefings or analyses of official
reports – which arguably might inform a
serious democracy – but of stories concerned with personalities, sexual scandal,
financial wrongdoing and celebrity gossip.
What makes the situation even worse from
the point of view of informed democracy is
that those newspapers that take the 'serious'
route sell far less well than those that follow
the 'popular' route. Television tends to
follow trends in print journalism and critics
claim that this is why television has been
subject to a 'dumbing down' in recent years.

## Next Steps agency

*See* executive agency.

## 'NIMBY' ('not in my back yard')

A derogatory acronym normally applied to
those whose self-interest is threatened by
development plans which would damage
the value of their property or quality of life.
The term is often applied to those who may
in other respects promote economic development, or be supporters of free market
capitalism, and are thus guilty of hypocrisy.
While no human being is perfect, politicians should be particularly careful to
avoid nimbyism, exposed as they are to the
glare of publicity in the media and political attack in parliament. There are some
examples of political nimbies, one such
being Nicholas Ridley, secretary of state
for the environment in Margaret Thatcher's
first government. In 1986 he had objected
to a planning application for new homes
near his residence, despite his granting of
permissions for other developments.

## 9/11, 2001

Day on which Muslim fundamentalist
terrorists hijacked four domestic airliners
flying out of Boston and flew two of them
into the twin towers of the World Trade
Center in New York. Of the other two one
hit the Pentagon and the other crashed
when passengers apparently overpowered
the hijackers. The towers collapsed and
over 3,000 people were killed, including
over 100 British citizens. Tony Blair immediately announced his support for US
president George W. Bush's declared war
on terrorism and made a speech proposing an attempt at a new world order at the
Labour Party conference on 2 October
2001.

*See also* terrorism.

## 1922 Committee

Name given to the committee which
emerged from a famous meeting in the
Carlton Club in 1922 of Conservative MPs
unhappy at the continuation of the party
in David Lloyd George's coalition government. The meeting ended both the coalition
and the leadership of Austen Chamberlain;
it thus established the independence of
Conservative MPs and their strength when
roused to express their discontent. The
committee meets every week and acts as a
conduit of opinion from the backbenches
to the leadership on general issues and
in specific policy areas from its various
subcommittees (which are attended by
party whips). It is maintained by some
commentators that it was the questioning
of Lord Carrington by the foreign affairs
subcommittee of the 1922 Committee
which forced him to resign after the
Falklands War. Academics Martin Burch
and Michael Moran argue (in an article in
*Parliamentary Affairs*, winter 1985,
pp. 1–15) that the tendency for Conservative MPs to come increasingly from state
secondary schools and to have local government experience tends to make them less
accepting of a single all-powerful leader.

## No Turning Back Group

Group of Conservative MPs established in 1983 by a group of passionate
Thatcherites, including Peter Lilley and
Michael Forsyth. The group calls for a
whole package of right-wing measures,
including extensive privatisation and
the virtual abolition of the welfare state.

POLITICS

Margaret Thatcher, unsurprisingly, was keen to attend its dinners and was generally supportive of its policy thrust but the group lost influence once John Major came to power in 1990.

### Nolan committee
The Committee on Standards in Public Life under its first chair, Lord Nolan. The committee was set up in response to a *Sunday Times* 'sting' operation whereby Graham Riddick MP and David Tredinnick MP were asked to put parliamentary questions in exchange for money. Their willingness to do so caused public outrage. Nolan reported in autumn 1995 and made a number of recommendations, including the need for MPs: to register their business interests with a new and powerful parliamentary commissioner for standards; to declare their income according to bands; and to be prevented from tabling questions and amendments on behalf of outside interests. In the ensuing parliamentary debate John Major opposed the recommendations but they were passed in any case.

*See also* Committee on Standards in Public Life; Neill committee; parliamentary commissioner for standards; Standards and Privileges Committee.

### nomination of parliamentary candidate
*See* candidate for parliamentary election.

### non-departmental select committee
Investigative committee of parliament not related to the work of a department. The best-known committee of this type is the Public Accounts Committee. The Public Administration Committee, chaired by Tony Wright, has carved out an enviable reputation for effective questioning of ministers and witnesses on often politically sensitive matters. Moreover, the Modernisation Committee has helped reform the practices of both chambers. Also in this category are the following: Broadcasting, Deregulation and Regulatory Reform, Environmental Audit, European Scrutiny, Information, Selection

and Standing Orders. In addition there are a number of other useful 'domestic' committees concerned with parliament itself: Accommodation and Works, Catering, Finance and Services, Standards and Privileges, Procedure, and Liaison. Finally, there are non-departmental select committees on Human Rights and Statutory Instruments, both joint committees of both houses of parliament.

### NOP (National Opinion Polls)
www.nop.co.uk
Established by Associated Newspapers in 1957 as a polling organisation used mostly by the *Daily Mail*. In 1979 MAI, owned by the Labour peer Lord Hollick, bought NOP, and merged it with another body but continued to use the NOP rubric.

### North Atlantic Treaty Organisation (NATO)
www.nato.int
A military and political alliance established in 1949. After the Second World War, the perceived threat of the Soviet Union encouraged Britain and then the USA to take defensive measures. Marshall aid was designed by the USA to strengthen European economies against the internal threat of communism. NATO was designed to counter the external threat of the Red Army. With the growing tension after 1947 from the orchestrated communist take-overs in eastern Europe, culminating in the fall of Czechoslovakia and the Berlin blockade, the idea of a collective security organisation for the west took shape. On 4 April 1949, 12 countries (10 European, plus Canada and the USA) signed a treaty which laid down that 'an armed attack against one or more of them in Europe or North America shall be considered an attack against them all'. Despite the formation of a retaliatory Warsaw Pact, NATO kept the peace successfully for 40 years and after the fall of the communist regimes in 1989 NATO extended an invitation to establish contacts with the organisation. Full membership remained a contentious proposal for some of the former communist

countries and a number joined, including Romania and Poland, with the Baltic states as well as the Ukraine also being spoken of as future members. But NATO found a role for itself in helping alleviate the crisis in the former area of Yugoslavia. Membership of NATO remains the bedrock of British defence policy and British forces are allocated to come under its command in certain crises. Led by the USA, its forces saw active service in spring 1999, the first time since its formation, when its airforces, mainly US, bombed Serbian military units in Kosovo. In 2003 a crisis developed over NATO support for Turkey in relation to the anticipated attack on Iraq.

*See also* Cold War; Marshall aid.

## north–south divide

The economic disparity between the generally more prosperous south of England and the less prosperous north, as well as Wales and Scotland. A report by Oxford Economic Forecasting in August 2000 predicted the south-east would outperform all other regions of Britain economically. Some northern MPs used the report to demand more action to help manufacturing in Labour heartlands. During 2000 the south-east was due to grow by nearly 4 per cent, while the north-east could expect only 2 per cent. Ronnie Campbell, chair of the northern group of MPs, called for regional assemblies to help regions work more effectively for assistance.

## Northcote–Trevelyan report, 1854

One of the most important reports ever published on the British civil service. Written by an obsessive reformer who later became permanent secretary to the Treasury (Trevelyan) and a future chancellor (Northcote), it was backed by the reformist prime minister William Gladstone. The report observed that 'Admission to the Civil Service' was 'eagerly sought after' by the 'indolent and incapable', whose 'abilities do not warrant an expectation they will succeed in the open professions'. Instead, the report recommended entry through merit in open

examinations and a separation of tasks into the 'intellectual' and the 'mechanical', which were to be undertaken by different classes of entrant. The report's recommendations were resisted initially but were eventually implemented. It took 50 years for the stratified system to form but it produced a durable model, which has arguably served the country well. It has introduced a powerful sense of public service for the able sons and daughters of the middle classes. In modern times this sense has been in marked decline as the products of Oxbridge have sought more financial rewards.

*See also* civil service; executive agency.

## Northern Ireland (Ulster)

The English invaded Ireland in the 12th century, followed by the Scots in 1315. As a consequence, Ireland became a strife-torn land for many centuries. Originally Northern Ireland was predominantly Catholic; however, it became more equally Protestant as Scots immigrants, appointed by City of London companies, were given land to settle and farm. The province played a crucial role in the Glorious Revolution, when William besieged Londonderry and emerged victorious from the Battle of the Boyne.

Heavy industry developed in Belfast in the form of shipbuilding and also textiles. Loyalist Ulster Protestants opposed the Home Rule movement in the 19th century. As the negotiations for Home Rule proceeded Ulster insisted on being treated separately under the effective advocacy of Sir Edward Carson. The Government of Ireland Act 1920 established a separate parliament at Stormont in Belfast for the six northern counties of Fermanagh, Armagh, Tyrone, Londonderry, Antrim and Down. In 1925 the Boundary Commission fixed the line between the north and south of Ireland. The 1937 Irish constitution embedded the notion of unification and Protestant northerners thereafter constantly feared these territorial claims, encouraged by IRA activity and the nationalist sympathies of the large (40 per cent) Catholic minority. Consequently politics in the province was dominated by the Protestants, to the detriment in political and employment terms of the Catholics, who reacted in the late 1960s with a civil rights movement. Civil rights marches in 1968 turned into riots and troops were sent in. The Provisional IRA emerged and wrought havoc in the early 1970s. Internment proved ineffective, as did most other measures, and in 1972 direct rule from London was introduced. Attempts to introduce power-sharing executives failed in 1974 and 1975–76, because of loyalist strikes. Over 3,000 people have died as a result of the violence since the late 1960s, until the Good Friday Agreement in 1998 offered new hope that power sharing might work. However, the tentative agreements reached persistently foundered on the subject of 'decommissioning of weapons' or, disarmament by the IRA.

*See also* Good Friday Agreement, 1998; Northern Ireland assembly.

### Northern Ireland assembly

Established as a result of the Good Friday Agreement of 1998. It has 108 seats and has devolved powers over domestic matters (plus an Irish dimension). After the first elections to the assembly, on 25 June 1998, the Ulster Unionist Party (UUP) had the most seats and David Trimble (its leader) became first minister. Sinn Fein, led by Gerry Adams, was given two portfolios in the administration, including Martin McGuinness as education minister. However, problems persisted, with the Unionists demanding the IRA decommission its arms. Trimble used a threat of resignation to pursue his objectives. His most acute political problem lies with his own party, which is implacably opposed to cooperating with partners who allegedly maintained strong terrorist links. In September 2002 the assembly was suspended. In May 2003 Tony Blair and Bertie Ahern, the Irish premier, sought to extract a definitive disavowal of violence from the IRA but Adams' form of words ultimately did not satisfy the British prime minister, aware as he was that Trimble's position would be vulnerable to a chal-

lenge from the Democratic Unionist Party (DUP), led by Ian Paisley, unless the renunciation was clear and absolute. Consequently elections were postponed from May to November 2003. These elections resulted in a squeezing of the centre in the form of the Social Democratic and Labour Party (SDLP) (lost 6 seats) and the UUP (lost one seat) and the strengthening of the extremes in the form of Sinn Fein (gained 6 seats) and the DUP (gained 10 seats). Some optimists hoped the closer interface between the hard-line Protestants and the nationalists might encourage cooperation through necessity but in the summer of 2004 this ideal seemed as far away as ever.

### Northern Ireland executive committee

Set up by the Good Friday Agreement in April 1998 as the executive arm of the Northern Ireland assembly. This body is composed of 12 members, including a first minister, deputy, and heads of department, including health, environment, education, economic development, agriculture and finance. David Trimble of the Ulster Unionist Party was elected first minister with Seamus Mallon of the Democratic and Labour Party (SDLP) as his deputy. The education portfolio was given, controversially, to Martin McGuinness, of Sinn Fein, who, it is alleged, once commanded the Londonderry brigade of the Provisional IRA. The executive was suspended in autumn 2002 and direct rule reintroduced.

### Northern Ireland peace process
*See* peace process.

### nuclear energy and waste
Nuclear power stations began to contribute to the National Grid in the 1960s but political opposition began to grow in the wake of worries that waste could not be processed satisfactorily and that genetic defects could be found in children living close to such plants. Following the Chernobyl accident in 1986 the industry was criticised bitterly by the environmental lobby

POLITICS

as unsafe. Given Britain's need to bridge the energy gap as North Sea oil runs out, however, nuclear energy has become a candidate for expansion despite the fact that it is the most subsidised form of energy and still cannot compete in the marketplace.

On 30 August 2004 it became known that, despite ministerial pledges that Britain would not become a dumping ground for nuclear waste, some 10 countries – including Germany, Japan and Italy – had been transporting nuclear waste to Britian for reprocessing by British Nuclear Fuels. The idea was to extract the uranium and plutonium and to send it back to the sender countries for reuse. However, the process did not produce the expected results and the waste ended up being stored in some 20 locations, including 10,000 tons in concrete bunkers in Drigg, Cumbria. The reasoning for this was that transporting it back to the originator countries was judged to be excessively expensive. Some environmental experts estimated a cost of £80 billion to maintain the waste over the next 100 years and that the high- and intermediate-level waste would not be safe for human contact for the next 200,000 years.

*See also* energy.

### nuclear weaponry

Britain acquired nuclear weapons just after the war in a bid to equip the country with the most up-to-date weapons. In the 1950s the Campaign for Nuclear Disarmament urged the unilateral abandonment of such weapons and was influential in winning Labour to its cause. However, Conservative victories in the 1980s stimulated a rethink and Labour came to accept a multilateral approach to disarmament – that is, it would take place only when other states disarmed as well. Currently nuclear weapons are available to British defence forces, the most powerful being the submarine-launched ballistic missile system, Trident.

*See also* Campaign for Nuclear Disarmament.

### Number 10, Downing Street
*See* 10 Downing Street.

O

### oath of allegiance
The swearing of allegiance to the crown. There have been several oaths of allegiance required at different times in British history, the first being in 1534 to ensure loyalty to Henry VIII and Anne Boleyn. The Test Act 1673 required all office holders to take one. Today, such an oath is sworn by MPs on first taking their seat. The Sinn Fein MPs Gerry Adams and Martin McGuinness refuse to take their seats as they feel they cannot take the oath of allegiance. However, both decided to take advantage of their parliamentary allowances and offices in Westminster in January 2002. The citizenship ceremonies introduced at Brent Town Hall in February 2004 involved an oath of allegiance to the queen.

### Office for National Statistics (ONS)
www.statistics.gov.uk
Established in 1996 in a merger of the Central Statistical Office and the Office for Population Censuses and Surveys. ONS provides the government's statistical service and regularly publishes reports on social and economic matters.

*See also* class.

### Office for Standards in Education (Ofsted)
www.ofsted.gov.uk
In charge of inspections of schools and tasked with raising standards. Under the Conservatives it was headed by Chris Woodhead, who became unpopular with teachers for his sweeping criticisms. He was kept on by Labour after 1997, possibly to assuage middle-class feelings, but he resigned in autumn 2000 to become a *Daily Telegraph* columnist.

### Office of Communications (Ofcom)
www.ofcom.org.uk
Regulator for communications industries – television, radio, telecommunications and

wireless communications services. Set up in 2002 this body replaced five media regulatory bodies: the Broadcasting Standards Commission, the Independent Television Commission, Oftel, the Radio Authority and the Radio Communications Agency. Ofcom employs over 1,000 people and has powers to control the behaviour and standards of media companies, including the BBC and Sky, as well as telecommunications companies, including BT. There was a row in July 2002 when the academic economist Lord Currie was appointed as the Office's first head: he was a Labour Party member and an advisor to Gordon Brown. The government defended the decision by pointing out that it had been made in accordance with the 'Nolan rules' in relation to public appointees and that Lord Currie had also advised the last two Conservative chancellors. The BBC is not bound by Ofcom, though calls for it to be so were voiced after the David Kelly affair and the Hutton inquiry.

### Office of Fair Trading (OFT)
www.oft.gov.uk
Established in 1973 to review commercial practices. It deals with mergers and cartels as well as a range of consumer affairs. It seeks to protect the consumer by preventing abuse, to provide information about fair trading regulations and to encourage competition and responsible supply. It issues licences for those offering consumer credit – 20,000 in 1998 – and monitors advertisements for fairness. The Competition Act 1998, which came into force in March 2000, greatly strengthened the OFT, giving it the power to levy fines of up to 10 per cent of turnover on companies involved in uncompetitive practices. The act stipulates criminal penalties for those obstructing the OFT in its monitoring of mergers and takeovers.

### Office of Government Commerce (OGC)
www.ogc.gov.uk
Formed in April 2000 as an independent office of the Treasury. It is responsible for much of the government's civil purchasing and project management previously offered by the Treasury Procurement Group, the Buying Agency, Property Advisers and Civil Estate, the Central Computer and Telecommunications Agency and the policy aspect of the Private Finance Initiative Taskforce. Its aim is to ease the process whereby business sells to government and to increase competition. The OGC has a chief executive appointed at permanent secretary level. It reports to the chief secretary to the Treasury.

### Office of Public Service (OPS)
This evolved out of various successive bodies with responsibility for the civil service. Initially the personnel and training functions were the preserve of the Treasury and its principal official was also head of the civil service. In 1968 the Civil Service Department (CSD) was created, along with the Civil Service College for training purposes. Margaret Thatcher, however, saw the CSD as too incestuously protective of civil service interests and in 1981 it was abolished. Its functions were subsequently redistributed to various agencies, ending up in the new OPSS in 1992 (which lost 'science' to become the OPS in 1995). The OPS, with its responsibilities for the Efficiency Unit, the Next Steps programme and the citizens' charter came under the responsibility of the Cabinet Office and was headed by the secretary to the cabinet, who ensured a more centralised degree of control over the public service. In 1998 the OPS was formally merged with the Cabinet Office.

### Office of the Commissioner for Public Appointments
www.ocpa.gov.uk
This body, independent of the Cabinet Office, was set up as the Public Appointments Commission by the Major government as one of the recommendations of the Nolan report. The aim was to monitor some 12,000 appointments made by ministers to public bodies, many of

them quangos. The first commissioner was Sir Leonard Peach. On 17 July 2002 the second commissioner to be appointed (in 1999), Dame Rennie Fritchie, criticised several Whitehall departments for ignoring the procedures she had laid down. She accused a number of departments, including the Treasury, Health and Culture, of failing to get independent assessors to sit on appointment boards. In addition, she criticised them for failing to ensure that jobs up for reappointment were made open to competition and for ignoring her own code of conduct for filling posts on merit.

## Office of Water Services (Ofwat)

www.ofwat.gov.uk
Set up by the Competition Services (Utilities) Act 1992 to regulate the privatised water companies.

## official gift

Gift given to a minister of the crown in the course of work. Ministers are frequently given such gifts. However, there is often a suspicion that they may be given in respect of favours either already given or anticipated. To guard against this, a limit of £140 is set for such items and any gift worth more than that has to be declared and, if the recipient wishes to keep it, the balance of value paid. In July 2004 Tony Blair decided to give back the guitar given him by rock star Bono when they met in May 2002 to discuss the AIDS epidemic in Africa.

## Official Secrets Act

Usually understood to refer to the two Acts of 1911 and 1936, which forbid anyone to pass on secret information, including information derived from being a servant of the crown, whether or not that information could be of any use to an enemy. Section I of the 1911 act covered spying but section II was broader, making it an offence for a crown servant to communicate official information to a person to whom it was not 'in the interests of the state or otherwise in the public interest' to do so. This covers all official documents and information. In theory this would cover, for example, the staff directory of the Ministry of Social Security. Reformers have railed against this illiberal statute but governments and bureaucracies find it convenient to keep secrecy wrapped more closely around the workings of British government than is the case in most similarly developed liberal democracies.

The Official Secrets Act 1989 attempted to clear up some of the confused areas of secrecy, but did not make the situation any more liberal. Its remit covers security, defence and international relations, as well as crime and its investigation. Any release of related information deemed 'harmful' to the public interest is a criminal offence and it is no defence to claim the information is in the public domain abroad. Those covered by the act include members of the security services, all civil servants, government contractors and journalists.

New Labour came into office in 1997 committed to removing secrecy from British government, but few believe radical or fundamental change has taken place, as evidenced by a limited Freedom of Information Act and the arrest in September 2000 of David Shayler, a former employee of the security services, who was charged under the Official Secrets Act for revealing an alleged plan to assassinate the Libyan head of state, Colonel Gaddafi.

## oligarchy

*See* iron law of oligarchy.

## ombudsman

www.ombudsman.org.uk
Popular name for the parliamentary commissioner for administration (PCA) (originating from Scandinavian practice). The office was established in 1967 to investigate maladministration by government departments and certain other bodies, including the Arts Council. Complaints have to be referred to the ombudsman by MPs but the ombudsman has no effective powers of enforcement.

One survey found that more than 10 per cent of MPs never referred cases to the ombudsman, while less than 10 per cent often sent papers for consideration. Most MPs prefer the direct approach to a minister, as they can keep the matter in their own hands and reap credit if successful. Usually complaints number about 1,000 per year and about 10 per cent of these are upheld. If the source of the upheld complaint is not remedied the ombudsman can report the case to parliament and the government will decide whether to act. In his annual report for 2001–02 Sir Michael Buckley, as ombudsman, said he had received 2,139 complaints, a 24 per cent increase on the previous year. The Department of Work and Pensions accounted for the largest number of complaints (693). Since 1967, the idea has been extended to other areas of government, with an ombudsman established for Northern Ireland in 1969, for the National Health Service in 1973, for local government in England and Wales in 1974, for local government in Scotland in 1976, and also a special ombudsman who reports to the European parliament in 1994.

### on message

Timely assertion of the official party line. Since the development of a mass electorate in the 19th century there has been a need for a party to appear united, and to convey the same message, at least in public. However, the growth of electronic media, especially television, has increased both the speed of communication and the need for politicians to synchronise their messages, as determined by the leadership and corps of special (media) advisors. These people now dominate election campaigning and party communications, especially since the New Labour victory of 1997. For many, Labour's then headquarters, at Millbank Tower, came to symbolise the party's concern with media presentation, in particular that Labour politicians be on message at all times. Infamously, for a while after 1997, Labour MPs were required by their whips to carry a pager so that they could be kept in touch with party thinking and policy and consequently be 'on message'.

### 'one nation' Conservatism

Strand of Conservative thinking which stresses the need for social harmony and measures which will help achieve this, like enlightened state welfare and egalitarianism. It originated with Benjamin Disraeli's novel *Sybil*, which talks of 'two nations', the rich and the poor. Since Disraeli's day the question has been much debated inside the Conservative Party. The balance between individualism and collectivism in the Conservative Party has varied, but in the wake of the First World War a concern with national cohesiveness predominated and a raft of social legislation ensued in the 1920s and 1930s which anticipated the so-called postwar consensus. The thrust of the approach was to ensure the unity of the nation was sustained. Some historians argue that the basis of the Conservative manifesto in 1945 was almost as collectivist as Labour's, although the voters did not perceive this to be the case. Margaret Thatcher was more interested in asserting the individualist element in Conservatism, though some of her close advisors, like John Biffen, contrived to be 'one nation' Conservatives as well as free market enthusiasts.

### open government

The principle that all government information should be freely available to the public. Following the *Spycatcher* case of 1988 the Conservative government passed the Official Secrets Act 1989. However, in practice the culture of secrecy was not changed and large amounts of information were still either unavailable to the public or very costly to elicit: *The Economist* (20 January 1996) reported that one inquirer was charged £2,000 for the provision of information and another £100 for photocopying. The Freedom of Information Act 2000 passed by Labour has disappointed many by its failure to allow disclosure of civil service advice to ministers.

### opinion poll

Systematic questioning of a representative sample of respondents. The opinion polls industry started life in the USA as a market research exercise for consumer products, and then moved to politics during the 1930s when Dr George Gallup developed a scientific approach to opinion measurement. Opinion polls successfully predicted the Labour Party landslide in 1945 and were soon embraced by the British press to the extent that polls have become an indispensable feature of every general election since. In particular, they are used by the press as barometers of government popularity, and the strength of leaders and their parties. There are five major polling organisations: MORI, ICM, NOP, Gallup and Harris. The British Institute of Public Opinion was founded in 1937 and its work was reported sparingly during the 1940s but increasingly thereafter as polling was seen to be an accurate predictor.

During the 1992 general election campaign it was calculated that 18 per cent of all newspaper front-page lead stories were based on polls. In that election all the polls predicted a close result but in the event they were proved wrong as the Conservatives romped home with a 7 per cent margin over Labour. Intensive studies as to what went wrong suggested the organisations had not properly analysed the 'don't knows' and those who refused to be interviewed. It seemed a disproportionate number of Conservative voters were included in these categories, thus producing the wrong forecasts. Corrective measures went much of the way to restore the reputation of opinion polls by the time of the May 1997 election, when 59 national polls were conducted by the polling organisations for the media. In 2002 pollster Peter Kellner set up YouGov, a polling company which uses the Internet as its means of eliciting views. Some criticised this approach as being skewed to middle-class respondents.

The Market Research Association (the pollsters' trade organisation) claimed the polls had performed reasonably well in the 2001 general election, with most predicting Labour's share at 45 per cent when it was actually 42 per cent; predictions of the Conservative vote were on average 1.7

per cent out and only 0.6 per cent out in the case of the Liberal Democrats. The BBC/NOP exit polls were reasonably accurate, with errors of between 2 and 12 in terms of predicted seat numbers. However, *The Economist* (16 June 2001) disagreed. It pointed out that during the campaign predictions varied by double-digit figures (for example 28 per cent for MORI). Furthermore, there was bias: every one of the 29 polls put Labour's lead above the actual final figure of 9 per cent. *The Economist* went on to point out that this was the third election in a row when Labour's share of the vote had been overestimated. It concluded the polling organisations needed to 'conduct a thorough review of their methods'.

*See also* exit poll; focus group.

## opposition

The second largest party in parliament. Given the provenance of British democracy from the institution of the crown, opposition carried a whiff of disloyalty to the monarch so, as government became more independent of the crown, the concept of 'Her Majesty's loyal opposition' became established, with a salaried leader plus an alternative team of government shadow ministers. However, the Conservative Party after 1997 failed to emerge as an effective opposition and the role was to a degree usurped by the media and elements within the governing party. In July 2004 the Liberal Democrats ran equal to the Conservatives in the polls. While Conservative leader Michael Howard was able to improve his party's morale in the Commons and test Tony Blair occasionally in debate, he proved less persuasive at winning round the voters.

On Wednesday [4 July 2001] sharp criticism was directed at PM Blair by his own MPs. With only 59% of voters voting the mandate of the new government was less impressive than in 1997 and restive elements in Labour were less constrained from expressing their dissatisfactions, especially over private–public partnerships (PPP).

Parliament too is in a more assertive mood and unwilling to be treated as a doormat any longer. (Michael White in the *Guardian*, 5 July 2001)

## opposition days

Days on which the subjects for debate in parliament are not decided by government. For 20 of the available days for debate the opposition leader has a choice of subject on 17 of them; the remaining three are decided by the leader of the third largest party (currently the Liberal Democrats).

## Orange Order

www.grandorange.org.uk
Established in 1795, the movement was a reaction to the threat of the United Irishmen and the Catholic secret societies associated with the Irish Rebellion (1795–98). Its organisation is via lodges and it has been heavily influenced by the freemasons. Today the order exists to defend and promote the interests of Protestants in Northern Ireland and on 12 July every year the Orangemen parade in celebration of William III's victory over James II at the Battle of the Boyne in 1690. Mid-July is thus the annual marching season, which provides a sparking point for trouble between the two communities. The parades in Drumcree, County Armagh, threatened the peace process in 1996 and 1997. The 1998 parade looked as if it might be accompanied by violence but the death of three young children in a fire bomb attack caused tempers to cool and the tension to pass. However, tension reappeared in subsequent years. In 2001 Drumcree was again the flashpoint, with its Orange Lodge insisting, as in previous years, that it had the right to ignore the government ban and march down the mainly nationalist Garvachy Road in adjoining Portadown.

## order in council

A legislative order made by the Privy Council under the royal prerogative, much used during wartime to achieve rapid changes when the traditional legislative procedures would be too slow. The orders

are issued in the name of the queen but in effect the lord president of the Council reads out a list of orders prepared by government and the queen says 'agreed' at regular intervals. The device is also used by the prime minister to protect measures from parliamentary criticism, such as the order giving Alastair Campbell the authority to instruct civil servants.

## Osmotherly rules, 1980

Series of rules governing civil servants, based on a memo by an assistant secretary in the Civil Service Department in 1980. These advise civil servants appearing before select committees not to allow themselves to become involved in anything politically controversial, for example advice to ministers, interdepartmental policy matters or information concerning foreign countries.

## Ouseley report, 2001

Report on major riots in Bradford city centre, by former chairman of the Commission on Race Relations, Lord (Herman) Ouseley. His report attracted considerable attention. The thrust of the recommendations was to break down the separateness of the different communities and to make 'Bradford citizenship' the top consideration, ahead of ethnic identity. The report focused on 'community fragmentation' along social, cultural, ethnic and religious lines throughout the Bradford district. Segregation in schools was seen as a symptom and a cause. Different communities tended to see others with suspicion and hostility. Political leadership had been weak, said the report.

> so-called community leaders maintain the status quo of control and segregation through fear and threats.

## outsider group

A term invented by Wyn Grant of Warwick University as a category of pressure group. Outsider groups are the corollary of Grant's insider groups and there are similarly three kinds: groups which seek closeness to the decision-making process; groups which lack the skills and resources to move closer; and ideological outsider groups, which deliberately place themselves beyond the values of Whitehall and the establishment. A good example of an outsider group is the Campaign for Nuclear Disarmament (CND), which, despite massive campaigning, failed to influence government policy whether Conservative or, more surprisingly, Labour.

*See also* insider group; pressure group.

## overload

A critique of a democratic government popular in the 1970s, whereby it was deemed unable to meet the mounting demands of a complex society. One analysis located the source of the problem in the civil service, where individual officers sought to advance their interests by expanding their departments as a means of enhancing their own careers, thus helping to cause excessive public expenditure, burgeoning numbers of civil servants and widespread inefficiency. Right-wing politicians prescribed privatisation and a new ethos for the public service which owed much to the private sector. Another attributed overload to the difficulty of coordinating the apparently infinite number of uncontrollable variables of which political problems are comprised.

## Oxbridge

Name produced by elision of the names of the two elite British universities. Oxbridge is important politically as so many of its products go on to dominate positions of power in Britain. On 1 November 1998 the *Observer* produced a list of the 300 most powerful people in the country and of them nearly one-third had attended either Oxford or Cambridge. As the paper commented:

> The Oxbridge system is a devastatingly efficient way of producing the nation's elites. The cosy Cambridge power club includes for example, the heir to the throne, the prime minister's press secretary, the permanent secretary to the Treasury, the Home Office and the Departments of Health and Social

Security, cabinet secretary Richard Wilson, the head of MI5, the Governor of the Bank of England and the director of the CBI.

Oxford, if anything, is even closer to the reins of power: its graduates include Tony Blair, Rupert Murdoch, David Miliband, Jonathan Powell, Peter Mandelson and Ed Balls. Oxbridge still, it would seem, runs the country. In 2000 Gordon Brown seized upon the case of Laura Spence, a state secondary schoolgirl who was refused a place at Oxford despite excellent A-level results. Brown claimed she was the victim of discrimination and elitism but the facts tended to prove him wrong, as other students turned down had equally good results and the college concerned had a good record for encouraging candidates from state schools.

## Oxford Union

The debating society of Oxford University, which has helped train some of the country's greatest politicians in public speaking. Being elected president of the Union has long been seen as an indication of political promise and possible career. For example, William Hague was, and performances as Tory leader after 1997 against Tony Blair at prime minister's questions attracted praise for their wit and good comic timing. When he stood down as leader in June 2001 Blair acknowledged Hague as a 'worthy and formidable opponent'.

# P

## paramilitary

A technical term for a terrorist military unit or organisation which claims to represent the two religious groupings in Northern Ireland. The Ulster Defence Association (UDA) is the best-known Protestant body and the IRA the best-known Catholic one. There had been occasional contacts between the British government and the

Provisional IRA since 'the troubles' began but none came to anything until the peace process initiated by the Conservative government in the late 1980s. These culminated in a series of negotiations chaired by US Senator George Mitchell, which involved the paramilitaries. Many believe their inclusion was the reason for the success of the peace process.

*See also* Continuity IRA; Irish Republican Army (IRA); Loyalist Volunteer Force; Provisional IRA; Real IRA; Ulster Defence Association; Ulster Volunteer Force.

**parenting class**
An initiative to curb crime based on the idea that parents of actual or potential offenders will benefit from some instruction in how to manage their children. Initial results were encouraging and so it was proposed to extend parenting classes to the parents of 3,000 young offenders held in secure facilities, to 'break the cycle of intergenerational criminality'. The white paper on the criminal justice system issued in July 2002 contained this along with many other ideas and policy proposals. In February 2004 it was announced that the government may use the law to force some parents to take parenting classes (*Observer*, 22 February 2004).

**parliament**
www.parliament.uk
Usually considered to comprise the House of Commons, the House of Lords and the monarch. The British parliament, held to originate in 1265, is often regarded as the 'mother of parliaments' though the Icelandic Althing from 930 is older. However, the British parliament is the usual model for large developed countries and has been very influential, not least because of the far-flung nature of the British Empire. The Norman kings used to convene a gathering of landowners called the curia regis, or great council, to which representatives of the shires were occasionally summoned. In 1265 Simon de Montfort (who had led a baronial revolt against Henry III but

who then needed a counter to their influence) summoned representatives from the boroughs as well as the shires and these two groups began to meet separately from the barons, thus establishing the embryos of the Commons and the Lords. Gradually parliament extracted from successive monarchs a number of rights in exchange for their support but they were still contested and it took the Civil War in the 1640s and the Glorious Revolution in 1688–89 to establish parliament's ultimate supremacy over the monarchy and the judiciary.

Two parliamentary groupings emerged in the 17th century, namely the Whigs and the Tories. The monarch began to invite their leaders to be ministers, depending on who commanded a majority in parliament. In 1707 the parliaments of England and Scotland were united and from 1801 to 1922 the Irish parliament too. Elections were fixed at every three years in 1694, every seven in 1716 and the current five in 1911. Parliament enjoyed a 'golden age' in the 19th century, when it was able to reject legislation and sack ministers on the floor of the House of Commons. However, the growth of disciplined parties made debates wholly predictable and 'majorities ruled'.

Critics argue that the massive majorities won by New Labour in 1997 and 2001, together with Tony Blair's apparent reluctance to consult the House, have brought parliament to a low position of power and prestige. A group of leading MPs, including Tony Wright and Gwyneth Dunwoody, were keen to persuade the then leader of the house, Robin Cook, that the balance of power between legislature and executive needed to be changed in the former's favour. A series of reforms occurred in the autumn of 2002, including a 7.00 p.m. finish to evening sessions, but the crucial balance of power in favour of the executive has not changed as a result.

**Parliament Act 1911**
One of the landmarks in British constitutional history, in that it originated in the Lords' rejection of David Lloyd George's People's Budget in 1909. The upper

chamber finally agreed to pass the 1911 measure only under threat that the king would create sufficient Liberal peers to ensure its passage. The act effectively made the Commons the more powerful chamber and the powers of the unrepresentative Lords were reduced to that of delay of one month for bills embodying financial proposals and two years for other bills, this being reduced to one year by the Parliament Act 1949. In addition the maximum time between general elections was reduced from seven years to five.

### parliamentary candidate
*See* candidate for parliamentary election.

### parliamentary commissioner for administration
*See* ombudsman.

### parliamentary commissioner for standards
www.parliament.uk/about_commons/pcfs. cfm
Set up in 1995 following the recommendations of the Nolan committee. The commissioner reports to the Select Committee on Standards and Privileges, which also adjudicates on the commissioner's reports. The commissioner also maintains the register of members' interests (but not the register of lords' interests, which is compiled by the Lords registrar under the authority of the clerk of the parliaments) and gives advice on the code of conduct and the Guide to the Rules Relating to the Conduct of Members.

The first incumbent was Sir Gordon Downey and he was busily employed from the outset considering the case of Neil Hamilton MP, who was accused of accepting cash for questions from the owner of Harrods, Mohamed al-Fayed. His successor was Elizabeth Filkin, a former chair of the Citizens' Advice Bureau. She established a tenacious style of investigation and press reports in late June 2001 suggested she had succeeded in offending some senior politicians. She had pursued inquiries against John Major and William

Hague regarding issues which some dismissed as trivial. The decision not to reappoint Filkin in January 2002 attracted considerable controversy. Her most famous investigation was into the loan of £300,000 made by Geoffrey Robinson MP to fellow Labour MP Peter Mandelson. She upheld two of the complaints against Mandelson, the outcome being his first resignation. She also investigated Robinson regarding undeclared financial interests from former business links with the disgraced Robert Maxwell. She experienced problems investigating accusations against Keith Vaz, regarding both the Hinduja brothers and his wife's business interests. Vaz, the member for Leicester East and minister for Europe, was cleared on several points but on others the commissioner indicated she had not received the cooperation she required. Vaz was re-elected in 2001 but lost his job in government.

### parliamentary counsel
Expert legal draughtsmen who put into words what legislators seek to do; they are in charge of the formal drawing up of bills, amendments to bills and statutory instruments placed before the legislature for approval. They are civil servants but usually qualified solicitors or barristers. In 1996 contracting out this activity to private practice was considered but not introduced.

### parliamentary democracy
*See* parliamentary government.

### parliamentary government
The mechanism producing both a government and democratic accountability. In Britain a general election must take place at least once every five years, at which voters elect a new House of Commons. The sovereign then invites the person who can command a majority in the House to become prime minister and form a government. This person is usually the leader of the largest party elected by the public but in February 1974 Edward Heath sought to form a government supported by the Liberals, then led by Jeremy Thorpe. The

bid failed when all 14 Liberal MPs rejected Heath's proposed coalition, and Harold Wilson went on to become premier of a minority government. Once an administration is formed it seeks to implement its manifesto promises, principally by means of legislation (public bills). The prime minister and other senior members of the government are responsible to the House of Commons, and ultimately to the electorate for their actions, policies and overall management of the country. Therefore, parliamentary government is responsible and accountable for its actions, two key features of the British political system. However, in recent years changes have taken place in these constitutional principles. For example, some have suggested that the development of executive agencies has weakened the principle of ministerial accountability; and Scottish and Welsh devolution has diluted the idea of a unified state run by a central government.

> The British, being brought up on team games, enter the House of Commons in the spirit of those who would rather be doing something else. If they cannot be playing golf or tennis, they can at least pretend that politics is a game with very similar rules. (C. Northcote Parkinson, 1962, British political scientist, expressing 'Parkinson's law' – work expands to fill the time available)

## Parliamentary Labour Party (PLP)

Members of parliament who accept the Labour whip in the House of Commons. Unlike the Conservative Party, Labour elects a Parliamentary Committee which the leader uses as the basis of the shadow cabinet. In this process each MP has as many votes as there are candidates and, since 1992, there must be at least four for women candidates. Once in government the leader is obliged to appoint the cabinet from those who held shadow cabinet posts, though later reshuffles can reflect the leader's choices. Until in government, the PLP contained well defined factional groupings: the 'soft left' Tribune Group and the harder-left Campaign Group, but these groups faded once it became clear

Tony Blair rewarded loyalty with government posts. However, the passage of years in power has led to dissatisfaction with the leadership and the groupings began to re-emerge, especially after the Iraq war in 2003.

Working-class representation in the PLP had declined from about 75 per cent in the interwar period to 13 per cent by 1997, while middle-class MPs increased in proportion of the whole, with two-thirds being graduates. In 1997, 101 women were elected but ethnic representation was still relatively low.

## parliamentary majority

A party's voting strength over and above other parties in the House of Commons. It is one of the cornerstones of the 'unwritten' constitution, because the leader of the largest party following a general election will be invited by the sovereign to form a government. Indeed, it is the voting strength and whipping system of the governing party which enables it to enact legislation and implement its manifesto commitments. The first past the post system of elections tends to produce majority governments, which can implement their legislation without having to form coalitions with other parties and make the inevitable compromises and 'deals' which proportional representation tends to foster. Critics of this system, for example the Liberal Democrats, point out that governments can be elected, and usually are, with much less than 50 per cent of the popular vote. They claim that this reduces the political legitimacy of an administration, a claim given greater force when governments are elected with very small overall parliamentary majorities (majority in parentheses): 1950, Labour (5); 1964, Labour (4); February 1974, Labour (33 short of an overall majority); and October 1974, Labour (3). Small overall majorities, or no majority at all, creates difficulties for government, as demonstrated after February 1974, when Labour soon lost its majority and was forced to rely first on Liberal support (the Lib–Lab pact), and then on the support of the Scottish National Party. Margaret Thatcher was fortunate in having substantial majorities, John Major less so in 1992, when he gained only a 21-seat majority and had to deal with a dissenting group of Eurosceptics. Tony Blair's 1997 administration was elected with a massive majority of 179, the largest since 1945; in June 2001 he succeeded again with a majority of 167, although from a limited turnout of only 59.2 per cent. Some pointed out that almost as many people did not vote in this election as those who voted in the governing party.

## parliamentary party

After the Reform Acts of 19th century, MPs were increasingly elected on party platforms and represented parties in addition to their constituents in the House of Commons. Today parties dominate the Commons, and to a lesser extent the Lords. The European parliament is dominated by coalitions of national parties. Both Conservative and Labour have well organised internal parliamentary structures, namely the 1922 Committee and the Parliamentary Labour Party (PLP) respectively, with managing committees, and others which shadow the major policy areas. Elections to the committees serving the parties are often quite fiercely contested. Internal party committees provide training for MPs specialising in particular issues and policies, as well as a line of communication between backbenchers and the leadership. Parliamentary parties used to elect the party leaders but in 1981 Labour introduced an electoral college that represented constituency parties, unions and the PLP to perform the function instead. In 1998 the Conservatives changed their procedures to one whereby the parliamentary party would identify a shortlist of two candidates but with the final vote delivered by the party members.

## parliamentary private secretary (PPS)

The lowest rung on the ministerial ladder. The PPS is part of a department's ministerial team and sits in on policy discussions but is given little to do that is of importance. He or she often acts as a conduit between the minister and backbenchers and is often little more than a message carrier. However, the importance of promotion to the post should not be underestimated; it is effectively that of 'apprentice minister' and can be the prelude to either promotion or renewed political oblivion.

## parliamentary privilege

The right MPs have to say whatever they like, within the bounds of parliamentary language, inside the confines of parliament, without fear of any court action being taken against them. It also includes the power of the House to prevent anyone impeding its work. 'Privilege' enables some MPs to make arguably slanderous statements in the Commons with impunity; saying them outside would lay them open to legal action. However, privilege goes beyond the individual MP to include the right of the House to regulate and control its own proceedings, as well as its power to punish MPs and others for breech of privilege. The Standards and Privileges Committee will examine misconduct and recommend punishment, ranging from suspension from the House to criminal prosecution. Even the testimony of witnesses to committees of the House is protected by privilege.

## parliamentary reform

*See* House of Commons reform; House of Lords reform.

## parliamentary session

Usually runs from November to November but can be altered. If an election is held in the spring, for example, then a long session can run through to the November of the following year (it has carried over in the past into December). Conversely, the calling of a general election can interrupt a session, producing a 'short' session. If the government's business programme is under pressure, the end of a session may be delayed. There are recesses at Christmas, Easter, Whitsun and summer. At the moment, both houses are experimenting with returning for two weeks in September, then rising for a three-week conference season, returning in October. Bills, if not passed by both houses, fall at the end of the session, though there is now some provision for carrying over bills from one session to another. In the Commons, this can be accomplished by the passing of a motion. The House of Lords has agreed that the carry-over should normally apply only to bills that have been subject to pre-legislative scrutiny.

## parliamentary sovereignty/ supremacy

It is important to note the distinction between sovereignty and supremacy. The former is used to describe the independence of the nation state from any outside authority and its special status in international law; the latter refers to the political authority which parliament exerts over the monarchy and courts. The legal entity of the United Kingdom comprises England, Wales, Scotland and Northern Ireland but it is a unitary state, not a federal one with defined powers for constituent elements. The explanation is historical in that England absorbed the peripheral states and made them subject to its parliament: Wales in 1536; Scotland in 1707; and Ireland in 1801 although in 1922 only the northern part of Ireland was retained. European Community law appeared to qualify British sovereignty in that it is held to be superior to British law but most constitutional lawyers would probably maintain that ultimately parliament could overturn European law and that sovereignty still resides with member legislatures until (if ever) the European Union becomes a genuine federation.

## parliamentary terms of address

In the Commons members are required to address their remarks to or through the speaker. Other members are referred to as 'honourable members' and members of the same party as 'my honourable friend'. MPs who are members of the Privy Council

are referred to as 'right honourable'. In the Lords members are 'noble lords'.

## participation

See political participation.

## partisan dealignment

Term associated with the work of the political scientist Ivor Crewe, among others, that describes how voters have become detached from their class-based or 'natural' party (the Conservatives for the middle classes, Labour for the working classes). The proportion of voters identifying closely with 'their' party fell from 38 per cent in 1964 to under 20 per cent in 1997; by 2001 the figure was closer to 10 per cent. Voters became more 'instrumental', choosing the party which they believed would most benefit their interests. This tendency hit Labour particularly badly as working-class support fell sharply in the 1980s, and shifted over to the Conservatives, particularly in the C2 or skilled manual categories. This view, however, was questioned by Heath, Jowell and Curtice in the mid-1980s, who suggested that most of the electorate still voted according to class; however, to prove this they had to redefine the class categories. By 1997 the allegiance of working-class voters had moved back to Labour, along with support from the middle classes. In that general election social groups A and B swung from Conservative to Labour by an average of 10 per cent. Those in groups C1, C2, and D and E swung by 21, 15 and 9 per cent, respectively. In 2001 A and B votes swung to Labour by 1.5 per cent and C1 votes by 2 per cent. However working-class votes swung to the Conservatives: 2.5 per cent of C2 votes and 6.5 per cent of D and E votes.

The overall effect of partisan dealignment is to make elections less predictable, with huge waves of support likely to wash first one way then the other. Votes are much more 'up for grabs' than at any time in the history of British politics.

## partition

The partition of Ireland in 1922 into Ulster and the Irish Free State. Partition can be seen from two perspectives. Nationalists see it as British imperialism, an attempt to maintain a foothold in Ireland having lost the war of independence. The religious and political differences, cited in justification for partition, are seen as a smoke screen for imperial interventions and impositions. The other view sees the partition as inevitable and necessary given the militant determination of Protestants in the north to retain a separate identity and the link with Britain.

## party election broadcast

Broadcast by a political party allowed during the course of an election campaign. Before 1998 broadcasts were allocated on the basis of: a party's voting performance in the previous election; or whether it was fielding at least 50 candidates. In 1998 a new consultation paper proposed to increase the required number of candidates to one-sixth of all seats (110). However, if a party is contesting seats in only one of the constituent nations of the UK then it would need to be contesting one-sixth of the seats available there to qualify for any broadcasts.

*See also* party political broadcast.

## party funding

A constant source of concern for all politicians. Running one of the main political parties costs upwards of £20 million a year and more in an election year. Both Labour and the Conservatives have tried hard to solve the problem but without total success.

Labour has traditionally derived its funding from trade unions but the political influence which unions exerted became a political liability and New Labour sought to reduce its dependence on them. The existence of direct funding, through the 'sponsoring' of members to support them financially, gave way after 1995 to 'constituency plan agreements', whereby unions contributed some money in exchange for representation on the constituency general management committee. New Labour did its best to increase individual donations and as the Conservative cause declined in the late 1990s Labour began to pick up wealthy supporters in business, the City and in the media. By 1994 unions donated only half of Labour's income. The party's national membership scheme also brought in substantial sums. The Ecclestone affair proved an embarrassment for Tony Blair and subsequent donations were accepted with more circumspection. David Sainsbury, publisher Paul Hamlyn and financier Chrisopher Ondaatje each donated £2 million in the autumn of 2000. Some said the gifts were squeezed in before the legal limits on donations began to be applied in February 2001.

The Conservative Party has traditionally been perceived as the 'rich' party and, indeed, business sources regularly provided the party with the wherewithal to fight expensive elections, often via 'front' organisations which fed funds through to the party indirectly for those who wished to keep their donations confidential. However, the Conservatives, with a declining membership, were forced to look further afield and ended up accepting money from some business sources abroad, for example the Greek shipping magnate John Latsis. These donations attracted adverse comment and were a gift to the Labour Party, which exploited the issue in the 1990s and linked it to 'sleaze'.

The Neill committee recommended that the amount of cash spent on elections should be capped and that regulations be introduced regarding donations to political parties and their identification. During the 2001 general election a cap of £20 million was placed on spending and neither party seemed to object; nor did the campaign seem especially 'cut price' from the voter's point of view.

In 1998 the Conservatives sought to escape their financial problems by appointing a Belize-based billionaire as their treasurer: Michael Ashcroft. He helped to erase Conservative debts but ran into criticism himself for his business dealings. More helpful perhaps were the rich donors who contributed millions of pounds over Christmas 2000. Stuart Wheeler, who made his money out of betting, donated £5 million and later Paul Sykes, a Eurosceptic businessman, donated several million pounds. However, the Electoral Commission released figures in April 2001 which revealed that Labour had received four times as much funding as the Conservatives in the February and March preceding the general election. Most of Labour's money came from the unions, including the GMB, AEEU, TGWU, MSF and USDAW. In addition, it received donations of £10,000 each from several businessmen, including Lord Haskins. In 2002 several unions threatened to sever their traditional financial support for the Labour Party on the grounds that the party no longer served union interests.

*See also* election campaign costs; Neill committee; Political Parties, Elections and Referendums Act 2000.

### party identification
*See* partisan dealignment.

### party list
*See* regional party list.

### party membership
In the 1950s it was reckoned both big parties had over a million members but the affiliated union members distorted this for Labour, while the Conservatives had many non-active members. In 2004 the figures were: Conservatives 320,000, Labour, 210,000 and Liberal Democrats 76,000. In 2002 the Greens claimed 5,000 – up from 3,500 in 1996 – and Plaid Cymru 11,000.

### party political broadcast (PPB)
Broadcast created by and issued on behalf of a political party. Parties are allocated airtime in relation to their performance in previous elections and the number of candidates they are fielding in an election. Not surprisingly, the lion's share goes to the three main parties. The very first PPB appeared in 1951, given by Lord Samuel for the Liberals; it was faded out as it overran its time. Anthony Eden presented the Conservatives' first PPB in the same year.

The politicians of the day were unskilled and tended to give awkward, stilted talks to the camera. Harold Macmillan was the first to show a flair for the medium of television, and was followed by the pipe-smoking Harold Wilson and folksy James Callaghan. Margaret Thatcher taught herself to be effective on television with help from her media guru Gordon Reece. In 1987 Labour produced a 'vox pop' broadcast that focused on Labour leader Neil Kinnock, directed by Hugh Hudson. This PPB pushed up Kinnock's personal ratings in the opinion polls and won praise from all sides; it stimulated a similar (though less praised) broadcast featuring John Major in the 1992 general election campaign. In 1997 John Major vetoed a PPB which represented Tony Blair as a Faust-like figure, prepared to sell his principles for electoral victory. PPBs seldom attract much interest and tend to attract small audiences.

*See also* party election broadcast.

### party system
The relationships between the political parties operating in a state. Unlike the one-party systems of the former Soviet Union and its eastern satellites, Britain, in common with other liberal democracies, offers voters a choice of party candidates in elections. Many European countries have multi-party systems (usually the result of a proportional system of representation), where more than two political parties either are competing for government or play a significant part in influencing government. Britain has been viewed as a two-party system, as either the Conservative or Labour party traditionally has control of the House of Commons. However, this was not always the case. Between 1929 and 1945 there were minority governments (1929–31) and coalitions (1931–45). It is only since 1945 that the 'two-party system' has been so clearly and well established but even then substantial third-party voting has taken place. Thus, since the 1970s the rise of the Liberals, Ulster nationalists and Scottish and Welsh nationalists has come to challenge this two-party control, most especially

in the mid to late 1970s. In the 1983 general election, the Alliance spectacularly pushed Labour into third place in a number of constituencies, and to many this signalled the beginning of the end of the two-party system. However, the breakthrough was short-lived and Labour recovered ground in the elections of 1987 and 1992, finally gaining office in 1997. Despite reservoirs of support for third parties the two-party domination of the House of Commons will probably continue unless there is a change in the first past the post system for parliamentary elections. Party systems in the Celtic assemblies are more complex and involve coalitions between Labour and the Liberal Democrats.

**paternalism**
The tendency of the state to take responsibility for important aspects of individual and group behaviour. Liberalism originally was predicated on the idea of limited government, that the state should not usurp areas of life that were the proper responsibility of the individual citizen. However, certain theorists, notably T. H. Green, argued persuasively that citizens were not properly free until they had equal opportunities to become self-reliant. From this beginning grew the whole structure of the welfare state and fears in the Liberal Party as well as the Conservative Party that the state in the 20th century has become too protective and too interventionist, threatening private liberties and inhibiting private initiative. Labour shed some of its paternalism before its 1997 victory but could not escape accusations of paternalism by the Conservatives, usually expressed as attacks on the 'nanny state'; examples given included the proposed ban on foxhunting and advice given on diet by the Ministry of Health.

**patriotism**
See nationalism.

**paymaster general**
www.opg.gov.uk
One of a number of non-departmental posts which the prime minister can use as he or

she wishes, whether in the cabinet or outside. At the time of writing it was a position in the Treasury with specific responsibilities for customs and excise, European and various other tax issues. Geoffrey Robinson occupied the post after 1997 but resigned over the controversy surrounding his loan to Peter Mandelson.

**peace process**
Short-hand term to describe the complex of initiatives, accommodations and rhetoric which moved Northern Ireland towards its latest period of peace. It was initiated by revelations in the *Observer* in 1993 that the IRA would be prepared to end its armed struggle. From this beginning, talks between the IRA, the Irish government and the British government ensued and took off when the former US Senator George Mitchell agreed to chair the peace negotiations. These eventually culminated in the Good Friday Agreement, which was signed by all sides in 1998. Only time will tell if this latest attempt at peace will be successful or just another false dawn in the violent history of Ireland.
*See also* Northern Ireland.

**Peacock report, 1986**
Report of a committee on the financing of the BBC. The Conservative Party in the 1970s and 1980s tended to view the BBC as excessively left wing. Consequently there was much support for the ending of the licence fee system of funding the BBC. Some Conservatives hoped such a recommendation would come from the Peacock committee, which reported in 1986, but it bitterly disappointed them by dismissing the idea that the BBC should accept advertising and by recommending that the licence fee be indexed to inflation.

**peak organisation**
An 'umbrella' body representing a collection of a certain type of pressure group. The Trades Union Congress, for example, covers trade unions, while the Confederation of British Industry represents the managements of the larger

POLITICS

economic enterprises. Peak organisations are especially valued by the European Commission as they help to streamline the consultation processes in Brussels.

## Peerage Act 1963

An act, called for by Anthony Wedgwood Benn, as he then styled himself, that enabled peers to surrender their titles. This allowed them to stand for the Commons. Benn was the first beneficiary but the second, ironically, was Lord Home, who became Alec Douglas-Home in 1964 in order to lead the Conservative Party and become prime minister.

## penal policy

The approach to punishing offenders. In Britain this has, since the 20th century, tended to be liberal, with some element of rehabilitation. However, Conservative policies after 1979 tended to be less so. Margaret Thatcher called for tougher sentences and Michael Howard, home secretary 1993–97, claimed that 'prison works', despite the fact that several judges asserted the opposite. As always, the younger generation are singled out for special treatment, with Conservative politicians frequently calling for tougher action to be taken against young offenders. To this end William Whitelaw, home secretary 1979–83, introduced the 'short sharp shock' approach, based on a recycled borstal model. Preventive remedies, though, were not wholly neglected and several programmes were initiated which attempted to make contact with young offenders and persuade them to mend their ways before periods in youth detention and then adult prison turned them into hardened criminals.

Neighbourhood Watch schemes became more popular from the 1980s onwards; there was also the appearance from that time of vigilante movements, whereby residents organise their own patrols and, occasionally, punishments (for example of paedophiles).

Labour used to take a more liberal line on penal policy, based on the belief that the sources of crime were to be found in poverty and social injustice. However, Tony Blair, as shadow home secretary in the early 1990s, changed this balance with his policy of attempting to be 'tough on crime, tough on the causes of crime'. After Labour's 1997 election victory, Jack Straw as home secretary was not notably more liberal than his Conservative predecessors and his successor in 2001, David Blunkett, was rumoured to have no ambition to be more liberal than Straw. In July 2001 he announced a new approach which suggested he might be, as it emphasised the rehabilitation of prisoners. Studies had shown that the changes in penal policy had not deterred the 100,000 core offenders who committed half of all crimes. Blunkett marked a break with the 'prison works' approach stating that: 'The aims of sentencing should be prevention, punishment and reparation, reducing crime and rehabilitation'. In May 2003 Blunkett announced plans to establish a new body, the Sentencing Guidelines Council, to set national guidelines for all offences.

See also crime; Prison Service; sentencing; vigilante movement.

## pension

State pensions began under David Lloyd George at the beginning of the 20th century, as payments to the elderly, which were met out of general contributions to the exchequer. More recently employers began to pay occupational pensions, from an accumulated fund. The government sought to encourage this practice by making contributions to such funds tax deductible. By the early 1980s pension funds, at 27 per cent, had become the largest holders of financial assets in Britain. In 1997 Peter Lilley, the social security minister, proposed a new scheme, whereby individuals would contribute towards their own pensions as the state pension increasingly declined as a proportion of the average income. Labour condemned the plan but could offer only a row between senior policy makers when in office. Frank Field, the minister entrusted with 'thinking the unthinkable' about welfare, suggested a second pension, of roughly the same value as the state one, funded by national insurance contributions and run by mutual societies. However, the chancellor, Gordon Brown, did not like it, as different-sized contributions, reflecting income, would be paid in for the same flat-rate pension. Higher payments for negligible extra benefits were judged unlikely to be acceptable and the scheme made no headway. Brown caused controversy in 1997 when he removed tax benefits paid to pension and insurance funds, thus taking for the Treasury an annual £5 billion out of pension funds, which a few years later were destined, in many cases, to run into deficit. Brown introduced 'stakeholder pensions' in 2001, a scheme targeted at lower income earners.

## People's Panel

A group of 5,000 people set up in 1998 to help government keep in touch with public opinion. In practice it had few functions and was wound up early in 2002.

## people's peer

Introduced in April 2001 in an attempt to make the Lords more representative of ordinary people. They were appointed by the House of Lords Appointments Commission – comprising four Lords and two commoners – chaired at the time by Lord Stevenson. The list was immediately ridiculed for being exclusive – seven knights and three professors were included as well as Lady (Elspeth) Howe, wife of the former Conservative chancellor. John Edmonds, the union leader, commented that 'The club remains as exclusive as ever'.

See also House of Lords; House of Lords Appointments Commission; House of Lords reform.

## permanent secretary

The senior official who runs each department of government in Whitehall. Permanent secretaries are often correctly characterised as being largely drawn from Oxbridge universities, though some, exceptionally, have no university experience.

They are the chief advisors to the ministerial heads of the departments and are responsible for the civil servants employed by them. Their pay in 2002 was a maximum of £179,000 but went up in that year to a maximum of £245,000.

## personal social services

Residential and visiting services to children, the elderly and others in need. In 1970 integrated social services departments were set up within local authorities to provide these services. These departments have responsibility for a range of people who are unable to look after themselves, especially children and children at risk within families.

## petition

See early day motion; political participation.

## Phillips report, 2000

Report into the outbreak of bovine spongiform encephalitis (BSE, or 'mad cow disease'). The report was critical of Stephen Dorrell and a number of other former Conservative ministers who had played down the risk of BSE-infected beef contaminating humans. John Major and some of his colleagues apologised, in the wake of the report, for their role in the BSE crisis.

## Phillis report, 2004

Independent review of government communications. Bob Phillis, chief executive of the Guardian Media Group, chaired an inquiry into government communication following the Jo Moore case, the political advisor who advised colleagues to use the disaster in the USA on 11 September 2001 as a good day to 'bury bad news'. His report recommended that: the Government Information Service should be disbanded; a permanent secretary should head a new communication service; the prime minister's communications team – one civil service and one political appointee – should report to the permanent secretary; there should be televised lobby briefings; the culture of secrecy should be

POLITICS

reduced; the media should separate comment from news; there should be special training for political advisors; the manipulation of government statistics should be ended. The government proved sympathetic to most of these suggestions.

*See also* Moore's email, 2001.

### Pinochet case, 1999–2000

General Augusto Pinochet, the former military dictator of Chile, on a visit to Britain, was arrested by British police in early 1999 in response to a request from a Spanish judge who was seeking to try the Chilean leader for crimes committed against Spanish nationals. Amnesty International, the group campaigning on behalf of those suffering at the hands of governments worldwide, was delighted, as were those on the left in Britain who had supported the Allende regime deposed by Pinochet with the help of the CIA. But other political figures, notably Margaret Thatcher and Norman Lamont, condemned the decision by home secretary Jack Straw to imprison a 'friend of Britain'. After considerable delay the general was found to be too ill to stand trial and was returned to his home country, where he may well have to face similar charges.

> The fact that Augusto Pinochet was arrested while travelling abroad – almost unthinkable just 16 months ago – has sent a powerful message: no one is above the law, even national laws protecting you from prosecution. (Amnesty International, 2 March 2000)

> Sometimes democracy must be bathed in blood. (Pinochet, when dictator of Chile, 1979)

### Plaid Cymru (Party of Wales)

www.plaidcymru.org

Party founded in 1925 by John Saunders Lewis. Its aim is independence for Wales within Europe and the United Nations. Its first MP was Gwynfor Evans, who won the Carmarthen by-election in 1966. By the end of the 1970s there were three Plaid

Cymru MPs but the proposed assembly for Wales was heavily rejected in the referendum held in 1979. Throughout the 1980s the party's MPs, including its leader Dafydd Wigley, kept the flame alight and in 1997 the referendum vote for a Welsh assembly was passed, albeit by a whisker. Welsh nationalism is more cultural and language-based than its Scottish equivalent. While the party was socialistic in the 1970s, it arguably moved to the centre and right during the 1980s and 1990s. Dafydd Wigley resigned as leader in the summer of 2000 to be replaced by Ieuan Wyn Jones.

### planned economy

To some extent the brainchild of John Maynard Keynes, who argued the economy could be managed to produce certain desirable goals like full employment. During the 1930s these ideas were supported by those who believed the USSR's planned economy was a success, but it was ridiculed by most Conservatives, a notable exception being Harold Macmillan. The Second World War appeared to reinforce Keynes' ideas, in that thorough planning of the economy achieved both full employment and victory. After the war the nationalisation of 20 per cent of the economy was initially thought to be a success but was soon judged to be inefficient and costly. Further government intervention in the 1970s was judged a failure and Margaret Thatcher came to power determined to 'roll back the state' in terms of economic planning. This aversion to planning characterised the 1980s and, while New Labour is not ideologically opposed to planning, it has not restored the machinery dismantled by its predecessor in government.

*See also* nationalisation; Keynes, John Maynard.

### planning

Britain has a system of planning permissions, whereby any organisation or person seeking to build or otherwise change the environment has to apply for permission to a planning authority, usually the local authority. Minor proposals – such as home extensions – are dealt with routinely by officials reporting to a council's planning committee. The same committee will closely consider any major proposal – such as a new supermarket – from either individuals or developers. The aim of such a system is to ensure that new developments do not clash with existing conditions or unacceptably offend against historical or aesthetic values. Consideration of the idea is then given and it is often possible for objectors to raise their cases at public inquiries chaired by a planning inspector. However, the system has come in for criticism, mainly from business. The public inquiry concerning the building of Heathrow's terminal 5 took 524 days, spread over five years. Consequently, revision of the system, to speed it up, was mooted by ministers in 2002, whereby parliament would decide on projects in principle and only the details would be worked out in public inquiries. The Commons Transport, Local Government and Regions Committee criticised this as 'unworkable' and 'deeply flawed' in July 2002, and predicted the emergence of a new generation of militant campaigners if ministers got their way.

**Plant report, 1993**
Labour Party report that recommended a change in the electoral system. It favoured a regional list system for the European elections and the 'supplementary vote' for Westminster elections, an amended form of the alternative vote. In 1998 the Jenkins committee also reported on electoral reform.

*See also* alternative vote; electoral reform; Jenkins report; proportional representation; supplementary vote.

**plebiscite**
*See* referendum.

**pluralism**
Term with both a descriptive and a normative or prescriptive meaning. As a description of a political system, the US political scientist Robert Dahl argued that in his country, where power is widely dis-

persed, major decisions are taken through a process of negotiation between competing groups, as no group holds a monopoly of power on all issues. The role of government is that of a neutral 'referee', who makes sure that all interest groups play by the 'rules of the game'. An alternative and contrasting view, however, is that government is best seen as a weathervane, turning in the direction which reflects the prevailing wind of group interests. In relation to the British system, journalist Paul Johnson in 1957 said that 'Cabinet ministers are little more than chairmen of arbitration committees'. The US expert on British politics, Samuel Beer, said much the same thing in his description of his 'new group politics'.

The normative or prescriptive element in the theory argues that group-based politics, despite its failings, is the guarantee of a free society, unencumbered by an oppressive or interfering government. However, critics have rounded on the theory, and have pointed out, for example, that some groups have more status, resources or contacts with decision makers than others. Government, it is argued, must accommodate the interests of powerful financial or business groups if it wishes to manage a capitalist economy efficiently and thus be re-elected. Moreover, many citizens do not belong to a pressure group, and thus may be shut out of the decision-making process; even those who do may not necessarily be effectively represented.

*See also* corporatism.

**plurality**
*See* first past the post.

**pocket borough**
Name given to a parliamentary constituency where the seat(s) were partly or wholly controlled by either an individual or a group, usually landowners. About 120 English borough seats were so influenced by private patrons in the 18th century and well over 300 by the beginning of the 19th century. The Great Reform Act 1832 helped to rid the electoral system of such features.

*See also* Great Reform Act 1832.

## police

The modern police force can be dated to Robert Peel's Metropolitan Police Act 1829. This established an organised system of police 'constables', whose job was to implement the law and prevent crime. They were to achieve this through regular street patrols. They wore a uniform but were armed only with a truncheon. The same system was introduced nationally in 1856 and by 1860 there were more than 200 borough or county forces in England and Wales, financed by public funds, though in Ireland the Royal Ulster Constabulary (renamed Northern Ireland Police Service after the Good Friday Agreement) took on a different form to take account of the special circumstances there. In the 20th century police foot patrols were seen as an important reassurance to the public and a deterrent to criminals, but in the 1960s motorised 'panda' car patrols were introduced, which led to the disappearance of the familiar 'bobby on the beat'. In the early 1980s inner-city riots and industrial disorder encouraged more centralised coordination of the police nationwide, the use of community styles of policing and increased powers of stop and search.

The large increases in pay for the police and huge increases in the law and order budget led to criticism of the police in the 1980s as the crime rate continued to soar and public confidence continued to slump. Further concern was expressed about the attitudes of police officers; for example, the Macpherson report (of the inquiry into the death of Steven Lawrence) stated that the Metropolitan Police, along with other public service organisations, were institutionally racist. Moreover, individual officers, and some units, have been accused of corruption and sexism. In 1995 Lancashire Constabulary was the first force to appoint a woman, Pauline Clair, as its chief constable. There are some 56 forces in the country, under the general control of the Home Office. By 2003 police numbers had risen to a record 131,000.

## Police Service of Northern Ireland

www.psni.police.uk

Police service set up as the Royal Ulster Constabulary (RUC) in 1922, when Ireland was partitioned. Few Catholics joined as they were mostly opposed to partition and the force became perceived as a Protestant stronghold: only 11 per cent of the force were Catholic in 1969; by the end of the century it was only 8 per cent. Consequently the RUC never enjoyed widespread support and its ability to control sectarian violence was therefore limited. In 1999 the Patten report urged a number of changes to the RUC, including a much-resisted change of name to Police Force of Northern Ireland as well as new symbols and flags. Sir Ronnie Flanagan, head of the RUC, described the name change as a 'great hurt'.

## policy community

Political science term to describe the way in which democratic governments make policy. According to this view, in each policy area there are actors who wish to have an input – ministers, professional lobbyists, group leaders and civil servants – who have a degree of mutual dependence. Such actors can move in and out of the community, depending on developments, but there will be some continuity. The community will sometimes unite against perceived threats.

*See also* policy network.

## policy formulation

How policy is formulated and decisions taken in the British system. There several theories on this. The 'pluralist' model, for example, emphasises the negotiation which takes place between different pressure groups or centres of power in the country. 'Corporatism', sometimes referred to as neo-pluralism, emphasises the decisions taken by elite members of key power groups and then presented to the legislature as necessary. The conventional Westminster model sees ministers taking advice from civil servants, making a decision, and civil servants carrying out their instructions, though few believe this actually happens.

Many commentators argue that civil servants, far from being compliant implementers of policy, regularly play a major role in formulation, implementation and, often, when they disagree, policy neutralisation. The 'ruling class' model follows the Marxist analysis that those taking the decisions subscribe consciously or unconsciously to the values of the economically dominant class.

An innovation introduced by the Labour government elected in 1997 is the use of consumer research devices, such as the People's Panel, as a way of better informing the development of policy (the Panel closed in 2000 after being judged a failure).

### policy-influencing legislature
One of the three types of legislature delineated by Philip Norton: the policy-making one, as in the USA; the policy-influencing one, as in Britain, which can occasionally modify or reject proposals; and those with no policy effect, like those in the former communist regimes of eastern Europe.

### policy network
An approach to the burgeoning area of policy studies, based on the idea of a policy community. The policy community comprises complex networks of people and groups who have input into policy. Actors win access through a willingness to accept the rules of the game. Professor Rod Rhodes from Newcastle University developed the idea of a looser 'network', as opposed to the more cohesive 'policy community'.

*See also* policy community.

### Policy Network
www.policy-network.org
International think tank set up in 2000 with the support of Tony Blair and Gerhard Schröder, among others. Peter Mandelson became its chair in September 2001 and described it as 'not like a conventional think-tank': it does not originate policy but rather 'enables policy-makers to meet and debate and exchange ideas so that policy is strengthened in practice'. He pre-

dicted he would use the new body to launch an attack on anti-globalisation protestors.

### Policy Unit (Downing Street)
Set up by Harold Wilson in 1974. It was first headed by Bernard, now Lord, Donoughue and was retained subsequently both by James Callaghan and by the Conservative administrations in the 1980s. John Hoskyns, a businessman turned Conservative supporter, headed it under Margaret Thatcher and tried to make it a forward-thinking strategic unit. However, its chief use has probably been as a source of non-departmental advice to the prime minister, which he or she can rely on as relatively disinterested. There were usually eight members in the unit, drawn from civil servants and the outside world, although in 2003 Tony Blair had 13 in his Policy Unit. After Hoskyns, Thatcher reduced the importance of the unit but John Major relied on it substantially and under him its leader, Sarah Hogg, actually wrote the manifesto for the Conservative Party in 1992. Tony Blair has invited journalists as well as think tank experts to join his Policy Unit. It is now seen as a de facto element in an emergent prime minister's department. David Miliband headed the unit until 2001 and then became an MP. Following the 2001 general election the prime minister's Policy Unit was merged with his Private Office, with Jonathon Powell in overall command.

*See also* prime minister's department.

### political advertising
The promotion of party, leader, policy or a combination of all three by use of commercially inspired advertising and marketing techniques. British electoral law does not allow paid broadcasting (unlike in the USA) but parties are given free airtime for party political broadcasts (PPBs) – issued between elections – and party election broadcasts (PEBs). Governments have often used the media surreptitiously to advance political messages. The Conservative 1989 white paper *Working for Patients* was backed by a £1.25 million campaign and in the same year water privatisation

was presaged by a £21 million campaign. Conservative government spending on advertising stood at over £200 million annually by the end of the 1980s.

## political advisor

Someone, often classed as a temporary civil servant, employed by a minister to provide essentially political advice. Traditionally a US phenomenon, it is customary for an incoming administration to install its supporters in key posts. During the 1970s Labour ministers began to appoint special advisors, for example Jack Straw was appointed by Barbara Castle and Bernard Donoughue became senior policy advisor to Harold Wilson and James Callaghan. John Major was keener than Margaret Thatcher on non-elected advisors, appointing 32, but the Blair government quickly put more than 50 in place, especially in posts with special media liaison functions. Before the 2001 general election there were 78 special advisors, who cost the taxpayer nearly £4 million, with the average salary being £56,000; around 30 work in the prime minister's office. Usually these jobs are not advertised but are the result of previous friendships and contacts. Anji Hunter – a close aide to Blair until she left for the private sector – had known Blair since school. When the 2001 general election was called the special advisors resigned. Some were reappointed or repositioned but others entered parliament, including David Milliband, James Purnell and Andy Burnham.

Some argue that importing a new 'tier' of government in the form of advisors is a good thing, making for more effective government and greater clarity, as the idea of a neutral civil service has in recent years been thrown into question. Others suggest that such appointments undermine open government by encouraging the employment of unelected, and therefore unaccountable, individuals, and expose senior politicians to the charge of 'cronyism' and patronage. Lord Butler of Brockwell, the outgoing secretary to the cabinet in 1997, was critical of the role played by political advisors under New Labour. Following the Jo Moore email scandal the Committee on Standards in Public Life chose to investigate the relationship between ministers, advisors and civil servants.

*See also* campaign strategist; Moore's email; prime minister's department.

## political agenda

Not all group or social concerns get into the arena of public or political debate. What defines something as political has been hotly debated by thinkers for many years; however, the political scientist Samuel Finer gives us a guide with his concept of the 'political predicament', as discussed in his *Comparative Government* (1970). This is where opinion is divided on a communal issue, or at least one which affects a substantial proportion of a community, and where an authoritative decision will have implications for all.

For example, plans to build a bypass on agricultural land in order to relieve a congested village will provoke intense and irreconcilable opinions from the groups concerned, and thus becomes a matter for the political agenda of the local people, the county council and ultimately the Department of the Environment. Competing groups will attempt to control the political agenda by controlling the media agenda. In 1997 Labour was perceived as dominating the media agenda with welfare and social policy, while the Conservatives could not shift attention away from a poor economic record and damaging stories of sleaze.

*See also* agenda setting; politics; power.

## political business cycle

Term used to describe the tendency of governments to arrange elections to coincide with upturns in the national economy and thus use a 'feel good' factor of voters to electoral advantage. In 1986 chancellor Nigel Lawson expanded the economy for a projected election in 1987, one which the Conservatives easily won. However, a government can survive unpropitious economic cycles; for example, John Major fought and won the 1992 general election against the

background of recession. Labour chancellor Gordon Brown claimed that he would
avoid boom and bust policies; however,
some observers saw signs that he prepared
the ground for the 2001 general election by
increasing public spending and leaving the
Monetary Policy Committee to take care of
interest rates.

*See also* boom and bust; Monetary
Policy Committee.

## political communications

The messages which link party or
government to the voter through the
central agencies of mass communication.
Historically, the press was the first of the
mass media, its origins being the tracts
and pamphlets of the early 17th century.
Indeed, in the 1750s political comment
was often part and parcel of popular folk
songs, which escaped the attention of the
authorities and the serious criminal charge
of sedition. During the 18th century, the
political class was deeply suspicious of comment; indeed, reports of debates had to be
smuggled out of parliament. Gradually the
principle of the free press was established, a
significant turning point being the abolition
of the Stamp Act, and today the principle
of a free press independent of government
control is jealously guarded by newspapers,
which retain the right to adopt political
positions critical of government. Newspaper
editors and many politicians insist that
statutory controls to protect the privacy of
prominent individuals would be a slippery
slope to press censorship. This having
been said, radical views which challenge
the political order in Britain are seldom,
if ever, supported in a national tabloid or
quality newspapers. Although spin doctors
and the prime minister's press secretary
provide stories via lobby correspondents to
the national dailies, broadcast media now
dominate the communications of political
parties and governments. Press conferences, news releases and ministerial statements
are timed to meet the deadlines of news
organisations and are often presented
against professionally designed exhibition
backdrops. Other instances of this direct
communication to the electorate is the
practice, extensively developed since 1997,
of ministerial announcements on policy initiatives being released to the media before
parliament has been informed, concern
about which was voiced in late summer
2000 by Betty Boothroyd, the retiring
speaker of the House of Commons.

These changes have been reflected in the
'Political Communications' series of books
(studies of British election campaigns
published since 1979). They bring together
senior politicians, campaign strategists,
media professionals and academics, who
provide specific insights into an election
campaign, the most recent edition being
*Political Communications: Why Labour
Won*, edited by John Bartle *et al.* (2001).

The development of the Internet and
email has increased the opportunities for
parties, governments and other campaigning organisations to communicate directly
with voters and other interested parties,
a trend that has led to a kind of 'virtual'
democracy. However, as with all open poli-
ties, it can be exploited by those opposed
to the very existence of democracy, like the
neo-Nazi organisation Combat 18, and to
a lesser extent far-right parties such as the
British National Party.

## political correctness
*See* political language.

## political culture
Popular attitudes towards politics in
general and, in particular, political
authority, the institutions of government
and national leadership. Public opinion
is what people think at any one point,
whereas political culture refers to
embedded attitudes. Gabriel Almond
and Sidney Verba's classic *Civic Culture*
(1963) explored how some societies breed
citizens who seem to trust their leaders and
feel an identity with their governments,
while others do not provide this basic
requirement, with adverse consequences for
their political stability. It is a fact that some
societies seem to demonstrate continuity of
characteristics. For example, Russia has

always been led by a revered authoritarian and it was arguably the political culture which contributed to the emergence under the Soviet Union of Joseph Stalin, a leader with similar characteristics to the tsars of old. Similar things might be said of Chinese politics, where Mao resembled the old-fashioned emperors he outwardly damned.

## political language

In *Politics and the English Language* (1947), George Orwell points to the use of language as an instrument of thought control, and in particular he warns against the use of terms which obscure meaning. In his 1949 novel *Nineteen Eighty-Four* he gave creative expression to this view in a nightmare vision of Britain, where the Ministry of Truth was responsible for propaganda, the Ministry of Love for internal control, and the Thought Police were always on the look-out for deviant individuals who gave themselves away by using the wrong expressions. While Orwell mainly had Stalin's terror in mind, his ideas have currency in the world of modern British politics. 'Political correctness', which began on US campuses in the 1980s, is the concern not to use expressions or words which offend minority groups such as women, members of ethnic minorities or others disadvantaged by social circumstances. The practice was adopted in Britain and has now been absorbed into mainstream discourse, especially by many business and government organisations. While some have ridiculed the more absurd examples of the practice (see, for example, Henry Beard and Christopher Cerf's *The Official Politically Correct Dictionary and Handbook*, 1993), others have suggested that language carries powerful emotional and psychological 'charges' which play their part in the transmission of ideological messages. During the 1980s and 1990s, new right concepts such as 'market forces' and 'freedom of choice' quickly invaded everyday speech; school heads became 'managers' and spoke of 'buying teachers' for their institution. With the election of a New Labour government, a new language or discourse seems to be emerging. Norman

Fairclough, Professor of Linguistics at Lancaster University, published a book entitled *New Labour, New Language?* (2000), which charts the way in which Labour politicians, Tony Blair in particular, are making use of a distinctive type of language which furthers the third way agenda.

## political marketing

A many-faceted phenomenon clearly different to advertising. Advertising is concerned with the promotion of an existing product, whereas marketing is concerned with identifying the concerns of customers (or voters) and then supplying a product or service that satisfies them. As an approach to politics, it uses marketing concepts such as 'packaging', 'positioning' and 'targeting', and investigates the behaviour of political parties, which now compete for votes from an increasingly choosy, volatile electorate. Margaret Thatcher was probably the first modern-day leader to be 'packaged', in her instance by campaign consultant Gordon Reece, for the 1983 general election. Following its disastrous performance in that election, the Labour Party under Neil Kinnock invited marketing and advertising consultants to advise on how the party could recover lost voters. People often associate Peter Mandelson with this revolution in the party's thinking, but the process began before his arrival as communications director for the Labour Party in 1985. Since then major changes have taken place in the party, including the development of New Labour, when Tony Blair, advised by political strategist Philip Gould, repositioned the party in the centre-ground of British politics. The party now uses focus groups extensively as tools by which to discover the motivational levers of voters. Although Labour won a landslide in the 1997 election, it is not at all clear whether this was wholly the result of changes in policy and presentation, or whether it was a by-product of voters' hostility to John Major's faction-ridden government, which was associated with sleaze and hypocrisy.

Since 1997 marketing has informed many aspects of the government's programme of modernising Britain, including the citizens' panels, encouraging a consumer focus in public service provision, introducing the 'best value' initiative for local government and making central government departments, including the Cabinet Office and Number 10, more 'consumer-friendly' to voters. This concern for establishing a dialogue with voter citizens is shared by all major parties, which regularly conduct market research. It is for this reason that the communication arts of marketing and advertising have become a growth industry in British public life. Jennifer Lees-Marshment's book *Political Marketing and British Political Parties* (2001) asserts that parties now conceive their political strategies in marketing terms. It follows that ideology is less important, that politicians tend to follow rather than lead the voters or 'consumers' and that eliciting what the voter wants through focus groups, polling and so forth has become a key aspect of creating political programmes. Lees-Marshment argues that Labour in 1983 had a 'product-based' message which was not attuned to voter demands and consequently failed. In 1987 the party moved to a 'sales-based' strategy but the product was too similar to that of 1983 and it failed again. The same thing happened again, though more narrowly, in 1992 but by 1997, under Blair, the product had been refashioned and remarketed, with the resultant landslide victory. However, Blair's determination to forge ahead with the hugely unpopular war on Iraq in March 2003 reveals that there are limits and exceptions to the extent to which New Labour bases its approach on marketing.

### Political Office
A section in 10 Downing Street. It deals with communication between the prime minister and the wider party machine, parliament and the country. The political secretary was a role which assumed great importance under Harold Wilson when Marcia Williams held it, though less so under Edward Heath, when Douglas Hurd held the post. The Political Office

is funded from party sources and not the public purse. In June 2001 the office was changed as Sally Morgan moved to the Lords and Anji Hunter became head of the Office of Government Relations – however, she left for a post in industry in late 2001. With this departure Tony Blair, in November 2001, brought Sally Morgan, now in the House of Lords and a junior minister in the Cabinet Office, back into Number 10 to replace Hunter with the title of director of political and government relations.

*See also* prime minister's department.

### political participation
To work efficiently, democracies are predicated upon a degree of participation. In practice this is generally minimal, apart from the act of voting in elections, in which generally 60–80 per cent engage within the UK; at local elections, however, the level – 30–40 per cent – is so low there has been some concern at the apathy shown. Figures released at the end of January 2002 revealed that the three major parties between them had memberships totalling a mere two-thirds of a million, or under 2 per cent of the population. Activist numbers are even lower.

There has been more activism in pressure groups over the past decades, with environmental ones witnessing sharp upturns in their memberships. Greenpeace, Friends of the Earth and the Royal Society for the Protection of Birds all increased their membership from 2000 to 2002.

Over 60 per cent of citizens have signed petitions on some issue; over 5 per cent have joined protest marches; and nearly 15 per cent have attended protest meetings of some kind. Studies show activism tends to increase with age – 24 per cent of 35–54-year-olds described themselves as politically active, compared with only 3 per cent of 18–24-year-olds in a poll reported in the *Guardian* in January 1998 – and with social class – the lower down the occupational hierarchy voters are, the less likely they are to be politically active. In an article in the *Guardian* in September

2001 Paul Whiteley of Sheffield University reported his study which had shown that 16 per cent of voters were certainly willing to demonstrate on an issue about which they felt strongly and another 18 per cent said they might be. Protestors were more likely to be middle class, younger and more highly educated than non-protestors. Only 15 per cent of working-class respondents were likely protestors, compared with 19 per cent of middle-class ones.

## Political Parties, Elections and Referendums Act 2000

Act limiting expenditure by parties on elections to £20 million per party. It also banned donations from abroad and limited anonymous donations to political parties to £5,000. It also established the Electoral Commission, to monitor the expenditure and income of political parties engaging in elections and referendums.

## political party

In democracies, organisations that seek to win sufficient public support to take control of the government. In the 19th century, when the electorate had been expanded, groups of politicians organised themselves to appeal to voters, so setting up party organisations and political programmes. By the end of that century political parties dominated the business of parliament. In the 20th century the struggle between the party of government and the main opposition party was made more formal and became the major daily feature of politics between elections. The Conservative Party was the first to organise and did so from its Tory provenance and base in parliament. The Liberal Party was somewhat similar. Labour, by contrast, originated outside Westminster – in an alliance of unions and socialist societies – and was designed to establish a foothold in the legislature. Consequently, the organisations of the two main parties in Britain have tended to reflect the centralised, 'top down' history of the Conservatives and the grass roots, 'bottom up' democratic origins of Labour. The political scientist Robert McKenzie argued

that despite Labour's apparent democratic organisation it was in reality led from the centre. Indeed, since the mid-1980s there has been increased centralisation in the Labour Party, which has come to embrace a corporate style of organisation and administration. The election of Tony Blair as a powerful individual leader and the need of the party to offer a united front to the voters have accentuated these centralising tendencies.

The nationalist parties in Wales and Scotland and the parties in Northern Ireland appeal to different factions in the political culture. In 1997 there were 123 registered political parties. In the 1997 general election, 3,724 candidates stood, of whom 1,592 polled less than 5 per cent of the votes in their constituencies and therefore lost their deposits of £500.

## political populism

A tendency to appeal to the opinions and preferences of ordinary people. The term takes its name from a US 19th-century movement when farmers expressed their disillusion that they had been let down by false political promises and left to drift into debt. More sophisticated politicians protest that such a populist political approach is irresponsible, as the mass of people are often ill-informed and likely to favour simple, short-term solutions to complex problems. British politicians often allow their policies or their rhetoric to become populist – the Thatcherite championing of capital punishment in the 1980s, for example – but they usually fall in line behind more responsible policies eventually, as in the case of home secretary Douglas Hurd's firm rejection of the death penalty during the key 1980s debates.

## political satire

It has long been a part of British political culture that the 'ruled' enjoy a laugh at the expense of their rulers. This tendency has competed with a deference to the 'upper classes', most noticeable in the tendency of some working-class voters to support the Conservatives. The barrier of deference was broken in the late 1950s and early 1960s by the publication of the magazine *Private Eye* and *Beyond the Fringe*, the satirical revue featuring Dudley Moore, Peter Cook, Alan Bennett and Jonathan Miller. This revue-style approach was later used again in the hugely popular ground-breaking television show *That Was the Week That Was*, screened in 1962 and 1963, which introduced David Frost and many others to the airwaves. In the 1980s the rubberised puppet television show *Spitting Image* made a huge impact on audiences with a variety of satirical sketches of the great and good. Other satirical offer-ings have included Harry 'loadsamoney' Enfield, who, for many, epitomised the greed of the 1980s. With the coming of the Blair government in 1997, and the inef-fectual Conservative opposition in the early years, some have argued that satirists were the only true opposition to the new wunder-kind, an example being Rory Bremner, with his brilliant, biting impressions.

## political socialisation
The process by which individuals acquire attitudes towards politics and the political system. The principal agents in this process include:
1  family, especially mother and father, as significant adults who introduce the child to adult authority;
2  schooling, where the hidden curriculum of rules, teacher authority and the examination system represent a type of micro political system;
3  peer group pressure;
4  the disciplines of work;
5  the mass media.

The subtle mix of factors and the development of the personality are probably more important than any individual factor. Moreover, while parents and schooling may leave a powerful impression, young people, perhaps in their first years at university, may rebel against a conservative upbring-ing, and become radicalised and enter student politics on either the left or right. In 1997, New Labour targeted first-time voters (18–29-year-olds), among other groups, with the result that they provided the party with one of its largest swings.

## Political Studies Association of the United Kingdom (PSA)
www.psa.ac.uk
The national body for professional academ-ics, graduates and others interested in the discipline. Membership is available to individuals and institutions (corporate membership). It publishes a monthly journal, *Political Studies*, and holds an annual conference, where members participate in workshops and seminars. These are collected and published in the journal *Contemporary Political Studies*. The year 2000 saw the 50th anniversary of the PSA. At the celebration dinner, lifetime awards were presented by Samuel Beer to Brian Barry, Bernard Crick, David Butler, Stanley Hoffman, Jean Blondel and Richard Rose.

## political violence
To some a logically inconsistent term, in that politics is the peaceful resolution of conflict. British politics since the Civil War has been characterised by its generally peaceful nature. This may be because the country solved many of its major problems sequentially and was not overwhelmed by ca-tastrophes as some other countries were. For example, the struggle between crown and church was over by the 16th century, that between crown and state by the end of the 17th and that between the aristocracy and bourgeoisie by the end of the 19th century. This is not to say British politics is always peaceful. Violence was used by government as well as by protestors during: the clashes between Mosleyites and opponents in the East End of London in the 1930s; the riots in the inner cities in the early 1980s; the miners' strike in 1984–85; and the riots over the poll tax in 1990. Northern Ireland, of course, saw extreme political violence from the late 1960s.

## politics
Best understood as a multifaceted phenom-enon involving the shaping and the sharing

POLITICS

of power and the non-violent resolution of conflict. As political scientist Harold Lasswell put it: 'who gets what, when and how'. For Bernard Crick, it is a moral imperative: 'politics is not just a necessary evil, it is a definite good. Political activity is a type of moral activity; it is a fine activity and it is inventive, flexible, enjoyable and human'. The study of politics dates back to Aristotle and Plato, and is regarded as the oldest of the social sciences. It is closely linked to history, law, sociology, economics, psychology, systems theory and behavioural science. It also has a number of sub-branches: political philosophy, political theory, political analysis, international relations and psephology.

> Politics is like boxing – you try to knock out your opponent. (Idi Amin, 1976)

> I reject the cynical view that politics is inevitably, or even usually, dirty business. (Richard Nixon, 1973)

> Politics is the art of acquiring, holding and wielding power. (Indira Gandhi, 1975)

> I used to say that politics was the second oldest profession and have come to know it bears a gross similarity to the first. (Ronald Reagan, 1979)

> It is evident that the state is a creation of nature and that man is by nature a political animal. (Aristotle, *Politics*, 350 BC)

> Politics is a strife of interests masquerading as a contest of principles. (Ambrose Bierce, *The Devil's Dictionary*, 1906)

> Where some people are very wealthy and others have nothing, the result will either be extreme democracy or despotism will come from either of these excesses. (Aristotle, *Politics*, 350 BC)

## Politics Association
www.politics-association.org.uk
Body set up by (Sir) Bernard Crick and others in 1969 to campaign for political literacy. It quickly became the professional body of politics teachers in schools and colleges and an active lobbyist for more political education, as well as a provider of a range of services to members. *Talking Politics* is the organisation's high-quality tri-annual journal.

## poll tax
*See* community charge.

## polyarchy
*See* pluralism.

## Ponting affair, 1985
*See* Ponting, Clive.

## Popular Front
Left-wing campaign in the mid-1930s de-signed to augment the defence of Republican Spain. It was an attempt to harness the activism of communists with the broader labour movement but the involvement of com-munism set it beyond the pale for the Labour Party leadership and they expelled Stafford Cripps and Aneurin Bevan for joining it. The left-wing magazine *Tribune* was estab-lished as part of the campaign.

## populism
*See* political populism.

## portfolio
Term used to describe the responsibili-ties undertaken by a minister. A minister might be said to have taken on the 'trans-port' or 'health' portfolio. Occasionally a prime minister will appoint an all-purpose non-departmental cabinet minister who is known as 'minister without portfolio'.

## postal voting
Experiments in the wake of the poor voter turnout in the 2001 general election revealed that postal voting tends to increase turnout by several percentage points. Accordingly wider experiments were tried in the local and European elections in 2004, when in some regions postal ballots were made compulsory and not optional. However, the original two areas designated were increased by the government to four, all of them in the north. The measures were criticised by the Electoral Commission and

by the Conservatives, who saw it merely as an attempt by Labour to increase turnout in areas where it would be of party advantage. Problems were encountered, including a failure to distribute voting forms in good time, as well as accusations of fraud and intimidation in certain areas, including Lancashire and Bradford. However, the experiment did succeed in raising turnout by an appreciable amount. In August 2004 the Electoral Commission concluded in a report that 'all-postal voting should no longer be pursued for use at UK elections'. The reasons given were that, despite the 5 percentage point increase in turnout it had produced, the experiment the previous June had been so beset with problems and alleged abuses that the public's faith in the new system had been badly damaged.

**postwar consensus**
Term used to describe the bipartisan agreement between Labour and the Conservatives formed during the war, which continued into peace and for the two subsequent decades. It grew out of a number of common experiences and values: the shared wartime alliance against a common enemy; successful government economic intervention; the blunting of ideological conflict caused by cooperation in the coalition government; the Beveridge report on welfare services; and the acceptance of Keynesianism as a new orthodoxy in macro-economics. The main elements of the consensus were: a mixed economy with a large public sector but retaining a wealth-creating private one; a welfare state providing services to all citizens irrespective of status; close cooperation with the trade unions and employers' organisations; and an acceptance of compromise and consultation as the best means of governing. What economic failure had not destroyed of the consensus by the mid-1970s, Margaret Thatcher did much to complete when she came to power in 1979. Her alternative agenda of promoting the free market was arguably so successful that it had convinced Labour to adopt it by the middle of the 1990s and thus created a new consensus.

By 2001 the Conservatives had moved from their policy of tight control on expenditure to one which was comparable to that of Labour, suggesting a leftward shift towards a new 'neo-Thatcher' consensus.

**poverty**
The lack of sufficient money to conduct a life of any comfort, either in absolute terms or in comparison with the rest of society. After the Second World War, many politicians assumed the welfare state had abolished poverty but during the 1960s academics like Peter Townsend and Colin Titmus revealed that widespread poverty still existed, especially in the inner cities. In the 1980s the concept was contested by Conservative ministers, who claimed that absolute poverty *had* been abolished; people classed as being in poverty then would not have been so classified earlier in the century. The Child Poverty Action Group has no such doubts, and stated in its 1996 study *Poverty: The Facts* that: 'Poverty blights the lives of around a quarter of the UK's population and a third of its children'. Calculations by social statisticians revealed that during the Conservative administrations of Margaret Thatcher and John Major the poorest 10 per cent of the population suffered an absolute decrease in income in real terms, while the richest 10 per cent enjoyed over a 50 per cent increase. The United Nations Human Development annual report in September 1998 stated that deprivation, chronic unemployment and low literacy levels had turned Britain into one of the most poverty stricken of the developed countries. It found that 9 per cent of Britons would not reach the age of 60, over one-fifth of adults were functionally illiterate and 13.5 per cent were below the internationally recognised poverty line (50 per cent of median disposable income). To reinforce such worrying figures about British poverty a further report by the Child Poverty Action Group in June 2000 asserted that:

1  10 per cent of children go without school meals, as their families cannot afford them;

2 differences in intellectual development between children in middle-class and poor families can be seen at 22 months;

3 2.5 million children live in households where income support is the only finance available;

4 63 per cent of children in single-parent families live in poverty.

In July 2001 the Labour government reported that the income gap had not closed during its years in power. Roy Hattersley in the *Guardian* (16 July 2001) deplored the fact that the 'poorest 10% of the population had fallen to 2.9% of overall income. The richest 10% still pocketed 27%'. He was especially concerned that the government claimed it did not matter if the income gap grew. Alistair Darling, when minister for social security, argued that income growth in absolute terms was the most important factor for the poor. Between 1994–95 and 1998–99, income growth after household costs was 10 per cent for the bottom decile and 13 per cent for the top decile. Martin Barnes of the Child Poverty Action Group insisted: 'Concern about the growing gap between rich and poor should not be dismissed as just the politics of envy. Increasing the incomes of the poor will not, in itself, deliver social justice if inequalities in health, education, well-being and opportunity remain'.

> Anyone who has struggled with poverty will know how extremely expensive it is to be poor. (James Baldwin, *Nobody Knows My Name*, 1961)

> Poverty makes you sad as well as wise. (Berthold Brecht, *Mother Courage and Her Children*, 1949)

> The child was diseased at birth – stricken with an hereditary illness that only the most vital of men can shake off. I mean poverty – the most deadly and prevalent of all diseases. (Eugene O'Neill, *All God's Chillun Got Wings*, 1924)

*See also* inequality; social exclusion.

### power

A defining quality of politics and arguably the core of the subject, but also one of the most hotly disputed concepts in social science. A baseline definition of power is given by the US political scientist Robert Dahl, whose intuitive idea of power 'is that A has power over B to the extent that he can get B to do something that B would otherwise not do'. Other interpretations demonstrate the complexity of the power relation. Bertrand Russell, the British mathematician and philosopher, stated that power is 'the production of intended effects'. Max Weber applied a sociological perspective: power is 'the probability that an actor in a social relationship will be in a position to carry out his own will despite resistance'. This points to the fact that power is the quality of a social relationship, not an absolute. As suggested by Hannah Arendt, a political scientist, power 'is not the property of an individual' but 'corresponds to the human ability not just to act but to act in concert'. Talcott Parson, one of the fathers of structural functionalism, elaborated the social roots of power by suggesting that it is 'a generalised facility or resource in the society, analogous to money, which enables the achievement of collective goods through the agreement of members of a society to legitimate leadership positions whose incumbents further the goals of the system'. Marxist writers like Nicos Poulantzas, however, prefer to focus upon class relationships; thus power is the 'capacity of a class to realise its specific objective interests'. Steven Lukes, a British political scientist, takes an altogether different approach: rather than focus on one definition he provides three 'faces' of power. The first 'face' is the ability of people, whether as individuals, groups or large institutions like government, to make decisions and get them implemented, an example of this being Jack Straw's proposals on law and order, which were successfully steered through the legislative process and became the Crime and Disorder Act 1998. The second 'face' of power is the control of the issues agenda or the list of issues which enter the policy arena, and more importantly those that do not. Pressure groups and political parties (the governing one in particular) have a major role in placing issues on the agenda, for example New Labour's manifesto commitment to promote policies which would sustain the environment and develop an integrated transport policy. It is unlikely that Labour, or any other mainstream party, would allow a proposal to abolish private transport to get on to the political agenda. Here, then, is an example of power, exercised in the negative sense, of keeping items off the agenda, in other words a form of non-decision making. The third 'face' of power is what Lukes calls 'the shaping of desires', achieved through the prevailing ideas and values of a society. He claims that this is the most insidious and pervasive demonstration of power, where individuals are trapped within a system of thought and are thus 'brainwashed' by an ideology which prevents them from seeing their real, 'objective' interests.

There are few minds to which tyranny is not delightful. (Samuel Johnson)

So that in the first place I put for a general inclination of all mankind a perpetual and restless desire of power after power, that ceases only in death. (Thomas Hobbes, *Leviathan*, 1651)

Tyrants seldom want pretexts. (Edmund Burke)

What luck for the rulers that men do not think. (Adolf Hitler)

The undesirable classes never liquidate themselves. (Joseph Stalin in reply to Lady Astor, who asked him when he was 'going to stop killing people')

As long as men worship Caesars and Napoleons, Caesars and Napoleons will duly rise and make them miserable. (Aldous Huxley, 1937)

I have no objection to politicians being interested in personal power. (Michael Foot, 1966)

Man is born to seek power, yet his actual condition makes him a slave to the power of others. (Hans J. Morganthau, US political scientist)

Power tends to corrupt and absolute power corrupts absolutely. (Lord Acton)

*See also* elite; hegemony; Marxism; pluralism; power elite.

## power elite
Term associated with C. Wright Mills' radical elite theory of the 1950s. Mills argued that a 'military industrial complex' existed in the USA. This was a network of elites, dominant in government, the military and industry, who served their own interests. More loosely defined, Britain has its own power elites, known as the 'establishment'. In keeping with classical elite theory, these constantly recruit new members to perpetuate the rule of the few over the many. Thus the old elites associated with the Tory party, judiciary and civil service have been reinvigorated with new people. On 1 November 1998 the *Observer* published a list of the 300 most powerful people in Britain.

## power sharing
Used to describe an executive for Northern Ireland in which representatives of the nationalists and the loyalists share power. This was tried in January 1974 after the 1973 Sunningdale Agreement but the loyalists opposed it, called a general strike, and the initiative foundered after only five months. A new initiative was established by the Good Friday Agreement, 1998, with David Trimble as the first minister and Seamus Mallon as his deputy. However, the executive did not last long as it sundered on the issue of the IRA abandoning its weapons; in the autumn of 2002 it was suspended and at the time of writing remains so.

## pre-legislative scrutiny
The consideration of a draft bill by a parliamentary committee before the bill is presented to parliament for its first reading. A number of bills are now subject to this process. Recently there has been a tendency for such 'draft bills' to be referred to ad hoc joint committees of both houses.

POLITICS

Examples in the 2003–04 parliamentary session include the joint committee on the draft civil contingencies bill and the joint committee on the draft gambling bill.

## prerogative powers

The legal powers and privileges of the sovereign. Many of them date back to medieval times, when the monarch had sweeping powers over all aspects of the nation's life. In the 16th century the scope of the prerogative was extended by Elizabeth I and included the appointment of ministers, the declaration of war, the signing of treaties and the summoning and dissolution of parliament. These powers became bones of contention under the Stuarts, who tried to exercise their powers while parliament sought to restrict them. This led to the English Civil War. The royal prerogative is now exercised only on the 'advice' of the minister responsible in virtually all cases; in other words, it has become the property no longer of the monarch but of the elected government.

## press

Newspapers first appeared in the 18th century with *The Times* and the *Observer*; mass circulation arrived in the late 19th century with the *Daily Mail* and the *Daily Express*. New technology eventually enabled the tabloids to sell millions of copies every day and reach the majority of the working class. There are presently three 'popular' papers – the *Daily Mirror, Star* and *Sun*; two 'mid-market' papers – the *Daily Mail* and *Daily Express*; and five 'qualities' – the *Guardian, The Times, Daily Telegraph, Independent* and *Financial Times*. In addition there are three popular Sunday papers, two mid-market Sunday papers and four qualities. After the Second Word War, the Conservatives commanded support from the majority of newspapers and in the 1980s this imbalance became even more pronounced. In the 1990s, however, the press began to realign, most dramatically in the case of the *Sun*, which switched its allegiance to New Labour as soon as the 1997 general election campaign started.

## Press Complaints Commission (PCC)

www.ppc.org.uk

Set up in 1991 to replace the Press Council (originally established in 1953). This industry body comprises editors and non-journalists as a result of the Calcutt committee's recommendations. The original concern related to low standards in tabloid journalism, as exemplified by press intrusions into privacy, inaccurate reporting and 'cheque-book' journalism. It was hoped the PCC would help put the industry in order through self-regulation by adherence to a 1991 code of conduct; few believe this has happened. Intrusions into privacy, for example, were thought to be a strong element in the road accident which killed Princess Diana in August 1997. The PCC has no real sanctions and newspapers can flout its rulings with impunity. However, complaints to the PCC rose from 1,500 in 1991 to 3,000 in 1997. In February 2002, the chair of the PCC, Lord Wakeham, resigned his post while he dealt with problems caused by his directorship of Enron, the massive energy conglomerate which crashed into near bankruptcy in January 2002.

## pressure group

An organisation that seeks to influence government policy on a specific issue. Two kinds are usually discerned: sectional groups, which defend the interests of particular groups in society (for example trade unions, the Confederation of British Industry, the British Medical Association); and promotional groups, which advocate a certain cause (for example the Child Poverty Action Group, the Lord's Day Observance Society). Pressure groups seek to apply pressure on decision makers (political parties, politicians, ministers, civil servants) in connection with their causes, and use a variety of methods, including the press, broadcasting and marches. Wyn Grant of Warwick University distinguishes between 'insider' and 'outsider' groups, depending on the closeness of their relationships to decision makers. Insider groups (those close to government) tend to be drawn into the policy process and may well exert influence and make compromises out of the glare of the media. Insider and outsider groups will use a range of tactics to get their view on the policy agenda, including newspaper articles, pamphlets, speeches, media interviews, marches, demonstrations, threats, civil disobedience and strikes. Sometimes different groups will join together in pursuit of a single objective. For example, in the autumn of 2000 a loose coalition of farmers, small businesses and independent road hauliers protested against the high level of fuel excise duty levied by the government and their actions led to a national fuel crisis. International pressure groups are increasingly attacking the process of globalisation. At a G8 summit in Genoa in July 2001 there were protests by anarchists (some violent), non-violent communists like Ya Basta from Italy, radical reformists from the Genoa Social Forum and Globalise Resistance. Moderates like Bob Geldof and fellow rock star Bono maintained they were 'negotiating' with world leaders to reduce third world debt but the more militant demonstrators claimed that their success in focusing attention upon such summits was the reason why the moderates were given an audience at all.

### Prevention of Terrorism Act 1974

First brought in as a temporary measure following the 1974 Birmingham pub bombings by the IRA. It gave wide powers of detention to the police, who were enabled to hold suspects for five days without trial and to ban them from the British mainland.

### prime minister

The head of the executive branch in the British system of government. The office emerged out of constitutional developments in the 18th century, when the new kings imported from Germany were unsure of the language and the politics of their adopted country. Robert Walpole was the first to exercise prime ministerial power via his strategic position as first lord of the Treasury (1721–42). He presided over the cabinet in the absence of the monarch and used his skills to become its dominant element. Pitt the Younger was the next to fill the role as head of the cabinet, itself embodying the shift of power from monarch to parliament which the Glorious Revolution had occasioned. In the 19th century it became the convention that the leader of the largest party in the Commons should be invited by the monarch to form a government, even though the latter could in theory invite anyone to do so. No member of the Lords has been prime minister since 1902, as they lack the necessary degree of political influence which membership of the Commons provides. During the 20th century the office grew in importance as successive premiers expanded its scope, especially David Lloyd George and Margaret Thatcher. The focus of publicity upon prime ministers and the image they give to their party ensure the office remains of key importance. Moreover, recent incumbents such as Harold Wilson, Margaret Thatcher and Tony Blair have sought to develop a presidential style, in keeping with their personalities, policy objectives and view of government.

*See also* first lord of the Treasury; Walpole, Robert.

### prime minister as president

Many observers have noticed how Tony Blair has developed his office towards something more approaching that of a president. In support they cite:

1 Blair's burgeoning private office, which is now closer to a White House staff than that which preceded it;

2 the use of White House titles like 'chief of staff';

3 his close relationship with George W. Bush and subsequent worldwide travel to assist the coalition forming after the 11 September 2001 terrorist attacks;

4 his tendency to keep cabinet meetings short and infrequent;

5 his preference for small, ad hoc meetings with advisors and concerned individuals rather than consulting widely to seek consensus.

## prime minister's department

Some experts advocate a fully fledged prime minister's department with perhaps a permanent secretary and a bevy of junior ministers and high-flying civil servants to staff it. While this would bring it into line with other chief executives in the USA and Europe, some argue the cabinet and its office perform many of the functions of such a department and fear such an innovation would act as a barrier between the prime minister and the rest of the government, especially leading members of the cabinet. On 9 June 2001 a lobby briefing from Number 10 insisted there would be no prime minister's department and that a separation would still exist between the Cabinet Office and Downing Street. However, there were some important changes:

1  Alastair Campbell, the prime minister's press secretary, moved from the 'frontline' to become director of communications and strategy. He would no longer conduct the daily lobby briefings, though he would meet the press from time to time. He would attend cabinet meetings and have such access to the prime minister as was necessary.

2  Daily briefings would be conducted by Godric Smith and Tom Kelly, both civil servants: they would be interchangeable and would each be known as the prime minister's official spokesman.

3  The Private Office and the Policy Unit would be merged under the control of Jonathan Powell, the prime minister's chief of staff.

4  A new office would be set up under Anji Hunter called the Government Relations Office. Blair's former political secretary Sally Morgan had been given a peerage and moved into government as a junior minister in the Cabinet Office (Hunter left Blair's service at the end of 2001 and was replaced by Sally Morgan).

5  The Policy Unit was merged with the private office under Jeremy Heywood after David Miliband became the MP for South Shields.

In addition, the prime minister is advised by:

1  The Social Exclusion Unit, under Moira Wallace, addresses long-term problems from its base in the Cabinet Office.

2  The Forward Strategy Unit looks at ways in which the civil service can improve its ability to deliver policies.

3  The Centre for Management Studies is headed by a former specialist academic in Russian studies, Ron Amann.

4  The Domestic Policy Directorate is headed by Suma Chakrabati, former head of the Policy and Innovation Unit.

5  The Delivery Unit has the remit to focus on delivery of services and is headed by a civil servant, Michael Barber.

6  Finally this network of policy advice is complemented by the Office of Public Services Reform, headed by a former Audit Commission official, Wendy Thomson.

In June 2002 it was reported that the incoming cabinet secretary, Sir Andrew Turnbull, changed the Downing Street machine to make it a 'reform and delivery team', by breaking up the various units and reducing the number of advisors, which had both mushroomed over the previous 12 months. The idea seemed to be that Sir Andrew would be in direct control of all advisors and would report to the prime minister, almost as the government's 'chief executive'. Sir David Omand was to be security coordinator as well as day-to-day manager of the Cabinet Office. Blair insists this degree of centralised control is necessary for him to do his job, yet others criticise a tendency which is making the British prime minister more and more presidential.

## prime minister's questions

A practice that dates only from the time of Harold Macmillan. From 1961 to 1997 the prime minister answered questions directly in the House during two 15-minute slots on Tuesdays and Thursdays. Soon these occasions became set-piece events that attracted a full attendance on both sides of the House and the intense interest of the media, which loved the party political and personal confrontation occasioned by it. Consequently, the House showed its less admirable side: the proceedings were characterised by much shouting and barracking; the exchanges were either insults or deliberately crafted sound bites; most of the questions were deliberately open-ended; and many were 'planted' by the whips into the mouths of compliant backbenchers to show the government in a good light. The leader of the opposition is allowed to ask six questions and the leader of the Liberal Democrats two. Tony Blair soon changed the rules: it now occurs once a week on Wednesdays at noon and takes 30 minutes. The same open-ended questions feature, however, and the occasion is still seen by both sides as a piece of party political jousting in which it is important to be seen to be winning debating points. Some MPs, however, not to mention commentators, see the event as a meaningless charade and waste of time. One new MP, Conservative George Osborne, argued in a television interview that prime minister's questions were something to be proud of: no other chief executive in the world subjects him- or herself to such a randomly searching weekly inquisition – certainly not the US president.

### prison numbers

In 2003 there were 75,000 inmates in British prisons and the projection was another 5,000 by the year 2006. Around 150–250 are imprisoned every week and 14,000 are forced to double up in prison cells designed for one. Overcrowding was a factor in the 26 mini-riots in prisons in 2003 and 28 hostage-taking incidents. Figures for 2001 revealed that, of those incarcerated in 1999, 61,000 were serving up to 12 months, 16,000 up to 36 months, 7,800 36–120 months and 481 life. The proportion of women prisoners is increasing in British prisons; women are generally incarcerated for minor offences, often some distance away from their homes, which makes family visits difficult. The government has sought to reduce overcrowding

through prison building and the use of prison ships berthed in southern ports. In an interview in February 2001 Sir David Ramsbottom, chief inspector of prisons, called for the reduction of the prison population by 20,000 or some 30 per cent through better community programmes. He insisted prison should be more rehabilitative.

> The opportunity to sleep nine hours a night and really relax has been extremely good for me. I ask you to disabuse yourself of any idea that prison is harmful. (John Stonehouse, former Labour cabinet minister jailed for corruption in 1975)

### Prison Service

www.hmprisons.gov.uk
An executive agency created following one the recommendations in Ibbs' *Next Steps* report. The service is entrusted with the custody, discipline and rehabilitation of offenders. It came to public attention in the early 1990s when Derek Lewis, chief executive of the Prison Service, was sacked by home secretary Michael Howard for alleged incompetence following escapes from certain prisons.

*See also* penal policy; prison numbers; private prison.

### private bill

A type of bill mainly introduced by companies and local authorities when they require legislative authority from parliament to undertake public works such as bridge or tunnel construction. Although their number declined in the 20th century owing to increased government involvement in national life, there has been a recent increase because of the greater involvement of the private sector in infrastructural projects. They often begin life in the House of Lords, due to the number of public bills passing through the Commons.

### *Private Eye*

www.private-eye.co.uk
Satirical fortnightly magazine. It began life in the fee-paying Shrewsbury School in the 1950s, where Richard Ingrams,

Willie Rushton, Paul Foot and Christopher Booker were involved in editing a school magazine. After national service Ingrams and Foot went to Oxford and met future collaborators, including Peter Usborne and John Wells. Usborne brought a knowledge of offset lithography to the magazine, which began to publish in the early 1960s. Early editions were filled with rather silly jokes, though it also reflected something of the ongoing rage for satire. It sold surprisingly well. Peter Cook and Nicolas Luard then provided more finance from the vantage point of the satire-based Establishment Club and the magazine was set fair. The first editor was Booker followed by Ingrams, to be followed later by Ian Hislop. Paul Foot provided, until his much-mourned death in 2004, the investigative journalism for what has developed into a highly successful publication.

### private finance initiative (PFI)

An approach inaugurated by the Conservative government in 1992 to finance public projects through private capital. Such projects included the Channel Tunnel rail link, the Skye Bridge and Bridgend Prison. One consequence of the scheme was to focus government activity more narrowly and cost-effectively. For instance, the Benefits Agency sold its offices in 1997 and then contracted out the office services it required. Labour, in keeping with its pragmatic approach to Tory policies, has made increasing use of PFI since coming to power in 1997. By September 1998, projects worth £10.5 billion had been agreed. A Prison Service report revealed that Altcourse Prison, built under PFI, cost £54,000 per prisoner, compared with £20,000 under the old system, which suggests that PFI can be hugely more expensive than purely public sector ventures, rather than the cost-saving exercise the government claims it to be. PFI projects are useful to the Treasury as they reduce the amount of debt the government would otherwise have to incur.

In a *Guardian* article (17 August 2001) Mark Seddon noted the use made by Labour of PFI projects. Under the Conservatives there were only 50 such deals over a five-year period. Since 1997 Labour had signed 300, worth £9.6 billion, and in the wake of its election victory in June 2001 promised a further 100 hospitals and 3,000 surgeries by 2010 financed through PFI.

*See also* public–private partnership.

### private members' legislation

One of the methods whereby back-bench MPs can initiate legislation in the Commons. The 20 MPs who have come top in the annual ballot have the opportunity on 20 Fridays in the session to debate bills they have themselves proposed. Despite the somewhat arbitrary nature of the process, some important human rights legislation – including abolition of capital punishment and the liberalisation of the laws on homosexuality – have been passed in this way and it remains an important route for ordinary backbenchers to make their contribution. In recent years private members' bills have been 'talked out' by certain MPs, for example the Conservative Eric Forth.

*See also* 10-minute rule bill.

### private notice question

A question which the speaker considers to be urgent and worthy of immediate discussion. In the past private notice questions have concerned the wreck of an oil tanker, a strike affecting essential services and threats to the liberty of the citizen. These questions are taken at the end of question time if the speaker agrees to the request in advance; the minister concerned always knows such questions are going to be put. Since 2003 these questions have been renamed 'urgent questions'.

### private office

Name given to the administrative unit which supports a minister, important official, or leader of the opposition. As part of their preparation for more senior office young members of the administration grade in the civil service have traditionally served for a year or two as the personal private

POLITICS

secretary of such a person. The prime minister's private office is especially sought after by ambitious officials and is staffed by the highest of the high-fliers of their generation. Robert Armstrong, who served as Edward Heath's private secretary, went on to be head of the civil service. Robin Butler had a similarly brilliant career.

### private prison

The Conservative government was attracted by the idea of private prisons, specially contracted from security companies to do the job previously performed by HM Prison Service. In 1993 Michael Howard, home secretary, announced 12 contracts for private prisons, to much Labour criticism. Reports of their efficacy had been positive in the USA but were mixed in Britain. Once in power Labour embraced the idea it had once opposed.

*See also* Prison Service; private finance initiative.

### private sector

Name given to the privately owned part of the economy. Labour eroded this after 1945 by nationalising 20 per cent of the economy but the Conservatives did their best to strengthen the sector after 1979 through privatisation, which returned most of the nationalised industries to the private sector. In addition, they sought to change the culture of these industries to one which favoured enterprise and cost-consciousness, in order to increase their own efficiency and profitability. After 1997 Tony Blair, in keeping with third way pragmatism, showed no hostility to private-sector provision of services if they served the consumer effectively. The result of these policies is that the country still employs most of its labour force in the private sector.

*See also* nationalisation; privatisation; public–private partnerships; public sector.

### privatisation

The sale of publicly owned enterprises to the private sector. The thrust for this policy emerged in the late 1970s when the Conservatives, hostile to state control

of industry, decided to reduce the size of the public sector, in line with new right thinking. The first major privatisation was British Telecom in 1984. This had originally been part of the General Post Office and then converted into a public corporation before being sold off to the public via a Stock Exchange flotation. This policy of establishing a separate corporation, making it profitable and selling it off became the norm and between 1982 and the early 1990s a raft of public sector industries were sold off in this way, including coal, gas, steel, forestry, electricity, water and the railways. By the mid-1990s privatisation had returned virtually all the nationalised industries to the private sector and generated huge revenues for the exchequer. Dr Madsen Pirie of the Adam Smith Institute listed the advantages of privatisation as 10-fold: government reduces its costs; private companies are able to raise money on the capital markets; the government can concentrate on core domestic policies and not on trading; private companies are more responsive to consumers, have better management, have higher capital spending and better industrial relations; and privatisation results in wider share ownership, more competition and choice, and lower prices. Needless to say, others contested these alleged benefits. Labour bitterly criticised the privatisations, citing, for example, the poor levels of service, and the pursuit of profit above public service. Labour promised to renationalise but in practice the party in power has not done so. Moreover, several state-owned enterprises have been earmarked by Labour for possible privatisation, including the Royal Mint. The National Air Traffic Services was partially privatised in 2000.

*See also* compulsory competitive tendering; market testing.

### Privy Council

www.privy-council.org.uk
Originally part of the King's Council, the Privy Council became the chief mechanism for governing the country until the 18th century. All the great officers of state were

members and it met whenever the monarch wished it. In the 18th century the cabinet, a smaller body, came to take over the functions of the Privy Council. The latter now survives mainly as a ceremonial body, membership of which is granted to cabinet members, senior backbenchers, senior opposition figures and even senior judges. The lord president of the (Privy) Council is a cabinet member, though the post holder often fulfils non-departmental duties, and more commonly in modern times combines the job with that of leader of the House of Commons. The Privy Council Office looks after bodies which hold a charter, such as universities, the appointment of high sheriffs and other appointments in the name of the crown. Privy councillors take an oath of secrecy, in the presence of the monarch.

The Judicial Committee of the Privy Council acts as a final court of appeal for Commonwealth. This function has survived many changes and reforms and applies to the following countries: Antigua and Barbuda, Bahamas, Barbados, Belize, Grenada, Jamaica, New Zealand, St Christopher and Nevis, Saint Lucia, Saint Vincent and the Grenadines, Tuvalu, the Sovereign Base Area of Akrotiri (in Cyprus); the United Kingdom overseas territories – Anguilla, Bermuda, British Antarctic Territory, British Indian Ocean Territory, British Virgin Islands, Cayman Islands, Falkland Islands, Gibraltar, Montserrat, St Helena and dependencies, Turks and Caicos Islands – and also the Republic of Trinidad and Tobago, the Commonwealth of Dominica, Kiribati, Mauritius. Finally, the Privy Council also hears appeals from the Brunei Court of Appeal by agreement with the Sultan.

## Procedure Select Committee
Committee that makes periodic reviews of legislative procedures and how they might be improved. For example, in 1978 its report recommended the new system of select committees, which have now become well established and shadow all the main departments of state, with wide terms of reference and powers to appoint specialist advisors. In 1979 Norman St John Stevas brought forward the recommendations in the form of parliamentary motions, which were then passed by 248 votes to 12.

## procurator-fiscal
A local public prosecutor in Scotland who is a qualified advocate or solicitor. Procurators-fiscal initiate preliminary investigations into criminal cases within the area over which they have jurisdiction. They take statements from witnesses and conduct any resultant prosecution. The Crown Prosecution Service performs these services for the rest of the UK.

## productivity
Normally taken as the value of goods or services divided by the number of hours of labour taken to produce them. High productivity is a long-term means of allowing unemployment to fall to low levels without risking inflation. Margaret Thatcher boasted in 1987 that Britain was back in the 'first division' in terms of economic productivity but studies in the late 1990s revealed the country was still trailing its major rivals. The productivity gap with the USA narrowed from the 1960s onwards and in certain industries it was exemplary. According to a measure called 'total factor productivity', which measures how efficiently both capital and labour are used, the USA and Germany are some 15 per cent in front of Britain and France 7 per cent ahead. No one is quite sure why British workers are less productive but when Japanese management is in control, as in Sunderland's Nissan plant, British workers can be the most productive in Europe. McKinsey points to low investment and poor worker skills as the main reasons for relatively low productivity in Britain.

## Profumo affair
One of the factors which marked the beginning of the end for the 1959 government of Harold Macmillan. War secretary John Profumo began an affair with Christine

Keeler, a high-class call girl, who was also having a sexual relationship with a military attaché at the Russian embassy. When called to account in the Commons he denied the relationship. When the truth emerged he was forced to resign, bringing the Conservative Party into disrepute. Lord Denning conducted an investigation into the affair. Profumo's political career was over but he gained some dignity and respect by devoting his life to charity work. The film *Scandal*, made in 1988, was based on the affair.

## programming motion
A procedure for speeding up the legislative process. This originated in the report of the Modernisation Committee in October 2002. It was subsequently accepted by the House of Commons for a trial period. The idea was to find arrangements for 'program-ming' legislation that were more formal than the usual channels (i.e. the whips) but more flexible than the guillotine motion. The new motion would be a proposal regarding: the committee option to be followed; the date by which the bill should emerge from the committee stage; and the time to be allowed on the report stage and third reading.
   *See also* act of parliament; guillotine motion.

## Progressive Unionist Party
www.pup-ni.org.uk
Protestant-based political party in Northern Ireland. Founded in 1979, it became known in the 1990s as the mouthpiece of the Ulster Volunteer Force. It took part in the 1998 Good Friday Agreement talks and supported it thereafter. In 1996 it won two seats in the Northern Ireland Forum; in 1998 it won two seats in the elections for the Northern Ireland assembly and in 2003 won one seat. In 2002 David Ervine replaced Hugh Smyth as leader.

## project (the)
Usually understood to be Blair's plan to forge a permanent alliance between Labour and the Liberal Democrats and thus keep the Conservatives out of power. According to Paddy Ashdown's memoirs, Tony Blair thinks that not including the Liberal Democrat leader in his first cabinet was his 'biggest mistake', as this move would have initiated the 'project'. However, Labour's huge majority and residual hostility to the Liberal Democrats in the Parliamentary Labour Party headed off this possibility. The personal chemistry which characterised relations between Ashdown and Blair was not replicated once Kennedy assumed the top job for the Liberal Democrats.
   *See also* third way.

## propaganda
Term used in the 1930s to describe the systematic distortion of truth as practised by the Nazi and Stalinist regimes. Its purpose was the internal control of the population and relations with external states. During the Second World War, the British national government coined the phrase 'propaganda through truth' to describe the activities of the Ministry of Information in its attempts to counter the physical and psychological threat posed by Hitler's Germany. Today, commentators prefer to use the term 'news management', as practised during the Falklands War in 1982, and the American-led Gulf War of 1991.
   *See also* political communications; political language.

## proportional representation
This is a voting system which produces seats in an assembly or parliament in proportion to votes cast. The regional list system is the most popular form of proportional representation in Europe, but the form favoured by some in Britain is the additional member system, which is used in Germany and which has been adapted for elections in the devolved assemblies of Scotland and Wales and the Greater London Authority. The single transferable vote system, used in Ireland and favoured by the Liberal Democrats, is not strictly

proportional, although it is often thought to be, as is the definitely non-proportional alternative vote. Northern Ireland has had proportional representation for local elections for several years. Reformers argue it is necessary for general elections in Britain to be fair and point out that elections to the European parliament are now all via this system.

*See also* additional member system; alternative vote; alternative vote 'top up'; Jenkins report; single transferable vote.

## Provisional IRA

Break-away faction of the official Irish Republican Army (IRA). When violence broke out between extremists in the late 1960s in Northern Ireland, the official IRA was accused of cowardice for not protecting the Catholic community. A much quoted contemporary piece of graffiti read 'IRA = I Ran Away'. By 1970 a more radical group (the 'Provos') had broken away from the official movement and soon became synonymous with the IRA as a whole. Events like internment in 1971 and Bloody Sunday in 1972 led to hugely increased recruitment to the paramilitary grouping, which continued its campaign of terrorism in pursuit of political goals until the Good Friday Agreement in 1998, when it seemed violence might be rejected as a vehicle for political change in favour of the ballot box. However, punishment beatings in the province continued and the refusal of the IRA to disarm prevented the newly formed Northern Ireland executive from functioning effectively.

## psephology

Name given to the study of elections. The first British psephologist is generally thought to be David Butler of Nuffield College, Oxford, who is the author or co-author of successive 'Nuffield' studies of general elections. Many others have subsequently joined him in this important subdivision of British political science.

## Public Accounts Commission

*See* National Audit Office.

## Public Accounts Committee (PAC)

www.parliament.uk/commons/selcom/pachome.htm

Parliamentary select committee, founded in 1861. For a long time the PAC was one of only two select committees and it is arguably still the most important and powerful. It examines how public funds have been spent and checks whether such spending has been for the purposes intended. It is served by the staff of the comptroller and auditor general and has real influence in the government service. In January 1994 the PAC issued its broadside against sleaze, *The Proper Conduct of Public Business*, a report which discerned what its then chair, Robert Sheldon, described as a noticeable decline in levels of public probity and integrity, which threatened the traditional 'incorruptibility' of Britain's public services. The chair of the PAC after 1997 was David Davis, who established a formidable reputation for getting things done. One study calculated that 95 per cent of the committee's recommendations were implemented under Davis's chairmanship.

*See also* National Audit Office.

## Public Appointments Commission

*See* Office of the Commissioner for Public Appointments.

## public bill

Any bill concerned with the interests of the public as a whole. There are two types of public bill: those promoted by the government and those promoted by private members. The former are government measures that are designed to implement manifesto promises – they take up 80 per cent of the parliamentary timetable. They are announced by the sovereign in the queen's speech at the opening of a new parliamentary session. Private members' bills have to compete for limited time and follow a separate procedure.

## public corporation

The legal entity for a nationalised industry. Public corporations usually have a charter that lays down their constitutions and the powers of the governing boards. The most important difference with public companies is that there are no shareholder rights. They are in theory independent of the state and responsible to the governing board, who are appointed by the government. Two of the first, established in the 1920s, were the Central Electricity Board and the BBC. Corporations have a sponsoring department in Whitehall which will oversee their activities and be accountable for them in parliament.

## public expenditure

The money spent by the government on public services. During the Second World War, public expenditure in relation to gross domestic product was over 60 per cent, and while it dropped to 35–40 per cent in 1945–50, it then rose to a peak of nearly 50 per cent in the mid-1970s. It hovered in the mid-40s during the 1980s, fell to under 40 per cent at the end of the decade and levelled off in the low 40s in the 1990s. The five biggest categories of public expenditure in 2000 were: defence (8.9 per cent in 1993), law and order (5.5 per cent), education (12.4 per cent), health (13.5 per cent) and social security (34.2 per cent).

## public expenditure survey

The annual process known as 'the survey' whereby the government reviews, confirms, allocates or reallocates funding between the spending departments. It involves all chief departmental officers as well as senior Treasury officials. The process starts in May with departmental submissions on desired expenditure. In June the cabinet sets the limits for the survey and nominates a subcommittee (named PX and chaired by the chancellor) to oversee the process. The chief secretary to the Treasury considers the submissions and responds with papers to the PX, which meets throughout the autumn. Recipients of funding are consulted beforehand and are informed of the outcome, though usually without any explanation. PX then submits its report to full cabinet, usually in November.

Allocations are then ready to be announced in the spring budget.

## public inquiry

These occur after major disasters, failures or embarrassments. They are designed to find the causes and advise on remedial action if at all possible; they are often chaired by senior judicial figures. Recent examples include Lord Justice Taylor's inquiry into safety at sports grounds, Lord Bingham's into the collapse of the BCCI bank and Lord Nolan's into standards in public life. Most public inquiries are set up at the behest of the prime minister or another government minister, who sets their terms of reference and their timeframes.

## public interest immunity (PII) certificate

Issued by government to prevent the release of secret documents where disclosure could threaten the national interest. These 'gagging orders' were little heard of before the arms to Iraq scandal in 1992, where a number of PIIs were overturned by the judge in the Matrix Churchill trial.

## public opinion

Since the dawn of the democratic age the views of the public have been considered important, not least because they are likely to influence the way votes will be cast at election times. In the past, popular opinion was thought to be so ill-informed it was frequently ignored, but the modern practice is to respect even ill-informed opinion and to measure it assiduously in public and private opinion polls. Public opinion on an issue seldom arises spontaneously – it is often the result of opinion formers, who operate in interest groups, the media and political parties. In an age of mass media, governments and political parties are highly sensitive to this phenomenon and try to monitor and predict the twists and turns of opinion through focus groups and other forms of opinion research. New Labour's People's Panel, among other devices, was a sophisticated attempt to monitor popular concerns; however, it was disbanded after a relatively short time.

## public opinion poll

*See* opinion poll.

## public–private partnership (PPP)

Collaboration between the government and the private sector, in theory to their mutual advantage and that of the public as well. PPPs became especially controversial when, after the June 2001 general election, Tony Blair announced his goal of 'world class' public services, which he felt could be achieved through the involvement of the private sector. In January 2000 Arthur Andersen Accounting released a report, commissioned by the Treasury, on 17 private finance initiatives (PFIs). It concluded that the 'average percentage estimated saving against the public sector comparator [i.e. traditional costings] for our sample of projects was 17%'. This finding was used by ministers to justify more projects but was furiously disputed by the unions and other critics, who pointed out that Arthur Andersen had made millions from the advice it had tendered.

The promise on public services had helped Labour win a second landslide in 2001 but worries continued that the £180 billion pledged to be spent on education, health and transport would not be enough. It was hoped the private sector would be able to help carry some of the financial and management burden. Much of the uproar focused on a report (*Building Better Partnerships*, 24 June 2001) by the Institute of Public Policy Research (IPPR), which envisaged substantial cooperation with the private sector. The IPPR report argued that the view that public services 'should always and everywhere be provided by the public sector' was wrong. However, it also maintained that private involvement should be limited to those occasions when public finance was not available or when current services were poor. Its main message was that ideological approaches were less attractive than pragmatic solutions. It urged the government to look beyond the PFI for a suitable model, as it had proved expensive in some cases. As *The Economist* noted (30 June 2001),

almost 20 per cent of public capital spending in 2001 was via the PFI route. PFI projects are attractive mainly because 'they allow spending departments to escape the Treasury's purse strings'. Trade unionists had visited the prime minister three weeks after the June 2001 general election victory to protest at plans to increase the role of private business in the public sector but had been roundly rebuffed.

On 11 July 2001 a MORI poll revealed that only one in nine of the general population believed the extension of private sector involvement would improve public services. Two-thirds said that better pay and conditions would be more likely to improve services. In February 2002 Tony Blair came under sustained pressure at the party's spring conference from trade unions objecting to plans to involve the private sector in public sector activities.

## public–private split: European comparisons

During the campaign for the 2001 general election Tony Blair emphasised how public services would face reform and greater involvement of private companies. Critics accused the prime minister of the Thatcherite mind-set of 'Public bad, private good'. However, European experience suggests there are ways of involving the private sector to the benefit of the public sector. *The Economist* (14 July 2001) reported that health services in the European Union spent about the same percentages of state funding as in Britain – about 5–7 per cent – but added up to 2 per cent from the private sector. Some experts claim Britain could achieve similar levels of health service to Germany, France and The Netherlands if the public were allowed to pay for private 'top-up' care. In France, for example, patients pay for their own care and then claim up to 85 per cent back from the state; however, doing this for simple visits to a general practitioner would not be easy to introduce in Britain.

## Public Record Office

*See* National Archives.

## Public Records Act 1958

Act that stipulates a 30-year delay in the
release to the public of some 40 categories
of government information. The reasons
may vary from state security to the embarrassment which might be caused to living
people. Some cabinet and other papers are
permanently secret.

## public school

Term used paradoxically for private
schools in England and Wales. Originally
the ancient schools, such as Eton, Harrow,
Rugby and Winchester, were intended
to provide education for the sons of poor
families but the quality of what they came
to provide led to their clients becoming
the rich and influential. Middle-class
people with money sought the cachet of
a prestigious education for their children
and the number of such schools expanded
in the 19th and 20th centuries. Roedean
and Benenden are examples of girls'
public schools. Some predicted the demise
of public schools after the Education
Act 1944 reformed the state secondary
education system. The resultant state-run
grammar schools – access to which was
via an examination taken at the age of 11
– certainly competed scholastically with
private education but postwar Labour
governments, in their desire to remove
selection in education, sought to phase
them out. Partly as a result, public schools
survived and then prospered as the quality
of state education was seen to be sub-
standard compared with private education.
This has produced a two-tier system of
education, with some 7 per cent of children, mostly from well-off backgrounds,
receiving an education which enables them
to win a disproportionate share of places
at the older prestigious universities and to
dominate the elite levels of government,
the professions, the civil service and most
other centres of power in Britain. A report
in May 2002 from the Organisation for
Economic Cooperation and Development
revealed that British public schools produce the best academic results of any in
the world.

## public sector

Economic functions controlled or funded
by government. After 1945 nationalisation
moved over 20 per cent of the economy into
the public sector but Margaret Thatcher
ensured privatisation 'rolled back the frontiers of the state' and enlarged the private
sector, which she admired, at the expense of
the public, which she disliked. This tended
to encourage a culture in which public was
seen as 'bad' and 'private' as 'good' (i.e.
more efficient and better managed). The
absence in the public sector of the con-
straining disciplines of profit making and
competition were particularly emphasised
by the right, while the left argued that
wastefulness was not the exclusive preserve
of the public sector and that profits were
irrelevant in the delivery of services like
health.

*See also* nationalisation; private sector;
privatisation; public–private partnership.

## public sector borrowing requirement (PSBR)

The difference between what the government spends and brings in via revenue and
therefore needs to borrow from the market.
Borrowing is done by selling certain kinds
of government stock, for example gilt-edged
stocks, national savings and local authority stocks and bonds. In the early 1990s
the Conservatives had to raise taxation to
cover a £50 billion PSBR which had built
up during the recession at the end of the
1980s. After 1997 the Labour government
made much of its financial virtue in paying
off government debt during its first term but
sceptics doubted the spending plans could
be fully implemented throughout Labour's
second term without recourse to some
expansion of government borrowing.

## public service agreement (PSA)

Agreement with government departments
made by the Treasury regarding the way
funding will be spent. PSAs appeared
after the 1998 comprehensive spending
review and set out what departments aim to
achieve in terms of priorities and direction
over a specific period. Similar agreements

are made with local authorities; in 2004, 60 of them had agreed 'local PSAs', which link national targets with local priorities. To provide incentives for improved performance, extra funding is made available if targets are met. Some commentators have seen in PSAs a device by the Treasury for controlling the work of departments.

# Q

## qualified majority voting (QMV)

A system of voting used in the European Union's Council of Ministers. It is a system of weighted voting which replaced the previous unanimity requirement (which gave each member a veto) and which is based on population sizes of member countries. Before expansion of the European Union in May 2004, Britain, along with the other large countries, had 10 votes. There were 87 votes in the Council distributed among members and a qualified majority required 62 votes to pass a proposal, instead of the mathematical majority of 44. Euro-enthusiasts seek extensions of QMV, while Eurosceptics are less keen on surrendering the veto. The Treaty of Nice 2000 adjusted the weightings to take account of new members, the new arrangements to come into force by November 2004: 345 votes in total on the Council, with the larger countries having 29 each, reducing down to 4 for Latvia and 3 for Malta. A qualified majority requires 255 votes and will have to represent 62 per cent of the EU population. Only a few subjects now carry the veto (i.e. require unanimity) apart from foreign and defence policy and justice and home affairs.

## quasi-autonomous non-governmental organisation (quango)

A body that is not attached to a government department and usually has no formal close contact with a minister but still performs a government function of sorts. Quangos are part of the 'shadow world' of government. According to the Whitehall manual *Non-Departmental Public Bodies*, there are three subdivisions:

1  Executive bodies, like the Medical Research Council, the Commission for Racial Equality and the Atomic Energy Authority. They are set up by statute and are headed by boards appointed by government. There are well over 300 such bodies, spending in total £12 billion per annum.
2  Advisory bodies, like the Bovine Spongiform Encephalopathy Committee, the Industrial Injuries Advisory Council and the royal commissions. There are over 800 advisory bodies, most of which comprise part-time experts.
3  Tribunals and other quasi-judicial bodies, like the Central Arbitration Committee, the Social Security Appeal Tribunals and the Value Added Tax Tribunal. These have delegated jurisdiction in a specialised area. There are around 70 such bodies plus another 130 or more which exist for monitoring the conditions of prisons and prisoners.

The Conservative government of 1979 denounced quangos but invented a number, which took over functions previously performed by central or local government. Labour furiously criticised them as undemocratic refuges for Conservative placement but did not dismantle them en masse once in power.

The Office of the Commissioner for Public Appointments, set up by Labour to ensure fairness in ministerial appointments to quangos, criticised a number of National Health Service trusts for packing their boards with Labour activists – in parallel to the accusation made by Labour against the Conservatives when they were in government.

## quasi-government

Those government institutions which are government funded but not staffed by civil servants. As the scope of government has expanded so rapidly since 1945, new bodies have sprung up to administer the enlarged public sector, including nationalised corporations and quangos. For example, independent specialised agencies include bodies like the Urban Regeneration Agency, which helps reclaim derelict urban areas. Critics accuse such 'government at arm's length' of not being properly accountable to parliament and subject to public control.

## queen's counsel (QC)

The elite of courtroom advocates. QCs originated in the 16th century under Elizabeth I, who wanted the best lawyers to advise her. Eventually the title became merely a form of promotion: QCs were able to earn more than ordinary barristers. However, in 2001 the Office of Fair Trading condemned them as 'uncompetitive' and the Bar Council, the body representing barristers, criticised the secretive way in which the lord chancellor collected information about candidates before awarding 'silks'.

*See also* judge.

## queen's (or king's) speech

Speech delivered by the monarch on the occasion of the state opening of parliament. It is not written by the queen but by government ministers, who are advised by civil servants. It lays down the legislative measures which the government intends to pass during the forthcoming parliamentary session. The speech is delivered by the queen in the House of Lords and the members of the House of Commons come through to listen, traditionally in silence. There then follows a six-day debate on the programme and the opposition tables critical amendments. Defeat on any resultant divisions (votes) causes the resignation of the government, as in 1924, when Stanley Baldwin's minority government was defeated by Labour and the Liberals on the king's speech and Ramsay MacDonald was invited to take over. In February 1974 Wilson issued his queen's speech for his minority administration,

daring the Conservatives to defeat it and precipitate another election, which might have improved Labour's position.

## question time (Commons)

This is of relatively recent origin but is now well established. It occurs Monday to Thursday at 2.30 p.m. and finishes at 3.30 p.m. MPs are restricted to eight questions in every 10 sitting days and never more than two on any one day. Questions must be precisely worded on areas which are appropriate for the minister concerned to answer; some areas, like arms sales and budgetary contracts, are ruled out of bounds. Most ministers appear on a rota to answer every four weeks. Usually about 20 questions are answered in each question time.

*See also* prime minister's questions.

## question time (Lords)

There are two types of questions in the Lords: starred and unstarred. The former are oral and non-debatable while the latter are written and can be the subject of short debates lasting no more than 20 minutes. Thus question time is usually shorter than in the Commons but answers to particular questions are in greater depth. Question time in the House of Lords takes place at the beginning of business on every sitting day except Fridays and may not exceed 30 minutes.

# R

## racism

A belief in the superiority of certain races over others, used as a justification for discrimination. The existence of the National Front, British National Party and other groups generally taking their inspiration from Oswald Mosley indicates that racism is a theme in British politics. Most commentators would suggest that racism is not a very powerful theme, but there is evidence to suggest there is considerable embedded racism in the culture of large institutions. This is especially so in the case of the police, and was referred to as institutionalised racism by the Macpherson report on the bungled investigation into the murder of Steven Lawrence in 1998. In a study by Warwick University in September 1998, of white respondents interviewed 16 per cent felt race relations were improving, 38 per cent thought that they were getting worse and 39 per cent felt that the situation was about the same. For black respondents the figures were 7, 79 and 14 per cent respectively, while for Asians they were 9, 50 and 33 per cent. Despite the fact that six black and Asian MPs were elected in 1997, rising to 12 in 2001, only 55 per cent of those eligible to vote from these communities were actually registered to do so. It is significant also that black people are twice as likely as whites to be unemployed, they are much more likely to be stopped and searched, to receive longer prison sentences and to die in custody. On 30 June 2001 a report to the United Nations from 11 British organisations led by Liberty claimed that 'politicians and the media alike have been encouraging racist hostility in their public attitudes towards asylum seekers…. In our view the recent race riots in Oldham and Bradford are to an extent directly linked to [this].' Lord Tebbit did not agree and accused the 'race relations industry' of being the 'main recruiting ground for the British National Party'.

See also British National Party; immigration; multiculturalism; National Front.

### radical
Term associated with the reformist movements of the 19th century, often the vigorously reformist wing of the Liberal Party. Radical movements had sprung up in England in the late 18th century and proposed fundamental reform of the British political and social order, similar to that which had taken place in revolutionary France and the American colonies. An even earlier form of radicalism was that of John Lilburne and his Leveller supporters, who were active in Cromwell's New Model Army in the middle of the 17th century. Historically in Britain, radicalism has been 'managed' or defused by gradual accommodation to pressure, as occurred during the 19th century when electoral reform took place from 1832. In the late 1970s and 1980s Margaret Thatcher was happy to use it to describe her own political beliefs.

### radio
Radio broadcasts were first introduced in the 1920s by the BBC, founded upon a mission to 'inform, educate and entertain'. It was used by Stanley Baldwin for political purposes with his folksy 'fireside chats'. Winston Churchill and the Ministry of Information were more interested in using radio to rouse the nation in the Second World War and his broadcasts inspired the country to survive the difficult years and win through against the might of Nazi Germany. After the war television increasingly came to dominate political attention, but radio still carries party political broadcasts and its current affairs coverage is widely listened to and admired. The *Today* programme on Radio 4 has been used by politicians to communicate directly with the one million or so people who listen to it every morning. Included in this number are members of Britain's political, media and economic elite, and of course students of politics.

### *Ragged Trousered Philanthropists*
Novel written in the early 1900s by Robert Noonan, under the pen-name Robert Tressell, set in Hastings and in a sub-Dickensian style, about the painting and decorating trade at the turn of the century. It dealt with: the poor standards of workmanship which private enterprise encouraged; the problems of poverty wages; and the plight of young unmarried women who become pregnant. It also contained arguments for an early kind of utopian socialism, which succeeded in convincing

thousands of people, including the future union leader Jack Jones, that they should convert to socialism and join the Labour Party.

### rail travel
*See* Network Rail.

### Ramblers' Association
www.ramblers.org.uk
Founded in 1935, a pressure group currently with some 130,000 members. It has campaigned for years for a 'right to roam' – freedom for walkers to traverse the 12 per cent of Britain classed as mountain, moorland, heath and common land.

*See also* right to roam.

### Rasmussen
www.rasmussenreports.com
US polling organisation which participated briefly in British politics in 2001, with some success. It worked for the *Independent* and introduced the novel idea of computerised interviewing by telephone (i.e. a disembodied voice seeking responses).

### rate support grant
A block grant given from the 1950s onwards by central government to local authorities to spend according to their needs. It was calculated to comprise a 'resources' element for small authorities, a 'needs' element based on population and a 'domestic' element to reimburse local government for rate reductions. The addition of a complex and superimposed formula in the 1970s undermined its utility and led to calls for reform. During the 1980s and early 1990s it was used by the Conservative government as a weapon to curb local government spending.

*See also* local government finance; rates.

### rates
A means of raising local taxes based on the notional rental value of the property owned (effectively, home occupiers had to pay in proportion to the size of their property). This was thought to be unfair by some politicians, as large families often paid no more than small ones or single people. Conservative governments after 1979 reduced the amount given to local authorities through the rate support grant and also 'capped' the amount local authorities could levy via the rates. In 1986, the Green Paper *Paying for Local Government* suggested the idea of a community charge (poll tax) which would, it was argued, more fairly reflect the link between voting and paying for local services. The charge was formally introduced in April 1990, and so the rates ended, only to be replaced three years later by the council tax.

*See also* community charge; council tax; rate support grant.

### Real IRA
Hard-line group which emerged in the wake of the Good Friday Agreement of 1998, committed to continuing the armed struggle against the British government. It was behind the Omagh bombing in 1998, which killed 29 people; it also exploded bombs in London, notably outside the BBC early in 2001. A *Sunday Times* article in July 2001 reported that MI5 operations against the group had weakened it significantly and reduced its capacity to obtain weapons from eastern Europe.

### realignment
The process by which movements in voter support for parties create changes in the party system. Four phases or periods of realignments can be identified in British politics:

1  In 1918, support for the Liberal Party declined, marking the beginning of the rise of the Labour Party. The reason for this can be found in the split between Herbert Asquith and David Lloyd George and the massive increase in the size of the electorate, when, for the first time, all adult males could vote (over the age of 21), as could women over the age of 30.

2  The revival of the Liberal vote in the early 1970s, marked by the Rochdale by-election, when the party took the seat from Labour. In the October

1974 general election, Liberal support had increased to 18 per cent, and the Scottish and Welsh nationalists received 2.6 per cent of the total vote. Since then third-party support in general elections has fallen below 20 per cent only once, in 1979.

3  In the 1983 general election, third-party support reached 31 per cent, the Alliance and others achieving 44 seats in the House of Commons. Indeed, up to the 1987 general election many commentators spoke of a significant realignment taking place in the party system, which would involve the Alliance displacing Labour as the second major party.

4  Labour's decline was halted at the 1987 general election and the party went on to win a landslide victory in 1997. However, third-party voting did not collapse, as the Liberal Democrats achieved 17 per cent and other parties 7.2 per cent in 1997, giving them a total of 75 seats in the House of Commons, the highest number since 1945. In 2001 the Liberal Democrats did even better in the general election, polling 18.8 per cent of the vote and garnering 52 seats.

Future realignments and their impact upon the party system are bound up with possible changes to the voting system used for parliamentary elections, the positioning of Conservative and Labour relative to the Liberal Democrats and tactical voting.

*See also* partisan dealignment; tactical voting.

### rebate
*See* European rebate to Britain.

### Reclaim the Streets
www.reclaimthestreets.net
A group that virtually took over the City of London in an anti-capitalist demonstration in June 1999. Many of the participants were prepared to use violence. One quoted in the *Observer* (31 October 1999) said 'We tried tree hugging at the Newbury bypass. It did get some great publicity but the road still got built. We lost. There are a lot of us who now recognise we can't pick

individual battles; we have to take on the whole system.' Activists arrived for the demonstration from all over the world – the Internet was used for their coordination. Similar demonstrations were expected on 1 May 2003 but in the event police out-numbered the demonstrators.

### 'Red Flag'
The anthem of the Labour Party for virtually the whole of its history. It was written in 1889 by Jim Connell. In 1997 it was downgraded at the party conference to a set-piece performance by a school choir after a rendition of the theme song for the 1997 campaign, 'Things Can Only Get Better'. When new converts joined the party, for example Peter Hain, news editors used to have fun focusing cameras on them during the finale singing of the 'Red Flag' to check whether they knew the words. They usually did not. The chorus is as follows:

> Then raise the scarlet standard high!
> Beneath its shade we'll live and die
> Though cowards flinch and traitors sneer
> We'll keep the red flag flying here!

### red lines
Policy areas on which Britain said it would not surrender sovereignty in the negotiations over the proposed new European Union (EU) constitution in 2004. In the face of sharp Eurosceptic criticism, the Labour government indicated that, while it supported the draft constitution in principle, it would not compromise domestic control over: tax and social security, labour laws, foreign and defence policy, crime and immigration, or voting systems within the EU. Britain's EU partners were concerned that if too many countries laid down similar 'red lines', agreement would prove impossible. Conservative opponents of the draft constitution dismissed the red lines as irrelevant.

### Redcliffe-Maud report, 1969
Report of the Royal Commission on Local Government Reform. The Commission was set up in 1966 to consider the structure

of local government in England outside Greater London. As local government had become, over time, a baffling patchwork, the report was not before its time. The commission accepted the need for local government and believed it should be efficient, adaptable and supported by the electorate. There were clearly too many fragmented units for efficiency but the commission could not agree on the best structure of reform. The majority report favoured 58 unitary authorities for the country outside London but a minority report urged the two-tier structure which was eventually introduced by the Conservatives in the Local Government Act 1972.

### Redistribution of Seats Act 1944

This established the boundary commissions and guaranteed minimum numbers of seats for Scotland and Wales, which were proportionally higher than for the rest of the country. This has benefited Labour; in 1987 it won 24 of the 36 Welsh seats and 50 of the 72 Scottish ones. In 1997 the Conservatives held no seats in either Scotland or Wales for the first time ever, although one was recovered in 2001.

### redress of grievance

Although Britain does not have an entrenched or 'written' constitution to protect individual citizens' rights, there are a number of channels available for the redress of grievance against government and other statutory authorities. The main ones are the MP; the parliamentary ombudsman; judicial review; the European Court of Human Rights; and tribunals. Under the various citizens' charters, users of public services such as the National Health Service can make a complaint about the quality of service.

### referendum

A special poll of the electorate, usually on a specific issue of public policy. Referendums have traditionally been alien to the British tradition of parliamentary democracy. At the time of writing there has been only one national referendum, in 1975 on whether

Britain should remain in the European Community; it was passed with a two to one majority. Regional referendums were held on devolution to Scotland and Wales in 1979. The former registered a majority in favour but not sufficiently large to meet the 40 per cent of the electorate required (quite a difficult criterion given the variability in turnout). The Wales vote registered a four to one majority against the proposal. In September 1997, however, the results were different: a heavy victory for devolution in Scotland and a very narrow one in Wales. Future referendums are promised on British entry into a single currency and any new constitution of the European Union, and on proposals to reform the electoral system. Although not a feature of constitutional practice in the past, it would seem a referendum is now standard practice before a major constitutional reform goes forward.

*See also* regional assembly.

### Referendum Party

Party founded by Sir James Goldsmith in 1996 to campaign for a referendum on British membership of the European single currency. Goldsmith allegedly spent £20 million on the campaign but received precious little in return, as the party failed to register more than 800,000 votes. The most that could be said for the party is that it made life difficult for those Conservatives who refused to support the referendum, as Labour did, and consequently lost votes to the Referendum candidates – and in some cases consequently lost their seats.

### Reform Act

Any of a series of acts from 1832 to 1928 affecting the franchise. The British political system has escaped the type of revolutionary movements which transformed the political order in France (1789) and Russia (1917). In the 19th and 20th centuries a series of Reform Acts enlarged the franchise. The Great Reform Act of 1832 increased the size of the electorate by nearly a half and abolished many of the archaic features of the system, like 'rotten boroughs'. The Reform Act 1867 further enlarged the electorate by nearly 90 per cent, and in 1884 it was enlarged still further to include working-class voters. In the 20th century most women aged over 30 were enfranchised in 1918 by the act that extended the franchise to nearly all men aged 21 or more; the age requirement for women was removed in 1928. The most recent reform was in 1969, when 18-year-olds were given the vote.

### regional aid

Labour governments in the 1960s believed in channelling government aid into regions with high unemployment but Conservative governments reduced this drastically, as it did not conform with their market-based philosophy. The European Union (EU), however, is keen to encourage development in particular regions and Britain has been a net beneficiary of such assistance: in the mid-1990s British citizens made up 20 million of the 50 million people living in some of the most economically deprived areas of Europe. In 1989 Britain had a standard of living 100.7 per cent of the EU average but this concealed a large variation, from 121 per cent for the south-east of England to 74 per cent for Northern Ireland. The north-east and Merseyside were other major recipients of EU funds, together with the Scottish Highlands and Islands Enterprise Area. EU grants mainly come from the European Regional Development Fund, the European Social Fund and the European Agricultural Guidance and Guarantee Fund. In addition, there are business loans and business support. Following the entry of 10 new members into the EU in 2004 regional aid to the UK is likely to decrease.

### regional assembly

Appointed assemblies set up in all eight English regions after the Regional Development Agencies Act 1998, which also set up the regional development agencies (RDAs). Over half of those appointed to these assemblies are elected councillors.

As a logical development of Scottish and Welsh devolution, the supporters of regional government suggest that the next step might be the creation of elected regional assemblies for all of the English regions. In May 2002 deputy prime minister John Prescott launched a white paper *Your Region, Your Choice*, which proposed more resources and flexibility for the RDAs and more powers to the unelected regional assemblies. It also set out how regions could have elected assemblies if this was endorsed in a regional referendum. The initial three regional referendums on regional assemblies scheduled for autumn 2004, by the summer of that year was reduced to one, in the north-east, scheduled for November.

### regional development agency (RDA)

Set up in 1999 in eight English regions. The ninth followed in London in July 2000. The RDAs aim to provide coordinated regional economic development and regeneration, reduce economic imbalances between regions and improve competitiveness. In 2001 chancellor Gordon Brown announced an increase of funding for the RDAs from £1.2 billion to £1.7 billion.

### regional government

*See* regional assembly.

### regional party list (voting system)

Introduced by the Labour government in 1998 for the election to the European parliament in 1999, this is a variant of the national party list system and as such is a significant move to proportional representation. Britain is divided into a number of multi-member constituencies to return the 78 MEPs: London (9 MEPs); South East (10); South West (7); Wales (4); West Midlands (7); North West (9); Scotland (7); North East (3); Yorkshire and Humberside (6); East Midlands (6); Eastern (7); Northern Ireland (3). Each party pre-selects a 'slate' or list of candidates in order of preference; voters then choose parties, not candidates. In other words the party has a major say in which of its candidates are 'elected', and for this reason many have criticised the system as

placing too much power in the hands of
political parties. Northern Ireland was not
included in the change, the province having
used the single transferable vote (STV)
system of election since 1979.

### register of members' interests

A register which records the financial
interests of MPs, including fees paid for
directorships and consultancies. In the 19th
century it was accepted that MPs would
have economic interests outside parliament;
indeed, it was seen as beneficial to democracy, mainly because government's links
with the economy were not as many-layered
as now. MPs paid by organisations to
speak for them in parliament were gradually
perceived as injurious to democratic government, as their contributions were tainted
by personal financial gain. Consequently, a
register of interests was introduced in 1975
on the basis of a parliamentary resolution,
although MPs were not obliged by law to
make such declarations. They are asked
to provide information under a variety of
headings: paid directorships, paid employment, trades and professions, clients,
financial sponsorship or gifts, overseas
visits, payment from abroad, land and
property and shareholding. Some MPs
refused to make declarations, like Edward
Heath and Enoch Powell, while others
made incomplete ones, by excluding, for
example, the size of fees received for consul-
tancy work. The blizzard of revelations
about MPs working for outside concerns
in 1994 prompted John Major to set up an
extra-parliamentary committee under judge
Lord Nolan to investigate standards in
public life. A new system was introduced as
a result of Nolan's recommendations which
obliged MPs to disclose earnings according
to income bands, forbade them from tabling
questions and amendments on behalf of outside interests, limited what they could say
in the chamber on behalf of such interests
and obliged them to register all details of
contracts with a powerful parliamentary
commissioner.

*See also* Nolan committee; parliamentary commissioner for standards.

### regulation

*See* Council of Ministers; delegated legislation.

### regulator

An office invented as a result of privatisation to ensure that the privatised industry
concerned does not operate inefficiently or
against the public interest. All the major
utilities have a regulator, such as Ofgem for
gas and electricity and Oftel for telecommunications. In Britain regulators: control
prices; specify operating requirements; set
rules of behaviour; and encourage competition.

### religion and politics

Following the Norman conquest, the
English church was integrated into the
Roman Catholic establishment. However,
in the 16th century Henry VIII broke with
Rome when the Pope refused to annul
his marriage to Catherine of Aragon.
Henry therefore set up an English church.
Religious persecution occurred during the
17th century but after that the role of the
church declined as an intense political issue,
except in Ireland. Religion is now generally
not a powerful cleavage in British society;
other divisions such as class have greater
effect. This is reflected in the fact that, with
the exception of Northern Ireland (where
national identity blends with religious affiliation), British politics is largely free of
religion. Nonetheless, most mainstream politicians are careful to claim a belief in God
and membership of a church. Margaret
Thatcher occasionally made speeches which
seemed to be related to the church but
more often she was responding to criticisms
from a church which soon became disen-
chanted with her individualistic philosophy.
Tony Blair is a high-profile member of the
Church of England but also attends mass
at Catholic churches (Cherie, his wife, is
Roman Catholic). When he was a student
Blair allegedly considered becoming a
priest. Some politicians have successfully
combined a political career with a commitment to the church; for example John
Gummer is a lay member of the General

Synod of the Church of England. Others attract publicity when they change churches (for example Ann Widdecombe, who converted to the Catholic Church).

> Politicians should not be preachers. (Enoch Powell)

## *Renewal*

www.renewal.org.uk

Blairite journal founded in 1993. Set up as a discussion forum for the Blairite modernisers, it boasts an appropriate board, comprising Patricia Hewitt, David Miliband and Margaret Hodge, as well as the less biddable Robin Cook, Alan Milburn and Clare Short. For most of its life the journal performed its role loyally but in August 2004 published a swingeing attack on the direction in which Tony Blair had taken the party. Particular criticism was aimed at: the similarity between the two main political parties; the collapse of trust in the party leadership; the mass exodus of members; and the disturbing similarity of Labour's decline to that of the Conservatives – loss of members, loss of councillors followed by the (threat of) a catastrophic flight of public support. The Iraq war was picked out as a major error and Gordon Brown's succession was mentioned as a desirable development.

> Tragically Blair still appears to believe that if he can only explain it one more time, we will get it. But Tony, we get the message – we just don't accept it.

## report stage

*See* act of parliament; legislative process.

## Representation of the People Act

*See* Reform Act.

## representative

Someone who, in political terms, is held to stand for or speak for a group of people from which he or she is drawn. This person may be appointed but more often, and desirably from the democratic point of view, is elected by some recognised process.

*See also* delegate.

## representative democracy

The system used in most advanced western economies, including Britain. As distinct from direct democracy, it involves electors choosing representatives to make law and form governments. Jeremy Bentham, James Mill and his son John Stuart Mill were the chief philosophical advocates of this form of government, which they believed was the best safeguard against bad rulers and 'sinister interests'. All three believed individuals were the best judge of their own interests and so it followed each must have a vote, although James Mill sought to restrict it to men over 40. In contrast his son urged universal suffrage in principle for all adult men and women, though only if they passed a literacy test, in a system which would give more votes to the educated classes. He believed participation in government through voting would contribute towards the moral education of society: 'Democracy creates a morally better person because it forces people to develop their potentialities'.

*See also* direct democracy; political participation; Bentham, Jeremy; Mill, James; Mill, John Stuart.

## republicanism

A strand of political thinking usually associated with Irish nationalists although the embryo of republicanism has long existed in mainland Britain, mostly in the Labour Party and sections of the press. Because of the monarchy's perceived popularity, republicanism has never been embraced by Labour's leadership. James Callaghan and Neil Kinnock were careful to bow in the direction of the crown and Tony Blair declared himself an 'ardent monarchist' in 2000 when Mo Mowlam suggested the royal family should move out of Buckingham Palace. However, in January 2002 the *Guardian* reported that a group of former Labour frontbenchers led by Roy Hattersley had formed the new All Party Parliamentary Republican Group. They met in secret to prevent Labour whips from intervening. Twenty Labour MPs were said to support it, plus Norman Baker from the Liberal Democrats.

## Research Department (Conservative)

Founded in the 1920s and revived by R. A. Butler after the Second World War. Three of its early members – Enoch Powell, Ian Macleod and Reginald Maudling – went on to serve in the cabinet. Its function was to undertake long-term research and help formulate policy. It also provides secretaries for the parliamentary committees of the party. From 1945 to 1975 it was a useful source of ideas and personnel but Margaret Thatcher tended to see it as a centre of consensual 'wet' influence and the more monetarist Centre for Policy Studies stole much of its role in the party. Future cabinet members who worked in the Research Department in the late 1970s included Chris Patten, William Waldegrave and David Howell. Chancellor Nigel Lawson, who once turned down the offer of directing the department, used to include its head in weekly policy discussions at the Treasury in the 1980s. Of its recent products, David Willets is perceived as someone destined for high office if the Conservatives return to power. It produces the invaluable campaign guides before general elections for Conservative candidates.

## reselection (of MPs)

The process whereby a constituency party confirms or revokes its support for a sitting parliamentary candidate. This practice is associated with all the main parties, but Labour is particularly noteworthy in this respect. In the late 1980s it subjected its sitting MPs to mandatory reselection before a general election, which, on occasion, resulted in deselection. In theory, the thinking behind Labour's system was to 'test' whether the MP had reflected constituency party interests; in practice during the early 1980s it reflected the agenda of left-wing party activists, who wanted to secure greater control over an MP's behaviour in the Commons, in line with the delegate theory of representation. However, under the leadership of Neil Kinnock the left was marginalised and

sitting MPs enjoyed greater independence. Under Tony Blair, the reduction of the block vote by trade unions at conference was applied also to the selection of candidates in 1995, where union influence could previously have been decisive. After 1995 and a close conference decision one member one vote (OMOV) was adopted for the selection of candidates. However, Labour's central party machine often intervenes in the selection of parliamentary candidates by local parties. The Conservatives tend to reselect automatically but in the case of Neil Hamilton, Central Office would probably have liked to intervene and force the Tatton MP to stand down. Under reforms introduced by William Hague after 1997 this kind of intervention is easier, though local autonomy is a strongly held principle in the Conservative Party.

*See also* deselection; National Executive Committee; candidate for parliamentary election.

## Respect (party)

New party set in 2004 focused on opposition to the Iraq war. One of the main founding influences was George Galloway, the former maverick Labour MP who passionately opposed the war against Iraq. Respect campaigned in the local and European elections in June 2004 and, while it did not win any seats in the latter contest, it polled a quarter of a million votes overall and did relatively well in Birmingham and in certain London boroughs, for example gaining 20 per cent of the vote in Tower Hamlets.

## restorative justice

Confronting criminals with their victims. This approach was pioneered in New Zealand, where it registered some success. The aim is to heal the wounds of the victim, offender and community through various forms of mediation between the victim and the offender, as well as reparation of the hurt caused. In spring 2003 home secretary David Blunkett announced that this theme would receive a new emphasis in coming years.

POLITICS

## returning officer

The officer appointed by local authorities to be responsible for and to supervise the count on election night. The sight of returning officers announcing results in front of the television cameras has become an essential aspect of British election nights.

## revisionism

The name given to the ideas of those in the Labour Party who disagreed with members who wished to extend the programme of Clement Attlee's 1945 Labour government into the 1950s and beyond. Those who conducted the rethink were intellectuals for the most part and included Hugh Gaitskell, Anthony Crosland, Denis Healey and Roy Jenkins. Harold Wilson pursued basically revisionist policies during the 1960s and 1970s but the left-wing backlash in the early 1980s so alienated voters it took a decade or so of a more full-blooded revisionism by Neil Kinnock and John Smith, but most of all by modernisers such as Tony Blair and Peter Mandelson, to reposition Labour in the electoral market to make victory possible again.

*See also* clause four.

## right honourable

*See* parliamentary terms of address.

## right to buy

The right of a council tenant to buy the house being rented. Margaret Thatcher's unerring sense of popular concerns was evident soon after 1979, when she identified the wish of many council house tenants to own their own homes. Accordingly the 'right to buy' policy was introduced, whereby tenants were allowed to buy their own houses at substantial discounts. It was criticised for reducing the housing stock and contributing to homelessness, but it was very popular with tenants and 1.7 million council houses were sold. However, the funds raised were returned to the Treasury, and local authorities were barred from using the receipts as a subsidy for general expenditure or to build additional houses.

*See also* council housing.

## right to roam

Slogan of the Ramblers' Association, expressing its objective of achieving freedom for walkers to use the 12 per cent of Britain classed as mountain, moorland, heath and common land. Such a right was in Labour's manifesto in 1997 but lobbying by the landed gentry caused the government to think again, especially after the Countryside Alliance's march in 1997 included opposition to it. Instead, the government decided on a consultation exercise; in this, 80 per cent of the over 2,000 responses favoured the 'right to roam'. Opposition continued in 1998 from the Country Land and Business Association, a 50,000-strong organisation that threatened to sue the government for the losses such a right would cause. Nonetheless, the measure was passed and celebrated by walkers in September 2004.

## riot

Term originally derived from Old French *riote*, meaning 'to have a good time'. Apart from the riots in the 1930s centred around Oswald Mosley, modern British political culture has not generally featured violence. Many commentators predicted riots in the streets when unemployment approached 3 million in the early 1980s. However, the streets remained surprisingly quiet until disturbances broke out in Toxteth, Liverpool, in 1981. Similar riots occurred in many British cities, including Manchester and London. Michael Heseltine produced a paper for the cabinet entitled *It Took a Riot* and advocated substantial expenditure to remove the social causes of the violence. His advice was rejected but Margaret Thatcher was at least momentarily worried by the apparent breakdown in law and order. Eventually peace returned but several areas of the country remained uneasily balanced on the edge of disorder for many years and, indeed, many still are. One of the most serious cases of rioting took place in Trafalgar Square as part of the anti-poll tax demonstrations in 1990; stewards lost control of the protest and the police, according to many protestors, actively provoked public disorder by their methods. In June 2001 riots broke out in Oldham, Burnley and Bradford; these had a racial component exacerbated by the activities of far-right parties like the British National Party.

*See also* anarchism.

## RMT
*See* National Union of Rail, Maritime and Transport Workers.

## rotten borough
Borough constituencies that sent MPs to parliament and that were so decayed they deserved Pitt the Elder's remark that borough representation was the 'rotten part of the constitution'. Examples include Old Sarum, which was a green mound populated by sheep, and Dunwich, which had been submerged for hundreds of years under the North Sea and whose patrons secured election through straightforward bribery or simple nomination.

## Royal Air Force
*See* armed forces.

## royal assent
Final stage of the legislative process after a bill has passed through both houses of parliament, when it thereby becomes an act. Queen Anne was the last monarch to deny the royal assent, in 1707 over the Scottish Militia Bill. The queen no longer gives the royal assent personally; since the passing of the Royal Assent Act 1967, commissioners in the Assent Office communicate the fact of assent to both houses of parliament.

*See also* legislative process.

## royal commission
Appointed by the sovereign, on the request of the prime minister, to investigate a matter of public concern. Royal commissions are usually chaired by a member of the 'great and the good' and therefore unlikely to produce anything too radical. They make recommendations for future action and can mark watersheds in the aspects of public life into which they inquire. Margaret Thatcher

did not establish any such bodies during her period in office, as she tended to believe she did not need research into what was wrong: she already knew this and merely wanted action to remedy it.

## Royal Commission on Criminal Justice
Set up by John Major in 1992, it produced 352 recommendations, including a suggestion for a new independent body to refer cases of miscarriages of justice to the Appeal Court.

## Royal Commission on Environmental Pollution, Transport and the Environment
Raised concerns in its 1994 report about the health implications of transport policy and recommended the halving of road building over the next decade plus the doubling of the real price of petrol. The Conservative government was unreceptive to the proposals but Labour deputy prime minister John Prescott was more sympathetic, though whether action will follow along such lines is still unclear. In September 2000 road hauliers and farmers led direct action against petrol taxation by blockading refineries. The public, it seemed, was not prepared to accept that high fuel prices were justified environmentally (or indeed in any other way).

*See also* fuel protest.

## Royal Commission on Local Government in England
*See* Redcliffe-Maud report.

## Royal Mail
www.royalmailgroup.com
The Post Office decided to change its name to Consignia in January 2001 on the grounds that its existing name no longer adequately described what it did. The change coincided with the transition of the Post Office to a government-owned public limited company in March 2001. Union critics complained that 350 years of history and the brand name 'Royal Mail' were being carelessly abandoned and that such

POLITICS

a move threatened a move to privatisation. Consignia reported financial problems early in 2002 – it allegedly lost over £1 million per day and was forced to consider the abandonment of second deliveries. Consignia announced restructuring plans which would entail 17,000 redundancies; some reports suggested the true figure was closer to 40,000. The name Royal Mail was subsequently reclaimed. In June 2004 a consumer watchdog claimed over 14 million letters were wrongly delivered every week.

### Royal Navy
See armed forces.

### royal prerogative
See prerogative powers.

### Royal Ulster Constabulary
See Police Service of Northern Ireland.

### royal wealth
Being a hereditary monarch in a democracy is something of an anomaly and the scale of royal wealth attracts criticism: why should the queen receive money via the civil list when she is already fabulously wealthy? Some estimates of her wealth include her palaces and art collection, which is inappropriate in that such items belong to the nation and are not convertible into any other form of wealth by the queen. An estimate of her wealth appeared in the *Guardian* in October 2001 and reckoned it to be £1.15 billion. This included:

1 property valued at £61 million;
2 racehorses worth £3.6 million (the queen owns 30 racehorses, which cost £500,000 a year to keep);
3 jewels worth £72 million (including the Cullinan diamonds, valued at £29 million);
4 cars valued at £7.1 million (the queen owns over a dozen cars);
5 stamps and medals worth £102 million (the queen has the biggest collection of stamps in the world, kept in 300 albums and 200 boxes).

### rule of law
The great constitutional lawyer A. V. Dicey defined this as one of the twin pillars of the British constitution and a principal element of a free and civilised society. Included in its provisions is the normative rule that governments must act within the law with respect to their own actions, as well as the treatment of individuals and groups. In particular, it posits an impartial judiciary which must also be independent in order to provide fair trials and freedom from arbitrary imprisonment. However, jurists and political scientists have criticised the doctrine on a number of counts. For example, parliamentary sovereignty could in theory override any prior law. Moreover, ministers of the crown enjoy certain quasi-judicial and legislative powers which may undermine a citizen's protection under due process of law.

### ruling class
Karl Marx argued that in stratified societies a ruling class owns the means of production and exploits and oppresses a subject class. Westergard and Resler, two sociologists, suggested in the 1970s that the ruling class amounted to 5–10 per cent of the population, and included owners of the means of production, chief executives of major companies, higher professionals and administrators, a large number of whom were major shareholders. Many of these people have similar social and educational backgrounds, usually having attended public school and Oxbridge, and go on to marry people with a similar background, thus perpetuating the class. Many have challenged this view as a simplistic explanation of the complex nature of economic and political decision making.

*See also* elite; meritocracy; pluralism; upper class.

# S

## safe seat
*See* marginal seat.

## Saint Kilda
Small group of islands in the Outer Hebrides notable politically only for the St Kilda parliament, which sat in the 19th century and comprised all the adult males on the island and conducted its proceedings purely in Gaelic. The island was evacuated in 1930, thus ending settlement.

## salariat
Term used – prefixed by 'higher' and 'lower' – by Oxford sociologist John Goldthorpe as an alternative to 'middle-class professional' in his analysis of social groupings. Both categories collectively were roughly equivalent to the groupings A, B, C1 according to the more widely accepted British Market Research Society's analysis. Others in Goldthorpe's scheme were 'routine clerical', 'petty bourgeois', 'foremen and technicians', 'skilled manual' and 'unskilled manual'.
    *See also* class.

## Salisbury doctrine
A rule that the Lords will not oppose a measure that has wide public support. It is named after the fifth Marquess of Salisbury, the Conservative leader of the Lords from 1945 to 1950 who formulated it. In practice, after the Second World War, this meant the Lords would oppose only Labour legislation that had not been mentioned in its manifesto. Margaret Thatcher invoked the doctrine in 1988 when she refused to accept the Lords' opposition to the poll tax on the grounds that it had been mentioned in the Conservative 1987 manifesto; the Lords responded that mere mention of 'reform of local government finance' was not the same as the 'poll tax' and that therefore the government did not have a mandate – but they passed it nevertheless.

## Salisbury Group
Right-wing intellectual grouping within the Conservative Party exerting influence through its journal, the *Salisbury Review*.

## Sandline affair
Case involving allegations of Foreign Office collusion with illegal arms supply by a British company. In May 1997, the Revolutionary United Front, headed by Colonel Johnny Koroma, took power from the elected President Kabbah in an armed coup. During the next nine months this junta indulged in widespread killings. In 1998 the legitimate government restored itself but it was alleged that the British-based Sandline firm (a private arms company, headed by a former British army officer) had shipped out £6 million worth of arms to help Kabbah regain power. This appeared to be in breach of a United Nations (UN) arms embargo, which Britain had supported. It was further alleged that Foreign Office officials had colluded with Sandline over the arms deal. The British military subsequently became involved when its forces were included in a UN force sent in to guarantee a peace agreement but which became embroiled in a civil war. In May 2000 British paratroops secured an airport and evacuated foreign nationals. The Commons Select Committee on Foreign Affairs' report into the Sandline allegations dismissed the charges but Robin Cook's 'ethical foreign policy' was called into question by the affair.

## satire
*See* political satire.

## Saville inquiry
www.bloody-sunday-inquiry.org
Set up in 2000 to investigate the deaths of 14 civil rights marchers on 'Bloody Sunday' in 1972. It reconsidered the ground supposedly covered by the 1972 Widgery report, the anodyne conclusions of which did nothing to assuage the sense of outrage felt by the families of those killed. That report had favoured the army and had been conducted in an adversarial manner.

By contrast, the Saville inquiry avoided those mistakes and summoned more than 900 witnesses, including senior politicians (for example Edward Heath), army officers and the soldiers who fired and killed the marchers. After three years of exhaustive hearings – the opening statement alone took 176 hours – the inquiry heard its last oral testimony in February 2004. So time consuming and expensive – at £155 million – was the process that it probably ruled out anything similar for some time. Time alone will tell whether the conclusions of the report will render the mammoth undertaking worthwhile; Lord Saville was expected to publish his report in early 2005.

*See also* Bloody Sunday.

### Scarman report, 1981

Following the riots in Brixton, Lord Scarman was appointed to investigate its causes. He focused on the absence of a police complaints procedure as a major reason for the breakdown in police–community relations. He came down in favour of measures to reduce racial discrimination, including positive discrimination.

### Scotland

A northern region of the British Isles of 79,000 km² (30,400 square miles) and a population of some 5 million. There were successive wars between England and Scotland but in 1603, when Elizabeth I died, the two separate kingdoms were united under a single monarch, as James IV of Scotland became James I of England. Scotland became part of the United Kingdom with the Act of Union in 1707. This was far from an 'annexation', as the agreement was to some extent negotiated and a degree of autonomy was allowed to the Scots to retain some of their independence. Scotland still retains its distinctive educational and legal systems and bank notes. This sense of identity fuelled the Scottish National Party (SNP), which began to attract support during the 1960s. There was substantial support for increased autonomy from Westminster in the 1970s but not enough to bring about devolution

in that decade. However, national feeling continued to grow under the Thatcher governments in the 1980s and beyond until New Labour came to power in 1997. This was evidenced by the large 'yes' in the referendum for a Scottish assembly in September 1997; the summer of 1998 saw increasing support for the SNP. In 1999, the queen opened the Scottish parliament in Edinburgh, signalling an era of (renewed) Scottish devolution and increased autonomy. In the 1999 elections to the Scottish parliament Labour was the biggest party but had to govern in coalition with the Liberal Democrats. Despite losses in 2003 the same coalition remained in power. As a consequence of devolution it is expected that the Boundary Commission will reduce the number of Scottish Westminster seats from 72 to 59.

*See also* devolution.

### Scotland Act 1998

*See* Scottish parliament.

### Scott report, 1996

The *Report of the Inquiry into the Export of Defence Equipment and Dual-Use Goods to Iraq and Related Prosecutions*. Sir Richard Scott was asked to inquire into the circumstances of the 1992 collapse of the Matrix Churchill trial of three British businessmen accused of selling arms to Iraq in contravention of government guidelines. The trial ended when a junior defence minister, Alan Clarke, admitted the businessmen had received an informal indication that their proposed sale could go ahead. The report uncovered a disturbing mixture of maladministration and several cases of departmental self-interest taking precedence over policy objectives. Several ministers, including William Waldegrave, as well as some officials were criticised, though Michael Hesletine, president of the Board of Trade at the time, emerged unscathed.

*See also* Matrix Churchill case.

### Scottish Grand Committee

Set up in 1981 to deal with Scottish legislative matters. Second and third readings of bills relating to Scotland were read in the committee, which often met in Scotland itself. Initially it comprised all Scottish MPs. During the Conservative years of government in the 1980s and early 1990s, therefore, it had a Labour majority. This led the Scottish secretary to point out to Labour members that Westminster had the 'absolute veto' and that the committee was not a 'Scottish parliament'. The committee survived devolution and in 2003 comprised 72 members, though bills relating exclusively to Scotland have been a rarity since the establishment of the Scottish parliament.

## Scottish Labour Party (SLP)

Set up in 1976 by Scottish members of the Labour Party who felt the then government's devolution proposals did not go far enough. James Sillars and John Robertson became members but continued to take the Labour whip until late in 1976. The party suffered entryism from the International Marxist Group and a very early bout of factionalism. Sillars saved his deposit in the 1979 election but the other two candidates did not. Sillars joined the Scottish National Party once the SLP was wound up.

## Scottish National Liberation Army (SNLA)

Militant faction seeking the end of English immigration into Scotland and the establishment of a Scottish republic. It was thought to be behind the sending of parcels containing toxic substances to a number of political figures in March 2002, including Cherie Blair. The chief suspect was Adam Busby, the founder of the SNLA, who lives in Ireland and has evaded attempts to extradite him. The organisation was involved in earlier hoax threats to poison water supplies in England and in sending hoax anthrax letters to Prince William.

## Scottish National Party (SNP)

www.snp.org

Founded in 1934 by John McCormick, who believed his country received a poor deal from the union with England effected in 1707. The party asserts that Scotland

could pay its own way through domestic taxes and pursue a policy of independence within the European Union. Its fortunes improved after the discovery of North Sea oil in the 1970s, when the proposition that this oil belonged to Scotland attracted support in a country beset with unemployment as traditional industries declined. In February 1974 it returned seven MPs and in October 1974 11 MPs – whose vote against Labour in 1979 precipitated the vote of confidence which then led to an election at which the party returned only two MPs. There were only three SNP MPs elected in 1992. In 1997 the SNP supported the 'yes' vote on the referendum for a Scottish parliament and it may be that Labour's policy of assuaging nationalist feeling with devolution paradoxically merely whetted the Scots' appetite for more autonomy. The SNP's standing in the polls was equal to Labour's in the autumn of 1998, which augured badly for Labour in the elections to the Scottish parliament scheduled for 1999. In the event the SNP emerged as the second largest party after Labour, with 35 MSPs. In 2000 Alex Salmond stood down as leader of the SNP and John Swinney took over. In the June 2001 Westminster election the SNP won 20 per cent of the Scottish vote (two points down on 1997) and five seats (one down on 1997). The election was something of a setback for the SNP, leaving it 8 percentage points down on the 1999 Scottish parliament elections in terms of votes received. In the May 2003 elections to the Scottish parliament the SNP lost eight seats; Swinney resigned in 2004 and Alex Salmond was re-elected as leader that September.

## Scottish parliament

As promised in Labour's 1997 manifesto, a referendum was held on two proposals: a Scottish parliament and a parliament with tax-varying powers. The voters approved the first proposal by 74 to 26 per cent, the second by 64 to 36 per cent. Turnout was 60 per cent. The Scotland Act establishing the parliament received its royal assent in May 1998. Just over a year later, on 6 May 1999, elections took place for the 129 members of the Scottish parliament (called MSPs) by the amended additional member system (AMS): 73 from constituencies plus 56 members by party list. Labour emerged the largest party but needed Liberal Democrat support, which came at a price: seats in the cabinet and an inquiry into student tuition fees, which eventually led to their abolition in Scotland. The parliament has legislative and executive powers, except in the following areas: UK constitutional issues, foreign affairs, defence and national security, macro-economic policy, employment, social security, and transport safety and regulation. Income tax could be varied by plus or minus 3 pence in the pound. Those powers not defined are devolved and become the responsibility of the Scottish executive, led by a first minister. The late Donald Dewar became the first first minister (he died in the autumn of 2000) and Jim Wallace (Liberal Democrats) his deputy. David Steel became presiding officer of the parliament. Jack McConnell took over as first minister and survived the second elections to the parliament on 1 May 2003. Labour lost six seats but the SNP fared even worse, losing eight. The Greens gained seven seats and the Scottish Socialists a surprising six seats. After four years of the parliament, voters did not seem to be especially pleased with the performance of the coalition. In June 2003 the secretary of state for Scotland was downgraded to a part-time job, when it was tacked on to that of the transport secretary but with political authority given to the new Department of Constitutional Affairs.

*See also* devolution.

**second chamber**
*See* House of Lords.

**Second World War**
A war with a profound effect on the development of Britain. Among the consequences were the fact that Britain, though triumphant, was now economically bankrupt, which ensured its days as a world

power were numbered. Despite this the experience of war unified the country and established a powerful myth of togetherness, sharing and equality, which was exploited by the Labour Party in the 1945 general election. Moreover, wartime social policy carried over into the peace with the founding of the National Health Service, social security and other elements of the welfare state during the 1945–51 Attlee administrations. Centralised planning of the economy, in particular of labour, fuel and manufacturing, which helped win the war, made Labour's programme of nationalisation more acceptable, as did a recognition that trade unions were part of the state and had a right to be consulted. Full employment in war nourished a desire for it in peacetime and the demand management theories of John Maynard Keynes were to underpin much of the economic thinking for the next 30 years or so. The public and the armed forces had been radicalised by a war fought against a barbaric system, Nazism, and many wanted a new start, which meant that the Conservative Party, despite the triumph of Winston Churchill, was discredited as the party of appeasement and unemployment. Finally, the carve-up of Germany and Europe at Potsdam and Yalta was eventually to lead, along with Marshall aid and the Berlin blockade, to Britain's membership of NATO in 1949, a military alliance led by the USA – an indication that the Cold War was already well under way.

**secondary legislation**
*See* delegated legislation.

**secondary modern school**
Established by the 1944 'Butler' Education Act, which introduced three types of secondary school – grammar, technical and secondary modern. Grammar and some technical schools were well resourced and catered for mostly middle-class children who had passed the 11 plus, an examination also introduced by the act. The majority of children, who failed, were condemned to a poorly funded education

in the secondary modern sector, where the teaching and the results were often dire. In the 1960s Labour decided to scrap the 11 plus and introduce comprehensive education as a substitute for grammar schools, secondary modern schools and technical schools; however, some areas retained these types of school.

## secondary picketing
Picketing by trade unionists of a place of work not directly involved in an industrial dispute. It was used extensively during the miners' strikes in 1972 and 1974 and during the public sector disputes in late 1978, now known as the 'winter of discontent'. To curtail union power, the Employment Act 1980 outlawed the practice, a measure which was retained by New Labour when it came to power in 1997.

## secrecy
Sir John Hoskyns, former head of Margaret Thatcher's Policy Unit, wrote that the culture of secrecy, sustained by the Official Secrets Act and the 30-year rule, was convenient for government by 'hiding peacetime fiascos as if they were military secrets or issues of national security, thus protecting ministers and officials from embarrassment'. Despite hopes of reform under New Labour, many have been disappointed by the relatively modest changes of Jack Straw's Freedom of Information Act 2000.

*See also* Freedom of Information Act 2000; Official Secrets Act; open government.

## secret ballot
*See* ballot.

## section 28
A clause of the Local Government Act 1988, accepted as an amendment, which made it illegal for local authorities to engage in the 'deliberate promotion' of homosexuality. This vague wording was used by some local authorities, claimed activists, to justify homophobic policies. Many teachers saw the clause as a veto on open

discussion of the issue in class and a barrier to their tackling of homophobic bullying. After 1997 Labour promised to repeal the section, but support for its retention proved surprisingly robust, especially in Scotland, where a privately funded poll suggested widespread support for its retention. It was finally repealed in November 2003.

## sectional interest group
*See* pressure group.

## Security Commission
www.cabinetoffice.gov.uk/security
Cabinet Office body tasked with investigating breaches in national security. It was established in 1964 to 'investigate and report upon the circumstances in which a breach of security is known to have occurred in the public service'. The Right Honorable Lady Justice Sloss was chair in 2004, supported by six other members. The members form a panel from which three or four, including the chair, are normally selected on each occasion when the Commission is invited by the prime minister to investigate a suspected breach of security.

## Security Service Act 1989
Placed MI5 on a statutory basis with a specified range of functions. In 1997 the latter were increased to include the prevention of crime and its detection. The act also set up a security services commissioner to monitor phone tapping and interference with property by the security services, and to deliver an annual report to the prime minister.

## security services
www.mi5.gov.uk
Britain's security services comprise MI5, the Security Service (the counter-intelligence agency for domestic matters), and MI6, the Secret Intelligence Service (the overseas intelligence service). The police have an internal agency called Special Branch and radio surveillance is carried out by SIGINT, Signals Intelligence. MI5 reports to the Home Office; MI6 collects intelligence on matters relevant to

the security of the state and reports to the Foreign Office. MI5 used to worry about the Communist Party but since that party's demise has focused on extremist political movements. Despite these different lines of accountability important matters can be taken direct to the prime minister when necessary. There are cabinet committees that overlook the security services: one, MIS, is chaired by the prime minister, and three, PSIS plus two others, by the cabinet secretary. Under the provisions of the Intelligence Services Act 1994 the Intelligence and Security Committee was set up to oversee the security services. In the mid-1980s there were about 10,000 people employed by the security services.

### select committee
www.parliament.uk/commons/selcom/cmsel. htm

An investigative committee of the House of Commons. Select committees have been used since Tudor times but more so recently. For much of the 20th century there were only two such committees, the Public Accounts Committee (PAC) and the Estimates Committee. These were supplemented by the Statutory Instruments Committee in the 1940s and in the 1950s by a committee dealing with the national-ised industries. Richard Crossman strove to expand their role in the 1960s but with limited success. It was not until the 1980s, when Norman St John Stevas was leader of the House, that real progress was made and a raft of departmental select committees were set up. The committees have powers to call for persons, papers and records; they may also hold hearings in public.

*See also* department select committee; non-departmental select committee; Public Accounts Committee.

### Select Committee on Science and Technology (Lords)
Set up in 1979 to replace the Commons committee of the same name which was dis-continued. The remit is wide – 'to consider science and technology' – and its inquiries have been assisted by the number of peers

with a distinguished scientific background. Between 1979 and 1991 the committee carried out 34 inquiries into issues such as hazardous waste disposal, space policy and the greenhouse effect. In 1992 the Commons decided to establish a new com-mittee on the same subject, so great was its importance.

### Selsdon Group
Formed in 1973 to champion free market policies in the Conservative Party. It took its name from the Selsdon Park Hotel at which the Conservative Party formulated its manifesto in 1970. Many of Edward Heath's critics felt he had departed from these principles and the group was designed to direct him back to the chosen path after his famous U-turns. It advocated privatisation, the scrapping of quangos, pri-vate initiatives in the welfare state and strict control of both the money supply and public expenditure. It was an important fringe group at party conferences in the 1980s.

### sentencing
A controversial aspect of penal policy, as few people can agree what punishment fits which crime. Parliament makes laws and the Home Office may issue guidelines on the maximum sentences for certain offences. Courts are allowed wide discre-tion based on the particular circumstances of each crime. Consequently there is not always consistency in the sentences handed down in different parts of the country. The Conservatives, influenced by the party rank and file, tend to favour tougher sentences, such as the return of the death penalty – though after much debate during the 1980s it was not readopted and is not party policy. Sentences for rape, robbery and the use of firearms did increase markedly dur-ing the middle of the decade. Tory home secretary Michael Howard was famous for adducing the simplistic claim that 'prison works' but criminologists and High Court judges tended to disagree strongly and on 10 September 1998 the Home Affairs Select Committee reported that the increase in the prison population of Britain – then

over 66,000 – was 'unsustainable' and that 20,000 inmates should be released and dealt with via community punishments. Its chair, Chris Mullin, said 'Prison is only an ineffective and very expensive means of containment'. In January 2003 the lord chancellor, Lord Irvine, and the lord chief justice, Lord Justice Woolf, caused controversy by suggesting that burglars should not necessarily be imprisoned for their first or second offences.

*See also* death penalty; penal policy; Prison Service.

## separation of powers

Montesquieu, the 18th-century French political theorist, developed a doctrine, first evinced in medieval Europe, that political power was too potent a force to be vested in one body or authority. So fearful was he that a despot or tyrant would come to overwhelm a kingdom that he examined the British parliamentary system and believed, wrongly, that he could discern three functions in government: law making, vested in the legislature; a judiciary which interpreted and judged the laws; and an executive which implemented the laws and performed other governmental functions. He believed the three elements should be kept separate and his ideas were taken up by the framers of the US constitution, who built into their fledgling political system clear separation between the Congress (the legislature), the Supreme Court (the judiciary) and the president (the executive), and an elaborate checking procedure between them, an arrangement which survives to this day. At the time he was writing, the political system in Britain (under George III) was rather different from his ideals, and this remains so today in a number of significant respects:

1  The executive or government is drawn from the legislature (the House of Commons) in that the government is formed by the largest party returned to the legislature in elections. Nearly all members of the cabinet are MPs.

2  The senior members of the judiciary sit as law lords in the House of Lords,

which is the highest court of appeal in Britain. (In 2003 the government initiated controversial proposals to set up a Supreme Court.)

3  Cabinet ministers have quasi-judicial and legislative powers, which enable them to make executive decisions without necessarily having to seek prior approval of parliament.

4  The lord chancellor used to be head of the judiciary, to appoint judges as well as QCs, to serve as a cabinet member and to preside over the House of Lords. This concentration of roles 'fused' the supposedly separate functions of government and attracted much criticism from reformers. In spring 2003 the government sought to resolve some of these anomalies by establishing: a secretary of state for constitutional affairs to take charge of the courts system instead of the lord chancellor; plans for a Supreme Court; and new procedures for appointing judges and QCs.

For these reasons, there is a 'fusing' rather than a separation of powers in Britain's political system. Despite this, advocates of the system maintain that there are extensive mechanisms of accountability and for the redress of grievance.

*See also* elective dictatorship.

## Septennial Act 1716

Act, passed by the Whigs, that extended the maximum period between elections from three to seven years. It contributed towards the greater stability of parliament and the authority of the House of Commons. The Parliament Act 1911 reduced the period to the present five years.

## Serious Organised Crime Agency

Planned new agency announced in the white paper *One Step Ahead* in 2004, and presented in the media as a kind of British equivalent of the US Federal Bureau of Investigation. Its aim is to find the big figures who run multimillion pound drug, vice and money-laundering rackets. Organised crime is believed to cost Britain £40 billion per year. The agency combines the National Crime Squad, the National Criminal Intelligence Customs and fraud investigations. The intelligence agencies support the work of the new agency, which, it is believed, will employ around 5,000 staff, including experts in finance and high technology.

### service (or tertiary) sector of the economy

The part of the economy which provides services to consumers, including tourism, leisure, financial services and information technology. As the manufacturing sector has declined, the service sector has expanded, so that it provided jobs for 70 per cent of the workforce in 2004. The service sector is more labour intensive and cannot cut costs as easily as manufacturing, where advances in production technology can reduce labour costs. Moreover, the service sector boomed in the 1990s while manufacturing declined, creating the 'two-speed' economy.

### Settlement
*See* Act of Settlement 1701

### Sex Discrimination Act (Election Candidates) 2001

Act that enabled political parties to use affirmative action to increase the selection of female representatives. The legislation is permissive and removes the possibility of prosecution under British law, though not European law. In 1996 all-women shortlists enabled more women to be adopted as candidates in the Labour Party – which contributed to a record number being elected in 1997 – but an employment tribunal in 1996 found this to be illegal. The act made such shortlists legal but it is up to individual parties to adopt the procedures they think appropriate.

### Sexual Offences Act 1967

Decriminalised homosexual acts conducted in private between consenting adults aged over 21 in England and Wales. The provisions of the act were extended to Scotland and Northern Ireland in 1982.

### shadow cabinet

The team of opposition politicians, drawn largely from the House of Commons, chosen to specialise in the various departmental portfolios of government ministers – in effect a 'government in waiting'. An election within the Parliamentary Labour Party in theory determines the composition of its shadow cabinet and the actual cabinet once the party is elected to office. However, in May 1997 Tony Blair left out two members of his former shadow cabinet on the grounds that there were not enough cabinet posts available. In the more hierarchical Conservative Party, the leader has the power to appoint cabinets and shadow cabinets. Appointment is eagerly sought by MPs, who recognise that a creditable effort in opposing their minister will reinforce their claims to office and possible promotion. Blair served in several shadow jobs – employment, Home Office and energy – before winning the leadership in 1994. The practice of creating an alternative 'government in waiting' from the biggest opposition party is not emulated in other systems. For example, it would be difficult to do this in a multi-party system or in the USA, where the executive is elected in the person of the president and the losing candidate is not even a member of any legislative chamber and has no status once the election is over.

### share ownership

Individual share ownership increased in the 1980s as millions of people bought shares in privatised industries. The Conservative government celebrated this as part of a change in the culture, a move to a 'people's capitalism'. However, shortly after buying them most people sold their shares to take a profit. The proportion of shares owned by individuals fell from over 30 per cent in the mid-1980s to just over 20 per cent in the early 1990s; the majority of shares are held by large financial institutions, especially pension funds and insurance companies.

### Sheehy report, 1993

Report into the management of the police force. Sir Patrick Sheehy, a prominent businessman, was asked by home secretary

Michael Howard to undertake the inquiry. The report criticised the top-heavy management structure of the police, overlapping responsibilities and promotion based on length of service, not merit or individual performance. It recommended: the abolition of three senior ranks; fixed-term, possibly 10-year contracts; performance-related pay; and less generous terms of sick pay. The Police Federation, the force's professional association, was incensed and attacked the report bitterly; even the former Labour prime minister James Callaghan, once a representative of the Federation, was called in to rubbish its 'dogmatic conclusions based on inaccurate analysis'. In the light of this robust response Howard agreed to ignore some of the more contentious proposals.

## Shelter
www.shelter.org.uk
National campaign for the homeless founded in 1966 by the former social campaigner Des Wilson. It campaigns for housing projects and undertakes studies of homelessness. Shelter has 300 voluntary groups throughout the country which give advice on housing and tenancy issues.

## silly season
Period in the summer when parliament is in recess, many politicians are on holiday and there seems to be very little hard news. This is traditionally when newspapers run apocryphal stories like 'man bites dog', or in August 2004 a story about two Greek athletes' failure to take a drugs test at the Olympic Games, which filled the headlines for several days.

## single currency
*See* euro.

## Single European Act (SEA), 1986
As soon as he became president of the European Commission in 1985, Jacques Delors became a catalyst for integration. He pushed for rapid movement towards the single internal market in Europe, defined by freedom of goods, people, capital and services. A single market was proposed for 1992 after the December 1985 European Council meeting in Luxembourg. During the following year it was ratified by the national parliaments. Geoffrey Howe as foreign secretary steered it through the British parliament with little fuss. The necessary British legislation was passed in July 1987, and the single market came into being in January 1993. It was a massive leap towards an integrated Europe since it strengthened the European parliament and established qualified majority voting in the Council of Ministers. However, it seems Margaret Thatcher, that great enemy of integration, allowed the act to pass because she was unaware of its importance for the future and its supranational implications.

## single transferable vote (STV)
The voting system used in the Irish Republic and much favoured by the Liberal Democrats as a model for Britain. The country is divided into multi-member constituencies, in which voters register their preferences from 1 to whatever the number of candidates there might be. To take a four-member constituency as an example, a quota is set at one-fifth of the votes cast, plus one. Only four candidates can possibly reach this quota figure. If any candidate reaches it after the first count they are elected but if they do not the next stage sees the elimination of the lowest-ranking candidate and a redistribution of the second preferences to all the others so that their votes are thereby increased. This continues until quotas are reached and then, if necessary, the other preferences are redistributed if quotas remain to be filled. Many consider the STV system is inappropriate for Britain as it would weaken the link between MPs and their constituents.

## sink estate
A council estate in which social problems such as unemployment, delinquency and vandalism are concentrated. It is calculated there are 2,000 such estates in Britain. This was exacerbated by the 'right to buy' policy, which led to 1.7 million council

houses – the best of them – being sold while 3.4 million remained, many of them of poor quality. Low pay or unemployment create a culture of despair and social exclusion in which groups of young men roam the estate, cause a nuisance to neighbours and get into trouble with the police. Initially the physical state of the housing was good but it then suffered years of neglect. The overall result is an estate in which no one wants to live, wrecked by crime and drugs: a 'sink estate' where 'problem families' are forced to live and bring up children, which establishes a set of vicious circles.

*See also* social exclusion; underclass.

## Sinn Fein

Gaelic for 'we ourselves'. The movement was founded in 1907 by Arthur Griffith as an Irish nationalist party. Over time it has become identified as the 'political wing' of the Irish Republican Army. It has more or less maintained this relationship though its leaders have found it convenient from time to time to distance themselves from the IRA's excesses. It steadfastly supported the armed struggle throughout the 1970s and 1980s, refusing to condemn terrorist atrocities, but eventually, in the early 1990s, its president, Gerry Adams, elected in 1978, decided the armed part of the struggle was not worth continuing. The result of this change of heart was the peace negotiations chaired by Senator Mitchell, which culminated in the Good Friday Agreement. In June 1998 elections were held for the resultant Northern Ireland assembly, which met on 14 September, Adams declaring he wished to 'make friends' with Ian Paisley. However, predictably, this friendship never materialised. In the November 2003 elections to the assembly, the need for closer relations between the nationalists and hard-line Protestants was heightened by the squeezing of the centre, which saw Sinn Fein gain six seats, the Democratic Unionist Party 10 and the Social Democratic and Labour Party lose six.

*See also* Northern Ireland; Northern Ireland assembly; Adams, Gerry.

## sleaze

Term that originated in the final years of the Major government of 1992–97. In November 1993 Major circulated a memo inviting ministers to come up with ideas around the theme of 'back to basics', which was the focus of his Conservative Party conference speech. Interpreted by some right-wingers and journalists as a campaign for a return to family values and traditional sexual morality, it backfired badly. Between October 1993 and February 1994 eight MPs, some of them ministers, were exposed by the tabloids as currently having or having had illicit sexual affairs. The scandals of 'cash for questions' followed shortly after, together with a number of other revelations. A poll on 12 February 1994 revealed that more than half the respondents believed the Conservatives gave an impression of 'sleaze'. It was a label which stuck to them right up until the general election in May 1997, and certainly made Labour's landslide easier to achieve. The defeat of MP Neil Hamilton by Martin Bell in the previously safe Tory seat of Tatton exemplified the problem the party faced. However, since then Labour has had its own problems with donations to the party from rich businessmen, in exchange, it is alleged, for special favours. One full of drama and intrigue concerned the Hinduja brothers, one of whom gained a British passport in an unusually short time following their sponsorship of the Faith Zone in the ill-fated Millennium Dome; the affair ensnared Peter Mandelson, the Northern Ireland secretary, who was forced to resign, for a second time, from the government in January 2001.

Labour's penchant for cosying up to business brought more grief in February 2002, when a letter from Tony Blair to the Romanian prime minister on behalf of an Indian businessman who had contributed to Labour Party funds was exploited by the Conservative Party. A poll published in the *Sunday Times* on 17 February 2002 suggested that 60 per cent of the public regarded Labour as 'sleazy and disreputable', compared with only 41 per cent who felt the same about the Conservatives.

## Smith Square

Westminster headquarters of the
Conservative Party for many years. In
the summer of 2002 Iain Duncan Smith
moved his office to the House of Commons,
thus freeing space in the former headquarters. William Hague had followed other
Conservative leaders and worked from an
office in Smith Square but Duncan Smith
decided a closer relationship with the
parliamentary party was necessary. In addition the party faced financial problems and
such a move saved thousands of pounds
in rent and rates. Following the accession
to the leadership of Michael Howard in
November 2003 it was announced that the
Smith Square building was to be sold. In
July 2004 Conservative Party headquarters
moved to Victoria Street, a short distance
away.

## Social Affairs Unit

www.socialaffairsunit.org.uk
Think tank founded in 1980 by Digby
Anderson, a right-wing journalist.
According to *The Economist* (6 May
1989), 'it is concerned less with advocating
free market economics than with promoting
social morality and preserving the social
fabric'. It has not been especially influential
since the fall of Margaret Thatcher.

## Social and Liberal Democratic Party

*See* Liberal Democrats.

## Social Chapter

Part of the Treaty on European Union
(TEU) signed at Maastricht in 1992. It
concerned employment policy and dealt
with such matters as workers' health and
safety, works councils, a minimum wage,
working conditions and other related
issues. These had not been received
sympathetically by the Conservative
government as they were thought to relate
to the sort of trade union demands which,
it was alleged, had caused British goods
to be overpriced and of poor quality. The
Conservatives under John Major negotiated
an 'opt-out'; a protocol was added to the
TEU to which 11 members subscribed but

not Britain. For a number of years Britain
was excluded from most social policy
measures, though some were binding,
including children's working time, equality
for pensioners and women's rights. In
1997 Labour accepted the Social Chapter
in its entirety as one of its first acts in
government.

## social class

*See* class.

## Social Contract

Agreement in 1975 between the Labour
government and the trade unions. It was
in response to a crisis that June which
had seen wages and inflation soaring. It
focused narrowly on wages, which unions
agreed to hold down to an agreed level, in
exchange for which their members would
receive benefits such as controls over
prices and rents. This fragile agreement
succeeded in bringing down inflation; it
continued until the autumn of 1978, when
the Trades Union Congress refused to
accept the government's wage guidelines
and the disastrous 'winter of discontent'
resulted.

## social democracy

*See* Social Democratic Party (SDP).

## Social Democratic and Labour Party (SDLP)

www.sdlp.ie
Northern Ireland political party formed
in 1970. It is moderately left wing and
favours eventual Irish unification, though
by peaceful means. Its leader up to 2001,
John Hume, consistently condemned the
terrorist tactics of the nationalists and
helped to encourage the peace process in
the late 1980s and early 1990s. Seamus
Mallon, as deputy leader of the party, was
made deputy to the first minister in the first
Northern Ireland executive, produced by
the elections in June 1998. (Mark Durkan
and Alasdair McDonnell are now the
leader and deputy leader, respectively.) In
the November 2003 elections the SDLP
suffered a disaster, losing six seats as the

centre was squeezed by the extremes of the Democratic Unionist Party and Sinn Fein.
*See also* Northern Ireland assembly.

## Social Democratic Federation

Britain's first Marxist party, formed in 1881 by H. M. Hyndman. For a while it recruited well, especially among middle-class intellectuals. It organised meetings in the 1880s and 1890s and was present at the foundation of the Labour Party in 1900. But its factionalism and dogmatism stunted its growth and its appeal waned; former members seemed to find a more agreeable home in the Communist Party of Great Britain, formed in 1920.

## Social Democratic Party

Political party in existence from 1981 to 1990. Social democracy is a blend of free market economics (economic liberalism) combined with a strong commitment to social welfare and the responsibilities of the state in this regard (social reformism or reformist liberalism). This type of thinking had existed uneasily alongside democratic socialist doctrines (for example nation-alisation) in the Labour Party, until the early 1980s. Matters came to a head on 1 August 1980, when Shirley Williams, David Owen and William Rodgers published an open letter to the Labour Party expressing their discontent at its leftward drift. When this drift accelerated and Roy Jenkins came on board to make up the 'gang of four', the formation of a new party was only a matter of time. In January 1981 the Social Democratic Party (SDP) was formed. Media interest was intense and many disillusioned Labour members were attracted by the new ban-ner. Labour supporters complained of betrayal. Opinion polls registered aston-ishing levels of support for the SDP: it attracted 70,000 members and won two sensational by-elections, at Crosby and Hillhead. In the Alliance with the Liberal Party it fought the 1983 general election, when it mustered an impressive 25.4 per cent of the vote, although only 23 seats. However, many of the defectors from the

Parliamentary Labour Party lost their seats and some of the forward momentum had been stalled. After the 1983 election Owen replaced Jenkins as leader of the SDP. In 1987 the Alliance needed nearly 40 per cent of the vote to win a majority and 30–34 per cent to hold the balance of power; it won 22.6 per cent and 22 seats, a major disappointment. Liberal leader David Steel called for merger negotiations but the SDP split into 'mergerite' and 'Owenite' factions. Owen resigned and at the 1987 conference the SDP voted to merge with the Liberal Party that year. Owen defiantly led a small rump SDP but it was hopeless and wound up in 1990. From euphoric beginnings the SDP ended up as a party of protest with limited appeal outside the middle classes. However, the experience had a salutary effect upon Labour and helped to nudge it back towards an electable position in the late 1980s and early 1990s.
*See also* Alliance; Liberal Democrats.

## social engineering

Changing the basic nature of human be-ings. Political philosophers have debated the intrinsic nature of humankind for cen-turies and some have suggested that it can be improved by changing social arrange-ments, a view propounded by Karl Marx, who stated that as 'environment creates consciousness', it follows that a change to the environment will change consciousness. This approach became known as social en-gineering. For the socialist utopians in the Labour Party this was seen as a mission to change the British people from selfish, com-petitive members of a capitalist society into cooperative, sharing members of a socialist one. Traditional Conservatives condemn 'social engineering' as an artificial interven-tion in the natural order which can only damage society, but Margaret Thatcher seemed to be doing something very similar with her efforts to create an 'enterprise society'. Despite the experience of failure, politicians seem irrevocably wedded to the idea that the acceptance of their political ideas will transform, invigorate and renew the nation, a visionary aim which underpins the project of Tony Blair and others.

## social exclusion
The inability of a poor section or 'underclass' of society to participate fully in the life of a community. The term, within the context of New Labour, neatly combines a sociological description with an ideological imperative: that those excluded have suffered an injustice which should be righted, and that those shut out should be included, possibly irrespective of their own wishes. The term is associated with Labour's approach to reforming welfare in Britain. When Tony Blair came to power in 1997 he formed the Social Exclusion Unit in the Cabinet Office. It produced a report in September 1998 on 2,000 run-down council estates, which called for more tenant-owned estates, an end to new estates which tend to break up communities and cheaper supermarket food to be made available to poor estates. Nearly £1 billion was allocated to the programme. In Whitehall 18 task forces were established to coordinate policy to tackle crime, education and youth disaffection.

*See also* poverty; sink estate.

## social justice
A fair and proper distribution within society of benefits and burdens. The idea that there should be social justice underlies much of the welfare state. It originates in the gulf between the rich and the poor, the powerful and the weak, and suggests the political 'playing field' ought to be level. Accordingly, advocates of social justice in Britain, usually in the Liberal and Labour parties, have called for redistributive taxation to fund free education, health and pensions. The Conservatives have argued that such ideas are false in that they substitute passive state dependence and moral decline for energetic self-reliance. Since Tony Blair became leader of the Labour Party in 1994, third way thinking recast the party's traditional commitment to welfare into a modern, critics would say pragmatic, safety net approach to the welfare state and social justice.

## Social Market Foundation
www.cpcs.co.uk
Think tank founded in 1989 by the Social Democratic Party luminary Robert Skidelsky, which survived the demise of its social democratic creators and became independent. The Foundation produced some influential work identifying where markets can be usefully applied to the public sector and where they cannot. The group has some links with Conservative thinkers like David Willets.

## social mobility
In May 2002 the Institute for Social and Economic Research at Essex University reported a study showing that social mobility had slowed in Britain in recent years. It seems that the sons and daughters of people who joined the middle classes in the 1960s are tending to block the ascent of children from working-class backgrounds by occupying the available middle-class jobs. Another causal factor is that people tend to marry within their own class and thereby close off another access route to potential new members of the stratum. According to the *Guardian*: 'Based on a 5000 strong sample of families which have been tracked and questioned repeatedly since the late 1950s the study finds that people with parents in better earning jobs are more likely to be in higher earning positions themselves and are more likely to marry someone with parents in higher earning occupations.'

## social security
*See* Department for Work and Pensions.

## social structure
*See* class.

## socialism
Originated out of the indignation created by the inequalities and suffering caused by early capitalism in the west. This critique, expressed most powerfully in Robert Tressell's novel *The Ragged Trousered Philanthropists* (1914), focused on: the exploitation of workers, who create wealth for the 'bosses'; the inequalities between workers who have

to bring up large families on a weekly sum their employer might spend on a single meal; the lack of responsibility bosses have for workers, who become a mere commodity; and the climate of brutal competition which infects and corrupts all concerned. Instead, early socialists in Britain, such as the Social Democratic Federation and the Independent Labour Party offered an alternative vision. This was of a commonly owned economy and workers who cooperated willingly in the creation of a better society, using free time to develop their individual talents and skills, and enjoy the full fruits of life. The foundation of the Labour Party and its successes after the First World War brought this ideal closer and it was refined into a set of policies based on nationalisation of the main economic enterprises plus improved social services. This programme was enacted by Clement Attlee's huge postwar majority but thereafter socialism was split between those who wished to continue nationalisation and create a command economy, and those revisionists who believed management of the economy through Keynesian techniques could bring the fruits of socialism without the fractures of destroying capitalism. This struggle reached its climax in the early 1980s with a full-blooded capitalist Conservative government. Left-wing activists made significant inroads into the Labour Party but the wider public was not impressed and its version of socialism received a blast of dismissive contempt by voters in 1983. From then on Labour inched away from socialism under Neil Kinnock; under Tony Blair socialism was a word very rarely used, even in Labour Party manifestos, in public and leadership speeches or by party activists in public. Margaret Thatcher swore one of her missions was to destroy socialism; while the Labour Party lived on to win famously in 1997 it is a moot point whether or not she succeeded.

### Socialist Alliance (SA)
www.socialistalliance.net
Umbrella organisation for left-wing parties which fought the 2001 general election. It was chaired by former Militant MP

Dave Nellist. Its manifesto was a scathing critique of New Labour as no better than Thatcherism, but did also put forward an 'alternative to the global unregulated free market'. Despite the effort expended in healing factional differences, the SA's six candidates garnered no more than 2 per cent of the vote in any contest.

### Socialist Labour Party
www.socialist-labour-party.org.uk
A left-wing socialist party launched by miners' leader Arthur Scargill in 1996. He was disgusted with what he saw as the anodyne revisionism of New Labour and wished to inject some 'real' socialism into the body politic. It subscribes to a fundamentalist programme of measures, including full employment, a four-day week, common ownership of the means of production and retirement at age 56. It attracted some publicity, but few votes in local and national elections. Scargill stood against Peter Mandelson, the sitting Labour MP for Hartlepool, in the 2001 general election but mustered less than 1,000 votes.

### Socialist League (SL)
Originally the International Marxist Group, the SL was founded in 1964 out of splits between feuding Trotskyites. Ken Coates was a leading figure, as was Tariq Ali. Prominent during student political action in the 1960s, the SL was more influenced by new left thinking, which stressed the importance of 'transforming consciousness' and the ending of 'alienation'.

### Socialist Party of Great Britain
www.spgb.org.uk
An unreconstructed Marxist party dedicated to world revolution and the destruction of capitalism, founded in 1904. It is against war but in favour of parliamentary democracy. Its attempts to get candidates elected have proved wholly unsuccessful.

### Socialist Workers Party
www.swp.org.uk
Trotskyite party founded by Duncan Hallas in 1950 as the International

Socialists. It changed its name in 1977. It existed as an non-entryist party that sought to influence the Labour Party. It was active in the Anti-Nazi League in the 1970s and the Right to Work Movement. Until his much-mourned death in July 2004, journalist Paul Foot was probably the best known member of the party.

### Society for the Protection of Unborn Children (SPUC)

www.spuc.org.uk
Classic 'cause' pressure group established to campaign against abortion, founded in 1966 to oppose the bill that became the Abortion Act 1967. Gynaecologist Aleck Bourne was a prime mover in this. Its aim is to 'uphold the principle of respect for the life of the unborn child'. It concentrates much of its work on parliamentary campaigns against euthanasia and embryo research, for example. The SPUC is funded by voluntary contributions and raises over £1 million annually.

### solicitor general

www.lslo.gov.uk
Since the 16th century, one of the two senior government legal officers, the other being the attorney general, both of whom lead for the government in major court cases as well as advise the government on legal matters.

### sound bite

Name given to short pithy statements which news editors use in bulletins. Having realised this, politicians now serve them up in a never-ending stream. In the late 1960s the average uninterrupted broadcast statement by a US presidential candidate was over 40 seconds. By 1996 it had shrunk to just 8 seconds. During election campaigns sound bites are even more important, as they can sum up the message for the day. Spin doctors try hard to dream up high-quality ones and then beg or bully news editors to include them on their television bulletins, watched in Britain by up to 20 million people each evening. Tony Blair was particularly good at inserting televisual

sound bites into his performances at prime minister's questions, as such high-profile jousting often wins news coverage. Some commentators voice concern that important political messages are being compressed into such short time spaces and possibly distorted in the process.

*See also* political marketing; political language; spin; spin doctors.

### sovereignty

The absolute power which states exercise over matters of government within their own borders. More a legal term than a behavioural reality, it has, however, become an emotive symbol for many patriots. Eurosceptics and opponents of the European Union (EU) are hotly opposed to what they see as a dilution of the essence of Britain's nationhood through membership of the EU. The supremacy of European law over domestic law rankles especially and led opponents in the 1970s, not to mention the present day, to argue for withdrawal. Constitutional experts assert that the ability of the nation to withdraw ultimately is the final guarantee of national sovereignty. Others argue the erosion of sovereignty by membership of international organisations like the United Nations and NATO, not to mention the international economy and other aspects of globalisation, make discussion of such matters redundant: in other words, why talk about complete control of the nation's destiny when it has not been within Britain's power for several decades?

*See also* parliamentary sovereignty.

### speaker

www.parliament.uk/works/speaker.cfm
Chief officer of the House of Commons. In the 14th century the speaker conveyed the wishes of the House to the king. For this service nine of the early speakers were executed, thus explaining the ritual show of reluctance by speakers to sit in their chair upon inauguration. Over the centuries the speaker ceased to play a political role and became an 'umpire' of proceedings, above the partisan fray. Elected by MPs, usually

on a non-partisan basis, the speaker has an authority which is jealously guarded, as Margaret Thatcher discovered in 1983 when she favoured Humphrey Atkins to succeed the legendary George Thomas, while the Commons insisted on a back-bencher, eventually the modestly effective Bernard Wetherill. Similarly, John Major wanted his colleague Peter Brooke in 1992 but the Conservative-dominated Commons chose Labour's Betty Boothroyd.

The speaker presides at sittings of the Commons, calls on members to speak and keeps their contributions within the rules of parliament and good order. He or she also decides on requests for emergency debates under standing order number 10 and private notice questions. MPs who offend against the rules can be repri-manded, suspended or even excluded. In the event of a tied vote in a division the speaker by tradition gives the casting vote against any amendment. The speaker's procession starts each day's proceedings after lunch. The speaker also heads the Commons Commission, which runs the House. At election times the speaker is traditionally returned unopposed, though this has attracted criticism from those who say constituents are thereby denied a choice and arguably effective representation. The colourful Betty Boothroyd stood down in 2000, after eight years in the job, and was replaced by Labour's Michael Martin, a former shop steward who attracted some criticism, centred on the fact that he was a Labour MP following a Labour MP, spoke with a broad Glaswegian accent and tended to make somewhat eccentric interventions. These allegations were angrily rejected by the speaker's supporters, who include chancellor Gordon Brown and a number of other Scottish members. By 2003 criticisms had virtually ceased.

*See also* deputy speaker.

## speaker's conference
Occasionally matters relating to arrange-ments affecting elections are considered in a conference chaired by the speaker, with representation from all parties. Examples

include consideration of changing the vot-ing system in 1917 and the lowering of the voting age in 1969.

## special advisor
*See* political advisor.

## special relationship
Term often used to describe the relationship between Britain and the USA. Despite the War of Independence which the USA fought in the 18th century to separate from the 'home' country, the two nations have a history of alliances against shared foes, including Germany in two world wars and the USSR during the Cold War. In addition, Britain supported the USA in a number of Cold War conflicts and the link was so close it helped explain why French leader Charles de Gaulle – suspicious of 'Anglo-Saxon' ganging up – vetoed British applications to join the Common Market in both 1963 and 1967.

The relationship has not always been smooth: the USA opposed Britain's Middle Eastern war in defence of the Suez Canal in 1956–57 and ignored Harold Wilson's advice over Vietnam. Margaret Thatcher was very close to US President Ronald Reagan, however, in his 'cold warrior' attitude to the USSR and Britain allied to the USA during the Gulf War in 1991. Tony Blair had a close relationship with Bill Clinton and was quick to establish good relations with George W. Bush in 2001. He displayed assiduous loyalty over most issues and his degree of support after the terrorist attacks on the USA on 11 September 2001 and the subsequent war against the Taliban in Afghanistan served to cement the alliance still further. However, many European countries were less enthusiastic and in 2003 Blair faced tension at home and abroad regarding his slavish support for the US-led invasion of Iraq.

## special standing committee
In 1980 the House sanctioned the creation of special standing committees to which a number of bills were referred. These

committees were allowed to hold up to four meetings before the normal standing committee stage, with three of them being public sessions in which witnesses could be questioned. The general conclusion from the experiment was that it was worthwhile but widespread use of the approach is yet to be made.

## Spectator
www.spectator.co.uk
Weekly journal of comment and analysis. Founded in 1828, it has established a reputation for good writing which has helped see it through occasional hard times. Its editors have tended to come from the right in post-war years and have included Ian Gilmour, Ian Macleod, Nigel Lawson, Charles Moore and Dominic Lawson. Predictably its policy line has tended to be right-wing independent but it can rock the boat a little, as when Lawson junior published in July 1990 a transcript of cabinet minister Nick Ridley's unflattering comments about Germany; Ridley was subsequently forced to resign. Lawson senior, in his memoirs (*The View From No. 11*, 1993), commented that Ridley made the remarks only because he had heard Margaret Thatcher saying similar things in private.

## speech from the throne
*See* queen's (or king's) speech.

## spin
The process by which messages are changed or otherwise massaged by politicians, especially by specialist spin doctors, to improve their acceptability to the public. The word is most closely associated with the refashioned New Labour Party, which revolutionised its media presentation during the mid-1980s under the influence of Peter Mandelson. However, most commentators agree the use of 'spin' in opposition was maintained in government, when it became counterproductive. In May 2002 both Mandelson and Tony Blair's press secretary, Alastair Campbell, admitted their party had relied too much on spin and called for a more open approach, in which

senior politicians would be more accountable to the voters. On 16 July 2002 Blair met the chairs of the select committees in a groundbreaking session. He agreed his government had been too obsessed with spin and attributed this to the 18 years of opposition, during which the 'announcement was the reality'. The session was judged a success by most – though not all – commentators and an effective way of being held accountable, thereby negating accusations of spin, and it has been repeated.

*See also* spin doctor.

## spin doctor
Media advisor to a politician who devises and manipulates messages to opinion formers in the media and hence voters. The phrase originates in the USA, where the science of managing the media began. One of the first spin doctors in Britain was (later Sir) Gordon Reece, who trained Margaret Thatcher in media presentation and, by accentuating her strengths and minimising her weaknesses, turned her into a formidable performer on the television. Bernard Ingham, her press secretary, became another highly respected though by many disliked figure – perhaps the inevitable fate of spin doctors. On the Labour side Peter Mandelson emerged in the 1980s as the master of the same black arts; he was able to understand the chemistry of the interaction between the media and the public and to make it work for Labour. Tony Blair's press secretary, Alastair Campbell, was another spinner in chief and his background in the tabloids gave him a special advantage. His coining of the phrase 'the people's Princess' for Blair to use in his supposedly impromptu speech after Diana's death was a perfect example of this skill in action.

During the run-up to the 2001 election there was some adverse comment about Labour's reliance on 'spin' and the feeling was widely expressed that the government relied too much on presentation and neglected delivery of promises. In a Radio 4 programme *Why Do People Hate Spin-Doctors?* (25 June 2001), Charlie Whelan, former controversial 'spinner' for chancellor

Gordon Brown, finished his presentation by unashamedly celebrating spin doctors and the role they had played in delivering a second huge majority to Labour, which would 'enable the enactment of the most radical programme of government for 50 years'. The Conservatives' communications director during the 2001 general election, Amanda Platell, was generally thought to have performed poorly and the effectiveness of Conservative media management over the previous decade was probably inferior to Labour's. Campbell was called more than once to give evidence on his role before a select committee and on each occasion did so with combative panache.

*See also* Moore's email; political communication; spin.

### sport

Harold Wilson used to suggest that he lost the 1970 election because voters blamed him for England's defeat by Germany in the World Cup soccer tournament in 1970. John Major recognised how important sport can be to the morale of the nation and did his best to support a number of sports, especially cricket. Minister of sport is a post in the Department for Culture, Media and Sport, and former cabinet minister Chris Smith argued in July 2001 that more big sporting occasions should be made available on terrestrial television and not limited to those who pay for cable television.

Sporting metaphors also pervade the political culture – for example, Harold Wilson likened his role as prime minister to a 'half-back providing the ball to the forwards to score' and Whitehall civil servants talking about 'close of play' and 'batting first' at meetings. Margaret Thatcher used to say she was 'batting for Britain' but the metaphor came back to haunt her in Geoffrey Howe's devastating resignation speech which effectively ended her tenure in power.

*See also* Department for Culture, Media and Sport; Wembley stadium.

### *Spycatcher* affair

Case involving the attempted banning in 1987 of the memoirs of a former intel-

ligence officer, Peter Wright, entitled *Spycatcher*, and elements of which breached the Official Secrets Act. In particular, he alleged that MI5 bugged and burgled its way around London, attempted to bug Number 10 Downing Street, and most sensationally of all tried to subvert the government of Harold Wilson in the mid-1960s. Legal injunctions launched by the government had the effect of banning the book and its newspaper serialisation in Britain, despite the fact that the book could be purchased in Moscow. Further action was taken against Wright in Australia and Sir Robert Armstrong, the cabinet secretary, was sent out to put the government's case. He proved to be no match for Wright's clever lawyer Malcolm Turnbull, who forced him to admit on one occasion he had lied or, in his own words, had been 'economical with the truth', a phrase that has entered the language as a serviceable synonym for lying.

*See also* Official Secrets Act; security services.

### stagflation

The combination of high inflation with high unemployment. It was once thought by economists that inflation stimulated economic growth, so that it would not be likely to cause unemployment. However, the British economy in the 1970s exhibited both record high inflation and soaring unemployment, which proved this assumption to be false.

### stakeholder society

Idea most closely associated with former *Observer* editor Will Hutton, whose book *The State We're In* (1995) became a best seller. The essence of the approach is the acceptance of a 'mutual reciprocity', that capitalism needs to be broadened from its neo-liberal individualism to encompass long-term social objectives for everyone, with rights given to citizens regarding education and training, job security and basic welfare; Germany is held up as a stakeholder society in operation. The corollary of these rights are the obligations citizens would shoulder regarding the need to create an internationally competitive economy and to save in order to minimise the welfare burden. The stakeholder society, along with communitarian ideas, was briefly hailed in the mid-1990s as Labour's 'big idea' but enthusiasm waned somewhat in the run-up to the general election in 1997, possibly because it lacked sharp definition and a clear plan for implementation.

## Stamp Act
Act passed in 1765 which attempted to raise sufficient tax from the American colonies to pay for their defence. The idea was to levy a charge ('stamp') on every publication and legal document issued in these colonies. The act was widely disobeyed and was repealed the following year but the upset caused helped precipitate the American Revolution.

## standard spending assessment (SSA)
A means of limiting local government spending through the setting of local authority grants via centrally defined calculations, introduced in 1990. This meant in effect central government was establishing the levels at which local government should spend; any spending beyond these levels constituted overspending and penalties could be applied. 'It amounts,' wrote David Wilson and Chris Game, 'to governments setting a ceiling for every council in the country, leaving locally elected politicians in the position of having the framework of their budgets, if not the detailed content, determined for them'. The Independent Audit Commission in 1993 studied the SSA and gave it only 2 marks out of 12: it was judged to be unaccountable and hard to understand.

## Standards and Privileges Committee
www.parliament.uk/commons/selcom/s&phome.htm
Commons committee set up in 1995, in the wake of the 'cash for questions' scandal, though the original function of the Members' Interests Committee was

subsumed into it. It set out the code of conduct for MPs, which was designed to assist members in discharging their duties. Complaints regarding breaches of the code are referred to the parliamentary commissioner for standards and also reported to the committee. In 2004 the committee was chaired by Sir George Young.
*See also* Committee on Standards in Public Life; parliamentary commissioner for standards; select committee.

## standards in public life
*See* Committee on Standards in Public Life; Neill committee; Nolan committee.

## standing committee
Committee established to consider a bill in detail as part of the legislative process following the second reading. Standing committees are set up afresh for each new bill and so are not really 'standing' or in any way permanent. Each comprises around 18 members and is constituted to reflect party strengths in the Commons. A bill is considered clause by clause and amendments are moved and debated, though none is allowed that is contrary to the underlying theme of the bill. If debate drags on in a partisan fashion, as it often does, the government can introduce a timetable or 'guillotine' motion, which often means the later clauses receive little or no close attention.

## Star Chamber
Originally used by medieval kings to administer their own, not always disinterested, brand of justice. In modern times the name has been attached to the cabinet committee which resolved disputes between the Treasury and spending departments. The meetings were chaired by the chief secretary to the Treasury. When John Major held this post, it was one of his boasts that the committee did not meet once, as all matters of expenditure had been resolved satisfactorily. The committee was abolished by the Blair government in 1997.

**state**
*See* nation state.

**statute law**
Term used for acts of parliament and subordinate or delegated legislation made under the authority of a 'parent' act. A distinction is made between public acts, which comprise those passed by the government of the day, as well as those initiated and piloted through by private members who have won a high place in the annual ballot, and private acts, which are prepared often by private interests, such as local authorities or private companies. Statutes may consolidate existing laws or amend them. Ultimately parliament can pass whatever law it wishes and cannot bind its potential future actions, although this has been severely curtailed by European Community law (which is superior to domestic statute law) and the European Court of Justice, as well as by devolution.

*See also* act of parliament; money bill; private bill; public bill.

**Statute of Westminster, 1931**
Enacted the decision of the 1926 Imperial Conference which gave full independence and equal status with the UK to the Dominions, namely Canada, Newfoundland, Australia, the Irish Free State, New Zealand and South Africa.

**statutory instrument**
*See* delegated legislation.

**stealth tax**
*See* indirect taxation.

**Stephen Lawrence inquiry**
*See* Macpherson report.

**Stevens inquiry, 1999– 2003**
Inquiry into allegations that collusion had occurred between the army and the police in Northern Ireland and Protestant terrorist groups to murder prominent Catholics. Foremost among the latter was Pat Finucane in 1989, a well known solicitor who defended many nationalists

against charges of terrorism. It had long been alleged that he had been murdered on army instructions, as he was too effective at doing his job. It emerged that the army Force Research Unit placed an agent, Brian Nelson, with the Ulster Defence Association, who, the report alleged, was responsible for at least 30 murders: in other words, these were state-sanctioned murders. Stevens condemned the practices he had unearthed and recommended a full review of procedures for investigating terrorist activities.

**Stormont**
After partition in 1922 the Northern Ireland parliament sat in Stormont Castle outside Belfast. After direct rule was introduced in 1972 it ceased to be used but came back into use in 1998 when the new Northern Ireland assembly was elected.

**subsidiarity**
Principle set out in Article 3b of the Maastricht Treaty (the Treaty on European Union, 1992). This was seen as providing a check on the centralising tendencies in the European Union (EU), as it stipulated that all actions that could be taken at the national level should be so taken, although the interpretation of the principle was not identical for each nation. To John Major this was a way of counteracting the fears of British Eurosceptics that a European super-state was emerging that would seriously undermine national sovereignty. In the technical language of the EU, it stated that the EU would take action 'in accordance with the subsidiarity principle, only if and in so far as the objectives of the proposed action cannot be sufficiently achieved by the Member States and can therefore, by reason of the scale or effects of the proposed action, be the better achieved by the Community'.

*See also* Maastricht Treaty.

**succession (to the throne)**
Under the Act of Succession Prince Charles will automatically become king upon his mother's death. He will not be

allowed to renounce his right to succeed
unless a special act of parliament is passed,
as in 1936. Some opinion polls have
indicated a preference from a section of the
population for Prince William to be king
and for the succession to jump a generation.
However, many have suggested that this
would be unwise, as the young prince has
already been burdened by the premature
death of his mother and is known to be
already less than enchanted with the life
of being a high-profile member of the royal
family.

## Suez crisis, 1956–57

A landmark in Britain's retreat as a world
power. It began when Egyptian leader and
pan-Arabist Colonel Nasser nationalised
the Suez Canal on 26 July 1956. The
canal had been owned by the Suez Canal
Company, controlled by British and French
interests. After abortive negotiations
Britain and France secretly conspired to
support an armed attack by Israel, the plan
being for the two European powers to intervene ostensibly as peacemakers to occupy
the canal and keep it open. Israel invaded
in October, followed by 8,000 Anglo-
French troops in November. However, the
action provoked intense dissent in Britain
and even more abroad. The USA refused
to support the initiative and threatened to
withdraw financial support for sterling on
the foreign exchanges. The military action
stopped on 6 November, western troops
were withdrawn and the United Nations
sent in a peacekeeping force. The whole
episode was a disaster for prime minister
Anthony Eden: it ruined his reputation,
his political career and his health. It also
demonstrated spectacularly how Britain's
world position had declined from the status
of a first-class world power to one almost
wholly dependent on US political and
military support.

> We are not at war with Egypt. We are in
> armed conflict. (Anthony Eden, 1956)

## suffrage

See franchise; Reform Act.

## suffragette

Campaigner for votes for women in the
early 20th century. Emmeline Pankhurst
and her daughter Christabel inspired and
led the Women's Social and Political
Union, established in 1903. It took the
First World War and the new role which it
brought women to help win them the vote
in 1918, though this was restricted to those
over 30 years of age and who met a property criterion. In 1928 all barriers between
men and women regarding the vote were
removed and there was equality.

## Sun

www.thesun.co.uk

Tabloid newspaper which emerged from
the ashes of the Labour-supporting *Daily
Herald* in 1964. It was purchased by
Rupert Murdoch, the Australian media
tycoon, who appointed Larry Lamb as it
first editor. Under the brooding tutelage
of its proprietor, Lamb established the
publication's profile as light on news and
heavy on trivia and titillation. The next
editor was the now legendary (for his
brash irreverence) Kelvin McKenzie, who
transformed the tabloid into the leading
British title, with a circulation of over 5
million per day. The political stance of the
paper was pro-Conservative in the 1970s
and 1980s, though this was probably more
a reflection of its proprietor's views. During
the Falklands War it was rabidly jingoistic,
and produced the notorious headline on 4
May 1982 'Gotcha', when the Argentinean
battle cruiser the *General Belgrano* was
sunk by the British submarine HMS
*Conqueror*. It also developed an expertise
in soft porn, with its daily topless page
three girl, and McKenzie was unafraid
of intruding into the privacy of many well
known people, especially Princess Diana.
In 1992 the *Sun* was sneeringly dismissive
of Neil Kinnock and did its best to destroy
his reputation, by using what the media
analyst Colin Seymore-Ure calls 'info-
fantasy', a mixture of comic book fantasy
and hard-hitting political comment. Other
media experts reckoned the *Sun* delivered
hundreds of thousands of votes to the

Conservatives in the election of that year, though others contest the extent of its own assessment that 'It's the *Sun* Wot Won It', delivered soon after the Conservative win. With John Major as prime minister in his second term, however, the editorial line became critical and almost as hostile as it had been to Kinnock. Murdoch and Tony Blair became friendly after 1995 and it was not too much of a surprise when, on 18 March 1997, the *Sun* came out strongly in support for Blair. Blair is said to lay great store by the good opinion of the tabloids and his former press secretary Alastair Campbell was recruited from their ranks. The honeymoon continued until 24 June 1998, when the paper ran a front-page headline 'Is this the most dangerous man in Britain?' over a picture of the prime minister, in relation to his stance on the European Union. When circulation began to dip a new editor, David Yelland, took over, with the alleged aim of taking the tabloid 'up market', to serve a supposedly increasingly sophisticated readership. During the 2001 general election the *Sun* sustained its support of New Labour but under Rebekah Wade, appointed editor in February 2003, has been more critical of the government.

### Sunningdale Agreement, 1973

A power-sharing initiative in Northern Ireland involving Catholics and Protestants but the latter bitterly opposed the part of the agreement which provided for the Council of Ireland and destroyed it by calling a general strike in the province. There were several other attempts to achieve a settlement: in 1975 (Constitutional Convention); in 1980 (Constitutional Conference); 1982 (Northern Ireland assembly); 1984 (New Ireland Forum); 1985 (Anglo-Irish Agreement). The Good Friday Agreement in 1998 is the latest attempt and so far the most promising.

### super class

Term invented by Andrew Adonis and Stephen Pollard in their book *A Class Act* (1997) to describe the new elite of top professionals and managers which is increasingly divorced from the rest of society: almost a complementary class to the 'underclass' at the bottom of society. Examples include Cedric Brown, the chief executive of British Gas who received a much publicised 75 per cent increase in his salary for running a private monopoly utility. Nick Leeson, the highflying Barings Bank trader, bankrupted his bank by reckless dealing, so that it was eventually sold for a mere £1. Nevertheless, his supervisors still received their bonuses. The authors trace the super class culture to the USA and argue it was imported during the 1980s, when it raised expectations and attracted the cream of Oxbridge graduates to go for jobs in law, accountancy or the City, rather than public service jobs like teaching or the civil service.

### supplementary vote (SV)

Electoral system similar to the alternative vote, in that the voter can record a first and second choice of candidate for a single-member constituency. If a candidate gets over half the first-preference votes then he or she is elected. If not, all but the top two are eliminated. Any second-preference votes for either of the top two candidates on the ballot papers for eliminated candidates are then duly allocated, and the person with the biggest share of the resultant vote is deemed to be elected. They system is used to elect the mayor of London.

*See also* alternative vote.

### supply-side economics

*See* monetarism.

### Supreme Court

In the USA, the highest court in the land for appeals against decisions and for interpretation of the constitution and the highest legal matters. In Britain such matters have been the preserve of the law lords in the House of Lords. Appeals must relate to a general point of law and are heard by a committee drawn from the 12 lords of appeal in ordinary. Critics of the British system have long argued for a separate arrangement whereby a Supreme Court is established; they argue that the judiciary should be independent of the legislature yet the law lords, as part of the legislature, precluded this requirement. In June 2003 critics had their way when the government declared its intention of setting up such a court, but on 5 November 2003 six of the law lords declared themselves opposed to the plan as 'unnecessary and harmful' and because 'the present system works well'. Only four of their lordships argued in favour of the proposal.

### swing

Measure used by psephologists to indicate movements in voting behaviour. It is calculated by adding the percentage of votes gained by one party to that lost by another and then dividing by two. For example, if the Conservatives lose 8 per cent at an election and Labour gain 6 per cent the average swing is half of 14 per cent, which is 7 per cent.

### swingometer

A relatively crude piece of machinery used by veteran political scientist Bob McKenzie in the 1950s and 1960s when commenting in BBC studios on general elections. It comprised a large arrow which swung to show how many seats would change hands between the parties, depending on the percentage swing from one to another. For example, a 1 per cent swing from Labour to Conservative usually indicated that 18 seats would change hands. In those early days it was easier to predict that percentage swings would be reflected across the country. During the 1970s and 1980s swings became less uniform. Moreover, television techniques advanced so that computer graphics replaced the swingometer in election coverage, which often featured the irrepressible Peter Snow using a lifelike House of Commons that would fill up with the requisite numbers of blue or red MPs, depending on swings or computer predictions.

# T

### tabloid press

These comprise the 'red tops', the *Sun*, *Daily Mirror* and *Daily Star*. The *Daily Mail* and the *Daily Express* are also tabloid size but are aimed at the so-called 'mid-market', comprising people in social class C1. The Sundays are also important, with the *News of the World*, *Sunday Mirror* and *People* shadowing the three daily tabloids. The three daily tabloids sell predominantly to C2, D and E groups. In 2002 the tabloids had over 7 million of the 13 million daily newspaper sales. The *Star* and *Sun* supported the Conservatives in 1992 and many experts believed their support, especially that of the *Sun*, swung hundreds of thousands of votes to the governing party – though such views are hotly contested by other experts. However, in the 1997 campaign a huge shift in press loyalty occurred and Rupert Murdoch's *Sun* swung behind New Labour, as did the *Star*. This meant that the previously close relationship with the tabloids no longer benefited the Conservative leadership as it had in previous elections, when the tabloids ran stories closely correlated with those of Central Office. Tony Blair's press secretary Alastair Campbell believed he was chosen for his job by Blair because 'We both acknowledge the significance to the political debate of the tabloids'. During the 2001 general election most of the tabloids supported New Labour again.

### tactical voting

When voters do not vote for the candidate of their preferred party but choose one who will most likely defeat their most disliked candidate. For example, in a seat held by a Conservative, Labour voters might choose to support the second-placed Liberal Democrat candidate as a way of defeating the Conservative. For tactical voting to take place electors usually need to have opinion poll information on which to base their calculations as to who is most likely to defeat the least wanted candidate. The practice is sometimes referred to as negative voting, in the sense that electors are not really making a positive democratic decision – they are in effect blocking or vetoing the choices of others. However, tactical voting can have important consequences. In the 1997 general election anti-Conservative tactical voting helped the Labour Party to gain a higher number of MPs (419) than it had expected, resulting in a parliamentary majority of 179. Part of this effect was the result of information published in the *Observer* before polling day. After the June 2001 general election, Peter Kellner wrote in the *Observer* that tactical voting was still significant and still hurt the Tories. In one seat Labour gained in that election, Dorset South, Ian Bruce, the sitting Conservative MP, actually increased his share of the vote but Labour's increased by much more and the Liberal Democrats' vote dropped from 20 per cent to 14 per cent. In nearby Totnes and Teignbridge it was Labour voters who switched and helped elect the Liberal Democrat candidate. Guilford and Ludlow were also gained by the Liberal Democrats through tactical voting and many of the latter party's majorities were boosted by the same effect.

### Taff Vale decision, 1901
Legal decision that badly affected the power of trade unions by making them liable for damages if sued in relation to actions by their officers. The Taff Vale Railway Company sued the railway workers' union after a strike and was awarded £23,000. This superseded the previous understanding that a union was not a legal corporation and could not be sued for the actions of its members. This decision, in the light of the Liberal Party's less than fulsome opposition, was one of the major reasons why the unions proceeded to seek independent Labour representation and to form the Labour Party.

### 'take note' motion
A motion on which the House of Lords debates reports from select committees or discusses topics on which the government would like to hear a view from the upper chamber.

### Tamworth manifesto, 1835
Election address by Robert Peel which is usually seen as the first manifesto. It is also taken to mark the emergence of the new Conservative Party from the more nebulous Tory group in parliament. Peel declared that he accepted the Reform Act of 1832 and favoured moderate reform which balanced the interests of aristocracy and commerce.

### task force
Body appointed by government to look into a particular matter, usually with a membership of civil servants and experts. New Labour came into office in 1997 with a flurry of task force creation in response to a myriad of different topics. Two hundred and thirty-eight such bodies had been set up within two years, and these employed a total of 1,500 people. Not all the task forces reported on time and their proliferation attracted much dubious comment and a feeling that they were an excuse for failing to deal with the issues in question. There was a task force on Near Earth Asteroids and Comets which reported in 2001 and a Northern Ireland Organised Crime Task Force was set up in 2000.

### taxation
The means whereby the government raises money in order for it to be able to provide services (public goods) such as the armed forces, education and the National Health Service. Income tax is a direct form of taxation which was first introduced in 1799. During the Second World War the standard rate rose to 50 per cent but the Conservatives brought it down gradually when in power to 23 pence in the pound by 1997. In 1998 it brought in £84.3 billion, or around a quarter of the £330.2 billion total expenditure. Corporation tax is a direct tax on company profits and brings in around £30 billion each year.

Indirect taxation, mainly value added tax (VAT), is preferred by the Conservatives, as taxpayers tend not to notice it as much as money deducted from wage packets. It is paid on the value added to a product at every stage of the production or distribution process. In 1998 it brought in £53.3 billion. Other forms of indirect taxation include the duties on goods like alcohol and tobacco – worth about £17 billion a year – and fuel excise duty, worth £21.5 billion in 1998. In the 1992 general election the Conservatives were able to alarm the voters into thinking Labour would put up taxation by large amounts, as they had done in the past to fund high government spending. When Labour lost that election the party decided to pursue a policy of low direct taxation and in 1997 promised not to increase spending above the Conservative level for at least two years into the next government.

Taxation is also one of the tools of macro-economic management and fiscal policy, although since the 1980s its role in this respect has largely been replaced by interest rates. Traditionally Labour governments have attempted to redistribute wealth by taxing higher earners and using the receipts to finance social security or other benefits, although New Labour claimed to have abandoned a policy of 'tax and spend'. Instead, the party sought to extract more revenue via indirect taxes such as the excise duty on petrol, which was bitterly criticised when the price of oil rose sharply in 2000 and again in 2004 (as some 75 per cent of the cost of petrol went to the exchequer). The Conservatives made much of these 'stealth' taxes in the run-up to the 2001 general election, claiming there had been 45 tax increases since 1997. Many critics of New Labour felt the party should have braved the consequences of supporting higher taxation during the 2001 election campaign. However, Labour chose not to and still adhered to a low-tax regime, despite the need to generate more income towards the end of its second term to fund its spending plans. The Liberal Democrats won some praise during their campaign for openly advocating higher taxes to fund public services.

*See also* income tax; indirect taxation; value added tax.

### televised debate
In the USA televised debates have long been a feature of presidential election contests. In Britain, however, there has never been a formal televised debate between a prime minister and a leader of the opposition in a general election campaign. The incumbent prime minister has generally shied away from giving opponents any advantage, though in 1997 John Major suggested such a confrontation as he was running behind Tony Blair and felt he had nothing to lose. In the 2001 general election campaign there were hopes a debate might be arranged but they foundered on the issue of participation by the Liberal Democrats, which the Conservatives felt would result in them being faced by two opponents instead of one.

### televising of parliament
First proposed in 1966 but then heavily defeated. While radio coverage was introduced into both houses in 1978 and television into the Lords in 1985, the Commons refused on the grounds that such a presence would destroy the unique, intimate atmosphere of the place. But opinion changed. If Margaret Thatcher had not been opposed, it would have become a reality before 2 November 1989, when the cameras, subject to various restrictions, were coyly allowed onto the floor of the 'mother of parliaments'. In January 1990 many of the restrictions were relaxed; in July of that year the Commons voted 131 to 32 to make the arrangement permanent.

### television
John Logie Baird's 1920s invention came into production in the 1930s. Television broadcasts were ceased during the Second World War and television was still secondary to radio after it. The 1953 coronation was the catalyst for television in Britain

and politicians realised its potential at about the same time. Winston Churchill had already appeared on US television, aboard the *Queen Mary* in 1951; later he agreed that cameras should televise his 80th birthday celebrations in Westminster Hall. In 1954 he took part in a secret television screen test at Number 10; the results were not positive, as he did not suit the medium. Harold Macmillan was arguably the first cleverly to exploit the medium, soon followed by Harold Wilson. After 1959 all election campaigns concentrated much expense and energy on transmitting political messages via the television sets most families owned. The BBC's monopoly was broken in the 1950s with the arrival of independent television. Prominent interviewers like Robin Day began to structure the coverage the medium gave to politics. Broadcasts became controversial; for example, Wilson objected bitterly to the BBC programme *Yesterday's Men*, on the Labour Party, produced in 1971. In the 1970s politicians began to take television even more seriously and Margaret Thatcher benefited from the services of a 'spin doctor', Gordon Reece, in adjusting her presentation to television. During election campaigns politicians try their best to make an impression in news bulletins with well turned sound bites.

## 10 Downing Street

www.number-10.gov.uk
Official London home of British prime ministers since the time of Robert Walpole. It is located in a row of 17th-century houses in Westminster. Number 11 is the home of the chancellor of the exchequer. The street is named after Sir George Downing (1623–84), who was an early secretary to the Treasury. In 1997 Tony Blair swapped sleeping accommodation with his chancellor neighbour Gordon Brown, as Number 10 had insufficient room for his three (later four) children. Portraits of all former prime ministers adorn the walls of Number 10,; a space awaits Tony Blair when he vacates the building.

*See also* prime minister's department.

## 10-minute rule bill

One of the methods whereby back-bench MPs can initiate legislation in the Commons. Revived in 1950, this device enables members to introduce a bill after question time on Tuesdays and Wednesdays, with a speech not exceeding 10 minutes. A speech of equal length is allowed in opposition and then the bill is put; if it is unopposed or passed it can progress further. The procedure is available to those MPs who are first in a queue at the Public Bill Office; it is valued in that the House is usually well attended for question time. The bill to abolish the death penalty and that which legalised homosexual acts were both introduced in this way.

## terrorism

A pejorative term used by state authorities and mainstream media to describe those 'extremist' and violent groups that they oppose and accuse of not subscribing to the liberal democratic consensus. However, these groups or their representatives may cross the line and sign up to democratic principles, and thus be rehabilitated by state authorities as recognised politicians, an example of this being Britain's recognition of former 'terrorists' as legitimate representatives of the people in Ireland, Cyprus, Palestine and, more recently, Northern Ireland. Political conflict in Britain is for the most part channelled through the system of parliamentary democracy and the operation of pressure groups in the policy-making process. However, the 'troubles' in Northern Ireland are a sharp reminder that this is not always the case and that some demands cannot be accommodated within the British political system.

*See also* Afghanistan; 9/11, 2001; Northern Ireland.

## Terrorism Act 2000

Came into force in February 2001 and replaced a range of temporary legislation relating to Britain and Northern Ireland. It gave, among other things:
1  a new definition of terrorism;
2  new powers to seize suspects at borders;

3  a new offence of inciting terrorism
   abroad from within Britain;
4  new extensions of rights to detain
   suspected terrorists;
5  a new offence of training terrorists.

### Terrorism Act 2001
Piece of legislation that complemented
the Terrorism Act 2000. It was passed in
December 2001 in the wake of the attacks
on the USA on 11 September 2001.
Its main provision was for the indefinite
detention of suspected terrorists but it also
contained clauses on the incitement of
religious hatred, hoax threats of terrorist
action, aiding the development of chemical,
nuclear, biological or radiological weapons,
the withholding of information regarding a
terrorist attack, refusing police requests to
remove hand and face coverings in public
order situations, and the financial support
of terrorist activities. The new act was
much criticised for its alleged breach of civil
rights and encountered difficulties during
its passage through the House of Lords.

### Thatcherism
Margaret Thatcher is one of the few prime
ministers to have an 'ism' attached to her
name. Her ideas were so clear and consistent everyone in government and probably
most voters understood them and either
loved or loathed them, as they did their
author. In essence Thatcherism reasserted
classical liberalism with traditional political authority, delivered in a populist and
assertive style of leadership. A set of policy
orientations, which later became known as
Thatcherism, were developed around this
ideological framework, and included:
1  tight control of the money supply to
   control inflation;
2  the notion that individual freedom is
   inseparable from the free enterprise
   economy;
3  the idea that market forces work
   automatically for the benefit of all;
4  the belief that capitalism works, and that
   state intervention destroys freedom and
   efficiency;
5  the belief that trade union power

endangers competitiveness and the
government's ability to run the country
in the interests of all;
6  the idea that state welfare is excessive,
   inefficient and saps the self-reliance of
   those who depend upon it.

Perhaps its greatest achievement was
to reshape the political terrain of Britain
and with it the Labour Party. Thatcher
continued to exert influence over the
rank and file of the Conservative Party
even after her departure from office; her
presence at the 1999 conference helped
to reinforce the rightward shift made by
William Hague towards the 'commonsense
revolution'. She also appeared prominently
during the 2001 general election campaign.
Experts considered the rightward shift
of the Conservatives to be a bad mistake
and that it ensured another beating at the
polls, and the presence of the former prime
minister during the campaign as another
mistake as she tended to speak 'off message'
and to remind voters of unhappy aspects
of her period in office. Others believed
Tony Blair's second general election victory
enabled him to move out from under the
shadow of Thatcherism, many of whose
tenets he had espoused in government. He
has made no secret of his admiration for the
formidable former Conservative leader.
  *See also* classical liberalism.

### think tank
A research and development organisation
which brings together academics, techno-
crats and politicians who wish to advance a
specific policy or ideological agenda. Think
tanks are often associated with the USA,
where there are more than 1,000 non-profit
political research institutes, with 100 based
around Washington, DC. Britain, however,
has had think tanks for over a century. Two
of the first were the Fabian Society (1884)
and the more academic Royal Institute of
International Affairs (1920). In the 1930s
two more, both academically orientated,
emerged: the Policy Studies Institute (PSI)
and the National Institute for Economic
and Social Research (NIESR). In the
1950s the first right-wing organisation,

POLITICS

the Institute of Economic Affairs (IEA), was founded, followed in the 1970s by the Centre for Policy Studies, the Adam Smith Institute and the Policy Studies Institute. In the 1980s the left contributed with the Institute for Public Policy Research (IPPR). In the 1980s and 1990s some more left-wing think tanks were founded, including Demos, the think tank closest to the Labour Party. In September 1996 the Centre for European Reform was set up by David Miliband, a member of the Downing Street Policy Unit (and minister after 2001). In the autumn of 1997 the Smith Institute was set up with chancellor Gordon Brown's support in honour of the former Labour Party leader John Smith. Robin Cook at the Foreign Office also got in on the act with the Foreign Policy Centre. All these recent think tanks were set up by New Labour but Catalyst is more in the Old Labour camp, with Lord Hattersley as the head of its editorial board. Unlike the Conservatives, who used them to prepare for their period in power, the Labour Party seemed in 1997 to have got into power first and then looked to the think tanks for ideas. During the early part of Labour's second term the think tank closest to the Labour government was the IPPR and its report on public–private partnerships caused controversy in June 2001.

### third-party voting

Voting for any party other than the two main ones in Britain's first past the post electoral system. Just after the Second World War the Liberal Party attracted only a fraction of the popular vote and the two big parties commanded 95 per cent. By the 1980s third-party voting had increased to over 20 per cent and in 1983 the Alliance polled 26 per cent for a mere 3.5 per cent (23) of the seats, strengthening the argument for electoral reform. Since then the nationalist parties have continued to prosper, though the voting system does not so severely penalise small parties where their vote is geographically concentrated.

*See also* tactical voting.

### third reading
*See* act of parliament; legislative process.

### third way

Term associated with Tony Blair's approach to politics, sometimes referred to as 'Blairism'. In September 1998 Blair published a Fabian pamphlet called *The Third Way*; it was an attempt to characterise his approach as neither old socialist nor Conservative, but a distinctively radical third direction. The pamphlet was received with doubt in most political circles. Critics claim that the third way was merely a clever piece of political pragmatism, in that it targeted disillusioned middle-class voters with a repackaged version of somewhat moderated Conservative economic policies. Supporters of third way politics suggest that Blair has a core of beliefs which qualify him as a progenitor of a new political movement. Moreover, these beliefs have found echoes in the work of social and political commentators such as Amitai Etzioni and Anthony Giddens, as well as the New Democrat thinking of Bill Clinton and the ideas of German chancellor Gerhard Schroeder. The third way is best understood as a set of themes or propositions:

1  It recognises that globalisation and new technology have created a world of rapid change, which requires new thinking and the application of treasured values in new ways.
2  It synthesises the best of old left and new right ideologies to meet the challenges of today. In particular, it combines the efficiencies of dynamic markets with social justice and inclusion.
3  It employs pragmatic and technological managerialism – third way thinking emphasises 'delivery' and it therefore follows that what matters is not public or private sector provision, but the quality of the provision, however sourced. (New Labour in office has indeed used the public, private and voluntary sectors, and various mixtures of all three at once, in the delivery of public services.)
4  It does not take a mechanistic view of the state as too big (new right) or too

small (old left), but rather asks whether it is doing enough in terms of regulation or policy initiatives, for example in the area of pensions or encouraging parental responsibility. It has become well known in Whitehall that Blair believes essentially in the 'non-ideological' notion of 'what works'.

5  It asserts that both the state and the market should serve the public interest. Citizens should expect high-quality services from both public and private sectors, which should serve the community fairly, efficiently and effectively. Thus, if market providers treat their workers unfairly or engage in uncompetitive practices, then reform should take place. Equally, if public services are inefficient, or do not respond to the needs of those they are there to serve, then government should bring about change.

6  It emphasises social inclusion. The third way rejects the idea that individuals have only themselves to blame for lack of success in life; it therefore insists that all have access to the full range of life resources, including health, income, work, education and public order. However, it also rejects the idea of equality of outcomes, where individual effort or merit is not recognised by additional income, social status or other rewards.

7  It offers a new contract between citizen and state. The third way emphasises the interdependence of individuals, groups and the state, each type of actor having rights but also obligations or responsibilities. Thus the state has a duty to provide work, or pathways into work or training, but equally the citizen is expected to take advantage of these opportunities, not only for individual improvement but also as a responsible citizen who has a duty to contribute towards society and the economy.

8  It also offers a new vision of politics. Third way thinking seeks to influence the political landscape, as did the Conservatives did in the early 1980s. It seeks to reshape the political agenda and establish a new consensus between all major political parties, and in so doing contribute to the governance of modern British society. In this sense Blair's third way has a powerful ideological agenda.

On 26 March 2002 'Bagehot' (David Lipsey) in *The Economist* wrote a valedictory piece in which he saw Blair's achievement through slightly different eyes: 'By turning Labour into New Labour, abandoning socialism, befriending business and promising not to squeeze the rich, Mr Blair has done more than build an election winning party. He has broken the tribal pattern of British politics in just the way the Social Democrats who broke from Labour in the 1980s hoped but failed to.… By finally breaking the old relationship between Labour and the interests it was created to represent, Mr Blair has twisted the whole of British politics into a new shape. It is the system he broke rather than the machine he built that makes his premiership so interesting.'

> The third way has been tested in the cauldron; those principles are still valid. However, some of the softer edges have been shown to be flaky. (Stephen Byers, *Guardian*, 14 January 2002)

*See also* political language.

## three-day week, 1974

A rationing of energy to industry announced by Edward Heath in January 1974 in an attempt to conserve energy. Supplies were being threatened by: the oil crisis caused by the price hikes determined by the Organization of Petroleum Exporting Countries; the industrial action of the miners' union; and the winter weather. The measure caused an atmosphere of crisis in the country but industrial production did not decrease initially – an indication of the degree of overstaffing which characterised British industry at that time. In February Heath called an election on the theme of 'Who Governs Britain?', which he lost, thus ending his time in Downing Street and setting the scene for the emergence of Margaret Thatcher.

*See also* miners' strikes, 1972 and 1974.

### three-line whip

Written instruction issued to MPs by the whips' office with three underlinings to indicate that voting for the party line on a debate is mandatory.

### Times, The

www.timesonline.co.uk
Daily newspaper nicknamed the 'Thunderer'. It was founded in 1785 as the *Daily Universal Register* and became *The Times* in 1788. It was owned by Lord Northcliffe from 1908 and then by J. Astor after 1922. The Thomson Organisation bought it in 1966 and then Rupert Murdoch's News International in 1981. *The Times* has always been the mouthpiece of the establishment and has pursued an independent Conservative line on most major issues. Murdoch lowered the price of the newspaper in the 1990s in an attempt to put the *Independent* out of business and to hurt the *Daily Telegraph*. *The Times* backed Labour for the first time in a general election in 2001.

### *Today* programme

www.bbc.co.uk/radio4/today
Early-morning Radio 4 programme introduced during the 1970s that has become something of a national institution. It commands an audience of over a million, who include many of the nation's political elite. Its presenters – the most well known of whom include John Humphrys, James Naughtie and (before her retirement in 2002) Sue McGregor – are famous for the tenacity of their interrogations and are regularly criticised for being rude or for interrupting excessively. In April 2002 the general secretary of the Labour Party, David Triesman, criticised the programme for allegedly treating politicians as if they were 'consummate liars trying to line their own pockets'. He went on to blame this tendency for encouraging disengagement from politics and apathy. Rod Liddle, the then editor of the programme, denied such a tendency and insisted '*Today* listeners expect to hear politicians challenged'. Margaret Thatcher, when prime minister,

once famously rang up the programme to comment live on something which she had just heard. On 29 May 2003, *Today* reporter Andrew Gilligan in a live interview accused Downing Street of embellishing the dossier on Iraqi weapons published by the government in September 2002, saying that the threat posed by Iraqi weapons of mass destruction (WMD) was exaggerated in order to justify the government's backing of the US policy of invading Iraq. This triggered the biggest crisis ever in relations between the BBC and the government.

### toleration

John Locke was the liberal philosopher in an age of religious conflict who advocated the advantages of toleration and compromise over dogmatism and conflict. British political culture has allegedly been characterised by a strong element of toleration ever since, though examples of racist bigotry and closed minds over a whole range of issues are not difficult to find and are revealed regularly in opinion surveys.

### top-up fee

Variable charge on students for their further education. This proposal caused much dissension in the Labour Party in the autumn of 2003 and was opposed, for example, by Estelle Morris when she was in charge of education. The proposal was to allow universities to increase the fees charged to students from just over £1,000 to £3,000. The condition was that they were to make special efforts to encourage students from disadvantaged homes. The key difference was that the funds raised were to go direct to the parent institution and not via the Treasury. Opponents argued that such a dispensation would allow elite universities to charge more and would open the way for variable salaries for academics instead of universal rates.

### Tory

The word was probably derived from Irish term *toraidhe*, meaning a brigand, cattle thief or outlaw. It was applied to supporters of the Duke of York (James II) in the 'exclusion crisis' of 1679–81, when great political energies were directed towards the exclusion of the Catholic son of Charles II from the succession. The Whigs supported exclusion whereas their opponents became associated with support for the Church and the king, and included many squires and large landowners. They were excluded from power by George I and George II for most of the 18th century, but George III decided to favour them. The French Revolution strengthened Tory principles and therefore their political profile in Britain. The term was still used abusively by Whigs to describe their opponents but gradually it came to be accepted as a non-pejorative term, especially after the Tory Benjamin Disraeli used it. Robert Peel preferred the term Conservative when he reorganised the party after the Great Reform Act of 1832 and the two terms are now used interchangeably, with the former being favoured by the right wing for its historical connotations.

## Tory Action

Right-wing grouping, active in the 1970s and 1980s, led by a former head of MI6, George Young. It held views on immigration close to those of the Monday Club and claimed to have several hundred members, who included about a dozen Tory MPs.
    See also Monday Club.

## Tory Reform Group

www.trg.org.uk
Set up in 1975 to defend the 'one nation' tradition within the Conservative Party, which was under fire from the new right. In the early 1990s it had around two dozen MP members.

## 'tough on crime, tough on the causes of crime'

Tony Blair sound bite produced when he was shadow home secretary in 1994. It was especially clever in that it combined the essence of 'Old' Labour's approach – that crime reflected an unjust social system – with the more populist and voter-sensitive New Labour: that criminals should be caught and punished, possibly severely.

## Trade Union and Labour Party Liaison Organisation (TULO)

www.labour.org.uk/tuloindex
Organisation established in 1994 that links nationally affiliated unions (currently 20) with the party. On 6 August 2004 TULO negotiated a series of commitments to the public services from Labour in exchange for continuing union support for the party. They included extending workforce protection in local government across all public services, an agreement to tackle unequal pay in local government and a commitment not to extend selection by ability in schools.

## trade unionism

Emerged in the 18th century with the appearance of mutual self-help organisations mostly for skilled workers. With the industrial revolution workers became more easily organised, especially in the 19th century, but employers were hostile and the Combination Acts (1799–1825) made trade union membership a serious criminal offence. The 'new model unions', which developed in the late 19th century, were reluctant to strike and sought rational settlement of disputes through negotiation rather than direct action. Membership grew in times of prosperity and slumped in depressions. In the 1920s the Transport and General Workers' Union (TGWU) had a third of a million members; by the mid-1970s this had grown to 2 million though it had slumped back to under 1 million by 2001. During the 1970s unions were instrumental in the fall of Ted Heath's government (1974) and it was said quite seriously that Hugh Scanlon of the Amalgamated Union of Engineering Workers and Jack Jones of the TGWU were the two most powerful men in Britain. Margaret Thatcher came to power determined to reduce their power for political and economic reasons. The sharp rise in unemployment in the early 1980s weakened the hands of unions, in that workers prove to be less willing to strike when their jobs are at risk. Legislation designed to make industrial action more difficult also contributed to their decline, but the single

POLITICS

most effective blow was the failure of the protracted miners' strike of 1984–85. Union membership slumped in the 1980s from 12 million to just over 7 million and the national political role they had played under Labour administrations had long since vanished. Under Tony Blair the unions were promised 'fairness not favours' and were lectured at the annual conference of the Trades Union Congress (TUC) on the need for modernisation by him in 1997 and by Peter Mandelson in 1998. On 1 July 2002 the *Observer* carried a report that Bill Morris of the TGWU was about to reach an agreement with the Liberal Democrats in coordinating opposition to the government's plans to increase the role of the private sector in the public services.

Several new union leaders surfaced during the early part of 2002 who threatened to be the 'awkward squad'. Tony Blair had himself blamed 'wreckers' for preventing his attempted reforms of the public sector at a conference in January 2002. It was clear to most observers that his later claim that he had meant the Conservatives was disingenuous – he had also meant those union leaders who disagreed with him. On 18 February 2002 the *Guardian* identified six members of this 'awkward squad': Dave Prentis of Unison, Britain's biggest union; Billy Hayes of the Communication Workers' Union (CWU); Mark Serwotka of the civil service union (PCS); Mick Rix of the Associated Society of Locomotive Engineers and Firemen (ASLEF); Bob Crowe of the RMT; and Andy Gilchrist of the Fire Brigades Union (FBU).

Unions are especially strong in the public sector; 60 per cent of this workforce are unionised compared with 19 per cent in the private sector. More surprising is that middle-class workers are more unionised than blue-collar workers. Younger workers seem apathetic regarding joining unions as well as political parties: only 18 per cent of the 18–29 age group are members of unions.

*See also* awkward squad; industrial relations; Trade Union and Labour Party Liaison Organisation; Trades Union Congress; unemployment.

## Trades Disputes Acts 1906 and 1927

The 1906 act removed the legal liability of unions for the actions of their members, thus reversing the legal significance of the Taff Vale decision of 1901. A further act passed in 1927, after the General Strike, banned general strikes and civil servants joining unions affiliated to the Trades Union Congress. It also required a positive decision on the part of members to 'contract in' to make financial contributions the Labour Party via union dues, rather than the automatic deduction which applied before the act. The result deprived the party of about one-third of its financial support until 1945, when the measure was reversed. Norman Tebbit's Employment Act 1983 required ballots to be held by trade unions to decide whether their members wished a political levy to be passed on to the Labour Party. In the event most union memberships confirmed the political contribution.

*See also* Taff Vale decision.

## Trades Union Congress (TUC)

www.tuc.org.uk

Founded in Manchester in 1868 to organise union activity more effectively and to hold annual conferences. Initially it involved only skilled workers but it grew in the later part of the 19th century as union activity increased. By 1900 it represented over 250,000 workers and by 1914 this figure had risen sharply, to 2.5 million. Militant activity during the First World War helped to increase membership to 6 million by 1920. The TUC was damaged by the failure of the General Strike in 1926, which discouraged it from politically related activity separate from its Labour links. During the Second World War union influence grew as leaders cooperated with government; Ernest Bevin, for example, who had been general secretary of the Transport and General Workers' Union before the war, became minister of labour in the wartime coalition government and a household name. Membership rose to over 8 million. Thereafter the TUC became for a time one of the 'estates of the realm' and was consulted and listened to as a matter of course. In the 1970s, however, union power was generally believed to be excessive and against the public interest. The 'winter of discontent' of 1978–79 was the culmination of this disaffection and Margaret Thatcher found a country not unreceptive to her measures to curb the trade unions during the 1980s. By the 1990s the TUC seemed to have accepted the legal framework created by the Conservatives (together with ballots for strikes and political donations) as normal. Its general secretary, John Monks, set about reforming the TUC's structure in the 1990s.

The TUC has a General Council and a body of officers who help coordinate union activity and resolve disputes. An annual conference is organised for each September. Following Labour's 2001 general election victory, trade union representatives visited Tony Blair in Downing Street in late June and frankly stated their hostility to attempts to introduce more private sector involvement in the public sector. He listened sympathetically but refused to move from his reform agenda. He did the same at Labour's spring conference, held in February 2002. On 3 July 2001, the *Guardian* reported that Blair would be seeing the unions 'five or six times a year' in order to defuse the growing conflict between the government and Labour's main donors. In 2004 the TUC had 71 unions affiliated and nearly 7 million members.

*See also* Trade Union and Labour Party Liaison Organisation (TULO); trade unionism.

## Transco
www.transco.uk.com
Privatised monopoly which owns the gas distribution network. It has come in for much criticism for poor maintenance and in June 2001 the Health and Safety Executive insisted Transco replace its mains equipment in Batley after an explosion killed a whole family. Clare Spottiswoode, the former gas regulator, accused the company of playing the game of demanding investment, not spending it and then giving it to shareholders in dividends.

## Transport and General Workers' Union (TGWU)
www.tgwu.org.uk
Formed from a merger of unions in 1922. It represents workers mostly in manual occupations in transport, construction, the public sector and agriculture. It has a famous history as the union once led by Ernest Bevin and has played an important role in Labour Party history, sometimes as a bastion of the right, for example under Bevin, and at other times of the left, for instance when Jack Jones was leader in the 1970s. In 2001 the leader was Bill Morris, who has been generally supportive of New Labour but has also been outspoken in his criticisms. The TGWU is now the second largest union after the public sector union Unison, and has a membership of just under 1 million.

### transport policy
Mobility has increased exponentially from 291 billion passenger kilometres in 1952 to 681 billion in 1992. The Department for Transport is responsible for the country's 2,700 km of motorways and 7,800 km of trunk roads. Strategic planning is undertaken by the core but maintenance and construction is undertaken by the Highways Agency. In 1997 it was included in deputy prime minister John Prescott's Department of Environment, Transport and the Regions. During his stewardship transport policy seemed to move against the car and in favour of public transport but this shift was not sustained in practice and environmentalists criticised Labour for not fulfilling promises. In September 1999 a poll revealed that 65 per cent of respondents felt the government had not improved public transport. In a poll published on 18 July 2001, two-thirds of respondents were in favour of paying more in tax in exchange for better public transport. Two-fifths ranked transport as their 'major' local issue, higher even than crime. Fifty-four per cent backed congestion charging, provided the money raised was ploughed back into transport improvements.

In 1997 the government promised a renaissance in public transport but by 2001 figures for the previous year indicated an increase in the miles travelled by motorists compared with the previous year. Given the number of vehicles on the road even a small increase in journeys brings about incalculable jams and related traffic problems. Experts argued that problems would continue to increase as long as motoring costs continued to fall and public transport costs to increase. Green groups accused the government of reneging on its promises, citing in evidence the new motorway projects initiated in 2001.

> Britain spends half as much on public transport as Germany, France and Italy. We have also some of the highest bus and train fares. Ageing rolling stock, vandalised buses and a Tube system where summer temperatures exceed the legal limit for transporting live animals make public transport the last resort for more and more commuters. (*Observer*, 31 March 2002)

> I will have failed if in five years there are not many more people using public transport and far fewer car journeys. It is a tall order but I want you to hold me to it. (John Prescott, 1997)

> If the railways don't improve, I take the blame – fine. At the next election I'm going to be judged by the quality of our travelling experience. (Stephen Byers, 14 January 2002; he was sacked later in the year)

*See also* Department for Transport; Network Rail.

## Treason and Felony Act 1848

Passed at a time when European capitals were being rocked by revolution and London by a surge in Irish nationalism. The act sought to make criticism of the monarchy in print an offence punishable by life imprisonment. Several prosecutions were made in the 19th century – especially against editors in Dublin – but none has been made since 1883, though historians judge it had a 'chilling effect' on the British press during Victoria's reign and inhibited open statements of republicanism into the 20th century. In June 2001 the editor of the

*Guardian* attempted to challenge the law and to claim it violated the Human Rights Act. Two senior law lords replied that the application for judicial review could not be allowed, though the reasoning was largely technical.

## Treasury

www.hm-treasury.gov.uk
The government department with responsibility for the economy. The Treasury has its origins in medieval times; since the 18th century the chancellor of the exchequer has been its senior member. By the 20th century it had become the most important department in the government and its head second in the hierarchy of importance. Its aims are: to provide the monetary and fiscal conditions necessary for continued economic growth; to run a stable financial system; to balance spending with taxation revenue; to advance Britain's overseas financial interests; and to manage the pay, conditions of service and industrial relations of the civil service. The Treasury has interests in all departments and especially big spending ones like defence and health. It constantly seeks to control public expenditure and consequently has few friends in the Whitehall spending departments. The Treasury also monitors 'delivery' of service – the mantra of Tony Blair's second term. It agrees performance targets with all the other government departments and does its best to ensure they keep to their side of these agreements. The Treasury also negotiates 'public service agreements' with departments, which are a collection of agreed targets for departments, agencies and local councils.

## Treaty of Accession, 1972

The treaty signed by prime minister Edward Heath in 1972 whereby the United Kingdom became a member of the European Community as of 1 January 1973.

## Treaty of Rome, 1957

The treaty which founded the European Economic Community. It was explicitly aimed at establishing institutions which would encourage the integration of Europe, in accordance with the wishes of its founding fathers Jean Monnet, Robert Schuman, Paul Spaak and others. The treaty was signed 25 March 1957 and it established the European Economic Community (the Common Market). There was also another Treaty of Rome of the same year, which set up the European Atomic Energy Community (Euratom). Once ratified by member parliaments the treaties came into force on 1 January 1958.

## Treaty on European Union, 1992
*See* Maastricht Treaty.

## triangulation
Name given to the US Democrats' strategy under Bill Clinton of 'neutralising' controversial policy areas by adopting positions which were midway between traditional Democratic ones and the Republican equivalent. It has been suggested that New Labour adopted a similar approach. Nick Cohen in his book *Pretty Straight Guys* (2004) suggested an example was New Labour policy on asylum seekers, which emerged as an issue on which the Conservatives were strong in the run-up to the 2001 general election, as Labour decided to be 'as nasty or nastier still' than the Conservatives. He concluded the result of triangulation of policies for the Labour Party was to move the political spectrum consistently rightwards.

## tribunal
An important quasi-judicial means of redressing a grievance. There are 68 tribunals, which decide, according to the *Times Guide to the New British State* (1995), on the 'rights and obligations of individuals to each other and to the state'. According to the *Guide* they are part of the 'peripheral state' and constitute non-departmental public bodies (NDPBs). They all have 'quasi-judicial powers in a specialised field of law', are served by over 22,000 appointees and include the Social Security Appeal Tribunal, the Disability

Appeals Tribunal and the Value Added Tax Tribunal. Probably the best known, however, are the employment tribunals. Applications to these – on issues such as unfair dismissal, discrimination and pay – have been increasing in recent years and the Confederation of British Industry was keen to reduce their role, as the average cost of defending a case for an employer is £2,000 per case plus 27 hours of management time. The Department of Trade and Industry proposed in 2001 that a charge be made of £100 for each applicant, in the hope that this would deter applications and produce a revenue stream of £12 million a year. However, exemptions would have reduced this amount substantially and there was such passionate opposition from MPs with union connections (and because the government was keen to appease the unions over the contentious involvement of the private sector in public services) that the proposal was dropped.

## *Tribune*
www.tribweb.co.uk
Socialist weekly newspaper founded in 1936 by wealthy Labour MP George Strauss and the socialist barrister and future chancellor Stafford Cripps, to advance the arguments for a popular front against fascism. Before the war it fell under the control of 'fellow travellers', who were communists in all but name, but was then edited by Aneurin Bevan and later by Michael Foot. The circulation of the journal was not great but it appealed to working-class socialists and received contributions from the likes of George Orwell, Barbara Castle and Ian Mikardo, as well as Cripps himself. After the war it gave its name to a group of left-wing MPs associated with Michael Foot initially and then Neil Kinnock. The group of MPs is no longer important but the publication *Tribune* still continues to play a role and might even be said to have offered a critical yet supportive voice to Tony Blair.

## tripartism
Term used to describe the close cooperation between government, employers'

POLITICS

organisations and trade unions from the 1950s to the 1980s. In 1961 the Conservative government created the National Economic Development Council (NEDC, or Neddy), a forum which included representatives of employers, trade unions and government. It met regularly to consider ways of improving economic growth. In the 1970s with the Social Contract some commentators predicted Britain was moving in the same direction as Germany: a corporate state or 'tripartism'. However, the Social Contract ended in the 'winter of discontent'. Critics saw tripartism as a form of undemocratic corporatism which excluded parliament and other interests, and Margaret Thatcher would have no truck with Neddies of any kind, although it was left to John Major to abolish it in April 1993.

See also corporatism.

### Trotskyism

The ideas associated with the Russian revolutionary Leon Trotsky. He urged a state of 'permanent revolution' as a means of achieving the fall of capitalism worldwide. Stalin had him assassinated in 1940. Followers of Trotsky sought to influence the Labour Party in the 1960s. Ted Grant had been a member of the Revolutionary Communist Party, which eventually transformed into the Revolutionary Socialist League. He joined up with Peter Taafe in Liverpool in 1964 and together they set up a newspaper called *Militant* and devised the tactic of entryism. This entailed members of their group joining a constituency Labour party and then attempting to take it over for the faction, to pursue left-wing policies. The ultimate hope was to lead the imminent revolution and direct it towards a Trotskyist vision of society. The activities of Militant were effectively countered during the 1980s and whatever Trotskyist activity continues in Britain is not very politically visible.

See also Militant Tendency.

### trust

Clearly, voters' trust in the government is a key factor in determining electoral success as well as, more generally, electoral turnout. Trust became a key issue under Tony Blair in the wake of the Iraq war, when he appeared to many to be not telling the truth. The *Observer* (15 February 2004) published a review of trust and the Blair government which revealed that, in the wake of the Hutton report on the death of Iraqi weapons expert Dr David Kelly, 54 per cent thought Blair had 'lied to the nation' over the threat posed by Iraq. In September 2003, 35 per cent of those polled thought Blair was trustworthy, while 58 per cent thought him untrustworthy. However, as pollster Bob Worcester pointed out, the matching figures for September 2000 were 37 and 56 per cent, respectively – and yet he still went on to win a landslide in the 2001 general election. Only 18 per cent of people in February 2004 thought politicians could be trusted.

> Trust you lose precipitately and regain glacially. You regain it by evidence, you cannot do it by rhetoric. (Bob Worcester, *Observer*, 15 February 2004)

### turnout

The percentage of registered voters who exercise their right and cast a vote (or spoil their ballot paper) in an election. Political scientists use turnout as one of the indicators of citizens' political participation in a nation's political system. It is also evidence for the degree of legitimacy that a system of government enjoys from the population. The performance of Britain in these respects is mixed. Turnout in British general elections is generally high, averaging around 70 per cent until the 1990s, although the figure has, on a trend, been falling since 1945. However, figures for local government contests and elections to the European parliament are far lower: in the 1999 European elections under 25 per cent of those registered to vote actually did so, though in 2004, with the assistance of postal voting, turnout was up to 39 per cent. Despite this, voting still remains, at least in Britain, one of the most significant ways by which citizens participate in the political life of their country. In the 2001 general election the turnout was the lowest since the birth of liberal democracy, at 59.2 per cent. (Although turnout was lower in 1918, those figures were distorted by the majority of voters who were voting for the first time.)

See also apathy; political participation.

## two-party system
See party system.

# U

## Ulster
See Northern Ireland.

## Ulster Defence Association (UDA)
Launched in 1971 (effectively as an umbrella organisation for such groups as the Ulster Freedom Fighters) in Belfast to protect Protestants from IRA violence. Based in the Shankhill area, the group has links with the Ulster Democratic Party. The leading figure is Johnny (Mad Dog) Adair, who was imprisoned for inciting sectarian attacks in the early 1990s, and who left the Maze Prison under the terms of the Good Friday Agreement in 2000, only to return in August of the same year for breaching the terms of his release. The UDA is suspected of involvement in drug racketeering and extortion, and has approximately 600 members.

## Ulster Freedom Fighters
See Ulster Defence Association (UDA).

## Ulster Unionist Party
www.uup.org
Unionist political party in Northern Ireland. It formed in 1905 and effectively ruled the province between 1921 and 1972. It is right wing on most issues and insists the province should be treated on a par with the rest of the United Kingdom. It hotly opposes any union with the Republic of Ireland. It was represented in Westminster after the 2001 general election by five MPs (down from 10 after the 1997 election) and eight peers. While opposing any drift towards eventual union with the south, the party proved willing to negotiate with all parties in the conflict, including the hated IRA and Sinn Fein. David Trimble, the party leader, became the first minister of the province after elections to the assembly in June 1998, and in September of that year met up with Gerry Adams, although he studiously avoided any symbolic handshakes. In June 2001 Trimble's position in the party came under fire when the party lost ground in the local and general elections to the more militant Democratic Unionist Party. Trimble threatened to resign as first minister in July if the IRA refused to disarm. He fulfilled his threat but resumed his role when the IRA seemed to move on decommissioning. In October 2002 the executive was suspended following the discovery of a Sinn Fein spying conspiracy in the Northern Ireland Office in Belfast. In November 2003, the UUP was eclipsed in the assembly elections by Paisley's hard-line Democratic Unionist Party.

## Ulster Volunteer Force (UVF)
Formed in 1966 with the same name as Carson's 1912 army, which was formed to fight Irish independence. It linked to the Progressive Unionist Party led by David Ervine. Gusty Spence was a hero figure who helped broker the loyalist cease-fire. Billy Hutchinson was another leading member. It has between 300 and 600 members.

## ultra vires
Being beyond one's legal powers or authority. In practice it means the actions of an individual or body has been beyond the legal authority granted by statute law. The term is specifically associated with the rulings from tribunals and judicial review, and is frequently applied to the actions of

POLITICS

local authorities and ministers of the crown which are adjudged to be illegal. Examples include *Conway* v. *Rimmer* (1968) and *Laker Airways* v. *Department of Trade* (1977). One of the most significant cases was *R.* v. *The Greater London Council* ex parte *Bromley* (1981), where the House of Lords upheld the decision of the Appeal Court that the Greater London Council (GLC) was acting beyond its powers in introducing a supplementary rate to subsidise fares on London Transport. This is historically important because judges became involved in party political squabbles between a Labour-controlled GLC and a Conservative council adhering to government policy.

## underclass

Name given by US writer Charles Murray to the poorest sector of society, often on minimum wage and/or welfare benefit, who subscribe to a set of values at odds with conventional society. He believes the sources of such a class can be found in unemployment, the lack of hope and expectation, and illegitimacy with its associated lack of male role models to influence growing children in a fashion supportive to society. After diagnosing such problems in the USA, Murray came to Britain and did the same; he wrote a number of influential articles in the *Sunday Times* in the 1980s. His term has subsequently entered the language of social debate. However, many sociologists dispute the term, particularly when applied to children in single-parent families, many of whom do not leave school to be on welfare benefits. Moreover, they suggest that it is a value-loaded term, heavily influenced by the ideas of the new right.

*See also* meritocracy; social exclusion.

## unemployment

In the 1930s unemployment soared to over 3 million and great hardship was suffered by families all over Britain, but especially in the north of England. During the Second World War full employment arrived of necessity and politicians, supported by Keynesian thinking, resolved that full

employment would continue into peacetime. For 30 years this more or less happened; in the mid-1970s unemployment was under 1 million, about the number of people likely to be unemployable anyway through disability, sickness or other non-economic reasons. However, full employment tended, by way of the law of supply and demand, to push up wages, which fuelled inflation. The Conservative government under Margaret Thatcher resolved to allow inefficient and non-competitive enterprises to fail and her policy of high interest rates to keep down inflation forced bankruptcies through the prohibitive cost of credit and the high exchange rate which it encouraged. During the 1980s unemployment rose to over 3 million and probably much more as the government resorted to a number of statistical sleights of hand to reduce the figures. Some commentators had predicted that a rate of 3 million unemployed would lead to riots and widespread social dislocation. This did not happen but there were riots in the inner cities in the early 1980s and the crime rate soared; this was almost certainly linked to unemployment, according to Home Office studies. Critics of the Conservatives maintain the valuable revenues from North Sea oil in the 1980s were lost paying unemployment benefit to those millions made unemployed by ineffective government policies. Levels edged down as the 1980s came to an end and during the 1990s were consistently below 2 million. Some economists claim this is the minimum level required by the market to keep inflation in check, though this is disputed by other experts. After 1997 the figure continued to fall until it was just under 1 million by the time of the 2001 general election (6.5 per cent of the working population). Studies submitted to the annual meeting of the British Association in September 2001 suggested the low unemployment rate in Britain masked a relatively large group of people who were classified as 'long-term sick' and claiming benefit. Seven per cent of the workforce was seen as economically inactive, compared with 2.1 per cent in Germany and 0.3 per cent in France. It seems that large groups of unemployed people may have deliberately moved on to sickness benefit, as it is more generous than unemployment benefit. If the 1.5 million claiming sickness benefit were included in the statistics, Britain would have a worryingly high unemployment figure.

## unilateralism

The giving up of nuclear weapons outside the framework of international (multilateral) agreements. In the 1980s, 'unilateralist' was used to describe a variety of different groups, prominent Labour politicians and others in Britain who were hostile to nuclear weapons. Although all unilateralists oppose the concept of nuclear force on moral or strategic grounds, the term is used to refer to a range of different positions on the issue. For example, one strand of unilateralism opposes Britain's membership of NATO as a military alliance, which, ultimately, has recourse to weapons of mass destruction. For pragmatists in the Labour Party, unilateralism was perceived by many, including Neil Kinnock, as an obstacle to winning a general election. For the 1992 general election the Labour manifesto removed all traces of its previous unilateralist stance, a position enhanced by the relaxation in tension between NATO and eastern Europe after the disintegration of the Soviet Union. The pragmatism of New Labour saw no reversal of the party's multilateralist position.

## union bashing

Colloquial term which entered the language in the 1980s and was associated with Margaret Thatcher's drive to reduce the powers and rights of the trade unions. Thatcher sought to do so as a means of allowing market forces to operate freely and to further the political objectives of the new right. The term, much used by trade unionists and Labour politicians in the 1980s, obscures the fact that Thatcher, a barrister by training, mainly used a raft of new industrial relations laws as a mechanism of reform. However, most commentators agree that one of her most significant acts was

the facing down of the most powerful trade union, the National Union of Miners, in its strike of 1984–85.

*See also* trade unionism.

## Union of Shop, Distributive and Allied Workers (USDAW)

www.usdaw.org.uk
Founded in 1947 to represent workers in shops, stores and transport, this union has over 300,000 members.

## Unison

www.unison.org.uk
The largest union in Britain, Unison was formed out of a merger of unions for health service, public service and local government workers in 1993. Half of its 1.4 million members are in the local government sector. Unison's leader, Dave Prentis, was greatly upset by the failure of the government to end 'two-tier' workforces, whereby private sector employees are brought in to perform former public sector jobs on lower rates of pay.

## unitary authority

A level of local government to replace county and district councils, first proposed by the Redcliffe-Maud report in 1966. It recommended the creation of 58 unitary authorities, in charge of all functions within their boundaries. The incoming 1970 Conservative government opted for two-tier authorities, which the public found confusing. After 1979 the Conservative government initiated a rethink and in 1992, under John Major, John Banham was appointed to the Local Government Commission in England with a brief to create new unitary authorities. The Welsh Office's internal review had already led to the replacement of 8 county councils and 37 district ones by 21 new unitary authorities. Scottish Office proposals also replaced 68 regional and district councils with 28 unitary ones. Banham's progress was uneasy and he was eventually sacked by John Gummer, secretary of state for the environment, in 1995. His successor, Sir David Cuckney, managed to increase the number of authorities recommended for unitary status but controversy remained and no wider reorganisation resulted from his tenure in the post.

*See also* Redcliffe-Maud report.

### United Irishmen (Society of)

Formed in 1791 as a revolutionary reform society. Initially it included Catholics and Protestants but it soon became strongly republican and in 1795 was driven underground. During the Irish Rebellion of 1795–98 the society tried to organise disaffected activists in England but it collapsed once the rebellion failed. Many of the group then emigrated to the USA.

### United Kingdom

The United Kingdom of Great Britain and Northern Ireland. It is not synonymous with 'Britain' in that Northern Ireland is not part of Britain but is part of the UK. The UK was established by the Acts of Union of 1536 (Wales), 1707 (Scotland) and 1800 (Ireland). England, united since 900, has 90 per cent of the population. The union with the whole of Ireland was broken in 1920 by the Government of Ireland Act, which partitioned the country, leaving the six northern counties as part of the UK and causing a civil war in consequence.

### United Kingdom crown dependencies

*See* Channel Islands; Isle of Man.

### United Kingdom Independence Party (UKIP)

www.ukip.org

A former fringe party which made an impact in the June 2004 elections to the European parliament. It was founded in 1993 by university lecturer Alan Sked, who later left the party and disowned its leadership. The party stands unambiguously on a platform of British withdrawal from the European Union. UKIP was overshadowed in the 1997 general election by the well funded Referendum Party, led by James Goldsmith, but in the 1999 Euroelections the party picked up 7 per cent of the vote to win three seats. At the general

election and regional assembly elections in 2001 the party performed poorly but by 2004 it had won about 30 local council seats and in June of that year spectacularly captured a rising tide of Euroscepticism, strengthened possibly by anti-immigrant sentiment, to claim 16 per cent of the vote and 12 seats. Studies showed that 45 per cent of UKIP's vote came from disaffected Conservatives and 20 per cent from former Labour voters.

### upper class

Term used to describe the aristocracy and upper stratum of British society. In the 19th century few would have quarrelled with this term but as the number of aristocrats reduced relative to the numbers of rich middle-class people and their influence receded, the term was avoided by social scientists as misleading. They prefer other categorisations and tend to refer only to the working and middle classes.

### urban development corporation (UDC)

Type of body set up in the 1980s by the Thatcher government to bypass local authorities, which were perceived as too respectful of planning regulations, obstructive of the wealth-creating process and insufficiently entrepreneurial. Consequently, development responsibilities were given not to local government but to UDCs, for example in Liverpool and the London Docklands. Local authorities therefore lost power to these well resourced quangos, which had considerable discretionary powers. Relations between UDCs and local authorities varied but in some cities, for example Manchester, they were generally productive of change and improvement.

### usual channels

Term used to describe the close working relationship between the whips' offices of all the parliamentary parties, though in practice it usually refers to those of the government and opposition. The latter are concerned to oppose the government, naturally, but their minority of parliamentary votes means they have to make arrangements with government on such matters as when key debates are going to occur and what type of debate is appropriate to the topic and occasion. Critics sometimes claim the relationship between the whips is too close and cosy and works to curtail inner party dissent.

## utilitarianism
The product of Jeremy Bentham and James Mill, further elaborated by the latter's son, John Stuart Mill. The thesis stated that whatever was conducive to producing happiness was 'good' and what tended to produce pain was 'bad'. Translated into political action it posited that 'The action is best which procures the greatest happiness of the greatest number'. Bentham argued it should be possible to calculate quite precisely the good and bad effects of an act: the 'felicific calculus'. Policy making could almost be an automatic process. Though crude and philosophically flawed, this approach has strongly influenced policy, especially welfare policy relating to prisons, new Poor Law and sanitary reform. Charles Dickens mocked the ideas of utilitarianism in *Hard Times* (1854), with his memorable character of Thomas Gradgrind.

# V

## Valuation and Lands Agency
http://vla.nics.gov.uk
Set up in 1993 by the Home Office, this provides a valuation list for the purpose of levying rates plus estate management and information on property in Northern Ireland.

## Valuation Office Agency
www.voa.gov.uk
Executive agency of the Inland Revenue in England, Wales and Scotland. The VOA has 85 offices and employs 4,000 people. Its functions are: to compile and maintain business rating and council tax valuations lists for England and Wales; and to advise ministers on property valuation matters.

## value added tax (VAT)
A tax of European provenance that was introduced in 1973 at a rate of 10 per cent. It is applied at each stage of the production process to reflect the resultant added value. Producers can reclaim it if their turnover falls under the VAT threshold. It was introduced to replace purchase tax and to make British taxation compatible with the European system. It is collected by Customs and Excise. A proportion of the tax collected – according to a complex formula – goes to finance the European Union (EU). In meetings of EU finance ministers in 1987 and 1992 it was agreed to levy a standard rate of 15 per cent and a maximum of 25 per cent throughout the EU.

## veto
A unilateral right to reject proposals. Although the veto is used by a number of states (for example the US president can exercise a veto) and international organisations (for example permanent members of the UN Security Council), the device is not recognised in the British system of government. The monarch's legal right to veto bills has not been used since 1707. However, the veto is important in Britain's relations with the European Union(EU); twice, in 1962 and 1967, French leader Charles de Gaulle blocked Britain's application to join the organisation. The veto was also used by Britain when John Major vetoed the candidate Jean-Luc Dehaene for the presidency of the Commission in succession to Jacques Delors at the Corfu summit in 1994. While the veto is not used much, the threat of its use can exert quite an ongoing influence.
*See also* qualified majority voting

## vigilante movement
Name given to the attempts by residents to police their own property as crime rates

soared in the 1980s and 1990s. Usually these amounted to no more than regular patrols to dissuade offenders, but occasionally they took the law into their own hands and delivered illegal punishments to suspects. The employment of security companies to undertake patrols is now a regular aspect of life on some estates. The dangers of vigilantism were vividly demonstrated in August 2000 when, following a 'name and shame' campaign on convicted paedophiles by the *News of the World*, residents on a number of estates attacked the homes of suspected child abusers, some of whom were innocent, including that of a consultant paediatrician, whom they mistakenly believed was a paedophile by virtue of her professional title.

## virtual politics

Term used to describe the virtual democracy which has developed with interactive media such as television and the Internet. Radio 'phone-ins', telephone opinion polls and email comments solicited by political parties and other organisations are now part of the 'wired' society. Only time will tell whether this interactive technology will expand or restrict democratic choices and the voice of the people.

*See also* e-voting.

## virtual representation

Idea associated with Edmund Burke, the conservative thinker who stated that it is possible for a group of people to represent others without them having been formally elected by ballot. Burke argued that there is a communion of interests between a section of people and those whose concerns they express in an assembly. This view was rejected by those in support of electoral reform in the debates which took place in the 19th century. After the Great Reform Act of 1832, and subsequent electoral reforms, the principle was firmly established that the people must give their approval for a candidate or government by means of secret and free ballots.

## voluntary sector

Comprises all those organisations that organise volunteers to work for specific social groups. Britain is unusual in having many such organisations, so much so that working for charities and small voluntary groups can be said to be part of the British way of life. In the 19th century these groups were the precursors to government action and the voluntary sector still works closely with government agencies. Most charities are funded by contributions but since its inception the National Lottery has channelled millions of pounds into the voluntary sector. In early 2001 chancellor Gordon Brown announced a programme of support for the sector.

## voting behaviour

After the Second World War voting behaviour appeared to be essentially about class divisions, with working-class people voting Labour and middle-class voters supporting the Conservatives. There was nonetheless a significant minority of working-class Conservative voters and certain sections of the middle class who were Labour supporters. However, most psephologists argued that this pattern started to change for a number of reasons:

1  Party loyalty began to decline, with the proportion of voters identifying strongly with either of the two main parties falling from 38 per cent in 1964 to 20 per cent and below this by 1997. This partisan dealignment made the outcomes of elections less predictable and meant voters were more amenable to persuasion.

2  Regional variations have long been discernible, with the north inclined to support Labour and the south the Conservatives. However, this pattern was altered in 1979–83, when both parts of the country swung to the Conservatives, and in 1997, when the swing was to Labour.

3  Third-party voting increased during the 1970s and the proportion supporting both main parties fell from 90 per cent in 1950 to only 70 per cent in 1983.

4  Mass media and television in particular assumed greater importance from the 1960s onwards.

5   In 1997, Labour turned the tide by attracting back not only former Labour voters but also formerly Conservative 'middle England'. Some on the left, such as Tony Benn, have argued that Labour would still have won with a socialist agenda – which would have presented the electorate with a real choice. However, it is unlikely for socio-economic and political reasons to see a return to the traditional two-class, two-party voting which characterised the postwar years.

*See also* partisan dealignment; third-party voting.

## voting system

The mechanism used to convert electors' choices of party or candidate into seats in assemblies, legislative and otherwise. Voting systems can broadly be divided into majoritarian, proportional and hybrid systems. All have advantages and disadvantages for majority and minority parties, and reflect different national and political traditions. Britain has the first past the post system, which has the advantage of producing strong executives but which suffers from discriminating against smaller parties and under-representing certain elements of the population.

*See also* additional member system; first past the post; regional party list; single transferable vote; third-party voting.

# W

## Wakeham report, 2000

Report of a royal commission established in 1999 to look at further reform of the House of Lords. Lord Wakeham's plan for the second chamber was essentially that it should not challenge the legitimacy of the Commons. Accordingly he proposed a 550-strong chamber with only a small proportion elected. The options outlined were: 65 regional members elected on election day; 87 regional peers; or 195 elected peers. One-third were to be elected at successive elections via closed party lists. The majority, however, would be appointed by an independent appointments commission, with the largest group of members still being nominated by political parties. The award of a peerage would no longer entitle the holder to membership of the upper chamber. Life peers would retain membership. The law lords would continue to sit in the upper chamber and the functions would remain the same.

*See also* House of Lords reform.

## Wales

Originally occupied by Celts from central Europe. What is now Wales became part of the Roman Empire about 50 AD and was a Celtic stronghold against the Saxons during the 'Dark Ages'. There was conflict with neighbours over the border for many centuries. Wales was formally joined to England in 1536 by an Act of Union after its conquest by Henry II. It now has 2.9 million people, 19 per cent of whom speak Welsh. The coal and iron industries developed in the south and a militant tradition of unionism was inaugurated. The main nationalist party, Plaid Cymru, is more cultural and language based than its Scottish equivalent.

The region returns 40 MPs to Westminster. Plaid Cymru seeks independence for the country but the Welsh people supported the devolved assembly by only a thin margin in the referendum vote in September 1997. The secretary of state for Wales was downgraded in June 2003 to a part-time role performed by the leader of the House of Commons, Peter Hain.

*See also* Plaid Cymru; Welsh assembly.

## Wapping

Part of London's Borough of Tower Hamlets, redeveloped since 1969. Its political significance is in the move to Wapping by News International from Fleet Street in

POLITICS

1986, when its owner, Rupert Murdoch, dramatically decided to outflank the print unions and unilaterally use labour-saving technology and cut production costs. Other parts of the press have benefited from Murdoch's decisive action. The result has been the weakening of the print unions' power and a renaissance in the press, with the launch of new titles.

### war cabinet
During wartime, political control has been best vested in a smaller body than the usual full cabinet. This happened in the two world wars as well as the Falklands War in 1982. David Lloyd George's war cabinet – the first modern one to be formed – included Labour's Arthur Henderson. Winston Churchill's first war cabinet numbered five and included Labour members Clement Attlee and Arthur Greenwood; later Ernest Bevin was brought in as well as Stafford Cripps. Margaret Thatcher's war cabinet included Cecil Parkinson, John Nott, William Whitelaw and Francis Pym, as well as Lord Lewin, the chief of the defence staff. Tony Blair's Iraq war cabinet contained John Prescott, Gordon Brown and Jack Straw, as well as Sir Michael Boyce, chief of the defence staff, the security chiefs of MI5 and MI6 and the occasional attendance of Alastair Campbell and chief of staff Jonathan Powell. Blair was criticised by the 2004 Butler report for holding meetings on Iraq which were over-casual and not minuted.
*See also* cabinet.

### war on terror
Tony Blair's determination to express political solidarity with the USA led him to go to war alongside George Bush in Afghanistan in 2001 and, to much greater domestic dissent, Iraq in 2003. After the Afghan war a number of British citizens were detained in the US Cuban base of Gauntanamo. In February 2004, it was announced that five were to be returned to the UK. However, the dozen suspects detained in Belmarsh Prison stayed in jail, with no clear explanation being given for the continued detention.

In the same month David Blunkett announced more stringent measures for the handling of suspected terrorists as well as more financial and personnel resources for the secret services.

### water privatisation
The sale of the 10 public water authorities in 1989. Opinion polls registered a 5 to 1 majority against the idea of privatisation when it was mooted but the public still turned out to grab the quick profit when shares were floated on the Stock Exchange. The National Rivers Authority (NRA) was created to take over pollution control, fisheries and protection of the environment. In 1996 the NRA was subsumed within the Environment Agency. In 1991 Ian Byatt, the head of the Office of Regulation for Water (Ofwat), was criticised for allowing rises of over 100 per cent in the domestic charges for water supply. Also criticised were huge self-awarded pay increases for the directors of these private monopolies. In September 1998 John Prescott, the deputy prime minister, imposed tough new restrictions on the water companies, including a 10 per cent reduction in water prices, an end to excess profits for shareholders and an insistence that more money be spent on environmental clean-ups.

### ways and means
*See* Committee of Ways and Means.

### wealth
Wealth is very concentrated in all developed capitalist economies and Britain is no exception. In 1992 the richest 1 per cent of the British population owned 18 per cent of all marketable wealth, or 29 per cent if the value of dwellings is subtracted (i.e. property values for ordinary families served to reduce the wealth gap). For the richest 10 per cent the figures were 49 per cent and 65 per cent, respectively. This distribution has remained similar for over half a century though some redistribution has occurred from the very rich to the merely rich, partly as a tactic to avoid death duties.
*See also* underclass.

# weapons of mass destruction (WMD)

Nuclear, biological or chemical weapons. Weapons of mass destruction were claimed to be in the possession of Saddam Hussein in the autumn of 2002, when Tony Blair was trying hard to find reasons for supporting US President George Bush's policy of 'regime change' in Iraq through military invasion. Invading merely to remove a vile dictator was arguably justifiable morally but not in terms of international law. Self-defence, however, was a legitimate casus belli – hence Blair's eagerness to prove British forces faced a danger from a possible Iraqi attack. His office produced a dossier in September 2002 based on intelligence reports which argued Iraq could launch an attack on Britain within 45 minutes: a clearly absurd claim but one which helped deliver a majority in the House of Commons for the eventual joint attack. However, the removal of Saddam did not lead to the exposure of such weapons and critics loudly accused Blair of fabricating reasons to go to war. BBC reporters were prominent in this process, citing 'senior intelligence' sources; in retaliation Blair's press secretary, Alastair Campbell, denied the charges and demanded an apology. Eventually an advisor to the Ministry of Defence, Dr David Kelly, a scientist and former Iraq weapons inspector, was named as the source of the story. He gave evidence to the Foreign Affairs Select Committee but denied being the source of the embarrassing parts of the BBC reports; shortly afterwards, at the centre of much media pressure, he committed suicide. In July Lord Hutton was appointed to make a full inquiry amid the most intense crisis of public trust in New Labour since 1997.

*See also* Hutton inquiry.

# welfare state

Term given to the battery of services supplied by the state since the turn of the century to improve the living conditions of the population. The National Insurance Act 1911, passed by David Lloyd George, introduced pensions for older people. The Beveridge report of 1942 committed the government to construct a welfare state after the war, with a whole battery of new benefits and services. To unemployment benefit was added sickness benefit, family allowances and family income supplement. As well as benefits disbursed by the Department for Work and Pensions there is free health care, compulsory state education for children aged 5 to 16, and personal social services. Welfare spending takes up the largest share of public expenditure and a long-running debate has been conducted in both main parties about the best means of welfare reform. Conservative politicians have long argued that the welfare state erodes self-reliance and the desire to fend for oneself, because it provides overgenerous benefits. Certainly, benefit fraud is widespread and both parties have sought to squeeze it out of the system. The right wishes to reduce welfare spending – social security spending at £100 billion is the biggest single item of government expenditure – by encouraging people at best to buy into private education and health or at worst pay a significant proportion of such costs personally. Labour came into power in 1997 talking of welfare reform but a clash emerged between Frank Field (minister for welfare reform in the Department of Social Security, 1997–98), who favoured cash transfers and no means tests, and others who favoured targeting benefits via means tests and adopting what were basically right-wing solutions. By 2000, despite some isolated changes to traditional Labour policy, such as the New Deal, no all-embracing or radical changes had been introduced.

# Welsh assembly and executive

Bodies for the devolved government of Wales. For historical and economic reasons, Welsh nationalism has developed as a cultural rather than as a political phenomenon – that is, mainly as a concern to preserve the Welsh language, sport, the arts and its nonconformist religion. It was therefore no surprise that the referendum on devolution held in September 1997 should have produced the narrowest of results: 50.3

per cent to 49.7 per cent in favour of the proposition. The assembly is composed of 60 members: 40 elected from existing parliamentary constituencies (using the first past the post system) and 20 using the party list system. In 1999 Labour won 28 seats; Plaid Cymru raided Welsh Labour heartlands to pick up 17; the Conservatives won 9; and the Liberal Democrats 6.

The assembly and executive (drawn from the majority party or coalition) has a number of devolved powers, including economic development, agriculture, forestry, fisheries and food, social services, education, the Welsh language and the arts. However, despite its nominal control of a £7 billion budget, unlike the Scottish parliament it cannot pass its own legislation or vary levels of taxation (other than council tax). In key areas final responsibility stays with Westminster: foreign affairs (including the European Union), defence, taxation, economic and finance policy, social security and broadcasting control. Welsh politics faced a series of crises during the first session of the assembly, which included the resignation of the leader of the Welsh Labour Party, Ron Davies, following a scandal involving an apparent 'cruising' incident on Clapham Common. Tony Blair was unhappy to endorse the popular but allegedly 'off message' Rhodri Morgan as his successor and an unseemly process of manipulation resulted in the Blairite Alun Michael being appointed first minister instead. In February 2000 Michael lost a no-confidence motion centring on matching funds from London for European Union regional aid. Michael resigned and was replaced by Morgan; Blair then let it be known he had misjudged the popular Welshman. After governing in a minority for a while Labour formed a coalition with the Liberal Democrats but after the 2003 elections Labour's 30 seats (including heartland retrievals) enabled the party to rule unencumbered by a coalition partner.

## Welsh Grand Committee
Established in 1960 but weaker than its Scottish equivalent. This is partly because

there is little legislation which relates specifically to Wales. New standing order regulations in 1996 made it possible for Welsh questions plus second reading debates and other debates to be held in the committee. However, this occurred only twice in the 1996–97 session (it did, however, enjoy a revival under Labour after 1997).

## Welsh nationalism
*See* Plaid Cymru.

## Welsh Republican Movement (WRM)
Small faction set up in 1949 in response to what some perceived as the passivity of Plaid Cymru. In 1949 some 50 of the party's senior members walked out to set up their own party dedicated to a more muscular approach to Welsh independence. The modern incarnation of the movement is Cymru Annibynnol (Independence for Wales), established in 1999. It seeks a 'new free Wales'.

## Wembley Stadium
The project to build a new national football stadium encountered funding problems as the Football Association, despite the millions made by the game, was unable to provide sufficient funding to make the idea viable. City banks were also wary of advancing cash as they doubted the financial viability of the new complex. The government was nervous of funding something which the public might think the sport itself should pay for; it was also afraid of another 'Millennium Dome' instance of spiralling costs and warring factions. The sports minister Kate Hooey was widely believed to have been sacked in June 2001 because she was unable to solve the problems surrounding the project.

## West Lothian question
A term associated with the Labour MP representing West Lothian, Tam Dalyell. In 1977 he questioned an aspect of the proposed devolution process (later abandoned) whereby over 100 MPs from

Scotland, Wales and Northern Ireland could influence legislation for England but English MPs would not be able to do the same in relation to the proposed new devolved assemblies. At the time of writing no solution has been found. Conservatives have suggested a separate parliament for England though this has attracted little support. Some point out that a similar position existed in relation to Stormont for 50 years (1922–72) and few complaints were made regarding that particular anomaly. Criticism may abate once the number of Scottish Westminster seats is reduced, by the Boundary Commission, from 72 to 59 in 2006.

### Westland affair, 1985–86

A dispute over the future of the Westland helicopter company. It gave a fascinating insight into the workings of cabinet government under Margaret Thatcher. The affair began when Michael Heseltine, the defence secretary, wanted the ailing enterprise to be taken over by a European consortium, while Thatcher and others favoured the US Sikorski company. Heseltine was convinced the matter was being kept off the cabinet agenda, to block discussion of the issue. Behind the scenes the argument continued but on 6 January 1986 a crucial action occurred: the deliberate leaking by an official at the Department of Trade and Industry (DTI) of a letter from the solicitor general, Sir Patrick Mayhew, to Heseltine pointing out 'material inaccuracies' in an earlier letter by Heseltine to Lloyds Merchant Bank. This leak was designed to damage the defence secretary's credibility over the issue but to leak a law officer's communication is illegal and that is when the real row started: who authorised the leak? At the time Leon Brittan at the DTI accepted the blame and resigned but he has subsequently admitted he received direction from the prime minister's office to release the information. In the cabinet on 9 January the issue was discussed and Thatcher tried to defeat Heseltine using all the advantages of her office. When it was obvious he had been isolated he claimed collective responsibility had been

violated, gathered his papers and walked out. Thatcher was probably happy to see the troublesome minister go but she could have called him back had he not seen journalists outside the door of Number 10 and, still angry, told them he had resigned. The crisis could have escalated to the point where the future of the government was threatened but an indifferent Commons speech by Neil Kinnock, as leader of the opposition, let the prime minister off the hook and the repercussions of the crisis were played down for the most part in a select committee where key participants in the drama were questioned, before the affair fizzled out. However, Heseltine used his freedom to campaign up and down the country for the time when he could stand as leader of the Conservative Party. When he finally did, in 1990, he was instrumental in removing Thatcher but failed to win the crown; this passed to the unassuming John Major.

### Westminster City Council

*See* 'homes for votes' scandal.

### Westminster Hall

A room, called the Grand Committee Room (adjoining Westminster Hall in the Palace of Westminster), has been used for some parliamentary debates since December 1999. The idea was experimental to begin with, to give MPs an additional forum in which to raise issues. The conduct of its business features the use of desks and microphones and is presided over usually by a deputy speaker. Topics chosen are usually non-contentious and votes are not taken. The practice has not won the media's attention and debates are as poorly attended as they are in the main chamber, but it has been made permanent as it enables MPs to place items of business before the government, as a junior minister replies to each debate. The initiative has increased the time available to MPs by 25 per cent.

### Westminster model

The much copied British form of liberal democracy, which gives executive power to the largest party after an election. This model has been much criticised for giving the government excessive powers between elections but is defended by those who prefer a strong executive rather than a coalition, which can cause immobility and lack of action. Defenders insist it is accountable to the voters, who can easily vote out the government if it proves inefficient or unpopular. The model has also been criticised for its lack of democratic credentials without proportional representation and its poor representation in parliament of women and ethnic minorities.

## wet

Contemptuous description given by Margaret Thatcher to those who supported the 'one nation' consensual approach to politics often associated with Benjamin Disraeli. Her brand of uncompromising free market monetarism was consequently described as 'dry', though this was less popular than the 'wet' designation, which some came to wear as a badge of pride rather than the shame intended. Prominent wets included Jim Prior, Peter Walker and Ian Gilmour. Others more on the right, like Chris Patten and Douglas Hurd, were perceived as somewhat 'damp' if not wholly wet.

## Whig

Term derived from 'whiggamore' and applied to those who opposed the king in the 'exclusion crisis' of 1679–81, when Charles II tried to ensure the succession for his Catholic brother James, Duke of York. The Whigs became a grouping in parliament devoted to promoting civil and political liberties and mild, controlled political reform. Between 1715 and 1760 there was said to be a 'Whig oligarchy' dominating all aspects of the political system; they supported the Great Reform Act of 1832. Eventually the Whigs were subsumed into the new Liberal Party during the middle of the 19th century.

## whip

An officer of a parliamentary party who ensures members know which side to vote in divisions and who also acts as a channel of information between the leadership and the backbenches. Whips are also used as a mechanism for reporting on MPs who fail to 'toe the party line' in Commons votes. Often the lowliest form of appointment for government parties the whips' office can also be an escalator to high office, as in the case of Edward Heath and Francis Pym.

*See also* chief whip.

## white paper

Statement of proposed policy by government. White papers are carefully constructed and often follow comments made by government inquiries, royal commissions or green papers circulated earlier. Pressure groups strive to influence white papers as they often, but not always, determine the eventual shape of legislation.

## Whitty report, 1985

Report, drawn up by Labour Party general secretary Larry Whitty, on how the Militant Tendency had infiltrated the Liverpool branch of the party and seized control of the local authority. It urged specific expulsions and presaged the coordinated assault which ended the Tendency's period of excessive influence.

*See also* entryism; Hayward report; Militant Tendency.

## 'winter of discontent'

The winter of 1978–79, when low-paid workers in the public and private sectors revolted against the government-proposed pay norm of 5 per cent and went on strike. The term was coined in the newspaper coverage of the time, and is a reference to the opening line in Shakespeare's *King Richard III* ('Now is the winter of our discontent'). Especially harmful to the nation's life was the strike by transport workers. The Labour leadership was weak at this time. James Callaghan returned from a conference in the West Indies, relaxed and calm, and was reported to have stated: 'Crisis, what crisis?' (In fact he did not use those precise words.) The impression that the trade unions were more powerful than the government proved

highly damaging to Labour and strengthened the arguments of Margaret Thatcher
that trade unions needed reform. When
the government lost a vote of confidence
following its defeat over a devolution vote
in March 1979, even Callaghan discerned
a sea change in opinion which swept the
Conservatives into office.

## Witangemot

Meeting of nobility with Anglo-Saxon
kings when the monarch sought counsel.
The Witangemot was the precursor to
parliament, which placed a check upon
unlimited royal power. Because this
ancient council represented the nobility,
the subsequent shape of the councils which
advised the monarch – the Lords and the
Commons – reflected similar representation
and provided the basis for representative
democratic government.

## Wolfenden report, 1957

Report of a royal commission on homosexuality and prostitution, chaired by John
Wolfenden. It recommended the legalisation
of homosexual acts between consenting
adults (aged over 21) if they were performed
in private. However, the law was changed
only in 1967 and reflected, in part, the
changing moral climate of the 1960s.

## Women's Coalition

www.niwc.org
Women's party in Northern Ireland. The
coalition was formed in 1996 as an attempt
to contribute a distinctive women's voice
into the negotiations concerning the future
of the province. It is cross-community
and involves Catholics and Protestants,
nationalists and unionists as well as others.
It is the only party in the world founded
by women to have elected representatives.
Unfortunately for them the Coalition failed
to win or retain seats in the 2003 elections
to the Northern Ireland assembly.

## women's movement

Although Mary Wollstonecraft advocated
women's political rights in 1789, it took
the direct action of the suffragettes, and

in particular Emmeline Pankhurst, to
win for most women over 30 the right to
vote in 1918, and then for all women over
21 in 1928. Reformist feminists argue
the Equal Pay Act 1970 and the Sexual
Discrimination Act 1975 achieved much
of what women were after and that the
political battle was being won when over
100 Labour women MPs were elected
in 1997, as there had also been a fundamental change in attitudes towards
women. Radical and Marxist feminists
say the battle against an inferior position
of women at work, in education and in
politics is only just the beginning of a more
thorough-going reformation of the social
order. The cutting edge of the women's
movement has been blunted a little by the
retirement from the political fray of leading
campaigners and the gradual opening up of
political and corporate elites to ambitious
women. Nonetheless, women are still faced
by major economic, cultural and psychological obstacles from a male-dominated
society. Margaret Thatcher remains the
only woman to have achieved the highest
political office of prime minister; she is the
exception which proves the rule. In 2001
women constituted 18.5 per cent of MPs in
the UK – better than the 11 per cent equivalent in France and 13 per cent in the USA
but worse than 31 per cent in Germany
and 43 per cent in Sweden. Percentages
in the Scottish and Welsh assemblies were
also better at 37 per cent and 42 per cent,
respectively. Many parties in European
Union countries use positive discrimination
in the form of quotas for women candidates.
*See also* feminism; inequality (gender).

## woolsack

A large red cushion upon which the lord
chancellor sat when presiding over debates
and other business in the House of Lords.
The accepted version of its provenance is
that it was placed in the House in the 14th
century during the reign of Edward III as
a symbol of how the country benefited from
the wool trade. It has no arms or backrest
and is thought to be uncomfortable to sit on
for long periods.

## Workers' Educational Association (WEA)

www.wea.org.uk

Founded by Albert Mansbridge in 1903. The Association sought to educate working men and women to give them a chance in an otherwise elitist educational system. In practice it provided day and night classes for thousands of working people over the years but perhaps its political significance was greatest for the many Labour politicians who worked as tutors at some time, including Richard Crossman, Neil Kinnock and R. H. Tawney.

## Workers' Revolutionary Party (WRP)

www.wrp.org.uk

Trotskyist party dating back to the Revolutionary Communist Party of the early 1940s. Gerry Healy was originally a member of the Revolutionary Communist Party but left to stimulate similar ideas in the Labour Party, and was expelled for his pains in 1959. He then concentrated on building up his own party, which became the WRP. It seeks government control of the economy as well as withdrawal from the European Union and NATO. It expanded in the 1970s, especially after the high-profile Vanessa and Corin Redgrave joined. As with all such parties, the WRP offers a disciplined cadre of activists to seize control once the final crisis of capitalism arrives. Training is undertaken in a Derbyshire mansion and in centres throughout the country. Gerry Healy was expelled in 1985 for sexual offences. The party is said to have assets worth £1.5 million. In the 2001 general election it fielded six candidates and polled 607 votes in total.

## working class

It is a truism that all adult British citizens who are in employment are working people, including Tony Blair, the governor of the Bank of England and counter hands in a MacDonald's fast-food outlet. However, when sociologists and others use the term 'working class' they are describing a section of the population who differ from others in terms of a number of socio-economic characteristics, including education, occupational status, housing tenure, lifestyle and life chances. Karl Marx and Max Weber were divided over the true nature of this group, the former claiming that they were those who had nothing to sell except their labour (the proletariat), the latter examining the characteristics of occupational status groups. Taking this Weberian form of analysis, the British working class have traditionally been those people employed for wages in return for their labour, in manual occupations where they work under the close supervision of others, and have little autonomy in the planning and control of their work.

In Britain at the turn of the 20th century, 80 per cent of the population were working class, while in 1998 the total of the C2, D, E groups was 46 per cent of the population. The social structure has been changing radically since the Second World War, as the occupational pattern has been transformed by changes in production technology and the labour market. Working-class jobs have disappeared, with traditional heavy industries such as mining, shipbuilding and iron and steel production being replaced by jobs in the burgeoning service sector of employment. Automation has replaced many routine assembly-line tasks in manufacturing, for example the car industry. The information revolution that has swept across many sectors of the economy and the labour market now demands workers who are competent in a range of transferable skills, including communications and information technology. The net effect of this, according to some sociologists, is the shrinkage of the traditional working class and the enlargement of the middle class. Some also detect a new grouping lying beneath the old working class and to some extent antipathetic to the values of mainstream society. US sociologist Charles Murray sees a new 'underclass', comprising older people, single-parent families and the long-term unemployed, who live on state benefits. Moreover, some of the individuals in these groups, in particular young unemployed males, make a life for themselves in the so-called black economy of petty crime and social security fraud.

*See also* class; underclass.

**working families tax credit (WFTC)**
Introduced by chancellor Gordon Brown in Labour's first term to help families in work but on low incomes. In the budget of March 2001 poorer families in work could claim under the new system a minimum of £214 per week, raised to £225 by October 2001.

**World War II**
*See* Second World War.

**World Wide Web**
*See* Internet.

**writ**
Originally a command of the sovereign but more commonly understood as an order of the court summoning someone to attend a hearing.

**xenophobia**
From the Greek, literally meaning fear of foreigners or strangers but in political usage more usually applied to a hatred or hostility towards people who are perceived or labelled as different and do not belong to the national or cultural group. As such, xenophobia is closely related to racism and extreme nationalism. It is thus a central feature of far-right belief systems. Some writers have suggested that it is associated with rapid social change in communities where traditional beliefs and practices are challenged by new forces. Ethnic minority groups are particularly vulnerable to xenophobic attitudes because they may have distinctive characteristics of language, dress, religious observance or physical

appearance. While Britain is generally devoid of xenophobic politics, there are occasions when the fear of foreigners or strangers is used, for example when Margaret Thatcher claimed that people had a fear of being 'swamped' by immigrants, or when Conservative politicians accused the Labour government of being soft on alleged bogus asylum seekers in the summer of 2000.

*See also* British National Party; fascism; National Front; nationalism; racism.

**YouGov**
www.yougov.com
Polling organisation specialising in Internet interactions. This body was set up by Stefan Shakespeare in 2002 and involves journalist Peter Kellner, broadcaster John Humphrys and former campaigner Des Wilson. It seeks to stimulate e-democracy and polls sample groups of 2,500–3,500 to seek opinion measures on a wide range of social and political issues. The *Daily Telegraph* regularly feature polls by YouGov (in preference to the once-favoured Gallup), employing Professor Anthony King as its analyst.

**Young Conservatives**
*See* Conservative Future.

**Young Labour**
www.younglabour.org
Youth body of the Labour Party. In the 1980s Labour's Young Socialists acquired a reputation for unruly behaviour and left-wing if not Militant political sympathies. In 1994 a new structure was introduced. It has an upper age limit of 27 and claims a membership of 30,000. Young Labour has no structure and no elected officers. Youth conferences occur every two years.

**yuppie (or yuppy)**

A colloquial term derived as an acronym for 'young urban professional'. The term, which came into use during the 1980s, refers to young, upwardly mobile professional people – implicitly those working and living in London. After the deregulation of the financial services in the City of London in the mid-1980s, yuppy-dom became a lifestyle term to denote a 'class' of big-earning, fast-living and aggressively acquisitive young people who cared only for themselves.

*See also* City (the); new right; Thatcherism.

# Z

**Zimbabwe**

Originally Southern Rhodesia, one of the three parts of the Central African Federation established in 1953. The federation was dissolved in 1963 but Rhodesia refused to accept democratic rule and declared independence unilaterally under prime minister Ian Smith. In 1979 Margaret Thatcher negotiated majority rule and Smith finally resigned.

However, Zimbabwe's president Robert Mugabe allowed many white-owned farms to be taken over by black 'war veterans' in 1999–2000, and further claimed that Britain still owed responsibility to black farmers dispossessed by the whites.

**Zinoviev letter, 1924**

Forged letter purportedly from Grigory Zinoviev, leader of the Communist International, calling for British workers to start a revolution. It was published in the British press shortly before the general election in 1924. The election had been called by Ramsay MacDonald's fragile Labour government. Labour had recognised the Bolshevik government in Russia and attracted the accusation from the right of being overly sympathetic with the revolutionary state. The use of the 'red menace' ploy contributed to Labour losing the election and the forgery was not revealed for many years.

**Zircon Affair, 1987**

A BBC film made by *Guardian* journalist Duncan Campbell about the Zircon spy satellite. Special Branch raided the Scottish offices of the BBC and confiscated the film. The Conservative government claimed the film compromised the country's security, while sceptics concluded they merely wished to conceal how far behind its timetable the project had fallen.

# People

**Note by author**

Inevitably there were problems in deciding whom to include and whom to leave out of this section. The aim has been to include the 'giants' of British political history from before the Second World War, such as Gladstone and Disraeli, and those who have since made or are making an important contribution to British politics. In addition, some leading British political scientists have been included. The use of the present tense has generally been avoided, because of the fast-changing nature of political careers.

# A

**Abbott, Diane (1953–)**

First black female MP (Labour). She was educated at Harrow County Grammar School and then at Newnham College, Oxford. She worked as a career civil servant but was active as a councillor in Westminster 1982–86 and was then elected MP for Hackney North and Stoke Newington in 1987. She has tended to be seen as a left-wing rebel in the Labour Party who has diverted some of her energies into becoming a media performer.

**Adams, 'Gerry' (Gerald) (1948–)**

Irish nationalist leader born in Belfast. He joined Sinn Fein and was interned and later imprisoned in the Maze for his IRA connections during the 1970s. He was first elected to Westminster in 1983 (for Belfast West). As Sinn Fein's president from 1983,

he took part in the negotiations surrounding the 1994–96 IRA cease-fire and the subsequent peace process that culminated in the Good Friday Agreement in 1998. He was elected to the new Northern Ireland assembly in July 1998. He was re-elected to Westminster in June 2001 for Belfast West with a majority of 19,342. Adams refused to take his Westminster seat because he felt he could not make the oath of allegiance. However, in a conciliatory gesture, he was allowed to use office facilities and take up Westminster allowances in January 2002.

**Adonis, Andrew (1963–)**

Political advisor. He was educated at Kingham School and Keble College, Oxford. He worked for Nuffield College, Oxford, the *Financial Times* and the *Observer* before he became an advisor to Tony Blair. He was seen as being especially influential on Labour's education policy, though he had a wider brief in practice, especially after being made head of the Policy Unit. His book *A Class Act* (1997) was an analysis of Britain's class system. He was a member of the Number 10 Policy Unit from 1998. In 2003 he was officially given a 'crosscutting policy role' as the prime minister's senior policy advisor on education, public services and constitutional reform.

**Aitken, Jonathan (1942–)**

Conservative MP and minister. He was educated at Eton and Christ Church, Oxford, where he studied law. He was personal secretary to Selwyn Lloyd 1964–66 and *Evening Standard* foreign correspondent 1966–71. He worked for Slater Walker in the Middle East 1973–75. He was Conservative MP for Thanet South

1974–83 and then Thanet East 1983–97. He was a member of the Select Committee for Employment 1979–82 and a director of TV AM 1981–88. He served as minister of defence procurement 1992–94 and chief secretary to the Treasury 1994–95. A *Guardian* article accused him of staying in the Paris Ritz hotel at the expense of a Middle Eastern arms dealer. He denied this and sued, with much talk about the 'sword of truth'. He came unstuck when his claim that his wife had paid his bill was proved wrong, as airline tickets showed she was in Switzerland at the time. A brilliant career was cut short, it would seem, through an apparent belief that he could lie and bluster his way out of trouble. He was sentenced in June 1999 to a term of imprisonment for perjury in the case he brought against the *Guardian*. On release he decided to study theology, having acquired an enthusiasm for it while in prison.

### Alexander, Douglas (1967–)

Labour MP and minister, and key election planner. He was educated at Park Mains High School, Lester Pearson College, Vancouver, Edinburgh University and Pennsylvania University. He worked as a researcher for Gordon Brown and as a solicitor before he became MP for Paisley South in 1997. He was Labour's election campaign coordinator from 1999 and orchestrator of Labour's 2001 general election campaign. He was minister of state for the Cabinet Office and chancellor of the Duchy of Lancaster from June 2003.

### Amos, Valerie Ann (1954–), Baroness

Labour politician and the first black woman to sit in cabinet. She was born in Guyana and educated at the universities of Warwick and East Anglia. After working in local government in London she became chief executive of the Equal Opportunities Commission 1989–94. She was given a life peerage in 1997 and became spokesperson on international development in the House of Lords as well as Tony Blair's 'envoy to Africa'. She stepped up to become

secretary of state for international development when Clare Short resigned in May 2003. She was then appointed leader of the House of Lords (where she had earlier served as chief whip) and president of the Privy Council in October 2003.

### Ancram, Michael (1945–)

Conservative MP and minister. He was educated at Ampleforth, and then Oxford and Edinburgh universities. He practised at the Scottish bar before he entered the House of Commons for Berwick and East Lothian in February 1974 (until October 1974), for Edinburgh South 1979–87 and for Devizes in 1992. He served in the Scottish Office as well as the Northern Ireland Office 1993–97, where he was judged to have been unusually effective. One of the few aristocrats left in the Commons, he stands, on the death of his father, to become the 13th Marquis of Lothian (he presently holds the courtesy title Earl of Ancram). He was chair of the Conservative Party 1998–2001 under William Hague. After the electoral disaster of June 2001 he responded to many colleagues who allegedly asked him to stand for the leadership. He espouses the 'one nation' brand of Conservatism and is widely seen as a moderate as well as a highly clubbable colleague. Some said his participation in the contest was an extension of the 'Stop Portillo' tendency and the support offered to him by Ann Widdecombe appeared to support this view. However, his bid failed when he polled only 17 votes in the second ballot and was eliminated. He was made shadow foreign secretary by Iain Duncan Smith in 2001 and he was the only person to retain his portfolio when Michael Howard took over as leader in November 2003. Following the House of Lords Act 1999, Ancram is entitled to continue serving in the Commons even after inheriting his father's title.

### Archer, Jeffrey (1940–), Lord

One of the most colourful and controversial figures of his day. He was Conservative MP for Louth 1969–74 before financial disaster led to near bankruptcy (which disbars a person from the House of Commons). To pay his debts he started writing novels and became hugely successful after *Not a Penny More, Not a Penny Less* (1975) became a bestseller. He was deputy chairman of the Conservative Party 1985–86 but resigned after being accused of giving money to a prostitute, Monica Coghlan. In 1987 he successfully sued the *Daily Star* over the allegation. Scandal also followed him in 1994, when it was alleged he used inside information via his wife's directorship of Anglia Television to make a large profit on the stock exchange. His biographer, Michael Crick, raised a number of questions relating to the veracity of his version of his education at Wellington and Oxford, where he was a noted athlete. He remained a stalwart supporter of his party and a close friend of both Margaret Thatcher and John Major. He was made a life peer in 1992; Thatcher had tried and failed to convince the Honours Scrutiny Committee that Archer should be made a peer in 1990 but his cricketing chum, John Major, succeeded in 1992. Attempts to make Archer a junior minister for sport failed when David Mellor refused to accept him. Archer put himself forward in 1998 as a candidate for the mayor of London but he withdrew from the party's selection procedure in late 1999 amid allegations that he had asked a friend to provide a 'cover' story in the 1987 libel case. His reputation in tatters, he seemed finished as a politician and as an influential member of the party. More unseemly publicity surrounded the perjury trial in the summer of 2001 when sordid details of Lord Archer's personal life were revealed to the world. His former secretary exposed him as a liar and a womaniser. The jury found him guilty of perjury and he was sentenced to four years' imprisonment, the judge observing that it was the most serious case of perjury he had 'been able to find in the books'. In the wake of the verdict the *Star* announced it would be seeking £2.2 million in damages for the libel action Archer's lies had caused it to lose. Archer eventually repaid most of the sums he had received.

It is most unlikely that he has been involved in any wrongdoing. Nothing would give me more pleasure than to know of his innocence. (Michael Portillo, July 1994)

This candidate is a candidate of probity and integrity. I am going to back him to the full. (William Hague, October 1999)

Lord Archer is my friend, has been my friend and will remain my friend. (John Major, April 2000)

He is not a Robert Maxwell figure, he is not someone who eats babies for breakfast. But there was something about Jeffrey, his ambition, and his inability to separate fact from fiction, that meant he was a ticking time bomb throughout his time in the Tory party. (David Mellor, July 2001)

### Armstrong, Hilary (1945–)

Labour MP and minister. She was educated at Monkwearmouth Comprehensive, West Ham College of Technology and Birmingham University. She was MP for North West Durham from 1987. She was opposition spokesperson on Treasury matters 1994–95; parliamentary private secretary to John Smith 1992–94; education spokesperson 1988–92, minister for local government in the Department of Transport and the Regions from 1997. From 2001 she was parliamentary secretary to the Treasury and chief whip. She encountered trouble in July 2001 when she was involved in the attempted sacking of Gwyneth Dunwoody and Donald Anderson as chairs (respectively) of the Transport and Foreign Affairs Select Committees. Backbenchers of all hues, including Labour, rebelled, and they were reinstated in the same month.

### Armstrong, Robert (1927–)

Cabinet secretary 1979–87 and head of the civil service 1983–87. He was educated at Dragon School, Oxford, Eton and Christ Church, Oxford. He joined the Treasury in 1950 and was principal private secretary to Roy Jenkins 1967–68; permanent private secretary to the prime

PEOPLE

minister under Heath and Wilson; and deputy under-secretary at the Home Office 1975–77. Then, the perfect establishment bureaucrat, he served Margaret Thatcher – though he was not politically sympathetic to her – through a series of crises, including the Ponting, Westland and *Spycatcher* affairs.

> It contains a misleading impression, not a lie. It was being economical with the truth. (Armstrong referring to a letter in the *Spycatcher* trial 1986 in New South Wales)

## Armstrong, William (1915–80)

Head of the civil service 1968–74. He was joint permanent secretary at the Treasury in 1962 before being given the top job in 1968. He became very close to Edward Heath and was closely involved with his anti-inflation strategy, many say too closely involved for a supposedly neutral civil servant. He was even dubbed the deputy prime minister by some critics. He suffered a nervous breakdown in the mid-1970s and retired soon after.

## Ashcroft, Michael (1946–), Lord

Conservative Party treasurer 1998–2001. Ashcroft became rich through financial dealings, principally in Belize (where he had spent much of his life), which he represented at the United Nations from 1998 to 2000. Controversy surrounded his appointment regarding the propriety of his finances and a court case for libel involving *The Times* was narrowly averted in 1998. His candidature for a peerage was initially rejected but approved once he made his home back in Britain. In June 2001 it emerged that he had served writs on two cabinet ministers, the foreign secretary and the international development secretary, Clare Short, under the European Convention on Human Rights. He argued that the government had breached his human rights by failing to prevent government documents from being leaked which formed the basis for hostile press stories. Ashcroft felt the leaks were part of a campaign to undermine his good name.

## Ashdown, 'Paddy' Jeremy John Durham (1941–), Lord

Liberal Democrat leader 1988–99. He was born in India and spent his childhood there and in Ulster before he joined the Royal Marines, when he served in the Special Boat Squadron and Northern Ireland. He gained a first-class honours degree in Mandarin at Hong Kong University and entered the diplomatic service but decided to stand as a Liberal for the Yeovil constituency, where he overthrew a Conservative majority in 1983. An astute and aggressive political operator he made his mark with his ability to speak directly and powerfully. He was made leader of the new Social and Liberal Democratic Party in 1988 (which in 1989 shortened its name to the Liberal Democrats). He eschewed 'equi-distance' between the two main parties in favour of 'constructive opposition' to Tony Blair's government and was rewarded with a seat on a cabinet committee and a prospect of his party's principal objective: electoral reform. However, Blair was always famously 'unpersuaded' on proportional representation and in September 1998 at the Labour Party conference made comments suggesting the much spoken of referendum on the voting system might be delayed for some time. Ashdown stood down as Liberal Democrat leader and was replaced by Charles Kennedy in August 1999. He was made a peer in 2001. In May 2002 he took on the task of International High Representative in Bosnia.

## Asquith, Herbert (1852–1928)

Liberal prime minister 1908–16. He was educated at City of London school and Oxford. He practised as a barrister before becoming MP for East Fife 1886–1918 and MP for Paisley 1920–24. He was home secretary 1892–95; chancellor 1905–08; leader of the Liberal Party 1908–1926; and secretary for war 1914. He was prime minister from 1908 but resigned in 1916 and became leader of the opposition. He was outmanoeuvred by David Lloyd George, who, for all his brilliance, succeeded in splitting his party between his own supporters and those of Asquith.

## Astor, Nancy (1879–1964)

US-born politician who in 1919 succeeded her husband as Conservative MP for Plymouth. She made history by becoming the first woman to win a seat in the House of Commons. Her interests lay in social problems, temperance and women's rights. She was a member of the pro-appeasement 'Cliveden set'.

## Attlee, Clement Richard (1883–1967)

Labour prime minister 1945–51. He was born in Putney and educated at Haileybury and University College, Oxford. He was called to the bar in 1905. His work in Stepney slums converted him to socialism. He lectured at the London School of Economics 1913–23 except for when he undertook war service, when he attained the rank of major. He was elected mayor of Stepney 1919 and then elected into parliament in 1922. He was parliamentary private secretary to Ramsay MacDonald 1922–24; junior minister for war 1924; member of the Simon Commission on India 1927–30; and postmaster general 1931. He then became deputy leader of the opposition 1931–35 and leader of the opposition in 1935. During the war he was deputy prime minister to Winston Churchill. Labour won a landslide in the general election of 1945 and Attlee thereafter presided over six years of Labour majority rule, during which the party nationalised the utilities, introduced the welfare state, gave independence to India and Burma (1947) and signed the NATO treaty, which joined Britain's defence to that of the USA. He served as leader of the opposition 1951–55 before he resigned and entered the Lords as the 1st Earl Attlee.

> I must remind the Right Honourable Gentleman that a monologue is not a decision. (Attlee to Churchill, 1945)

> He is a sheep in sheep's clothing. (Churchill on Attlee)

> He seems determined to make a trumpet sound like a tin whistle.... He brings to the

fierce struggle of politics the tepid enthusiasm of a lazy summer afternoon at a cricket match. (Aneurin Bevan on Attlee)

> I am a diffident man. I find it hard to carry on a conversation. But if any of you wish to come and see me, I will welcome you. (Attlee to his junior ministers, 1945)

> I have none of the qualities which create publicity. (1949)

> Democracy means government by discussion, but it is only effective if you can stop people talking. (1962)

## Avon, Lord

See Eden, Anthony

# B

## Bagehot, Walter (1826–77)

Born in Somerset, studied mathematics at University College London. He was called to the bar in 1852 and succeeded his father-in-law in 1860 as editor of *The Economist*. His *English Constitution* still remains one of the most perceptive analyses of British politics and has been reissued many times, most notably in an edition introduced by Richard Crossman. He advocated many constitutional reforms in his writings, including the introduction of life peerages.

## Baker, Kenneth (1934–), Lord

Conservative politician and cabinet minister. He was educated at Magdalen College, Oxford, then did national service 1953–55 as a lieutenant in the Gunners. He was a member of Twickenham Borough Council, was elected MP for Acton in 1968 and later for Mole Valley. He was a junior minister in the Civil Service Department 1972–74 and parliamentary private secretary to the leader of the opposition (Edward Heath) 1974–75. He was minister for information technology 1981–84 and local government 1985–6; education secretary 1986–9; chancellor of the Duchy of Lancaster; chair of the Conservative Party 1989–90; and home secretary 1990–92. Baker was one of the most articulate and persuasive of Margaret Thatcher's ministers; he served her faithfully despite being a committed Heath-ite when younger. When chairman of his party his greatest coup as a 'spinner' of news was in the 1990 local government elections, when his insistence that the poll tax worked was apparently vindicated when Wandsworth and Westminster, 'flagship' councils with exemplary low charges, increased their majorities. The (admittedly pro-Tory) press accepted this version of events and neglected to emphasise the huge losses made by the party countrywide.

## Baldwin, Stanley (1867–1947)

Three times Conservative prime minister (1923–24, 1924–29, 1935–37). He was born into a wealthy family with interests in iron and steel manufacturing, and educated at Harrow and Trinity College, Cambridge. He entered the House of Commons in 1908, was president of the Board of Trade 1921–22 and chancellor 1922–23. He was unexpectedly selected as prime minister when Andrew Bonar Law retired through ill-health. He managed to be the dominant personality in his party for over a decade through cultivating a relaxed, pipe-smoking, and reliable image: 'the man you can trust'. He was, however, a tough politician: he led the revolt against David Lloyd George in October 1922, overcame the threat of the Trades Union Congress during the General Strike in 1926 and forced King Edward VIII to give way over the abdication crisis in 1936. He was the first senior British politician to become familiar with the media and he mastered perfectly the art of the confidential talk to the nation via radio. He goes down as an under-rated prime minister of resilience and generally sound judgement, though his insistence on returning to the gold standard

was unwise and his complacent attitude towards the rise of fascism myopic. In 1937 became Earl Baldwin of Bewdley.

> I hate elections, but you have to have them – they are medicine. (1931)

## Balfour, Arthur (1848–1930)

Conservative prime minister 1902–05 and foreign secretary 1916–19, when he issued the Balfour declaration. He was born in Scotland and educated at Eton and Cambridge; he initially combined politics with scholarship and wrote *A Defence of Philosophic Doubt* (1879). He was elected to the House of Commons at the age of 26 and was soon made personal secretary to his uncle, then foreign secretary, the Marquess of Salisbury. Balfour was made president of the Local Government Board 1885 and soon after secretary for Scotland and then chief secretary for Ireland 1887–91, where he strongly opposed Home Rule. He became first lord of the Treasury in 1891 (before that title became synonymous with the office of prime minister) and led his party in the Commons while his uncle was prime minister in the Lords. When Salisbury resigned in 1902 Balfour became prime minister. A destructive battle followed in the Conservative Party, with Joseph Chamberlain (colonial secretary in Salisbury's government) pressing imperial preference and being opposed by the advocates of free trade, and Balfour resigned as prime minister (though not as party leader) in December 1905. The Conservatives mustered only 156 seats in the 1906 general election. Balfour lost his seat but was soon in again as the member for the City of London. As leader of the opposition his patrician style was not well received; he encountered a 'Balfour Must Go' movement and in 1911 he resigned the leadership. However, David Lloyd George brought him into the wartime government eventually as foreign secretary, as which he issued the Balfour declaration in 1917 and played a role in the Versailles peace treaty in 1919. He managed to serve again in Stanley Baldwin's government as lord president of the Council 1925–29. He left office in 1929, having served 27 years in the cabinet, and died soon afterwards.

> I would rather take advice from my valet than from the [Conservative] party conference.

> Nothing matters very much, and few things matter at all.

## Balls, Ed (1967–)

Former advisor to chancellor Gordon Brown. He was educated at Oxford. According to the *Observer* (25 February 2001) he 'is one of the handful of people the chancellor will listen to, he is a prime mover behind the Americanisation of economic policy'. Regarded as the 'deputy chancellor', he saw every key Treasury paper and was an advocate of welfare to work and promoting individual opportunity. A 'closet Keynesian', said the *Observer*, who 'believes in income redistribution'. On 1 July 2004 he was made Labour candidate for the safe seat of Normanton.

## Barber, Anthony (1920–), Lord

Conservative chancellor under Edward Heath. He was educated at Retford Grammar School, Oxford, and was a barrister before being elected for Doncaster 1951–64 and then Altrincham and Sale 1965–74. He began his ministerial career as a whip, moved on to the Treasury, and then became the minister of health and chairman of the Conservative Party 1967–70. He was chancellor of Duchy of Lancaster in 1970 and chancellor of the exchequer 1970–74. He was generally reckoned to have precipitated the inflationary spiral of the 1970s as a result of high borrowing. He was made a life peer in 1974.

## Barber, Brendan (1951–)

General secretary of the Trades Union Congress (TUC) from 2003. He was educated at St Mary's College grammar school, Crosby, then spent a year on Voluntary Service Overseas (VSO) before going to City University, where he was president of the Student Union. He worked for a while as a university researcher before he joined the TUC in 1974. He became a head of section one year later and head of press in 1979 and deputy general secretary in 1993.

## Barnett, Joel (1923–), Lord

Labour politician who devised the Barnett formula. He was educated at Manchester High School. He became an accountant and businessman in Greater Manchester after serving in the Royal Army Service Corps and the British military government in Germany. He was MP for Heywood and Royton 1964–83 and entered the House of Lords in 1983. He was a member of the Public Accounts Committee 1961–71 and its chair 1979–83. He served as shadow Treasury spokesman 1970–74 and chief secretary to the Treasury 1974–79, with the last two years as a cabinet member. He devised the 'Barnett formula': the basis on which public expenditure was to be divided between the constituent countries of the UK. He was known for his canny, folksy style, his right-of-centre opinions, his tough negotiating with departments on behalf of the Treasury and subsequently for his revealing memoirs, which were said to be a favourite of Margaret Thatcher.

## Barry, Brian (1936–)

Distinguished British political scientist who has been Lieber Professor of Political Philosophy, Columbia University, New York, since 1998. He was educated at Taunton School, Southampton University and Queen's College, Oxford, and was Rockefeller Fellow, Harvard, 1961–62. He worked at the universities of Keele, Southampton, Oxford, Essex (1969–72), Chicago (1972–83), the California Institute of Technology (1982–86), European University, Florence (1986–91) and the London School Economics (1987–98). He won the Johan Skytte Prize in Political Science 2001 and the W. J. M. Mackenzie Prize (of the Political Studies Association) for the best book in the previous year, 1989 and 2001, for *Theories of Justice* and *Culture and Equality*.

## Beaverbrook, Max (1879–1964), Lord

Newspaper magnate, historian and Conservative politician. He was born in Ontario, Canada (as William Maxwell Aitken), moved to Britain in 1910 and in same year entered the Commons for Ashton-under-Lyne; soon afterwards he became parliamentary private secretary to his friend Andrew Bonar Law. Under David Lloyd George he was made minister of information in 1918. In 1916 he took over control of the struggling *Daily Express* and made it the newspaper with the largest circulation of his generation. He founded the *Sunday Express* in 1921 and bought the *Evening Standard* in 1929. During the Second World War he was made minister of aircraft production and displayed unusual energy and effectiveness. He held the post of minister of supply 1941–42, but his political career fizzled out after the war. His newspapers stoutly supported the Empire and tended to be opposed to an integrated Europe. Beaverbrook was one of the great original 'press barons', who probably did not fulfil his own dreams of power and effectiveness. The fact that he had close friends among left-wing journalists and politicians – including the likes of Michael Foot and Aneurin Bevan – attests to his charm and ability to rise above his own prejudices.

> I learnt one thing from my father – and that was to hate, to hate! (1935)

> He is a magnet for all young men and I warn you if you talk to him no good will become of it. Beware of flattery. (Clement Attlee warning junior ministers against Beaverbrook, 1945)

## Beckett, Margaret (1943–)

Labour MP and cabinet minister. She was educated at Notre Dame High School, Norwich, and studied metallurgy at Manchester College of Science and Technology before she became a research assistant to the Labour Party 1970–74. She was elected MP for Lincoln in 1974,

lost her seat in 1979 but re-entered parliament in 1983 as MP for Derby South. She went through a period of closeness to the hard left in the early 1980s (which is still remembered with some bitterness by older Labour MPs). She soon forgot her leftist past though and held a number of posts with evident competence before becoming deputy leader of the Labour Party from 1992 to 1994 and briefly (acting) leader in 1994 when John Smith died. She shadowed social security, the Treasury and trade and industry, and was made president of the Board of Trade in 1997. She was moved to leader of the House in July 1998, played an active part in the 2001 general election campaign and was made the new secretary for environment, food and rural affairs in the reshuffle following the election.

## Beith, Alan (1943–)

Liberal MP. He was educated at Macclesfield School and Balliol College, Oxford, and was a lecturer in politics at Newcastle University. He won Berwick upon Tweed at a by-election in 1973. He was deputy leader of the Liberals from 1985 and deputy leader of the Liberal Democrats from 1992. He was chief whip for the Liberals 1976–85; served as Treasury and home affairs spokesman and served on the Treasury and Civil Service Select Committee. He was appointed chair of the select committee set up to scrutinise the Lord Chancellor's Department in January 2003.

## Bell, Martin (1938–)

Independent MP, 1997–2001. He was educated at Cambridge and joined the BBC in 1962. He became an award-winning foreign correspondent in Washington, Berlin and Vienna, as well as a war correspondent, notably in Bosnia, where he was celebrated for his bravery and his trademark white suit. In 1997 he decided to fight Tatton as an 'anti-sleaze' candidate. Complete with white suit, he campaigned against former Conservative trade minister Neil Hamilton, the MP at the centre of the 'cash for questions' scandal. He won by a majority of 11,000 and served as an effective constituency MP in a job he came to enjoy. However, he was forced, in line with his stated 1997 intention, not to stand in 2001. Instead, he fought Brentwood and Ongar in 2001 and, while his campaign against the alleged infiltration of local Conservatives by a religious faction was effective, his opponent, Eric Pickles, won by a majority of 2,800 – down from over 10,000 in 1997.

## Benn, Hilary (1953–)

Labour MP and minister. He was educated at Holland Park Comprehensive School and the University of Sussex, where he studied Russian and East European Studies. He worked for trade unions in the 1980s and became active in local politics. He stood for Ealing North in 1983 and 1987. He was head of policy and communications at the MSF union and in 1997 became special advisor to education secretary David Blunkett. He was elected to the Commons in 1999 for Leeds Central and became a junior minister in the Department International Development in June 2001; he became minister of state in May 2002 after a sojourn in the Home Office, May 2002–03. His accession to the cabinet meant three generations of his family had served in this way: his father Tony and his grandfather before that.

## Benn, Tony (1925–)

Labour MP, cabinet minister, diarist and left-wing ideologue. He was originally known as Anthony Wedgwood Benn, son of Viscount Stansgate. He was educated at Westminster and New College, Oxford. He was Labour MP 1950–60 but was then barred from the Commons when he inherited his father's title. He fought this and succeeded in changing the law so that he could re-enter the Commons in 1963. In Harold Wilson's first governments he was postmaster general 1964–66 and minister of technology 1966–70. In opposition 1970–74 he shadowed trade and industry and briefly held this ministry after

Labour's 1974 election victory, until Wilson moved him to the less sensitive position of secretary of state for energy 1976–79, because of concern at the left-wing stance his ambitious protégé had uncompromisingly adopted. In opposition after 1979 he led the left wing of the Labour Party and was responsible, according to some critics, for much of the internecine fighting which characterised Labour in the early 1980s and helped keep the party out of power. His attempt to become deputy leader in 1981 narrowly failed and he lost his seat in 1983 but came back for Chesterfield in 1984. He challenged Neil Kinnock for the leadership in 1988 but failed by a wide margin. He remains true to his left-wing ideals but is now seen with affection, even by his opponents, as a great radical dissenter, a wonderful speaker and (important to the Tories) scrupulously polite, whose time for leadership passed decisively in the mid-1980s. His prolific diaries, culled from the tape recordings he assiduously made on every aspect of his varied life, provide a unique insight into British political history. He stood down as MP for Chesterfield in June 2001 to 'devote more time to politics'.

## Bentham, Jeremy (1748–1832)

Political thinker and author of 'utilitarianism'. He was a child prodigy who entered Queen's College, Oxford, aged 12 and entered Lincoln's Inn three years later. His fame, however, was established not at the bar but as the creator of the philosophy of utilitarianism, which is based on the premise that the aim of all legislation should be the achievement of 'the greatest happiness for the greatest number'. He invented a model prison named the Panopticon and a special school, the Chrestomathia. He travelled widely in Europe and wrote on economics, politics and penal reform. He founded University College London, where his clothed skeleton was preserved and remains on public view.

## Bevan, Aneurin ('Nye') (1897–1960)

Labour minister of health after the Second World War, whose energy and speaking talent made him a rival to Hugh Gaitskell for the party leadership. He was born in Tredegar as one of a miner's 13 children; he himself entered the pits aged 13. He became active in the miners' union and led the Welsh miners during the 1926 General Strike. He was elected Independent Labour Party member for Ebbw Vale in 1929 and joined the Labour Party in 1931. In the Commons he soon established a reputation as a brilliant orator, whose wit excoriated the Conservatives and anyone else he disagreed with, including some in his own party, which expelled him for a while for supporting the Popular Front campaign. As part of that campaign he had been a co-founder of the left-wing magazine *Tribune*. During the war he criticised Winston Churchill for 'conducting wars like a debate and debates like a war'. In 1945 he was made minister of health and was instrumental in establishing the National Health Service in 1948. As minister of labour in 1951 he resigned over the imposition of prescription charges and led a left-wing faction of 50 or so MPs against the leadership of Clement Attlee and then the 'desiccated calculating machine' Hugh Gaitskell (who easily defeated him in the 1955 leadership contest). He was passionately opposed to nuclear weapons but abandoned his stand in the 1957 conference when, as shadow foreign secretary, he claimed Britain could not go 'naked into the conference chamber' (to negotiate arms reductions with the Soviet Union).

No attempt at ethical or social education can eradicate from my heart a deep burning hatred for the Tory Party.... So far as I am concerned, they are lower than vermin. (4 July 1948)

The language of priorities is the religion of socialism. (Labour Party conference, 8 June 1949)

Like an old man approaching a young bride – fascinated, sluggish, apprehensive. (On the Allies' advance into Italy, 1943)

He was like a fire in a room on a cold day. (Constance Cummings on Bevan)

## Beveridge, William Henry (1879–1963)

Liberal academic and thinker credited with framing the modern welfare state. He was born in India of Scottish descent and educated at Charterhouse and Balliol College, Oxford. Initially a journalist he became an authority on unemployment insurance and compiled his report *Unemployment* in 1909. At the Board of Trade he became director of labour exchanges 1909–16 and then director of the London School of Economics 1919–37 and master of University College, Oxford 1937–45. He served on many official committees and chaired the one which produced the famous report associated with his name in 1942, *Social Insurance and Allied Services*. This was a comprehensive blueprint for social insurance for the whole of the national community. It was endorsed by the wartime government and provided the basis for the postwar welfare state. Beveridge was elected to the House as a Liberal MP in 1944 but lost his seat in 1945; he was made a peer in 1946.

Ignorance is an evil weed which dictators may cultivate among their dupes, but which no democracy can afford among its citizens. (*Social Insurance and Allied Services*, 1942)

## Bevin, Ernest (1881–1951)

Trade union leader and Labour foreign secretary 1945–51. He was born to poor parents in Somerset, who abandoned him at an early age. He first worked as a van driver in Bristol and soon entered the world of the trade union movement, which he did so much to form into its modern shape. He became a paid official of the Dockers' Union at the age of 30. His brilliant conduct of a case in front of a wage tribunal earned him the title of 'the dockers' KC'. He amalgamated over 30 unions to form the massive Transport and General Workers' Union (destined to become the largest union in Europe) and became its general secretary 1921–40. He was active in the 1930s on the Macmillan Committee on Finance and Industry, where he absorbed early Keynesian ideas. In 1940 he became minister of labour, when he achieved near complete mobilisation of the workforce, and served in the war cabinet. He was foreign secretary in Clement Attlee's postwar government, when he was scrupulously loyal to his premier and the architect of the formation and Britain's membership of the North Atlantic Treaty Organisation. Unlike many in his own party, and by no means a left-winger, he soon perceived the USSR as a potential threat to the peace achieved in 1945. Bevin was not without idealism, as many of his speeches attest, but he was essentially a realist, used to tough negotiations, who would not allow Soviet claims to obscure the USSR's advance into eastern Europe. The original John Bull of British trade unionism, he died in office in 1951, mourned by Labour politicians and Foreign Office officials alike.

> The most conservative man in the world is the British trades unionist when you want to change him. (1927)

> I do not know whether Marx really educated anybody. What he did was to confuse me. (House of Commons, July 1948)

> The familiar saying is that Bevin always treated the Soviet Union as if it were a breakaway faction of the Transport and General Workers' Union. (Kingsley Martin, when editor *New Statesman*)

> A speech from Ernest Bevin on a major occasion had all the horrid fascination of a public execution. If the mind were left immune, eyes and ears and emotions were riveted. (Michael Foot)

### Biffen, John (1930–), Lord

Conservative MP and cabinet minister. He was born the son of a Somerset tenant farmer and was educated at his local grammar school, followed by Jesus College, Cambridge. He worked in industry and for the Economist Intelligence Unit before winning the seat for Oswestry in 1961. A 'one nation' Tory, he became a supporter of Enoch Powell's economic ideas, a convinced Eurosceptic and a close advisor and confidant of Margaret Thatcher. She made him chief secretary to the Treasury, trade and industry secretary and then leader of the House of Commons. In 1986 he began to question the direction of her leadership – he preferred a team approach and was sacked in 1987 after the Conservatives' general election victory of that year. Bernard Ingham, Thatcher's press secretary, responded famously to his dissent by describing him as a 'semi-detached' member of the cabinet. Biffen responded by calling Ingham 'the sewer and not the sewage', though they had cordial personal relations in retirement. He was made a life peer in 1997.

### Bingham, Tom (1934–), Lord

Law lord. He was educated at Oxford. As lord chief justice 1996–2000 he tended to reinforce the rights of the accused: he opposed cuts in legal aid on grounds it would disadvantage the poor; he opposed the plan to remove the right of men on rape charges to cross-examine their accusers; and he argued that sections of the Prevention of Terrorism Act 1989 violated the presumption of innocence in a 'blatant and obvious way'.

### Birt, John (1944–), Lord

Director general of the BBC. He was born in Liverpool and educated at St Mary's College, Oxford. Initially he worked for London Weekend Television, where he developed the philosophy that current affairs coverage should provide the background to politics and also met and became friends with Peter Mandelson. When he moved to the BBC there was much criticism – some of it virulent – that he used management jargon to disguise swingeing cuts and a deprofessionalisation of the Corporation, referred to by critics as 'Birtism'. However, he defended his policy vigorously and won the trust of government, both Conservative and Labour. He was raised to the peerage in 2000 and performed an advisory role on crime for a while, though evidence of any influence remained slight. In the summer of 2001 Birt was given a role in helping to reform Whitehall, which was widely perceived as failing to 'deliver' the results government wanted. Tony Blair then asked him to assist in the field of transport, where he was commissioned to think 'blue sky' thoughts on how related thorny problems could be resolved. His suggestion that toll-paying motorways be built alongside existing ones was not well received and subsequently his profile has rarely risen above that of a 'Tony's crony'.

### Black, Conrad (1944–)

Press magnate. He was educated at Carleton, Laval and McGill universities. He was the third most powerful press magnate in the world, with interests in Canada and the USA, and owner of *Telegraph* newspapers and the *Spectator*. He failed to win control of the *Independent* in 1994. He was close politically to Margaret Thatcher and became a peer in 2001, though his home government in Canada objected to the elevation. In 2004 Black was forced to give up control of the *Telegraph* and it was sold to the financiers and newspaper owners the Barclay bothers.

### Blair, Cherie (1954–)

Recorder since 1998 though probably best (perhaps unfairly) known as Tony Blair's wife. She was educated at Seafield Grammar School and the London School of Economics. She was called to the bar in 1976 and specialised in public and employment law and human rights after joining Matrix chambers. She was thought to earn in the region of £200,000 a year. Cherie was reckoned to have been a better lawyer than her husband and she too had political ambitions at one time, though these took second place to those of her husband. In the autumn of 2002 she was involved in 'Cheriegate' when the *Daily Mail* and other tabloids revealed she had bought two flats in Bristol (one for her student son, Euan) partially on the advice of convicted conman Peter Foster, boyfriend of her style advisor Carole Caplin. The story ran for longer perhaps than it merited.

### Blair, Tony (1953–)

Labour leader from 1994 and prime minister from 1997. He was born in Scotland; educated at Fettes College and St John's College, Oxford, where he studied law. He was always a rebellious pupil but showed more interest in Christianity than politics until he left university. He was called to the bar in 1976. He sought a parliamentary seat and fought a by-election in Beaconsfield before he won the safe seat of Sedgefield in 1983. He shadowed the Treasury, trade and industry and energy before 1988, employment in 1989 and home affairs in 1992. After the death of Labour leader John Smith in 1994 he was elected leader and did much to 'modernise' the party; this included abolishing clause four of Labour's constitution and steering the party into the electable centre-ground on economic and social policy. He was helped by colleagues such as Gordon Brown and key advisors such as Peter Mandelson. His stunning general election victory in 1997 gave him unparalleled power in his party; Blair was highly telegenic and his performances on television helped to win the landslide victory. As prime minister his high poll ratings lasted for many months into his premiership but critical voices began to be raised regarding his bevy of advisors, including his press secretary, Alastair Campbell, upon whom, it was alleged, he placed a disproportionate reliance for advice, at the expense of cabinet and parliament. On 9 September 1998 a *Guardian* ICM poll revealed what the newspaper announced was the true end of the 'honeymoon', with a 'disaffected electorate beginning to view him as just another politician'. His personal ratings then appeared to plummet for trust and effectiveness as prime minister. He won the 2001 general election by another landslide but on a worryingly low turnout. As 2002 progressed he came in for criticism for excessive use of 'spin' and for offering such uncritical support for George Bush. By the spring of 2003 Blair had faced near fatal opposition from his side of the House to his plans for foundation hospitals and university top-up fees but these were small beer compared with party as well as wider opposition to the US plan to invade Iraq. The Iraq war and its barbaric aftermath became a running sore in Blair's standing, damaged as it already was by the repercussions of the David Kelly affair, the Hutton and Butler reports. By the autumn of 2004 there was open talk of Blair being replaced as leader, possibly by Gordon Brown.

> Labour is the party of law and order in Britain today. Tough on crime and tough on the causes of crime. (Labour Party conference, 1993)

> Ask me my three main priorities for government, and I tell you: education, education, education. (Labour Party conference, 1996)

> We are not the masters. The people are the masters. We are the servants of the people … what the electorate gives, the electorate can take away. (1997)

> I now have more respect for judgement than intellect. (Attributed to Blair by John Prescott and cited as a sign of his increasing wisdom, BBC2 programme, 4 May 2003)

## Blunkett, David (1947–)
Labour MP and cabinet minister, remarkable for the fact that he is blind. He was educated at Sheffield University and later lectured in industrial relations at Barnsley College of Technology. He was leader of Sheffield City Council in the 1980s before he became a Labour MP in 1987. He was opposition spokesman on health, education and employment and chairman of the party 1993–94. He was made secretary of state for education in 1997 and judged to have angered teaching unions by his support for chief inspector of Ofsted, Chris Woodhead. Blunkett was home secretary from June 2001, a post in which he was controversial in pursuing relatively hard-line authoritarian policies on crime and antisocial behaviour.

Mr Blunkett grew up blind in dreadful poverty, the son of a factory foreman who died in an accident and whose family did not have enough money to give the grave a headstone. (*The Economist*, 12 January 2002)

## Bogdanor, Vernon (1943–)
A professor at Oxford from 1996 and an expert on the British constitution. He was educated at Bishopshalt School and Queen's College, Oxford. He was a fellow of Brasenose College, Oxford, from 1966. He was special advisor to the Select Committee on European Communities and to foreign governments, including those of the Czech Republic and Israel.

## Bonar Law, Andrew (1858–1923)
Conservative prime minister 1922–23. He made money through being an iron merchant in Glasgow and became a Conservative MP in 1900. He was colonial secretary in Herbert Asquith's wartime coalition and chancellor in David Lloyd George's 1916–19 cabinet and later became lord privy seal. In March 1921 he retired through ill-health but came out of retirement to help defeat Lloyd George's coalition government in 1922. He then resumed the position of party leader and became prime minister in October 1922 but the following May was again forced to resign because of ill-health. One of the least known or lauded prime ministers this century, he also deserves to be known as the politician who helped end the ministerial career of the greatest politician of his time – Lloyd George.

> I must follow them, I am their leader.

> I am afraid I shall have to show myself very vicious, Mr Asquith, this session. I hope you will understand. (When leader of the House, 1912)

> If I am a great man, then a good many of the great men of history are frauds. (During the Ulster crisis)

## Booth, Cherie
*See* Blair, Cherie.

## Boothroyd, Betty (1929–), Baroness

Speaker of the House of Commons 1992–2000. She was educated at Dewsbury College of Commerce and Art. She entered the House for West Bromwich West in 1974, served variously in the whips' office and on select committees before becoming deputy chairwoman of the Ways and Means Committee 1979–87, the second in line to the speaker. Boothroyd was a colourful character whose used to dance as a Tiller Girl in the war. She developed an effective blend of humour and firmness to keep the House on the civilised side of the unruliness it frequently threatens. Her command of the House was much admired also in the USA, where video clips from the House's proceedings stimulated considerable interest. In 2000, to general acclaim, she retired from the speakership and went into the Lords.

## Bourn, John (1934–)

Comptroller and auditor general from 1988. He was educated at Southgate Grammar School and the London School of Economics. He worked as a civil servant in the Air Ministry, Treasury and Civil Service College but his main career was in the Northern Ireland Department, where he became deputy secretary 1982–84, and the Ministry of Defence, where he rose to deputy under-secretary (defence procurement) 1985–88. He was not afraid to make highly critical reports on government activity, whether Conservative or Labour.

## Boyce, Michael (1943–)

Admiral and chief of general staffs (CGS). He was educated at Hurstpierpoint School and Britannia Royal Naval College, Dartmouth. He joined the Royal Navy in 1961 and had a distinguished career as a submariner and then staff officer. He was first sea lord before he became CGS. He was thought to be sceptical on US missile policy. He resigned in July 2002.

## Brandreth, Gyles (1948–)

Conservative MP and diarist. He was educated at Bedales and New College,

Oxford, where he was president of the Oxford Union debating society. He built a career in television, the theatre and writing, especially novels and children's books. Many would have thought him an unlikely politician but he entered the House as MP for Chester in 1992 and became a government whip 1995–97, but was defeated in the 1997 general election. He earns a small footnote in political history through his witty and perceptive diaries published as *Breaking the Code* (1999), which were widely praised.

## Branson, Richard (1950–), Sir

Entrepreneur whose gift for publicity led politicians to seek his support. He was educated at Stowe School. He first made money through founding Virgin Records but moved swiftly into air travel, radio, pensions and other enterprises, not all of which proved successful. Political parties wooed him and he gave low-level support to Tony Blair in 1997. There was some talk later that he might stand for London mayor but nothing came of it. In August 2000 his People's Lottery initially defeated Camelot as the agency to run the National Lottery for the next seven years but later he saw this victory overturned in the Court of Appeal.

## Bremner, Rory (1961–)

Britain's premier political satirist. He was educated at Wellington College and King's College, London. He was lauded with awards from BAFTA, RTS and elsewhere and was the nation's favourite impressionist and satirist of politicians. Along with fellow satirists John Bird and John Fortune, his Channel 4 programme became a 'must see' event for anyone interested in British politics who also had a sense of humour; this, fortunately, seemed to include most of the politicians pilloried on the shows.

## Bright, John (1811–89)

One of the leading Radical Liberals of the mid-19th century, speaking out for trade, peace and reform. He was born in Rochdale and became a leading member of the Anti-Corn Law League after 1839, when he gained a reputation as a brilliantly fiery speaker. After 1843 he was MP for Durham. Later he represented Birmingham and campaigned for what became the second Reform Act (1867). He was briefly president of Board of Trade in 1868 but retired through ill-health in 1870. He returned to office in 1881 as chancellor of the Duchy of Lancaster.

### Brittan, Leon (1939–), Lord

Conservative politician who became a cabinet minister and then a European commissioner. He was educated at Cambridge and Harvard, and qualified as a barrister. He became a Conservative MP in 1974 and from 1979 held office under Margaret Thatcher: chief secretary to the Treasury 1981–83 and home secretary 1983–86. He resigned in 1986 over the Westland affair, though most insiders believed him to have taken the blame for the actions of others. He became a European commissioner in 1989, with responsibility for competition policy, and was vice president of the Commission 1995–99. Brittan was not afraid to criticise his Eurosceptic party (though with no discernible effect).

### Brown, George (1914–85), Lord

Unpredictable, quick-tempered foreign secretary under Harold Wilson 1966–68. He left school at 15 to become a van driver. He became an official of the Transport and General Workers' Union and established himself as a robust critic of the left. He entered the House in 1945 and gained junior office. He was minister of works in 1951. His talents suited opposition. He defended the leadership against 'Bevanism' and was elected deputy leader in 1960. He lost to Harold Wilson in the Labour Party leadership election following Hugh Gaitskell's death in 1963. He became secretary of state for economic affairs in 1964. His National Plan for the economy, however, was never really practical or acceptable to the cabinet. He was moved to the Foreign Office, where he pursued his enthusiasm for Europe and hostility to US involvement in Vietnam. He resigned in 1968 over his exclusion from a key economic decision. He went to the Lords after his defeat in 1970 as Lord George- Brown but was not offered office again and he became a critic of the government. He joined the Social Democrats in 1982.

### Brown, Gordon (1951–)

Labour politician and chancellor from 1997. He was educated at Edinburgh University, where he gained a first-class history degree and then gained a doctorate. He entered the House in 1983 for Dunfermline East. At the age of 38 and already a party 'heavyweight', his destructive debating and media-friendly style placed him top of the party's shadow cabinet poll. In 1994, it was rumoured, he agreed to stand down as the successor to Labour Party leader John Smith, in favour of his friend and colleague the even more telegenic Tony Blair, with whom he had been assiduously 'modernising' the Labour Party. Once in office in 1997 he immediately gave the Bank of England the right to set interest rates, advised by a Monetary Policy Committee. He soon established a reputation as the 'iron chancellor', partly because he insisted on restraining public expenditure for two years. However, in July 1998 he delighted 'Old' Labour by announcing substantial increases in planned social spending over the forthcoming three years. His press advisor Charlie Whelan was criticised for exceeding his authority and misrepresenting Brown's policies as well as urging Brown's advancement to the detriment of other colleagues. Labour's general election victory of June 2001 was widely attributed to Brown's sound record on the economy. He retained his position as chancellor, though talk of rivalry with Blair continued.

### Brown, Nick (1950–)

Labour politician and chief whip from 1997. He was educated at Tunbridge Wells Technical School and Manchester University. He was a legal advisor to the GMB union before he entered the

Commons in 1983 for a Newcastle constituency. He served as Treasury opposition
spokesman under Labour leader John
Smith. Brown has been seen as a loyal
supporter of Gordon Brown. In office after
1997 he had a difficult time at the Ministry
of Agriculture, Fisheries and Food
(MAFF), both through the tail-end of the
crisis over bovine spongiform encephalitis
('mad cow disease') and the epidemic of
foot-and-mouth disease in 2001, which he
was perceived to have handled ineptly. In
June 2001 he lost his job at MAFF, which
was subsumed into a new ministry, but was
appointed to the ministry of work and pensions as minister for work.

### Brown, Simon (1938–), Lord Justice

Intelligence services commissioner since
2000. He was a judge of the High Court
Queen's Bench Division 1984–92 and lord
justice of appeal from 1992. He was appointed commissioner for security services
under the Security Act 1994 and then for
intelligence services under the Regulation
of Investigatory Powers Act 2000.

### Burke, Edmund (1729–97)

Great Conservative thinker who opposed
the French Revolution. He was born in
Dublin and educated at Trinity College.
He became secretary for Ireland but is
better known as the major philosophical
founder of modern Conservatism. He was
horrified by the French Revolution and
asserted that humans are not able to change
their basic nature; thus change has to be
slow and gradual, and continuity between
past, present and future is essential for
stability. He also supported the right of
the American colonists to oppose taxation
without representation and insisted the
duty of an MP is not to reflect the views of
constituents but to use judgement on their
behalf in the government of the country.

> All government – indeed every human ben-
> efit and enjoyment and every prudent act – is
> founded on compromise and barter. (1775)

> The only thing necessary for the triumph of
> evil is that good men do nothing.

### Butler, David (1924–)

Political scientist. He was educated at St
Paul's and New College, Oxford. He became a fellow at Nuffield College, Oxford,
where he established himself as the 'father'
of modern psephology, the study of voting
behaviour. He has appeared regularly on
television and has written, with a variety of
collaborators, the series of Nuffield studies
on British general elections.

### Butler, (Frederick Edward) Robin (1938–), Lord

Able British 'mandarin' who rose to be
head of the civil service. He was educated
at Harrow and University College, Oxford.
He joined the Treasury in 1961, was principal private secretary to Edward Heath
1972–74 and Harold Wilson 1974–75;
then principal private secretary to the prime
minister 1982–85, permanent secretary
at the Treasury 1985–87, secretary to
the cabinet and head of the civil service
1988–97. He served five prime ministers
in all, including Tony Blair for a short time
before retiring and being raised to a life
peerage. In February 2004 was called back
from retirement to chair an inquiry into the
intelligence upon which the decision to go
to war against Iraq had been based. He
was the archetypal smooth mandarin, with
the traditional upper-middle-class background, who, in the classic mode, seemed
to achieve his success effortlessly.

> The deal is that you give people very con-
> siderable power for five years and then they
> can be thrown out. And, in the meantime,
> if things get bad enough, there are ways of
> getting rid of them. That is the deal of our
> constitution. (1998)

> What can a few special advisers do against
> thousands of civil servants? We'll swat them
> like flies. (Butler quoted in *The Times*, 3
> February 2004)

### Butler, Richard Austen ('Rab') (1902–82)

Conservative politician, cabinet minister,
thinker and candidate for leadership who

never quite made it. He was educated at Marlborough and Cambridge, where he became a fellow before he entered the Commons for Saffron Walden in 1929. He served as a junior minister before becoming minister of education 1941–45. His name is still associated with the Education Act 1944, which reorganised secondary education and introduced the much criticised 11 plus examination. He was chancellor 1951–55 before he went on to become a liberal home secretary 1957–62. Harold Macmillan believed him to be unsuited to leadership at the very top and did his (successful) best to frustrate Butler's efforts to achieve the premiership. Consequently Butler failed to win the succession to Anthony Eden in 1957, losing out to Macmillan, who also prevented him gaining the prize when he retired through ill-health in 1963. Butler served briefly as foreign secretary under Alec Douglas-Home. In 1964 he became master of Trinity College, Cambridge, and a peer. He was one of the most able and thoughtful Conservative politicians of his generation, very much of the consensual school but ultimately perhaps lacking the steel, and the luck, to become prime minister.

## Byers, Stephen (1953–)

Labour politician and cabinet minister. He was educated at Chester City Grammar School and Liverpool Polytechnic. He became a lecturer at Newcastle Polytechnic before becoming MP for Wallsend in 1992. He was education spokesman in opposition. After the 1997 general election he became a junior minister in education and employment, then in July 1997 he moved to the Treasury as chief secretary. Byers was an earnest Blairite high-flier and was even mentioned as a potential future leader, though critics complained that he had little charisma. In June 2001 he moved to secretary for transport and local government, where he inherited problems from deputy prime minister John Prescott, who had had responsibility in this area. Byers ran into heavy criticism from the right and from the world of finance for declaring Railtrack

bankrupt and appointing a receiver. He also attracted criticism for supporting the private–public partnership favoured by chancellor Gordon Brown for the London Underground. His cup of woe overflowed in February 2002 when he faced a scandal involving his political advisor Jo Moore and his press secretary Martin Sixsmith. To make matters even worse he was blamed for a financial crisis involving the National Air Traffic Services (NATS). Byers survived one crisis of confidence in the autumn of 2001 through the support he commanded from the Labour backbenches over his Railtrack moves, which forced the privatised company into a kind of renationalisation. However, such support could not stop the gaffes and alleged misleading statements to the Commons taking their toll and in May 2002 he resigned and returned to the backbenches.

# C

## Callaghan, James (1912–), Lord

Labour prime minister 1976–79. He was born in Portsmouth. He joined the civil service in 1929, became involved in trade union matters, and served in the Royal Navy during the war as a midshipman. He was elected MP for South Cardiff in 1945 but rose to prominence in the 1960s when he was chancellor 1964–67 and home secretary 1967–70. In Harold Wilson's second administration he was foreign secretary 1974–76 and after Wilson's surprise resignation became prime minister 1976–79. As premier he operated with relaxed aplomb and survived some awesome financial crises as well as the two-year period when he had to operate with the support of the Liberals (the Lib–Lab pact of 1977–79). His decision to peg wage increases to 5 per cent in 1978 proved unacceptable to the Trades Union Congress and the so-called 'winter of discontent' of industrial unrest resulted. This destroyed the authority of the government and the notion that it could keep the unions in check. Callaghan lost the 1979 general election but remained as leader of the opposition until 1980, when he resigned. He took up a seat in the Lords in 1987. He was the only prime minister to have served beforehand in all three of the great offices of state and he proved remarkably effective as the incumbent of Number 10. As his luck ran out towards the end of the 1970s, when events began to engulf him, his political judgement as to when to go to the country deserted him also.

> Crisis? What crisis? (*Sun* headline, 11 January 1979, which wrongly quoted the prime minister at a press conference in which he had actually said 'I don't think that other people in the world would share the view that there is mounting chaos')

> You can never reach the promised land. You can march towards it. (1978)

## Campbell, Alastair (1950–)

Famously tough press secretary to Tony Blair from 1994. After Oxford Campbell entered journalism, specialising in the tabloids: he was political editor for the *Daily Mirror* and *Today*, where he was a colourful Fleet Street figure known for a taste for alcohol and a quick temper. In 1994 he became Blair's press secretary – technically a civil servant though his role was intensely political. He quickly gained a reputation for aggression towards the Conservative press and fierce loyalty to his boss, which virtually equalled that of Bernard Ingham, Margaret Thatcher's formidable equivalent during the 1980s. Some commentators described him as the second most powerful man in the government – the 'deputy prime minister', even though in June 1998 he assured the Public Administration Committee he was no more than a humble 'mouthpiece'. In 2000 he was given a new title – director of communications and strategy – and a less conspicuous role, as the chore of daily press briefings was given to his deputy, Godric Smith. In the summer of 2002 New Labour was engaged in a bit-

ter war with the media and some, including Roy Hattersley, a former deputy leader of the party, blamed some of the trouble on a press secretary who had outlived his usefulness and should go. By the summer of 2003 Campbell had been hit by the aftermath of the war on Iraq, when attention focused on how the case for war had been presented. Campbell himself was accused by the BBC of having 'sexed up' an intelligence-based dossier issued in September 2002 to justify the attack on Iraq. Campbell demanded an apology but the exposure of the BBC's source, Dr David Kelly, an advisor to the Ministry of Defence, was quickly followed by his tragic suicide. This prompted the Hutton inquiry, out of which Campbell emerged officially exonerated but hardly spotless. However, he had already resigned in September, apparently of his own volition, though the criticism occasioned by Hutton made his going opportune. He denied his diaries – quotations from which had an explosive effect at the Hutton investigations – were intended for publication, but few believed him. His decision to take to the 'road' with a stage show in January 2004 was initially successful though attendances dropped off.

> G[eoff] H[oon] and I agreed it would fuck Gilligan if that was his source. (Campbell's diary, read in evidence to the Hutton inquiry, 22 September 2003, in which he and the defence secretary agreed the exposure of David Kelly's name would help his side of his row with the BBC)

> This is diary writing – it doesn't actually express what is going on. It's me, at the end of the day, scribbling whatever comes into my head. (Evidence to Hutton, 22 September 2003)

## Campbell-Bannerman, Henry (1836–1908)

Liberal prime minister 1905–08. He was educated at Glasgow High School and Cambridge. He was Liberal MP for Stirling Burghs 1868–1908 and held junior office in the War Office and Admiralty before becoming secretary for war 1892–95. He became leader of the Liberal Party when Herbert Asquith was seen as too young for the job and managed to hold a divided party together during the Boer War, which he and David Lloyd George opposed. When the Conservative prime minister Arthur Balfour resigned in December 1905, thinking the Liberals would be even more divided than the Conservatives, Campbell-Bannerman took office. He proved an astute and effective manager of his party and led it to the historic 1906 landslide election victory. The unassuming typical Liberal, 'CB' ended up leading a great reforming administration and succeeded in harnessing the talents of the likes of Asquith and Lloyd George. He resigned in 1908 through ill-health and died shortly afterwards.

### Carey, George (1935–)

Archbishop of Canterbury. He was educated at Bifron Secondary Modern School, Barking, and King's College, London. He was appointed archbishop in 1991, as someone with an evangelical tinge to his Christianity. He took a conservative line on homosexuality in the 1998 Lambeth Conference votes. He was succeeded in 2002 by Rowan Williams.

### Carrington, Peter (1919–), Lord

Conservative politician much in office in the late 20th century. He trained in Sandhurst and won the Military Cross in the Second World War. He held junior posts in government in the early 1950s before becoming high commissioner to Australia 1956–59, first lord of the Admiralty 1959–63 and leader of the House of Lords 1963–64. He was defence secretary under Edward Heath 1970–74 and briefly energy secretary in 1974, while also chairman of the Conservative Party 1972–74. He was foreign secretary 1979–82 but resigned over the Falklands crisis. He became secretary general of NATO 1984–88. Carrington was one of those competent, loyal, aristocratic Conservatives who devoted their lives to public service and occupied Tory cabinets out of a sense of noblesse oblige.

It was appropriately in character that he should tender his resignation over the Falklands when, arguably, others were more responsible.

### Cash, Bill (1940–)

Conservative MP and noted Eurosceptic. He was educated at Stonyhurst College and Oxford, and went on to practise as a solicitor. He was known essentially as a monomaniac Europhobe who was central to the rebellions over this subject during John Major's troubled years as prime minister (1992–97). Colleagues complained he bored them relentlessly on his pet subject and consequently many were surprised, especially on the moderate wing of the party, when in September 2001 the new Conservative leader, Iain Duncan Smith, appointed him to a senior shadow job, claiming it would require a much wider knowledge than merely things European. Under Michael Howard, however, he did not receive any preference.

### Castle, Barbara (1911–2000), Baroness

Labour cabinet minister during the 1960s and 1970s. She was educated at Bradford Girls' Grammar School and St Hugh's College, Oxford. She worked as a journalist before the Second World War and entered the House of Commons in 1945 for Blackburn. She was a supporter of Aneurin Bevan and a chair of the Labour Party in the 1950s. She served as minister of overseas development 1964–65, transport 1965–68 (where she introduced the breathalyser and the 70 mph limit) and employment and productivity 1968–70. She was minister of health and social security 1974–76 but was not a favourite of James Callaghan and returned to the backbenches when he came to power in 1976. She acted as vice chair of the socialist group in the European parliament 1979–84 and campaigned for better pensions during the 1990s. As a much-respected Labour veteran, the New Labour hierarchy allowed her to have her say but chose to disregard her advice. She was ennobled in 1990.

## Chamberlain, Austen (1863–1937)

Conservative chancellor 1903–05 and 1919–21, leader of the party 1921–22, and foreign secretary 1924–29. He was the eldest son of Joseph Chamberlain and was educated at Rugby and Trinity College, Cambridge. He was returned as MP for East Worcester in 1892 and soon began to climb the ladder into the cabinet. In the wartime coalition government he was secretary for India 1915–17. Following Andrew Bonar Law's resignation he was elected leader of the Conservative Party 1921–22. He was opposed to backbench pressure to end the coalition government with the Liberals, but in 1922 the famous meeting in the Carlton Club voted to take Law and Baldwin's advice to end it. While foreign secretary 1924–29 he negotiated the 1925 Locarno pact, which many thought was a guarantee against a renewed outbreak of war, and for which he was awarded the Nobel Peace Prize in 1925. He was a sensitive man who somewhat misjudged the political climate of his times and consequently arguably missed being made prime minister.

> A man who played the game and always lost. (Winston Churchill's acid comment on Austen Chamberlain)

> All governments are pretty much alike, with the tendency, on the part of the last to be the worst. (1911)

## Chamberlain, Joseph (1836–1914)

Liberal politician and secretary of state for the colonies 1895–1903, who split his party over Irish Home Rule. He was educated at University College School, which he left aged 16, and then went to work for Nettlefolds screw factory, from which he retired in 1874 a wealthy man, aged 38. He began his political career as a Radical councillor and then mayor of Birmingham 1873–76, where he made a reputation as something of a 'machine politician', even in those days. He entered the House of Commons for Birmingham via a by-election in 1876 and by 1880 was president of the Board of Trade and then president of the Local Government Board in 1886, but was seen in cabinet as an extremist by some. He resigned over William Gladstone's Home Rule plans for Ireland and went on to lead a faction called the Liberal Unionists, who were destined to merge with the Conservatives. In the Conservative government of 1895 he was colonial secretary but, unlike the Radical Liberals, supported the Boer War. He resigned in 1903 to advocate tariff reform to protect British industries from foreign competition. In 1906 he suffered a stroke, which drove him out of public life, though he lived on for several more years. He was one of the great talents of 19th-century politics but never quite fulfilled his potential.

> The day of small nations has passed away. The day of Empires has come. (1904)

> The manners of a cad and the tongue of a bargee. (H. H. Asquith on Chamberlain, 1900)

## Chamberlain, Neville (1869–1940)

Conservative chancellor 1923–24 and 1931–37, and prime minister 1937–40. He was the son of Joseph Chamberlain by second marriage. He was educated at Rugby and Mason College, Birmingham, and became a successful businessman in his own right before serving as lord mayor of Birmingham 1915–16. Then he entered national politics as Conservative MP for Birmingham Ladywood. He was a minister in his early 20s and then chancellor until 1924, followed by a period as minister of health. In 1931 he was appointed chancellor again and remained in the post until 1937, when he became prime minister. He was out of his depth in foreign affairs and was unable to gauge the danger of Hitler – he believed a policy of appeasement was morally and politically justified. In 1938 he returned from Munich with an agreement which he thought offered 'peace in our time' but it soon fell apart and he was forced to declare war: the direct opposite of his policy objective. As the war went against Britain in the early months the

Conservative Party turned against him and in a crucial vote of confidence he could muster a majority of only 80 instead of the party's 200. He therefore resigned as prime minister (though not as party leader) before ill-health forced him to allow Winston Churchill to take over, with historic consequences. He died, of cancer, a broken man, six months later.

> How horrible, fantastic, incredible it is that we should be digging trenches and trying on gas-masks here because of a quarrel between people in a faraway country of whom we know nothing. (Reference to Czechoslovakia in a radio broadcast, 27 September 1938)

> This is the second time in our history that there has come back from Germany to Downing Street, peace with honour. I believe it is peace for our time. (From a window in Number 10 Downing Street, on returning from Munich, 30 September 1938)

## Charles, Prince of Wales (1948–)

Heir to the throne. He was educated at Gordonstoun School and Cambridge University. He also studied Welsh at Aberystwyth University for a while in 1969. Faced with the problem of a high public profile and the longevity of his mother, Charles busied himself with the Prince's Trust, which seeks to put young people into worthwhile work. He also advocated traditional opinions on architecture and conservationist ones on the environment. His disastrous marriage to Diana left him appearing more the sinner than the sinned against, though since her death the press presented him more favourably as a father trying desperately hard to bring up his two sons in a loving fashion. His affair with Camilla Parker Bowles was not popular with the public and he tried to usher her into the public limelight discreetly, possibly to prepare the way for a more permanent connection.

## Churchill, Winston (1874–1965)

Heroic, world famous, long-serving statesman whose career spanned two centuries and included most of the senior political offices. He was the son of Lord Randolph Churchill and was educated at Harrow and Sandhurst. He joined the 4th Hussars in 1895 and fought at Omdurman. He reported the Boer War as a journalist. He became Conservative MP for Oldham in 1900 but joined the Liberals in 1904 and served in junior office before becoming president of the Board of Trade 1908–10 and home secretary 1910–11, first lord of the Admiralty 1911 and munitions minister in David Lloyd George's wartime government 1917, war minister 1919–21 and, from 1924 when he rejoined the Conservatives, chancellor until 1929. During the 1930s he inveighed against the spinelessness of the national government in the face of the threat of fascism and as a result of his furious assaults on appeasement was regarded by his party as a dangerous maverick.

In 1939 he returned to the Admiralty in Neville Chamberlain's wartime coalition government and when Chamberlain fell in 1940 Churchill took over as prime minister. This was the greatest period of his career, perhaps of any British political career, when he promised the country nothing except 'blood, toil, tears and sweat'. After working closely with the Allies and under his inspiring leadership, in which his gift of oratory ranked as a major weapon in the war, Britain eventually emerged triumphant. However, a country transformed by war denied him re-election and he led the opposition – not with conspicuous distinction – until 1951, when he became prime minister again. He finally retired in 1955. During this final phase he was sick and for a while, after he suffered a stroke, the government was run discreetly in his name. As well as a great orator he was also an accomplished writer and journalist. He wrote enthralling histories of the English-speaking peoples and the Second World War. He was awarded the Nobel Prize for Literature in 1950.

> I have nothing to offer but blood, toil, tears and sweat. (4 June 1940)

> We shall fight them on the beaches, we shall fight them on the landing grounds, we shall

fight them in the fields and streets. (4 June 1940)

If the British Empire and Commonwealth last for a thousand years, men will say, 'This was their finest hour'. (Anticipating the Battle of Britain, September 1940)

From Stettin in the Baltic to Trieste in the Adriatic, an iron curtain has descended across the Continent. (Fulton, Missouri, 5 March 1946)

Victory at all costs, victory in spite of all terror, victory however long and hard the road may be, for without victory there is no survival. (1940)

Give us the tools and we will finish the job. (1941)

## Clark, Alan (1928–99)

Conservative politician, historian and diarist. He was educated at Eton and Christ Church, Oxford, and became a member of the Household Cavalry, and a barrister. He was MP for Plymouth Sutton 1974–92, then retired from politics, but he decided to return in 1997, for Kensington and Chelsea. He was a junior minister for employment and defence, where, as a minister of state, he admitted the defendants in the Matrix Churchill affair had been 'tipped the wink' by the government regarding how to sell arms to the Middle East which ended up in Iraq. He is best known for his witty and scandalous diaries, published in 1993 and later televised. His abilities were not taken as seriously by the higher echelons of the party as he took them himself.

## Clark, Charles (1950–)

Labour MP and cabinet minister. He was educated at Highgate School and King's College, London, as well as Cambridge. He was president of National Union of Students in the 1970s. He was elected to the House of Commons for Norwich South in 1997, after working as chief of staff to Neil Kinnock. In 1999 he became a Home Office minister and he was soon tipped as a 'coming man' and even possible

future leader. He was promoted to cabinet in 2001 as party chair. This resembled Conservative practice – Clarke was paid a cabinet minister's salary but by the Labour Party and not the taxpayer. He saw his role as assisting the delivery of the election promises by reconnecting the government with the party membership (which was falling). Critics pointed out that the party already had a chairperson elected by the party's National Executive Committee. He was appointed to secretary of state for education when Estelle Morris resigned unexpectedly in autumn 2002.

## Clarke, Kenneth (1940–)

Conservative politician and versatile cabinet minister. He was educated at Nottingham Grammar School and Cambridge University. He practised as a barrister before being elected MP for Nottingham Rushcliffe in 1970. He became a member of the 'one nation' Bow Group and served as junior minister under Edward Heath 1970–74 but won senior office under Margaret Thatcher. He became health secretary in 1988. Under John Major, he was home secretary 1992 and chancellor of the exchequer 1993–97. He stood for the leadership of his party in 1997, in the wake of its general election defeat, but was defeated by William Hague, even though he made a surprising alliance with fellow candidate John Redwood. In the wake of the 2001 general election defeat Clarke was initially absent on a business trip to Vietnam in pursuance of his (not uncriticised) role as deputy chairman of the British American Tobacco Company. However, he returned to declare his candidature in late June, though refused to compromise on his robustly pro-Europe views. In the first ballot he polled a disappointing 36 and came third. In the second round he increased his votes to 39 but few expected his winning 59 in the third ballot on 17 July. Some predicted more civil war over Europe with a right-wing Iain Duncan Smith pitted against him for the party members' ballot. However, the ballot by party members, used for the first time by the Conservatives to elect a leader, found heavily for the Eurosceptic, more right-wing Duncan Smith in September 2001.

## Cobden, Richard (1804–1865)

Early Radical Liberal. He was born in Sussex but educated in Yorkshire, and settled in Manchester as a calico merchant in 1831. He became an advocate of free trade. He contested the Stockport seat in 1837 on a free trade ticket but lost. He became the most prominent member of the Anti-Corn Law League and was returned for Stockport in 1841. He spoke regularly against the Corn Laws, which were repealed in 1846 once Peel, leader of the Conservatives, was won over. With John Bright he opposed the Crimean War and Henry Palmerston's foreign policy in China. He supported the North during the US Civil War. He was one of the great radical politicians of the 19th century and was dubbed 'the apostle of free trade'.

## Cook, Robin (1946–)

Labour MP and foreign secretary. He studied at Edinburgh University and trained as a teacher before becoming MP in 1974 for Edinburgh Central; after 1983 he represented Livingston. He served in the shadow Treasury team 1980–83, before taking on health and social security 1987–92. After Labour leader John Smith died in 1994 he became spokesman on trade and industry and then, under Tony Blair, foreign affairs 1994–97. From 1997 he was foreign secretary. Generally seen as the cleverest member of Labour's front bench, he lacked television appeal and his divorce and remarriage (1997/98) earned him unflattering publicity. The general opinion of commentators – though the view was contested – was that this fearsomely intellectually able man under-performed in office and was prone to misjudgements. He introduced an awkwardly 'ethical dimension' into foreign policy, although many diplomats doubted whether the national self-interest could be reconciled with consistently high moral principles. His

negotiation of the end of the Kosovan war was regarded widely as a success. In June 2001 his demotion to leader of the House and Jack Straw's appointment to Cook's old job was the surprise of the post-election reshuffle. There were some early signs that in his new role he might seek to strengthen parliament against the executive. His reforms in autumn 2002 were welcomed by reformers but few felt the balance of power had been altered. In March 2003 he resigned over the imminent war in Iraq and made an impressive, principled speech in support of his decision. He thereupon became a measured critic of the government's foreign policy from the backbenches.

> Our foreign policy must have an ethical dimension. (1997)

## Cranbourne, Robert (1946–), Viscount

Conservative leader in the Lords. He was educated at Eton and Christ Church, Oxford. He entered the House of Commons in 1979 for Dorset South. He spent some time in Afghanistan resisting the Soviet occupation. He served as a junior minister in the 1980s and then returned to the backbenches until John Major elevated him to the Lords via a 'writ of acceleration', necessary as his father, the Marquess of Salisbury, was still a sitting member. He became Conservative leader in the Lords with a place in the cabinet in 1994. He made several speeches opposing Labour plans to end the role of hereditary peers when the Conservatives were in government. In a volte face in December 1998 he conducted a series of secret meetings with Number 10 Downing Street and reached a compromise agreement whereby he accepted a two-stage abolition of peers; during the interim stage 92 hereditary peers would continue to sit and vote. When his party leader, William Hague, heard of these unauthorised meetings and agreements – the events were exposed very publicly at prime minister's questions on 3 December 1998 – he was both embarrassed and angry. Cranbourne was sacked immediately, though still retained the support of some Tory peers.

### Crewe, Ivor (1945–)

Political scientist. He was educated at Manchester Grammar School, Exeter College, Oxford, and the London School of Economics. He became professor of government at Essex University in 1982 and its vice chancellor in 1995. He has been a leading British psephologist who has appeared regularly on television, especially during election campaigns. His book with Anthony King on the history of the Social Democratic Party was received with critical acclaim. He received the Political Studies Association's Isiaih Berlin Prize 2004.

### Crick, Bernard (1929–), Sir

Political scientist. He was educated at Whitgift School, University College, London, and Harvard, McGill and Berkeley universities. He lectured at the London School of Economics and became professor at Sheffield and Birkbeck. He was joint editor of *Political Quarterly*, chaired Labour's working party on citizenship and was a joint founder of the Politics Association in 1969. His books include *In Defence of Politics* (1962) and a praised biography of George Orwell (1980). He was knighted in 2002.

### Crick, Michael (1958–)

Investigative BBC2 *Newsnight* reporter and author. He was educated at Manchester Grammar School and Oxford. He started work for Independent Television News in Washington before moving to the BBC's *Panorama* and then *Newsnight* programmes. He has written praised biographies of Arthur Scargill, Michael Heseltine and, most famously, Jeffrey Archer, in which he exposed much of the fantasy on which the Conservative peer's life had been based. He entered the news in October 2003 by submitting a dossier accusing Iain Duncan Smith of employing his wife Betsy on tax payers' money as a secretary when there was no substantive job performed.

### Cripps, Stafford (1889–1952)

Labour MP and minister. He was educated at Winchester and New College, Oxford, where he showed brilliant promise as a chemist but chose the law. He then became the youngest barrister in Britain and went on to make his fortune out of patent and compensation cases. He became solicitor general in 1930 but refused to join Ramsay MacDonald's coalition, preferring to support a succession of left-wing causes, culminating in the Popular Front campaign to rally a broad swathe of support against Nazism. For this he was expelled from the Labour Party and he sat through the war as an independent. He served as ambassador to Moscow 1940–42 and then returned to hold a number of posts, including minister of aircraft production. He became president of the Board of Trade in 1945 and chancellor in 1947, when Hugh Dalton was forced to resign for leaking budget secrets. He presided over a period of austerity, which he seemed to relish. He lost political credibility when he devalued the pound in 1949. He became ill from overwork in 1950 and retired.

> There, but for the grace of God, goes God. (Winston Churchill on Cripps)

> He has all the virtues I dislike and none of the vices I admire. (Churchill on Cripps again)

### Cromwell, Oliver (1599–1658)

Revolutionary English politician and general. He was born into lesser gentry from Huntingdon. He became an MP in 1629 and his conversion to Puritanism followed in the 1630s. He led the parliamentary resistance to Charles I. In the Civil War he was responsible for the cavalry forces – called Ironsides – which contributed towards a decisive victory at Edgehill in 1642 and Marston Moor in 1644. Along with Fairfax he was the creator of the New Model Army, which won decisive victory at Naseby in 1645. Following the execution of Charles he declared a republic in 1649. He became lord protector in 1653, when he dismissed parliamentary government for a number of years. He was a harsh ruler in some respects, executing the radical Levellers and crushing the Irish rebellion of 1649–50, not to mention the Scots at Dunbar in 1650 and Worcester in 1651. He brooked no parliamentary interference and was essentially a dictator during the period of his 'protectorship'. He was successful militarily against the Dutch and the Spanish. He refused those who pressed him to become king, though he was one in all but name. He introduced a high degree of religious toleration and was responsible for the readmission of the Jews into the country in 1655. When the crown was restored in the person of Charles II, Cromwell's body was dug up from Westminster Abbey and 'ceremonially executed'. He is a contradictory figure in British history: devout and unambitious yet ruthless and dictatorial.

Necessity hath no law. (1654)

I need pity. I know what I feel. Great place and business in the world is not worth looking for. (1650)

The people would be just as noisy if they were going to see me hanged. (In response to a friend who pointed to the cheering crowds)

## Crosland, Anthony (1918–77)

Labour politician and writer on socialism. He was educated at Oxford, where he also taught after war service. He became an MP in 1950. His seminal revisionist text *The Future of Socialism* (1956) argued that Keynesian economics made socialist revolution unnecessary, as the fruits of revolution could be won without one. His passion was equality and he believed it could be won largely through reforming the education system. As education secretary 1965–67 he tried but his vision of comprehensive schools eventually failed to deliver his dreams. He also served in the cabinet at the Board of Trade 1967–69, local government and planning 1969–70 and environment 1974–76, and as foreign secretary 1976–77. His premature death

denied Labour his great talents at a time when arguably they were sorely needed.

If it's the last thing I do I'm going to destroy every fucking grammar school in England and Wales and Northern Ireland. (Quoted by his wife, Susan, 1982)

## Crossman, Richard (1907–74)

Labour politician, journalist and writer. He was educated at Winchester and New College, Oxford, where he taught for a while for the Workers' Educational Association, before leading the Labour group on the city council 1934–40. He joined *New Statesman* in 1938 as a journalist and worked in psychological warfare during the war before being elected Labour MP for Coventry East in 1945. His brilliance in debate, criticising Labour's foreign policy, earned the anger of Ernest Bevin and Clement Attlee. In the 1950s, ever the rebel, he became a leading supporter of Aneurin Bevan. Harold Wilson made him a minister of local government 1964–66 and leader of the House 1966–68, where he initiated some reform of the select committee system, and social services and health 1968–70. He edited *New Statesman* 1970–72 and wrote a classic introduction to Walter Bagehot's *British Constitution* in 1963. His *Diaries of a Cabinet Minister* (published in three volumes, 1975–77) proved a goldmine for historians and lovers of Labour political gossip in equal measure.

I view this able and energetic man with some detachment. He is loyal to his own career but only incidentally to anything or anyone else. (Hugh Dalton on Crossman, 1941)

## Currie, Edwina (1946–)

Colourful junior health minister under Margaret Thatcher. She was educated at Liverpool Institute for Girls, St Anne's College, Oxford, and then at the London School of Economics. She was a lecturer 1972–81 before becoming active as a Birmingham city councillor, where she specialised in social services and housing.

She was MP for Derbyshire South 1983–97. She became a junior minister at education and health 1986–88 but lost the latter job after unwisely describing the British chicken industry as being infected with salmonella, thus damaging the egg industry. Despite her expectations she failed to win office again but won attention through her broadcasting and her novels (the best-known being *A Parliamentary Affair*, 1994). In 2002 she caused a sensation when her published diaries revealed she had conducted a four-year affair with John Major, before he became prime minister. She was a clever and interesting politician whose reach perhaps exceeded her grasp.

# D

## Dacre, Paul (1948–)

Editor in chief at Associated Newspapers and editor the *Daily Mail*. He was educated at University College School, Leeds, and Leeds University. He succeeded to the editorship on the death of David English in 1998 and sustained the tabloid's position as the second (to the *Sun*) best-selling daily newspaper, with over 2 million daily sales. His newspaper is reportedly regularly read and respected by Tony Blair. Dacre was credited with being able to 'feel the pulse of middle England' and was known for campaigns like that over the death of Stephen Lawrence.

## Dalton, Hugh (1887–1962)

Labour politician and cabinet minister. He was the son of the chaplain to Queen Victoria. He was educated at Eton, King's College, Cambridge, and the London School of Economics before serving in the First World War. He was a Labour MP from 1924 to 1931 and then again from 1935. He was minister for economic warfare 1940 and president of the Board of

Trade 1942. In 1945 he became chancellor of the exchequer but disclosed the contents of the 1947 budget to a journalist before his speech to parliament and, in the honourable custom of the time, resigned. He was made a life peer in 1960. One of the founding fathers of modern Labour, he was influential in economic and foreign policy. An extrovert with a high self-regard, he attracted enemies as easily as friends but had a record of encouraging younger colleagues to advance themselves, including Hugh Gaitskell. His diaries have been a rich source for historians; his biography by Ben Pimlott has been highly praised.

## Dalyell, Tam (1932–)

Formidable old Etonian Labour backbencher with reputation for persevering with his campaigns. He was educated at Eton and King's College, Cambridge, and then trained and practised as a teacher before he entered parliament for West Lothian 1962–83 and Linlithgow 1983. The 'backbencher's backbencher', Dalyell had no experience of office and little of shadow office either. Rather, he has channelled his formidable talents of research and perseverance into particular campaigns like the one on the circumstances surrounding the sinking of the *General Belgrano* in the Falklands War and the discovery of the authors of the Lockerbie disaster. He took over from Sir Edward Heath in 2001 as the father of the house.

## Darling, Alistair (1953–)

Labour MP and minister. He was born into a Conservative family and was educated at Lorretto School and Aberdeen University. He served on Lothian Regional Council 1982–87. After being elected Labour MP for Edinburgh Central in 1987 he was opposition Treasury spokesman. In government after 1997 he was an impressive chief secretary to the Treasury before he moved to become secretary of state for social security after the reshuffle in July 1998. He was made secretary for work and pensions in June 2001. In June 2002 he took over from the sacked

Stephen Byers at transport, to attempt to sort out Labour's possibly most intractable policy area. He was given the 'part-time' job of spokesman for Scotland in June 2003 when the residual functions of the secretaries of state for Scotland and Wales were subsumed into the new Department of Constitutional Affairs. He is a clever, competent minister, good with media skills, and tipped for further promotion.

## Davies, Clement (1884–1962)

Liberal politician and leader. He was born in Llanfyllin, Montgomeryshire, and educated at Cambridge. He was elected for his home county in 1929 and served until his death. He was leader of the Liberal Party 1945–56 and in 1951 refused Winston Churchill's offer of a post as education secretary, to avoid his party being subsumed, as had the National Liberals, into the Conservative Party.

## Davies, Gavyn (1952–)

Chairman of the BBC 2000–04. He was educated at both Cambridge and Oxford. He had a hugely lucrative career as an investment banker for Philips and Drew, Simon and Coates, and then Goldman Sachs, where sale of shares made him a very rich man. He was attached to the Policy Unit of Number 10 Downing Street 1974–79 and subsequently was a regular advisor to governments of both main parties. The Conservatives complained bitterly when in 2001 he was appointed as chairman of the BBC, as his wife, Sue Nye, worked for chancellor Gordon Brown and Davies was known to be a generous donor to the Labour Party, just as the BBC's then director general, Greg Dyke, was. Davies defended himself by saying he had worked for governments of both left and right and was able to suspend personal bias in a professional capacity. His role in the BBC was anticipated when he chaired a committee into the future funding of the BBC in 1999. The previous chairman, Sir Christopher Bland, had been a well known Conservative supporter. Davies was forced to resign when the Hutton report criticised

the BBC in the wake of the row caused by Andrew Gilligan's controversial broadcast on 29 May 2003 regarding the government's presentation of the case for war with Iraq.

## Davies, Ron (1946–)

Former Labour secretary of state for Wales whose flourishing career was sadly ended by scandal. He was educated at Barasleg Grammar School, Portsmouth Polytechnic and Cardiff University. He was a teacher and tutor for the Workers' Educational Association 1968–74 before he became a councillor and then MP for Caerphilly. He served in the whips' office and as shadow spokesman on Wales. He became secretary of state 1997–98 and was instrumental in setting up the Welsh assembly. After serving as a member of the Welsh assembly from 1999, he decided to resign from politics after a bizarre scandal involving a late-night walk on Clapham Common in an area frequented by gays.

## Davis, David (1948–)

Conservative MP and leadership hopeful in 2001. Of Polish Jewish descent, he went from humble beginnings in a council house to study at grammar school, then Warwick and Harvard universities. He was a successful businessman at Tate and Lyle. He entered the House in 1987 for Boothferry, was made a whip in 1990 and became Foreign Office minister of state for Europe under John Major 1994–97, who hoped Davis's Eurosceptic views would help him sell the idea of the European Union to fellow MPs. After the Conservative defeat in the 1997 general election he became a highly regarded chair of the Public Accounts Committee, 95 per cent of whose recommendations were accepted by government during his time in the chair. After the 2001 election defeat of his party he stood as a candidate in the leadership contest, when he was widely seen as a 'dark horse' but he came joint last with Michael Ancram. He decided to drop out shortly afterwards. Iain Duncan Smith made him party chair but in July 2002 he was sacked amidst some damaging circumstances involving accusations of a dilatory attitude and residual designs on the leadership. He was re-established as deputy leader but was seen by many as a less than loyal member of the shadow cabinet as the chorus of complaint against Duncan Smith grew in 2003. When the latter was defeated in the vote of confidence in October 2003, Davis, after some hesitation, decided not to stand for the leadership and stood aside to allow the 'coronation' of Michael Howard.

### Day, Robin (1923–2000)

Leading television interviewer of his day. He served in the artillery during the Second World War and then studied law at Oxford and was called to the bar in 1952. He worked as a broadcaster for Independent Television News 1955–59 and then joined BBC's *Panorama* 1967–72 and played a leading role as an interviewer and political commentator, especially during election campaigns. He fronted the BBC's *Question Time* for many years. He was arguably the first interviewer to shake off the deferential attitude towards senior politicians and brought to them a freshness and irreverence, not to mention abrasiveness, which others have assiduously copied and developed.

> But why should the public, on this issue, as regards the future of the Royal Navy, believe you, a transient, here-today and, if I may say so, gone-tomorrow politician, rather than a senior officer of many years? (October 1982, during an interview with the Conservative secretary of state for defence John Nott, while pursuing a line of questioning regarding cuts in defence expenditure – Nott then walked out of the interview)

### de Chastelain, John (1938–), General

Head of the Independent International Commission on Decommissioning in Northern Ireland. Son of American mother and Scottish father, he was educated in Fettes School, Edinburgh, and then moved to Canada when aged 18, and entered the

Canadian military. He soon rose through the ranks and distinguished himself before becoming his country's ambassador to the United Nations in 1993. In 1995 he was invited by Senator Mitchell to head up the new Commission.

### Delors, Jacques (1925–)

French politician of the left who became president of the European Commission in 1985 and was reappointed in 1988 (a term extended until 1995). Given his length of time in office he is rightly seen as one of the major influences on the evolution of European political and economic integration. Accordingly he was disliked by the Conservative Europsceptics, including Margaret Thatcher, and the *Sun* newspaper, which once led with the headline 'Up Yours Delors'.

### Denning, Tom (1899–1999), Lord

One of the most distinguished judges in postwar British public life. He was educated at Oxford and called to the bar in 1923. He became a High Court justice in 1944 and was made a lord of appeal in ordinary in 1957. He led an inquiry into the Profumo affair in 1963. He was Master of the Rolls 1962–82 and the author of many controversial judgements. He believed judges should make the right decisions on behalf of individuals now and 'not leave it to Parliament years afterwards'. Consequently he was more than once overruled by the Lords.

> We shouldn't have all these campaigns to get the Birmingham Six released. If they'd been hanged they'd have been forgotten and the whole community would have been satisfied. (1990)

### Dewar, Donald (1937–2000)

Labour MP and minister. He was educated at Glasgow Academy and Glasgow University. He was a silkily clever and ambitious Scottish politician who became his country's first first minister after the votes for the assembly in 1999. Labour scandals in Scotland in the early years of the assembly did not help his cause and the Scottish National Party posed a constant threat to his dreams. Following a period of ill-health, he died in the autumn of 2000.

### Dicey, Albert Venn (1835–1922)

Author of the definitive work on the constitution *Lectures Introductory to the Study of the Law of the Constitution* (1885). He was Vinerian professor of jurisprudence at Oxford. His work emphasised the rule of law and the supremacy of parliament and was instrumental in creating the much imitated Westminster model of liberal democratic government. He was fervently opposed to Irish Home Rule.

### Disraeli, Benjamin (1804–81)

Conservative prime minister 1868 and 1874–80. He was privately educated but trained as a solicitor. Of Jewish origin but baptised in boyhood, he was a best-selling novelist as well as a leading politician (*Coningsby*, 1844, and *Sybil*, 1845, being his best-known works). He became leader of the Young England movement, was critical of industrialism and advocated an alliance between the aristocracy and the working class. He became well known for his acidic criticism of Robert Peel's repealing of the Corn Laws. He led the Conservative Party after Peelites left and was made chancellor in 1867, piloting the second Reform Act through parliament. As prime minister he helped secure ownership of the Suez Canal for Britain and pleased Queen Victoria by making her Empress of India. He was judged to have achieved a diplomatic triumph at the Congress of Berlin in 1878, which settled disputes between the Russians and the Turks in the Balkans. For many Tories his name remains synonymous with 'one nation' Toryism. He is the most exotic and unusual man to achieve high office, let alone become prime minister as leader of the Conservative Party.

Though I sit down now, the time will come when you will hear me. (Following the derisive reaction to his maiden speech in the Commons, 1837)

I will not go down to posterity talking bad grammar. (Correcting *Hansard* proofs on his deathbed)

At the top of the greasy pole. (Describing his position as prime minister, 1868)

A Conservative government is an organised hypocrisy. (1845)

England does not love coalitions. (1852)

He is a self-made man and worships his creator. (John Bright on Disraeli)

### Dobson, Frank (1940–)

Labour MP and minister, and latterly critic of Tony Blair's government. He was educated at Archbishop Holgate Grammar School, York, and the London School of Economics. He worked for the Central Electricity Generating Board 1962–70 before becoming a local councillor in Camden 1971–76, when he was council leader 1973–75. He was the MP for Holborn and St Pancras after 1979. He had various shadow portfolios before he became health secretary 1997–99. He left office to stand as Labour mayoral candidate; however, the leadership's hope that he would stop Ken Livingstone winning the election as an ex-Labour independent was dashed. As a backbencher he opposed the Iraq war and was the leader of the campaign against foundation hospitals.

### Donaldson, John Francis (1920–), Lord

Cambridge-educated British judge specialising, when a barrister, in commercial law. He was made a judge in 1966, justice of appeal 1979–82 and Master of the Rolls 1982, in succession to Lord Denning. He achieved a high profile in 1971 when he became president of the National Industrial Relations Court, which was regarded by unions and Labour alike as a Conservative anti-union instrument. He sat on the crossbenches in the House of Lords.

## Douglas-Home, Alec (1903–95), Earl of Home

Conservative prime minister. He was educated at Eton and Oxford, where he was elected head of the prestigious 'Pop'. He entered parliament in 1931 and served as secretary to Neville Chamberlain during the appeasement years. In the 1950s as the Earl of Home (after 1951) he had junior office and was then promoted to foreign secretary 1960–63, as which he was successful and popular. He astonished the political world when he emerged out of the then undemocratic 'magic circle' system of appointing Conservative leaders and became the compromise candidate between rivals R. A. Butler and Reginald Maudling. He went on, with the support of Harold Macmillan – who wished to stop Butler – to become prime minister in November 1963, when he renounced his peerage and won Kinross at a by-election. As premier he was popular with his party but perceived as ineffectual and out of touch with ordinary people, a deficiency exploited effectively by Harold Wilson in the 1964 general election campaign. He served as leader of the opposition until 1965 and then as foreign secretary under Edward Heath 1970–74. He became a life peer in 1974. He was the only senior politician of his day to have played county cricket.

> The doctor unfortunately said I was fit. (On taking office as prime minister, 1964)

> There are two problems in my life. The political ones are insoluble and the economic ones are incomprehensible. (1964)

> After half a century of democratic advance, the whole process ground to a halt with a fourteenth earl. (Harold Wilson on the new Conservative prime minister, Sir Alec Douglas-Home, 1963)

## Dugdale, Thomas (1897–1977)

Conservative minister of agriculture. He is usually quoted as the minister who resigned in recognition of his ultimate responsibility for mistakes made by his officials, in his case in 1954, over the reselling of land, Crichel Down, requisitioned during the war. In more recent times few ministers have emulated his behaviour despite dire mistakes in their departments.

## Duncan Smith, Iain ('IDS') (1954–)

Conservative MP and party leader. He was educated at Sandhurst and became an MP for Chingford. He was shadow defence spokesman under William Hague and he decided to stand in the elections for Conservative leadership after Hague stepped down in June 2001. His advantages included support from the right, including Margaret Thatcher and Norman Tebbit, but disadvantages included lack of name recognition and, in the television age, his baldness. He believed the party had to broaden its appeal while remaining true to its traditions. He did well in the first ballot, winning 39 votes, coming second behind Michael Portillo. In the second ballot he edged up to 42, and in the final ballot on 17 July he failed to beat Ken Clarke but came second to him with 54 votes (to the ex-chancellor's 59). The stage was then set for the choice for 330,000 party members, who now, under rules introduced by Hague, had the opportunity to vote on the two candidates produced by the parliamentary party: Duncan Smith was resolutely right-wing – opposing gays in the military, in favour of education vouchers, a supporter of caning in schools and a Eurosceptic – while Clarke was defiantly pro-Europe, pro-euro and more liberal on most social issues. Duncan Smith won easily. As leader he initially steered a right-wing course but then signalled a shift to the centre on social policy in 2002. He seemed to be leading his party into the centre-ground but in February 2003 became embroiled in a crisis when he sacked a former Portillo supporter as executive head of the party organisation. This caused a major crisis of confidence and contributed towards polls which suggested most voters did not know what the party stood for. After talk of a leadership challenge in autumn 2002 it was assumed a good Tory performance in the 2003 local elections would be crucial for his continued leadership. In the event the party won well over 500 seats and Duncan Smith hailed a great victory – but the rumblings against him did not altogether cease. At the 2003 party conference at Blackpool there was much talk of a leadership challenge but his speech, more aggressive and rehearsed, won support in the hall and some improvement in the polls: 'the Quiet Man is turning up the volume' he claimed. In the longer term, however, the speech was seen as over-coached and risible. Support continued to ebb away and on 28 October 2003 Sir Michael Spicer, chair of the 1922 Committee, announced that the requisite 25 letters had been received asking for a vote of confidence in the leader. Duncan Smith made an inspired speech to the party's MPs the next day but he lost the vote of confidence 60 to 90. The problem with the Hague leadership rules was that Duncan Smith won the leadership battle in 2001 with the support of only a third of the parliamentary party and it took his failure as leader to reveal that it is support in the legislature which still really counts. He declared that he was considering a new career as a writer but must have been desolate when the *Telegraph*'s reviewer judged his first novel as 'terrible, terrible, terrible'. Michael Howard took over from Duncan Smith unopposed. However, IDS took great pleasure in March 2004, when the Commissioner for Standards in Public Life exonerated him of any wrongdoing regarding the employment of his wife as a secretary. 'Betsygate', as the row was dubbed, centred on whether his wife actually put in enough work to justify the £15,000 a year of public money she was given.

## Dunleavy, Patrick (1952–)

Professor of politics at the London School of Economics from 1989. He was educated at St Mary's Grammar School, Sidcup, and Corpus Christie College, Oxford, followed by Nuffield College, where he became a research fellow 1976–85. He was the author of many influential works on British politics and an advisor to the Jenkins commission on the reform of the electoral system.

## Dyke, Greg (1947–)

Director general of the BBC 2000–04. He was educated at Hayes Grammar School and York University. His early career encompassed TV AM 1965–83, London Weekend Television 1987–91, GMTV 1993–94 and Pearson Ltd 1995–99. His appointment at the BBC was controversial in that he was a known Labour supporter and donor. In the summer of 2000 he made a widely publicised speech criticising the legacy of his predecessor, John Birt. He was ranked by the *Guardian* as the second most important person in the media for taking the BBC 'by the scruff of the neck to raise morale, rejuvenate the ratings and seize control of digital terrestrial television following ITV Digital's collapse'. He was forced to resign by BBC governors in February 2004 when the Hutton report criticised the reporting and editing of news stories in the wake of Andrew Gilligan's accusatory broadcast on 29 May 2003. In his memoirs, published August 2004, Dyke bitterly attacked New Labour and accused Blair of either incompetence if he did not understand the 45-minute claim or lying if he did, when he 'duped' the country into the Iraq war; Alastair Campbell he called a 'deranged, vindictive bastard'.

# E

## Eden, Anthony (1897–1977)

Conservative foreign secretary and prime minister. He was born to an upper-class landed family, and educated at Eton and Christ Church, Oxford. He was awarded the Military Cross during his war service in 1917. He went on to stand for parliament in 1923 and represented Warwick and Leamington for 30 years. He was a junior minister in the Foreign Office 1931 and foreign secretary 1935 but resigned over the policy of appeasement towards Fascist Italy and Nazi Germany. After Winston

PEOPLE

Churchill replaced Neville Chamberlain as prime minister he again served as foreign secretary, from December 1940, when he helped to negotiate all the major wartime and immediate postwar agreements. He was deputy leader of the opposition from 1945 and then went back to the Foreign Office in 1951. In 1955 he succeeded Churchill, at long last, as prime minister. However, his premiership was not as celebrated as his service in the Foreign Office. In November 1956 he ordered British and French forces to occupy the Suez Canal Zone in the wake of an invading Israeli army, which provoked a furious political protest at home and in the United Nations as well as Washington. Eventually the USA's threat to withdraw support for the pound, combined with his ill-health, forced Eden to climb down humiliatingly over Suez and to withdraw. He resigned in January 1957 and became a peer in the early 1960s.

> He is forever poised between a cliché and an indiscretion. (Aneurin Bevan on Eden)

> Beneath the sophistication of his appearance and manner, he has all the unplumbable stupidities and unawareness of his class and type. (Bevan again on Eden)

## Elizabeth II (1926–)

Monarch, head of state. She was educated privately at home. She succeeded to the throne when her father died in 1952; her coronation was the first major public event to be televised. She has been revered as a slave to duty and has escaped many of the scandals which surrounded the royal family during the 1980s. However, the death of Diana in 1997 revealed the family in an unflattering light and the queen as a possibly unfeeling and vindictive woman. The queen looked to reform the royal family so that it could become once again the centre of the nation's affections.

> The British constitution has always been puzzling and always will be. (Elizabeth II, 1995)

> Please don't be effusive. (To prime minister Tony Blair on the speech he was about to

make to celebrate her golden wedding, 18 November 1997)

> I for one believe there are lessons to be drawn from her life and from the extraordinary and moving reaction to her death. (Broadcast from the Palace on the evening before the funeral of Diana, Princess of Wales, 5 September 1997)

## Erskine May, Thomas (1815–86)

Famous clerk of the House of Commons who wrote *Parliamentary Practice*, the bible of anyone wishing to discover the complexities of parliamentary procedure. It is regularly updated and currently exceeds 1,200 pages.

# F

## Falconer, Charles (1953–), Lord

Labour peer and minister. He was educated at Fettes with Tony Blair and became a successful barrister. He was made a life peer early in the Blair administration and took a pay cut when appointed solicitor general. The appointment was criticised, as Falconer's only apparent political qualification for office was having shared a flat with Blair when they were both young barristers. In July 1998 he moved to the Cabinet Office and was chairman of many cabinet committees, where his ability and judgement were allegedly greatly valued by the prime minister. He sailed into a gale of criticism when placed in charge of the Millennium Dome. The financial and other aspects of that fiasco were frequently blamed on him as the minister responsible but he resolutely refused to resign. In June 2003 was made the new secretary of state for constitutional affairs, a combination of the old Lord Chancellor's Department and the residual functions of the secretaries of state for Wales and Scotland. Again the 'Tony's cronies' jibe was frequently deployed but Falconer chose to ignore them, claiming his record in office was good. His easy charm certainly helped him to deflect criticism in a way denied to his predecessor, Lord Irvine.

## Falkender, Lady
*See* Williams, Marcia.

## Field, Frank (1942–)
Pressure group leader turned Labour MP and a prolific author on poverty and welfare issues. He was educated at St Clement's Dane Grammar School and Hull University. He was director Child Poverty Action 1969–79, the Low Pay Unit 1974–80 and MP for Birkenhead from 1979. He was chair of the Social Services Committee for many years, in which role he won widespread admiration. He was made minister for welfare reform in the Department of Social Security 1997–98 but his brief to 'think the unthinkable' proved short-lived as his proposals were too costly for the Treasury to support and he departed, not without a degree of bitterness, to the backbenches.

## Filkin, Elizabeth (1940–)
Former parliamentary commissioner for standards. She was educated at Clifton High School and the University of Birmingham. She worked for London local authorities, Liverpool University, the Citizens' Advice Bureau, London Docklands Development Corporation and the Inland Revenue before becoming parliament's watchdog in 1999. Her job was to report to the House of Commons Committee on Standards in Public Life. She soon established a reputation as a tough investigator who was no respecter of political rank: she investigated, among others, John Reid, Peter Mandelson, Geoffrey Robinson and Keith Vaz. However, she began to attract criticism for being allegedly 'politically naive' and a process began whereby she was marginalised and then effectively sacked in 2001 when she was told to reapply for her job. She resigned in protest amid accusations

that parliament had sought to rid itself of a watchdog whose bite was too fierce for its liking. Her successor was Philip Mawer, appointed in February 2002. On 16 February 2001 she told the *Guardian* she would be 'going down the Job Centre on Monday' as she had no job to go to.

## Foot, Michael (1913–)
Labour politician, scholar and journalist. Son of Liberal MP Isaac Foot, Michael was educated at Leighton Park School, Reading, and Wadham College, Oxford. During the war he worked as a journalist on left-wing publications and for the right-wing, Beaverbrook-owned *Daily Express*. He was elected for Devonport in 1945 and defeated in 1955 but returned for Ebbw Vale (the constituency of his idol, Aneurin Bevan) in 1960. He was thereafter a perennial rebel over expenditure, industrial relations and Vietnam in the 1960s. He stepped up to real power in 1974 as employment secretary. Under James Callaghan he became lord president of the Council and leader of the House, as well as a key conduit between the left and right in the party, then dangerously wide apart. Aged 67 he was elected as leader of the Labour Party in 1980 and there began three tortured years when Margaret Thatcher was supreme and Foot synonymous with a discredited and largely ungovernable left-wing Labour Party. He lost the 1983 election heavily and gave way to Neil Kinnock but continued campaigning, writing and espousing his many causes. Possibly the most brilliant public speaker and parliamentarian of his day as well as one of the most cultured and civilised politicians of the century, he was widely popular in many sections of the party, but suffered from a poor media image.

> The members of our Secret Service have spent so much time looking under the bed for Communists, that they haven't had time to look in the bed. (On the Profumo affair, 1963)

> It is not necessary that every time he rises he should give the impression of being a

semi-house trained polecat. (On Norman Tebbitt, 1978)

### Forsyth, Michael (1954–), Lord

Conservative MP and cabinet minister. He was educated at Arbroath High School and St Andrew's University (where he was president of the Union). He was MP for Stirling 1983–97 and junior minister in the Scottish Office before becoming secretary of state for Scotland in 1995. He was known to be a staunch Thatcherite and was created a life peer in 1997 (as Lord Drumlean).

### Fox, Charles James (1749–1806)

Whig politician with reputation as a radical. He was son of Baron Holland, entered parliament in 1769 as a supporter of the monarchy but crossed to the Whigs in 1774. He led the opposition to Pitt the Younger's war of intervention against the French Revolution, which he supported. He was made foreign secretary in 1782 (so becoming the first office holder) and again in 1806. He succeeded in abolishing the slave trade.

> How much the greatest event it is that has ever happened in the world! and how much the best! (On the fall of the Bastille, 1789)

> I will not close my politics in that foolish way. (On being offered a peerage)

### Fox, Liam (1961–)

Conservative MP. He was educated at St Bride's High School and Glasgow University, where he qualified in medicine. He was elected MP for Woodspring in 1992 and soon made a mark as a lively right-winger. He shadowed health under Conservative leader Iain Duncan Smith but helped Michael Howard with his leadership campaign in November 2003. He was joint Conservative Party chair from November 2003.

### France, Elizabeth (1950–)

Commissioner for information from 2002. She was educated at Beauchamp's School,

Leicester, and University College Wales, Aberystwyth. She entered the elite grade of the civil service and by 1986 had risen to be in charge of the Criminal Justice and Constitutional Department. She was data protection registrar 1994–2002.

### Friedman, Milton (1912–)

US monetarist economist who argued in *Free to Choose* (1980) that in order to control inflation governments should control the supply of cash and credit in the economy through the manipulation of interest rates. Many governments and right-of-centre politicians were influenced by him, not least Margaret Thatcher, Keith Joseph and Nigel Lawson, who applied a brand of monetarism closely related to Friedman's ideas. He won the Nobel Prize for Economics in 1976 and advised the governments of Chile and Israel.

> There's no such thing as a free lunch.

> A society that puts equality – in the sense of equality of outcome – ahead of freedom will end up with neither equality or freedom.

### Frost, David (1939–)

Broadcaster and interviewer. He was educated at Oxford and began his career by presenting *That Was the Week That Was* in the 1960s. He went on to *The Frost Report* and his current *Breakfast with Frost*. He assisted the trend towards irreverent, sharp questioning which began with Robin Day in the late 1950s.

# G

### Gaitskell, Hugh (1906–63)

Labour MP, minister and party leader. He was born to a middle-class family and educated at Winchester and Oxford. He became a socialist in the 1920s and an adult education tutor before teaching economics at the University of London.

He worked as a civil servant with Hugh Dalton during the war and was elected for Leeds South in 1945. After junior posts he replaced Stafford Cripps as chancellor in 1950. His 1951 budget proposed massive rearmament in response to the Korean War, which provoked Aneurin Bevan and Harold Wilson to resign their ministries. Bevan led a faction in the party but lost the battle to succeed Clement Attlee in 1955, when Gaitskell won, with the support of the unions. Gaitskell lost the 1959 general election and was rebuffed over unilateralism at the 1961 Labour Party conference. However, he reacted passionately and overthrew the decision at the following year's conference. Gaitskell was brilliant intellectually though he lacked the charisma and common touch of his rival, Bevan. He died suddenly and tragically in 1963 but left his disciples in the form of Anthony Crosland and Roy Jenkins. He was very much a moderate socialist, was in favour of scrapping clause four of the party's constitution, and led the way to the revisionist approach which dominated the 1960s and 1970s Labour governments.

> There are some of us Mr Chairman who will fight, fight and fight again to defend the party we love. (Labour Party conference, 1960)

## Galloway, George (1954–)

Labour MP expelled in 2003 for persistent rebellious behaviour. He was educated at Harris Academy, Dundee, but left school aged 16 and worked for a tyre factory before becoming active in politics. He became Labour chair in Scotland when 26, and later became chair of the charity War on Want. He raised its profile but there were some doubts about its finances. In 1987 he defeated Roy Jenkins to become MP for Glasgow Hillhead (later Kelvin). He espoused several causes in the Middle East, including that of the Palestinians and sanctions against Iraq under Saddam Hussein. He met the Iraqi dictator several times and was accused, somewhat unfairly, of being his apologist. On 23 October

2003 Labour expelled him for allegedly urging soldiers to disobey orders during the 2003 war against Iraq. He set up the anti-Iraq war Respect party, which contested the European and local elections in June 2004. He was one of the most brilliant natural orators in the House of Commons and, given a different career trajectory, might easily have fulfilled his ambition of becoming a foreign office minister.

> Sir, I salute your courage, your strength and your indefatigability and I want you to know that we are with you. (In a televised meeting with Saddam Hussein, 1994)

## George, Eddie (1938–), Sir

Governor of the Bank of England 1993–2003. He was educated at Dulwich College and Cambridge University. A lifetime employee of the Bank he developed a reputation for cool judgement and reliability. After 1997 he and members of the Monetary Policy Committee were given responsibility for fixing interest rates. In an interview he once admitted to be hopeless with his private finances and estimated the cost of a pint of milk at £1. He was nicknamed 'Steady Eddie' but could make gaffes, as when he said unemployment in the north was a price worth paying for low inflation.

## Giddens, Anthony (1938–)

Director of the London School of Economics and professor of sociology at Cambridge. He is said to have influenced New Labour thinking in the 1980s and 1990s. He was educated at Hull, the London School of Economics and Cambridge. He became a fellow of King's College, Cambridge, in 1969. He is the author of many books on sociology, which have been influential worldwide. His book *The Third Way* (1998) was said both to express and influence New Labour's approach to politics.

## Gilligan, Andrew (1968–)

BBC defence and diplomatic correspondent 1999–2004. Gilligan was educated at a comprehensive school in south-west London before going on to Cambridge University. He worked for the *Sunday Telegraph* for five years as its defence correspondent and joined the BBC in 1999. He was unusual in that his BBC reports sometimes involved seeking news exclusives rather than merely reporting news. This practice proved problematic on 29 May 2003 when he was interviewed on Radio 4's *Today* programme and claimed an intelligence source had told him the government had deliberately embellished the intelligence dossier produced in September 2002 on Iraq's weapons of mass destruction, a document used to justify the war on Iraq launched in 2003. Soon the name of the informant, Dr David Kelly, came out and his subsequent suicide led Tony Blair to set up the Hutton inquiry into the circumstances leading to Kelly's death. Hutton's report, in January 2004, heavily criticised the BBC's news editing procedures and led to the resignations of the corporation's chairman, director general and, on 30 January 2004, Gilligan.

### Gilmour, Ian (1926–), Lord

Conservative cabinet minister who was too 'wet' for Margaret Thatcher. He was educated Eton and Balliol College, Oxford. He served in the Grenadier Guards before being called to the bar in 1952. He edited the *Spectator* 1954–59. He was MP for Norfolk Central 1962–74, Chesham and Amersham 1974–92. He was a junior defence minister in Edward Heath's government and lord privy seal under Thatcher 1979–81. He wrote several books on British party politics and was made a life peer in 1992.

### Gladstone, William Ewart (1809–98)

Liberal prime minister. He started his political life as a reactionary high Tory and served in government at the Board of Trade under Robert Peel, whose high-mindedness made a great impression on him. His sympathy with Italian nationalism influenced his views on foreign policy. His first ministry (1868–74) initiated landmark reforms

in the army, civil service and local government as well as taxation and education. He came out of retirement to fight, successfully, the Conservative seat of Midlothian in an attack on Benjamin Disraeli's foreign policy in the Middle East. His inspiring speeches revealed how politicians can win power through appeals to the mass electorate. He returned to be prime minister in 1880–85, 1886 and 1892–94 but the Irish Home Rule question was a constant distraction to the 'Grand Old Man' in his later years. One of the greatest politicians of his age in terms of both his administrative and his speaking abilities, he was notable for injecting his own high-minded morality into the lifeblood of the nation's politics.

> My mission is to pacify Ireland. (On hearing he was to become prime minister, 1868)

> He has not a single redeeming defect. (Disraeli on Gladstone)

> He speaks to me as if I were a public meeting. (Queen Victoria on Gladstone)

### Goldsmith, James (1933–97)

Wealthy businessman who established the Referendum Party. He was born in Paris though educated in Britain. He developed a network of publishing and food companies but became rich through being a financier, cleverly selling stocks before the mid-1980s crash and buying when prices were low. He was calculated to be worth over £1 billion and owned a huge estate in Mexico. He was elected as a member of the European parliament 1995–97 and intervened in the 1997 British general election with his lavishly funded Referendum Party, which argued against closer European integration. The party ran candidates all over the country but was perceived by voters as a fringe oddity for the most part and it had little overall impact on the outcome. Shortly afterwards the charismatic and highly controversial Sir James died of cancer. He was also well known for his aggressive libel action against the satirical magazine *Private Eye* in the 1970s. He was knighted in 1976.

## Goldsmith, Peter (1950–), Lord

Labour peer. He was educated in
Liverpool Queen's School and Cambridge
University as well as University College,
London. He was called to the bar in 1972
and became a QC in 1997. He sat as a
recorder from 1987 and a deputy High
Court judge after 1994. He was created
a life peer in 1999 and made a privy
counsellor in 2002. He served as chairman of the bar in England and Wales and
was chairman of the International Bar
Association. In 1996 he was the prime
minister's personal representative at the
Convention for Fundamental Rights. He
was attorney general from June 2001, and
became embroiled in controversy when his
advice that the war on Iraq was legal was
subsequently challenged.

## Gordon Walker, Patrick (1907–80), Lord

Academic and Labour foreign secretary in
the 1960s. He was educated at Wellington
and Oxford. He worked as a university lecturer before he became MP for Smethwick
1945–64 and Leyton 1966–74. He held
junior office under Clement Attlee, then
was foreign secretary 1964–65 and minister for education and science 1967–68.
He was defeated in Smethwick in the 1964
general election by an opponent who played
the 'race card' but was appointed foreign
secretary nevertheless when Reg Sorensen
accepted a peerage from Wilson so Gordon
Walker could (eventually) be elected to the
Commons.

## Gould, Philip (1950–)

Tony Blair's aide and pollster. He was
educated at Knaphill Secondary Modern,
East College, London, the University of
Sussex, the London School of Economics
and the London Business School. He
worked as a marketing consultant in the
1970s and 1980s before he assisted the
Labour Party. He founded Philip Gould
Associates in 1985 and was a partner
of Gould, Greenberg, Carville Ltd from
1997. He married Gail Rebuck, head of
Random House publishers. Memos to

and from Blair in 2000 were leaked and
provoked bad publicity, as they suggested
Blair was anxiously obsessed with short-
term popularity. Gould is generally seen as
the champion of focus groups in Labour
campaign strategy, and in his book *The
Unfinished Revolution* (1998) he defends
them as aides to democratic government.

> The New Labour brand has been badly
> contaminated. It is the object of constant
> criticism and, even worse, ridicule. (Memo
> to Tony Blair, May 2000, leaked to press)

## Grade, Michael (1943–)

Chairman of the BBC after April 2004.
He was educated St Dunstan's College,
London. Undoubtedly highly imaginative
and talented in his field, Grade has been
a somewhat maverick figure in the British
media. He began his career as a journalist
with the *Daily Mirror* and then moved to
London Weekend Television in 1973; he
became director of programmes in 1977.
Next he was BBC1's controller 1986–88
and director of programmes in 1987. He
moved to become Channel 4's chief executive 1988–97. When he failed to obtain the
key jobs he wanted – mostly at the BBC
– during the 1990s he switched careers
to become chief executive of Camelot in
1997 and then chairman 2000–04. His
appointment by Tessa Jowell as the BBC's
chairman in 2004, following the upheavals
of the Huttton report, was controversial
– the *Daily Mail* attacked him as 'pornog-
rapher in chief' at Channel 4 – but the
appointment was welcomed in the media
and on the left.

## Green, T. H. (1836–82)

Philosopher and social theorist. He was
educated at Rugby and Oxford. He was influenced by the German idealists Kant and
Hegel. Not a prolific writer, his influence
was disseminated more through his lectures
and teaching. He did not go the way of
Hegel in idealising the state but insisted
on individual responsibility and rights. He
put forward the view that to be free one
had to have the opportunity to fulfil one's

potential – a crucial element in thinking, a century later, on the welfare state.

## Greer, Germaine (1939–)

Leading Australian feminist academic, author and broadcaster. She was educated at universities in Melbourne and Cambridge, and lectured at Warwick University. Her *Female Eunuch* (1970) portrayed marriage as a legalised form of slavery and she attacked the way in which women's sexuality was misrepresented and denied by males. Later in her career her early radicalism was modified a little.

## Grimond, Joseph (Jo) (1913–93)

Liberal MP and party leader in the 1950s and 1960s. He was educated at Eton and Balliol College, Oxford. He married Herbert Asquith's grand-daughter. He practised as barrister and fought in the Second World War. He was elected MP for Orkney and Shetland from 1950 and was leader of the Liberal Party 1956–67. During this time the number of Liberal MPs doubled: he thereby ended the decline in Liberal fortunes which began when David Lloyd George split the party in 1916. He was made a life peer in 1983.

> I look forward to the day when there is a strike not because a firm has introduced automation, but because it has not. (1956)

## Gummer, John Selwyn (1943–)

Conservative MP and cabinet minister. He was educated at King's School, Rochester, and Selwyn College, Cambridge, where he was chair of the Cambridge University Conservative Party and Federation of Conservative Students. He was MP for Suffolk (Eye) 1979–83 and Suffolk Coastal 1983. He served as a junior minister at agriculture and employment before he became secretary of state for the environment 1993–97. He was also chairman of the Conservative Party 1983–85. He was one of the faithful Thatcherite ministers who served during the 1980s; he reinforced her enthusiasm for the environment, and won plaudits even from the green lobby.

He famously once fed a beefburger to his daughter in front of the press during the crisis over bovine spongiform encephalitis ('mad cow disease'), to demonstrate the safety of British beef. He was also well known as a member of the General Synod of the Church of England, 1979–92.

# H

## Hague, William Jefferson (1961–)

Conservative MP and party leader 1997–2001. He was educated at Wath Comprehensive School, near Rotherham. He received a standing ovation when aged only 16 after an address to the Conservative Party annual conference. He moved on to Oxford, where he was president of the Union and attained a first-class honours degree. He became a McKinsey management consultant and then an MP in 1989. He served as parliamentary private secretary to Norman Lamont 1990–93, became a junior minister and then secretary of state for social security and secretary of state for Wales 1995–97, when he met his wife, Ffion. Initially he was approached by Michael Howard to run with him as deputy leader in the 1997 leadership fight but he decided to stand in his own right after Kenneth Clarke and John Redwood tried to form a united front. He came through to win the contest decisively on the third ballot, by 92 votes to Clarke's 70. He became thereby the youngest party leader since William Pitt the Younger. Many commentators thought little of Hague's performance as leader during his first year but he reorganised party structures and developed a sharp style at prime minister's questions, which frequently rattled the normally serene Tony Blair. After an initial attempt to introduce a species of 'compassionate Conservatism', Hague swung to the right and presided over a Thatcherite 'commonsense revolution' in 1999, which sealed the fate of his party at the 2001 general election. His anti-Europe stance may have led to Tory gains in the 1999 European elections but this was on a low poll. During the 2001 general election campaign Hague decided to stress issues like (bogus) asylum seekers, taxation and the perils of Europe, especially joining the single currency. Almost certainly as a result, Conservative support barely rose above 30 per cent throughout the campaign: about the level of the party's core vote. On 7 June 2001 the Conservatives' representation rose by only one seat, to 166, while Labour had won 412 and had a majority of 167. Immediately in the wake of the defeat – despite widespread tributes to his resilience and courage – Hague resigned his position, leaving the field open for rivals to contest the leadership. Hague was the first Conservative leader since Austen Chamberlain in 1922 not to become prime minister.

> People work and save hard to own a car. They do not want to be told they cannot drive it by the deputy prime minister whose idea of a park and ride scheme is to park one Jaguar and ride away in another. (1999)

## Hailsham, Lord (Douglas Quintin Hogg) (1907–2002)

Leading postwar Conservative lawyer, thinker and cabinet minister. He was educated at Eton and Christ Church, Oxford, where he was president of the Union. He was a fellow of All Souls 1932, and from 1938 to 1950 served as MP for Oxford City. He succeeded as the 2nd Viscount of Marylebone in 1950 and served as first lord of the Admiralty 1956–57, education minister 1957, lord president of the Council 1957–59 and 1960–64, minister for science and technology 1959–64 and chairman of the Conservative Party 1957–59. He then renounced his peerage in order to become eligible for the leadership of the Tory party after Harold Macmillan resigned and was re-elected to the Commons in a by-election for Marylebone. He was made a life peer in 1970 and became lord chancellor 1970–74 and 1979–87. He was

thus one of the longest-serving Conservative grandees, with a fine legal mind and a combative political style slightly out of step with his party, though he served both Edward Heath and Margaret Thatcher loyally. He was also a distinguished writer on politics and the constitution. In the mid-1970s he claimed the ability of Labour to introduce radical reforms on the basis of well under half of the electorate's vote indicated Britain had become an 'elective dictatorship', where the majority in parliament delivered too much power to the government. However, his enthusiasm for reform disappeared once he was back in government.

> A great party has been brought down because of a squalid affair between a woman of easy virtue and a proven liar. (In a television interview with Robert McKenzie about the Profumo affair, 13 June 1963)

> Mercy is not what every criminal is entitled to. What he is entitled to is justice. (1975)

> The best way to win an argument is to start by being in the right. (1960)

## Hain, Peter (1950–)

Labour MP and minister. He was born in South Africa but his family were forced to leave in 1966. He was educated at Pretoria Boys High School, the University of London and Sussex University. He later took part in anti-apartheid activities, especially against rugby links with his home country. He was chairman of the Young Liberals 1971–73 and was active with the Anti-Nazi League (as its press officer). In the 1970s he worked for a number of unions. He contested Putney for Labour in the 1980s but was elected for Neath in South Wales in a by-election in 1991. He served in the whips' office and was spokesman on employment matters as well as Welsh affairs. Once Labour gained power in 1997 he served in the Welsh Office and the Department of Trade and Industry and was minister for Europe in the Foreign Office, before becoming secretary of state for Wales. In June 2003 was given the job of speaking for Wales in cabinet and the

Commons as well as being leader of the House. He was seen as a streetwise, loyal, thoughtful but ambitious minister marked down for further promotion in the cabinet.

### Hamilton, Neil (1949–)

Conservative junior minister who was embroiled in the 'cash for questions' scandal in the mid-1990s and sensationally defeated by Martin Bell in the 1997 general election. He was educated at Amman Valley Grammar School and University College Wales, Aberystwyth, then studied law at Cambridge. He worked as a barrister until he was elected for Tatton in 1979. He served as a junior minister in the Department of Trade and Industry. The *Guardian* claimed he had regularly accepted favours and cash from the owner of Harrods, Mohamed al Fayed, in exchange for asking parliamentary questions on his behalf and other lobbying activities. Hamilton declared he would sue (he had sued the BBC for libel in the mid-1980s and won, over an accusation that he had fascist tendencies). However, in October 1996 Hamilton pulled out of the action through lack of money and the *Guardian* responded by calling him a 'Liar and a Cheat' on its front page. In the 1997 general election the BBC war correspondent Martin Bell stood against Hamilton – who was supported by his formidable wife, Christine – in this rock-solid Conservative seat and won it by a majority of 11,000; Bell served only one term as an MP and the constituency returned to the Tories in the 2001 general election. In August 2001 a bizarre follow-up to the Hamiltons' notoriety occurred when a single mother in Essex claimed both Hamiltons had been involved in an incident in which she was raped. Both Neil and Christine hotly denied the story and, after huge media interest, the police decided there was no case to answer and dropped their inquiries.

### Hardie, Keir (1856–1915)

One of the founders of the Labour Party. He worked in the mines from childhood and became an organiser of the men and

a journalist. He was defeated as a parliamentary candidate in Mid Lanark in 1888 but sat for West Ham South 1892–95 and then Merthyr Tydfil 1900–15. He founded and edited *Labour Leader* and handed it to the Independent Labour Party in 1903, which he chaired 1893–1900 and 1913–14. He supported the formation of a separate Labour Party. He was a dedicated pacifist and opposed the Boer War and the First World War.

### Harmsworth, Alfred (Lord Northcliffe) (1865–1922)

Newspaper magnate. He was born in Ireland and rapidly rose to prominence in the emerging newspaper business at the end of the 19th century. He founded the *Daily Mail* in 1896, when it was priced a halfpenny. This prompted the launch of the *Daily Mirror* in 1903. He then acquired the *Observer* and in 1908 *The Times*. He was openly political and attacked the government of the day, especially Herbert Asquith and Horatio Kitchener in the First World War.

### Harmsworth, Harold (Lord Rothermere) (1868–1940)

Younger brother of Alfred Harmsworth and owner of the *Daily Mirror* after 1914. He controlled Associated Newspapers for 10 years from 1922 and was one of the 'press barons' who featured so strongly in politics at the start of the 20th century.

### Haskins, Christopher (1937–), Lord

Special advisor on rural policy and chairman of Northern Foods. He was educated at Trinity College, Dublin, then worked for Fords in Dagenham before moving to Northern Foods. He was a member of several government task forces set up after 1997 and had a controversial role as a government advisor on agriculture, as he was himself a farmer.

### Hattersley, Roy (1932–)

Labour cabinet minister and journalist. He was educated at Hull University and was a journalist and local politician before entering the Commons in 1964. Always pro-Europe, he served as a minister in the Foreign Office 1974–76 and then as cabinet minister for prices and consumer protection 1976–79. He was opposition spokesman on the environment and home affairs in the 1980s and was elected on the so-called 'dream ticket' to be deputy party leader 1983–92 to Neil Kinnock. His age was probably why he was not appointed to office on Labour's return to power in 1997. However, witty, perceptive and fluent he continued his prolific journalistic and broadcasting career, often appearing as a left-wing critic of New Labour, which is an irony as throughout his political career the left regarded him as hopelessly revisionist and right-wing. On Sunday 24 June 2001 he wrote an article in the *Observer* highly critical of Tony Blair. He called for a 'counter-coup' against New Labour to restore the party's principles. He attacked Blair for being contemptuous of ideology and described the pursuance of 'social justice' a 'vacuous platitude'.

> One by one the policies which define our philosophy have been rejected by the Prime Minister. (*Observer*, 24 June 2001)

> Opposition is four or five years' humiliation in which there is no escape from the indignity of no longer controlling events. (1995)

## Hatton, Derek (1948–)

Deputy leader of Liverpool council 1983–87. He was educated at Liverpool Institute and Goldsmith's College, London University. He briefly followed his father to become a fireman before finding a profession closer to his political instincts: a community social worker. Study in London introduced him to the world of local politics and he carried this experience back to Liverpool, where he met Peter Taafe, who led him to support the Trotskyist Militant Tendency, a group which, while outwardly democratic, strove to take over the Labour Party from within. He became deputy leader of Liverpool council in 1983 (though most saw him as the effective leader himself), leading a left-wing programme for jobs

and housing. He led the fight for the council against the Thatcher government's attempts to starve left-wing councils of funding. Hatton, who had become a bogey figure for the right-wing press, clashed bitterly with the Labour leadership and was denounced at the 1985 conference by Neil Kinnock in a famous speech. By 1987 the fight was lost and Hatton departed politics; he used his loquacious talents to become, variously, a public relations consultant, after-dinner speaker and local radio broadcaster.

> People have often accused me of being a show-off, a showman, someone who loves hogging the limelight. I suppose there's a degree of truth in it too. (1988)

## Hayek, Friedrich von (1899–1992)

Austrian-born British economist. After being director of the Austrian Institute for Economic Research 1927–31 he moved to become Tooke Professor at London University 1931–50. He was appointed professor at the University of Chicago 1950, then worked in Frieburg 1962–69. His work was a reaction to Keynesianism, especially his *The Road to Serfdom* (1944) and *The Constitution of Liberty* (1960). His work demonstrates a passionate opposition to controls on the economy from the government. He saw Britain as a bulwark of freedom, which took the regulatory 'road to serfdom' in the late 19th century. He jointly won the Nobel Prize for Economics in 1974. He influenced Conservative leaders Keith Joseph, Nigel Lawson and Margaret Thatcher, along with his colleague Milton Friedman, and was partly responsible for the monetarist stance of the party during the 1980s. Thus he was one of the people who changed the way politicians think about economics.

## Healey, Denis (1917–), Lord

Labour MP and cabinet minister. He was educated at Bradford Grammar School and Balliol College, Oxford. He served in the army during the war, rising to the rank of major, and won distinction as a beach master at Anzio. In 1945 he became secretary to the International Department of the Labour Party, where he made myriad contacts all over Europe and influenced the evolution of Ernest Bevin's anti-Soviet stance, which ultimately led to Britain joining NATO in 1949. He entered the House via a by-election in 1952 in Leeds South East (later Leeds East, which he held until his retirement in 1992). He helped refashion the 'revisionist' version of Labour's socialism during the 1950s and was a supporter of Hugh Gaitskell. Harold Wilson made him minister of defence, in which post he initiated cuts, restructurings and the crucial 'east of Suez' withdrawal. He was then shadow foreign secretary 1970–74 and on Labour's return to power chancellor 1974–79, when he weathered horrendous political storms as inflation roared uncontrolled and the dissenting left wing of the Labour Party almost undermined the government. He stood for the party leadership in 1981 but was beaten by Michael Foot, by 139 votes to 129 (he subsequently served Foot loyally in opposition). He must have been sympathetic to the aims of the breakaway Social Democratic Party in 1981 but resisted any temptation to join and continued as shadow foreign secretary until 1987, when he retired to the backbenches; he left the Commons in 1992 and was made a life peer. Healey was a natural politician who revelled in extroverted performances in front of the media. Brilliant intellectually – and with intense interests in music, literature, philosophy and languages – he suffered fools not at all and made enemies as a result, which may explain why this most able of politicians did not achieve his just reward of being party leader. It is sometimes said he was the 'best prime minister we never had'.

> That part of his speech was rather like being savaged by a dead sheep. (Replying to a Commons attack by Sir Geoffrey Howe, 14 June 1978)

## Heath, Edward (1916–)

Conservative prime minister 1970–74. He was the son of a carpenter and domestic

servant. He was educated at Chatham School, Ramsgate, and Balliol College, Oxford, where he was president of the Oxford Union. He had a distinguished war record and returned to enter parliament in 1950 for Bexley (Old Bexley and Sidcup after 1974). His maiden speech was a call for European unity and this ideal informed the whole of his career. He moved up through the whips' office, and served as chief whip 1955–59. In 1960 he was appointed lord privy seal, in charge of negotiations for entry into the European Community. Under Alec Douglas-Home he was at the Board of Trade, where he abolished resale price maintenance, which won him credit in his party; this, along with his humble origins and similar age to Harold Wilson, helps to explain his victory in the first democratic election (within the parliamentary party) for a Conservative leader: 150 votes to Reginald Maudling's 133. He developed a right-wing alternative to Labour and had the opportunity to put it into practice after he surprisingly won the 1970 election. However, his initial attempts to impose his 'Selsdon' programme ran into trouble and he resorted to full-blooded Keynesianism investment. This came unstuck when the unions refused to accept his reforms, as well as his prices and incomes policy, and oil prices rose sharply. The record number of days lost in strikes and the troubles in Northern Ireland, not to mention the stand-off with the miners, were not overshadowed by Heath's successful negotiation of entry into the European Community in 1972. He called a 'Who governs Britain?' election in February 1974 and lost narrowly to Wilson. His government was regarded by many Conservatives as unsuccessful and after his second general election defeat, in October 1974, he was challenged by Margaret Thatcher as leader and lost in the 1975 leadership election. He never forgave Margaret Thatcher for standing against him and remained a dissenting presence on the backbenches throughout her period in opposition and then in government. His somewhat curmudgeonly style and tense appearances on television prevented this talented and capable politician from fulfilling his true potential. Despite his well publicised love of music and yachting, the electorate never warmed to him. He went on to become the father of the House in 1997, but retired in 2001.

It is the unpleasant, unacceptable face of capitalism. (On the Lonrho affair in the Commons, 15 May 1973)

From 31 December, they [most industrial and commercial premises] will be limited [in the use of electricity] to three specified days each week. (Commons, 13 December 1973)

I am not a product of privilege, I am a product of opportunity. (1974)

If politicians lived on praise and thanks, they'd be forced into some other line of business. (1973)

Power, which has the ability to mellow some of those who achieve it … in Heath's case changed his personality overnight. When prime minister he became authoritarian and intolerant. (Journalist James Margach, 1978)

## Henderson, Arthur (1863–1935)

Labour cabinet member and party leader in early years of the 20th century. He left school aged 12 to work in an iron foundry and became active in the Ironfounders' Union. He was Labour MP for Barnard Castle 1903–18, Widnes 1919–22, Newcastle East 1923, Burnley 1924–31 and Clay Cross 1931–35. He served as Labour leader in the Commons 1908–10 and 1914–17, chief whip 1914, education minister 1915–16, as a member of the war cabinet 1916–17 (resigned 1917), chief whip again 1920–24 and 1925–27, home secretary 1924, foreign secretary 1929–31 and leader of the opposition 1931–32. He was perceived as a wise and committed socialist who tried manfully as foreign secretary to achieve disarmament.

## Hennessy, Peter (1947–)

Political scientist and historian. He was educated at Marling and St John's College, Cambridge, the London School of Economics and Harvard University. He worked as a journalist on *The Times*, *Times Higher Education Supplement*, *Financial Times*, *The Economist*, *New Statesman* and *Independent*. He founded the Institute of Contemporary British History and became a well known broadcaster. He has been professor of modern history at Queen Mary and Westfield College, London University, since 1992. His books include: *Cabinet* (1986), *Whitehall* (1989), *Never Again: Britain, 1945–51* (1993), *The Hidden Wiring: Unearthing the British Constitution* (1995) and *The Prime Minister: The Job and Its Holders Since 1945* (2001). He is an innovative academic who developed his journalistic skills into an extravagant gift for narrative history writing.

## Heseltine, Michael (1933–), Lord

Conservative MP and cabinet minister. He was the son of a wealthy businessman; he was educated at Shrewsbury School and Oxford, where he was president of the Union. He served as MP for Tavistock 1966–74 and for Henley from 1974. He became rich from property and publishing (Haymarket Press) – he was a millionaire by the time he was 30. He held junior office under Edward Heath and served in Margaret Thatcher's cabinet as secretary of state for environment from 1979; he maintained his close concern for Liverpool and its surrounds following his support for government action after the 1981 riots. In 1983 he moved to defence and he fought an effective battle against the Campaign for Nuclear Disarmament and the protestors outside Greenham Common. In 1986 he clashed with his prime minister over the fate of the Westlands helicopter company and her refusal to accept his European consortium solution. In December 1985 the clash became public when he walked out of the cabinet and accused Thatcher of unfairly and unconstitutionally keeping the item off the cabinet agenda. Thatcher – always suspicious of Heseltine's ambition to be prime minister – survived the crisis but Heseltine did not languish on the backbenches. Instead he began an unofficial campaign for the leadership, travelling the country to speak at party meetings. He was not shy about pointing out that his green paper on local government finance when at Environment had ruled out a poll tax as unfair before the government unwisely pressed through its introduction as the community charge for local government finance. When in October 1990 Geoffrey Howe resigned as foreign secretary and accused Thatcher of poor leadership, Heseltine decided the situation was such that his earlier pledge not to stand against her could safely be ignored. He mustered 152 votes on the first ballot to her 204; she was four short of the majority required by party rules. His ambition to be prime minister was thwarted, however, when John Major came through to win the resultant contest with Heseltine and Douglas Hurd. He served as secretary of state for environment under Major, when he abolished the hated poll tax, and then as president of the Board of Trade. He lost some credibility when he accepted the Coal Board's recommendation to close 30 pits and was forced under pressure to rescind the decision. He recovered well from a mild heart attack in 1993 and was regarded as the most likely successor to Major. However, he decided to support Major when he resigned his leadership of the party in July 1995 and dared opponents to stand against him. In the event Major won but Heseltine 'won' the post of deputy prime minister and much power over policy formulation. He fought a vigorous election campaign in 1997 but his heart condition prevented him from standing in the leadership contest which followed his party's defeat. Famously ambitious, this colourful and able politician had accepted that deputy prime minister was the highest position he would attain when he retired from the Commons in 2001. He was subsequently made a life peer.

> I knew that 'He who wields the knife never wears the crown'. (On his failure to win the leadership contest he initiated against Thatcher in November 1990)

The market has no morality. (1988)

Polluted rivers, filthy streets, bodies bedded down in doorways are no advertisement for a prosperous and caring society. (Speech to Conservative Party conference, 1989)

### Hewitt, Patricia (1948–)
Labour MP and cabinet minister. An Australian by birth, she was educated at Canberra High School, the Australian National University and Newham College, Cambridge. She worked for a number of pressure groups, including Age Concern and the National Council for Civil Liberties, as well as Andersen Consulting, before being elected MP for Leicester West 1997. She was soon appointed a junior Treasury minister and then moved to the Department of Trade and Industry before she entered the cabinet for the same department in 2001 as secretary of state and minister for women.

### Heywood, Jeremy (1962–)
Civil servant. He was educated at Bootham School, York, Oxford, the London School of Economics and Harvard University. He then became a Treasury civil servant who worked in Washington for the International Monetary Fund 1988–90. He worked closely with Norman Lamont when he was chancellor as his personal private secretary 1991–94. He was in charge of securities and markets policy in 1997 when he transferred to Number 10 as liaison with his department on economic and domestic briefs. Thereafter he became principal private secretary to Tony Blair.

> One of the most important chefs in Blair's kitchen cabinet. (*Sunday Times*, 26 September 1999)

### Hill, David (1947–)
Tony Blair's director of communications from 2003. He was educated at King Edward VI School, Birmingham, and Brasenose College, Oxford. He was assistant to Roy Hattersley 1972–74, policy advisor in the Department of Prices

and Consumer Protection 1976–79; head of staff for the deputy leader of the Labour Party (Hattersley again) 1979–83, and director of campaigns and communications for the Labour Party 1991–93. He was generally regarded – especially by Roy Hattersley – as a 'safe pair of hands', who was also popular with the press.

### Hislop, Ian (1960–)

Editor of *Private Eye*, writer and broadcaster. He was educated at Ardingley College, and Magdalen College, Oxford. He became a 'disciple' of Peter Cook and Richard Ingrams (former editor of *Private Eye*) and served as deputy editor 1985–86 before becoming editor in 1986. Initially he intended to do the job only for two years but he decided to stay longer. He survived a number of expensive libel cases to make the magazine financially stable.

> I have more influence as an editor of the *Eye* than I would have as a backbench MP. (At a book signing in Manchester, 1998)

### Hoare, Samuel (Viscount Templewood) (1880–1959)

Conservative cabinet minister in the 1930s. He was educated at Harrow and Oxford. He was elected MP for Chelsea 1910–44 and served in the Air Ministry 1922–29 and India Office 1931–35, before becoming foreign secretary 1935, first lord of the Admiralty 1936–37 and home secretary 1937–39; he was lord privy seal 1939–40 and ambassador to Spain 1940–44. His part in the Hoare–Laval plan in 1935 to concede much of Abyssinia to Italy was believed to have neutered the League of Nations' attempts to act collectively. He was a committed supporter of appeasement and continued to defend it even after the war had ended. Also, perhaps surprisingly for a Conservative at this time, he was a vigorous opponent of capital punishment.

### Hobbes, Thomas (1588–1679)

One of the greatest British political philosophers. Educated at Oxford, he kept himself by tutoring the sons of the rich, including Charles II during his exile in Paris in 1642. Hobbes can be understood only within the context of the civil strife of his time. His great work *The Leviathan* (1651) was posited on the social contract idea, that in a state of nature life would be 'solitary, nasty, brutish, and short'. To achieve some sort of decent life it was necessary for people to create civil government and Hobbes believed a powerful king – and his power had to be absolute – should be supported by the populace, provided the king could deliver effective law and order. The significance of these ideas was that, in a climate where support for the divine right of kings was in decline (Charles I had been beheaded in 1649), his formulation provided a basis for authority without a religious underpinning. Hobbes lived a vigorous and prolific life, dying at the age of 91.

> During the time men live without a common power to keep them all in awe … the life of man [is] solitary, poor, nasty, brutish, and short. (*Leviathan*, 1651)

> I put for a general inclination of all mankind, a perpetual and restless desire after power, that ceaseth only in death. (*Leviathan*, 1651)

### Hobhouse, L. T. (1864–1929)

Social and political theorist. He was educated at Oxford University and became a fellow at Merton College. He wrote for the *Manchester Guardian* for a while and became a social philosopher of the left. His writings marked the completion of the shift of left-wing thought from economic liberalism to paternalism, in which he saw the state as an 'overparent' providing the 'basis of the rights of a child, of his protection against neglect, of the equality of opportunity which he may claim as a "future citizen"'. Hobhouse prepared the intellectual ground for what later became the welfare state.

### Hobson, J. A. (1858–1940)

Liberal economist. He was educated at Oxford. He believed that capitalism was fatally flawed – because it produced a rich minority who accumulated unspent profits,

which led to under-consumption. This
tended to create slumps and booms and
the phenomenon whereby surplus wealth
was invested abroad, thus creating overseas
economic interests, colonies and then
imperialism. He suggested the solution was
the redirection of resources from the rich
to the poor via progressive taxation. His
thinking anticipated that of John Maynard
Keynes and was especially attractive to
socialist politicians.

**Hogg, Douglas Quintin**
*See* Hailsham, Lord.

**Hoggart, Simon (1946–)**
Journalist and broadcaster. He was educated Hymer's College, Hull, Wyggeston
Grammar School, Leicester, and King's
College, Cambridge. He joined the
*Guardian* in 1968 and undertook most roles
there – reporter, columnist, political editor
– until he became parliamentary correspondent and daily sketch writer. Whether
he is as accomplished in his present role as
his predecessor, Michael White, is a topic of
*Guardian* reader debate. Since 1996 he has
also chaired, with some aplomb, the highly
rated *News Quiz* on Radio 4.

**Hoon, Geoff (1953–)**
Labour MP and cabinet minister. He was
educated at Nottingham High School and
Jesus College, Cambridge. He was a barrister before he became an MP for Ashfield
1992. He also served as a member of
the European parliament 1984–94. He
shadowed the solicitor general and information technology, then, after Labour came
to power in 1997, served as minister of
state in the Lord Chancellor's Department
1997–99 and secretary of state for defence
from 1999. He has been viewed as a
competent Blairite but, in the perception
of critics, another colourless New Labour
operative. He had, by general consent, a
'good war' against Iraq.

**Howard, Michael (1941–)**
Conservative MP and minister and leader
of the Conservative Party from November

2003. He went to Cambridge University,
where he was president of the Union. He
was called to bar in 1964 and elected
MP in 1983. He held several junior
posts before entering cabinet in charge of
employment 1990–92 and environment
1992–93. He was a somewhat controversial home secretary, 1993–97, when he
was known as a 'prison works' advocate
and a high-profile politician who was
found to have exceeded his legal powers
as a minister some eight times. In 1994 he
introduced his Criminal Justice and Public
Order Bill, which, among other things:
modified a suspect's right to remain silent;
introduced new measures against terrorists;
gave tougher penalties for young offenders; gave new powers for the police to evict
squatters and stop trespassers; and reduced
the amount of paperwork required of police
officers. He also initiated the building
of six new prisons. His dismissal of the
director of prisons, Derek Lewis, brought
him up against his shadow, Jack Straw, a
debating contest between two barristers
which he easily won. However, when he
stood for the leadership of his party in the
wake of the Tories' 1997 defeat, his former
junior minister, Ann Widdicombe, ruined
his chances with a series of criticisms in
which she alleged there was 'something of
the night' about him. He performed badly
in the contest and the person whom he
had invited to stand with him as deputy
leader, William Hague, eventually won
it on his own. Some were surprised when
Iain Duncan Smith ('IDS') gave him the
brief of shadow chancellor after 2001,
but he performed well against Gordon
Brown – so well that many believed he
would make a better leader than the much
criticised IDS. When dissatisfaction with
the latter reached its height in the autumn
of 2003, Howard was seen as the competent, experienced heavyweight, who
could rescue the Conservatives electorally.
When IDS lost a vote of confidence on 29
October 2003, Howard was widely seen
as his most credible replacement. Possible
candidates stood down so that he was the
only person available for the competition,

which consequently became a 'coronation' on 6 November 2003. His first few weeks as leader were deemed a success by most commentators. He proved effective at prime minister's questions; he appointed a credible and smaller team of shadow ministers, when he managed to involve most of the previously alienated 'heavyweights'; he struck a more conciliatory note on social issues; and pledged, perhaps optimistically, in February 2004 to maintain or increase spending on public services, if elected, but to effect eventual tax savings through cutting down on wasted expenditure. As summer closed in 2004, Howard was forced to contemplate polls which in some cases showed his party level with the Liberal Democrats.

> Prison works.... I know what causes crime: criminals. (When home secretary in John Major's government)

> There is tidal wave of crime in this country. I am not going to ignore it. I am going to take action. Tough action. (As home secretary to Conservative Party conference, 1993)

> I am proud of Britain's history as a safe haven for refugees over the centuries. People have always wanted to come to Britain, as my own family did.

> I'm probably a bit more mellow than I was. (6 November 2003)

> There is something of the night about him. (Ann Widdecombe placing the kiss of death on her former boss's then leadership ambitions, 2001)

## Howe, Geoffrey (1926–), Lord

Conservative chancellor, then foreign secretary, to Margaret Thatcher, who finally turned on his patron. He was educated at Winchester and Cambridge. He was a Conservative MP from 1964, was knighted in 1970, and served as solicitor general 1970–72, at trade and consumer affairs 1972–74, as chancellor 1979–83, foreign secretary 1983–89 and deputy prime minister 1989 (effectively a demotion). He resigned in 1990 and precipitated the fall

of Thatcher. Always diffident – Healey famously said debating with him was like being 'savaged by a dead sheep' – and loyal, Howe also was highly ambitious and his years of accepting his prime minister's dismissive scorn were revenged in his brilliant resignation speech, when he ridiculed Thatcher's management of the cabinet and the issue of Britain's relations with Europe. As chancellor he pursued a rigidly deflationary policy which produced a deep recession. He was created Baron Howe of Aberavon upon his retirement from the Commons.

> It is rather like sending your opening batsmen to the crease only for them to find that the moment the first balls are bowled, their bats have been broken before the game by the team captain. (Resignation speech, 13 November 1990)

## Hume, John (1937–)

Leader of Northern Ireland's Social and Democratic Labour Party and Westminster MP. He was educated at St Columb's College, Derry, and St Patrick's College, Maynooth. He was a strong advocate of peace in Northern Ireland via democratic consent; he took a risk in joining in talks with Sinn Fein leader Gerry Adams in 1988. This dialogue helped create the Good Friday Agreement in 1998. He won the Nobel Peace Prize in 1998, shared with David Trimble.

## Humphrys, John (1943–)

Presenter of the *Today* programme on Radio 4, *On the Record* and newsreader. He was educated at Cardiff High School. Since the death of Brian Redhead, Humphrys has been, along with James Naughtie, the voice of this daily wake-up programme for the nation's chattering classes. His tenacious questioning style made him unpopular with certain politicians. Others see him as an adornment to the nation's life. In his Mactaggart memorial lecture in August 2004 Humphrys savaged the 'seedy and cynical' television which was 'coarsening society'. He reserved some of his sharpest criticism for reality television shows like *Big Brother* and concluded by questioning whether Mary Whitehouse, the long-time 'clean-up TV' evangelist much mocked by liberals, had not been right all along.

> The bad television of today (compared to 'the old days') is worse. It is not only bad – it is damaging, meretricious, seedy and cynical.

### Hunter, Anji (1955–)

'Special assistant for presentation and planning' to Tony Blair and a key member of his kitchen cabinet. She was educated at Oxford, where she sustained her childhood friendship with the future prime minister; she ran his office from 1986 to 2001, when she left government service to work in industry. She was seen as guarding the door to Blair's office.

> She is no fawning Blair babe, but one of Britain's most powerful women. (*Sunday Times*, 26 September 1999)

### Hurd, Douglas (1930–), Lord

Conservative MP and cabinet minister. He was born into lesser landed gentry and educated at Eton and Cambridge. He joined the diplomatic corps in 1952; he learnt Chinese when posted in China. He joined the Conservative Party Research Department in 1966 and served as an office manager to Edward Heath and then as his political secretary after Heath became prime minister 1968–74, after which Hurd entered the House of Commons. Under Margaret Thatcher he was Northern Ireland secretary 1984, home secretary 1985 and foreign secretary 1989–95. He stood as a candidate in the leadership election in 1990 but mustered only 56 votes on the second ballot. He became a peer in 1997. Unusual in a world of driven politicians, he also writes occasional novels, usually political thrillers.

### Hutton, Brian Edward (1931–), Lord

Lord of appeal in ordinary from 1997. He was educated at Shrewsbury School,

Oxford University and Queen's University, Belfast. He was called to the Northern Ireland bar in 1954 and the English bar in 1972. He served as lord chief justice in Northern Ireland 1988–97. He chaired the inquiry in 2003 into the death of Dr David Kelly, the scientific weapons advisor to the Ministry of Defence who committed suicide in July 2003. He reported on 28 January 2004, when he cleared ministers and civil servants of any wrongdoing regarding the circumstances leading to Kelly's death and allocated most of the blame to the BBC, which thereupon suffered the resignations of its chairman and director general. The press generally greeted the report with scepticism and criticised his excessively narrow interpretation of the inquiry's remit; the press also made the accusation of a 'whitewash' of the establishment by a classic establishment figure.

### Hutton, Will (1950–)

Economist, journalist and social commentator. He was educated at Chislehurst and Sidcup Grammar School and Bristol University. He entered the BBC and worked as a radio producer at Radio 4 before moving to television to feature on *The Money Programme* and *Newsnight*. He was named Political Journalist of the Year in 1993. He became editor of the *Observer* in 1996. He is best known for his mammoth critique of British institutions, *The State We're In* (1995), in which he developed the thesis of a partnership between employees, employers and others in modern capitalism (the stakeholder economy).

# I

### Ibbs, Robin (1926–)

Author of the *Next Steps* report. He was educated at Toronto University and Trinity College, Cambridge. He served as a lieutenant in the Royal Navy 1947–49 then practised at the bar 1949–52. He joined ICI in 1952 and became a director 1976–80 and 1982–88. He was head of the CPRS 1980–82, of the Efficiency Unit 1983–88 and author of the *Next Steps* report, which established executive agencies. He was also associated with many banking and business concerns, as well as several public bodies, like the Top Salaries Review Body 1983–89.

**Ingham, Bernard (1932–), Sir**
Redoubtable press secretary to Margaret Thatcher during the 1980s. He was born in Yorkshire and educated at Hebden Bridge Grammar School. He worked as a journalist on local papers before he moved to the *Guardian* 1962–67 and then into government service as a press advisor in the 1970s, when he rose to under-secretary at the Department of Energy under Tony Benn 1978–79. In 1979 he became chief press secretary to Thatcher and became nationally known for his gruff yet highly competent performances at press conferences and in the media. He also managed to become one of Thatcher's closest and most trusted advisors. He was knighted in 1990.

**Irvine, Alexander Andrew Mackay (1940–), Lord**
Labour peer and minister. He was made lord chancellor after Labour's victory in 1997. He was educated at Hutcheson's Grammar School, and Glasgow and Cambridge universities. He lectured at the London School of Economics 1965–69, was called to the bar in 1967, became a QC in 1978 and a deputy judge in the High Court in 1987. He was Tony Blair's head of chambers when Blair (as well as Cherie Booth, his future wife) practised as a barrister. He was made a life peer in 1987 and served as shadow lord chancellor 1992–97 then lord chancellor after Labour's 1997 election victory. He proved a controversial member of Blair's cabinet, though it was rumoured that Blair depended upon him for advice. He chaired several cabinet committees and his undoubted

influence encouraged him to compare himself in a public talk to Cardinal Wolsey. His aloof manner won him few friends and his expensive refurbishing of the lord chancellor's rooms in the Lords, especially the heavy wallpaper, attracted much criticism and satirical comment. He remained unrepentant and predicted the nation would be 'grateful' for his foresight. In January 2000 he was at the centre of the 'wigs for cash' scandal when he invited senior lawyers – whose future advancement he could determine – to a fund-raising dinner for the Labour Party. On a more positive assessment, he did drive through the devolution legislation in 1997/98 which led to the first Scottish parliament in three centuries. In addition he introduced the revolutionary Human Rights Act 1998. In June 2003 Blair removed his former boss as part of his restructuring of the judiciary. The 1,400-year-old office – much criticised for involving the law-making function with the law-implementing judiciary – was replaced by the Constitutional Affairs Department. Irvine was known to oppose the measures and this possibly helps explain why it was pushed through with indecent haste.

# J

**Jackson, Ken (1937–)**
General secretary of Amicus 1995–2002. He was educated at St Joseph's School, Wigan. In 1956 he joined the Royal Air Force as a technician and later was an electrician in the engineering industry. He became an official of the electrical union (EEPTU) in 1966 and rose through the ranks to be president in 1992. He was general secretary of the Amalgamated Engineering and Electrical Union before heading up the new union, Amicus, in 1995. He was known as Tony Blair's 'favourite trade unionist' for his loyal support of the prime minister.

## Jay, Margaret (1940–), Baroness

Labour peer. She was educated at
Blackheath High School and Somerville
College, Oxford. She was the daughter
of James Callaghan and at one time was
married to Peter Jay the journalist and
broadcaster. She was a *Panorama* reporter
and a director of the National Aids
Trust. She gained a peerage in 1992 and
served as a whip in opposition. A highly
sociable socialist, she describes herself as
a 'moderniser'. She was made leader of
House of Lords in July 1998 and was put
in charge of reform of that chamber. She
oversaw the abolition of hereditary peers
in 1999 but decided to give up her cabinet
post in June 2001.

## Jenkins, Roy (1920–2002), Lord

Apparently ageless Labour politician
with a passion for Europe who joined the
Social Democratic Party (SDP) and then
the Liberal Democrats. He was born in
Wales to a mining family, though his father
was a Labour MP. He was educated
at a local grammar school and Balliol
College, Oxford, where he took a first in
modern greats. He was the youngest MP
when elected for Central Southwark in
1948 and sat for the Stechford Division,
Birmingham, 1950–76. He served as minister for aviation 1964–65 before gaining
the Home Office. He then swapped offices
with James Callaghan in 1967 to become
chancellor. He became deputy leader in
opposition, when he rebelled against his
party's opposition to Europe. He was home
secretary again 1974–76. He then left
Westminster politics in 1977 to become
president of the European Commission,
until 1981. He was a founder member of
the SDP and part of its joint leadership
1981–82 before he stood down in favour of
David Owen. He won Glasgow Hillhead
for the SDP in 1982, lost it in 1987 and
then was made a peer. He was elected
chancellor of Oxford University in 1987.
A noted journalist and biographer, Jenkins
was one of the 1930s-educated polymaths,
like Denis Healey, who led the Labour
Party after the war. He was very able

intellectually and as a minister but his aloof
manner belied his humble origins. His passionate advocacy of most things European
discouraged the support he might otherwise
have commanded. He was a powerful
figure in British and European politics
for a generation. In 1997 he was asked to
chair Labour's commission into the voting
system and produced a controversial report
recommending the alternative vote 'top-up'
system. In his final years he became an
intimate advisor to Tony Blair.

## Johnson, Boris (1964–)

Editor of the *Spectator* and Conservative
MP known for his sense of humour. He
was educated Eton and Balliol College,
Oxford. He became a journalist at *The
Times* and the *Daily Telegraph* before
assuming the editorship of the right-lean-
ing *Spectator* in 1995, where he helped to
increase circulation. He became MP for
Henley on Thames in 2001, though still
appeared on the comedy news programme
*Have I Got News for You* from time to
time.

## Jones, Digby (1955–)

Director general of the Confederation
British Industry after 2000. He was edu-
cated at Bromsgrove School and University
College, London, where he studied law.
He became a solicitor in 1980 and more
recently worked for business consultants
KPMG.

## Jones, Jack (1913–)

Leader of the Transport and General
Workers' Union (TGWU) in the 1970s.
He was born in Liverpool and left school
at 14 to work on the docks and in engineering before moving into union activism;
after reading Robert Tressell's *Ragged
Trousered Philanthropists* at this time he
was converted to socialism. He fought in
the Spanish Civil War and was wounded
in 1938. He became district organiser in
Coventry before moving up in the organisation and becoming general secretary of
the TGWU 1969–78 at the same time as
Hugh Scanlon was leading the engineering

union. Between them they dominated the union scene in the 1970s and were often described as the two most powerful men in the country, responsible for making the unions too powerful and provoking the backlash by Margaret Thatcher's administration. Jones served on the General Council of the Trades Union Congress 1968–78 and, much respected throughout the world of politics, dedicated his retirement to campaigning for a better deal for old-age pensioners.

### Joseph, Keith (1918–94)

Leading postwar new right ideologue and Conservative cabinet minister. He was educated at Oxford University and he practised as a barrister before becoming a Conservative MP in 1956. He was secretary of state for social security 1970–74 under Edward Heath and he might have become leader but for an ill-advised speech which appeared to advocate eugenics. However, his elaboration of a 'common ground' in the mid-1970s, which he claimed was to the right of the postwar consensus and on to which he urged his party to move, was justified by future events. He became one of Margaret Thatcher's most closely trusted policy advisors in opposition and in government served as secretary of state for education 1981–86. He founded the Centre for Policy Studies with Thatcher in 1975.

> It needs to be said that the poor are poor be-cause they don't have enough money. (1970)

### Jowell, Tessa (1947–)

Labour MP and minister. She was educated at Aberdeen, Edinburgh and London universities. She was MP for Dulwich from 1992 and served as junior minister in education 1998–2001 and health 1997–98. Since 2001 she has been secretary of state for culture, media and sport.

# K

### Kaufman, Gerald (1930–)

Leading postwar Labour politician whose long years in opposition denied him the chance of senior office. He was educated at Leeds Grammar School and Queen's College, Oxford. He then worked for the Fabian Society and various newspapers before becoming press officer to the Labour Party, when he worked for a while in Downing Street after 1966. He was elected MP for Ardwick in 1970 and then Gorton from 1983. He served as a junior minister for environment and industry before becoming minister of state for industry 1975–79. He was shadow home and foreign secretary in the 1980s. He was an able politician with a wicked wit and good ministerial record but was too young to achieve high office in the 1960s and too old to return to office after 1997. He was the author of the much quoted *How To Be a Minister* (1980). In 1992 he became chairman of the Culture and Heritage Select Committee and, despite his well known hostility to such committees, proceeded to chair it with great panache and effectiveness.

> The longest suicide note in history.
> (Kaufman's much quoted comment on Labour's 1983 manifesto)

### Kavanagh, Dennis (1941–)

Professor of Politics at the University of Liverpool from 1996. He was educated at St Anslem's College, Birkenhead, and Manchester University. He then taught at the universities of Hull and Manchester before becoming professor at Nottingham 1982–95 and then Liverpool. His writings include *Political Culture* (1972), *Thatcherism* (1986), studies of the prime minister and cabinet and a series of Nuffield election studies co-authored with David Butler.

### Kavanagh, Trevor (1943–)
Political editor of the *Sun* from 1983. He was educated at Reigate Grammar School, then emigrated to Australia. He joined News International in 1974 and returned to Britain in 1978. He took over as political editor of the *Sun* in 1983 and became one of the country's most influential journalists. He was known to be a supporter of Thatcher and her policies, and to have opposed Rupert Murdoch's switching of support to Tony Blair in 1997.

### Keeler, Christine (1942–)
Model who conducted a dual affair with the minister of war, John Profumo, and a Soviet naval attaché, Eugene Ivanov, in 1963, which raised questions of state security. Profumo denied the affair in the House and when his deceit was revealed he resigned. The scandal damaged the final months of Harold Macmillan's government.

### Kelly, David (1944–2003)
Government advisor whose suicide on 18 July 2003 precipitated an acute crisis for the BBC's relations with government and for public trust in Tony Blair's New Labour regime. He was the son of an officer in the Royal Air Force. He was born in the Rhondda but moved to Tunbridge Wells. He was educated at Oxford, where he studied agricultural science. He moved into microbiology and subsequently worked at the Ministry of Defence's Porton Down 1984–92, engaged in biological warfare research. In the 1980s he worked for the government as a weapons inspector in Russia and then for the United Nations 1994–99 as a weapons inspector in Iraq. Some experts claimed he was pre-eminent in his field, not just nationally but worldwide. However, he had doubts in 2002 about the government's determination to use the supposed threat of Iraqi weapons of mass destruction to justify going to war with that country. When such weapons failed to appear at the end of the war his conversations with BBC journalists fed into reports that a 'senior intelligence' source had claimed the government had 'sexed up' intelligence reports to help justify the war on Iraq. He was soon identified and subsequently gave evidence to the Foreign Affairs Select Committee but in July 2003, as the media frenzy grew, committed suicide. Lord Hutton was appointed to head the judicial inquiry into the affair.

### Kemp, Peter (1934–), Sir
Senior civil servant who master-minded the 'Next Steps' reform of the civil service. He was educated at Millfield and Royal Naval College, Dartmouth. He entered the civil service in 1967, serving in the Department of Transport before moving to the Treasury and then the Cabinet Office. He rose to second permanent secretary at the Treasury and was engaged on the Next Steps reform as project manager within the Cabinet Office during the late 1980s. He left the service in 1992.

### Kennedy, Charles (1959–)
Liberal Democrat MP and leader of the party. He was educated at Lochaber High School, Fort William, and the University of Glasgow, where he was the president of the Union. He was a Fulbright scholar and lecturer at Indiana University. He was elected MP for Ross, Skye and Inverness for the Social Democratic Party in 1983 and was president of the Liberal Democrats 1990–94. He won the contest to replace Paddy Ashdown as leader in August 1999 but was initially thought by some to be too diffident and a bit too lazy to be an effective leader. However, his laid-back style went down well in the 2001 general election campaign and he led his party to a good result. His opposition to the Iraq war in 2003 was well judged and his party benefited politically, for example winning the Leicester South by-election in July 2004, when many Muslims deserted Labour to vote in a Liberal Democrat.

### Kennedy, Helena (1950–), Baroness
Labour life peer and QC. She was educated at Holyrood Secondary Grammar and Glasgow University. One of the country's leading female lawyers, she has

headed government inquiries, sits on important bodies and, perhaps crucially, is a close personal friend of the Blairs.

## Kerr, John (1942–)

Civil servant. He was educated at Glasgow Academy and Oxford. As a diplomat he served in Moscow and Rawalapindi as well as being permanent representative to the European Union 1990–95. He was ambassador to the USA 1995–97. He was permanent under-secretary to the Foreign Office and head of the Diplomatic Service after 1997. He became a close advisor to Tony Blair in the aftermath of the terror attacks on the USA on 11 September 2001 but retired at the end of that year.

## Keynes, John Maynard (1883–1946)

Economist. He was born into an academic Cambridge family and studied at Eton and King's College, Cambridge, where he became one of the so-called Bloomsbury Group of intellectuals. He lectured at Cambridge in economics then served as a member of the Royal Commission on India. He advised the Treasury during the First World War and was opposed to the peace terms, which he criticised in his *Economic Consequences of the Peace* (1919). He attacked Winston Churchill's restoration of the gold standard in 1925. He was influenced by J. A. Hobson's under-consumption theories and developed them in response to the unemployment in the 1930s, most famously in his *General Theory of Employment, Interest and Money* (1936). His view that recessions could be combated through investment to stimulate growth was revolutionary and was not initially widely accepted. His idea that the economy could be planned influenced US president Roosevelt's New Deal and many thinking politicians in both main political parties, such as Harold Macmillan and Hugh Dalton, began to study his ideas and adapt them. During the Second World War his views gradually became orthodoxies and the 1945 white paper on employment embodied his views of the achievability of full employment. He was one of the architects

of the international economic order agreed at Bretton Woods (1944–46), which established the International Monetary Fund. He also helped form the Vic-Wells ballet and the Cambridge Arts Theatre. One of the truly great intellects of his time, or any time, he achieved more in one lifetime in the field of economic thought, public affairs and the arts than a team of gifted people might reasonably hope to achieve. His contributions to economics revolutionised government not only in Britain but all over the world. The problems of inflation in the 1970s initiated a reaction against Keynesianism and for a while monetarism eclipsed it, but the fundamental analyses and ideas were not jettisoned and live on as tools of analysis if not articles of faith.

> They [Conservative MPs] are a lot of hard faced men who look as if they have done well out of the war. (Quoting a Conservative politician, often thought to be Stanley Baldwin, in *Economic Consequences of the Peace*, 1919)

> I work for a government I despise for ends which I think criminal. (1917)

## Kiley, Robert (Bob) (1935–)

Commissioner for transport for London from 2001. A US citizen, he was born in Minneapolis and educated at Notre Dame University, Indiana, and Harvard University. He began his career in 1963 as a CIA agent and remained with it until 1970. He was deputy mayor of Boston, 1972–75, chief executive of Massachusetts Bay Transportation Authority, Boston, 1979–83, chairman of the Metropolitan Transportation Authority, New York, 1983–90, and president of New York Chamber of Commerce, 1995–2000. He then came to Britain and served as chairman of London Transport January–July 2001, appointed by Ken Livingstone, but his opposition to the Treasury's plan for the London Underground led to his dismissal after only 10 weeks in post, though he remained commissioner for transport for London.

## Kilroy-Silk, Robert (1942–)

Former Labour MP, chat-show presenter and prominent member of the United Kingdom Independence Party. He was educated at Saltley Grammar School, despite failing the 11 plus, and then the London School of Economics. He was elected Labour MP for Knowsley in 1970 and surprised some of his colleagues by predicting he would soon lead the party and become prime minister. In 1985 he was deselected by his Militant-dominated constituency party. He then turned to the media and became the presenter of *Kilroy*, a successful and long-running morning chat-show with an emphasis on shocking viewers. In January 2004 he was dismissed by the BBC for making anti-Arab remarks in a newspaper column but, again undeterred, in June 2004 he successfully stood as a candidate in the European elections for the United Kingdom Independence Party; his new party garnered 17 per cent of the national vote. Some predicted he would soon go on to challenge former Conservative MP Roger Knapman as leader of the party.

> Robert has never really lost his love of politics. He wants to influence things, to shake up opinion formers. (Liz Barron, former editor of *Kilroy*)

## King, Anthony (1934–)

Professor of government at Essex from 1969 and a member of the Committee on Standards in Public Life after 1994. He was educated at Queen's University, Kingston, Ontario, and Magdalen College, Oxford (he was a Rhodes scholar). As one of the leading political scientists in Britain, King analyses polls regularly in the press and provides shrewd commentary on television on election nights. He wrote *The Birth, Life and Death of the Social Democratic Party* (1997) with his Essex colleague Ivor Crewe.

## Kinnock, Neil (1942–)

Labour leader who lost the general elections of 1987 and 1992 before becoming a

European commissioner. He was the son of a coalminer and was educated at University College, Cardiff, before becoming a tutor with the Workers' Educational Association, and then Labour MP for Bedwellty in 1970 and then, from 1983, Islwyn. He immediately became a champion of left-wing policies and made a name as a powerful speaker. He was elected to Labour's National Executive Committee in 1978 and the shadow cabinet in 1980. Michael Foot's election to the leadership reflected the leftward swing of the party, which went down to a disastrous defeat in the 1983 general election. In its wake Kinnock, the popular left-wing rebel, was favoured in the elections for a new leader. His was the first election under the rules introduced in 1980 which gave 70 per cent of the decision to extraparliamentary constituency parties and trade unionists. He was successful and was initially welcomed as a dynamic force. However, his movement towards the centre-ground in response to the new right-wing Thatcherite agenda annoyed some of his erstwhile left-wing supporters and his performances in parliament were not judged impressive; Margaret Thatcher, in particular, seemed to treat him with contempt at prime minister's questions. His assiduous efforts to gain control over the party's machinery paid some dividends and in 1986 he appointed Peter Mandelson as its communications director. Both men moved the party even further towards the centre and poll ratings began to improve. However, the 1987 general election proved a bitter disappointment. He persevered with even more centrist policy reviews and further moves to neutralise the electorally embarrassing left-wing groups, especially Militant, which he had excoriated triumphantly at the 1985 Labour Party conference. By 1992, with John Major as premier and the economy deep in recession, it seemed his time had come. But it was not to be and Labour – despite appearing to be marginally ahead in the polls – lost yet again. Kinnock resigned and John Smith took over. When making his election victory speech in 1997, Tony Blair was careful to acknowledge the debt he owed to Kinnock as the man who had prepared the way. Kinnock went on to become the European commissioner for transport in 1994 and eventually became a vice president of the Commission (up to November 2004). He was a gifted party politician who used his hugely likeable personality to build a power base in the unions and constituencies. However, he was let down by a tendency to be prolix in media interviews and muddled when making crucial speeches in the House. Maybe his renunciation of so many left-wing opinions strained the electorate's credulity. He is historically significant as the man who presided over the introduction of political marketing and managerialism into the modern Labour Party.

> If Margaret Thatcher wins on Thursday, I warn you now not to be ordinary, I warn you not to be young, I warn you not to fall ill, I warn you not to grow old. (To supporters in Bridgend as the general election campaign closed, 8 June 1983)

> The grotesque chaos of a Labour council – a Labour council – hiring taxis to scuttle round the city handing out redundancy notices to its own workers. (Attacking Militant councillors in Liverpool, in his party conference speech at Bournemouth, 1985)

> I have a lot of sympathy with him. I too was once a young bald Leader of the Opposition. (On William Hague, 3 October 1999)

# L

## Lamont, Norman (1942–), Lord
Conservative chancellor under John Major who took the country out of the European Exchange Rate Mechanism (ERM). He was educated at Cambridge, after which he worked for the Conservative Research Department and in the City as a merchant banker and journalist. He was elected as

Conservative MP for Kingston on Thames in 1972. He served as financial secretary to the Treasury under Margaret Thatcher in 1986 and was promoted to the cabinet in 1989. Following Thatcher's departure in 1990 he managed Major's election campaign and was rewarded with the chancellorship. His credibility in this office was shattered by Black Wednesday, in September 1992, when Britain was forced to leave the ERM. However, membership of the ERM was the prime minister's policy, too, and perhaps because of this Lamont kept his job, in the face of clamorous criticism, until the following year, when he was replaced by Ken Clarke. His resignation speech was bitter – he accused Major of giving the impression of being 'in office but not in power'. On the backbenches he became ever more Eurosceptical and supported General Pinochet throughout the former Chilean dictator's period of arrest in Britain.

## Lansbury, George (1859–1940)
Leader of the Labour Party during the 1930s. He was an activist for reform and against poverty before he entered politics. He was elected as MP for Bow and Bromley in 1910 but he resigned in 1912 and was not elected again until 1922. He founded the *Daily Herald* and edited it for a while. He became the Labour leader after the debacle of the 1931 election robbed the party of so many leading figures (Labour gained only 52 seats after Ramsay MacDonald had formed the national government coalition with the Conservatives). He was a successful leader for much of the time but his pacifism was inappropriate as Hitler's power was on the increase. At the 1935 party conference he suffered a devastating personal assault over his pacifism from the trade unionist Ernest Bevin and resigned shortly afterwards.

## Lawson, Nigel (1932–), Lord
Conservative chancellor whose resignation from the government in 1989 anticipated and helped hasten Margaret Thatcher's own fall a year later. He was educated at

Westminster school, and Christ Church, Oxford. He worked as a speech writer to Alec Douglas-Home 1963–64 and edited the *Spectator* 1966–70. He was elected Conservative MP for Blaby in 1974.

By 1977 he was an opposition Treasury spokesman. He served as financial secretary to the Treasury 1979 and energy secretary (in cabinet) 1981. In 1983 he was made chancellor and served for six years. He reformed the tax system but was best known for lowering the top rate of income tax to 40 per cent. He was opposed to the poll tax. He argued strongly for membership of the European Exchange Rate Mechanism as the best guarantee against inflation and for growth. Thatcher was advised differently by Sir Alan Walters and a clash ensued in 1989. When Thatcher refused to dismiss her advisor Lawson resigned sensationally and the first stage of Thatcher's downfall was completed. He laid the foundations for the Conservative election victory of 1987 with his 1986 budget. However, his reputation was damaged by his unwise reduction of interest rates in the late 1980s, which fuelled inflation; the resultant high rates produced the recession which damaged John Major's government in the early 1990s. He also had a reputation for arrogance and for alienating colleagues. He worked for a bank after his retirement and took his seat in the Lords in 1992. His memoirs, *The View from Number 11* (1992), provided a fascinating insight into economic policy making during his years as chancellor.

### Letwin, Oliver (1956–)

Conservative MP and shadow minister. He was educated at Eton and Trinity College, Cambridge. He was elected MP for Dorset West in 1997. This cerebral Conservative politician (who has written books on philosophy) made an embarrassing gaffe during the 2001 election when he made an incautious remark about his party's tax-cutting plans as shadow chief secretary to the Treasury; he was nonetheless promoted under Iain Duncan Smith to shadow home secretary. He was tipped as

a possible replacement leader at the time of Duncan Smith's removal in November 2003 but bowed out of the contest in favour of the popular choice, Michael Howard, who then made him shadow chancellor in 2003.

### Liddell, Helen (1950–)

Labour MP and secretary of state for Scotland 2001–03. She became MP for Airdrie and Shotts in 1997. She served as junior minister for transport, energy and competitiveness, and at the Treasury and Scottish Office before stepping up to the cabinet. She was a famously tough operator but after devolution was not left with much of a departmental remit and left the cabinet in June 2003.

### Lilley, Peter (1943–)

Conservative cabinet minister in the 1990s, made deputy leader after the 1997 election defeat. He was educated at Dulwich College and Clare College, Cambridge. He worked in finance during the 1960s and became an MP in 1983. He served as parliamentary private secretary to chancellor Nigel Lawson 1985–87 and was then economic secretary 1987–89; financial and economic secretary 1989–90 and secretary of state for trade and industry 1990–92 and social security 1992–97. He was a quiet, even uncharismatic politician but formidably clever, with a talent for policy initiatives. He was not unambitious, as he demonstrated by standing for leadership in 1997, though he withdrew after the first ballot. He shadowed Treasury under William Hague then moved in 1998 to become deputy leader but was sacked after two years and returned to the backbenches.

### Livingstone, Kenneth (1945–)

Mayor of London from 2000 and Labour MP for Brent East 1987–2000. He was educated at Tulse Hill Comprehensive and Philippa Fawcett Teacher's Training College. He was a Lambeth councillor 1971–78, vice-chair of housing 1971–73 and 1978–82, and chair of Camden Council 1978–80. A lifelong, though idiosyncratic, left-winger, he was leader of the Greater London Council 1981–86, when he stoutly resisted the Conservative government's decision to abolish the Council. He stood as a candidate for the Labour leadership in 1992 but had no deep support in the party. He was a frequent critic of Labour's leaders, especially Tony Blair and Gordon Brown. His decision to stand as the mayor of London was in defiance of the Labour Party, whose official candidate he had failed to become; he stood as an independent and was expelled from the party. After a noisy campaign he defeated Frank Dobson (Labour's candidate) by a comfortable margin on 4 May 2000. His achievements in his first years as mayor were slight and were constrained by his battle with the Treasury on the future of the London Underground. He attracted some bad, though short-lived, publicity in June 2002 when it was alleged he had been involved in a skirmish with a journalist at a London party. The apparent success of his brave London traffic congestion charges in February 2003 strengthened his reputation. He was re-elected in June 2004.

> He was never a leftwinger. What passed for his philosophy was the devout belief that a day without a mention on the front page of a national newspaper was a day wasted.... He is not fit to be mayor of London. (Roy Hattersley, *Guardian*, 8 July 2002)

## Lloyd George, David (1863–1945)

British chancellor and then wartime prime minister (nicknamed the 'Welsh wizard'). He was born in Manchester, the son of a schoolteacher who died when David was young, and brought up in rural North Wales by his uncle Lloyd. He became a solicitor but won the seat of Carnaervon Boroughs for the Liberals in 1890 at a by-election and then held the seat for 55 years. In 1905 he was made president of the Board of Trade, then took over from Herbert Asquith as chancellor and in 1909 submitted his famous tax-raising budget which precipitated the reform of the Lords with the Parliament Act 1911. He passed more social legislation, including the National Insurance Act 1911. During the First World War his administrative skills were needed to improve the supply of munitions. He was secretary for war 1916. When Asquith refused to accept a small war cabinet he resigned and out of the resultant crisis Lloyd George emerged as prime minister. The Liberal Party never really recovered from the split this occasioned between Lloyd George and Asquith. He was energetic in modernising the government machine – he set up a five-man war cabinet (the first ever formed) and invented the Cabinet Office. He clashed with field marshall Douglas Haig but could not get rid of him. In 1918 he led the coalition government to a landslide but it was largely a victory for the Conservatives rather than the Liberals. Lloyd George had a presidential-style role and treated his ministers badly, particularly George Curzon, his foreign secretary. In 1922 he fixed a temporary peace in Ireland at the price of the Black and Tans' excesses in the postwar period. In October 1922 Conservative MPs' loss of faith in the 'Welsh wizard' was such that they voted to end the coalition. Lloyd George was meanwhile selling political honours and building a political war chest but he never returned to high office, even though he lived throughout the interwar years. The main reason for this failure was the lack of trust he inspired and his tendency to create divisions. He espoused Keynesianism before most of his contemporaries and was at all times perceived as a powerful figure. He refused an offer of a post by Winston Churchill in his wartime government. He is one of the two or three greatest political figures of the 20th century and few have equalled his mastery of the political arts.

> You mean Mr Balfour's poodle! It fetches and carries for him. It bites anybody that he sets it on to. (To H. Chaplin MP, who claimed the House of Lords was the watchdog of the constitution, 26 July 1907)

> What is our task? To make Britain a fit country for heroes to live in. (24 November 1918)

How these dukes harass us. They're as expensive to keep as a dreadnought and not half as useful. (1909)

I do not believe you could point to any case where men work better for the state than they work for syndicates. (1919)

I hate fences. I always feel like knocking down every fence I come across. (1915)

He could not see a belt without hitting below it. (Margot Asquith on Lloyd George)

He did not care in which direction the car was travelling, so long as he remained in the driver's seat. (Lord Beaverbrook on Lloyd George, 1963)

He spent the whole of his life in plastering together the true and the false and therefore manufacturing the plausible. (Stanley Baldwin quoting Carlyle to attack Lloyd George)

## Locke, John (1632–1704)

One of greatest figures in British political philosophy, who helped provide some of its essential character. He was educated at Westminster School and Christ Church, Oxford, where he studied philosophy. At first he was interested in science and actually qualified with a medical degree. Descartes' thought, however, stimulated his thinking, which continued to develop while he worked for his patron the Earl of Shaftesbury, who became lord chancellor in 1672. When the Earl died Locke fell from favour; he retired to Holland, where his writing prospered. His *Two Treatises of Government* appeared in 1690 and drew on most of the advanced thinking of the time. He was keen to refute the idea that the monarch had any God-given right to rule: on the contrary, the monarch had a duty to provide good, if strictly limited, government and, if he did not, might be legitimately removed. However, Locke was no democrat and while he believed people to be basically rational and cooperative he did not trust democratic assemblies. He was in favour of a separation of powers and favoured a tolerant approach towards Dissenters. He

is often seen as the father of the liberal enlightenment and a huge influence on the formation of liberal democracy in Britain and elsewhere, especially the USA, where his views influenced the colonists to seek independence.

# M

## MacDonald, Gus (1941–)

Labour peer and minister. He left school aged 14 to work as an apprentice machine fitter in a Glasgow shipyard and evolved into a left-wing activist who became a journalist for *Tribune*. He worked as circulation manager before he moved to the *Scotsman* and then Granada Television, where he worked as a presenter and senior executive before becoming director of programmes with Border Television in 1985. In July 1998 Donald Dewar invited him to become a minister in the Scottish Office. There was an immediate outcry – echoed by disappointed Scottish Labour MPs – that New Labour was again appointing its 'cronies' to top jobs. However, MacDonald was deemed to be an energetic, tough and effective minister – he was, after all, used to running large organisations. He served as chancellor of the Duchy of Lancaster 2001–03 within the Cabinet Office, charged with the 'enforcer' role in relation to government policy.

## MacDonald, Ramsay (1866–1937)

First Labour prime minister. He sprang from the most humble of origins as the illegitimate son of a Scottish farm labourer and received only a rudimentary education. He moved to England when 18 and flirted with the idea of becoming a Liberal MP but in 1894 joined the Independent Labour Party. He was secretary to the Labour Representation Committee, formed in 1900, and, thanks to the pact with the Liberals which he negotiated, became MP for Leicester in 1906 along with 28 other early Labour MPs, a group which he came to lead by 1914. Ideologically MacDonald was no revolutionary; he was more an evolutionary socialist and a vague one at that. However, his resignation as leader and his opposition to the war gave him an undeserved reputation for radicalism, something which helped his subsequent career. He was elected MP for Aberavon in 1922 and elected chairman of the Labour Party. He became prime minister in a minority government in January 1924. This short period in power achieved little but did, as MacDonald hoped, reassure doubters that Labour was not made up of revolutionary Bolsheviks. He became premier again in 1929 but had to face the mounting financial crisis of the day. A committee recommended to the cabinet a package of deep cuts in pubic spending, including unemployment benefit. The cabinet was unable to agree. MacDonald saw the king but returned having been persuaded to lead an all-party government to deal with the crisis. MacDonald went ahead but the majority of his party, who did not follow his lead, regarded him as a traitor. These feelings were compounded when the resultant general election returned MacDonald's coalition but almost wiped out Labour. MacDonald was the prisoner of the Conservative majority in parliament and cabinet and achieved little of note, degenerating into a pathetic figure. He was defeated in his Seaham seat in 1935 but returned for the Scottish Universities 1936–37. MacDonald's life story is one of the most unusual in British political history. From the most crippling of starts in life he became the architect of the Labour Party and then three times prime minister. However, he lacked the intellectual weight to deal with the fearsome economic problems which beset his times and was weakened by an overweening vanity. He is seen in retrospect by his party as a renegade and a disgrace – a poor reward, perhaps, for his remarkable contributions to the genesis of the Labour Party.

Sit down man, you're a bloody tragedy!' (James Maxton to MacDonald, 1933, as he was making one of his last speeches to the Commons)

If God were to ask me and say 'Ramsay, would you rather be a country gentleman than Prime Minister?' I should reply, 'Please God, a country gentleman'. (1930)

### Macleod, Ian (1913–70)

Leading Conservative politician who died before fulfilling his potential. He was educated at Fettes, Gonville and Caius Colleges, Cambridge. He was injured in the Second World War and suffered from rheumatoid arthritis. He worked in the Conservative Research Department 1948–50. He became MP for Enfield West in 1950 and was appointed minister of health following a brilliant attack on Anuerin Bevan in the House, and minister of labour in 1959. The Marquess of Salisbury, a Tory grandee of the old school, described him once (May 1961) as 'too clever by half' – a serious 'crime' in the party at the time. Along with Enoch Powell he refused to serve under Alec Douglas-Home (Macleod had supported R. A. Butler). He was editor of the *Spectator* for a while in the 1960s as well as shadow chancellor and was briefly chancellor before his death (from a heart attack) in 1970. Macleod was one of the most brilliant minds in postwar British politics, blessed with exceptional debating skills. He was a founder member of the 'one nation' group of Conservative MPs. His death was a huge loss to the Conservative Party in the 1970s; he was held up as a model by Conservatives of the centre left, like John Major.

Equality is a futile pursuit, equality of opportunity is a noble cause. (1969)

### Macmillan, Harold (1894–1986)

One of the most successful British prime ministers, 1957–63. He was educated at Eton and Balliol College, Oxford. He served in the Grenadier Guards and was injured three times in the First World War, bearing his serious third injury with typical sangfroid, by reading classical Greek in no-man's land. His experience in the war and his service as Conservative MP for Stockton 1924–29 and 1931–45 during the Depression deeply affected his political philosophy: he became a paternalist Keynesian, advocating a *Middle Way* – the title of his 1930s book – of government regulation and intervention in a free enterprise economy. He served as a junior minister in 1940 and then was attached to Allied Forces in the Mediterranean, where he met future US president Dwight Eisenhower. He lost his Stockton seat in 1945 but won a by-election in Bromley and went on to become a leading opposition spokesman. In 1951 he became a cabinet minister for housing and managed to achieve his own ambitious target – 300,000 – for house construction. He was rewarded with defence in 1954 and became Eden's foreign secretary in 1955 and chancellor in December of the same year. However, the Suez debacle ruined Anthony Eden and Macmillan, who had been an enthusiast for going in quickly, became equally keen to pull out when US support was not forthcoming. Despite his lack of consistency, he was preferred in the ensuing Conservative Party leadership process to his rival, R. A. Butler, and became prime minister. His gift in the highest office was to exude calmness and confidence, sentiments belied by his intense inner nervousness and an unhappy personal life. His laid-back campaigning included shrewd use of modern media and he won handsomely in the 1959 general election. His reputation as 'Supermac', however, did not last long and he ran into economic difficulties as well as failing to achieve, as a result of De Gaulle's veto, his goal of joining the Common Market. In 1962 he tried to reverse growing unpopularity by sacking one-third of his cabinet in the so-called Night of the Long Knives. Now 'events', as he ruefully observed, took over and the Profumo affair took its toll. In October 1963 he entered hospital with prostatitis and prematurely resigned (he had over 20 years left to live). From his hospital bed he choreographed the fight for

the succession, when he ignored Butler. He first favoured Lord Hailsham and then, when he proved excessively histrionic at the party conference, Alec Douglas-Home. And so this unlikely, mild-mannered aristocrat – and Macmillan admired the aristocracy intensely – briefly became prime minister with Macmillan's blessing. Macmillan lived out an active retirement, writing memoirs and acting as chancellor of Oxford University. He accepted a hereditary peerage in 1984 and caused a stir when he criticised Margaret Thatcher's privatisation policies as 'selling the family silver'. He clearly did not enjoy seeing his consensual 'middle way' being overturned by one of his successors as party leader.

> Let us be frank about it, most people have never had it so good. (Party rally, 21 July 1957)

> I thought the best thing was to settle up these little local difficulties, and then turn to the wider vision of the Commonwealth. (Referring to the resignations of Treasury ministers before flying off for a Commonwealth tour, 7 January 1958)

> The wind of change is blowing through this continent [Africa], and whether we like it or not, this growth of national consciousness is a political fact. (Capetown, 3 February 1960)

> Events dear boy, events. (In reply to a young journalist who asked what kept him awake at night when prime minister)

### Major, John (1941–)

Successor to Margaret Thatcher as Conservative prime minister, 1990–97. He was born the son of a trapeze artist and, unlike either Edward Heath or Margaret Thatcher, did not go to university. He did attend grammar school but left at 16. He joined Standard Bank and worked in Nigeria before a serious accident encouraged him to come home. He was elected Conservative councillor for Lambeth, was adopted for the safe Tory seat of Huntingdon and entered the Commons in 1979. After junior office as a whip, then as a junior minister in social security, he became one of Thatcher's favourites; he was made chief secretary to the Treasury in 1987 under Nigel Lawson. In July 1989 he took over from Geoffrey Howe at the Foreign Office and then from Lawson as chancellor that October. When Thatcher fell he stood in the resultant leadership contest and, as one of her proposers in the contest she lost, inherited some of her mantle in the perceptions of Conservative MPs. He won the contest in the second ballot by 185 votes to Michael Heseltine's 131 and Douglas Hurd's 56. He soon belied his apparent strong Thatcherism by revealing a moderate Conservatism, not hostile to the public sector, but the main thrust of his programme in terms of privatisation and welfare reform was still essentially Thatcherite. After an extended 'honeymoon' he soon attracted criticism for being weak and vacillating but the economic recession did more to damage him. In 1992 he called an election which most expected him to lose but his defiant electioneering and clarity compared with Neil Kinnock's more passionate but opaque style for Labour proved decisive and, in spite of the polls, which showed Labour slightly in front throughout, he won by a 7 per cent margin, though with a majority of less than 30 in the Commons. His first disaster in his new government was Black Wednesday, in September 1992, when Britain withdrew from the European Exchange Rate Mechanism, which destroyed his party's reputation for economic competence. Divisions over Europe exacerbated the Tories' poor image. However, he won respect and credit for persevering with Northern Ireland, where he combined with Irish premier Albert Reynolds to initiate a process which ultimately led to the Good Friday Agreement in 1998. To answer critics within his own parliamentary party he resigned as leader in July 1995 and stood again for his own job, when he won by a margin that did not still criticism. His government staggered on until 1997, riven by splits and discredited by evidence of corruption, sexual peccadilloes and

incompetence. Few were surprised when he lost by a landslide but the scale of his defeat reflected the deep pit into which the Conservatives had slipped. He resigned as leader after the election, to be replaced by William Hague. He stood down from parliament in 2001. A decent, competent politician who became prime minister at a time when the Conservatives' long tenure in power had reduced their majority and splits over Europe were, arguably, making the party unleadable.

> So right, OK. We lost. (On election night, 1 May 1997)

> Margaret has been at her happiest confronting political dragons: I choose consensus. (1999)

> Fifty years from now Britain will still be the country of long shadows on county grounds, warm beer, invincible green suburbs, dog lovers, and – as George Orwell said – old maids bicycling to Holy Communion through the morning mist. (1993)

> In the next 10 years, we will make changes that will make the whole of this country a genuinely classless society. (1990, soon after becoming prime minister)

### Mallon, Seamus (1936–)
Deputy leader of the Social Democratic and Labour Party (SDLP) 1979–2002 and MP. He was educated at Brothers Abbey Grammar School, Newry, and St Joseph's College of Education. He was elected for Newry and Armagh in 1986, though he had become deputy leader of the SDLP in 1979. He was deputy first minister of the Northern Ireland executive following elections to the assembly in the province in June 1998.

### Mandelson, Peter (1954–)
Labour MP and minister. His grandfather was Labour MP Herbert Morrison. He was educated at Hendon County Grammar School and St Catherine's College, Oxford. As a student he was a member of the Young Communist League and notoriously earned an MI5 file as a result.

He worked for the Trades Union Congress and for London Weekend Television as a producer. He was made Labour's director of communications in 1985 and was a close ally of Neil Kinnock in moving the party into the centre. He played an important role in the 1987 general election and a bigger one in 1992, when he himself was elected MP for Hartlepool. He advised Tony Blair on his leadership campaign in 1994 following John Smith's death, though secretly. In 1997 he became minister without portfolio in charge of monitoring policy delivery and the ill-fated Millennium Dome. In 1998 he was made secretary of state for trade and industry but was forced to resign that autumn when it became known he was the secret recipient of a large house loan from fellow (Treasury) minister Geoffrey Robinson. In 1999 he came back into the cabinet as secretary of state for Northern Ireland. He prospered until it was alleged he had intervened on behalf of a Dome contributor, one of the Hinduja brothers, to advance his application for citizenship. The story attracted much criticism and eventually he was forced to resign by Blair. He never accepted any guilt and remained bitter despite his continued contacts with Blair. In July 2004 Blair announced that his old friend was to be sent to Brussels as the UK's European commissioner. Some criticised another example of cronyism, while others reflected that the 'Prince of Darkness' was at least three hours' travel away from Downing Street.

> New Labour is extremely relaxed about people becoming filthy rich. (1998)

> I'm a fighter and not a quitter. (Speech at Hartlepool, June 2001)

## Manning, David (1949–)

Civil servant and foreign policy advisor to the prime minister. He was educated at Ardingly Hall, Oxford University, John Hopkins University and in Bologna. He had appointments in eastern Europe, India, Moscow, Israel (as ambassador), the Cabinet Office 1985–90 and was British

representative to the Contact Group on Bosnia. He came to public attention following the terrorist attacks in the USA in September 2001 as someone advising Tony Blair on foreign policy at the highest level.

## Marquand, David (1934–)

Political scientist and author. He was educated at Emanuel School and Magdalen College, Oxford. He worked at the University of California 1955–59, was a leader writer for the *Guardian* 1956–62 and then worked at the University of Sussex 1964–66. He was MP for Ashfield 1966–77 and parliamentary private secretary to the minister for overseas development 1967–69. He contested a seat for the Social Democratic Party in 1983. He was a professor at Salford University 1978–91 and Sheffield University 1991–96, and then became master of Mansfield College, Oxford 1996–2002. His books include *Ramsay MacDonald* (1977), *Social Theory and Radical Change* (1982), *Thatcherism* (1987) and *The Unprincipled Society* (1988). He won the Sir Isaiah Berlin Prize for Lifetime Contribution to Political Studies in 2001.

## Martin, Michael (1945–)

Speaker of the House of Commons from 2000 – the first Roman Catholic to have held the office – and Labour MP for Glasgow Springburn from 1979. He was educated at St Patrick's School, Glasgow, and was later a councillor, a trade union officer and a sheet-metal worker. He served on a variety of House committees and was deputy speaker 1998–2000. He was parliamentary private secretary to Denis Healey. His strong Glaswegian accent and general conduct in post have been criticised by some in his own party. His friends and defenders include Gordon Brown and Tam Dalyell, who tend to dismiss such criticism as 'southern snobbery'.

## Marx, Karl (1818–83)

Revolutionary intellectual, author of international communism, who spent much of his life studying and writing in England. Of

Jewish extraction, he was educated at Bonn and Berlin universities, where he became one of the 'Young Hegelians'. He emigrated to Paris in 1843 (after being warned that his militant journalism might lead to his arrest), where he became a revolutionary and friend of Friedrich Engels – with whom he wrote *The Communist Manifesto* in 1848. He believed that the social group, or class, which controls the means of production effectively controls society. He argued that this was true of all stages in history and that each dominant class provokes opposition from a subordinate class, making all history the story of class conflict. In the 19th century he argued a small group of property-owning capitalists (the 'bourgeoisie') were dominant at the expense of a huge working class (the 'proletariat'). He predicted that the latter would (inevitably) eventually rise up and overthrow the former, thus creating a classless society. He also ordained that it was the duty of enlightened people to assist in the revolution, which would end exploitation and usher in a new era of dignity and happiness for those who suffered from the workings of capitalism. He moved via Brussels to London and began his research in the Reading Room of the British Museum, which led in 1867 to the first volume of *Das Kapital*. Engels helped support the impoverished Marx and his family during these years. He is buried in Highgate Cemetery. Despite basing much of his work on British experience, Marx never exerted much influence on British politics, apart from the tiny Communist Party of Great Britain and the more peripheral fringes of Labour's left wing.

## Maudling, Reginald (1917–79)

Leading Conservative politician who served as chancellor and was a leadership candidate. He was educated at Merchant Taylor's School and Merton College, Oxford. He practised at the bar and was elected to the Commons in 1950 as MP for Barnett. He held a succession of junior and senior posts in the 1950s, principally at the Department of Trade. In 1962 he became chancellor after Harold Macmillan's 'Night

of the Long Knives' and retained this post under Alec Douglas-Home. He was widely expected to win the party leadership election when the latter stepped down (the first election for Conservative leader) but was beaten by Edward Heath, by 150 votes to 133. He was home secretary under Heath in 1970 but resigned when his business partner, John Poulson, was investigated for corruption. He briefly held shadow office under Margaret Thatcher until she sacked him in 1976. He escaped expulsion from the House – a reflection of his popularity – following censure in respect of his dealings with Poulson.

> We're a Conservative country that votes Labour from time to time.

## Maxwell, Robert (1923–91)

Media tycoon and Labour politician who proved to be a fraud as well as a bully. Originally Ludwig Hoch, Maxwell was a Czech who served in the Second World War and then settled in Britain. A born survivor, fluent in several languages, he worked for intelligence, possibly for the east as well as the west. He set up Pergamon Press, which established his reputation as a brilliant businessman. He was elected Labour MP for Buckingham 1964–70 but retained extensive business interests in the media. In 1984 he became chair of the Mirror Group and did his best to influence editorial policy. A man never to do things in half measure, he left this world in dramatic style: his body was found floating alongside his luxury yacht in 1991 near the Canary Islands; the conclusion of suicide seemed to follow from the parlous state of his business finances, but many have disputed this and conspiracy theories abound. After his death it was discovered he had emptied the pension fund belonging to *Daily Mirror* employees in a vain attempt to save his business empire. After his death he was initially praised as a generous and brilliant businessman, known and respected by the world's most powerful leaders, but as revelations emerged he was condemned as a fraudster, bully and hypocrite.

## May, Theresa (1956–)

Conservative MP and former party chair. She represented Maidenhead after 1997. She shadowed education before 2001, when she was generally judged to have been ineffective. As transport spokesperson, her opposition to Stephen Byers won her some commendations and she was made the first ever woman Conservative Party chair, in succession to David Davis, in July 2002. She quickly became identified as a leader of the 'moderniser' faction in the party, controversially urging it to lose the label of 'the nasty party'. She was the only woman selected in Michael Howard's shadow leadership team in 2003, becoming shadow secretary of state for the family.

## Mayhew, Patrick (1929–), Lord

Conservative cabinet minister under Margaret Thatcher, who proved a tenacious Northern Ireland secretary. He was educated at Tonbridge and Balliol, Oxford, where he was president of the Union in 1952; he was a barrister before becoming MP for Tunbridge Wells 1983–97. He was a junior minister in the Home Office and for employment before becoming successively solicitor general, attorney general and then secretary of state for Northern Ireland from 1992. He was a key player in the events leading to the Downing Street Declaration, itself the precursor to the Good Friday Agreement in 1998.

## McCartney, Ian (1951–)

Labour MP and minister. He was state educated and then worked variously as a seaman and a manual worker for local government. He served as a local councillor in Wigan 1982–87 and was elected MP for Makerfield 1987. After a number of shadow jobs at health, employment, education and social services he became minister of state at the Department of Trade and Industry 1997–99, the Cabinet Office 1999–2001 and for work and pensions 2001–03. From 2003 he was a minister without portfolio and Labour Party chair. Short of stature but with dynamic energy, this Scotsman provided a vital link between the government and the unions and was a credible loyal connection between 'New' and 'Old' Labour.

## McGuinness, Martin (1950–)

Sinn Fein leader who joined Gerry Adams in supporting the peace process that culminated in the Good Friday Agreement, 1998. Catholic born in Derry's Bogside, he joined the IRA in the 1960s and became a senior officer in Derry. In 1972 he joined Gerry Adams in talks with Northern Ireland secretary Willie Whitelaw. His close relationship with Adams was a crucial element in the process towards peace and the Good Friday Agreement, with McGuinness seen as the 'hard' negotiator, with credibility with the IRA, as opposed to Adams' more subtle and political approach. In September 1998 it was announced he would be 'liaison officer' between Sinn Fein and the body set up to oversee decommissioning of paramilitary weapons. He was made minister of education in the new Northern Ireland executive after 1998, though his period in office was soon interrupted when the executive was suspended.

## Meacher, Michael (1939–)

Labour MP and minister, and allegedly the most 'green' member of New Labour. He was educated at Berkhamstead and New College, Oxford. He was elected MP for Oldham West and Royton in 1970 and served in junior capacity at the Departments of Trade and Industry and Health and Social Security 1974–79. He was seen as a left-wing ally of Tony Benn in the early 1980s but moved back into the centre under Neil Kinnock. In opposition he shadowed employment, transport, social security and then environmental affairs. He was minister of the environment 1997–2001 but then returned to the backbenches. In August 2002 he was left out of the official delegation to the world environment conference in Johannesburg but was reinstated when green groups said they would pay his fare themselves.

## Mellor, David (1949–)

Former Conservative cabinet member turned broadcaster and journalist. He was educated Swanage Grammar School and Cambridge. He became a barrister and was made a QC in 1978. He served as MP for Putney 1979–97, a junior minister in the Home Office and Foreign Office under Margaret Thatcher and chief secretary to the Treasury 1990–92 before becoming secretary of state for national heritage under John Major. He was forced to resign in 1992 after a scandal involving an actress with whom he had an affair. After he lost his seat in 1997 he became a member of the football task force 1997–99.

## Meyer, Anthony (1920–2002)

Conservative backbencher who earns a footnote in history for standing against Margaret Thatcher in the 1989 party leadership election. He was educated at Eton and New College, Oxford. He fought in the Second World War in the Scots Guards, then worked in the Treasury and Foreign Service (Paris, Moscow). He became MP for Eton and Slough 1964–66, West Flint 1966–83, Clywd North West 1983–92. He was a pro-European backbencher with an unexceptional career but was notable for standing against Thatcher in 1989 in the annual leadership contest. He mustered only 30 votes but, with an equal number abstaining, he helped show that his party was unhappy with its leader; she was deposed a year later.

> I question the right of that great Moloch, national sovereignty, to burn its children, to save its pride. (In a speech against the Falklands War, 1982)

## Michael, Alun (1943–)

Labour MP and minister, and first minister in Wales. He was educated at Colwyn Bay Grammar School and Keele University. He worked as a journalist before becoming MP for Penarth from 1987 and Cardiff South from 1997. He was spokesman for Wales in opposition then after 1997 served initially as Home Office junior minister

before taking over from Ron Davies as secretary of state. When Davies was no longer leader of the Welsh Labour Party he was controversially 'installed' by the party machine (according to most commentators) as Davies's successor and thereafter as first minister of Wales. Following problems over government funding for Wales he resigned and was replaced by the more popular Rhodri Morgan. He was made minister of state in the Department of Environment and Rural Affairs in June 2001.

## Milburn, Alan (1958–)

Labour MP and minister. He was educated at John Marley and Stokesley Schools (Newcastle and Cleveland, respectively), and Lancaster and Newcastle universities. He was elected MP for Darlington in 1992 and was opposition spokesman on health and Treasury matters 1995–97. He was chief secretary to the Treasury 1998–99 and secretary of state for health 1999–2003. Former left-wing firebrand turned Blairite, he is widely seen as competent and tough but perhaps lacking in personality. He surprised the world of politics in June 2003 by suddenly declaring he was giving up front-line politics to bring up his young family. Nonetheless, he was appointed to the cabinet again in September 2004, as chancellor of the Duchy of Lancaster, in which role he was to develop policy for the next general election.

## Miliband, David (1965–)

Labour advisor turned MP. The son of Ralph Miliband, a Marxist academic, he was educated at Oxford University and the Massachusetts Institute of Technology. He was made head of the Downing Street Policy Unit in 1998. He left Number 10 in June 2001 to become a Labour MP and, tipped as a high-flier, was made a junior education minister (for schools) in 2002. He helped to set up the Centre for European Reform.

## Mill, James (1773–1836)

British liberal political philosopher. He was ordained in 1798 and moved from

Scotland to London, where he worked as a
journalist and became an admirer of Jeremy
Bentham and part of his 'utilitarian' school
of thought. Mill helped form University
College London in 1825. He worked for
the British India Company while writing
books which included *Elements of Political
Economy* (1821).

## Mill, John Stuart (1806–1873)

One of the most famous political thinkers
and a founder of liberal thought as well as
the concept of representative democracy.
Son of James Mill, this remarkable child
prodigy, taught by his father, was similarly
a follower of Jeremy Bentham. He joined
his father at the India Office and retired
prematurely in 1858 to write. After a nervous crisis relating to his cloistered childhood
he rediscovered equanimity and wrote *On
Liberty* (1859), followed by *Considerations
on Representative Government* (1861)
and *Utilitarianism* (1863). He defined
freedom as the right to do anything which
did not impinge on another's freedom
and argued for the protection of liberties
against both the power of government and
popular democracy. He developed the case
for: electoral reform – he favoured a form
of proportional representation; improved
living conditions for the working class; and
representative government – he argued
that participation in the political process
was the best education in citizenship. Mill
was the intellectual father of Britain's
liberal democracy. He was elected to the
Commons in 1865 and campaigned for the
enfranchisement of women. He is probably the best-known British liberal thinker
worldwide.

> The Conservatives ... being by their law of
> existence the stupidest party. (1861)

> The only freedom worth the name is that
> of pursuing our own good in our own way.
> (1859)

> The liberty of the individual must be thus far
> limited; he must not make himself a nuisance
> to other people. (1859)

## Mitchell, George (1933–)

US politician who played a crucial role
in achieving the 1998 Good Friday
Agreement in Northern Ireland. He
was educated at Bowdoin College and
Georgetown University. He served in the
US army in counter-intelligence, then
worked as a lawyer in the US Department
of Justice 1960–62 and in public office in
Maine. He became a US senator in 1982
and was re-elected in 1988. He was made
majority leader in 1988 but surprisingly
retired in 1994. He accepted an invitation
to chair the peace commission in Northern
Ireland and performed a delicate job with
great sensitivity up to the Good Friday
Agreement in 1998. He won praise from
all sides.

> I never said it would be easy– and that was
> an understatement. (1998)

> Peace, political stability and reconciliation
> are not too much to ask for. They are the
> minimum that a decent society provides.
> (1998)

## Monks, John (1945–)

General secretary of the Trades Union
Congress (TUC). He was educated
at Dulcie Technical High School,
Manchester, and Nottingham University.
He joined the TUC after university and
worked his way up through the ranks, serving as deputy general secretary 1987–93
before becoming general secretary after
1993. He was seen as a moderate 'moderniser' and a skilled diplomatic operator who
was less than happy with New Labour's
plans to introduce more private sector
involvement in the public sector.

## Moore, Charles (1956–)

Leading right-wing columnist and editor
of the *Daily Telegraph*. He was educated
at Eton and Trinity College, Cambridge.
He worked for *Daily Express*, the *Sunday
Telegraph* and *Daily Telegraph* and as
editor of the *Spectator* and then of the
*Telegraph* from 1995. He was nicknamed
'Lord Snooty' by some, after the comic
character.

## Morgan, Piers (1965–)

Former editor of the *Daily Mirror*. He worked for the *Sun* before he moved to the *Mirror*, where he did not prevent the *Daily Mail* from overtaking its ailing circulation of 2.3 million daily; the *Mirror* is still the third best-selling daily newspaper. He suffered some bad publicity when he was associated with some suspect share reporting by two of his financial journalists. He was sacked in May 2004 for publishing pictures of British servicemen abusing Iraqi prisoners which turned out to be fakes.

## Morgan, Sally (1959–), Baroness

Labour peer and Downing Street aide. She was educated at Belvedere Girls' School, Liverpool, and Durham and London universities. She was a teacher 1981–85, student organiser in the Labour Party 1985–87, director of campaigns and elections in the Labour Party 1993–95, head of party liaison for the leader of opposition 1995–97 and political secretary to the prime minister 1997–2001. She was briefly a minister of state in the Cabinet Office before she became director of political and government relations based in Downing Street in 2001.

## Morris, Bill (1938–), Sir

General secretary of the Transport and General Workers' Union (TGWU). He was educated at Mizpah School, Manchester, Jamaica. In 1954 he moved to Handsworth, Birmingham, and joined the TGWU in 1954. He was deputy general secretary 1986 and was elected general secretary 1991 and re-elected 1995. He retired in 2003.

## Morris, Estelle (1952–)

Labour MP and minister. She was educated at Whalley Range High School, Manchester, and Coventry College of Education, then worked as a teacher. She was active in local government before entering the House and was leader of Warwick District Council 1979–81. She was elected MP for Birmingham Yardley in 1992, became a junior education minister after

1997 and then secretary of state in 2001. However, after just more than a year in the post she resigned, claiming the demands of the job were beyond her. She was later made minister for the arts but declared in September 2004 that she would not contest the next election.

## Morrison, Herbert (1888–1965)

Leading Labour politician who helped develop the policy of nationalisation. Self-educated, he helped to found the London Labour Party and became leader of the London County Council from 1934. He did much to establish transport in the capital and to protect 'green belt' land from development. He was elected an MP in 1923 and helped formulate Labour's policies on nationalisation. He served in Winston Churchill's war cabinet as home secretary. After Labour's 1945 election victory he was deputy prime minister 1945–51 and leader of the House. He succeeded Ernest Bevin as foreign secretary for a few months after the latter's resignation but was not a success in the post. He was defeated by Hugh Gaitskell in the party leadership contest in 1955. He was made a life peer in 1959. His grandson is Peter Mandelson.

## Mosley, Oswald (1896–1980)

Gifted British politician who became leader of the 1930s fascist movement and failed to achieve any power. He was born into a landed family and educated at Winchester and Sandhurst. He was elected Conservative MP in 1918, retained his seat as an independent in 1922 and 1924 and then joined the Labour Party, when he made a name for himself as a left-wing rebel. He served as chancellor of the Duchy of Lancaster in the 1929 Labour government, when he was in charge of tackling unemployment, the major problem of the day. His Mosley Memorandum was a proposal to spend money on public works and anticipated much Keynesian thinking. His ideas were rejected and he resigned. He formed the socialist New Party in 1930, lost his seat in 1931 and then looked to other routes to power. He was clearly

PEOPLE

influenced by the fascist movement on the
Continent and set up the British Union of
Fascists in 1932. His Blackshirts took part
in violent rallies, which contained strong
anti-Semitic overtones. Their excessive violence in demonstrations in 1934 and 1936
led to the passing of the Public Order Act
1936. Mosley's demeanour as a political
leader seemed to ape that of Adolf Hitler
in appearance, style and manner of political
meeting. However, the British political
culture was not receptive to such messages
and he never prospered. During the war
he was interned, though he was released
on health grounds in 1943. He attempted
to be active in politics after the war and in
the late 1950s stood unsuccessfully for the
Commons. A vigorous and imaginative politician, he could have achieved much but his
desperate wish to acquire power by whatever
means ultimately destroyed his career.

> Jewish international finance, the nameless,
> homeless and all powerful force which
> stretches its greedy fingers from the shelter of
> England to throttle the trade and menace the
> peace of the world.

> I am not, and have never been, a man of the
> right. My position was on the left and is now
> in the centre of politics. (1968)

## Mottram, Richard (1946–)

Civil servant. He was educated at Edward
VI Camp Hill School, Birmingham,
and Keele University. He worked in the
Ministry of Defence, the Cabinet Office
and Office of Public Service and Science
before moving to be permanent secretary
in the Department of Transport, Local
Government and the Regions in 1998.
He was involved in public controversy in
February 2002, when his minister, Stephen
Byers, sacked his head of communications,
Martin Sixsmith. The latter claimed he
had not offered his resignation and an
unseemly public dispute ensued, with Sir
Richard insisting he had told Sixsmith his
'position was untenable' and that the ex-
BBC man had agreed to resign as long as
Jo Moore (with whom he had difficulties)

did the same and that his resignation did
not appear to blame him for any wrongdoing. Sir Richard's highly unusual
statement was published in the press on 26
February 2002. Shortly afterwards he was
moved to become the top mandarin at the
Department of Work and Pensions.

## Mowlam, Mo (Marjorie) (1949–)

Labour MP and cabinet minister with
the popular touch. She was educated at
Conodon Comprehensive, and Durham
and Iowa universities. She lectured at
Florida University before becoming MP for
Redcar in 1987. She was shadow Northern
Ireland spokeswoman then, after 1997,
secretary of state for Northern Ireland.
She is credited with playing a big part in
obtaining the Good Friday Agreement in
1998 but was replaced by Peter Mandelson
and took over the Cabinet Office job once
performed by Jack Cunningham. She left
the House in 2001 to do different things.

> You can't switch on peace like a light.
> (1999)

## Mulgan, Geoff (1961–)

Head of policy at 10 Downing Street. He
was educated at Oxford University and
the Polytechnic of Central London. After
working for Gordon Brown as an advisor
1990–92, he founded the independent
think tank, Demos, in 1993. He became a
member of the Cabinet Office Performance
and Innovation Unit before joining the
Downing Street Policy Unit, where he was
responsible for the social exclusion issue. In
June 2001 it was announced he was to be
head of policy, charged with undertaking
'blue skies policy thinking for the prime
minister' and 'strategy projects at request'.

## Murdoch, Rupert (1931–)

Media tycoon with a big stake in the
British media, who decided to support
Tony Blair in 1997. He was educated at
Geelong Grammar School and Oxford
University. He then worked for a while on
the *Daily Express* before returning to his
homeland, Australia, to run the paper he

inherited, the *News* in Adelaide. Using this as a base he bought newspapers in Hong Kong and the USA, as well as others in his home country. In Britain his News International owns *The Times*, *Sunday Times*, *News of the World* and the biggest-selling British tabloid, the *Sun*. He also moved into satellite television with Sky TV in Europe, Fox in the USA and Star TV in Asia. He owns Random House and other publishing interests. He was known for astute though legal tax avoidance, for his ruthless use of the law to advance his business interests (as occurred when he broke the power of British trade unions by moving to Wapping and employing new technology in defiance of the print unions), for his wooing of politicians, and for his editorial intervention to influence the content of the newspapers he owns. Murdoch is one of the world's most influential media moguls. He is clever at maximising his influence, for example inviting Tony Blair to address his company's executives in 1995. The *Sun* supported Blair in 1997 and since then commentators have discerned a desire by Blair to retain Murdoch's support – Blair allegedly assisted him in 1998 by contacting the Italian prime minister on a business matter on Murdoch's behalf. More traditional Labour supporters are deeply troubled by the Blair–Murdoch connection. The *Sun* supported Blair in the 2001 general election and Murdoch was an early visitor to Number 10 after the victory.

## Murphy, Paul (1948–)

Labour MP and minister. He was educated at St Francis School, Abersychan, and Oriel College, Oxford. He worked as a technical college lecturer. He became MP for Torfaen in 1987. He served as minister of state at the Northern Ireland Office 1997–99, where his ability was noticed. He was opposition spokesperson on Wales 1988–94, Northern Ireland 1994–95 and defence 1995–97. He was secretary of state for Wales from 1999 but devolution had not left his department much to do. He was moved to take charge of the Northern Ireland Office in October 2002.

# N

## Naughtie, James (1951–)

Nationally known, along with John Humphrys, as the voice of Radio 4's *Today* programme. He was educated at Keith Grammar School, Aberdeen University and Syracuse University, New York. He worked for a variety of newspapers but principally the *Guardian* before he joined the BBC to present *The World at One* and then from 1994 *Today*. He wrote a study of Gordon Brown and Tony Blair entitled *The Rivals* (2000).

## Neville-Jones, Pauline (1939–), Dame

Chair of the Joint Intelligence Committee 1993–94. She was educated at Leeds High School and Oxford University (Harkness fellow 1961–63). She was a career member of the Diplomatic Service 1963–96. She was seconded to the European Commission, where she acted as chef de cabinet to the budget and financial institutions commissioner Christopher Tugendhat. She became political director of the Foreign Office 1994–96 and led the British delegation to the Dayton negotiations on peace in Bosnia. She was made a governor of the BBC in 1998. Anticipating the Butler report, in 2004 she said that responsibility for any intelligence failure rested ultimately with the prime minister.

## Norton, Philip (1951–), Lord

The leading academic authority on parliament. He was educated at King Edward's Grammar School, Louth, Sheffield University and the University of Pennsylvania. He has written over 20 books, including *The Conservative Party* (1996) and *Legislatures* (1990). He served as president of the Politics Association for many years and in 1998 was elevated to the House of Lords as a Conservative peer – one of the few political scientists in the upper chamber.

**Nott, John (1932–)**
Conservative MP and minister. He was educated at Kings Mead, Seaford, and Trinity College, Cambridge, where he was president of the Cambridge Union. He was called to the bar in 1959 and worked as a merchant banker 1959–66. He was MP for St Ives 1972–83, and served as a junior minister in the Treasury under Edward Heath, and under Margaret Thatcher as secretary of state for trade 1979–81 and defence secretary 1981–83, during the Falklands War. After leaving politics he filled a number of jobs in the City.

# O

**Oakeshott, Michael (1901–99)**
English philosopher who influenced the Conservatives. He was educated at Cambridge, where he also taught, 1929–49. He moved to the London School of Economics in 1950 as professor of political science. His *Experience and its Modes* appeared in 1933 and *Rationalism in British Politics* in 1962. He was sceptical of ideological approaches and trusted a pragmatic approach to politics.

**O'Donnell, Gus (1952–)**
Civil servant. He was educated at Salesian College, Warwick University and Oxford University. He became a career civil servant who was moving smoothly upwards when he was made press secretary to John Major. He resigned in 1993 and returned to the Treasury to head the monetary group and became a member of Gordon Brown's inner circle on the economy as chief economist at the Treasury.

**Omand, David (1947–), Sir**
Civil servant. He was educated at Glasgow Academy and Cambridge University. He started his civil service career in the Ministry of Defence and moved

to head Government Communications Headquarters at Cheltenham and then became permanent secretary at the Home Office. He was mentioned as a candidate to take over from Sir Richard Wilson as cabinet secretary in April 2002 but was eventually – after a period of ill-health – given the job of security coordinator as well as day-to-day manager of the Cabinet Office. He was centrally involved with the David Kelly affair and gave evidence to the Hutton inquiry in 2003.

**Orwell, George (pen name for Eric Blair) (1903–50)**
English political writer. He was born in India and educated at Eton. He spent the early 1930s empathising with and writing about people living in oppressed circumstances before he fought in Spain on the Republican side (as depicted in *Homage to Catalonia*, 1938). He was associated with left-wing socialist ideas and groupings but was a firm opponent of communism and the USSR. Apart from his influential and prolific journalism he wrote two world-famous books inspired by the Soviet Union: *Animal Farm* (1945), a satirical parody; and *Nineteen Eighty-Four* (1949), a dystopian view of the future. His was a genuinely honest and perceptive voice with lasting relevance.

> Most revolutionaries are potential Tories, because they imagine that everything can be put right by altering the shape of society. Once that change is effected – as it sometimes is – they see no need for any other. (*Inside the Whale*, 1940)

> War is peace. Freedom is slavery. Ignorance is strength. (Example of 'doublespeak', *Nineteen Eighty-Four*, 1949).

**Owen, David (1938–), Lord**
One time Labour minister and leader of the Social Democratic Party. He was educated at Cambridge University, where he studied medicine. He became Labour MP for Plymouth Sutton in 1966 and held the seat until 1974; thereafter he held

Plymouth Devonport until 1992, when he stood down. He had junior posts held in health and defence, then became second in command at the Foreign Office until Anthony Crosland died and he took over, aged 39, 1977–79. At this time many spoke of him as a future leader but he became disaffected with Labour's drift to the left, especially in the wake of the 1979 general election, and he formed the so-called 'gang of four' (with William Rodgers, Shirley Williams and Roy Jenkins) to form the Social Democratic Party (SDP), which was initially led by Roy Jenkins, and which in the autumn of 1981 joined up with the Liberals to form the Alliance for electoral purposes. Owen led the party after 1983 and insisted on leading it even after a majority of members voted to merge with the Liberals in 1987. In 1991 he offered John Major support in exchange for the Tories not fielding candidates in the constituencies of the two remaining MPs loyal to his banner. Even when this could not be done Owen declared his support for the Conservatives. He resigned from the House of Commons in 1992 and was given a role in the former Yugoslavia, promoting peace, though little came of his efforts. Owen was one of the most able of politicians of his generation but his self-confidence, bordering on arrogance, alienated many potential allies and a life of the highest achievement passed him by.

The price of championing human rights is a little inconsistency at times. (1977)

We are fed up with fudging and mudging, with mush and slush. We need courage, conviction, and hard work. (Labour Party conference, 1980)

# P

## Paine, Thomas (1737–1809)

Revolutionary writer. Born in Norfolk, he was first a corset-maker, then a sailor and later a schoolmaster. In 1774 he arrived in Philadelphia and almost at once argued for American independence, and even served for a while in the US army. He returned to Britain in 1887, where he wrote *The Rights of Man* (1791/92), which supported the French Revolution. He fled to Paris, where he became a deputy to the National Convention. His views were unacceptable, however, even to his French hosts and he was imprisoned until 1796, when he wrote *The Age of Reason* (1794). He returned to the USA in 1802.

Government, even in its best state, is a necessary evil; in its worst state, an intolerable one. Government, like dress, is the badge of lost innocence; the palaces of kings are built upon the ruins of the bowers of paradise. (1776)

Of more worth is one honest man to society, and in the sight of God, than all the crowned ruffians that ever lived. (1791)

## Paisley, Ian (1926–), Reverend

Uninhibited Protestant leader in Northern Ireland famous on the 'mainland' for his intractability but respected by his own community. He was born in Armagh, Northern Ireland, and educated at Ballymena Technical High School and Belfast Reformed Presbyterian Theological College. He was ordained in 1946 and set up his own Free Presbyterian Church of Ulster in 1951. He gained a doctorate from an American university which did not entail a thesis and was not widely recognised in Britain. In the 1960s he became involved in the politics of the province as an outspoken activist on the Protestant side. He was imprisoned for a while in 1966 following his behaviour during a riot. He founded the Democratic Unionist Party

(DUP) in 1972 and represented North Antrim in its name. In 1979 he was elected to the European parliament. Paisley always provoked strong reactions. He was strongly opposed to any move which hinted at an eventual unification of Ireland and maintained a powerful suspicion of Catholics and the Dublin government. For many Protestants he was the authentic voice of unionism; for others he epitomised the bigotry and inflexibility which made Northern Ireland a political tragedy. Those who hoped hard-line Protestantism might fade as a result of the peace process were disappointed in November 2003 when the DUP won an extra 10 assembly seats, placing Paisley at the head of loyalist representation and making compromise with Sinn Fein even less likely – Paisley declared the elections spelt the end of the Good Friday Agreement.

> The Mother of all Treachery. (On the Good Friday Agreement, April 1998)

> Trusting in the God of our fathers and confident that our cause is just, we will never surrender our heritage. (1968)

### Palme Dutt, Rajani (1896–1974)

Leading intellectual in the Communist Party of Great Britain (CPGB). He was the son of an Indian doctor and a Swedish mother. He was suspended from Oxford for opposing the First World War. He joined the CPGB in 1920 and established the *Labour Monthly*, which he edited until his death. He served on the executive committee of the party 1923–65 and was responsible in part for the party's slavish obedience to the Moscow line. He was also active in the communist international body, the Comintern, as well as the Communist Party of India. He willingly stood in to take the place of the dissenting Harry Pollitt in the chaos caused in 1939 when Stalin decreed the war against Hitler was an 'imperialist' war which communists should resist. Palme Dutt never lost his allegiance to the USSR and remained loyal to it, throughout the convulsions caused by the

invasion of Czeckoslovakia and the growth of Eurocommunism in the 1970s.

### Pankhurst, Emmeline (1857–1928)

Founder of the suffragette movement. She was born in Manchester. She founded the Women's Franchise League in 1889 and the Women's Social and Political Union in 1903, along with her daughter Christabel Harriette (1880–1958). She embraced violent methods for her struggle and went on hunger strike in prison several times.

### Parkinson, Cecil (1931–), Lord

Thatcherite loyalist cabinet minister whose career was badly damaged by an affair with his secretary. He was educated at Royal Lancaster Grammar School and Emmanuel College, Cambridge. He was in management at Metal Box Company then a chartered accountant, founding Parkinson Hart Securities in 1967. He was elected at a by-election in 1970 as MP for Enfield West and served as parliamentary private secretary to Michael Heseltine 1972–74 and then became a whip. He was opposition spokesman on trade and then in 1979 a junior minister in the Department of Trade and Industry (DTI). He was made chairman of the party by Margaret Thatcher in 1981 and paymaster general. Popular in the party, he successfully led the election campaign in 1983 and sat in the cabinet for the DTI but was overwhelmed by the scandal involving his lover, Sarah Keays, who bore his child. After much vacillating he decided to stay with his wife and lost much credibility within his party and the country. Margaret Thatcher brought him back to serve as energy minister 1987–89 and transport minister 1989–90. He resigned the day Thatcher resigned and returned to business but, despite leaving the Commons in 1992, was still involved in politics. Most commentators were surprised when William Hague made him party chairman again in 1997.

### Parris, Matthew (1949–)

Well known Conservative MP who reinvented himself as a successful journalist, author and broadcaster. He was educated at Waterford School, Swaziland, and Clare College, Cambridge, as well as Yale University. He worked in the Foreign Office and then the Conservative Research Department and the office of Margaret Thatcher. He was MP for West Derbyshire 1979–86, then left the Commons to become the presenter of *Weekend World* and a columnist on *The Times* and other newspapers. In November 1998 he caused uproar by saying 'Peter Mandelson is certainly gay'. Parris maintained this was an unexceptional thing to say as the *News of the World* had 'outed' him in 1987 but he lost his column in the *Sun* as a result and attracted criticism from those who pointed out that, as long as he served as an MP, he had not divulged that he, too, was gay.

### Patten, Chris (1944–)

Conservative cabinet minister and governor of Hong Kong. He was educated at Balliol College, Oxford. He joined the Conservative Research Department (CRD), then worked in the Home Office and Cabinet Office. He directed the CRD 1974–79 and entered the House as MP for Bath in 1979, after which he served as junior minister in a number of departments before becoming minister for overseas development 1986 and environment 1989. He lost his seat in 1992 and became the last governor of Hong Kong before returning to Britain to speculation as to his ambitions in Conservative politics. In the end he became a European commissioner in charge of external affairs, courtesy of Tony Blair. He criticised the 2001 Conservative campaign and joined Leon Brittan as a pro-European critic of his former party.

### Paxman, Jeremy (1950–)

Formidable interviewer and BBC presenter of current affairs television programmes. He was educated at Malvern College and St Catherine's College, Cambridge. He worked variously for the BBC, mostly on current affairs programmes, as well as Breakfast Television but is most closely associated with *Newsnight*, which he began

to present in 1989. Feared by many politicians for his deliberately lofty intellectual style and tenacious questioning, he once won an award for his persistence in repeating the same question to home secretary Michael Howard 14 times in a vain attempt to elicit a clear answer. Paxman is also an accomplished author, with a number of volumes to his name.

### Pepys, Samuel (1633–1703)

English diarist. Pepys was administrator of the Royal Navy. His diary 1660–69 provides a unique insight into the atmosphere of the day, with many entries covering corruption, scandals and court gossip. He thereby set a tradition which ever since other politicians and public people have sought to extend.

> I went to Charing Cross, to see Major General Harrison hanged drawn and quartered; which was done there, he looking as cheerful as any man could do in that condition.

> I see it is impossible for the King to have things done as cheap as other men.

### Philby, Kim (1912–88)

British intelligence officer and Soviet spy. He became a communist while at Cambridge in the 1930s and a Soviet agent in 1940. His real use to the USSR, however, came later when he was liaison officer in Washington, 1949–51. He was unmasked as a double agent and asked to resign but fled to the USSR in 1963 when it became public knowledge that he had warned the spies Guy Burgess and Donald MacLean in the early 1950s that they were about to be exposed. He became a Soviet citizen and a general in the KGB.

> To betray, you first have to belong. (1967)

### Pimlott, Ben (1945–2004)

Britain's leading political biographer and professor of politics and modern history, Birkbeck College, London University. His biographies *Harold Wilson* (1992), *Hugh Dalton: A Life* (1995, Whitbread

Biography Prize) and *The Queen: Biography of Elizabeth II* (1996) have been acclaimed as superlative examples of this elusive art. He died, much mourned, of leukaemia in 2004.

> The best political biographer now writing. (Andrew Marr)

### Plant, Raymond (1945–)

Professor of politics at Southampton University and Labour peer. He was educated at Grimsby Havelock School, King's College, London, and Hull University. He was a senior lecturer in philosophy at Manchester University and then professor of politics at Southampton University. He was made a life peer in 1989 (Lord Plant of Highfield) and subsequently Neil Kinnock asked him to study alternative electoral systems for Britain. He is the author of several books on political philosophy.

### Pollitt, Harry (1890–1960)

Former general secretary of the Communist Party of Great Britain (CPGB). He was born in Droylsden, Lancashire, and educated in local schools; he left school aged 13 to work in a Benson's mill but later became a boiler maker. Despite working 53 hours a week, Pollitt attended evening classes and became active in union affairs and socialist campaigning. He joined the fledgling CPGB in 1920 and in 1929 became its respected general secretary. Under him membership rose from 3,000 at the start of the 1930s to 18,000 by the end of that decade. In 1939 he refused to obey the Moscow line that the war against Hitler was to be opposed and in consequence stood down from his post, when he was replaced by Rajani Palme Dutt. However, after the USSR joined the war in 1941 he was reinstated. He stood down as general secretary in 1956. In 1971 the Soviet Union named a ship after him.

### Ponting, Clive (1946–)

Civil servant in the Ministry of Defence who, in 1985, passed secret information to Labour MP Tam Dalyell about the sinking of the *General Belgrano* in the Falklands War. He was prosecuted under the Official Secrets Acts; Ponting defended himself on the basis of being responsible not primarily to his minister but to parliament. He was found not guilty by the jury, who had been specifically directed to convict by the judge. The case highlighted the ambiguity of a civil servant's duty – whether to his/her minister or to parliament and the public – when something in the national interest is involved. To clarify the matter, the head of the civil service, Sir Robert Armstrong, issued a statement which asserted that the 'duty of the individual civil servant is first and foremost to the minister of the crown who is in charge of the department'. After leaving the civil service Ponting settled in Wales, and became a writer and academic.

### Portillo, Michael (1953–)

Conservative MP and minister. He was educated at Harrow and Peterhouse, Cambridge. He worked for the Conservative Research Department 1976–79 and was a policy advisor on energy 1979–81. He then worked for an oil company 1981–83. He was elected MP for Enfield Southgate in 1984 and served as a junior minister at the Department of Health and Social Security and for local government and transport before becoming chief secretary to the Treasury 1992–94 and then secretary of state for employment 1994. In the small hours of election night, 2 May 1997, he was defeated by Steven Twigg, his young Labour opponent, giving birth to the humorous question among Labour supporters 'Were you up for Portillo?' He was therefore unable to stand in the ensuing leadership contest after John Major resigned, which most commentators think he would otherwise have won. Portillo attempted at the Conservative Party conference later that year to refashion his brand of Conservatism, offering a much more 'one nation' version than the right-wing attitudes he supported when a minister. In the autumn of 1998 he presented a television programme called *Portillo's*

*Progress*, in which the new, non-arrogant, voter-friendly ex-minister talked to a range of people about why the Conservatives lost the election. In 1999 he was elected for Kensington and Chelsea and almost immediately became shadow chancellor. In the aftermath of the Conservatives' defeat in 2001 he did stand for the leadership of his party, advocating a gentler, more inclusive form of Conservatism. However, his admission in 2000 that he had indulged in homosexual experiences when at Cambridge lost him the support of certain sections of the party. In the first round of the contest he polled 49 seats, in the second ballot 50 and by the time the third and final ballot came it was clear his candidature was in trouble, but his third place on 53 votes was a shock to everyone and in its wake he announced he was standing down from 'front line' politics, though continuing his role as a backbench MP. In June 2002 the Conservative grouping Conservative Change was formed to advance his political cause. Portillo announced in November 2003 that he would not be contesting the next election.

> You cannot ditch policies that succeeded so convincingly that they were adopted by our opponents. (1999)

## Powell, Enoch (1912–98)

MP, cabinet minister and writer. He was educated at King Edward School, Birmingham, and Trinity College, Cambridge. A brilliant scholar, he became a professor at Sydney University aged 25. He joined the Conservative Party Research Department in 1945 and was elected for Wolverhampton South West in 1950. He served a year as a junior Treasury minister before resigning over levels of public expenditure. He became minister of health 1960–63 but refused to serve under Alec Douglas-Home, as he had supported R. A. Butler for the leadership. He himself stood for the party leadership in 1965 but mustered only 15 votes, coming third. However, he became best known for his unorthodox but well argued ideas: an early form of

monetarism at odds with the postwar consensus; withdrawal from east of Suez; opposition to Britain's joining the Common Market; against capital punishment; and opposition to continued immigration. His views on race – most vividly expressed on 20 April 1968, when he said he foresaw 'rivers of blood' in British city streets – were unacceptable to Edward Heath and he lost his chance of office in the 1970–74 administration. In 1974 he believed he helped Labour win its narrow victory by urging voters to support Labour as the party most likely to withdraw from Europe. In October 1974 he was elected for South Down as an Ulster Unionist, a seat he held until 1987.

> As I look ahead, I am filled with foreboding. Like the Roman, I seem to see the Tiber foaming with much blood. (Speech to Conservative Political Centre meeting in Birmingham, 20 April 1968, when he dramatically put race on the political agenda and indicated his future maverick tendencies)

> An almost unlimited faith in the ability of people to get what they want through price, capital, profit and a competitive market. (On his economic beliefs, 1968)

> If we had a presidential system, on polls I would no doubt be a candidate. (1974)

> For a politician to complain about the press is like a ship's captain complaining about the sea. (1984)

> All political lives, unless they are cut off in mid stream at a happy juncture, end in failure, because that is the nature of politics and human affairs. (1977)

> I was born a Tory. I am a Tory and shall die a Tory.

## Powell, Jonathan (1956–)

Chief of staff to the prime minister. He was educated at Oxford and Pennsylvania universities. He originally pursued a diplomatic career, like his brother Charles, who for several years advised Margaret Thatcher but was persuaded to join Tony Blair in 1995 and acted as his fixer, making crucial contacts with civil servants in the government machine. After the departure of Alastair Campbell (Blair's press secretary) in 2003 he was made the prime minister's chief of staff and was rated as the person with the most intimate influence within the Blair government. He was made head of Number 10's combined private office and Policy Unit when he was officially responsible for 'leading and coordinating operations across Number 10, reporting to the Prime Minister'.

### Prescott, John (1938–)

Labour MP and deputy prime minister from 1997. He was first secretary of state after 1997. He was born in Prestatyn, North Wales, and educated at Ruskin College, Oxford, and Hull University. He served in the merchant navy 1955–63, when he was a steward and also an officer in the National Union of Seamen. He was elected as a Labour MP in 1970. He was also elected to the European parliament in 1975 and, though then opposed to the concept of Europe, became Labour group leader 1976–79. In the shadow cabinet he served as spokesman for energy, employment and transport. He became deputy leader in 1994 and deputy prime minister with the job of secretary of state for environment and transport. His 1998 transport white paper, which suggested cars should be used less, caused controversy and was, according to some reports, opposed by the prime minister. He retained his post after the June 2001 general election, surviving the celebrated incident when he punched a Welsh demonstrator who threw an egg at him. Prescott, given his working-class provenance and no-nonsense style, is seen as something of the left-wing conscience of the party, as well as not especially bright. The latter judgement is almost certainly unfair and the former may underestimate his ambition to be eligible for the highest office should Tony Blair stand down.

> People like me were branded, pigeon holed, a ceiling put on their ambitions. (On failing his 11 plus)

> We did it! Let's wallow in our victory! (Speech to the Labour Party conference, September 1997)

> John Prescott is the best deputy leader Labour has ever had. (Roy Hattersley, *Guardian*, 9 August 2004)

> Our Willie Whitelaw. (Peter Mandelson on Prescott, 2004) .

### Prior, James (1927–), Lord

Conservative MP and minister. He was educated at Charterhouse and Pembroke College, Cambridge. He was MP for Lowestoft 1959–83 and Waveney 1983–87 and served as parliamentary private secretary to several cabinet ministers during the 1960s. He rose quickly under Edward Heath and served Margaret Thatcher as employment secretary 1979–81 and Northern Ireland secretary 1981–84 but was always seen as too 'wet' for the Iron Lady. He chaired General Electric Company 1984–98. He was made a life peer in 1987.

### Profumo, John (1915–2001)

Conservative defence secretary at the heart of a scandal which helped bring down Macmillan in 1963. He initially denied his involvement with Christine Keeler, a glamorous young woman who also shared her favours with a Soviet naval attaché. When exposed he was forced to resign and the scandalous aftermath damaged Macmillan's government. He devoted the rest of his life to charity, becoming administrator of the social and educational settlement, Toynbee Hall, in 1982. When he died, Profumo was the last remaining MP who had voted against Chamberlain in the 1940 debate which presaged Winston Churchill becoming prime minister.

### Pym, Francis (1922–), Lord

Conservative MP and cabinet minister. He was educated at Eton and Cambridge. He served in the Second World War. He became a Cambridgeshire MP in 1961 and served as chief whip 1970–73, secretary of state for defence 1979–81 and foreign secretary 1982–83. He was associated with the liberal wing of the Conservative Party and clashed with Margaret Thatcher over a number of issues before bowing out of mainstream politics, perhaps before his full contribution had been made. He was made a life peer in 1987.

# R

### Rawnsley, Andrew (1962–)
Associate editor and chief columnist of the *Observer*. He was educated at Lawrence Sherif Grammar School and Cambridge University. He then worked for the BBC and the *Guardian* before the *Observer*. He presented and produced several television programmes and wrote *Servants of the People* (2000), the widely accepted though highly controversial account of New Labour in power, in which he detailed Tony Blair's obsession with presentation and the rivalry between him and his chancellor, Gordon Brown.

### Raynor, Derek (1926–), Lord
Long-time advisor to Margaret Thatcher on efficiency in government. He was educated at City College, Norwich, and Selwyn College, Cambridge. He joined Marks and Spencer in 1953 and rose to be its managing director 1973–91. He started to advise the prime minister on efficiency in government in 1979 and for a number of years headed the Efficiency Unit in the Cabinet Office. The Whitehall expert Peter Hennessy writes in his book on *Whitehall* (1989) of 'Raynerism', so profound was his impact upon the civil service culture.

### Redwood, John (1951–)
Leading Conservative MP and cabinet minister. He was educated at Oxford University, then worked for a merchant

bank before his intellectual brilliance led to him heading Margaret Thatcher's Policy Unit in 1983. He was Conservative MP for Wokingham from 1987 and served as a junior minister for trade until he was made secretary of state for Wales 1993–95. He resigned from cabinet in 1995 and stood against John Major when he recontested the party leadership. His support was sufficient to encourage him to stand again in the contest following his party's election defeat in 1997. In 1998 he shadowed trade and industry under William Hague.

### Reece, Gordon (1929–)
Influential public relations consultant and political advisor. He was educated at Ratcliffe College and Downing College, Cambridge. He was a television producer 1960–70 and an advisor to Margaret Thatcher 1975–79, during which time he transformed her image to one that was more acceptable on television. He was director of publicity at Conservative Central Office 1978–80.

### Reid, John (1947–)
Labour MP and minister. He was educated at Stirling University (PhD). He became the MP for Hamilton North in 1987 (previously named Motherwell North and Beshill). He served as minister of transport 1997–99, minister of state defence 1997–98 and secretary of state for Northern Ireland 2000. He was a tough Scottish political operator, an effective Labour government advocate and apologist on the media. He was brought in to cover after the forced resignation of Peter Mandelson and was leader of the House after the resignation of Robin Cook and then health minister after Alan Milburn resigned in June 2003.

### Reith, John (1889–1971), Lord
First director general of the BBC (1927–38). Born in Scotland, he was educated at Glasgow Academy and Gresham School, Holt. He began life humbly as an engineering apprentice but found his métier in radio communication. In 1922 he became

the first general manager of the BBC and managed its transition to a public corporation in 1927. He resisted the attempts by politicians and business people to exert influence and pursued a high-minded mission for the BBC to 'educate, enlighten and entertain'. His influence helped make the BBC an international template for public service broadcasting. He served as minister of information in 1940 and then minister of works 1940–42 before falling out with Winston Churchill, who once described the imposing but dour Scot as 'that wuthering height'.

### Riddell, Peter (1948–)

Leading columnist and commentator on British government. He was educated at Oxford. He worked on the *Financial Times* and *The Times*, of which he was the assistant editor. He is a highly respected authority on British government and politics and the author of several much-praised books, including *Honest Opportunism* (1993) and *Parliament Under Pressure* (1998).

### Ridley, Nicolas (1929–93)

Thatcherite Conservative cabinet member. He was educated at Oxford and became a Conservative MP in 1959. He held junior posts until Margaret Thatcher made him secretary of state for transport 1983–86, moved to Environment 1986–89, where he had responsibility for the hated poll tax, and then to trade and industry 1989–90. He resigned after making unflattering remarks about Germany, for example that the European Exchange Rate Mechanism was a 'German racket to take over Europe' and that Britain might just as well have given in to Hitler. Ridley was very close ideologically to Thatcher and some felt that he said what she could not say in public.

### Rimington, Stella (1935–), Dame

Former director general of MI5 and the world's first female head of national security. She was educated at Nottingham High School for Girls and Edinburgh University. She joined MI5 in 1969 and rose to be its director in 1992; she retired in 1996. She favoured a more public face for the secret service but was herself criticised for publishing her memoirs, *Open Secret* (2001). She responded to this exclusion from her previous 'insider' status by calling for a reform of the Official Secrets Act.

### Robertson, George (1946–), Lord

Labour MP and secretary of state for defence in 1997 then secretary general of NATO. He was educated at Dunoon Grammar School and Dundee University. He then worked as a trade union official before being elected MP for Hamilton in 1978 (Hamilton South from 1997). He served as shadow spokesman for Scotland, foreign affairs and defence before entering government. He was perceived to have been calm and effective during the Kosovo crisis and became secretary general of NATO (1999–2003) shortly after its conclusion. He was made a life peer in 1999.

### Robinson, Geoffrey (1938–)

Labour MP and paymaster general sacked by Tony Blair in the wake of the first ministerial resignation of Peter Mandelson. He was educated at Emmanuel College, Cambridge, and Yale. He was a Labour Party researcher in the 1960s, worked for British Leyland in the 1970s and became chief executive of Jaguar 1973–75, as well as an unpaid director of the Meriden motor cycle cooperative 1978–80. He was MP for Coventry North West from 1976. He made a considerable fortune in the 1980s through his engineering company TransTec. He was made a minister by his friend Tony Blair but was criticised by the Conservatives for his alleged failure to register all his financial interests. A connection with the disgraced tycoon Robert Maxwell also figured in the criticisms made in the press and by the opposition. Blair, however, seemed to believe he was perfectly acceptable as 1998 drew to a close. Robertson made a loan to Mandelson of £330,000 to assist a house purchase but was embroiled in the crisis which arose when it transpired

Mandelson had not told his permanent secretary at the Department of Trade and Industry of the loan, even though his department was investigating Robinson's finances.

## Rodgers, William (1928–), Lord

Labour MP who became one of the 'gang of four'. He was educated at Oxford, served as general secretary of the Fabian Society 1953–60, then was elected MP for Stockton on Tees in 1962. He held a series of junior posts in the 1960s and 1970s, including transport minister 1976–79. He was a strong pro-European and was unimpressed with the left. He joined the gang of four in 1981 and helped found the Social Democratic Party (SDP). He lost his seat in 1983 but served as vice president of the SDP 1982–87 and was influential in the Alliance. He withdrew from politics in 1987 to become director general at the Royal Institute of British Architects. He stood down as leader of the Liberal Democrats in the House of Lords in 2001.

## Rose, Richard (1933)

Leading British political scientist and director of public policy at the University of Strathclyde. He was educated at Clayton High School, Missouri, USA, John Hopkins University, the London School of Economics 1953–54 and Oxford University 1957–60. He worked as a journalist in the USA 1955–57 then lecturer at Manchester University 1961–66 before moving to Strathclyde 1966–82. Rose has been possibly the most prolific author in his subject since the war and has displayed an extraordinary and distinguished eclecticism, writing highly original studies of psephology, urban problems, public policy, the territorial dimension, as well as books on the presidency in the USA, Russia and Europe. One of his books (*Do Parties Make a Difference?*, 1998) daringly suggested parties had little effect upon politics; now every textbook on British politics includes a rebuttal of this well argued but flawed thesis.

## Rothermere, Viscount (1968–)

Succeeded his father, Vere, in 1998 as owner and chairman of the *Daily Mail* and General Trust as well as being hugely rich through property. He has been a big player in the media though was still unsure about investing in broadcasting after losses with Channel One TV.

## Rushdie, Salman (1947–)

Celebrated novelist. He was educated at Catholic School, Bombay, Rugby and King's College, Cambridge. He won the Booker Prize (1981 for *Midnight's Children*) but his fourth novel *Satanic Verses* (1988) was condemned in February 1989 by the Iranian religious leader Ayatollah Khomeini, who pronounced a fatwa against the author. He then lived for nine years in secret, making virtually no public appearances until February 1993, when he announced he was coming out of hiding. According to Rushdie over 20 hit squads during this period sought to fulfil the fatwa. On 26 September 1998 Iran announced it had withdrawn its support for the fatwa but danger still persisted for the author from extremist enemies.

## Russell, Bertrand (1872–1970)

Philosopher and mathematician of Welsh extraction, who became known as a tireless campaigner for peace and disarmament. He was the second son of Viscount Amberley, the third son of prime minister Lord John Russell. He was educated privately and at Trinity College, Cambridge, where he was awarded a first in mathematics and philosophy. He worked briefly as a diplomat and an academic before writing the first of many books. His joint work with Alfred North Whitehead, the three-volume *Principia Mathematica* (1910, 1912, 1913), became a landmark and his pupil Ludwig Wittgenstein went on to achieve similar groundbreaking works in philosophy and logic. He was imprisoned for his pacifism in 1918 but renounced it in 1939, on the eve of the fight against fascism. He won the Nobel Prize for Literature in 1950. In the 1950s he became obsessed with nuclear weapons and assumed a leading role in the Campaign for Nuclear Disarmament. He retired to live the last years of his long and highly productive life in North Wales.

> Envy is the basis of democracy. (1930)

> Few people can be happy unless they hate some other person, nation or creed.

> The trouble with the world is that the stupid are cocksure and the intelligent full of doubt.

# S

## Saatchi, Charles (1943–); Saatchi, Maurice (1946–)

Brothers who owned the Saatchi and Saatchi advertising agency. Political parties had used advertising agencies before but the involvement of Charles and Maurice Saatchi's agency, already well known in their field in the late 1970s, as the advisors of the Conservative Party, marked a new departure in British politics. It was Gordon Reece, Margaret Thatcher's media advisor, made director of publicity in 1981, who employed the firm, and gave it full responsibility for all aspects – from press and poster advertising to television. Managing director Tim Bell got on well with Thatcher and the 1979 election saw the famous poster of a long dole queue (in reality dragooned Young Conservatives) under the caption 'Labour isn't working'. The firm worked for the party again in the 1983 and 1987 general elections but in 1992 there was disagreement and after the 1997 general election debacle for the Tories the party parted company with the agency, which had by now lost some of its previous international lustre and had split due to disagreements between the two Saatchi brothers. Maurice was elected joint chairman of the Conservative Party in 2003. He was made a peer in 1996 for his services to politics via the Conservative Party. He became a Treasury spokesman in the upper

house in 1999 and on the Cabinet Office after 2001. Charles became renowned for his collection of modern art and was less active politically.

## Sainsbury, David (1940–), Lord

Labour peer, minister and patron of centre-left politics. He was educated at Eton, Cambridge and Colombia. He was hugely rich from his family's supermarket business, was elevated to the Lords by Tony Blair and made a trade minister. He had previously funded the Social Democratic Party as long as David Owen was involved but shifted allegiance to New Labour in the 1990s – he donated £2 million in late 2000 to the party.

## Salmond, Alex (1954–)

Scottish National Party (SNP) MP and leader. He was educated at Linlithgoe Academy and St Andrew's University. He worked as an economist before entering politics, as MP for Banff and Buchan in 1987. He became SNP leader in 1990. He fought for the devolved assembly in Scotland 1997–99, as he believed it a halfway house to full independence. He proved an effective speaker and media performer. He resigned as leader of the party in the autumn of 2000. He was elected to the Scottish parliament in 1999 but left in 2001 to lead the SNP at Westminster. After the resignation of John Swinney as party leader, in September 2004 Salmond was re-elected, four years after he resigned the post, to reverse the party's decline.

## Sampson, Anthony (1926–)

Journalist and author. He was educated Westminster School and Christ Church, Oxford. He served in the Royal Navy 1944–47 and then became a journalist, mostly with the *Observer* but also with *Newsweek* and other publications. He also made a number of radio and television programmes, for example *The Midas Touch* (BBC2, 1992). He is best known for his prolific output of books, especially *The Anatomy of Britain*, which first appeared in 1962 (and has been updated regularly since); he inspired many future journalists and students of British politics (including this author). His other books have addressed topics as varied as banking and the oil and arms industries; he also wrote biographies of Harold Macmillan and Nelson Mandela.

## Sands, Bobby (1954–80)

IRA hunger striker. He was born in a loyalist area; the Catholic Sands family was twice intimidated into moving by loyalists, in 1962 and 1972. Bobby also was forced by loyalists to give up his job as a coach builder. He joined the IRA in 1972 and served time in Long Kesh for possession of firearms. In 1976 he rejoined the IRA upon his release and became active in his community. In 1977 he was sentenced to 14 years for possession of a handgun. He led the 'dirty protest' in the H Block of Long Kesh Prison and began his hunger strike against prison conditions in March 1980. He stood as a candidate on behalf of the strikers in the Fermanagh and Tyrone by-election that April and was elected but on 5 May died of hunger. Throughout, Margaret Thatcher refused to compromise with Sands and the hunger strikers, who undoubtedly won a significant propaganda victory by their actions.

## Scanlon, Hugh (1913–2004), Lord

Former general secretary of the Amalgamated Union of Engineering Workers (AUEW). He was educated at Stretford Elementary School, Manchester, and the National Labour College. He worked as an instrument maker before becoming a shop steward and full-time union official. He became president of the AUEW 1968–78 and member of the General Council of the Trades Union Congress 1968–78. In the 1970s during times of high inflation and the Social Contract, he was linked with Jack Jones of the Transport and General Workers' Union as one of the 'two most powerful men in the country'.

> Of course liberty is not a licence. Liberty in my view is conforming to majority opinion. (1977)

## Scargill, Arthur (1938–)

Union leader and founder of the Socialist Labour Party. He left school at 15 to work in the mines. He became president of the National Union of Mineworkers in 1982, though he had been a militant activist in the union long before that, especially as the organiser of flying pickets in the 1972 and 1974 miners' strikes. He is best known as the instigator of the doomed miners' strike 1984–85, when he sought to use his union as a political battering ram against the government of Margaret Thatcher. His strategic sense was much criticised during this strike but his predictions of pit closures and the plans to run down the industry proved prescient. As a fervent opponent of Blairism he formed the left-wing Socialist Labour Party in May 1996 but its electoral success was scant. He stood in Hartlepool, the constituency of Peter Mandelson, in the general election of June 2001 but mustered under 1,000 votes.

> The capitalist society belongs to the dustbin of history. The ideal of a socialist society belongs to the youth of today and to the future. I have seen the vision of the socialist tomorrow and it works. (1975 – he was not more specific as to where he had seen this socialist 'vision')

> Parliament itself would not exist in its present form had people not defied the law. (To the Select Committee on Employment, 1980)

> I wouldn't vote for Ken Livingstone if he were running for the mayor of Toytown. (May 2000)

## Scarman, Leslie (1911–), Lord

High Court judge 1961–73, Appeal Court judge 1973–77 and lord of the appeal in ordinary 1975–86. He was reformist on divorce laws and called for a bill of rights in 1974. He is best known for his eponymous report on the Brixton riots in 1981.

> A government above the law is a menace to be defeated. (1992)

> The people as a source of sovereign power are in truth only occasional partners in the

constitutional minuet danced for most of the time by Parliament and the political party in power. (1989)

## Scott, Richard (1934–)

Judge. He was educated Michaelhouse College, Natal, and the University of Capetown, South Africa, Trininty College, Cambridge, and Chicago University. He was called to the bar and became a QC in 1975. He served as judge in the High Court of Justice, Chancery Division, and as lord justice of appeal 1991–94. He was the chairman of the arms to Iraq investigation 1992–96, which produced the Scott report (1996).

## Selwyn Lloyd, John (1904–78), Lord

Conservative cabinet minister. He was educated at Fettes and Cambridge, then became a barrister in Liverpool. He stood as a Liberal in 1930 but switched to the Conservatives. He rose to the rank of colonel in the Second World War. He was elected Conservative MP for Wirral in 1945 and served as minister of supply and defence 1954, foreign secretary 1955 (when he defended Anthony Eden's Suez debacle), chancellor 1960 but was purged by Macmillan in his 'Night of the Long Knives'. He was later lord privy seal, leader of the House 1963–64 and speaker of the Commons 1971–76. He was made a life peer in 1976.

## Shore, Peter (1924–2001), Lord

Leading Labour MP and cabinet minister. He was educated at Quarrybank School, Liverpool, and Cambridge University. He served as a flying officer in the Royal Air Force before he joined and then headed Labour's Research Department in Transport House. He was elected MP for Stepney in 1964, served as parliamentary private secretary to Harold Wilson and then as junior minister for technology under Tony Benn. In 1967 he was surprisingly promoted into the cabinet as secretary of state for economic affairs. His department was weak, however, and he was shifted to deputy leader of the House – Wilson is said to

have commented 'I over promoted him. He's no good.' He polled only 39 votes in the shadow cabinet elections in 1970. During the 1970s he became associated with opposition to the Common Market. This helped his popularity in a party shifting leftwards and he polled 105 votes in the 1971 shadow cabinet elections. He became environment secretary in 1976 and in 1979 stood as a leadership candidate of the left; he was eliminated after the first ballot. In 1983 he mustered only 3 per cent of the vote. For the rest of his life he was seen as a principled elder statesman to the right of the party with a powerful antipathy to Europe. He became a life peer in 1997.

## Short, Clare (1946–)

Labour MP and cabinet minister. She was educated at St Paul's Grammar School, Birmingham, and the universities of Birmingham and Keele. She has been MP for Birmingham Ladywood since 1983. She was seen as something of a maverick member of Labour's otherwise well disciplined cabinet, as secretary of state for international development, because she was given to encouraging debate, for example on the legalisation of certain drugs, and she made disparaging remarks about the islanders of Montserrat when they demanded compensation following the volcanic eruption in 1997. While given to blunt speaking, she was regarded as an excellent minister in her post and did much to raise the profile of international development. She was known to be unenthusiastic about the proposed war on Iraq in early 2003. In March 2003 she threatened to resign but was persuaded to remain in the government by Tony Blair, for whom the resignation would have been embarrassing. However, she resigned that May over the minor role allowed for the United Nations in the reconstruction of Iraq. She added wider and quite bitter criticisms of Blair's style of government in public statements around this time.

Having met all these ministers and MPs in the civil service, I knew they had feet of clay. If they could do it, I could do it.

### Skinner, Dennis (1932–)

Left-wing MP known as 'the Beast of Bolsover' for his fearless, uncompromising style. He was educated at Tupton Hall Grammar School and Ruskin College, Oxford. He worked as a miner in Parkhurst and Galpwell collieries before entering the Commons in 1970. He was a member of Labour's National Executive Committee 1978–96 and vice chair of the Labour Party 1987–88. Usually sitting in the front row of the Commons, he is well known for his direct and memorable interventions on the side of his unchanging socialist principles; he is therefore not a favourite with New Labour but, as with all such nationally known rebels, his effectiveness has tended to decline in inverse proportion to his popularity.

### Smith, Adam (1723–90)

Scottish philosopher and economist. He was educated at Glasgow and Oxford. In the middle of the 18th century he became a member of the group surrounding the philosopher David Hume as a professor of logic at Glasgow. He then moved to London, where he wrote *An Inquiry into the Nature and Causes of the Wealth of Nations* (1776), an analysis of successful economics and an attack on medieval mercantile protectionism and monopolies. Smith's work was hugely influential and provided the basis of classical liberalism; he is still acknowledged by modern neo-liberals as their inspiration.

> Little else is requisite to carry a state to the highest degree of opulence from the lowest barbarism, but peace, easy taxes and a tolerable administration of justice; all the rest being brought about by the natural course of things. (1795)

> It is not from the benevolence of the butcher, the brewer or the baker, that we expect our dinner, but from their regard to their own interest. We address ourselves not to their humanity but their self love, and never talk to them of our necessities but of their advantages. (1776)

> That insidious and crafty animal vulgarly called a statesman or politician, whose councils are directed by the momentary fluctuations of affairs. (*Wealth of Nations*, 1776)

### Smith, Chris (1951–)

Labour MP and minister. He was educated at George Watson's College, Edinburgh, and Pembroke College, Cambridge, and Harvard University. He became MP for Islington South and Finsbury in 1983. He was Treasury and then environment spokesman in opposition, and secretary of state for culture media and sport 1997–2001. He was the first openly gay cabinet minister. He lost his job in the June 2001 cabinet reshuffle.

### Smith, Godrich (1965–)

Civil servant. He was educated at Perse School and the universities of Oxford and Cambridge. He worked for the charity Sane 1988–91 before joining the Government Information Service, where he became a senior press officer 1995 and then a deputy press secretary in Downing Street 1998–2001. In 2001 he was made the prime minister's official spokesman.

### Smith, John (1938–94)

Labour MP and party leader. He was educated at Glasgow University and called to the bar in 1967; he became a QC in 1970. From 1970 he was Labour MP for North Lanarkshire (renamed Monklands East in 1983) and held junior posts in Harold Wilson's governments. In 1978 he was appointed secretary of state for trade by James Callaghan. In 1979 he was made opposition spokesman on trade, energy and then industry before he became shadow chancellor in 1988. His shadow budget in 1992 proposed some tax increases and was dubbed by the Conservatives a 'tax and spend' extravaganza. This was clearly a misrepresentation but the voters were influenced and Labour lost the election. When Neil Kinnock then resigned as Labour leader John Smith took his place. Labour MPs were relieved to have a leader who always performed well in debates and at prime minister's questions. He was tragically struck down by a heart attack in 1994 and was succeeded by Tony Blair.

> I am a doer and I want to do things but there is always the terrible possibility in politics that you might never win. (1992)

### Snowden, Philip (1864–1937)

Labour chancellor in the interwar years. He was educated at elementary school. He joined the civil service but was disabled in a cycling accident and forced to leave. He became an MP in 1906 and served as chancellor in 1924 and 1929, when he pursued orthodox economic policies which did not alleviate the depression afflicting Britain. He resigned from the national government in 1932 over free trade. He was one of the genuinely talented early prophets of socialism, who found the world far less tractable once he was in power rather than when he was fighting for it.

> This is not socialism. It is Bolshevism run mad. (On Labour's election manifesto, 1931)

### Spedding, David (1943–)

Head of MI6. He was educated at Sherborne and Oxford and spent his whole career in the security service. He became head of MI6 in 1994. He had to face the embarrassment of the former MI6 man David Shaylor revealing secrets about the service. He also helped to adjust the service to a non-Cold War world.

### St John Stevas, Norman (1929–), Lord

Conservative MP and cabinet member. He was educated at Radcliffe School and Fitzwilliam College, Cambridge (where he was president of the Union), Christ Church, Oxford (where he was secretary of the Union) and Yale University. He qualified as a barrister and lectured at Southampton University and Merton College, Oxford, 1953–57. He worked for *The Economist*

from 1959. He was MP for Chelmsford 1964–87. In shadow cabinet 1974–79 he served as education spokesman and shadow leader of the House. He was appointed chancellor of Duchy of Lancaster, leader of the House and minister for the arts 1979–81 under Margaret Thatcher. A witty and media-friendly politician, Norman St John Stevas was a favourite of Thatcher initially and was able to push through certain reforms of parliament under her aegis, especially the reform of the select committees. However, he was on the 'wet' side of the cabinet politically and compounded this disadvantage with his witty disloyalties to his leader, which, some say, contributed to his early political demise. He was considered to be a Conservative expert on the constitution. He was made a life peer in 1997 as Lord St John of Fawsley.

### Steel, David (1938–), Lord

Liberal MP and party leader. He was educated in Kenya and Edinburgh. When he was first elected in 1965 he was the youngest MP. He sponsored the bill which made abortions legal in 1967. He became Liberal chief whip in 1970 and succeeded Jeremy Thorpe as party leader in 1977. As leader he formed the Alliance with the Social Democratic Party in 1981. The two parties merged in 1988 but Steel did not seek its leadership. He became a life peer in 1997 and presiding officer of the Scottish parliament 1998–2003.

> Go back to your constituencies and prepare for government. (To the Liberal Party conference, 1985)

### Strathclyde, Thomas (1960–), Lord

Conservative peer. He was educated at Wellington and the University of East Anglia. He served as a junior minister in the Scottish Office and at the Department of Trade and Industry during the early 1990s. He acquired a reputation as a bon viveur but was also a shrewd politician. He became Tory leader in the Lords in December 1998 when Conservative leader William Hague chose him to replace

Viscount Cranboune after the latter's secret deal with Tony Blair over Lords reform.

# T

## Straw, Jack (1946–)

Labour MP and cabinet minister. He was educated Leeds University and was president of the National Union of Students 1969–70. He was called to the bar in 1972 and served as a councillor for Islington 1971–78. He became MP for Blackburn in 1979 and was Labour spokesman on Treasury and economic affairs. He was in the shadow cabinet for education 1987–92, environment 1992–93 and home affairs 1994–97. Not the most admired member of Tony Blair's cabinet initially, he won much credibility as an outwardly tough home secretary 1997–2001, who maintained a more liberal agenda in practice. He gained credibility in 1997 when his son was tricked by a tabloid into supplying soft drugs and he took the matter and his son to the police. He was surprised, pleasantly, to be given the Foreign Office portfolio in June 2001, though he found himself overshadowed by Tony Blair, especially after the events of 11 September 2001.

## Sutch, 'Lord' (with its prefix 'Screaming'), David (1940–1998)

Leader of the Monster Raving Loony Party. He was born in Kilburn, the son of a policeman. He became a plumber, rock singer (of questionable ability) and then political party leader, ending up as the longest-serving leader – albeit of a joke party – by the time of his death. He became a constant and colourful feature of television election and especially by-election broadcasts, often standing against party leaders to maximise the publicity gained. He stood 39 times for parliament, polled 15,000 votes and lost £10,000 in deposits. His high-point came in May 1994, when his party's candidate polled 554 votes in the Bootle by-election to the Social Democratic Party's 155, which persuaded David Owen that it was time to wind up his party. His other major achievement is probably to have been the reason for parliamentary deposits being raised from £150 to £500.

## Tatchell, Peter (1952–)

Campaigner for homosexual and civil rights. He was born in Australia but was educated in Mount Waverley High School, London, and the Polytechnic of North London. He worked as a social worker. He stood unsuccessfully as Labour candidate for Bermondsey in a controversial by-election in which his sexuality was a major issue. He helped found Outrage in 1990 and led many high-profile demonstrations. He began to target Robert Mugabe for civil rights violations towards the end of the 1990s and bravely attempted to arrest him for torture in February 2003 during the African dictator's visit to Paris.

## Tawney, R. H. (1880–1962)

Socialist philosopher and economist. He was born in Calcutta and was educated at Balliol College, Oxford, where he became a fellow in 1918 and wrote several volumes on economic history. He was active in the Workers' Educational Association (WEA), an active Christian and a passionate advocate of equality. He was a professor at the London School of Economics 1931–49. His works include *The Acquisitive Society* (1920), *Religion and the Rise of Capitalism* (1926) and *Equality* (1931). His influence in the Labour Party was considerable, especially his emphasis on equality.

> Freedom for the pike is death for the minnow. (*Equality*, 1931)

> Private property is a necessary institution, at least in a fallen world; men work more and dispute less when goods are private than when they are common. But it is to be tolerated as a concession to human frailty, not applauded as desirable in itself. (1926)

## Taylor, Ann (1947–)

Labour MP and minister. She was educated at Bolton School, and Bradford and Sheffield universities. She was MP for Bolton West 1974–83 and Dewsbury after 1987. She shadowed various ministries in opposition before becoming chief whip 1998–2001, president of the Council and leader of the House of Commons 1997–98. She returned to the backbenches in 2001.

### Taylor, Matthew (1961–)

Head of Number 10's Policy Directorate from 2003, officially charged with policy planning and strengthening policy links between Number 10 and the Labour Party and 'the wider policy community'. He was educated at Emmanuel School, Clapham, and Southampton University, where he followed in the footsteps of his father, Laurie, in studying sociology. He became assistant general secretary of the Labour Party and then director of the Labour think tank Institute for Public Policy Research, a post which he retained.

### Tebbit, Kevin (1946–), Sir

Civil servant. He was educated at Cambridgeshire High School and Cambridge University. Unlike his famous cousin Norman, he took a politically neutral career route by joining the civil service in 1969. He was assistant personal private secretary to the secretary of state for defence 1973–74, principal at the Ministry of Defence 1974–79, a member of the UK delegation to NATO 1979–82, counsellor at the Washington embassy 1989–91, head of economic relations at the Foreign Office 1992–94, under-secretary at the Foreign Office 1997 and head of Government Communications Headquarters 1998 and permanent under-secretary for the Ministry of Defence after 1998. He was questioned by the Hutton inquiry, when he sought to distance himself from the decision to allow David Kelly's name to become public; the Hutton report cleared him as well as Tony Blair of any wrongdoing.

### Tebbit, Norman (1931–), Lord

Famously combative Conservative cabinet minister. He left school at 16 to work as a journalist and after national service

became an airline pilot. He went on to lead the Airline Pilots' Association. He became Conservative MP for Chingford from 1970. Margaret Thatcher liked his clear mind and unrelenting right-wing politics, as well as his aggression as a debater – something which did not appeal to older colleagues like Edward Heath, who deplored Tebbit's style. He was employment secretary 1981–83 and trade and industry secretary 1983–85 but his career was almost ended by the bomb placed by the IRA in Brighton in 1984, when he was injured, though his wife Margaret more seriously. In 1987 he became chancellor of Duchy of Lancaster and chairman of the Conservative Party, but in the latter role fell out with his prime minister over election strategy. Some suggested she suspected Tebbit was interested in taking over as party leader and that this provoked her enmity. He retired to backbenches in 1987, where he established a strong anti-Europe profile. He was made a life peer in 1992. His (in)famous brutal rudeness served to conceal an infinitely subtle political mind and an administrative ability which won the admiration of his civil servants.

> He [Tebbit's unemployed father] did not riot. He got on his bike and looked for work. (Blackpool Conservative Party conference, 15 October 1981)

### Thatcher, Margaret Hilda (1925–), Baroness

Leader of Conservative Party 1975–79 and prime minister 1979–90. She was educated at Grantham Grammar School and Oxford University, where she studied chemistry (and became president of the Conservative Association). Her father was a local small shopkeeper and councillor – later mayor – and exerted substantial influence upon her. She worked in industry before studying for the bar and marrying wealthy businessman Dennis Thatcher. She was MP for Finchley 1959–92. She served as junior opposition spokesman in the late 1960s. In 1970 she became education secretary in the cabinet. She stood against

Edward Heath in the Conservative Party leadership contest in 1975 following his two election defeats in 1974. Those who supported her on the first ballot, which she won by 130 votes to 119, did not expect her to win but voted for her in protest against Heath's lofty style of leadership. She won on the second ballot. Initially she did not do well as leader of the opposition; she was, after all, an avowed free market enthusiast and the senior Tory MPs were still largely 'Heathite' supporters of the postwar consensus. And she was female. However, she concentrated, with some success, on changing policy and improving her performances in the House and the media. Her general election success in 1979 was greatly aided by the imploding Labour Party after the 'winter of discontent' of 1978–79. She won the election handsomely and set about leaving her mark on the country. Her insistence on letting inefficient businesses die a natural death, combined with high interest rates, produced high unemployment and social division but her heroic conduct of government during the Falklands War ensured she won the 1983 general election, aided by an economic recovery and a hopelessly divided Labour Party under Michael Foot. During her second ministry she won the battle of the extended miners' strike, 1984–85. She also pressed on with her discovered policy of privatisation, as the public flocked to buy shares they could later sell at a profit. She also worked her way through the establishment – the universities, the BBC, the Church, and many of the professions – doing her best to destroy protective practices and monopolies. She won her third election in 1987 but overstepped herself by seeking to reform not only the welfare state but local government finance with the ill-fated community charge, or poll tax. From here she gradually lost touch with voters. Her second ill-fated mission was to attack what she believed as a creeping centralisation around the European Community – the 'Belgian Empire' as she is alleged to have called it. Her bungled reshuffles in 1989 and 1990 alienated some of her closest colleagues and things came to a head in 1990 when she attacked the European Community and angered her long-suffering deputy prime minister, Geoffrey Howe. His devastating resignation speech, in which he attacked her style as much as her policies, triggered a challenge to her in the annual leadership election by the famously ambitious Michael Heseltine. She received 204 votes to his 152; she was just four short of the margin she required. She consulted with her cabinet, the majority of whom advised her to resign, which she did on 21 November 1990. She backed John Major in the resultant leadership election, though criticised him when things went wrong. She thereafter spent much of her time in retirement lecturing and raising money for her Margaret Thatcher Foundation. She said she had no remaining leadership ambitions but allowed the occasional hint that she was still available. Her effect on the politics of Britain was immense and her achievements unchallengeable though still controversial. She privatised nearly 20 per cent of the economy; she greatly reduced the power of trade unions; she abolished a tier of local government (the metropolitan counties); she won a tense war against Argentina against many predictions; she introduced market forces into much of the public sector, including the health and education services; and she restrained the progress towards European integration. In terms of government she demonstrated that determination and will and sheer ability can still fundamentally change this conservative and tradition-bound country. To be hated by many and regarded with distaste by even more, including members of their own party, is a price most politicians seem willing ultimately to pay.

The Lady's not for turning. (Speech to Conservative Party conference, Brighton, 10 October 1980)

Ladies and gentlemen, I stand before you in my green chiffon evening gown, my face softly made up, my fair hair gently waved.... The Iron Lady of the Western World. Me? A cold warrior? Well yes, if that is how they wish to interpret my defence of values and freedom fundamental to our way of life. (To Finchley constituency, 31 January 1976)

The President of the Commission, M. Delors, said at this conference the other day that he wanted the European parliament to be the democratic body of the Community, he wanted the Commission to be the executive, and he wanted the Council of Ministers to be the Senate. No. No. No. (In the Commons on her return from the Rome summit, 3 January 1990)

I don't mind how much my ministers talk as long as they do what I say.

Let me make one thing absolutely clear. The NHS is safe with us. (Speech to Conservative Party conference, Brighton, 8 October 1982)

I usually make my mind up about a man in ten seconds and I very rarely change it. (1970)

If someone is confronting our essential liberties, if someone is inflicting injuries and harm – by God, I'll confront them! (1979)

Most of us have stopped using silver every day. (1970)

## Thorpe, Jeremy (1929–)

Leader of the Liberals 1967–76. He was educated at Oxford and became a barrister before entering the House of Commons for North Devon in 1959. Witty and articulate, he had his moment of glory in 1974, when the Liberal vote was the highest in 50 years and the party won 14 seats. Rumours began to circulate in the early 1970s that Thorpe had possibly had a relationship with a former male model, Norman Scott. It subsequently became clear that Scott had been receiving money from the Liberal Party via one of its MPs, Peter Bessell. The allegations were repeated by an emotional Scott when he appeared in court in 1976, with the result that Thorpe stood down as leader. In May 1979 he lost his North Devon seat and in June stood trial for the attempted murder of Scott. It transpired that a former pilot, Andrew Newton, had been hired to shoot Scott but

had bungled the attempt, shooting his dog, Rinka, instead. Thorpe and three other accused were acquitted. Thorpe's lawyer did not let Thorpe give evidence and in the wake of the trial there was some scepticism about the verdict. Thorpe's career was destroyed by the scandal and he left politics to live quietly in the south-west. Some time later he was diagnosed with Parkinson's disease.

## Trimble, David (1944–)

Ulster Unionist MP and leader. He was educated Bangor Grammar School and Queen's University, Belfast, where he later lectured in law. He was MP for Upper Bann from 1990 and became leader of the Ulster Unionist Party in 1995. He worked hard to engineer the Good Friday Agreement in 1998, when many of his party were suspicious and tended to take the line of Ian Paisley, though less raucously, that the agreement was a sell-out. He skilfully persuaded his party to support the process and the resultant agreement and won the Nobel Peace Prize in 1998, jointly with John Hume, leader of the Social Democratic and Labour Party, for his efforts. He resigned as Northern Ireland's first minister in July 2001 in response to the IRA's failure to disarm, though he maintained his position as party leader and the hope that moderation might triumph eventually. However, the delayed elections to the Northern Ireland assembly in November 2003 saw his party lose much ground to Paisley's Democratic Unionist Party. The defection of key members of his own party to the hard-line Protestants further weakened his position from 2004.

Once we are agreed our only weapons will be our words, then there is nothing that cannot be said, there is nothing that cannot be achieved. (September 1998)

## Turnbull, Andrew (1945–)

Cabinet secretary and head of home civil service from 2002. He was educated at Enfield Grammar School and Cambridge University. He entered the civil service via the Treasury in 1970. He served as principal private secretary to Margaret Thatcher and was praised by Tony Blair for his work in developing the Office of Government Commerce and Partnership UK before being appointed as secretary to the cabinet in late 2002. He was as seen by some commentators as the 'establishment' candidate.

## Turner, Adair (1955–)

Director general of the Confederation of British Industry 1995–99. He was educated at Cambridge University and was president of the Union in 1976. He worked for McKinsey and Co. and was a director of Chase Manhattan Bank and of Merrill Lynch. He was a public figure associated with the centre-ground.

# W

## Wakeham, John (1932–), Lord

Conservative MP and peer, minister, and chair of the Press Complaints Commission (PCC). He was educated at Charterhouse. He served as a cabinet minister under both Margaret Thatcher and John Major, as chief whip 1983–87 and as leader of the House of Commons 1987–88 and of the House of the Lords 1992–94, having been made a life peer in 1992. He chaired the commission on reform of the Lords and produced a formula for a largely appointed new chamber. He was appointed chair of the PCC in 1995 but resigned in February 2002 when Enron, the energy conglomerate of which he was a director, collapsed.

## Waldegrave, William (1946–), Lord

Famously clever Conservative cabinet minister whose reputation was damaged by his involvement in the arms to Iraq affair. He was educated at Eton, Corpus Christie College, Oxford, and Harvard University. He was a member of Central Policy Review Staff (a think tank) 1971–73,

and advisor to Number 10 Downing Street 1973–74 and to the leader of the opposition 1974–75; he then worked for GEC 1975–81. He was Bristol West MP 1979–97 and secretary of state for health 1990–92. Waldegrave was criticised by the Scott report for his role in the Matrix Churchill trial and the arms to Iraq affair.

## Walden, Brian (1932–)

Former Labour MP turned television presenter and interviewer. He was educated at West Bromwich Grammar School, and Queen's and Nuffield Colleges, Oxford (he was president of Oxford Union 1957). He was MP for Birmingham All Saints 1964–74 and Ladywood 1974–77, then worked as a television presenter on *Weekend World* 1977–86, as well as a columnist for the *Evening Standard* and a number of broadsheets. He was a gifted young politician who was perceived by many Labour MPs as too self-seeking; he left to pursue a successful career in the media.

## Wall, Stephen (1947–)

Civil servant. He was educated Douai School and Cambridge. He joined the Foreign Office in 1965, and served in Africa, Washington and at the European Union. He was press officer to Number 10 Downing Street 1971–77, ambassador to Portugal 1993–95 and to the European Union 1995–2000. He then became head of the European Secretariat in the Cabinet Office and the prime minister's advisor on European foreign policy. He has been one of the most influential diplomats in the political system.

## Walpole, Robert (1676–1745)

Usually reckoned to be the first British prime minister (1721–42). He was educated at Cambridge and became a Whig MP in 1701. He became secretary for war in 1708. He spent some time in prison on corruption charges in 1712 but was recalled by George I as chancellor in 1715 and returned to the post in 1721. About this time he became known as the 'prime minister' – a sobriquet he resisted. Both George I and George II found him indispensable until policy misjudgements led him to resign in 1742.

> Madam, there are fifty thousand men slain this year in Europe and not one Englishman. (To Queen Caroline on the War of Polish Succession, in which England had refused to take part)

> All those men have their price. (On parliamentarians, 1798)

> They now ring their bells but will soon wring their hands. (On the declaration of war on Spain, 1739)

### Walters, Alan (1926–), Sir

Economic advisor to Margaret Thatcher. He was educated at Alderman Newton's School, Leicester University College and University College London. He lectured at Birmingham University before he became a distinctly monetarist professor of economics at the London School of Economics and then John Hopkins University 1976–91. He served as a member of various commissions before serving as the prime minister's economic advisor 1981–84 and 1988–90. Walters was the cause of a long-running row between chancellor Nigel Lawson and Thatcher as he advised her against joining the European Exchange Rate Mechanism.

### Webb, Sidney (1859–1947); Webb, Beatrice (1858–1943)

Social reformers and left-wing intellectuals. Sidney was educated privately, then at the Birkbeck Institute and the City of London College. Both husband and wife played a formative role in the Fabian Society and the early years of the Labour Party. Sidney helped to write its constitution in 1918 and its manifesto for the 1918 election. He entered the Commons in 1922 and, after becoming Lord Passfield in 1929, was secretary of state for the colonies 1929–31. Sidney was a prolific journalist and author, and was chair of the editorial board of the *New Statesman*. He married Beatrice (a wealthy heiress) in 1892 and they

collaborated closely on research and writing, and both helped to set up the London School of Economics in 1895. They both visited the USSR in the 1930s and, like George Bernard Shaw, proved vulnerable to Soviet propaganda when they declared that Joseph Stalin's dictatorship represented a 'New Civilisation'.

> Old people are always absorbed in something, usually themselves. We prefer to be absorbed in the Soviet Union.

### White, Michael (1945–)

Broadcaster and columnist. Educated at Bodmin Grammar school, and University College London. He was made political editor of the *Guardian* in 1990. He has been rated by some as arguably the paper's most distinguished sketch writer.

### Whitelaw, William ('Willie') (1918–99)

Veteran Conservative cabinet member. He was educated at Winchester and Cambridge. He served with distinction in the Second World War. He entered the House of Commons in 1955 and served as secretary of state for Northern Ireland 1972–73 and for employment 1973–74 and home secretary 1979–83. He stood for leadership of the party in 1975 when he was widely deemed to be the strongest candidate, but loyalty to Edward Heath prevented him from standing in the first ballot as Margaret Thatcher had, thereby establishing the momentum which saw her elected on the second ballot. He was deputy to Thatcher and displayed a similar loyalty, though he was one of the few advisors she allowed to be honestly critical of her policies. It was often said that once she lost him as her close advisor her policy judgement declined.

> It is never wise to appear more clever than you are. It is sometimes wise to appear slightly less so. (1975)

> The Labour Party is going around the country stirring up apathy. (May 1983)

## Widdecombe, Ann (1947–)

Conservative MP and minister. She was educated at La Sainte Union Convent, Bath, Birmingham University and Lady Margaret Hall, Oxford. She worked as a university administrator before she entered parliament for Plymouth Devonport in 1983, then Maidstone 1987–97 and Maidstone and Weald from 1997. She served as a junior minister in employment and as minister of state in the Home Office, in charge of prisons. An unusual, combative politician, she clashed with Michael Howard, her boss at the Home Office, over prison management. During the contest for Conservative Party leader in May 1997 she made a speech in the House of Commons in which she attacked Howard with her observation that there was 'something of the night' about him; his bid for the leadership was effectively torpedoed. Her obvious ability combined with a forthrightness verging on aggression won her the shadow health position in William Hague's shadow cabinet in 1998. She considered standing for the leadership in the wake of the party's 2001 general election defeat and Hague's resignation but lacked sufficient support in the parliamentary party.

> As for Michael Portillo … I can hardly believe that it has all worked out so perfectly. (On the defeat of Portillo's challenge for the leadership, which she hotly opposed, and his subsequent retirement from front-line politics, 2001)

## Wilkes, John (1727–97)

Archetypical political radical. He was educated at the University of Leiden, to avoid the Anglicanism of Oxford and Cambridge. He was elected to parliament in 1757 at a by-election. He was accused shortly afterwards of libeling the king's speech in number 45 of his weekly essay paper but argued successfully that he was protected by parliamentary privilege. Wilkes soon became a champion of liberty in the public view, especially after the king had him expelled from parliament. He was returned in 1768 for the seat of Middlesex.

He then surrendered to the courts and was imprisoned for two years. He was released in 1770. He was then elected an alderman of London and went on to become lord mayor in 1774, then once again was returned for Middlesex. He opposed the American War of Independence and the mob in the anti-Catholic Gordon riots. His support for Pitt the Younger tended to lose him radical support. His colourful, rakish life and rebellious attitudes created an early template for flamboyant radicalism.

> Nothing has been so obnoxious to me through life, as dead calm.

> That will depend, my lord, on whether I embrace your principles or your mistresses. (To the Earl of Sandwich's comment, 'Egad sir, I do not know if you will die on the gallows or of the pox.')

## Willets, David (1956–)

Clever Conservative minister and thinker, nicknamed, by friend and foe alike, 'two brains'. He was educated at King Edward's School, Birmingham, and Christ Church, Oxford. He worked as an assistant to Nigel Lawson in 1978 and in the Treasury 1978–84. He moved to the Policy Unit in Number 10 Downing Street and then was director of the Centre for Policy Studies 1987–92. He was MP for Havant from 1992; he served as a whip and in the Office of Public Services in the Cabinet Office. He was paymaster general 1996–97 and then shadow employment spokesman 1997. Under Michael Howard, he was made shadow secretary of state for work and pensions and welfare reform.

## Williams, Gareth (1941–2003), Lord

Welsh barrister and Labour leader of the House of Lords. He was famously born in a taxi between Mostyn and Prestatyn. He was educated at Rhyl Grammar School and Cambridge. He was called to the bar in 1965 and became a QC and then recorder from 1978. He became a Labour peer in 1992 and shadow spokesman for legal affairs from 1997. He served as a junior minister at the Home Office 1997 and minister of state 1998, deputy leader of the Lords and attorney general 1999, and leader of Lords from 2001.

> This almost irreplaceable figure was universally popular because the steel of his radicalism and the iron of his logic were covered with the velvet of his deft articulacy and the sheen of his sparkling wit. (*Guardian* obituary, 22 September 2003)

### Williams, Marcia (Lady Falkender) (1932–)

Personal secretary to Harold Wilson when he was prime minister and rumoured to exercise great influence over him. She was educated at Queen Mary College, London University, then worked at Labour headquarters before she became Wilson's private and political secretary 1956–73. She was given a life peerage in 1974.

### Williams, Shirley (1930–), Baroness

Labour secretary of state for education 1976–79 and member of the 'gang of four' who founded the Social Democratic Party (SDP). Born to political scientist George Catlin and writer Vera Brittain, she was likely to favour public life and an education at Oxford and Columbia universities did not discourage her. She was MP for Hitchin 1964–74 and Hertford and Stevenage 1974–79. She was a steadfast supporter of the revisionist Labour line associated with Hugh Gaitskell. She was also fervently pro-Europe. She held junior posts in Harold Wilson's 1966 government and was elected to the shadow cabinet in 1971; she was secretary of state for prices and consumer affairs 1974–76, then education secretary 1976–79, as which she pressed on with the comprehensive project. In 1980 she stated she would leave the party if it committed itself to leaving the European Community, and thereupon formed the Social Democratic Party along with Bill Rodgers, Roy Jenkins and David Owen. She was elected president of SDP in 1982, after she had won the Crosby by-election in 1981. She lost the seat in 1983 and went on to support the merger with the

Liberals to form the Liberal and Social Democratic Party (later renamed the Liberal Democrats). She joined the Lords in 1993 though she worked at Harvard University. She was the third member of the 'gang of four' to become leader of the Liberal Democrats in the Lords, in November 2001.

> The saddest illusion of revolutionary socialists is that revolution itself will transform the nature of human beings.

### Wilson, Harold (1916–95)

Labour prime minister 1964–70 and 1974–76. He was educated at Wirral Grammar School and Oxford, where he shone and became secretary of the Liberal Association. He was director of economics and statistics in the wartime civil service for the Ministry of Fuel and Power. He was on brink of choosing an academic career but chose Labour politics instead, being returned for Ormskirk 1945 and then for Huyton, Liverpool, 1950–83. By 1947, aged 31, he was already president of the Board of Trade and did much to remove wartime controls on economic activity. He resigned in 1951 with Aneurin Bevan in protest against health cuts. Some speculate he was establishing left-wing credentials for a future attempt on the leadership, though when younger he seemed unambitious. He fought Hugh Gaitskell for the leadership in 1960 but lost; he succeeded after the death of Gaitskell in 1963, in a party without the left-wing firebrand Bevan, who had died in 1960. He established himself as a dynamic Kennedy-type figure in the early 1960s and won the 1964 general election, though only by four seats. He succeeded brilliantly in managing his tiny majority and in 1966 won a landslide victory. Then his problems started, with devaluation and inflation plus relative economic decline and abortive attempts to reform the Lords and the trade unions, as well as join the Common Market. His administration's rather few achievements included the Open University, liberalisation of laws on homosexuals and the abolition of the death penalty. His defeat in the 1970 general election was unexpected, as his poll position had been promising. In opposition his party moved to the left, especially on Europe. He strove to maintain party unity and was rewarded by the victory over Edward Heath in February 1974, after the miners had weakened Heath's credibility, and the narrow victory in October 1974. He defused the split over Europe with a referendum, in which membership was endorsed by two to one. In 1976 he resigned dramatically. Perhaps the most astonishing thing about it was that there was no shocking scandal underlying it – the reason seemed to be mere boredom with public life; some have suggested he already knew he was suffering from Alzheimer's, the disease which eventually killed him. His final honours list, which rewarded businessmen, marred his reputation and it continued to decline for several years until new biographies by Ben Pimlott (1992) and Philip Zeigler (1993) revived it somewhat. One of the cleverest and most pragmatic of Labour politicians, he resembled David Lloyd George in trying to please too many people and ending up being distrusted by almost everyone.

We are re-defining and we are re-stating our socialism in terms of the scientific revolution.... The Britain that is going to be forged in the white heat of this revolution will be no place for restrictive practices or out-dated methods on either side of industry. (Speech to the Labour Party conference, Scarborough, 1 October 1963)

Smethwick Conservatives can have the satisfaction of having topped the poll, of having sent a member who, until another election returns him to oblivion, will serve his time here as a parliamentary leper. (Referring to Peter Griffiths, who defeated Patrick Gordon Walker in a racist campaign, 4 November 1964)

It does not mean, of course, that the pound here in Britain in your pocket or your purse or your bank has been devalued. (Announcing the devaluation of the pound, 20 November 1967)

A week is a long time in politics. (Probably used in a lobby briefing, 1964)

Selsdon Man is designing a system of society for the ruthless and pushing, the uncaring.... His message to the rest of us is: you're out on your own. (Referring to the Tory policy meeting at Selsdon Park, Croydon, 1970)

One man's wage rise is another man's price increase. (When opposition leader, 1970)

If I had the choice between smoked salmon and tinned salmon, I'd have it tinned. With vinegar. (1962)

If Harold Wilson ever went to school without boots, it was merely because he was too big for them. (Harold Macmillan on Wilson's much-vaunted poverty-stricken childhood)

### Wilson, Richard (1942–), Sir

Civil servant. He was educated at Radley and Cambridge. He served as cabinet secretary and head of home civil service 1998–2002. He subsequently became master of Emmanuel College, Cambridge. He was a self-effacing, urbane mandarin.

There are occasions when you have to say 'bollocks' to ministers. (February 2000)

### Wollstonecraft, Mary (1759–97)

One of the first feminist writers. She married one of the so-called English Jacobins, William Godwin. She wrote *A Vindication of Rights of Man* (1790) and *A Vindication of the Rights of Women* (1792), which advocated equality of the sexes, especially in education.

### Woolf, Harry (1933–), Lord Justice

Lord chief justice of England and Wales after 2000; Master of the Rolls, 1996–2000. He was educated at Fettes and University College London. He was called to bar in 1954, served as a captain in the army from 1955 and practised law after 1956. He chaired an inquiry into prisons in 1990, which attracted much publicity, though only some of its recommendations were implemented. His report into civil justice when Master of the Rolls was more successful and inaugurated profound changes to civil litigation procedures.

### Worcester, Bob (1933–)
Chairman of Market Opinion Research International (MORI) from 1973. He was educated at Kansas University before he became a consultant with McKinsey and Co., 1962–65. He joined MORI in the late 1960s and quickly became identified as the public face of the polling organisation as well as pollsters in general. In addition to being a visiting professor at City University and the London School of Economics, as well as Strathclyde University, he has authored several books and regularly writes in the broadsheet press, and appears on television and radio current affairs programmes.

### Wright, Anthony (1948–)
Labour backbencher and political scientist. He was educated at Kettering Grammar School, the London School of Economics, Harvard University and Balliol College, Oxford. He lectured in politics at Birmingham University, and was MP for Cannock after 1992. He has written several well received books on political philosophy and British politics. He was chair of the Public Administration Committee 1997–2001. He has been a (not uncritical) Blairite 'moderniser' and advocate for reform of parliament.

# Y

### Yelland, David (1963–)
Editor of the *Sun* from June 1998 to January 2003. He was educated at grammar school in Yorkshire and at Lancashire Polytechnic. He started his career as a business reporter, and proved hardworking and prescient. He was a surprise choice as

replacement for Stuart Higgins as editor of the *Sun*. He followed a pro-Labour line, though only up to a point – he branded Tony Blair the 'most dangerous man in Britain' in August 1998 for his pro-European stance.

> I don't think the Blairs are *Sun* readers. (July 2000)

### Yeo, Tim (1945–)
Conservative MP and member of the shadow cabinet. He was educated at Charterhouse and Cambridge and worked in business until he was elected MP for South Suffolk in 1983. He served as a junior minister under John Major but resigned after a scandal involving an affair. After 1997 he shadowed agriculture for a while and then trade and industry under Tory leader Iain Duncan Smith. He was occasionally seen as a possible leadership contender from the left of the party. He was the party's spokesman for health and education after November 2003 – a wide area in which he had responsibility for convincing voters that his party cared deeply about public services. In the summer of 2004 Michael Howard redistributed the health and education portfolios and made Yeo shadow spokesman for the environment.

### Young, Hugo (1938–2003)
Leading political columnist. He was educated at Ampleforth and Balliol College, Oxford, where he studied law. He worked for the *Sunday Times* as political editor before moving to the *Guardian*, where he established a reputation as a profound analyst of British politics in his twice-weekly columns. His Radio 4 programmes (such as *The Thatcher Phenomenon* and *No, Minister*) were well received and his book *One of Us: Life of Margaret Thatcher* (1989) was widely regarded as the best biography of her. He died, lamented by colleagues and readers alike, in September 2003, having continued writing his column until the last week of his life.

# Websites

**Britain and Europe**
Britain in Europe campaign
www.britainineurope.org

Campaign against Britain joining the single currency
www.bfors.com/

Council of the EU
http://ue.eu.int/en/

European Central Bank
www.ecb.int/

European Commission
www.europa.eu.int/comm/

European Court of Justice
http://curia.eu.int/

European Parliament
www.europarl.eu.int/

Treasury site on the euro
www.euro.gov.uk/

UK Office of the European Parliament
www.europarl.org.uk/index.htm

University Association for Contemporary European Studies
www.uaces.org/


**Constitution and monarchy**
British monarchy
www.royal.gov.uk/

Constitution Unit at University College London
www.ucl.ac.uk/constitution-unit/

House of Commons within the British constitution
www.leeds.ac.uk/law/teaching/law6cw/hc-1.htm

**Elections and voting behaviour**
National Election Studies
www.umich.edu/~nes/

UK Data Archive
www.data-archive.ac.uk/

**Judiciary, police, crime**
Court Service
www.courtservice.gov.uk/

Crown Prosecution Service
www.cps.gov.uk/

Home Office Research Development Statistics
www.homeoffice.gov.uk/rds

Law Society
www.lawsociety.org.uk

Police service
www.police.uk

**Local government**
Improvement and Development Agency
www.idea.gov.uk

Local Government Association
www.lga.gov.uk

Local Government Information Unit
www.lgiu.gov.uk

Office Deputy Prime Minister
www.odpm.gov.uk

## Ministers, departments and civil servants

Civil service
www.cabinet-office.gov.uk/cservice/index.asp

Directgov – public service information
www.direct.gov.uk

Guide to government department websites
www.parliament.uk/directories/hciolists/hmg.cfm

# Bibliography

**General works of reference**
Axford, B., *et al.*, *Politics: An Introduction*, Routledge, 1997.
Butler, D. and Butler, G., *British Political Facts 1900–1994*, Macmillan, 1994.
Crystal, D., *The Cambridge Biographical Encyclopaedia*, 2nd edition, Cambridge University Press, 1998.
Gardiner, J. (ed.), *Who's Who in British History*, Collins and Brown, 2000.
Heywood, A., *Politics*, Macmillan, 1997.
*Hutchinson Encyclopedia of Britain*, Helicon, 1999.
*Hutchinson Softback Encyclopaedia*, 3rd edition, Softback Preview, 1996.
*Macmillan Encyclopaedia*, Guild Publishing, 1981.
Magnusson, M., *Chambers Biographical Dictionary*, 1990.
*Oxford Dictionary of Quotations*, Oxford University Press, 1996.
*Oxford World Encyclopaedia*, Oxford University Press, 1998.
*Parliamentary Yearbook and Diary, 2000*, Blake Contracting Publishing, 2001.
Pritchard, J., *The Penguin Guide to the Law*, 2nd edition, Guild Publishing, 1986.
Urmson, J. O. and Ree, J. *The Concise Encyclopaedia of Western Philosophy and Philosophers*, Routledge, 1993.
*Who's Who*, A. and C. Black, 1998.

**General politics sources**
Day, A., *et al.*, *Political Parties of the World*, 4th edition, Cartermill, 1996.
Kavanagh, D. (ed.), *The Oxford Dictionary of Political Biography*, Oxford University Press, 1998.
McLean, I. (ed.), *The Concise Oxford Dictionary of Politics*, Oxford University Press, 1996.
Pilkington, C., *The Politics Today Companion to the British Constitution*, Manchester University Press, 1999.
Roberts, G. and Edwards, A., *A New Dictionary of Political Analysis*, Edward Arnold, 1991.
Robertson, D., *The Penguin Dictionary of Politics*, Penguin, 1993.

**British history**
Gardner, J. and Wenborn, N. (eds), *The History Today Companion to British History*, Collins, 1995.
Kenyon, J. P., *A Dictionary of British History*, Secker and Warburg, 1981.
Lee, C., *This Sceptred Isle*, BBC, 2000.
Schama, S., *A History of Britain*, BBC, Vol. I 2000, Vol. II 2001, Vol. III 2002.
Trevelyan, G. M., *English Social History*, Pelican, 1979.

**General British politics**
Budge, I., *et al.*, *The New British Politics*, Longman, 1998.
Coates, D. and Lawler, P. (eds), *New Labour in Power*, Manchester University Press, 2000.

Coxall, B. and Robins, L., *Contemporary British Politics*, 4th edition, Palgrave, 2003.

Dunleavy, P., *et al.* (eds), *Developments in British Politics 6*, Macmillan, 2000.

Holliday, I., *et al.* (eds), *Fundamentals in British Politics*, Manchester University Press, 1999.

Jones, B. (ed.), *Political Issues in Britain Today*, 5th edition, Manchester University Press, 1999.

Jones, B. and Kavanagh, D., *British Politics Today*, Manchester University Press, 2003.

Jones, B., *et al.*, *Politics UK*, 5th edition, Pearson Education, 2004.

Kingdom, J., *Government and Politics in Britain: An Introduction*, 3rd edition, Polity, 1991.

Roberts, D. (ed.), *British Politics in Focus*, Causeway Press, 2003.

## Specific issues, policy areas and topics in British politics

Abercrombie, N., *et al.*, *Contemporary British Society*, Polity, 1988.

Adonis, A., *Parliament Today*, Manchester University Press, 1993.

Adonis, A. and Pollard, S., *A Class Act: The Myth of Britain's Classless Society*, Hamish Hamilton, 1997.

Alderdson, J., *A New Cromwell: The Centralisation of the Police*, Charter 88, 1994.

Almond, G. A. and Verba, S., *The Civic Culture*, Princeton University Press, 1963.

Almond, G. A. and Verba, S. (eds), *The Civic Culture Revisited*, Little, Brown, 1980.

Althusser, L., *For Marx* (transl. B. Brewster), Penguin.1969.

Amery, L. S., *Thoughts on the Constitution*, Oxford University Press, 1947.

Arblaster, A., *The Rise and Decline of Western Liberalism*, Blackwell, 1984.

Armstrong, P., Glyn, A. and Harrison, J., *Capitalism Since 1945*, Blackwell, 1991.

Armstrong, P., Glyn, A. and Harrison, J., *Capitalism Since World War II*, Fontana, 1984.

Audit Commission, *Passing the Buck: The Impact of Standard Spending Assessments on Economy, Efficiency and Effectiveness*, HMSO, 1993.

Audit Commission, *Realising the Benefits of Competition: The Client Role for Contracted Services*, HMSO, 1993.

Audit Commission, *We Can't Go On Meeting Like This*, Audit Commission Publications, 1990.

Auerback, M. M., *The Conservatism Illusion*, Columbia University Press, 1959.

Bagehot, W., *The English Constitution*, Fontana, 1963 (first published 1867).

Baggott, R., *Pressure Groups Today*, Manchester University Press, 1995.

Bains, M. A. (chairman), *The New Local Authorities: Management and Structure*, HMSO, 1972.

Baker, K., *Turbulent Years: My Life In Politics*, Faber, 1993.

Baldwin, R. and Kinsey, R., *Police Powers and Politics*, Quartet, 1982.

Balogh, T., 'The apotheosis of the dilettante: the establishment of mandarins', in Thomas, H. (ed.), *Crisis in the Civil Service*, Anthony Blond, 1968.

Banton, M., *Promoting Racial Harmony*, Cambridge University Press, 1985.

Bar Council, *Quality of Justice: The Bar's Response*, Bar Council, 1989.

Barberis, P. (ed.), *The Whitehall Reader*, Open University Press, 1996.

Barker, R., *Politics, Peoples and Government*, Macmillan, 1994.

Barnett, A., *Iron Brittania*, Allion and Busby, 1982.

Barnett, A., Ellis, C. and Hirst, P., *Debating the Constitution*, Polity, 1993.

Barron, J., Crawley, G. and Wood, T., *Councillors in Crisis*, Macmillan, 1991.

Batty, K. and George, B., 'Finance and facilities for MPs', in Norton, P. (ed.), *Parliament in the 1980s*, Basil and Blackwell, 1985.

Baxter, J. and Koffman, L. (eds), *Police, the Constitution and the Community*, Professional Books, 1985.

Beard, H. and Cerf, C., *The Official Politically Correct Dictionary and Handbook*, Grafton, 1992.

Beer, S. H. *Britain Against Itself*, Faber, 1982.

Beer, S. H., *Modern British Politics*, Faber, 1965.

Bell, D., *The End of Ideology*, Free Press, 1960.

Benn, M., 'Policing women', in Baxter, J. and Koffman, L. (eds), *Police, the Constitution and the Community*, Professional Books, 1985.

Benn, M., *et al.*, *The Rape Controversy*, National Council for Civil Liberties, 1983.

Benn, T., *Arguments for Socialism*, Penguin, 1979.

Benn, T., 'Manifestos and mandarins', in *Policy and Practice: The Experience of Government*, Royal Institute of Public Administration, 1980.

Bentley, A. F., *The Process of Government*, Harvard University Press, 1967 (first published 1908).

Bentley, M., *Politics Without Democracy, 1815–1914*, Fontana, 1984.

Berlin, I., 'Two concepts of liberty', in Berlin, I., *Four Essays on Liberty*, Oxford University Press, 1970.

Beveridge, W. (chairman), *Social Insurance and Allied Services*, HMSO, 1942.

Birch, A. H., *Small Town Politics*, Oxford University Press, 1959.

Birkinshaw, P., *Freedom of Information: The Law, the Practice and the Ideal*, Weidenfeld and Nicolson, 1988.

Birkinshaw, P., *Reforming the Secret State*, Open University Press, 1991.

Bishop, M., Kay, J. and Mayer, C. (eds), *The Regulatory Challenge*, Oxford University Press, 1995.

Blake, R., *The Conservative Party from Peel to Thatcher*, Fontana, 1985.

Blunkett, D., *On a Clear Day*, Michael O'Mara, 1995.

Boaden, N., *Urban Policy Making*, Cambridge University Press, 1971.

Boddy, M. and Fudge, C. (eds), *Local Socialism: The Way Ahead*, Macmillan, 1984.

Bogdanor, V., *The People and the Party System*, Cambridge University Press, 1981.

Bognador, V., *Politics and the Constitution: Essays on British Government*, Dartmouth, 1996.

Bognador, V., *The Monarchy and Constitution*, Oxford University Press, 1997.

Bottomore, T., *Elites in Society*, Penguin, 1964.

Bower, T., *Maxwell: The Outsider*, Aurum Press, 1988.

Box, S., *Deviance, Reality and Society*, Holt, Rinehart and Winston, 1971.

Brand, J., *British Parliamentary Parties: Policy and Power*, Oxford University Press, 1992.

Brett, E. A., *The World Economy Since the War: The Politics of Uneven Development*, Macmillan, 1985.

Bruce, B., *Images of Power*, Kogan Page, 1992.

Bruce-Gardyne, J., *Mrs Thatcher's First Administration*, Macmillan, 1984.

Bull, H., *The Anarchical Society*, Macmillan, 1977.

Bunyan, A., *The History and Practice of the Political Police in Britain*, Quartet, 1977.

Burch, M. and Holliday, I., *The British Cabinet System*, Prentice Hall/Harvester Wheatsheaf, 1996.

Burnham, J., *The Managerial Revolution*, Putnam, 1942.

Butler, D., *British General Elections Since 1945*, Blackwell, 1995.

Butler, D. E., Adonis, A. and Travers, T., *Failure in British Government: The Politics of the Poll Tax*, Oxford University Press, 1994.

Butler, D. and Butler, G., *British Political Facts, 1900–1994*, Macmillan, 1994.

Butler, D. and Kavanagh, D. (eds), *The British General Election of 1987*, Macmillan, 1987.

Butler, D. and Kavanagh, D. (eds), *The British General Election of 1992*, Macmillan, 1992.

Butler, D. and Kavanagh, D. (eds), *The British General Election of 1997*, Macmillan, 1997.

Butler, D. and Rose, R., *The British General Election of 1959*, Macmillan, 1960.

Butler, D. and Stokes, D., *Political Change in Britain*, Macmillan, 1969.

Butler, M., *Europe: More Than a Continent*, Heinemann, 1986.

Cabinet Office, *The Citizen's Charter: Raising the Standard*, Cm 1599, HMSO, 1991.

Cabinet Office, *Open Government*, Cm 2290, HMSO, 1993.

Cabinet Office, *Review of Fast Stream Recruitment*, HMSO, 1994.

Cabinet Office, *The Civil Service: Continuity and Change*, Cm 2627, HMSO, 1994.

Cabinet Office, *Development and Training for Civil Servants: A Framework for Action*, Cm 3321, Stationary Office, 1996.

Callaghan, J., *Great Power Complex*, Pluto, 1997.

Callaghan, J., *Time and Chance*, Collins, 1987.

Camilleri, J. A. and Falk, J., *The End of Sovereignty?*, Edward Elgar, 1992.

Cannadine, D., *The Decline and Fall of the British Aristocracy*, Picador, 1992.

Cannadine, D., *In Churchill's Shadow*, Penguin, 2003.

Castells, M., *The Urban Question*, Edward Arnold, 1977.

Castle, B., *The Castle Diaries, 1974–6*, Weidenfeld and Nicolson, 1980.

Cawson, A., *Corporatism and Political Theory*, Basil Blackwell, 1986.

Cecil, H., *Conservatism*, Thornton Butterworth, 1912.

Chandler, J. A., *Local Government Today*, 2nd edition, Manchester University Press, 1997.

Chandler, J. A., *Public Policy-Making for Local Government*, Croom Helm, 1998.

Clark, A., *The Tories: Conservatives and Nation State 1922–1997*, Weidenfeld and Nicolson, 1998.

Clark, A., *Diaries*, Phoenix, 2000.

Cockerell, M., *Live From Number 10: The Inside Story of Prime Ministers and Televison*, Faber and Faber, 1988.

Cohen, N., *Pretty Straight Guys*, Faber and Faber, 2004

Crick, M., *Michael Heseltine*, Hamish Hamilton, 1997.

Crossman, R., *Diaries of a Cabinet Minister*, Hamish Hamilton, Vol. I 1975, Vol. II 1976, Vol. III 1977.

Curran, J. and Seaton, J., *Power Without Responsibility*, Fontana, 1981.

Day, R., *But With Respect*, Orion, 1993.

Dell, E., *A Strange Eventful History*, Harper Collins, 1999.

Denver, D., *Elections and Voting in Britain*, Palgrave, 2003.

Donoughue, B., *The Heat of the Kitchen*, Politico's, 2003.

Dynes, M. and Walker, D., *The Times Guide to the New British State*, Times Books, 1995.

Ferguson, N., *Empire*, Allen Lane, 2003.

Franklin, B. (ed.), *Televising Democracies*, Routledge, 1992.

Garner, R. and Kelly, D., *British Political Parties Today*, 2nd edition, Manchester University Press, 1998.

Geddes, A. and Tonge, J., *Labour's Landslide*, Manchester University Press, 1997.

Geddes, A. and Tonge, J., *Labour's Second Landslide*, Manchester University Press, 2002.

Giddens, A., *The Third Way: The Renewal of Social Democracy*, Polity Press, 1998.

Hennessy, P., *Never Again, Britain 1945–51*, Cape, 1992.

Hennessy, P., *Whitehall*, Secker and Warburg, 1988.

Heseltine, M., *Life in the Jungle*, Coronet, 2000.

Heywood, A., *Key Concepts in Politics*, Palgrave, 2000.

Hogwood, P. and Roberts, G., *European Politics Today*, 2nd edition, Manchester University Press, 2003.

Howe, G., *Conflict of Loyalty*, Pan, 1994.

Hutton, W., *The State We're In*, Vintage, 1996.

Jenkins, R., *Churchill*, Pan, 2001.

Kavanagh, D. and Seldon, A., *The Powers of the Prime Minister*, Harper Collins, 1999.

King, A. (ed.), *New Labour Triumphs at the Polls*, Chatham House, 1997.

Lawson, N., *The View from Number 11: Memoirs of a Tory Radical*, Corgi Books, 1993.

Little, R. and Whickam-Jones, M. (eds), *New Labour's Foreign Policy*, Manchester University Press, 2000.

Ludlam, S. and Smith, M. (eds), *New Labour in Government*, Macmillan, 2001.

Lyn, J. and Jay, A., *The Complete Yes Prime Minister*, BBC, 2003.

Marquand, D., *The Progressive Dilemma*, Phoenix, 1999.

McIlroy, J., *Trade Unions in Britain Today*, 2nd edition, Manchester University Press, 1996.

McQuail, D., *McQuail's Mass Communication Theory*, 4th edition, Sage, 2000.

Naughton, N., *Local and Regional Government in Britain*, Hodder and Staughton, 1998.

O'Brien, C. C., *Edmund Burke*, Vintage, 2002.

Paxman, J., *The English*, Michael Joseph, 1999.

Paxman, J., *The Political Animal*, Michael Joseph, 2002.

Perkins, A., *Red Queen*, Macmillan, 2003.

Pilkington, C., *Representative Democracy in Britain Today*, Manchester University Press, 1997.

Pilkington, C., *The Civil Service in Britain Today*, Manchester University Press, 1999.

Pilkington, C., *Britain in Europe Today*, Manchester University Press, 2001.

Pilkington, C., *Devolution in Britain Today*, Manchester University Press, 2002.

Pimlott, B., *Harold Wilson*, Harper Collins, 1992.

Rawnsley, A., *Servants of the People: The Inside Story of New Labour*, Hamish Hamilton, 2000.

Rentoul, J., *Tony Blair: Prime Minister*, Time Warner, 2001.

Ridley, N., *My Style of Government: The Margaret Thatcher Years*, Huchinson, 1991.

Rivlin, G., *Understanding the Law*, Oxford University Press, 2004.

Sampson, A., *Who Runs This Place?*, John Murray, 2004.

Sevaldsen, J. and Vadmand, O., *Contemporary British Society*, Akedimisk Forlag, 1997.

Silk, P. and Walters, R., *How Parliament Works*, Longman, 1998.

Taylor, R., *The Trade Union Question in British Politics*, Blackwell, 1993.

Tebbitt, N., *Upwardly Mobile*, Futura, 1991.

Thatcher, M., *The Downing Street Years*, Harper Collins, 1995.

Thomas, G., *Government and the Economy Today*, Manchester University Press, 1993.

Thomas, G., *Prime Minister and Cabinet Today*, Manchester University Press, 1998.

Thorpe, J., *In My Own Time*, Politico's 1999.

Toynbee, P., *David Walker: Did Things Get Better?*, Penguin, 2001.

Watts, D., *Political Communication Today*, Manchester University Press, 1997

Westlake, M., *Kinnock: The Biography*, Little, Brown, 2001.

Williams, M., *Inside Number 10*, New English Library, 1972.

Young, H., *One of Us: Life of Margaret Thatcher*, Macmillan, 1989.

Young, H., *Supping with the Devil*, Guardian Books, 2003.